ESTIMATING TILE COVERAGE

Square feet	Number of tiles needed			
	9″ x 9″	12″ x 12″	6″ x 6″	9″ x 18″
1	2	1	4	1
2	4	2	8	2
3	6	3	12	3
4	8	4	16	4
5	9	5	20	5
6	11	6	24	6
7	13	7	28	7
8	15	8	32	8
9	16	9	36	8
10	18	10	40	9
20	36	20	80	18
30	54	30	120	27
40	72	40	160	36
50	89	50	200	45
60	107	60	240	54
70	125	70	280	63
80	143	80	320	72
90	160	90	360	80
100	178	100	400	90
200	356	200	800	178
300	534	300	1200	267
400	712	400	1600	356
500	890	500	2000	445
600	1068	600	2400	534
700	1246	700	2800	623
800	1424	800	3200	712
900	1602	900	3600	801
1000	1780	1000	4000	890

Tile waste allowances		
1 to	50 sq. ft.	14%
50 to	100 sq. ft.	10%
100 to	200 sq. ft.	8%
200 to	300 sq. ft.	7%
300 to	1000 sq. ft.	5%
Over 1000 sq. ft.		3%

CEMENT, MORTAR AND CONCRETE MIXES

Cement

Use	Portland cement (bags)	Sand (cubic feet)
Setting flagstones	1	2½
Masonry surfacing	1	2½
Stucco	1	2½
Filling tree cavities	1	2

Mortar

Use	Mortar cement (or add 10% lime to portland cement)	Sand (cubic feet)
Brick and block laying	1	2½
Repointing brick	1	2
Stucco (in place of cement)	1	2½
General masonry patching	1	2 to 2½

Concrete

Use	Portland cement (bags)	Sand (cubic feet)	Gravel (cubic feet)
Foundation footing	1	2	4
Floors	1	2	3
Foundation walls	1	2½	4
Walks (heavy traffic)	1	1½	3
Walks (light traffic)	1	2	4
Stairs	1	2	4
Cast posts, lintels and other forms	1	1½	3
Setting posts	1	2½	4

(partial left table)

	hat you get
	1 5/8 x 2 5/8
	1 5/8 x 3 5/8
	1 5/8 x 5 5/8
	1 5/8 x 7 1/2
	1 5/8 x 9 1/2
	3 5/8 x 3 5/8

WATER-CEMENT RATIO

Use the specified number of gallons of water per sack of portland cement for the following concrete work:

Basement floor	5½	Patio floor	5
Cast posts, forms	5	Sidewalk (light traffic)	5
Driveway	5	Sidewalk (heavy traffic)	4½
Footing	5½	Stairs	5
Foundation wall	5	Topping for house floor	4½

Deduct the following from the amount of water to be used, depending upon the condition of the sand:

if the sand is slightly damp to the touch but leaves only a slight amount of moisture on your hand	¼ gallon per bag
if the sand is damp and leaves your hand wet and covered with some grains of sand	½ gallon per bag
if the sand is very wet and drips water	1 gallon per bag

AMERICA'S HANDYMAN BOOK

AMERICA'S

HANDYMAN BOOK

BY THE *Staff* OF
THE FAMILY HANDYMAN

CHARLES SCRIBNER'S SONS
NEW YORK

INTRODUCTION

As the world grows smaller but life more complex, the majority of men find themselves forced into some type of career specialization. Gone forever are the days of those who hoped to "embrace all knowledge and parts thereof." In fact, so specialized have we become that the simple phrase, "do it yourself," has a distinct and unique meaning in our every-day vocabulary.

In one sense, "do it yourself" reflects an attitude inherent to Americans, who historically pride themselves as a people possessing an abundance of initiative and self-reliance . . . but in another sense, it represents a protest against the restrictions of specialization, of standardization and mechanization, of red tape and high prices. It is often easier to do it yourself, when you can, and usually much more economical, exciting and rewarding.

The early Colonial homesteader is America's outstanding example of a man forced by necessity into mastering a variety of skills. He was a literal "Jack of all trades," and the craftsmanship with which he handled his simple tools and materials is attested to today by the value placed on the rare products still in existence from his crude workbench. An authentic object of Early Americana is now a treasure, not only because of its antiquity and inherent good workmanship but also because it was hand made. There is still an intrinsic something about work done with one's own hands that sets it apart, makes it exclusive and not merely one more item rolling off an assembly line, given a stock number and stacked alongside others exactly like itself.

In the 1800's, miscellaneous work and odd jobs fell to the lot of men called handymen. Sometimes they were itinerant and made their living as they traveled about the countryside; some of them made reputations for themselves, by word of mouth, and built tidy little businesses. But, as times changed, so did occupations. As industry grew, the demand for specialized, skilled labor increased, and gradually the handyman became just a memory of the horse and buggy days. Homeowners were able to call in the services of a variety of tradesmen—a carpenter, a plumber, an electrician, a painter, a gardener or a mason, plus a wide range of experts on such subjects as fireplaces and chimneys, floors, doors and windows, insulation, siding, etc.

In the late 1940's, as a result of World War II, prices and labor costs boomed. Further, there was a woeful lack of adequate and suitable housing for the exploding population. Young couples, in their desperation for shelter, were buying or renting homes that were too small for their growing families. Builders, in a seller's market, too often put the absolute minimum into their houses and the problem of repairs was ever present.

As it became difficult, if not impossible, for many millions of homeowners to afford the cost of outside help, the term "do it yourself" began to be heard. At first it carried a note of banter, as if the very idea were somewhat outlandish. Possibly it was, for a people so long unused to the idea . . . and, further, they didn't know *how* to do it themselves. They had no "how-to" information with which to begin. How many knew how to build in shelves, expand storage space, add rooms in an attic, fix a sagging floor or mend a leak in a roof? Who could clean out a chimney, pour concrete or paint a house?

Sensing a new market, the tool manufacturers began to produce light-duty stationary and portable power tools, heretofore mainly made for heavy-duty industry. First came a popular version of the quarter-inch electric hand drill, followed immediately by a list of accessories that made it one of the most versatile tools ever conceived. Realizing that a full workshop of separate stationary power tools would be beyond the average homeowner for reasons of cost as well as lack of space, the toolmakers evolved a series of combination tools, the first being a table saw-drill press-lathe with a common source of power. There soon followed a combined table saw and jointer, and again accessories appeared to increase their versatility. A precision instrument in industry, the radial-arm saw was brought out in a version especially for the new "home handyman." It, too, became a combination tool with the addition of many conversion accessories.

Other manufacturers began to prepare lines suited for use by the amateur. Wallpapers pre-pasted and trimmed appeared on the market; new paints, easy to work with and quick drying; pre-finished wallboard panels in standard sizes; complete window and door assemblies, ready to install; a variety of floor and wall tiles of all sizes and shapes, easy to cut and work with; new, fast-acting adhesives; lumber in standard sizes . . . these are but a few of the many new products that gave momentum and incentive to the idea of "doing it yourself," and the homeowning populace soon took keen notice.

But, while some manufacturers gave directions for the use of their products, the writing was in the language of the professionals and the homeowner was thoroughly bewildered. He faced problems concerning his house and property for which he knew no answers and had no ready, easily understandable source of "how-to" information.

One of these homeowners was a young publisher, Arnold E. Abramson. He and his growing family had just moved into an early 18th Century Colonial home, and the needed repair and restoration work seemed overwhelming. Thus, acutely aware of the problem, he began to develop in his mind the idea of *The Family Handyman* . . . a publication that would devote itself exclusively to the guidance and instruction of the growing army of baffled, non-expert homeowners. Gradually the nucleus of a staff was gathered. A rare few were found who did have the "how-to" at their finger-tips; then came the writers who could interpret the technicalities into simple, every-day language; and, finally, the artists who could further condense complexities into drawing and diagram relatively easy to understand. *The Family Handyman* was thus born and shortly became the most popular magazine in the do-it-yourself field.

From the first issue (January, 1951), the emphasis in preparing material for the magazine has been on simple, step-by-step language, avoiding the technical phrase and professional jargon. No effort has been spared to maintain this clarity and to guide the new homeowner-handyman in the best use of his tools, the best selection of materials to use, the best and most economical way to do a job. Step-by-step photo series abounded in every issue; simple line drawings and diagrams explained such intricacies as rabbeting, dadoing, wiring, furring out a wall and hanging a door.

After ten years of publishing, Arnold Abramson's original formula for his homeowner-handyman readers has changed little. *The Family Handyman*'s editorial content can be divided into three major categories:

> the preventive maintenance which prolongs the life of the home
> the repairs that eventually become necessary
> the improvements that increase comfort, convenience and value

This is the basis on which AMERICA'S HANDYMAN BOOK has been organized. The book contains the most basic material published in *The Family Handyman*, carefully compiled by the editors over a two-year period of time. First, Chapter 1, "The Tools of the Trade," introduces the reader to the hand tools and light-weight portable power tools most essential to his workbench. Actually, there is little in the book that cannot be done by the use of these tools alone, but, for those who want to go further, Appendix A, "The Home Workshop," deals with stationary power tools. The use of materials—paint, wood and masonry—is covered in detail in Chapter 7.

Appendix B, "Attic and Basement: Opportunities for Expansion and Improvement," was incorporated in view of the space problems that beset the majority of American families today and appear certain to continue. Wise and planned use of all available space in the home reaps many rewards, and the transformation of an unfinished basement or attic into a usable living area is one of the most logical and economical ways of solving family space problems.

Chapters 2 through 6 contain maintenance and repair information vital to the upkeep of every home. These chapters are the real core of the book and have been planned to withstand the test of time and changing home plans. They will long serve as a fundamental reference and guide for all do-it-yourself homeowners.

The Family Handyman
New York, New York
June, 1961

ACKNOWLEDGMENTS

I would like to extend very special appreciation to those members of *The Family Handyman* staff, past and present, whose enthusiasm and spirit through the years have made invaluable contributions: Phillip H. Scheller, Editor, often known affectionately as "Mr. Handyman"; Franc L. Roggeri, Art Director, who has given his unstinting attention to all photography, artwork and layout since the magazine's inception; Morton Waters, Editor, whose years of editorial guidance have been a continual source of inspiration; Tom Smith Roots, contributing artist, whose adroit line sketches say more than words; Harold J. Highland, Editor, whose expert advice could always be counted on; and Dorothy M. Sheehan, Assistant to the Publisher, who faithfully steered the compilation of AMERICA'S HANDYMAN BOOK through to completion. Without her determination, publication of this book would have been difficult.

Also, special tribute is made to Viola Sperka who so ably caught the essence of the material in the typography and layout of the book; and finally, but certainly not least, to Scribner Editor Donald Hutter, through whose wise liaison and supervision the book emerged into reality.

Arnold E. Abramson, Publisher
The Family Handyman

CONTENTS

THE TOOLS OF THE TRADE

*Hammers · Nails · Screws and Screwdrivers · Hand Saws ·
Braces and Assorted Bits · Big Pliers and Little Nippers ·
Wrenches · Files for Metals and Rasps for Wood · Planes ·
Chisels · Levels · Vises and Clamps · Measuring · Sanding
(Abrasives) · Adhesives · Care of Your Tools · Grounding
Power Tools · The Quarter-Inch Drill · Drill Bits · Portable
Power Saw · Power Sander · Sabre Saw · Router*

Eons ago when one of our remote ancestors discovered how to chip a keen-edged shard off one flint rock with another, the first cutting tool was born. And with the maul he made by lashing a stone to a broken branch, the caveman had two tools. Although we've come a long way since those first crude implements, cutting and impact tools (i.e., hand tools) still form a most important part of any tool collection.

With a few basic hand tools and several planks across two sawhorses for a temporary bench, the home handyman is well on his way to becoming an expert in many fields. The next step in his expansion of equipment leads to portable power tools—lightweight, motor-driven tools with greater strength and versatility—and, finally, the man who undertakes large and continual projects (usually home improvements and additions as well as repair and maintenance) will want to go on to stationary power tools.

In any selection of tools, it is far better to buy a few, carefully chosen and of good quality, than many of an inferior grade. According to old-timers, you have only to "heft" a tool to tell the difference—the good hammer becomes an extension of your own arm as you swing it; the well-made saw follows straight through the cut without effort. With proper care and use, a good tool will be a lifetime investment.

Having the tools themselves is not quite enough, however. Still needed is a place to use them and a place to store them—a workshop—and the first requisite of every workshop is a sturdy workbench. With only the most basic tools, construction of the workbench on the following page becomes possible, and your workshop is off to a good, sound start.

HAMMERS

Hammers are made in many sizes and shapes to handle the multitude of jobs assigned to them. The basic type, of course, is the claw hammer. The head is metal, the handle wood. But even claw hammers vary in shape, and also in quality. The claw may be

1

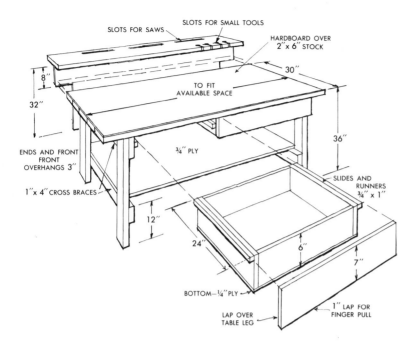

SLOTS FOR SAWS
SLOTS FOR SMALL TOOLS
HARDBOARD OVER
2" x 6" STOCK
8"
32"
30"
TO FIT
AVAILABLE SPACE
36"
¾" PLY
ENDS AND FRONT
FRONT
OVERHANGS 3"
SLIDES AND
RUNNERS
¾" x 1"
1" x 4" CROSS BRACES
12"
24"
6"
7"
BOTTOM—¼" PLY
LAP OVER
TABLE LEG
1" LAP FOR
FINGER PULL

BASIC WORKBENCH

The secret of a satisfactory workbench may be summed up in one word—stability. No matter how small it must be, heavy timbers and rigid joints will lend it the inertia that gives stability under impact. This workbench is doubly sturdy, with its heavy legs and 2" top braced with a ¾" plywood back.

Regardless of the total length of the bench, do not space leg trestles more than five feet apart. Drawers are proportioned to fit this space and are constructed simply. The top overhangs at the front and ends of the bench to accommodate clamps needed when working on long pieces.

sharply curved, in which form its major function is to pull out nails, or nearly straight, a variation which not only pulls nails but also separates boards which have been nailed together. This type can be used to split boards along the grain.

The metal head may be cast iron, which is quick and easy to make. But since cast iron breaks on impact, the best head is made of drop-forged steel, which is practically indestructible. Straight-grained hickory is best for the handle and will last a lifetime if protected against dry rot with linseed oil and against gouges and saw cuts while on the job.

The handle is inserted in a hole in the head, and one or more wedges are driven down into the grain end of the handle, expanding it tightly into the head so that it can't fly off.

CLAW

HEAD

HANDLE

NECK

FACE

A hammer is designed with a definite "balance." That is, maximum impact is provided if the hammer is held properly—at the curved indentation in the handle near its heavy end—and freely swung instead of jabbed at a nail. Wherever possible, arrange your work to use a hammer in this way and you will be amazed at the ease with which the job gets done.

For tight corners and overhead work, of course, this method isn't always possible. Vary the grip if the position demands it. It is important that the exact center of the hammer face strikes the nail on the head and that the direction of the blow is exactly in line with the direction of the nail.

A representative of each of the following types of hammers will equip your workshop for every common need:

1. Claw hammer for general carpentry.
2. Tack hammer, preferably magnetized, for tacks and brads.
3. Mason's hammer for working with brick, stone or concrete.
4. Ball peen hammer or No. 4 sledge for hand drilling in masonry and other heavy work. The broader face of the sledge affords more protection to the drill-holding hand than the peen.

If you are going to specialize, then the addition of others—such as the plastic-faced hammer—may follow as the need for them arises.

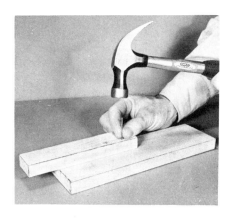

Two types of claw hammer: (left) the standard claw used for withdrawing nails and (right) the straighter claw which can be used to separate boards or as a splitting wedge.

Wedges driven into end grain of handle secure head in place so it can't fly off.

Extra weight of sledge drills faster.

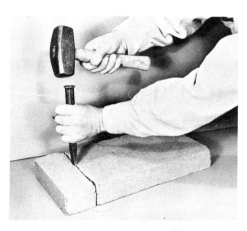

Light sledge goes hand in hand with cold chisel.

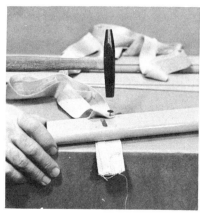

Lightweight tack hammer has dozens of uses for driving small fasteners.

Mason's hammer scores mark, deepens score to split stone. The square end chips points.

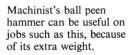

Machinist's ball peen hammer can be useful on jobs such as this, because of its extra weight.

NAILS

The common nail is called "common" because it is the most practical means for fastening pieces of wood together easily, quickly and inexpensively. Glue is neater, screws are stronger, and either one combined with correct joinery becomes stronger still. But 99 per cent of all the homes of the nation are fastened together with nails because they are quicker and easier to handle.

There are hundreds of different kinds of nails, each kind with its own assortment of sizes. They range from railroad and boat spikes down to brads so fine that a thousand barely make a pound. However, less than a dozen sizes and kinds will serve the needs of the average handyman. Choosing the right nail and driving it right makes the difference between the finished work holding together or falling apart.

Nails hold by friction, that is, the pressure of wood against the shank of the nail. Just how well they hold depends upon three things: the condition of the wood, the shape and texture of the nail, and the size of the nail in relation to the size of the wood.

First, consider the condition of the wood. If it is soft, the nail will drive in easily, but it will also pull out easily. The harder the wood, the more difficult to drive a nail, but the harder it will be held. There is one notable exception—splitting. Hardwoods split more easily than soft. Starting with softwoods like balsa and pine, through rock maple and oak, and on to ironwood and teak, you come to a point where a nail thick enough to be driven without bending is also thick enough to split the wood. In other words, some woods are so hard that they cannot be nailed without drilling a pilot hole first. When you reach that necessity, it is more practical to use a screw.

Dry wood splits more readily than does wet wood, which often cannot be split at all. When a nail is driven into wet wood, there is a good chance that after the wood dries it will shrink, leaving the nail loose.

The second consideration is the shape and texture of the nail. The more exterior surface of the nail in contact with wood, the greater the holding power. In addition, many types of nails have ridges or spirals along the shank, both of which increase the nail's holding power and also the tendency to split the wood into which it is driven. A long, thin, pointed nail goes in more easily, holds well, but is more apt to split the wood. Blunt-pointed nails, or those blunted by the hammer before driving, have less splitting action but more holding power. The common diamond-pointed nail is the best compromise.

Many types of nails are coated with a special glue. When driven into wood, the heat of passage melts the glue and in a few minutes the nail is glued in fast. If you drive these nails part way, they will freeze in that position and will bend if you try to drive them deeper later on. Also, they will be difficult to pull out. It is best to drive coated nails all the way at once. Nails coated with powdered rosin will react in somewhat the same way.

The final consideration is the size of the nail in relation to the size of the wood. Obviously, a spike will split a thin, dry slat. A good rule is to choose a common nail which will not penetrate all the way through the last piece of wood. If the wood is extremely dry, choose a coated box nail of the same length as the common nail. If you are fastening a thin board to a thick one, use a nail that is long enough to go through the thin piece and two-thirds of the way through the thick one. This standard can apply to virtually all mixed-size carpentry and all normal household work except the laying of hardwood floors (where special steel-cut nails are used) and the fastening of wood trim. Since nearly all trim is made of softwood, long, slim nails are used. There is little load on the nail, and often the nail must reach through an empty space before reaching the foundation to which the trim is actually fastened.

Locating the right spot in which to drive the nail is also of vital importance. Driving *across* the grain is usually the correct procedure. It holds better and is

CHOOSING NAILS. Nails are ordered by penny number, or "d." Once based on price per nail, this number is now related only to length. The table below shows length of nail in relation to this number and the number of nails of that size you get per pound. In deciding what length of nail to use, rule-of-thumb calls for setting the nail two-thirds of its length into the second of two pieces to be joined. Use the thinnest possible nail in very dry wood to avoid splitting. Pre-drill holes for larger nails, particularly in hardwoods. Avoid using rusty nails as they may bend or break.

Table of Nail Sizes

Penny Number	Length in Inches	Number per Pound		
		Common Nails	Box Nails	Finishing Nails
2	1	876	1010	1351
3	1¼	568	635	807
4	1½	316	437	548
5	1¾	271	406	500
6	2	181	236	309
8	2½	106	145	189
10	3	69	94	121
12	3¼	64	87	113
16	3½	49	71	90
20	4	31	52	62
30	4½	20		

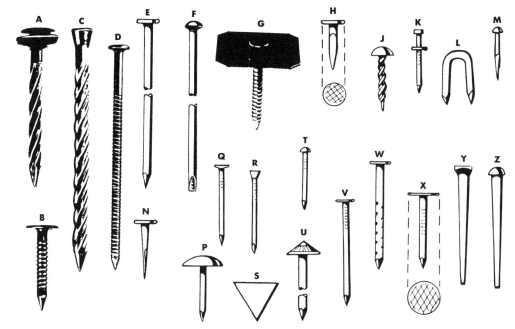

SPECIAL-PURPOSE NAILS

A spiral roofing nail with washer
B spiral flat-headed tack
C spiral flooring nail
D spiral asbestos-shingle nail
E flat-head gutter spike, non-rusting
F round-head gutter spike, non-rusting
G washered roofing nail
H checkered-head carpet tack

J round-head screw nail, slotted
K duplex head, easy to pull out
L wire staple for fencing
M oval-head tack, ornamental use
N flat-head common household tack
P upholsterer's tack, ornamental head
Q blued lath nail, also for panels
R brad for thin woods, delicate work

S glazier's point for windowpanes
T escutcheon nail for door hardware
U leakproof nail, seals its own hole
V shingle nail; copper, galvanized
W barbed asbestos-shingle nail
X double-length checkered roofing nail
Y steel-cut flooring nail
Z common-cut nail, round head

COMMON NAILS—ACTUAL SIZE

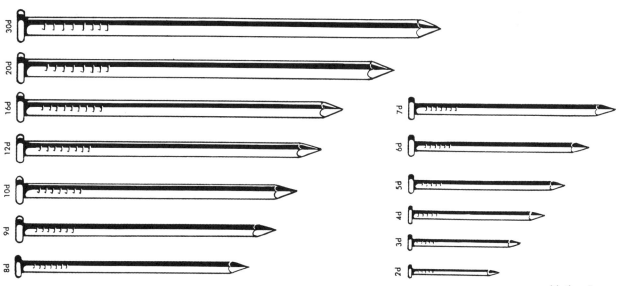

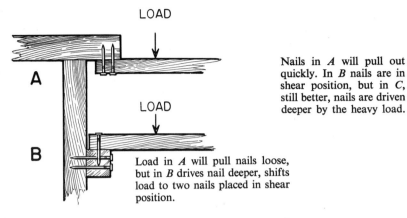

LOAD

LOAD

Load in *A* will pull nails loose, but in *B* drives nail deeper, shifts load to two nails placed in shear position.

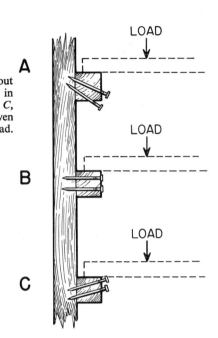

Nails in *A* will pull out quickly. In *B* nails are in shear position, but in *C*, still better, nails are driven deeper by the heavy load.

less apt to split. Driven *along* the grain, the nail is easily pulled out. Any shearing stress placed on a nail so driven will split the wood. A nail placed too close to the end grain will split out. Placed too near the edges of the board, it will also produce splits. A single nail will permit a certain amount of swing in the joint, but two nails, not placed in the same grain line, will eliminate swing and more than double the strength.

Although we have discussed nails in relation to their holding power against pulling outward, nails should never be used for that strength alone. The nail should be so placed that strain against it is crosswise, not along its length. A nail can be pulled out, but it is extremely difficult to shear it off. Place all nails in your construction work so that this principle is observed. With the exception of trim, which carries little load, all structural joints can be made so that the weight and live load will drive nails deeper or force the load against their shear angles. If you find a spot where this is not possible, something other than simple nailing strength is needed. Use angle irons, straps, bolts or some additional means of securing. Study the sketches to note the right-and-wrong techniques. They'll assure safety on your building projects.

Long finishing nails must often pass through empty space to find an anchor.

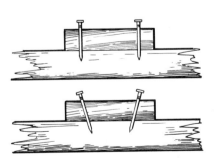

Nails straight in are easily pulled up, but when angled reinforce one another.

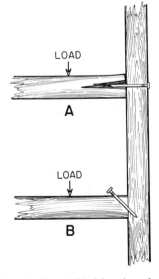

Load on *A*, when nail is driven in end grain, splits wood, but in *B* the load drives the nail deeper into stud.

6   THE TOOLS OF THE TRADE: Nails

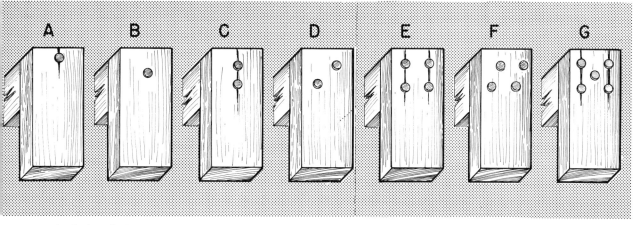

A—bad; nail close to end splits wood.   B—good.   C—bad; both nails in same grain splits wood.   D—perfect.
E—weak; same cause as C.   F—correct nailing.   G—too many nails, will hold no better than B.

SCREWS AND SCREWDRIVERS

Screws. While 90 per cent of all carpentry can be completed by the use of common nails, the remaining 10 per cent requires some special fastening device and, in most cases, it will be wood screws which are called upon. Screws are specifically recommended in the following instances: (1) when the work may have to be taken apart at some future date; (2) when greater holding power is required of the joint; (3) when it is important that the finished job be unmarred.

Screws should always be used when the pull of the load is to be directed along the *length* of the fastening devices. A nail in such a position will pull out but a screw will hold tightly.

Since there are literally hundreds of types of screws from which to choose, selection of the right one is important. Screws are not, like nails, identified by length alone. A screw has two dimensions: the diameter of the shank just below the head is the number of the screw, and the length is indicated in inches or fractions of an inch.

In choosing a screw for a specific purpose, first select the proper head style for the job. Round heads will remain exposed and can actually become a part of the decorative scheme; otherwise they must be used where they will remain unobtrusive. Flat heads will either be countersunk flush with the surface or buried deeper and concealed by wood putty or filler.

When selecting a screw by its number, remember that the number indicates thickness only and that the length must also be specified. Use a thin screw for hardwood, a screw with a thicker shank for softwood. A flat-head screw is measured by its over-all length; a round-head screw is measured from point to the base of the slot in the screw head. Select a maximum length that will not pass entirely through the wood. At the same time, remember that, as with nails, the maximum area of wood fiber gripping the screw provides the maximum holding power. In determining the safety limit to be placed on a single screw, consult the table. It provides a guide for selection when 1″ of screw thread is embedded in wood *across* the grain. This, of course, means 1″ in the *holding* piece of wood. For ½″ of embedded screw,

SAFE LOADS FOR SCREWS. Screws are used instead of nails when greater holding power is needed. The "power" referred to is in an outward direction, opposite that in which the screw point is aimed. In other words, outward pull against the threads is holding power.

The quality of the wood into which the screw is driven has a definite bearing on its ability to hold. Screws hold best in hardwoods. A glance at the table shows the differences.

The table also indicates safe loads for each 1″ of screw *thread* inserted into the "holding" piece of wood. For a screw set with threads ½″ into the holding piece, reduce the safe load figure by 50 per cent. Remember that the threads of a wood screw represent ⅔ the total length of the screw. Setting into end grain reduces holding power 40 per cent.

Screw Number	4	8	12	16	20	24
In Oak	80 (lbs.)	100	130	150	170	180
In Yellow Pine	70 (lbs.)	90	120	140	150	160
In White Pine	50 (lbs.)	70	90	100	120	140

Example: a No. 20 screw set with threads 1″ into the cross grain of oak will hold 170 pounds; set into white pine, it will hold 120 pounds; set into the end grain of white pine 1″, it will hold 72 pounds; but if set into the end grain of white pine only ½″, it will hold only 36 pounds. To increase load limits, use additional screws.

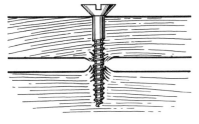

Screws need pilot holes. Without them, fibers of two joined boards pushed and pulled toward the joint will keep these two faces from joining tightly (sketch). A pilot hole through both boards permits the screw threads to draw both pieces tightly together. Devices for making pilot holes are shown. The Screw-mate (in use on right) matches the screw outline. Straight drills for the root section of the screw are used only in softwoods.

use one-half the load shown. For 2″ of embedded screw thread, double the load value. When the screw is set *with* the grain, use 60 per cent of the indicated load figure.

In softwood, it is sometimes necessary to make only a short indentation as a starting hole for the screw, and your screwdriver plus wrist action will sink it into place. Larger screws require pilot holes. For softwoods such as pine and spruce, drill a hole only half as deep as the threaded part of the screw. For hardwoods such as oak, maple and birch, drill the hole as deep as the screw. When using exceptionally large screws in hardwoods, first drill a pilot hole that is slightly smaller than the threaded part of the screw; then use a second drill (of the same diameter as the unthreaded portion of the screw) to enlarge the hole at the top.

To speed up the driving action on setting screws, it has long been customary to soap the threaded end of the screw. The idea was that this made driving the screw easier, and this is correct. However, soap eventually turns to a form of glue and cements the screw into the hole. It also produces rust on steel screws, corrosion on brass screws. As a result, withdrawing the screws later is almost impossible. It is far better to use candle wax or graphite. Don't use oil—it will stain and penetrate the wood grain for some distance around the screw head.

Since a screw is often used with the idea that it may later be removed and replaced, it is well to bear in mind that, when withdrawn, it will leave a much larger hole than will a nail. Before the screw can be replaced, the hole must be filled to provide a firm gripping area. You can fill it with wood putty and reset the screw in this new material, or use plastic plugs, driven into the old screw holes. Both provide an excellent base. Also, you can use a longer screw for replacement.

To remove a tight screw, be sure to use a screwdriver blade with perfectly parallel sides and one which fits the screw head exactly. If turning the blade counterclockwise does not loosen the screw, reverse the direction (which will drive the screw in a bit further) and then again turn counterclockwise. By working the screw both ways, you will often find that it will back up a bit more each time until it is entirely out.

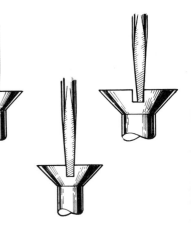

In setting screws, choice of a screwdriver is important. Unless the blade of the driver matches the slotted head of the screw, the head will be torn to bits by the force of the blade. The screw cannot be fully set in, nor can it be easily withdrawn. Make sure the screwdriver bit fits the screw slot (center). At right the screwdriver is too small, permitting head to be mangled. At left, rounded screwdriver (used too often as a chisel) cannot turn the screw without shredding the head or slipping out of the slot.

HOW TO MEASURE WOOD SCREWS AND TAPPING SCREWS

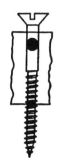

To determine sizes of screws, lay screws flat within parallel lines shown at right.

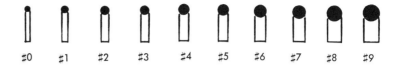

#0   #1   #2   #3   #4   #5   #6   #7   #8   #9

ACTUAL SHANK SIZES

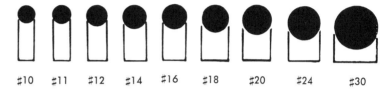

#10   #11   #12   #14   #16   #18   #20   #24   #30

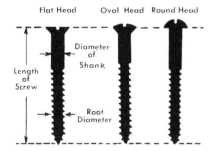

Flat Head   Oval Head   Round Head

Length of Screw

Diameter of Shank

Root Diameter

Unlike nails, which are measured only by length, screws are measured by length and by the diameter of the shank which is not tapered.

In ordering screws, therefore, specify the *length* wanted, allowing the threads to be two-thirds placed in the second of the two pieces to be joined, and also the *gauge number*, which will determine the diameter of the shank.

When driving screw into end grain, use a dowel across grain to hold screw threads.

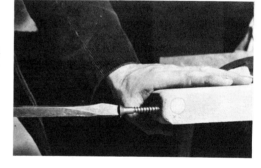

Old screws with battered heads can be salvaged with a metal-cutting saw blade.

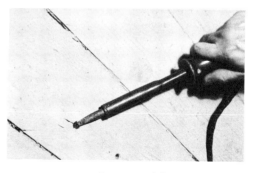

Wood screws frozen in place can be freed by soldering iron applied to head.

Screwdrivers. The screwdriver will be one of the most essential tools in your tool kit and, used correctly, it will contribute much to keeping your home in tiptop shape.

A quality screwdriver has a tip of high-grade steel which will not become burred easily, and its sides are almost parallel. Most screwdrivers may look somewhat alike, but they vary considerably in the jobs for which they are made. The use of the right size for a particular screw will cut down considerably on time and effort involved on any job. A screwdriver's size is designated by its blade—a 7″ screwdriver has a 7″ blade, and so on. Naturally, those with heavier tips are specifically designed for heavy jobs, those with narrow-tipped blades are made for more delicate work. There is no such thing as an all-purpose screwdriver—the screwdriver must be suited to the job, and you always use the *longest* screwdriver convenient for the job. There are combinations which utilize one handle and several different blades, and these are fully practicable for a variety of jobs. The four types of screwdrivers most generally used are:

1. The common screwdriver—available in a wide variety of sizes, each for specific screws. Remember that the tip of the screwdriver must fit the screw slot. If too wide, the blade tip may ruin the wood around the head of the screw. If the tip is too narrow, there is a good chance that it will slip and chew up the head of the screw.

2. Spiral ratchet and ratchet screwdrivers—may be used with blades of various sizes. Use these to drive in screws or to extract them; they work semi-automatically, much faster than the ordinary screwdriver. The handle of the ratchet type turns back and forth but the ratchet allows the blade to turn only in the direction you set.

3. Phillips screwdrivers—used only with Phillips screws. The head of each Phillips screw has two slots which cross at the center, guiding the blade of the screwdriver to the right location.

4. Offset screwdrivers—used where there isn't sufficient space to use the common screwdriver. One offset type has two blades at opposite ends, made at right angles to the handle.

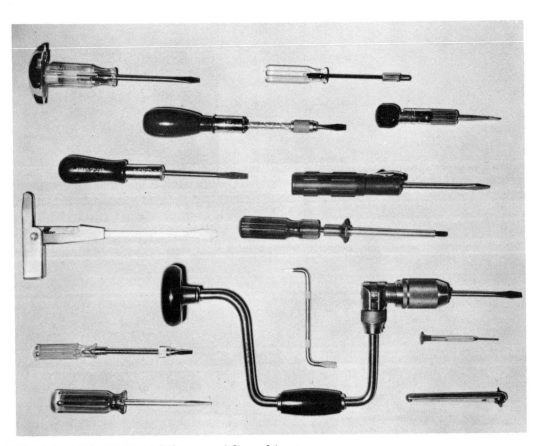

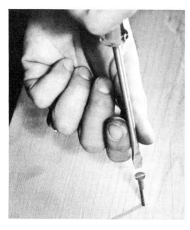

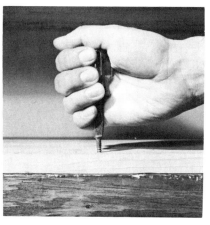

In driving a screw, hold the handle of the screwdriver firmly in your right hand; use your left hand to grasp the blade just over the screwdriver tip.

For removing a screw, or driving in a screw in confined areas, you will find that a common screwdriver of the "stubby" type is ideal for the job.

In extremely confined areas, it may be impossible to use any screwdriver but the offset type. This has two blades, both at right angles to the handle.

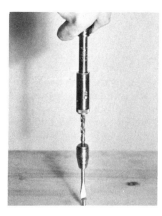

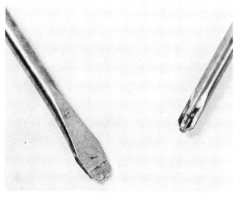

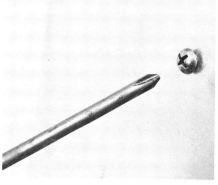

The spiral ratchet type considerably speeds up driving a screw. Simply set the blade in the screw slot, steady the blade, and push to drive the screw.

Never use screwdrivers with damaged tips like these (common and Phillips types). These rounded edges will "chew up" any slot, may slip and injure you.

This Phillips screwdriver can be used only with Phillips screws. The head of each screw has two slots which cross each other, obviating slipping of blade.

For removing a tight screw, it may be necessary to use a heavy-duty type of screwdriver with a square shank. Use a wrench on this shank to turn screw.

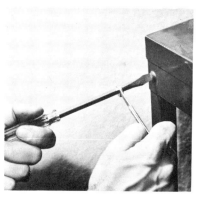

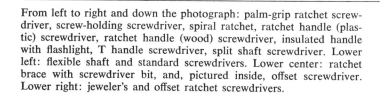

From left to right and down the photograph: palm-grip ratchet screwdriver, screw-holding screwdriver, spiral ratchet, ratchet handle (plastic) screwdriver, ratchet handle (wood) screwdriver, insulated handle with flashlight, T handle screwdriver, split shaft screwdriver. Lower left: flexible shaft and standard screwdrivers. Lower center: ratchet brace with screwdriver bit, and, pictured inside, offset screwdriver. Lower right: jeweler's and offset ratchet screwdrivers.

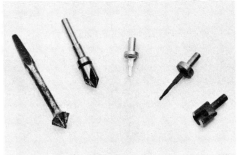

Do not tap on the handles of common screwdrivers. Use the type favored by mechanics; it has a shank which goes all the way through the handle to the top.

These are various types of countersinking bits (for sinking screws) and a plug cutter for making plugs of wood to conceal screws.

Special screwdrivers help out in a tight spot. This one makes a one-hand operation possible. Tension of split blades holds screw while you guide it.

There are also heavy-duty types of screwdrivers with square shanks. You can use a wrench on the shank and apply enough force to turn and loosen large, rusted screws.

In use, the handle of the screwdriver should be held firmly in your right hand, the head of the handle should be against your palm, and your thumb and fingers should grasp the handle near the ferrule. To drive the screw *in*, turn the handle clockwise. To remove the screw, turn it in the opposite direction.

A screwdriver does not have to be sharpened, but occasionally it must be ground on an emery wheel or the sides must be filed with a flat file. Never bevel the tip of a screwdriver. When filing the blade, use a good vise, and make the tip straight across the end. It must be at right angles to the sides and shank. Make certain that the faces of the blade near the tip

are parallel to each other. This is a vital point; if it is neglected, the blade will slip often and jump out of the screw slot.

HAND SAWS

The saw is one of the most basic tools of any home workshop. It is generally the first tool needed for a job after the work has been measured. There are many different kinds of saws, each of which is designed for a particular job. With the right saw, the handyman will find most jobs easier to do and the results better.

The first saw in your rack should be a crosscut saw; the second, a utility tool that will do the job of both a compass saw and a hack saw. Afterwards, as you expand your collection, add the special saws to do the specific jobs at which they're best.

SAW POINTS

You can learn to identify a wood-cutting hand saw by the number of teeth per inch and the manner in which the teeth are set. The *crosscut* saw—used to cut wood *across* the grain—has from 6 to 12 teeth per inch. The teeth are pushed outward, alternately by the "set", and each tooth is beveled on both its forward and rear edges. The *ripsaw*, designed to cut wood *along* its grain, has 4, 4½, 5, or 5½ teeth per inch.

These teeth also extend outward, alternately, but each tooth is sharpened straight across on the short forward and longer tapered rear edges. A straightedge, laid on the points, should touch every tooth. The blade should taper slightly from the toothed side to the back to prevent the saw blade from binding in a cut.

Continued use wears down teeth unevenly so that not all meet the wood.

With a metal file you can level teeth, fitting them to identical size and set.

USING THE CROSSCUT SAW

No handyman can start work without a crosscut saw. For fine work, use one with 12 points to the inch. For all-around chores, try the 8-point, which might, on occasion, be used for ripping.

Mark the line of cut, hold the saw $\frac{1}{16}''$ to the scrap side of the mark at an angle of 45°. Hold the saw at right angles to the board face with the knuckle of the left thumb (below). This may scratch the knuckle on the first tries, but you learn quickly to hold the saw properly and not force it. Push forward with the arm, not the hand or wrist. The return stroke is made without downward pressure. Use the full length of the blade. If forced by wrist action, the saw will leave the straight lines and bind in the curved cut.

If you do stray from the line, withdraw the saw and resume cutting at the point where you left the mark, guiding the strokes with a slight twisting motion.

Support the cut-off piece or, in falling, it will tear. If the wood is green or full of sap, coat the blade with machine oil—or, if the wood is to be stain-finished, with paraffin, which will not mar the wood.

For precision, clamp a straightedge guide to the work and follow it instead of a standard pencil mark. With practice, a pencil line can be followed easily, however, and the straightedge method dropped. Always hold the saw *lightly*.

The crosscut saw has a lot of uses besides straight cutting of wood. In a miter box built on the spot, it makes all angle cuts accurately. It can also be used to cut light metals such as aluminum (as shown here), if necessary.

RIPPING

While the all-purpose, 8-point saw can be used to rip lumber along the grain, the 4½- to 5½-point ripsaw does it better and faster. The saw is held at an angle of about 60°. As with cross-cutting, support both work and scrap.

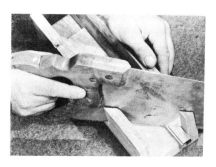

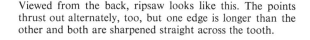

Seen from the back, crosscut teeth look like this. They are set alternately, with both biting edges beveled. The edges are of approximate equal length.

Viewed from the back, ripsaw looks like this. The points thrust out alternately, too, but one edge is longer than the other and both are sharpened straight across the tooth.

Side view shows even teeth, edges beveled to each side, notches even.

Side view of rip teeth reveals the straight-across filing on forward edges.

THE BACK SAW

This is the saw you need for accurate cutting in cabinet work. The back saw has anywhere from 18 to 32 small teeth per inch, and they are not sharply set. The edge it cuts is almost smooth, always straight. The big brother of the back saw is known as a miter-box saw. It is longer and usually used with a miter box of some sort. The back saw is 12″ to 14″ long, the miter-box saw from 20″ to 30″ long. Use these saws for cutting moldings to angles, for mitering, for accurate joints.

A good trick when cutting moldings or miters is to cut 1° *less* than the desired angle. The pressure necessary to force the two pieces together will make a tighter joint.

KEYHOLE AND COMPASS SAWS

These close relatives have a very specialized job to do. They are tapered so they can enter a drilled hole and move about in all directions from that point. Their purpose is to make cutouts in the center of a piece of wood without cutting the edges. The compass saw, a rugged 8-pointer, tapers to a point, while big brother keyhole, finer-toothed at 24 points, is longer and not always sharply pointed at the end. Many makers include an assortment of interchangeable blades to fit a single handle. In some cases the handle also rotates, making circle-cutting easier from a given position. Use the big-toothed shorty for plywood cutouts, the finer-toothed blades for cutting plastics.

THE COPING SAW

This thread-thick, spring-steel-tough blade is held in a rectangular frame. It can be held at any angle, can work its way along a straight line, turn a right-angle corner, or cut circles. It is particularly useful in face-matching molding cuts. The blade has 17 points which produce a fairly smooth surface. Breakage of blades is high owing to forcing, so keep a supply on hand. Tension on the blade is produced by turning the handle. The blade may be set to aim the teeth in any direction—an aid to circle-cutting.

For intricate cutouts and many hobby projects, the coping saw is indispensable, but it's also a must for the handyman's utility kit.

 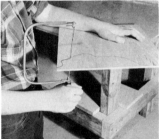

FOR REAL UTILITY

Small, resembling the keyhole saw and the hack saw, the utility saw has multiple uses all around the house and shop. It cuts metal as easily as a hack saw. Its fine teeth make it ideal for plastic cutting. It does passably well cutting curves and will do as well as the coping saw on some intricate cuts. It's a good item to tuck into the tool tote box.

THE HACK SAW

A hack saw blade can fit into a No. 11 shoe, but it's tough enough to cut through steel. In fact, cutting metal is its principal function. No other tool will cut the armor from electrical cable as easily. And you will find a hundred other uses for your hack saw around the house.

Blades are fitted with from 18 to 32 points per inch. Use the coarse variety on armored cable, copper tubing, soft metals. Use the fine-toothed type for cutting plastics of all kinds or for smoother edges on metals. Keep an assortment of blades on hand.

Your wife will also find a hack saw useful in cutting frozen foods.

There is considerable debate over the direction in which the teeth should point when the hack saw is in use. The usual method is to aim the teeth away from your hand, toward the work. Pressure is applied on the forward stroke. Since this causes the blade to skid on rounded metal surfaces, many prefer the teeth aimed the other way to take pressure on the "pull" stroke. A neat compromise is the use of two blades, one aimed each way. This speeds up cutting but makes the cut far wider.

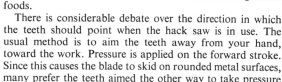

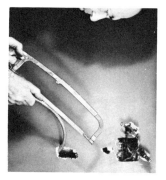

BRACES AND ASSORTED BITS

In its chief role as a drilling tool, the brace is an absolute "must" for every tool kit, large or small. It is not only an essential shop tool; it is an every-day tool for many home maintenance projects as well.

An electric drill is a supplement to—not a substitute for—the brace. The average electric drill is limited, without special bits, to drilling holes up to the diameter of ¼", and the depth of the holes is also limited. There is practically no limit to the diameter or depth of holes which can be produced with a brace, using one of the wide assortment of bits.

A brace has an adjustable chuck which receives bits from ¼" up to 1⅛" in diameter, and it will also handle expansive bits of various types that will cut holes up to 3" in diameter. A well-balanced brace with a heavy-duty ratchet is best. A ball-bearing head for easy turning and long wear, a self-opening chuck with automatic centering, and a deep-sweep frame for maximum leverage are features of the better makes. The chuck should grip round-shanked as well as square-shanked bits. The ratchet feature, of course, makes working in close quarters possible where half turns and quarter turns are all the clearance allows. With a reverse ratchet, you can easily remove tightly set screws.

The value of the brace is multiplied by building a collection of special-purpose bits as the need for them arises. In addition to assorted standard auger bits, one of the first you will find use for is the expansive bit. Some makes are marked on the spur or cutter, with a graduated scale for accurate setting. A depth-gauge bit can be set to drill holes to exact depth—essential in dowel work, setting adjustable shelf pegs and many forms of cabinet work.

Standard auger bits range in size from ¼" to 1⅛" and are numbered in order from 4 to 18. Each number indicates a size $\frac{1}{16}$" larger than the preceding one. Lengths are from 6" to 8", but special bits are made up to 18" in length. For greater depth, an extension rod can be inserted with the auger in the far end. This is often used in wiring an existing building and saves opening walls.

Two additional items to be added to the collection are the countersink bit and the screwdriver bit. The latter will prove immensely helpful in driving screws, particularly when a large number must be driven or when the wood itself is hard. Also, in withdrawing screws that are tightly set, the screwdriver bit proves itself a great aid.

In drilling holes with a brace, there are a few practical rules to follow. Center the screw tip of the bit accurately. To drill a hole without a slant to either

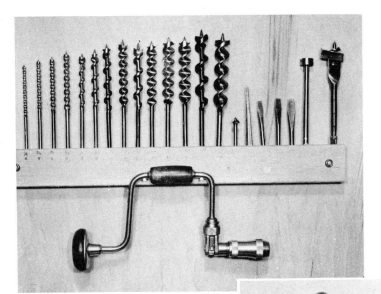

Brace and complete assortment of augers, plus special-purpose bits, all properly stored in 2 × 3 block, bored part way through and marked as to size of augers.

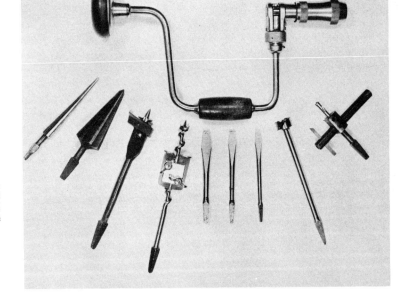

Special-purpose bits, from left to right, include: two reamers, expansive bit, depth gauge on bit, three screwdriver bits, and two types of circle-cutting bits, adjustable to 3″ diameter circles.

side of the intended line of bore, use a jig or make one yourself from a block of wood which can be clamped to the work. Since the screw tip is apt to tear the reverse side of a piece of wood as it comes through, either back up the work with a piece of scrap wood and drill into it, or pull back the augur and drill through from the other side. In this case, allow the screw tip to emerge just enough to indicate the point for drilling from the reverse side.

The spurs on bits are brittle so that they will keep a sharp cutting edge. They can be damaged by banging against each other if tossed loosely in a drawer. It's better to form the habit of racking them up, in order of size. To keep both brace and bits in good working order, oil the brace at indicated points periodically. Bits should also be oiled before storing them after use because rust quickly blunts sharp edges and damages the screw tips.

In boring a hole, back up work with a scrap board and drill through into it to avoid tearing back of stock with emerging tip.

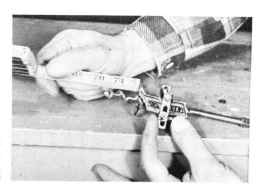

Depth gauge is fastened to bit at desired point, measured from bottom of gauge to tip of the spur.

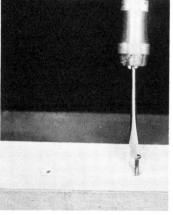

Screwdriver bit, on a ratchet brace, will set screws rapidly and effortlessly, and will also withdraw tightly set screws.

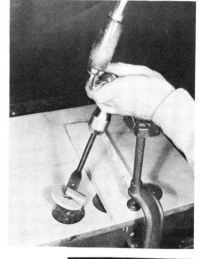

Adjustable expansive bit has screw tip for pilot hole, cutting spur on outer end. This operation should proceed from one side halfway, then be completed from other side.

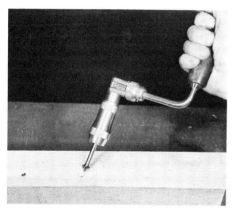

Countersink bit reams top of hole so that flat-head screws can be recessed below the surface and so concealed from view.

Always center screw tip accurately on the point where center of hole should be. For accuracy, make pilot hole with center punch.

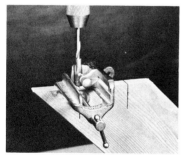

Auger bit held in vise can be sharpened, and burrs can be removed, with a fine file. An exacting job, but it keeps bits in shape.

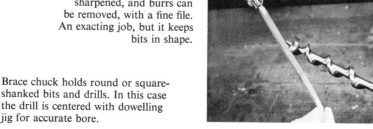

Brace chuck holds round or square-shanked bits and drills. In this case the drill is centered with dowelling jig for accurate bore.

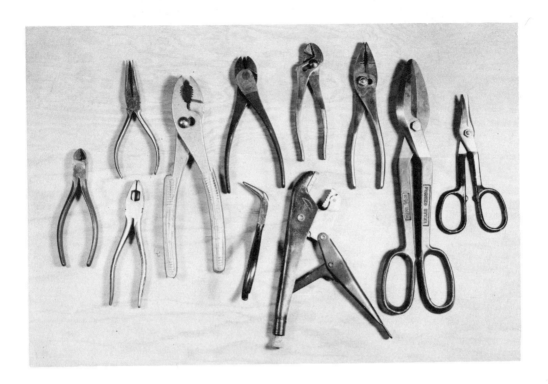

BIG PLIERS AND LITTLE NIPPERS

Basically, pliers were designed to hold materials with a firmer grip than mere fingers can provide. But they have been adapted to such jobs as bending metal, cutting wire or nails, stripping insulation from wire, holding hot substances without injury to the hands and providing insulation against electric currents. Thus, the work of pliers may be divided into three categories: gripping, cutting, and reaching.

For gripping, use the usual slip-joint type of pliers. Add a larger pair as a supplement and you'll find it will often double as a wrench or a vise. One of 8″ would be about right. You might add a somewhat thin-nosed one with plastic or rubber-covered handles as a protection for wiring work.

Cutting pliers are more varied in design. End-cutting nippers and combination wire-cutting, wire-stripping pliers are valuable aids to the handyman. The wire-stripping device has a notch inside the jaws

through which wire is drawn to remove its insulating covering.

For reaching and holding, there are thin, long-nosed types, capable of reaching into tight spots where fingers cannot go. Some are needle-nosed to pick up tiny objects, others are flat- or duck-billed and hold flat objects firmly and securely. Don't use them for pulling out nails or the finely finished jaws may spread in opposite directions, making the pliers useless for their intended functions.

There are also a number of pliers with angled noses. Some of these are designed for reaching into the

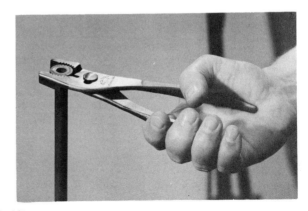

Heavy-duty slip-joint pliers are useful in holding materials with firmer grip than fingers provide.

close confines of TV and radio innards. Others multiply your grip several times by allowing full power in awkward spots.

Pliers generally require little care other than a light coating of oil to prevent rust. Misuse will result in dulled edges, broken tips and loosened pivots. If the nose has been broken, the pliers can sometimes be salvaged in grinding the tip. In grinding, keep the tool's temperature low by dipping it frequently in cool water so as to avoid loss of temper in the steel. Grind one side at a time, then level both sides until the nose is restored to shape.

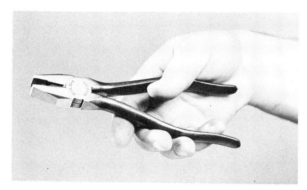

Hold pliers with handle in palm of hand, using the thumb as a cushion. Little finger opens pliers.

Certain pliers are suited to the job of nail cutting. Others are not designed for it and will nick, break.

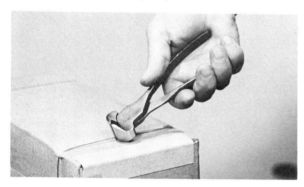

End-cutting pliers will snip through wire of all kinds, cut nails off flush with surface.

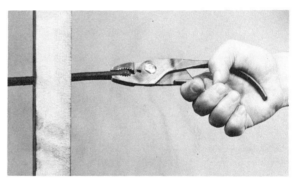

Curved handles on this type provide added gripping strength for forearm, do much extra work.

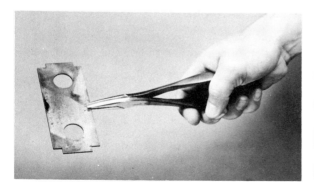

Duck-billed or flat-nosed pliers are ideal for holding fine or flat bits of metal when heated.

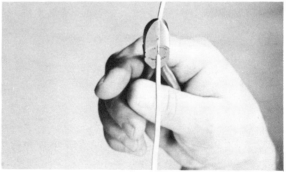

Combination wire-cutting pliers and insulation strippers; wire is being slipped through a hole to clean it of insulation.

This fine pair of spring-back pliers will be ruined if used to cut heavy-stranded cables. Try another!

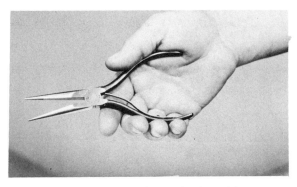

Needle-nosed pliers—handy for getting into tight corners, picking up delicate objects and parts.

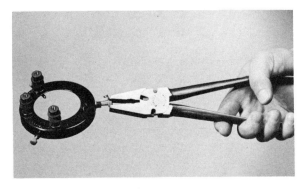

Long-handled pliers with multiple duties will prove useful on many handyman chores and electrical work.

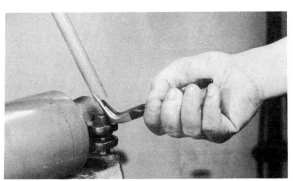

Bent-tip needle-nosed pliers work well in particularly confined areas.

WRENCHES

A wrench is patterned after the human hand with thumb and forefingers extended. In this position, you can turn objects in either direction. When the going becomes difficult, your fingers part and you need something stronger. Steel enters the picture in the form of a wrench.

Since pipes and nuts and other objects you may have to turn are quite varied as to size and shape, an assortment of wrenches has been developed. While the whole collection isn't needed around the house, your tool kit should include at least four types. They are: an adjustable, open-end wrench, a monkey wrench with its flat, smooth parallel jaws, a Stillson wrench for turning pipe (or better still, a pair of them, one to hold and one to turn), and a set of nonadjustable, open-end wrenches. Among the odd fellows of the wrench world, you'll also find essential the Allen wrench for recessed-head screws and the parallel-jawed pliers.

The majority of the wrenches mentioned are used to turn nuts of some kind, square or hexagonal. The very first requisite of the wrench is that it fit snugly against opposite sides of the nut. Unless it does, turning will wear off the corners of the nut quickly and it will become round. In working with pipe, a Stillson wrench is used. This tightens up under pressure and the teeth of the wrench bite into the pipe. Since turning a pipe tightly into a fitting can also turn the fitting and cause damage to extensions of the line, one wrench should be used to hold the fitting rigidly and the other to make the turn. If greater leverage is needed to open a stubborn pipe joint, a length of pipe may be slipped over the Stillson handle to lengthen it. Do *not* use a Stillson on chromed fittings where the teeth may cause damage. The plumbing

Open-end wrenches in graduated sizes provide just the right-sized opening for all sizes of nuts. Always choose the one that fits snugly over the sides of the nut. In this instance, the bolt is held fast by a pair of pliers in the other hand.

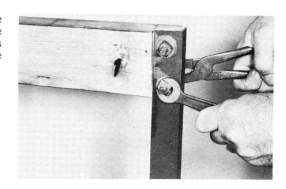

The adjustable open-end wrench is a timesaver, fitting an assortment of nut sizes on the job. Works as well on hexagonal nuts as on square types when tightened.

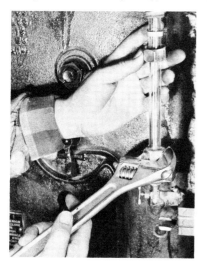

The Stillson is the plumber's wrench, fit for heavy duty. It slides around a pipe, its teeth grip deeply. In places where a joint is "frozen", pipe length slips over handle for leverage.

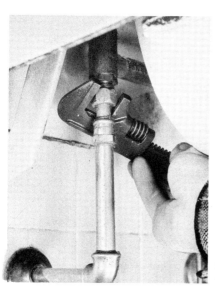

Monkey wrench, with parallel jaws, is also useful on plumbing where hex nuts are met with as part of pipe-joint unions.

When turning one pipe into another, two wrenches are necessary, one to hold fixed pipe rigid, one to turn new piece.

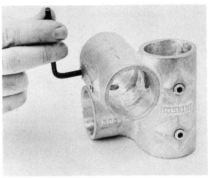

Allen wrench (or hex wrench) fits inside recessed-head screws to turn them. The leverage is provided by bend in shaft.

field has developed a number of special wrenches, among them the chain wrench for tight spots and the basin wrench for remote corners, to mention just two of them.

A nut, to be effective, must hold fast where placed. Though drawn up tight, it may vibrate loose. One way to prevent this is by use of a lock washer. Also, you can coat the threads with a special liquid that hardens and prohibits the nut from vibrating, though a wrench may loosen it.

When tightening a nut into wood, the wood may easily be damaged. As the wood shrinks, the nut is left free and its hold is reduced. To prevent this, a metal washer should be placed under the nut.

Keep a can of penetrating oil near the wrench rack in your tool shop. Fed into a rusted nut-bolt combination, it will penetrate and free the joint of rust, and you can loosen the nut then without twisting the bolt out of shape. Also, use the same lubricant on moving wrench parts to keep your wrench in tiptop condition.

FILES FOR METALS AND RASPS FOR WOOD

Files may be divided into two main groups—those used on wood and those used on metal. The kind used for smoothing and shaping wood are called wood rasps. The metal-cutting types are the true files.

Two rasps, one long and one short, will prove adequate to the needs of the average homeowner. A good type of rasp is curved on one side, flat on the other, and provided with two narrow, flat edges. The length is a matter of convenience and the size of the user's hand. There are many tight corners where the convenient, long-stroke, larger rasp will not fit.

While coping, keyhole, jig and band saws may be used with skill to the point where near perfection is possible, a neat, smooth curve or circle requires hand

retouching, and here is where the rasp goes to work. A few light strokes remove saw marks, imperfections and errors. Cutting notches, rounding edges and shaping irregular curves can be done quickly and accurately by use of the rasp, with no other tools needed. The roughing-out is done with the heavy-toothed end; then the rasp is reversed and the job finished with the finer teeth. Virtually no sanding is needed on such work if the rasp is properly used.

Small pieces should be clamped in a vise, the outline of the cut carefully marked and the rasp drawn with even strokes across the wood surface. Freehand work becomes possible as practice with the rasp creates confidence and skill.

The home handyman will want a rough-and-smooth, or wood and cabinet combination, wood rasp; the rough and smooth surfaces are usually found at opposite ends of the same tool, each grade extending to a center line. For the average home workshop, the rasps should include a middle or half-way in round and triangular shapes, a smooth-grade square file, a coarse half-round, a second-cut flat, and a smooth file of any obtainable shape. These should provide just about all answers for the usual needs. More intricate shop work on metals would require a wider range in all shapes and grades of fineness.

Working in the shop, the home handyman will find a set of files worth a dozen other implements. Constant use of files will keep all other cutting tools in working shape, putting keen burr-free edges on plane, chisel, saw, hatchet, drawknife, and ax. Garden tools such as hoes, spades, mowers, and clippers will do their work faster and with less effort on the part of the user when the edges are kept sharp by filing.

In repair work, there are dozens of jobs where the file will serve as no other tool will. Among them are such simple tasks as smoothing the ends of pipe cut with a hack saw, cutting through bolts which have rusted in place, substituting for a hack saw in cutting BX electric cable, reaming holes in metal for larger bolts, shaping scrap metal for patchwork. Again, when soldering and welding, the file is the first tool to pick up to remove rust and clean surfaces for a good bond between metals.

Files are made in a wide assortment of shapes. There are rattail, square, and triangular files, flat, half-round and combinations of these. There are files with flat edges and others with sharp edges to be used for cutting. While the full complement may not be needed by every handyman, at least seven should be kept available—the rattail or round, triangular, half-round, flat, square-tapered, the mill file and the wood rasp. Files, graded by the spaces between the teeth, are classified as rough, coarse, middle, halfway, bastard, second-cut, smooth, and superfine. These will be found in two forms: those with a single set of parallel lines of sharp edges set at about 25° across the file face, called mill files; and those with two sets of lines crossing each other, the second set of lines set at about 45°.

Your files and rasps can be kept in top shape if you protect them from rust by light oiling and keep the teeth free of debris by light wire-brushing.

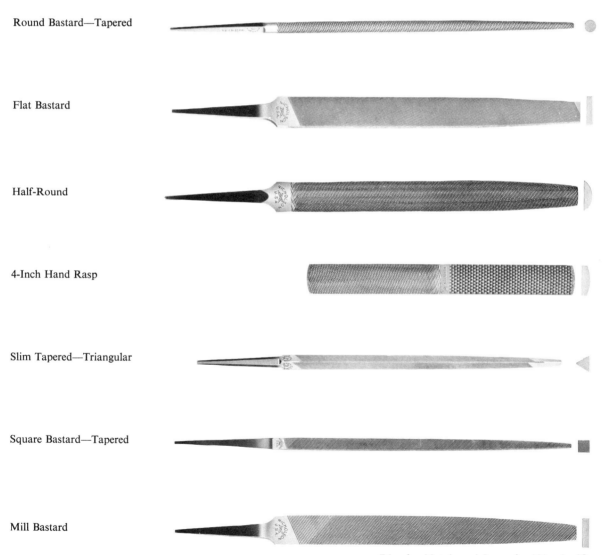

Round Bastard—Tapered

Flat Bastard

Half-Round

4-Inch Hand Rasp

Slim Tapered—Triangular

Square Bastard—Tapered

Mill Bastard

Files for Metals and Rasps for Wood   23

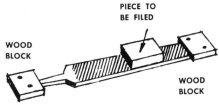

USING A METAL FILE

When working on small metal pieces, a bench vise is indispensable. A good light, proper elevation of the work, and a steady hand contribute to a good job. For one not skilled in draw filing, it may be better to secure the file on a bench with blocks and draw the work over it. Move work toward the tang (handle) end of the file, then lift up and start over.

RASPS

A wood rasp is far more coarse than a metal file. It takes away wood particles at a rapid rate. Yet its shape—a square edge, a flat back, and a curved face—makes it adjustable to almost any desired surface. Once you've used a rasp, you'll never be without it again. The handy double-ender has one end coarse, one much finer for real smoothing. Next time you are making wood joints, cut a tenon slightly oversize, then shape it to a snug fit with a rasp. Or polish off poorly cut dovetails the same way.

For rounding edges in simulation of aged colonial pieces the rasp is also handy. In addition, it will dress up scrolled pieces of trim.

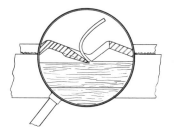

THE FILE THAT PLANES

Not quite a rasp, yet close enough to be a cousin, is this planelike device. It removes strips like shavings instead of particles. Yet it is used on the same jobs as a rasp, while it has all the control of an old-time plane.

PLIABLE RASP

With a surface as rough as a coarse wood rasp, but thin enough to be pliable, this piece of tough metal is wrapped around a block or stick and put to work. It shapes surfaces as readily as a rasp—and the holes keep the surface free from clogging.

KEEPING FILES IN GOOD SHAPE

Metal files are apt to clog with bits of plastic and very soft metal. This is easily cured by brushing along the scored lines with a stiff-bristle brush. After using *any* file, coat it lightly with fine machine oil. This stops rust —the one thing that can dull a file faster than the hardest steel.

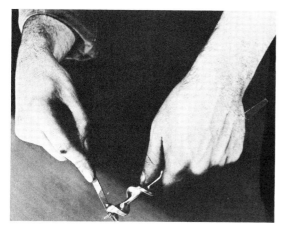

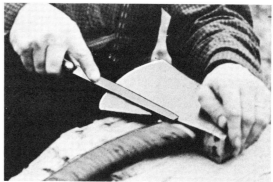

Augers may be kept clean by a few strokes of a file across the bevels.

Outdoor cutting tools, also, may be kept in top shape by filing.

PLANES

No carpentry can proceed very far without the use of a plane, which is simply a knife whose cutting ability is limited and directed as to width and depth. This controlled knife is highly essential to such operations as smoothing, trimming, and shaping pieces of wood. While freehand whittling requires skill and artistry, the controlled cutting of a plane blade makes precision work possible for skilled and unskilled alike.

Selection of the right plane for each job of carpentry is shown in the illustrations on the next page. The average workshop should have at least three planes—jack plane, smooth plane and block plane. For good joinery, add the dado plane, rabbet plane and plow. Or, for really fancy work, invest in a combination plane with which you will be able to make by hand virtually all shapes which can be turned out on a jointer-planer machine.

Remember that the plane is a knife, and to cut properly a knife must be sharp. Take your plane apart to become familiar with its parts: the lever cap, which is flipped upward to reduce tension on the blade and release it; the frog, which holds the blade to the body; and the blade itself. Examine

the edge of the blade as you would a knife. If nicked or dulled, it requires sharpening, and this must be done correctly. The bevel must be retained at 20° to 30°. With a circular motion, rub the back of the blade on an oil stone, held flat. The edge must be held at the correct angle against either an abrasive

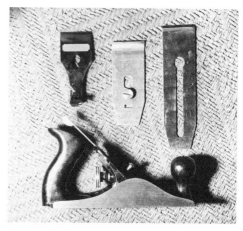

Steel-bodied plane with its three removable parts. Adjusting wheel and lever are not removed for sharpening.

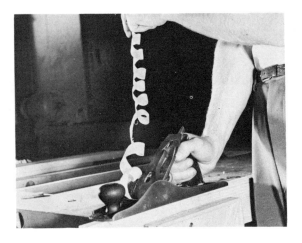

Sharp plane, properly adjusted, will peel off a shaving of equal thickness the full length of the planed board.

To plane down an uneven surface, first use short strokes across the raised portion only, before reducing the rest.

When planing knotty board, stroke to knot from opposite sides to prevent gouging adjoining wood and knot itself.

When planing end grain, stroke from each end toward center to prevent ripping edges. Note bevel to mark depth of cut.

Use jack plane for making bevels, as its length will guide the plane to an even stroke along the marked lines.

Combination plane with its variety of knives permits forming numerous shapes along edges and surfaces in one operation.

wheel or an oil stone. Replace the blade so it protrudes only slightly when the adjusting wheel is at maximum. Then retract the blade until the plane is to be used. In this way, you cannot dull or nick the blade when you lay the plane down.

CHISELS

Wood-chisel blades are uniform in shape, the edges of the larger ones being beveled to reduce their weight. The blades are ground off to a slant of 20°. Usually, a new chisel blade is heavily covered with a protective plastic coating which peels off for use. Beginners need a set of four: $\frac{1}{4}''$, $\frac{1}{2}''$, $\frac{3}{4}''$ and $1''$ widths. These will handle most jobs.

One of the most common jobs for a chisel is cutting a mortise or "gain" for the recessed leaves of hinges. After marking the hinge outline, hold the chisel vertically, beveled side toward the scrap, and tap it down into the mark. Score all around. Then turn the chisel so the bevel side rests on the wood and tap it along the grain, removing very thin slices of wood at a time. Continue until the exact thickness of the hinge leaf has been removed. When making a gain in a plywood veneer door, cut out the soft wood of the stile first, then remove the thin veneer strip. This method prevents marring the veneer with too deep a cut.

In cutting a gain for a cabinet-door hinge, first check the grain of the wood carefully. If it is not truly even, cut the gain as shown below. The first vertical cuts are made to outline the hinge, then a number of scored cuts are made through the scrap at equal distances. Remove part of the scrap with bevel side down, then smooth off the gain with the chisel laid flat on the wood, bevel side up. This last step is done without the use of the hammer.

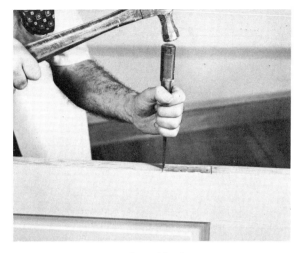

Cutting a Mortise

Cutting through Veneer

Removing Scrap in Chips

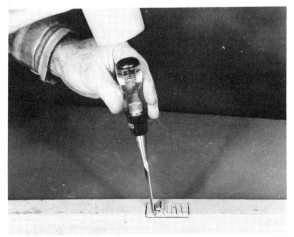

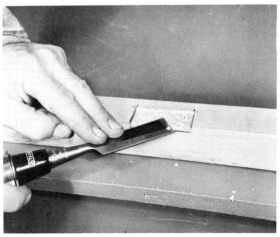

In cutting into plywood, cut only the depth of one ply with vertical cuts, remove that layer and cut those following one at a time. Many pieces you make with your shop tools will call for beveled edges. A plane does this neatly, but if the bevel is not the full length of the piece, the chisel is called upon. With pencil lines as a guide, and with a steady hand, the bevel is as neatly made as if done with a plane. Keep the beveled side of the chisel on the wood and, using hand pressure only, cut along the grain.

While tool lovers may shudder at the sight, you can use your chisel to remove putty from a window frame. Cut under the putty, using a light pressure to avoid gouging the wood. Keep the bevel side on the wood as a further precaution. You may dull the chisel by cutting into rock-hard putty—in which case it will need sharpening for further use. *Never* use your chisel in place of a screwdriver. It will turn the screws, but screws will also chew little pieces out of the blade. Store your chisels in racks or wrap each individually in protective coverings for storage. If left to lie in a drawer, they may become nicked.

OTHER WOOD CHISEL USES

Joining pieces of wood at angles calls for many special joints for strength; many are formed at least in part with a chisel. Aside from power tools, no other implement can do the work.

A mortise is cut like a hinge gain, only deeper and in the center of the wood. The job is done in a succession of identical steps, each series deepening the mortise until the desired depth is reached.

A dovetail—one of the strongest joints possible—is made by cutting diagonally into the wood with a saw, then removing the scrap with a chisel. It is important that the chisel be slightly narrower than the smaller dovetail base. While the entire dovetail can be made with the chisel, the saw cuts speed the work.

To form lap or tenon joints, the work is started with saw cuts, as with dovetails, but the finish must be done with a chisel. Use the same technique as with gains—scoring the scrap with closely placed cuts to avoid cutting too deeply on irregularly grained wood. Be sure to use a chisel narrower than the width of the cut.

DOVETAIL

TENON   LAP JOINT

COLD CHISELS

Still another group of chisels—the cold chisels—must have a place in your collection. These are used to cut metals and masonry.

No masonry repair job will progress far without a cold chisel. Cracks must be widened to provide a "key" for the patching material to be added. Use a chisel width suited to the job. These chisels are of unusually tough steel and cannot be broken.

Inside the house, a cold chisel is used to cut through plaster when patching is necessary or for new installations in walls.

The same chisel used to cut concrete can also cut and split stone.

Wear heavy gloves—at least on the chisel-holding hand—as a protection in case you miss the chisel with the hammer. And, when cutting masonry, goggles are a good investment for eye protection.

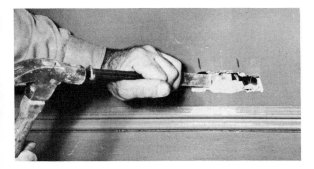  

LEVELS

Very few of the walls in your home are truly vertical. More than likely the floors slope, too. You won't be aware of these facts until you try to put up wallpaper which has a striped pattern or until you try to match a built-in to a wall and it comes out all askew.

You won't be able to do much at all in the way of successful remodeling or redecorating without a level to establish true vertical and horizontal dimensions as new starting points.

If you have been using the little level set in the short leg of your try square, you probably noticed that it is difficult to check a long span. It's a handy thing for small work in the shop, but a bigger level is better for bigger chores. It's a good idea to have one on hand about 1½' to 2' long—one which will take both horizontal and vertical readings on separate dials. Such levels are made of hardwood or a light metal such as aluminum or magnesium. The wood variety does well in a shop, but those of metal are best for masonry work and outdoor construction since they are unaffected by moisture.

For a large outdoor project, you can clamp your level to a long wood or metal straightedge to span considerable distances, a trick which is useful in foundation and masonry wall construction. But there is another way to level up these larger projects, too. In fact, there are several other ways. One, called a line level, consists of a very small level which is fitted with hooks that enable it to slide on a tight line. You use the line as your guide. Or, to make two remote points level, try the type consisting of a thin hose, filled with a colored liquid, which is attached to two indicators at the ends. Fasten one end at the desired height, and the other end will indicate that height by the rise or fall of the fluid.

Metal beam level cannot be distorted by weather or temperature; a special type also indicates degree of slope—useful for many operations.

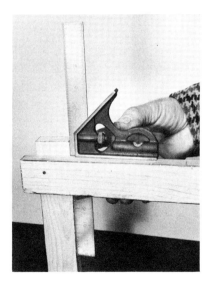

Any try square usually has small level in one "leg." Fine for short distances, it is not practical for wide spans.

Not even the simple job of putting in preformed shelves can be done correctly without use of a level to check the vertical as well as the horizontal lines. If the supports (right) are not "true," shelves (below) cannot be level.

Levels 29

VISES AND CLAMPS

Sometimes, though you measure accurately and assemble properly, the finished product may turn out to be just a distortion of the original intent. Crooked cuts, uneven edges, poor joints—these are typical of the bungled job. When a piece of wood is held firmly in a vise for cutting and planing, and when the assembled piece is firmly and accurately clamped when joined, the results are likely to improve 100 per cent.

Selection of a vise depends on the type of work being done. The primary requirements are that it be strong, firmly mounted and accurate in the meeting of the jaws. It must grip tightly, hold fast without marring, and to save annoyance, operate smoothly and rapidly. Some vises are mounted on the bench with turn screws, others with wood screws set in holes or slots. Some are embedded in notches and cuts in the bench itself. For multipurpose duty, those giving a variety of holding surfaces and positions lend themselves best to handyman activities. One of the types, pictured directly below, may be swung up or laid over. Another has extra, removable jaws which hold pipe for cutting and threading.

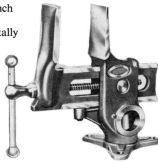

Typical home workbench vise which works both vertically and horizontally

When board is held in vise for planing, the workmanship improves.

Woodworking vise for end-of-bench use is handy for home workshops.

Some bench vises may be converted by adding special jaws to hold pipe.

There is no substitute for a pipe vise when threading pipe ends.

The big difference between vises and clamps is that clamps are portable and move about on the job while the vise is stationary. Both, however, perform the same basic function of applying equal pressure from opposing ends toward the center. Both employ the screw as a means to apply controlled pressure in measurable amounts.

For large jointing, such as building up a wide glued board from several small ones, the bar clamp is

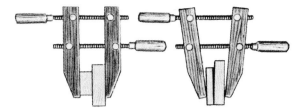

Hand screw clamps require care in applying pressure. Turn both screws at once.

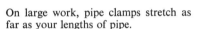

On large work, pipe clamps stretch as far as your lengths of pipe.

When gluing little boards to make big ones, bar clamps are a real asset.

Entire pieces of furniture may be glued if you have enough clamps.

used. This consists of a long bar, flat or round, with a movable tail-stop held to the bar and a sliding head equipped with a screw turned by a handle or wheel. It is a simple matter to provide yourself with a large stock of these bar clamps by buying just the tail-stop and head to fit a specified pipe diameter, then buying scrap pipe in assorted lengths to go with these essentials. The pipe need only be straight and smooth. Press screws are simple mechanisms which, when braced properly, are turned by a handle on the screw end to apply pressure on flat work.

There are hundreds of types and makes of clamps in addition to these, but this group will provide most of the necessary equipment for the average home-owner. A stock of assorted C-clamps is the only suggested addition.

With all clamps and vises, it is well to remember that heavy pressures crush softwoods. To prevent injuries of this sort, which may ruin a project, large blocks are used to distribute the pressure over a wider surface. Provide yourself with a stock of blocks, assorted sizes, thicknesses and lengths, preferably of hardwood such as maple or gum. For vises, of course, thin strips of plywood will often do the trick.

MEASURING

Before any sort of project is undertaken, measurements of materials must be made—accurately. Starting with a 1' ruler, a folding rule for greater lengths and a tape which rolls up into a pocket-size case,

the careful home handyman will quickly graduate to more complicated measuring tools, and these will spell the difference between a good job or one badly made. By all means include in your tool chest various squares, fixed or adjustable. And, if you are apt to shy away from complicated arithmetic, try the framing-square substitute which does the figuring for you right on its arms. How to use the various devices is shown pictorially.

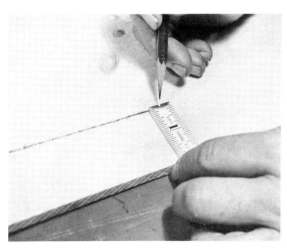

1. Straight-line mark, for rough cut, needs only a pencil in the indent of the rule, and a finger held at the mark and run along board edge. →

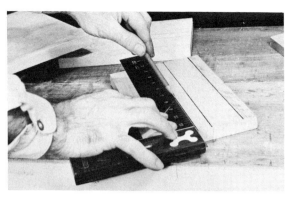

2. More accurate mark requires straightedge plus angle guide—in this case a mark of 90°, or at right angles, to the guiding edge of board.

3. Same angled guide rule makes it possible to mark right on around the piece to be cut, tells at a glance if board is "true" all around.

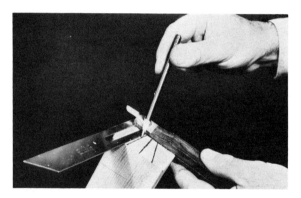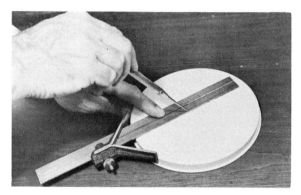

4. Adjustable guide can be preset to desired angles and, when set screw is tightened, will hold angle for repeated markings and reverses.

5. No question about locating the center of a circle when this device is employed. Two legs, resting on circumference, indicate radius line, and any two intersecting lines mark the center.

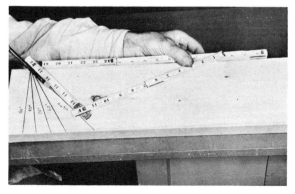

6. A steel square is an invaluable aid in laying out angles to be cut in rafters.

7. Folding rule can be used in place of framing square for various angled cuts, but lacks accuracy owing to flexibility of rule joints.

SANDING (ABRASIVES)

Sandpapering should be a major factor in all handyman operations. There are few jobs around the house where sandpaper does not play an important part, no matter whether on wood, metal, plaster or fabricated materials. Various minerals applied to paper, cloth or fiber backings are used to make sandpapers; yet not a single grain of sand goes into any of them. The minerals used are as follows:

Flint—actually white quartz, similar to white sand in appearance and largely responsible for the descriptive name of sandpaper. It is not as hard or as tough as the other minerals used.

Garnet—a red quartz, heat-tempered to increase its hardness. This is the ideal abrasive for wood sanding.

Emery—tougher than garnet, but with a poor cutting edge. It is primarily used in polishing metal to remove rust, grease and dirt.

Aluminum oxide—also a product of the electric furnace, a shiny black, brittle abrasive. It is excellent for work on wood or metal, on enamel and lacquer, on glass, marble or leather. When used with a waterproof backing and a sanding lubricant, this is the ideal paper for satin finish on shellac, varnish and lacquer.

After having been mined or manufactured, these abrasive materials are crushed, screened to size and applied to adhesive-coated backings. When applied *closed*, no space remains between particles and the backing is completely covered. When applied *open*, space is left between particles on the backing. This permits dust and other materials removed by sanding to fall free of the paper. It does not clog. A noted example of this type is the coarse abrasive used for floor refinishing.

The correct use of sandpaper starts with the selection of the right kind of grit, the right size of grit and the correct backing. The choice may be made as follows: (1) To remove thick varnish or paint coats preparatory to refinishing, use the very coarse grade. (2) For rough sanding of raw wood to remove irregularities, saw marks, dents and gouges, use coarse. (3) For smoothing operations after the use of coarse grade, use medium grade. (4) For final bare wood finishing, use the fine grit.

Open coating (middle two) removes old paint finishes; closed coating smooths wood surface, hard finishes.

Wrong way to sand by hand. Fingertip pressure produces uneven streaks in wood surface.

Correct hand sanding without block requires flat palm, closed fingers, uniform pressure.

Best way: use sanding block for an even surface, with a smooth professional finish.

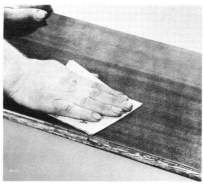

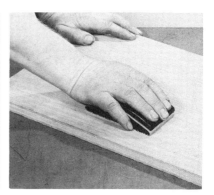

Sanding (Abrasives)   33

ADHESIVES

A good adhesive must do two things—adhere to the surface to which applied and cohere to itself. On those surfaces which are porous, the glue penetrates so that it sticks to the surface. Then the glue remaining outside the pores must adhere not only to that inside the pores but to the object to which this material is to be attached. This is true when used on wood, fabric and leather. When you try to glue together less porous materials such as glass, plastic, metal and glazed tile, the glue must adhere to the outside only. Then it must adhere to a similar coating of the same adhesive applied to the other material. Not all glues and adhesives have this latter ability.

The rules for good gluing are simple: (1) choose

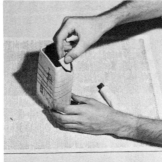

You can use synthetic thermoplastic resin glue to mend china, glassware. It may not hold up under heat or repeated dishwashing, so it's best only for bric-a-brac, art pieces.

Cement only two pieces together at a time, then let stand 24 hours before adding each next piece. This way you won't strain the glue with weight, move pieces out of place.

Liquid animal and fish glues have long been used on wood joining, where they have great strength. Liquid form makes them easy to apply and to store for future use.

Clamping is necessary with liquid fish and animal glues. Use scrap blocks or strips to keep clamps from marring wood.

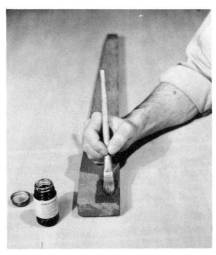
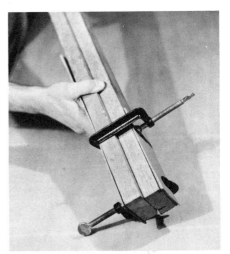

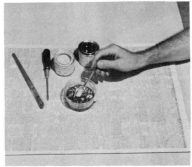

Accurate measuring is important when mixing synthetic thermosetting resin glues. Mix the activating powder into resin, using disposable implements.

This type of glue has a working life of about 4 hours. Don't mix too much, and unless you throw away containers, wash them out quickly within the 4-hour limit.

the right glue, (2) follow the manufacturer's directions carefully, and (3) give the adhesive a chance to "set." If you place a great strain on the pieces before then, the joint may separate and the job has to be done again.

Follow the chart for the proper selection of glue. It will show why some of your previous gluing projects may have failed. Metal-to-metal bonding presents a special problem since a greater strain is expected and the glue itself must do the holding. Contact and epoxy resins are the best choices. Ornamental metals, carrying no great weight, can rely on rubber-base cement. Needless to say, both metal surfaces must be thoroughly clean and ample time must be allowed for setting.

One word of caution: some adhesives can be

Selecting the Right Adhesive

Adhesive	Characteristics	Drying Time	Heat Resistance	Moisture Resistance	Uses (Primary in **boldface** type) (Secondary in lightface type)
Paste	white, semi-fluid, safe for children, brittle when dry	slow	little	none	**Paper,** some tight-weave fabrics
Vegetable glue natural resin	clear to pale yellow, safe for children, fluid, brittle when dry	slow to medium	little	little	**Paper, cardboard, close-weave fabrics**
Animal and fish glue	liquid, clear to amber, brittle when dry	slow	slight	little	**Wood,** paper, cardboard, close-weave fabrics
Casein glue	powder for mixing or in prepared liquid mix, clear to pale yellow, dries hard and brittle	medium fast	good	little	**All wood,** wood to cement and plaster; heavy fabrics, leather to wood
Casein-latex	flexible when dry, usually clear, will not stain	medium fast	good	good	**Repairs,** good on metal, glass, fabrics, ceramics, leather, some plastics, felt
Thermoplastic resins (synthetic)	usually powder for mixing on job (some are prepared for use); will damage some plastics, rubber and lacquers	fast	little	little	**Leather, paper,** non-plastic fabrics, wood, china, glass
Thermosetting resins (synthetic)	usually powder for mixing; light shade, won't stain	medium fast	very good	excellent	**Wood (boats),** fabrics, paper, cardboard
Contacts	thick fluid, spread with toothed applicator; cannot be separated	very fast	very good	excellent	**Plastic laminates to wood** and for joining unlike materials
Mastics	heavy paste, usually dark, spread with toothed applicator	slow to medium	little	little—some are waterproofed	**Application of floor tiles, wall materials to furring, ceiling tiles to plaster, floor linoleum, ceramic and plastic tiles**
Rubber cement	may be thinned with solvent, dries clear, may be re-softened with solvent	fast	little	excellent	**Paper,** some fabrics, books
Rubber-base adhesives	light or dark, heavy fluid for trowel application or from tubes	fast	good	excellent	**All-purpose mending,** will join unlike materials of all kinds

dissolved with solvents or other chemicals, some cannot. Consequently, keep these points in mind when handling adhesives:

1. If you get an adhesive on your hands, be sure to wipe it off before it sets. Some types will set in a matter of seconds.

2. Some adhesives, once joined to themselves—notably contact bonds—cannot be separated once they've touched. This leaves a ruined piece of work if the joining was faulty. It can't be undone for a new start.

3. Adhesive spilled on material is always bad. The solvent in some plastic-base adhesives will destroy other plastic materials. Adhesion of dried mastics to various surfaces may never be undone without damage. In other words, be careful.

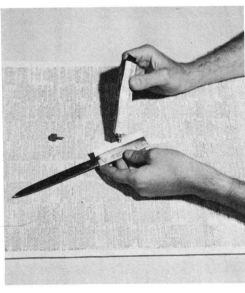

Clear household cement can be used to attach leather to metal, as with this leather handle on a metal letter opener. Give leather a primer coating first.

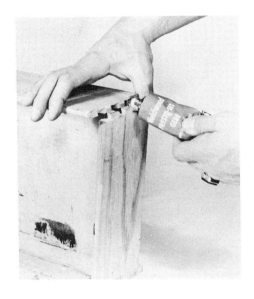

Polyvinyl acetate glues are easy to use, often sold in tubes. Good for gluing any porous materials but do not have great strength, can weaken under heat and moisture.

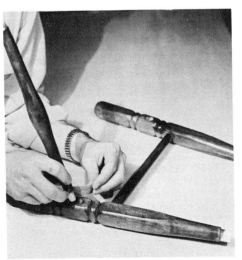

Liquid animal and fish glues are good for furniture mending. Remove old glue first, apply thin coat, let become tacky and apply second coat, then join and clamp.

If chair rung fits loosely, wrap the end with glue-soaked cloth and join, then apply a rope windlass and tighten up as a clamp. Protect wood from marring by rope.

1. Contact cement permits joining plastic laminate sheets to plywood or other surfaces. A toothed spreader distributes even coat of bond over the entire surface.
2. Apply a coat of the contact bond to the back of the laminate sheet as well. Allow both to dry until tacky. About ½ hour is enough, up to 2 hours in confined areas.

3. To avoid trouble, cover the plywood, all but a narrow strip down the side, with kraft paper, then rest laminate on it. When aligned, withdraw the paper so that bonds unite.
4. Press the two together with a small roller (even a rolling pin will do the trick) to insure proper contact all over. No clamping is necessary.

Marred tops of old furniture can be covered with laminates by using contact adhesive. Be sure old surface is free of wax, oily polish, flaky paint scale.

Although mastic is used mainly to set tiles, it can also be used to set wall and ceiling materials on flat surfaces. Spread mastic with toothed trowel, press material into mastic.

Adhesives 37

1. You can put up panel materials of all kinds with contact adhesives on furring strips. Position of the strips is located on the back of the panel stock, adhesive applied there.
2. Furring strips are then coated with the same bond. Both applications are allowed to become tacky before the sheet is put carefully into position. Paper is not used here.
3. Once contact is made, use a block and a hammer and lightly tap along all seams to insure firm union between bond of both surfaces. Positive adhesion is certain.

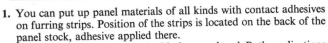

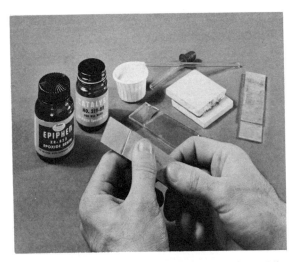

Epoxy resin adhesives are mixed at the time of use. Like materials or unlike materials can be glued. All joints become waterproof, heatproof. Careful measuring of mix is needed; containers should be disposable since adhesive won't come off.

As an example of what modern adhesives can do, these nails attached to metal plates adhere to masonry walls to hold furring.

Pressure-sensitive adhesives, or rapid-dry types, will hold fixtures on glazed tiles or glass. Hook will hold weight in minutes.

Whereas many plaster menders used to fail through fall-outs, adhesive applied first now holds plaster patch securely in cracks.

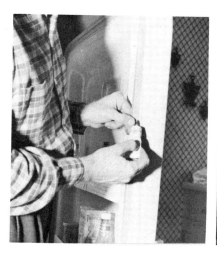

Ordinary glue won't hold rubber to steel, but to put the gasket back on your refrigerator, rubber-base adhesive works very well.

Mastics for holding down tiles and linoleum are well known. They spread with a toothed trowel, exposing floor between ridges.

Rubber cement, often confined to office routine, has a household use, too. Solvent that thins it makes paper removal possible.

Contact adhesives are versatile, will work on wood. Here, split on curve of sled is mended with contact cement and temporary clamping device. In this case, the clamp simply pulls surfaces together; adhesive holds on contact.

CARE OF YOUR TOOLS

Rustproofing. Rust is the archenemy of tools. You will have to contend with it sooner or later. It cuts down the efficiency of the tools and, consequently, the quality of your work. Rust prevention is a most important part of the care of your tools. These photographs show how rust is removed and various preventives applied. The methods are simple and fast and well worth the time.

1. Before applying any protective coatings, rust must be removed. Rust remover is good for light formations on any tools.

2. Steel wool is often used to remove rust from tools; as you rub add a few drops of cutting oil, available in hardware stores, to surface.

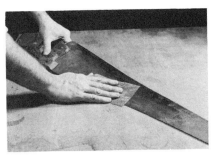

3. Rust may be removed from hand saws and other tools by using emery cloth. Later, apply a protective rust-preventive coating.

4. Pitch must be removed from saw blades before applying oil or petroleum jelly. Use special removers, available in hardware stores, for this.

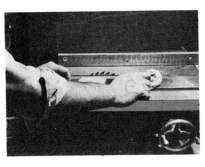

5. A small block of paraffin is very inexpensive. Use it for coating saw tables to prevent rust formation in the future.

6. Ordinary paste wax offers protection, too, against rust. Surfaces must be clean before applying wax or any other coating.

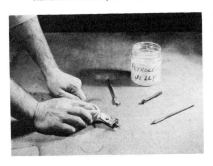

7. Petroleum jelly is an excellent rust preventive. Light grease is just as suitable; apply with cloth.

8. You can use a pressurized oil spray on tools not handled often. Acrylic sprays may be used as well as the oil.

9. Brush or spray metal bluing (Prussian blue, diemaker's blue) on tools not handled constantly.

Sharpening Cutting Edges. No tool designed for cutting will please you when it fails to cut. It will mar your work and make work of what should be fun. The basic material used in sharpening is an abrasive—either a file, sandpaper, or abrasive stones. If, during the sharpening process, these become so clogged with bits of metal that they are no longer effective, you can remove many of the metal particles with gummy wallpaper cleaner, adhesive tape or a strong magnet run along the abrasive surface. Any nonmagnetic metal particles which are firmly imbedded can also be cleaned out with a very fine wire brush.

Oil and water are often used in sharpening operations. It isn't so much that the abrasive needs the lubrication as the fact that the presence of the liquids reduces the heat of friction during the process. Too much heat anneals hardened metals, takes the temper out of steel. Oil or water prevent this damage and help form and keep a keen edge.

Once you have gone to the trouble to sharpen a cutting edge, protect it. A knife, a chisel or a saw newly sharpened and then flung among others will be quickly ruined. Make a place for each of these tools so that they can be stored where nothing can touch the blades or damage the edges.

TONE UP GARDEN TOOLS

A busy hoe needs a keen edge. Hammer out burrs on a solid surface, then go to work to reshape the cutting edge with a file. File away burrs on the top edge, making the bevel entirely on the outer surface which scrapes along the ground. A few strokes while the hoe's in use, this time with a Carborundum stone, will keep the tool in perfect condition.

KEEPING THE LAWNMOWER FIT

No mower can cut grass with a dull blade. It merely chews off the grass, leaving it brown-tipped and ugly. Sharpen the rotary-mower blade, held in vise, with a mill file, whether the blade is metal or plastic. A few strokes of a Carborundum stick will put a keen edge on the bed knife of your reel mower—all the sharpening it should need for a season.

SHARPEN EDGERS AND SHEARS

Hand-powered grass clippers and trimmers must be razor-sharp to save your arm muscle. A file to put on a new edge, and a fine-grained Carborundum stone to keep it sharp, will do the job for you. Like the job of sharpening shears, this one can be botched. Be sure to keep the beveled edges on the outer surfaces. The meeting edges should be sharp, without bevel.

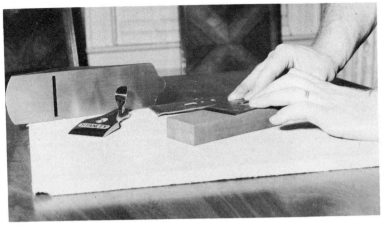

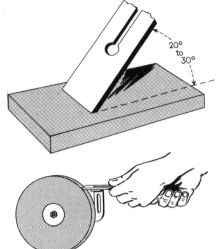

SHARPENING A PLANE

A plane blade must be sharp or it will gouge, must be free of burrs or it will leave streaks. Your plane requires resharpening at intervals. The job is done as shown here.

1. Lay the blade flat on an abrasive block and remove burrs with a rotary motion.

2. Lay beveled side against stone at a 20° to 30° angle and again use rotary motion to sharpen.

3. If preferred, a drum sander, grinding wheel, or other power-operated abrasive surface may be used. Be sure to hold tool firmly and at correct angle. After sharpening on power grinder, finish up on oiled stone—coarse grit first, then fine.

SHARPENING A CHISEL

As with the plane blade, sharpen a chisel by first removing nicks and burrs, holding the back of the blade flat on a stone. Then reverse and sharpen the beveled side. Here too, a rotating grinding wheel or sanding disc may be employed. But the final touch-up is a brief honing on an oil stone.

WHAT EVERY BOY KNOWS ABOUT KNIVES

A jackknife is a boy's first friend, and he soon learns the basic fact that use makes it dull. Then he learns that rubbing it on a rock makes it sharp again. Experts say the best way to sharpen a dull knife is with a Carborundum stone stroked as shown. Then keep it in shape with a few strokes on a sheet of sandpaper, tacked to the workbench, each time the knife is used.

SHARPENING THE HOUSEHOLD CUTLERY

While kitchen pin-up sharpeners will do much to keep carving and paring knives keen, now and then a thorough overhaul of the cutting edges is necessary. Start with a grinding wheel to remove nicks and to provide the concave "razor"-shaped edge. Keep the angle of the blade slight—not over 20°—to avoid rounding edge.

Finish up with fine-grit Carborundum sticks, drawing the blades across the abrasive away from —never toward—the sharp edge. Sharpen both sides of the blade. Use a light touch even on the toughest steel.

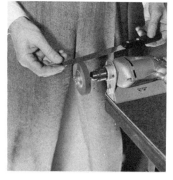
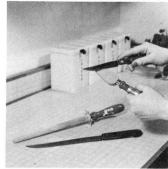

GROUNDING POWER TOOLS

All power tools, particularly portable power tools, should be grounded *every* time you use them. Grounding is a safeguard, for if the tool "shorts" and becomes "hot" or "live" with electricity, the current will pass through a grounded tool instead of through the user. Grounding is especially necessary when working in a damp basement, outdoors in grass, or around plumbing and heating pipes.

1. Some devices designed to save you from shock: 3-prong plug, 3-way female-plug extension cord, 2-prong plug with pigtail to ground wire to grounded pipe.

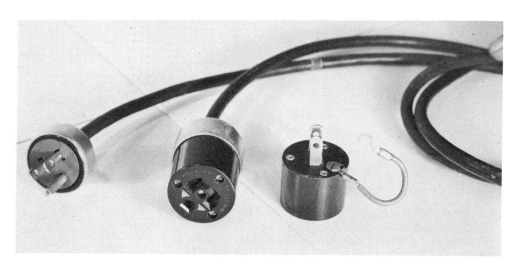

→

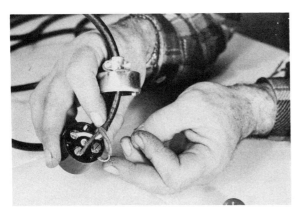 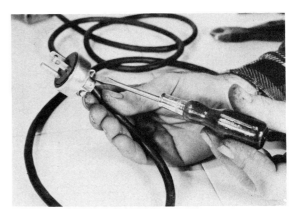

2. 3-wire cord of power tool may be fitted with pigtail on the third off-color screw.
3. Plug may also be provided with special round prong for insertion into 3-way outlet.

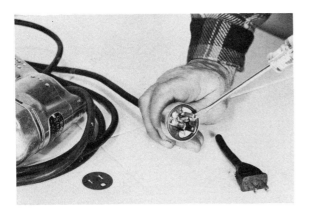 

4. If tool cord has 2-prong plug with pigtail, this can be removed and new plug added.
5. Plug with side pigtail is grounded to special type of screw on center of outlet plate.

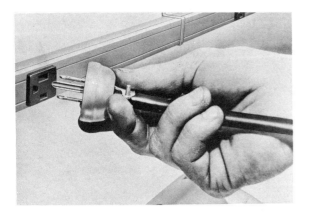 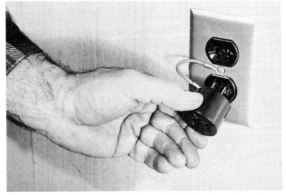

6. 3-prong plug can be fitted into grounded wall outlet designed to match with it.
7. Standard outlet can be fitted with 3-prong adapter, third wire grounded to screw.

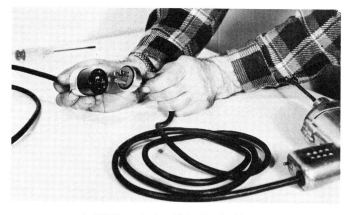
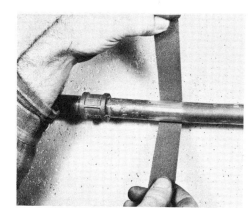

8. While tools should be fitted with ground, extension cords should also be equipped for grounding.
9. If electric system uses BX cable, ground to it; if not, ground to water pipe. Sand pipe clean, then . . .

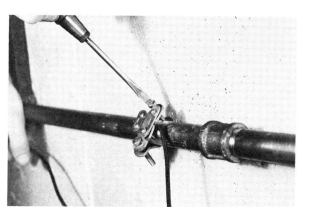
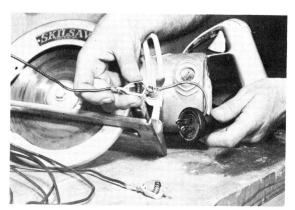

10. . . . attach ground wire to sanded area with special screw-type clamp to hold it fast.
11. Ground wire from pipe is attached to pigtail of cord, or to tool, or to both.

THE QUARTER-INCH DRILL

For the home handyman, the ¼″ electric drill, among all power tools, rates supreme. By using inexpensive accessories, it will saw wood, drive screws, rough-sand and finish a cabinet, sharpen a knife, mix paint, cut hedges, and more. It's a "do-everything" tool whose usefulness grows on you.

Most drills for home use have universal motors, that is, they will work on both DC and AC currents (any cycle).

A chuck is on the work end of the drill. It holds drill bits and varied tools. A geared key chuck is practically a must on all electric drills. In general use, any speed from 1,800 to 2,500 rpm is all right. All speed selections by the manufacturers are compromises, since there is no ideal speed for general use. The labels on home craft drills giving power ratings are of dubious value. Amperage ratings, as a means of comparison, are useless. There are no established standards for rating nonindustrial drills. Electric drills have universal motors which deliver different power under different loads, and the horsepower is not constant.

In operation, a drill which is hot to the touch is an overloaded drill and needs a rest. Lack of air will cause overheating, so be sure vent holes are dirt-free. In average use, drills require greasing once a year. First remove the front gear housing and wash out the old grease with kerosene, then half fill with fresh, medium-weight auto grease. Other defects common to drills, and their remedies, are shown in the photographs on pages 47 and 48.

Always keep your drill bits sharp. This will reduce

the load on the motor. Should the motor stall, don't click the switch on and off in an effort to restart it. Get to the core of the trouble instead, or the motor may be seriously damaged.

A jig-saw attachment makes decorative cutting and valance making easy. This unit will cut 1¼″ pine and the softer metals, and starts its own hole. Don't push the jig-saw—let the motor do the work. You need, for jig-sawing, a speed of about 2,000 to 2,500 rpm.

This orbital sanding attachment adjusts to fit almost any ¼″ drill made and is designed for fine sanding and finishing. It uses one-third of a standard sheet of abrasive paper—aluminum oxide open coat is recommended. Rubbing felt can be used (with rottenstone or pumice) in place of abrasive sheets for rubbing varnish.

On such jobs as running BX cable through beams and studs, there is rarely enough space to get the drill into position to make the hole. A right-angle drive is the answer to this one: this unit takes any size of chuck up to ½″ and has a 2-to-1 speed reducer.

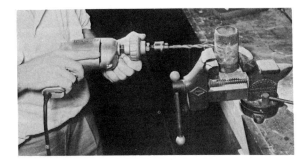

When you need more power than your drill can deliver, a 5-to-1 speed reducer will multiply the torque. It's similar to putting a car into low gear to get more push at the rear wheels. This is the answer if you must drill holes in steel.

A 5″ flexible sanding disc is one of the first accessories you should buy. It's considered a rough sander, but with a little practice you'll achieve much better results later on. Get a variety of abrasive discs. Let the speed of the disc do the sanding and don't press down. Start and stop the disc off the work. If you don't, you'll get swirls that are difficult to remove.

1. The first sign of overloading is heating. Is drill too hot to touch? Rest it. Lack of air often causes overheating. Clear vent holes of any blocking dirt.

2. In average use, drills require greasing once a year. Remove front gear housing, wash out old grease with kerosene. Half fill with fresh, medium-weight auto grease.

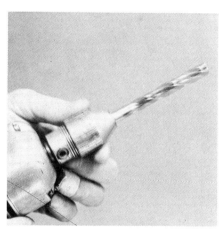

3. Excessive play in chuck spindle eventually will cause serious damage to drive gears and the motor itself. Remedy by replacing spindle bearing with new one, as follows.

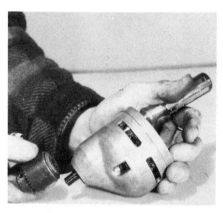

4. Remove the gear housing, jam the gear with a screwdriver, and remove the chuck by turning it to the left. The gear may now be slipped from the housing.

5. "Pressed fit" bearing is removed by filing a dowel to size and tapping bearing out. Replacement parts are available from factory or through hardware dealer.

6. Tap new bearing into place with help of wood scrap and the large gear, reversed, after first ascertaining that new bearing is smooth and free of burrs.

The Quarter-Inch Drill   47

ARMATURE

8. Sometimes motor won't run because of a defective switch. Disconnect wires *A* and *B* from the switch and connect their bare ends, thus bypassing switch. If motor now runs, switch is at fault. If motor still balks, investigate brushes.

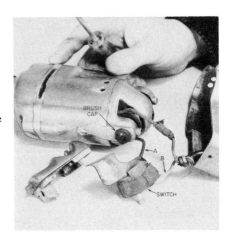

BRUSH CAP

A

B

SWITCH

7. If motor won't run, check cord by bending it with current on. Check plug and outlet for obvious breaks. With current on, spin chuck. If motor then runs, but without pep, there's a broken wire in the armature. Replace armature.

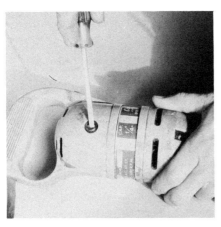

10. If motor becomes hot, even when under no load, suspect a short in field coil or armature. Only a shop can test for such shorts. Without equipment, you can test only by replacing suspect parts.

9. In some models, brushes are accessible by removing caps on outside. In other models, brush caps are inside (see 8). If burned, chipped, or worn to within ¼″ of springs, brushes should be replaced. Springs should be lively and unbroken.

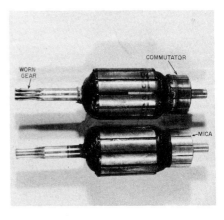

WORN GEAR

COMMUTATOR

MICA

11. Sometimes motor failure is due to break in field coil. Test is made by running electricity through the coil to a light bulb. Bulb's failure to light indicates break in coil wire. Be careful with bare wires.

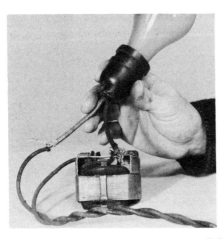

12. If motor runs and chuck does not turn, armature shaft gear has worn off. Replace armature. Excessive brush sparks indicate high mica dividers. Use hacksaw blade to undercut them below level of copper.

DRILL BITS

No matter what the project, drilling holes is frequently an important part of it. Selection of the drill especially suited to the job makes all the difference between good results and bad. Properly speaking, the part that makes the hole is a drill bit, and it is rotated by a drill, either hand-powered or electrically operated. Drill bits fall into two major classes: slow-speed auger-style bits and high-speed drill bits which are usually electrically operated. The former are used almost entirely in braces or hand-powered devices. The high-speed drill bits can be rotated in a number of ways, some by hand, some by power. Then there is the long list of specialty bits for specific purposes.

To acquaint the handyman with a drill bit and to identify each section, an enlarged sketch is shown here. Not all of the terms are important to boring a hole, but the reasons behind the variations help in choosing the right type for the specific job. In general, sharply tapered points are for rapid piercing of soft materials. Blunt points are intended for slower penetration of tough materials. When the material to be drilled is soft, the size and angle of the flutes and rake are designed to carry away the scrap rapidly so the hole is kept clean, thus avoiding stalling the bit. When drilling metal, for example, only tiny fragments are removed on each revolution, so the angle and size of these portions of the bit are designed accordingly.

The considerable variation in drill bits, showing these changes in design, is indicated in the large photograph on the next page. Different makers of drills do their own engineering and develop what they consider the best tool for each job. Finally, there is the group of drills for specific purposes, such as making holes in hard or soft metal, glass or ceramic tile and plastics. The purpose for which each is designed is indicated by the shape of the bit.

It is not enough to simply make a hole with a drill. The hole must be the right size and, since two objects are to be joined, there must be two matching holes, one in each piece of material, and the line through the centers of the holes must be straight. If the two materials are of equal density, it is easiest to clamp them together and drill through both in one

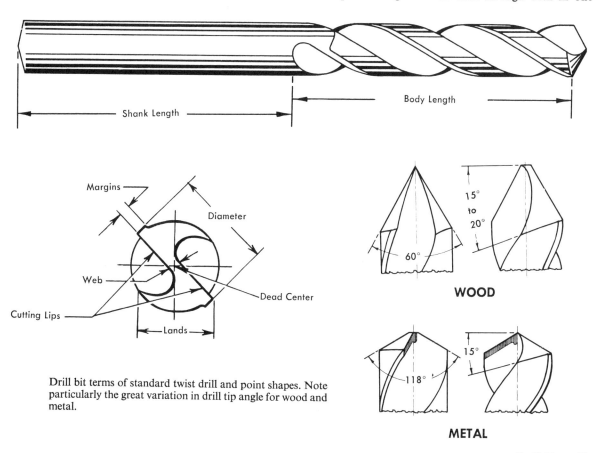

Drill bit terms of standard twist drill and point shapes. Note particularly the great variation in drill tip angle for wood and metal.

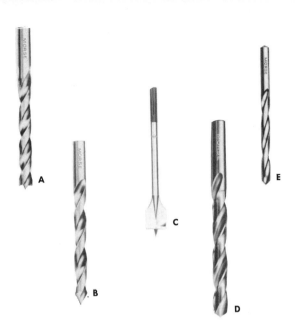

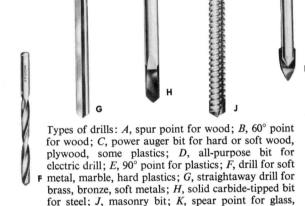

Types of drills: *A*, spur point for wood; *B*, 60° point for wood; *C*, power auger bit for hard or soft wood, plywood, some plastics; *D*, all-purpose bit for electric drill; *E*, 90° point for plastics; *F*, drill for soft metal, marble, hard plastics; *G*, straightaway drill for brass, bronze, soft metals; *H*, solid carbide-tipped bit for steel; *J*, masonry bit; *K*, spear point for glass, glazed ceramic tile, porcelain.

operation. When a hole must be at a right angle to the surface being drilled, a jig is needed to guide the bit because your eye alone is not precise enough.

In determining the hole size, consider the material. If it's rigid, such as steel, the fastener cannot expand or bite into it. The hole must, therefore, match the size of the fastener. In the case of wood, however, where a screw is to be fitted into the hole, the hole itself must be smaller than the screw so that its threads have something to grip. A bolt with a diameter of $\frac{3}{16}''$, for example, requires a hole of the same diameter in steel, or slightly larger, whereas a hole in softwood may be as much as a third smaller than the diameter of the screw. In hardwoods, it is best to use a drill bit which outlines the shape of the screw (see photo). In soft metal, the hole may be made slightly smaller and a self-tapping screw used since this type threads the hole by itself.

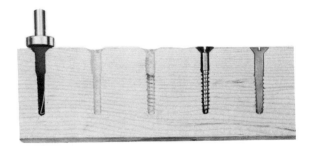

Drill bits may be used to match screw shapes—particularly useful in hardwoods. Bit makes hole to fit screw, also provides for countersetting, can make recess for plug in hole.

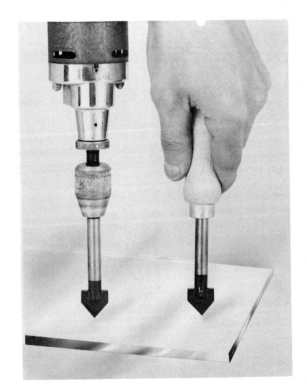

Drill specially designed to bore holes in glass may be operated by hand or in electric drill chuck. Bit will also drill concrete, brick, cinder blocks, tile, and hard plastic.

Hole-cutting saw acts like drill but cuts perfect plugs for reinsertion if desired. The attachment is adjustable to various hole sizes as needed.

Adjustable drill-guiding jig can be clamped to work. The various holes fit an assortment of drill bit sizes. With this device, hole alignment becomes a precise matter.

PORTABLE POWER SAW

With a portable power saw, wood can be cut at least ten times faster than by hand, and the cuts will be far more accurate and look much better. Saws range from little ones, weighing 6¾ pounds and cutting to a depth of 1¼", to large 12" units, weighing 34 pounds. It's best to buy the smallest that will do the job. An inexpensive saw will cut 1⅞" deep; that is sufficient for more than 97 per cent of the cutting you will do. If you do have to cut deeper, it's simple to reverse the wood and saw across it to meet the first cut.

For the man who does his work in an apartment or the homeowner who plans only small jobs, the small 4" diameter saw is completely adequate. It can cut up to 1¼". A variety of blades are available, and adjustable guides can be added.

Calculate the distance of the saw plug-in from the power source. If you will be working at a considerable distance, use an extension cord of sufficient wire size to prevent a drop in power voltage. For distances up to 35', use a No. 14 wire or heavier; up to 100' use a No. 12 wire or heavier. Extension

cords in specific sizes can be purchased with that purpose in mind.

Don't overwork your light-duty saw. Cut the pieces one by one, as you measure and mark them, rather than do all the marking at one time and the cutting at another. Never force the blade into the work; an easy, steady pressure is best. Start the saw and listen to it come up to full speed before you enter the wood, and then let it cut its way through—you just guide and engineer the job. Any time the cut seems to bind the blade, force a screwdriver or wedge into

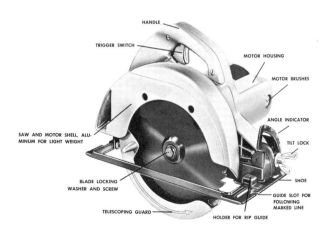

Rip cut—made along wood grain—in this case with cutting guide attached to saw.

Bevel cut—on this cut the diagonal is cut through the wood by tilting the saw blade to the desired measured angle.

Compound miter—this is a miter cut at a diagonal across the grain, plus the bevel cut. The miter is made on the line, the bevel by tilting the saw blade.

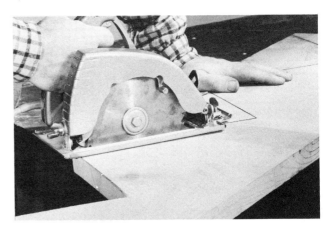

Stringer cutting—here, cuts meet at right angles. Follow marked lines only to their ends, then complete cuts with hand saw—circular blade will cut beyond marked line and weaken the stringer.

Always support work being cut!—this is the first rule in handling a portable power saw.

Cutting corrugated non-wood stock—fiber-supported plastics are cut with abrasive disc substituted for saw blade.

Crosscut—cut across wood grain.

Pocket cut—this is used to cut a section from the center of a board. Rest saw on its forward edge and press rotating blade slowly into wood. Remove saw and repeat on all four sides.

the cut behind the blade to keep the cut open. Make especially sure your work is well supported. Any movement of the board being cut binds the blade or deflects it from the guide line.

And don't let the motor overheat. If you find the motor housing too hot to touch, stop sawing and do something else while the motor cools because further use will cause motor damage. As with all cutting tools, always use a clean, sharp blade and keep an extra on hand. Clean the blade with kerosene to soften the pitch and gum it will pick up in cutting unseasoned wood. Wiping the blade with kerosene prior to cutting such wood prevents gumming during use.

Portable saw blade teeth cut upward, leaving the best edge on the bottom side of the cut. In cutting plywood, do the marking on the back surface and work with the better face down to protect it. On thinner grades and veneers, this practice is an absolute must. Plan your cutting so that the broader base remains on the supported section as the cut is made —this is usually to the left side of the blade. If pos-

sible, use guides; they provide far more accuracy than only a marked line.

For general crosscutting and ripping, a combination blade will work well. If you have a large amount of one kind of work, change to the appropriate blade. A crosscut blade works best on plywood and in cutting across wood grain. For large quantities of ripping, switch to a ripsaw blade. A miter blade gives a much better, smoother finish to the cut. Use this where the appearance of the cut is important— for example, on such work as exposed edges and grain ends.

In addition to the cuts shown in the photographs, you can make rabbets along board edges with two cuts to the measured depth at right angles to each other. Also, you can make dado cuts by setting the blade to the desired depth, making two parallel cuts and removing the scrap with a chisel. You may also utilize special washers to complete these cuts, attaching them to the spindle next to the blade.

Combination Crosscut and Rip Blade

Most popular blade, good for all-around work, suited to both operations and for use on plywood.

Rip Blade

Best when a lot of ripping along wood grain is to be done. Teeth are larger, specially set for this job.

Crosscut Blade

Best for all crosscut work, excellent for plywood. Also a good blade for cutting hardboards and similar composition materials.

Combination Miter Blade

For smooth cuts, miter work, interior trim, this blade is best. Teeth are not set, width of cut is small, edge of cut is smooth.

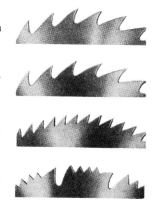

POWER SANDER

When the family handyman goes shopping for a power sander, he may very well ask for "a sander to do everything about the house," and it no more exists than does the perfect house or the cure-all pill. In general, there are three kinds of power sanders: disc, belt and finishing. Each kind has its own advantages and disadvantages since each was designed for a specific purpose.

Disc Sanders. All disc sanders have a circular rubber pad mounted at right angles to the drive

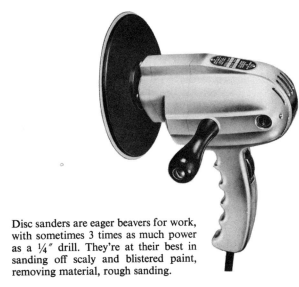

Disc sanders are eager beavers for work, with sometimes 3 times as much power as a ¼" drill. They're at their best in sanding off scaly and blistered paint, removing material, rough sanding.

spindle of the motor. The abrasive discs are attached by a flange and screw that threads into a steel rod which is held by the drill chuck. Discs are easy to change and, in the 5"- and 6"-diameter sizes, the choice of grits (degree of roughness) is great.

Disc sanders usually have an rpm in excess of 3,000, and their main function (by design) is to remove stock rapidly and roughly. If you have a lot of paint to remove or a large amount of wood to sand off, the disc sanders will do it best. They are not designed, and hence not recommended, for finish work. All too many new owners of disc sanders attack (and "attack" is the only word) a sanding job as if they planned to push the sanding disc through the work. The results are swirls, gouges, clogged or torn discs and a motor that gets overheated. Sanding with a flexible disc is best done with speed, not pressure. If the tool is slowing down so that you notice it, ease off. For best results, keep the disc nearly flat and moving over the surface lightly. Keep three grits on hand—coarse, medium and fine—and use the right grit for the right job. On really stubborn jobs like outside window ledges and much-painted porch floors, where discs keep loading in seconds, try a No. 3½ open-coat disc. It's long-lasting and loads very little. All disc sanders can be used as polishers. Just remove the abrasive and cover the pad with a lamb's-wool bonnet.

Belt Sanders. A belt sander should not be considered by the handyman who plans to have only one kind of sander. By and large, belt sanders are for heavy-duty work over large, flat surfaces. The port-

able types are excellent for smoothing large, flat areas preparatory to finishing. In the shop, a stationary belt sander may be pressed into use for joining work as well as finishing. Instead of being guided over the work, the work is pushed against the whirling belt. For most of its jobs, the belt sander will use medium- and fine-grit abrasive belts, and they can remove a lot of material quickly. Belt widths are available from 2" to 4", with lengths from 21" for the 2" width to about 28" for the 4" width.

Belt sanders are convenient but not vital tools for the family handyman. Basically they are used for removing material, but with proper abrasives can do finishing. With a suitable bracket (made by most manufacturers), they can be side-mounted for doing smaller, more exacting work—becoming, in effect, small fixed-belt sanders.

Finishing Sanders. Finishing sanders have many names—orbital, reciprocal, straight line, vibro and flat—but they all have one purpose in common, that of providing a surface with a fine finish. They won't remove paint rapidly or do a good job of taking down wood, but they will provide a smooth, fine surface.

With finishing sanders, the abrasive is laid flat on the surface to be finished and moved with very short, rapid strokes in all directions. The tool has a wide variety of uses owing to this versatility. The choice of abrasives is equally broad, but since finer work is the chief purpose, medium, fine and very fine grits are likely to be used with it. Use a medium grit for smoothing plaster patchwork and dry-wall taped joints. Use fine and very fine grits for furniture finish-

ing. A "sand screen" abrasive cloth may also be used for such purposes after it has been cut and fitted over the sander pad.

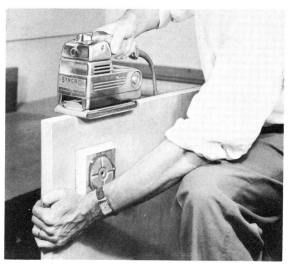

Orbital sanders are as close to an all-purpose sander as anyone (limiting himself to one type only) can buy. They are fair at removing materials and are very fine finishing tools. They are easy to control in any position.

Kind of Material	To Remove Some Material—and for a Fair Finish		For a Fine Finish	
	Abrasive Paper	Size of Grit	Abrasive Paper	Size of Grit
Softwoods Cardboard wallboard Untempered hardboard	Cabinet paper garnet (open coat)	½ to 2/0	Finishing paper garnet	3/0 to 5/0
Most plastics	Wet paper, "C" weight (Silicon carbide)	120 to 220	Wet paper "A" weight (Silicon carbide)	240 to 600
Hardwoods Tempered hardboard (Masonite) Plasterboard joints	Cabinet paper (Aluminum oxide)	60 to 100	Finishing paper (Aluminum oxide)	120 to 180
Soft metals (mostly non-ferrous)	Cabinet paper (Aluminum oxide)	80 to 100	Wet paper (Silicon carbide)	150 to 320
Hard metals (mostly ferrous)	Metal working cloth (Aluminum oxide)	80 to 100	Metal working cloth, with oil (Aluminum oxide) Crocus cloth for very fine finish	150 to 320
Paint and varnish	Cabinet paper (Aluminum oxide) Open coat	60 to 120	Wet paper (Silicon carbide)	240 to 400

When refinishing furniture, remove the old varnish or shellac first with a good chemical remover, for an abrasive rough enough to remove finish may also scar the wood, and the use of finer abrasives will be of no help since the grit will load in the first few seconds. Change grits often. Don't try to do a job from start to finish with one grade of abrasive. Use a finer and finer grit as the job progresses. This doesn't mean you have to waste paper. Save the sheets you change and use them on another job. And on really fine work, don't use a fresh sheet. Run a fresh sheet on some scrap for a moment and then use it. Fine finishing paper may sometimes have an abrasive clump on it which will leave swirl marks with orbital sanders. Always be sure the paper is on tight; otherwise its efficiency will be lost.

SABRE SAW

Unique among power tools is the sabre saw, a hand-held motor which sends a slender blade in and out of its guard at high speed. It is fairly quiet in operation, not much noisier than the average electric drill.

If the price of the tool isn't justified by the amount of work you plan to do, you can buy a sabre-saw attachment for a ¼" electric drill. It works out fine —not as well as a sabre saw itself, but well enough if the price is an important factor.

The sabre saw lets the handyman add that extra fillip to his work. Scrolls, valances and cutouts involve cutting curves. If the project is small, the portable sabre saw does it quickly and easily. If the work piece is large, the portable sabre saw is probably the only tool that can do it, for the sabre operates outside the range of the jig saw and the band saw in the size of the work it can handle.

It's fine for on-the-job work. Since it's lightweight (most models weigh less than five pounds), it can actually cut a valance from a straight board which has been nailed in place. If your shop is small, this may be the only way you can do the job on a long board. Large-scale scallops just aren't possible if you have to maneuver a long board over a fixed saw blade on a table.

This versatile tool is in a class by itself; it can do stunts which no other type of saw can duplicate. For instance, suppose you built accurately a right-angled unit such as a cabinet or a set of

COMMON TYPES OF BLADES

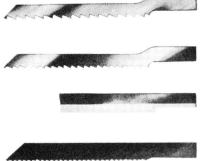

Coarse-toothed blade for wood cutting. Cuts rapidly, has some "set." Best where rough edge on cut surface is not objectionable.

Fine-toothed wood-cutting blade. Less "set" and finer teeth, not as apt to rip grain of plywood, leaves softwood edges ready for final sanding.

Knife blade. This has no teeth, but is designed primarily for cutting such things as leather, rubber, linoleum, Celotex, and other fibrous materials.

Nonferrous-metal cutter. This one cuts aluminum, brass, copper, and most other metals (not iron and steel). Also cuts Masonite, Formica, asphalt tiles.

Heat-treated blade cuts steel and iron. In effect, converts the sabre saw to a power hack saw. Best, too, for plastics, since it leaves smoother edges.

Taper ground blade for wood has no "set." Leaves absolutely smooth edges ready for jointing or final finish. Cuts more slowly, but saves time.

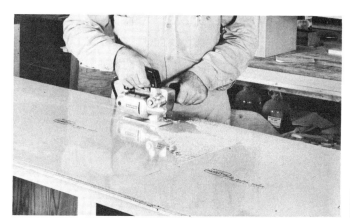

Sabre saws are provided with blower device that clears marked line of sawdust. V-notch in shoe also aids in guiding tool along straight lines or curves.

Above right: One of hundreds of practical uses of the sabre saw—cutting into baseboard without making a pilot hole, for the purpose of inserting a new outlet box.

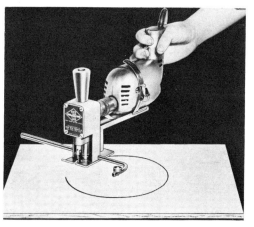

Sabre-saw attachment with circle-cutting guide uses ¼″ drill as power source and makes quick job of cutting hole from plywood of ¾″ thickness.

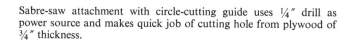

For the precision-minded craftsman, guide clamped to work is followed by sabre saw to cut materials at precise angles. Shoe is made to fit guide.

With a little practice you'll get the knack of holding saw properly; then try the one-hand method, holding work as required on any substantial support. Model here cuts ¾″ ply.

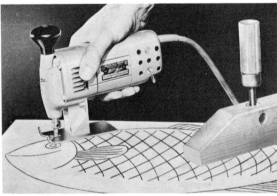

If you're a beginner, clamp down the work and use two hands, one as shown and the other on the front control knob to hold the saw tight against the work.

Sabre saw, mounted upside down under table, becomes a jig saw which can be handled in the usual manner, only feeding stock into the saw instead of saw into the stock.

shelves and, upon installation, you discover that the walls are crooked and your built-ins don't fit. With your sabre saw you can trim the units to match the crooked wall or corner. Or suppose you want to cut a hole in the middle of a sheet of plywood, hardboard or a Formica-covered counter top. You don't have to scout around for a suitable drill and make corner holes through which the standard coping or keyhole saw can work. The sabre saw makes its own entry hole right on the marked line.

Again, imagine handling a large cutout made from a single 4-by-8 sheet of stock in a scrolled pattern. How are you going to turn a 4-by-8 around and around to meet your jig- or hand-saw blade? It can't be done, but the sabre saw will travel around the pattern in all possible directions easily and quickly. Then too, if you want a jig saw on a table in a

hurry, just turn the saw upside down, anchor it and let the blade work through a table top. You can build this top for yourself or buy it. Take the saw off its mountings and it's back on duty as a portable again.

When you use a sabre saw, first make sure the switch is off, then plug it in. Hold the tool firmly and turn on the switch. Place the guide on the piece to be cut and line up the blade with the marked line. Gently push the saw forward along the line—otherwise the tool may vibrate and wander. Until you have had a bit of practice with it, clamp the wood down tightly (unless its weight holds it in place) and use both hands to hold the saw. Push down on the forward knob if your model has one, otherwise use both hands on the case. Later, you'll become familiar with one-hand operation.

ROUTER

Reproduction of the finest details of noted furniture craftsmen is possible with a router. Beautifully carved and curved moldings, inlay work, mortises for hinges and all sorts of exacting work become almost routine. The router works not only on wood but on other materials as well—plastics, hardboards and Formica. Inlays and molded edges can be made from most of these with a router.

Nearly everything a router does can be broken down into a series of simple operations which can be learned quickly. The motor driving the router is small but quite efficient. Its great work ability comes from its very high speed, 20,000 rpm or even more.

fancy edge of a valance or table top, but it also permits the constant repetition of that pattern without variation.

In as simple an operation as putting up shelves, a router can be of great help. It will speedily cut a dado groove on opposite side supports. The shelf can then be slipped into the grooves and nailed or screwed and glued. Such shelves will be far stronger than those put together with nails or screws alone. And, since the router can make a curved as well as a straight groove, you can insert corrugated plastic sheeting just as easily as a flat shelf. For another example, you can make a groove along the edge of a board and also make a tongue on another board edge and join the two.

Some of the jobs these cutters can do: (left to right) rabbet, V-rabbet, spindle bead, concave cut, convex face, thumbmold, combined concave-convex, surface bead, corner bead, chamfer.

All routers have the same general type of chuck to hold shaped cutters. In fact, nearly all brands of cutters will fit into all routers.

At first, all you will need is the router itself, a set of basic bits and a guide. Later on, you might want to add a complete dovetailing outfit. All routers are essentially the same, and there are only good ones and better ones. There are no bad ones. They require practically no maintenance. There is not even much variation in design. The motor is vertically mounted, with no belts or gears or complex machinery. It fits into a base which permits adjustment in the distance between the cutter and the work. When attachments are added, you can suspend the router as an over-arm cutter for carving, drilling and other fixed-tool attachment work. You can also convert it to a powered plane with a multiple assortment of blades, and it can become a grinder and a dovetailing machine. When the wide assortment of blades is added, the shapes that can be cut are almost limitless. Cutters, in many cases, have as one part of them a noncutting pilot which acts as a "follower" and as a cutting limit. This not only allows cutting the

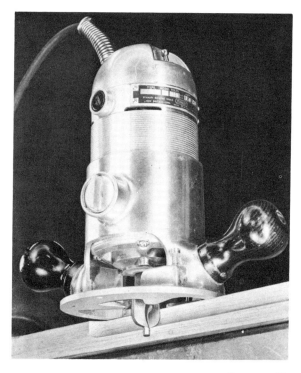

Router making a cove molding. Note that non-cutting pin on bottom of cutter governs depth of cut.

Dovetailed end, bottom dado groove, and rabbeted edges—all made in a single drawer side with router.

Parallel grooves for slide-in shelving are one of the basics of routing.

For wider dado cuts, make repeated cuts alongside one another until desired width is attained.

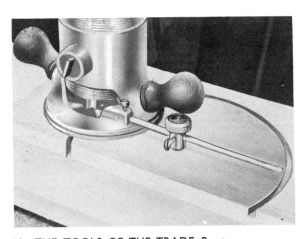

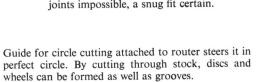

End dovetailing is easy. The guide makes mismated joints impossible, a snug fit certain.

Guide for circle cutting attached to router steers it in perfect circle. By cutting through stock, discs and wheels can be formed as well as grooves.

Among the many types of joints that a router will make are: mortise and tenon; cross laps; rabbets and dados, plus combinations of both; and the dovetail joint. Dovetail jointing with a router is one of the most satisfactory jobs you can do. You will need a special set of accessories, but with it you can easily make sturdy drawers.

In addition to joints of all kinds, the router has one special trick of its own—recessing. This allows you to make recessed platters and trays of all kinds and shapes. Or, by a similar process, you can make inlays of wood or tile for table tops and chess, checker and assorted game boards.

Making a recess panel requires repeated cuts closely spaced. Depth control is handled by means of a board rested on edges of cutout, with router cutter extended through a hole.

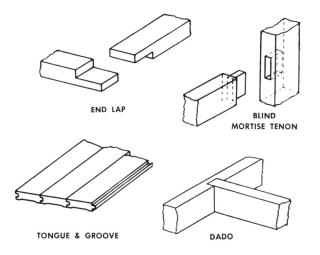

END LAP

BLIND MORTISE TENON

TONGUE & GROOVE

DADO

For the beginner, a guide clamped over the work guarantees straight cuts across wide boards.

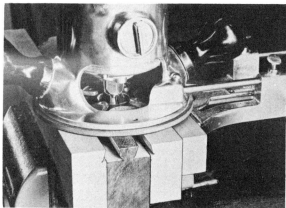

For joining two boards to make a wider one, a dovetail on edges to be joined assures permanent joint. Cut groove along one edge of one of the boards. Then make a "tongue" on the edge of the second board, clamping it between scrap stock as shown. Same cutter is used.

CHAPTER 2

THE INTERIOR OF THE HOUSE

Floors and Stairs · Walls and Ceilings · Doors · Windows

This chapter deals specifically with the basic structural condition of the rooms within your house. It considers the elements necessary to *any* room—simply enough, its floors and walls, its windows and doors. Whether your house is a mansion or a cottage, ornate or simple, these elements constitute the visible background of every room in your home.

A comfortable, livable home is not dependent upon the dictates of fashion or decorating trends. You cannot conceal a sagging floor or a window that won't raise, a sticking door or flaking plaster on the wall. First, before any room can be really enjoyable or any decorating truly effective, all structural parts must be solid and firm, floors properly supported, stairways safe, walls smooth, windows easy to operate and doors functioning properly.

The home handyman will discover, in the following pages, that maintenance of the interior of his home, when taken step-by-step as in the ensuing detailed directions, is not only easy but amply rewarding. His home will be safer, more attractive, and he will find himself saving on the family budget time and time again.

FLOORS AND STAIRS Floor repairs · Replacing a threshold · Concrete floors · How to lay finish wood flooring · How to lay a wooden floor over concrete · Finishing and refinishing floors · How to lay floor tiles · Ceramic tile floor · Installing and repairing linoleum · Stairs

A sound floor is more than just an attractive asset to a home. It's an actual safety factor. A floor with rotted and warped boards, for instance, may cause a serious fall, and a poorly finished floor is a trap for dust and germs. The same is true of the stairs in your home—if they're too steep or if the treads are worn and uneven, eventually someone is likely to trip.

Proper floor and stair maintenance begins with a solid, level underfooting. Sagging floors may indicate a serious weakness developing in the structure of the house, and sometimes the only satisfactory way to restore the floors in an older home is by a thorough overhaul. The addition of extra supports may be needed, the complete removal of boards (or other flooring material) no longer serviceable may be necessary, and this in turn will mean laying an entirely new floor.

On the other hand, some older floors can be made as good as new by the simple replacement of a few damaged boards or the application of a new finish coat. Although concrete floors are usually cold, a basement can quickly become a useful family room with an over-flooring of tile or wood. Stairs which are too steep can be widened, the steps respaced. You may even have room to make an extra landing.

Whether your floors are old or new, the final protective finish given them will make the difference between warped, splintery, and cracked floors or ones which are easy to care for, smooth, and trouble-free for years to come.

People walk over their floors every day but seldom know what really lies underfoot. The parts of floors that are always hidden are brought into view by the accompanying diagram. By knowing just what floors consist of and how the many components are put together, the homeowner is in a better position to understand and maintain his own house.

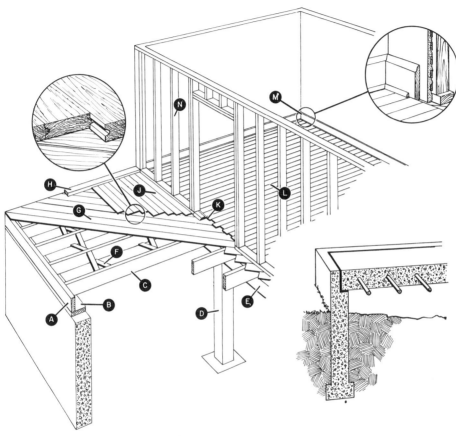

A	Header, connects joists	**D**	Post, supports girder
B	Sill or plate, supports wall and joists	**E**	Girder, supports central load
C	Joist, supports flooring	**F**	Bridging, braces joists

G	Subflooring	**M**	Baseboard, conceals wall-floor joint
H	Sole, supports studs	**N**	Stud, supports wall, upper floor, roof
J	Finish flooring		
K	Threshold		
L	Finish flooring		

While this cutaway drawing shows a typical floor, there are many variations. Subflooring may be laid at right angles to the joists instead of diagonally, for example, and bridging may be omitted from your floors. In some houses, the supporting wall over the girder may be placed directly on the girder instead of on the subflooring. Flooring is not necessarily laid in two different directions as shown here, in which case a threshold or saddle is not needed, as its function here would be to cover the joint between the flooring of the two rooms. In any event, these are the most likely details you will uncover when you lay a new floor in your home.

Lower right view is that of concrete slab floor with radiant-heating tubing exposed. This type is common in one-floor ranch-style homes. Floor may be covered with wood flooring nailed to furring strips, or covered with asphalt tiles.

FLOOR REPAIRS

Flooring defects can be divided into two groups—damage to the finish or flaws in the flooring itself. The first group requires a trip to the paint store as a starter. Defects in the second group require some carpentry.

Sagging Floors. You don't usually notice low spots in your floors or pay much attention to those that shake when walked over or jumped on—not if you have lived with them for a long time. Such floor troubles develop so slowly that they're hardly noticeable as you gradually become accustomed to them. However, there comes a time when, for safety's sake alone, repair and correction are necessary.

Timber shrinkage over a period of years, warping and twisting of floor joists and the occasional failure of a timber to stand live loads account for most of the trouble.

These conditions on the first floor of a house are usually curable, often with very little effort or expense. The plan of the house and the extent of the trouble govern the ease with which corrective measures can be accomplished. A typical first-floor structure consists of a girder laid across the central area of a basement, resting on the foundation at its ends and supported by one or more posts in the midsection. At right angles to and supported by the girder are the floor joists, themselves supported at their outer ends by the foundation or house sill. At right angles, or on a diagonal to the joists, are laid the rough flooring boards and across this subfloor the finish floor boards are nailed.

Sagging in the floor can be traced to one or more of the following causes:

1. Warped or shrunken floor joists which allow the floor and subfloor boards to sag to the new level.

2. Sagging girder due to supporting posts having been pressed into the ground through failure of the footing under the posts.

3. Crumbling foundation under the outer ends of joists or girder, allowing the floor to sag at the end rather than the center.

A floor with a bounce to it (and this trouble is usually accompanied by considerable squeaking) may be caused by these same failures. However, in this case, the nails holding down either the finish floor or the subfloor may have pulled loose from the joists and the floor is depressed only to the joist level when there is weight on it.

Less common is the floor that bounces owing to the fact that the joists are too small to carry the weight on the floor and a live load causes the entire floor structure to vibrate. This type is really dangerous, but rare.

Examination of first-floor timbers is relatively easy where there is a basement with the substructure exposed. Floors over crawl spaces are easily checked also, if no insulation has been applied. Have someone walk over the floor above and check carefully which part of the floor and which supporting timbers vibrate. Check the foundation at points where joists and girders rest. Brick is usually the first foundation material to show signs of crumbling, then poor quality concrete, then stone. Where the house is supported on piling and the "foundation" is actually

SETTING UP A BASEMENT POST TO SUPPORT A SAGGING FLOOR

1. Use star drill to make 1"-deep holes for bolts to hold down base plate.

2. Tighten bolts in lead expansion anchors set in the drilled holes.

3. Set assembled post over lugs on base plate. Weight holds post in place.

a ring of heavy timbers supported on posts or piles, this timber may be rotted or damaged by termites.

Cures for floor troubles of this nature follow these steps:

1. Where the joists have warped, shrunk or sagged but remain sound, hardwood wedges may be driven between the subflooring and joists. They will push the lower areas upward to a level equal to the surrounding floor. They will also prevent further vibration where a loose floor is responsible and they will cure squeaks as well.

2. Where bridging is lacking, cross bridging of 1-by-3″ or 2-by-3″ stock may be applied to add rigidity to joists. This will stabilize a shaky floor, add strength to a weak one.

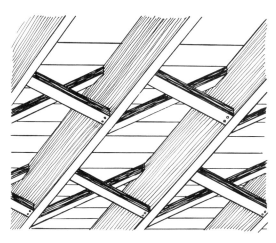

3. If a girder unsupported in the middle has sagged, it must be propped up. Since the basement floor will not carry such a load, a new footing must be placed beneath the support. A hole is dug from 18 to 24″ deep and from 18 to 24″ square. Fill it with concrete and, after it has set, erect a 4-by-4″ or 6-by-6″ post on it and wedge it tightly under the girder. In place of such a timber, an iron column may be used. For this purpose, special jacks are employed to push the girder back to level and the column is placed in position; then the jacks are removed.

4. If the girder is already supported but footings have crumbled, new footings must be made. Support the girder on temporary beams, remove and replace the old footings and erect a new supporting column of timber; then remove the temporary timber.

5. Where the foundation has crumbled under the ends of joists or girders, temporary timbers are rested on planks on the cellar floor, wedged beneath the floor support, and driven tight until the floor is raised to the necessary level. Then the damaged foundation

is cut out with hammer and cold chisel (in the case of brick, concrete or stone) to such a point that new material may be inserted. Brick is suggested since it's the easiest to handle. The damaged foundation is cut back to accommodate units of brick that are cemented into place. When the mortar has dried thoroughly, the temporary supports can be removed and the joist or girder allowed to rest on the new base.

6. Where a girder or the joists rest on a wood sill supported by the foundation, piles or posts, and the sill is damaged, replacement is necessary. There is only one solution—call your contractor. He will use some method of supporting the entire house during the time that it takes to replace this sill. Obviously, this is not your kind of work.

Bridging, diagonally nailed between joists, adds strength and rigidity to weak floors.

In two-story houses, a sagging second floor, which is also the ceiling of the first floor, presents an entirely different and more complex problem. As a rule, these joists are completely enclosed by ceiling material below and flooring material above. The trouble is not uncommon where an attic has been converted to additional living space, since an unusual load is placed on floors probably not originally designed to carry it. Correction here depends upon the most convenient method of approach. If lower-floor plaster is damaged, it may be best to remove it all, strengthen the joists with bridging and 2-by-4's spliced along the lower edges of the joists, and then replace the ceiling. Additional joists may be installed between the existing ones to carry part of the new load on the second floor. The only other approach to this second-floor problem is through removal of the flooring to get at the cause of the trouble in the joists.

Simple sagging in second floors due to timber shrinkage, but where the timbers remain sound and strong, can be remedied by removing the finish floor, inserting furring strips between it and the subfloor, and replacing the finish flooring. The strips must be planed and tapered to correct for the sag and placed at right angles to the finish flooring. Check repeatedly with a level as the work progresses.

REPAIRING DAMAGED WOODEN FLOORS

1. Sagging, bouncy floors can be helped by driving 2 × 6 or 2 × 4 braces snugly between joists against subfloor. Toenail at each end to joists, then drive screw nails down from above into brace.

2. Warped boards—particularly wider ones—can be flattened by first soaking them, then setting countersunk screws or screw nails through their outer edges into subfloor. Sanding is the only other method.

3. Boards that have cracked along grain may be helped by forcing glue into the cracks with putty knife. This treatment stops cracks from lengthening. Use glue-and-sawdust mixture for wide cracks.

4. New floor laid with green or wet lumber develops cracks as wood dries. Fill cracks with glue-and-sawdust, plastic wood, or wood-fiber putty if floor is to have clear finish. Otherwise, use putty under paint.

5. Rotted or damaged section requires replacement. Process involves several steps. First, cut length of flooring to size of piece to be removed. Bevel one end of replacement piece at a 45° angle.

5a. Mark length of replacement piece on section to be removed. Using large bit, cut hole in each corner of section right up to edge of board and marked line. Do not cut into subfloor.

5b. Split damaged piece end to end between holes along grain. Use a sharp 1″ chisel and hammer or mallet. Be careful not to damage tongue and groove of adjoining piece.

5c. Undercut the remaining piece of the damaged board at a 45° angle. The beveled end of the replacement board will fit snugly under it and make a smooth, tight joint.

5d. Plane off underside of groove on replacement piece so it can be fitted over the tongue of the adjoining board. If not cut away, replacement board can't be fitted.

5e. Insert beveled end of replacement under beveled end of old section, then press into place carefully. Tap down, using a block to avoid marking new piece.

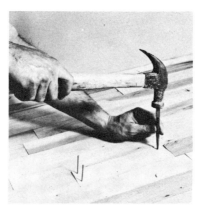

5f. Drill at least 4 pilot holes for screw nails or finishing nails. Without pilot holes, flooring would be split. Use drill slightly smaller than nail size. Do not drill in center.

5g. Drive in finishing or screw nails, then countersink heads. If replacement board is thicker than old flooring, plane or sand down flush with rest of floor.

5h. If new piece is lighter, or of a different grain pattern, you may make it match by darkening with stain, orange shellac, or crayon rubbed in with alcohol.

REPLACING A THRESHOLD

Probably no one spot in the entire house is subject to as much wear and tear as the thresholds, those pieces of lumber directly below the doors. When worn, a gap develops between door and floor and nothing other than complete replacement of the threshold can prevent rain, wind, dust and drafts from entering.

First, to remove the old threshold, swing the door wide open. If it doesn't clear the threshold, remove it by taking the pins out of the hinges. Next, remove the door stop. Pry it away from the jamb gently,

starting at the bottom and lifting ¼″ at a time to prevent cracking. A floor or glazier's chisel will do a neat job, as will a pry bar or regular wood chisel. A screwdriver, however, will gouge the wood.

In most standard door openings, the threshold can be removed once the door stop is out. If not, take a chisel and split the threshold, or saddle, as it's sometimes called. If the door jamb rests on the saddle, use a back saw and cut flush with the jamb through the saddle (see sketch, next page) or pull it out entirely.

By using the old threshold as a pattern, cut the new one to the same length and lower it into position.

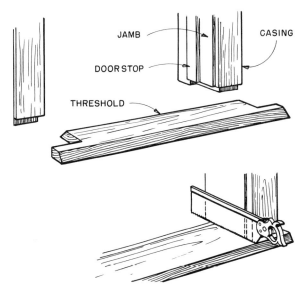

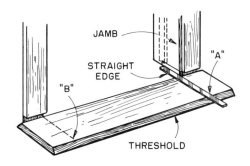

from the front edge of the door stop (edge nearest you when you're outside the house) to the outside wall. (This is distance **X** and **Y** in the sketch.)

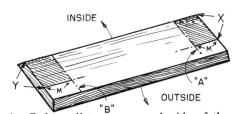

If the old threshold was under the jamb and you removed it completely, you can slide the new one into position. However, before securing the new one, it is best to spread roofing asphalt with a trowel or putty knife between threshold and floor. This helps to waterproof the area.

The new threshold may be thicker than the old one. If you've cut away under the jamb, use scrap lumber to fill in the space and then fit the new threshold flush against the jamb, disregarding the fact that it originally fitted under it. Also, when replacing the door stop, it may be necessary to trim the ends to match the new threshold if it has a different shape from the old one.

Mark off these distances on each side of the new threshold along lines A and B from the inside edge of the threshold (side nearest the inside of the house). With a try square, draw lines across the new threshold at these points. (These are lines M in the sketch.) Using a crosscut saw, cut out the shaded areas shown in the sketch. The threshold will now fit into the door opening with the protruding ends resting against the casing or the outside wall.

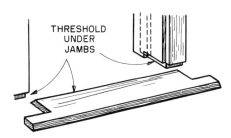

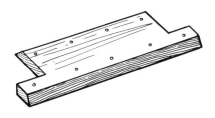

If you don't have the old one in one piece to use as a model, measure and cut the new one as follows: lay the new threshold outside the door so that it extends evenly on both sides. Rest the straight edge flush against the door jamb and draw a line across the threshold. Do this on both door jambs. (Lines A and B indicate these markings in the sketch.) Next, measure along the jamb on each side the distance

For oak or hardwood thresholds, drill small holes through the shoulders, that imaginary line along the top edge where the slope at the ends joins the top. These holes should be $\frac{1}{16}''$ in diameter or slightly smaller than the size of a $2\frac{1}{2}''$ finishing nail. It's best to stagger holes on the opposite sides of the center line. Drive nails all the way through, countersink the heads and fill the holes with wood filler.

CONCRETE FLOORS

While a concrete floor would seem to be about as durable as any building material could possibly be, the list of ways in which such floors can break down is quite long. Some defects are caused by mistakes made at the time the floor was laid. Others develop because of exterior pressures and stresses. And still more trouble can arise from continued heavy usage. A list of some of these defects might include:

1. A dusty surface that no amount of sweeping will improve.

2. A sandy, pitted surface with small gravel constantly being dislodged.

3. Unevenness—bumps and depressions.

4. Cracks—hairline and some much wider and deeper.

5. Dampness—ever-present, owing to seepage through from below or condensation of moisture from the air.

6. Stains such as oil spots, paint stains and an assortment of discolorations due to use.

The first three are the result of poor workmanship right from the start. Too little cement in the mixture leads to a "sandy" surface later. Too much water allowed to run off rapidly from the wet surface produces a similar result, as does freezing before the cement has cured. Excessive troweling, which brings the cement to the surface and leaves it there, will result in a dusty surface not improved by sweeping. Hasty work and failure to level the floor during the laying process will, of course, leave the surface irregular.

The presence of water under pressure beneath a floor is usually the cause of cracks. When the floor is laid below grade, an excavation is often made below existing water tables and it's up to the concrete floor to shut the water out. If the concrete is too thin or not properly reinforced, pressures from below push it up and cracks develop. Even when properly built, such a floor will remain cold, and if the air in the room is moist, the moisture will condense on the colder surface—the floor—and leave it wet. These are the two basic causes of a wet basement, the most common ailment of many homes.

At one time, solution to the first two problems was difficult. Etching the floor with acid to receive another inch or so of cement was the common treatment. Now the "dusty" floor is treated with sealer paints, not only clear in color but also available in a variety of shades. These paints may be in the silicone group, the epoxy-resin base materials or latex-base paints. All work wonders.

Should the floor be excessively sandy and pitted, a bonding agent may be painted on, and over that as little as ¼ to ½" of new cement may be spread.

This same method will solve the problem of bumpy, uneven or poorly sloped floors. The amount of new cement added need be only enough to bring the entire floor level with its highest point.

Treatment of a cracked and broken floor, usually accompanied by some flooding, is more difficult but the approach is similar. For minor breaks, cement putties may be used to seal the cracks in less than five minutes. If the floor is weak, however, such attempts result in new breaks nearby. Stronger measures are needed—usually at least 1½ to 2" of new cement reinforced with wire applied over the old floor after application of a bonding coat. This makes up for the lack of sufficient depth of the original floor.

The only probable cure for condensation on a subgrade cement floor is adequate ventilation and reduction of humidity in the air by way of dehumidifiers.

Stains, of course, are often unavoidable. Concrete and cement are quite porous. Anything spilled on them penetrates and becomes very difficult to remove. Oil stains may be slowly removed by softening the oil with gasoline (dangerous in confined areas) and then applying a poultice of a powder-like material such as plain cornstarch or dry portland cement. This is put on about 1" thick, allowed to remain 24 hours and then swept up. Most of the oil is absorbed by this method and a thorough scrubbing with a strong detergent takes up the rest. Other stains are often removed with muriatic acid, which softens the cement momentarily and must be rinsed off with a lot of water. The acid is strong and dangerous to use, and the rinse must have a drain to flow into. These points make the process of stain removal so limited that it is often better to consider the application of a coating of deck enamel to conceal all stains.

HOW TO LAY FINISH WOOD FLOORING

The handy homeowner experienced at working with wood should be able to lay a wood floor with completely satisfactory results. Here are a few wise preliminary precautions:

1. If the walls or ceiling of the room to be floored have been recently plastered, defer floor installation until the plaster has thoroughly dried.

2. Arrange, if possible, to have the flooring delivered during dry weather.

3. At least four or five days before installation, pile the flooring loosely in a ventilated area heated to approximately 70°.

These precautions, by protecting the wood against absorption of excessive moisture, will minimize subsequent expansion and contraction of the wood and help assure a permanently trouble-free floor.

Before beginning installation, sweep the subfloor

clean, nail down any loose boards, and drive down any protruding nails. Then cover the subfloor with building paper, preferably 15-pound asphalt-saturated felt. Run the strips in the same direction to be taken by the wood. For the most attractive appearance, this is usually along the longest room dimension.

1. Walls may not be perfectly true at all points. Use a string as guide in lining up the first course. Stretch the string between nails at opposite ends of the room at equal distances from the wall. Place a long piece of flooring with groove edge nearest the sidewall and groove end nearest the endwall. Keep it at a uniform distance from the string, leaving expansion space of about ½″ from the wall. The space should be no more than will be covered by the shoe molding. Bottom edge of baseboard comes just above floor level. Face-nail the flooring piece progressively at 10″ intervals. Then toenail the tongue edge. Follow the same procedure for succeeding pieces in the course, toenailing the tongue end of each piece.

2. Lay each succeeding course by fitting groove edges of flooring pieces into the tongue edges of the preceding course. Toenail, as illustrated here, but do not face-nail. For 25/32″-thick flooring one 7d or 8d flooring nail is nailed every 10″ to 12″. Countersink nails.

3. Whenever it is necessary to cut a piece to fill out a course, place it in reversed position for measuring, as shown here. In this way you will be more certain of cutting off the tongue end. The groove end is needed for joining with the tongue end of the previous piece.

4. For the most attractive appearance, avoid grouping joints closely. Joints in adjacent rows should be at least 6″ apart. To effect this arrangement, lay out pieces for the next few courses as you go along. Professionals nail while standing.

5. After every three courses, place a piece of scrap flooring against a tongue in the last course. Strike the scrap piece with a hammer. Repeat at similar intervals to drive nailed flooring up snugly. Using scrap piece protects tongues from breakage.

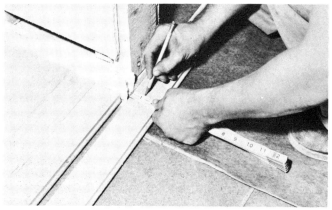

6. To fit flooring around jutting places like a door frame, place strip flush against the frame, as shown. Measure open space between face edge of the previous piece and groove edge of strip to be installed. Mark strip accordingly on each side of the frame and saw out the piece. Flooring will fit snugly around obstacle.

7. Last two courses cannot be toenailed because of insufficient space. Fit in the next-to-last course without nailing. Face-nail the last course, pulling it up tightly with a crowbar or chisel. Protect baseboard with cardboard. If shoe molding won't cover remaining space, cut strips of flooring with ripsaw and face-nail them in.

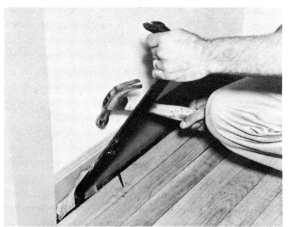

8. Give the floor at least two sanding traverses, the first with No. 2 sandpaper on the machine, the second with No. ½. Keep the machine moving whenever power is on, to avoid gouging the wood. Use an edger (a small sander) near walls and small areas. Floor sanders can be rented cheaply in most communities.

HOW TO LAY A WOODEN FLOOR OVER CONCRETE

By using mastic and nailing screeds, you can install a wooden floor right over the concrete floor of your basement and achieve a complete "living room" effect. Tongue-and-groove finish flooring is the only kind that can be laid effectively with this method, which was developed by the manufacturers of oak flooring. It's best to buy the flooring in advance and stack it indoors for at least four or five days so that the wood has a chance to adjust to interior humidity and heat conditions.

First spread a waterproof variety of mastic on concrete. A tight vapor barrier must be obtained.

Press short pieces of 2 × 4s into the mastic in rows 12″ apart. Stagger and lap these screeds 4″ to 6″.

Flooring strips are laid at right angles to screeds. Long 2 × 4 against wall supports ends of flooring.

Nail floor strips to all screeds. This ties screeds together where they overlap and strengthens floor.

FINISHING AND REFINISHING FLOORS

No matter what type of floor you intend to finish, two basic rules must always be observed: (1) prepare the surface carefully to insure good results, and (2) be sure that wood floors are firm, sanded smooth, and thoroughly dry.

Wax is possibly the worst bugaboo in finishing floors. No finish will dry satisfactorily over it, so make sure every bit of wax accumulation is removed with turpentine or a commercial wax remover. Floor polish is in the same category and also should be completely removed. In further preparation, all loose boards must first be fastened, broken or badly split boards replaced, and protruding nail heads set.

Sanding. As a rule, you'll find it easy to rent a floor sander from a local shop. If the floor is covered with varnish, paint, or shellac, using a sander is the easiest method of removing the old finish. Don't try to save time by skipping on the sanding operation or by handling the sander carelessly. The latter will gouge your floors. Three "cuts" are suggested for sanding: a coarse grit (3½) for the first sanding, a medium grit (1½) for the second, and a fine grit (2/0) for the final operation.

Always sand with the grain, that is, lengthwise with the floor boards. Since it is impossible to sand with the grain of the wood on parquet floors, use only finer grits on the sanding machine and take special care. With new floors, three sanding operations are also recommended, but use finer grits—medium-coarse, fine, and extra-fine.

Use an edge sander along baseboards, on stair treads, and in other areas inaccessible to the drum sander. All dust must be removed from the floor, ledges, and baseboards with a vacuum cleaner or dry mop before applying a new finish.

1. Before sanding a floor prior to refinishing, go over it carefully with a hammer and nail set and countersink all visible nail heads. They'll ruin sander and paper.
2. To make sanding your room edges easier, remove shoe mold along the baseboards. You can then sand all the floor without damaging either the baseboard or molding.
3. If there are areas where the floor is high or bulged upward, plane them smooth. The sander might ride over such areas without reducing them to a level with the rest of the floor.

→

4. Powered sander, rented, is run from end to end of the wood flooring, never across the boards. *Never* stop sander in one spot with sandpaper in contact with the floor!

5. Edger, also a rental tool, gets up close. Guard protects shoe mold. Your disc sander on a drill will also do this job. Use medium-grit paper for the main work, then fine.

6. No round sander can get into a square corner, so eventually you get down to hand work. Sandpaper on a block will do the trick if you haven't an orbital sander.

7. For super-smooth floor finish, use a disc sander to remove "trees"—short, treelike fibers thrust up from the first sanding. Floor treated in this way needs less seal.

8. Vacuum floor next, removing every trace of sanding dust. If left on floor and in small cracks, dust blends with the sealer and prevents an even penetration.

Fillers. On close inspection, such hardwoods as oak will be seen to be covered with millions of tiny pin-point holes. Such woods are referred to as "open grain." Obviously, any liquid finish is going to run into these holes rapidly. To economize on expensive finishes, a filler is first applied.

A filler is a pastelike substance painted on along the grain, wiped off across the grain with a cloth, using a light touch so as to leave a deposit of filler in the pores of the wood. Most fillers dry rapidly. Some are wiped off across the grain immediately after application; others are allowed to "set" about five minutes before being wiped off. Commercial fillers are available in either a neutral (colorless) form or a variety of pigmented tones. A homemade form of filler might consist of thinned varnish, plaster-of-Paris, and the pigment.

Since such finishes as varnish, shellac, and plastic are clear, the wood they cover is exposed to light. In most rooms, this exposure is irregular and the floor is apt to take on a blotchy effect. A filler containing a pigment is undamaged by light exposure and allows the floor to maintain an even tone throughout the room.

A filler is rarely used along with floor sealers, which already include not only the needed pigment but often a filler as well. Neither is a filler used on close-grained woods such as maple.

Paint and Varnish Removers. If, for some reason, you cannot use a power sander, the old finish may be removed with a solvent type of paint and varnish remover or an alkaline remover that also acts as a bleaching agent. The solvent type of remover is easy to use and does not raise the grain. Brush on a heavy coat and let it stand undisturbed until the finish softens. Then remove it with a stiff putty knife and #2 steel wool. Several applications may be necessary if the old finish is particularly heavy. Wash the surface thoroughly with turpentine and wipe dry with clean cloths.

If the floors are dark with age and wear, an alkaline remover and bleach will be more effective than the solvent type of remover. But the alkaline remover must be made up in a solution of hot water (and applied hot). This will cause the grain to raise, entailing sanding after the finish has been removed. With the solvent type of paint remover there is always some danger that the wax generally found in these liquids will remain in the floors; hence, it's a good idea to scrub them afterward with a strong floor cleanser. Rinse with clear water and wipe with a clean cloth. Do not attempt painting or finishing until the surface is thoroughly dry.

Finishes. A finish should be hard, tough and durable, lasting for years rather than for months. Choose a finish that is easy to apply and dries quickly. It should be easy to keep clean and to "touch up" traffic areas so that eventual worn spots may be recoated without further sanding.

Enamel is rarely used over a first-class hardwood floor because it will hide the beauty of the grain. However, it also hides imperfections and provides color for the floor. For new work, apply two or three coats (the first coat thinned) of floor enamel. For refinishing, first spot-coat bare patches, let dry and then apply one or two coats of enamel.

If you want to retain the beauty of the grain of your floors but wish to add color, use an oil stain. Apply it to the bare wood as the label directs, brushing it on a few boards at a time with the grain. The longer the stain is allowed to remain on the wood, the darker it will become. The depth of color is easily controlled by wiping off excess stain when the desired shade has been reached. Filling is not a "must," but if you intend to use it be sure to stain the floor first; otherwise the stain cannot penetrate the wood evenly. Staining and filling may be combined into one operation by adding a sufficient amount of oil stain to paste wood filler for the desired color effect. This mixture should be brushed on *with* the grain, allowed to remain until it dulls (5 or 10 minutes), and then rubbed *across* the grain with burlap or any coarse cloth to pack the filler into the pores and to remove excess. Allow it to dry thoroughly, sand lightly by hand, then clean with a turpentine-moistened cloth and apply the finish coats.

Varnish stain will do the job of staining and varnishing in one operation. It is faster and easier than staining and varnishing in separate steps, but does not produce the beauty and clarity obtained by using varnish on an already stained surface. It will, however, with a minimum of effort, bring new life and color to old, worn, and discolored floors. Also, you may on occasion wish to change a darker finish to a lighter one. This can be done without removing the old finish. Simply apply a coat of ground color and when this is dry, apply one or two coats of the lighter varnish stain in the exact color you want.

Shellac is fast-drying and very easy to apply. White shellac darkens wood less than orange shellac. Therefore, if you want to keep as much of the natural tone of the wood as possible, use white shellac. Shellac is usually packaged in a 4- or 5-pound cut (a mixture of 4 or 5 pounds of shellac gum dissolved in one gallon of alcohol). Always thin this to a 2- or $2\frac{1}{2}$-pound cut before using it on floors. *A few thin coats of shellac are far superior to one or two thick coats.* In fact, thick coats of shellac are responsible for most of the complaints regarding use of this material. A thick coat does not have the resiliency of a thin coat; whether it is used as a final finish or as an undercoat for varnish, a thick (and hence, brittle) coat will crack and cause the finish to fail. Shellac deteriorates in time and should be purchased fresh for each major job. It can be easily used to "touch up" worn areas. A shellacked floor can be given additional protection that will greatly increase its life if you wax it regularly—weekly or at least monthly. Periodically, remove old and soiled wax with warm water and mild soap suds. When dry, apply another thin coat of wax. As with shellac, be sure to keep the coats thin.

Varnish is another widely used floor finish, but its extreme slow-drying is often considered a handicap.

APPLYING FINISHES

Left: Penetrating floor sealer may be applied with cloth or brush. When pigmented, it adds color. Penetration is $\frac{1}{4}''$ deep. Final finish is floor wax. Nothing else goes on.

Right: Since floor sealer may not penetrate evenly, a certain amount may remain on the surface. Remove this with fine steel wool pad on disc sander.

Left: The penetrating sealer finish is waxed. To simplify the job, use the disc sander with brush attachment. Similar wax application may be made over shellac-varnish finishes.

Right: Two coats of a good plastic finish will cover the floor, also. This is a clear, hard finish requiring no wax and lasting many years without refinishing of any kind.

The length of drying time is invariably linked to the durability of the varnish, and the "quick-drying" type should, as a rule, be avoided. For new work, use a coat of thinned shellac or varnish as a sealer, then apply finish coats of varnish without thinning. Make certain that newly varnished floors are protected from dust, lint, etc., until they are at least tack-free. Most floors require three coats of varnish. The usual drying time, at normal temperature and humidity, is 24 hours for each. For refinishing, apply one or two coats of varnish, sanding lightly between coats. Varnish is superior to shellac in water resistance, but it darkens in time. Dirt and grime may hurt the finish, and if soap is used for cleaning, it should be used sparingly and thoroughly removed after use. Periodic waxing will be very helpful in prolonging the life of a varnish finish.

Unlike shellac and varnish, which are surface coatings, sealers penetrate *into* the wood. There is very little surface film to scratch or mar. No filler is necessary with sealers. If color is desired, a pigmented sealer may be used—then two coats of clear sealer especially formulated for floors. Apply the sealer generously with a brush, mop or cloth. After about 15 minutes (before it becomes sticky), wipe clean with fresh cloths. Allow overnight drying, sand lightly with 2/0 sandpaper and apply a second coat. Periodic waxing will be found helpful, too. A sealer finish will not scratch or chip, and worn spots may be "touched up" without showing laps. The sheen of a sealer finish is particularly attractive.

A plastic finish is a surface coating especially formulated for its clearness and durability. It will yield a pleasant sheen or a brilliant high gloss if (as a third coat) it is thinned, as per directions, with a reducer. Various epoxy-resin finishes are known to outlast varnish. In any worn areas, "touching up" is easily done without the danger of showing lap marks. Some plastic coatings provide a high-gloss effect, others a satin finish.

Finishing Concrete Floors. First clean the concrete thoroughly, removing any soap or grease with a lye solution. Next, etch the floor with a commercial etching solution (follow the manufacturer's directions). Use three coats of rubber-base paint especially formulated for floors. The first coat may be thinned a bit; use the paint for the next two coats as it comes from the can and apply each successive coat only when the previous coat is perfectly dry to the touch. After application of the final coat, wait one day before using the floor for normal service. If the traffic is heavy, wait three days.

HOW TO LAY FLOOR TILES

Covering a floor with tiles (asphalt, vinyl, cork or rubber) is a job that can be badly botched if it gets off to a poor start. All floor irregularities must be eliminated at the very beginning—otherwise the tiles, because of their flexibility, will become molded to them. Follow the photographs on the next page for floor preparation. First, however, you should estimate the number of tiles you will need; to do this, compute the square footage of the room. As an example, suppose the room size is 253 square feet and you plan to use the common 9-by-9″ size of tile. First find the number of tiles needed for 200′, the number needed for 50′, and then the number for 3′. The total is 451. Check the table below for "tile waste allowances." It shows that you will need an additional 7 per cent, or 32 tiles. Thus, a total of 483 tiles will be needed.

Square Feet	Number of Tiles Needed			
	9″ × 9″	12″ × 12″	6″ × 6″	9″ × 18″
1	2	1	4	1
2	4	2	8	2
3	6	3	12	3
4	8	4	16	4
5	9	5	20	5
6	11	6	24	6
7	13	7	28	7
8	15	8	32	8
9	16	9	36	8
10	18	10	40	9
20	36	20	80	18
30	54	30	120	27
40	72	40	160	36
50	89	50	200	45
60	107	60	240	54
70	125	70	280	63
80	143	80	320	72
90	160	90	360	80
100	178	100	400	90
200	356	200	800	178
300	534	300	1200	267
400	712	400	1600	356
500	890	500	2000	445
600	1068	600	2400	534
700	1246	700	2800	623
800	1424	800	3200	712
900	1602	900	3600	801
1000	1780	1000	4000	890

Tile waste allowances		
1 to 50 sq. ft.	14%
50 to 100 sq. ft.	10%
100 to 200 sq. ft.	8%
200 to 300 sq. ft.	7%
300 to 1000 sq. ft.	5%
Over 1000 sq. ft.	3%

1. Wood floors in good condition need little preparation other than countersetting visible nails and planing down raised areas and splintered boards. Sweep clean.
2. Badly scarred floors, or rough subfloors, can best be prepared for tiles with an underlayment.

3. The underlayment is placed rough side up, joints left open about $\frac{1}{32}''$ to allow for expansion. Stagger joints so that nowhere will four corners meet at one point.
4. Underlayment is nailed down with resin-coated or grooved nails spaced at 4″ intervals along edges and over surfaces. Chalk lines help to space nails.

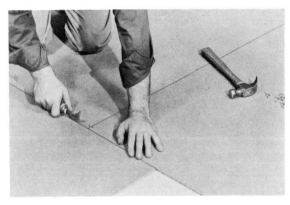

5. Filler for masonry or wood consists of 1 part cement, 1½ parts mastic, and 3 parts sand over nailed-down chicken wire. Use ½″-thick lath screeds to maintain level floor.

Tile Removal. Putting down floor tiles is easy, but getting them up again is often another matter. In trying to remove one tile for replacement, a dozen might be damaged. The easiest and quickest way is to use the broad-flame nozzle of a propane torch and play the flame, held about 6 inches away from the tile, over the whole center area of the tile. The heat softens the adhesive underneath, and then a putty knife or scraper will pry it loose easily. Work from the center to the edges and stop there so the adjoining tiles will not be damaged. The adhesive under these adjacent tiles may be softened, but if pressed tightly against the floor for a few seconds, they'll be firmly reseated. Then you can lay a new tile in the open space and press it into the still-soft adhesive.

NOW YOU ARE READY FOR TILES

1. With the floor in good shape for tiles, locate the center point of each of two opposite walls. Connect the two points with chalk lines across middle of room.

2. Measure to the center of the line and, with a framing square, draw a line at right angles to the first. You can use a floor tile instead if you have no square.

3. Lay out two rows of tiles from the crossed lines to the walls. These are not cemented down, since the purpose is to see how the tiles will fit in place.

4. If the space between the last tile and the wall is over 8″ or under 2″, move the center line over. The space between the last tile and wall should be about 4½″.

5. If necessary, move the line running in the opposite direction as well. The idea here is to avoid having a strip of tile about 1″ wide along the walls at either side. →

6. Now for the adhesive. A brush is used with the type shown here, but other types, such as mastic, require a trowel.

7. With average humidity, the cement will get tacky in about 15 minutes. If you can touch it and it doesn't stick to your fingers, it's ready for the tiles.

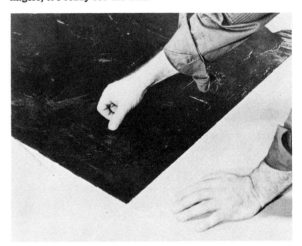

8. Still working only ¼ of the room, start laying tiles flush with the chalk lines. Butt tiles together but do *not* slide them into place. Just lay them down.

9. The tricky part comes when you reach the wall—two tiles are needed now, call them *A* and *B*. Lay tile *A* over the last one laid, and lay tile *B* against the wall. Draw a line on *A* along outer edge of *B* with a pencil.

10. Tiles are brittle and break easily if cold. When stored or warmed to room temperature (70°), they are workable and may be cut easily with a pair of scissors.

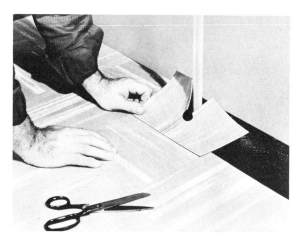

11. Put the cut-off piece into place against the wall. This cutting is repeated along both walls until the area is filled. Then start on the next ¼ of the room.

12. When a cutout has to be made, make a paper pattern. Transfer the pattern to a tile and cut with a scissors. Slit allows close fit behind the pipe.

CERAMIC TILE FLOOR

In just three steps you can lay a ceramic tile floor in the bathroom which will endure as long as the house itself. The first task is to take up the old floor covering, whatever it may be. After that, take up the wood top floor and expose the subfloor. Remove all nails and debris and check the subfloor carefully for signs of rot, warped boards and damaged spots. If any boards need replacing, do it at this time, for the new tile floor will cover the subfloor permanently.

As part of the preparation, remove the door from its hinges and the threshold, or saddle, so that the tiles may be laid in a straight line between the inside door casings. Remove the shoe molding and baseboard so that the tiles may extend to the wall.

Finally, consider other obstacles on the floor. Usually radiators can be jacked up slightly, or at least enough to lay the tile beneath them. Water pipes will have to be surrounded with tile. Permanent fixtures will also be encircled with the tile.

The second step is laying the tile. Begin by spread-ing a layer of heavy waterproof paper over the entire area, overlapping at least 2″ at every joint, and turning up the edges from ½ to ¾″ at walls and around fixed objects. Tack down the paper suffici-ently to prevent moving it while working. Over the paper lay a fine-mesh metal plaster lath, tacking it down over its entire surface at 6″ intervals with rust-proof nails. The lath must be absolutely rigid. Cut the lath with tin snips or wire cutters and fit it closely against the wall and in the corners. To fit around pipes, cut as shown in the sketch below.

Next comes the cement, a mixture of 1 part port-land cement, 2½ to 3 parts sand and just enough water to make a sandy mixture. Avoid too much water, as tiles will completely sink into a watery cement. Spread the cement to the depth of ¾″ and level it off. If you have a large area to cover, divide it into sections with grounds (¾″ boards that will be used as a guide in levelling off the cement) and lay only one section at a time. Grounds are removed as work progresses, so do not drive nails in such a way that the grounds cannot be easily removed.

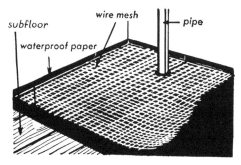

Cut wire mesh to fit around obstructions.

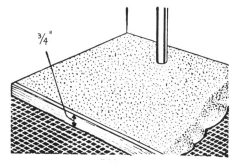

Grounds divide sections for working ease.

Tiles of this type, sometimes called mosaic tiles, are usually sold in one or two square-foot "sheets," already pasted at correct spacing on sheets of paper. Lay the first sheet on the cement, paper side up, in one corner. Lay the next alongside, keeping the same spacing between sections as is observed on the ones pasted to the paper. Continue until the area is covered.

Sooner or later you will come to spots where tiles must be cut. They can be broken by first scoring each side with a glass cutter, then snapped with a pair of pliers. Ragged edges are flaked off by little nips with the nose of the pliers. Irregular and curved lines are formed in the same way. Nip off the surface side carefully to a marked line and remove the rough lower sections at will. Slate and stone cutters, or power-driven Carborundum discs, speed the process of cutting tiles but are by no means necessary.

With the tiles laid in place, leveling off begins. Use a length of 2-by-4 with a perfectly flat side and a hammer. Lay the flat side against the tiles and tap gently on the wood with the hammer, sinking the tiles into the cement. Move the stick slightly and tap again until the entire surface has been gone over. Check your progress with a spirit level to see that no valleys or ridges are created. Where individual tiles protrude, tap them down. During the tapping process, the paper to which the tiles were pasted will come loose. Remove it and wipe the tiles with a damp cloth, taking care that none are dislodged.

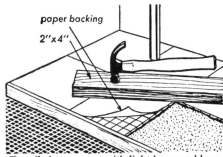

paper backing

2"x4"

Tap tile into cement with light hammer blows.

To fill the cracks between the tiles, make a second mixture of cement; a 1:3 mix, but thinned with water to a creamy paste. Pour it over the tiles and work into the cracks with a paint brush. Mop up the excess, then wipe the tiles clean with a damp cloth frequently rinsed. If you have laid the floor in sections, repeat the entire process until all tiles are laid.

At entrances, lay the tiles in a straight line drawn between the door casings. At this point, you will discover that you have raised the level of your bathroom floor. This is due to the ¾″ of cement plus ¼″ of tile. The old wood floor was less thick. To make an adjustment between the tile floor and the floor of adjoining rooms, spread a tapered layer of cement across the threshold and lay the wooden saddle or threshold over the cement. It will no longer be level across the top, but its curved surface is designed to adjust such differences.

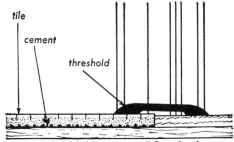

tile

cement

threshold

Threshold bridges unequal floor levels.

If you decide to replace the baseboard, lay a ½″ ribbon of calking compound around the entire edge of the bathroom on the tile and press the new baseboard into this compound to provide a watertight joint. Quarter-round shoe molding may, of course, be either nailed into the baseboard or omitted.

If there are left-over traces of cement on the tiles and it has hardened, make a solution of 10 per cent muriatic acid and water and wash the floor with it. The acid softens the cement to permit removal. Wear rubber gloves and be careful in handling the acid. Read the directions carefully. If the mortar between the tiles has become soiled, wash the floor with sodium hypochlorite or with any chlorine cleansing liquid.

INSTALLING AND REPAIRING LINOLEUM

Laying Linoleum. Start to lay a linoleum floor by first taking everything movable out of the room. Pry up the trim around the baseboard at the floor level with a screwdriver or broadnose pinch bar. Then paste single sheets of newspaper together to fill nearly every clear space in the room. Run the edges right up square with the walls. At complicated places, such as door jambs, cut and paste small strips of paper to an exact fit. Check the pattern carefully and then remove the paper from the floor. Turn it upside down on the underside of the linoleum (which should be laid flat for a day or so before working on it) and trace its outline with a sharp pencil. Then cut around this with ordinary household scissors or a trimming knife. A single-edge razor is handy in tight spots.

After the linoleum has been cut to fit the newspaper pattern, lay it out on the floor to see if it fits exactly. Make any adjustments that might be needed; laying linoleum is similar to laying individual tiles. Be certain to apply a liberal quantity of paste where the seams join. And don't make the seams too tight; swelling linoleum will cause the strips to buckle. It is best to leave about $\frac{1}{16}''$ between each strip at the seams.

Nail the trim molding back into position along the baseboard. Cut metal edging with a hacksaw and nail it over the linoleum at door sills or places where the linoleum meets a wooden surface.

Patching Linoleum. When linoleum wears thin around the kitchen sink, the back door, or under the table, you can replace it, choosing your color and design so that the patch becomes an attractive decoration in the room. All that is needed for this small job is a ruler, a hammer, some small nails, a putty knife, a linoleum knife, the linoleum patch and paste. Then follow the photo series below.

PATCHING A WORN-OUT SPOT

1. Make desired pattern and use it as a guide to cut old linoleum with a knife. Take piece to dealer; use it as guide for thickness of replacement. Buy new piece about 1″ larger than worn sample.
2. Use 4 or 5 small nails to hold patch in place; do not drive nails all the way in. Cut along edge and remove extra old linoleum. Clean out space. Use paper underneath to raise new linoleum level with old, if necessary.

3. Remove nails and linoleum; apply the cement generously to floor or both sides of paper, if used. Fit patch in position. If linoleum is warm, it will lie flat; otherwise, use weight to hold it down while cement is drying.
4. When cement is dry, some edges may be higher than the rest of linoleum. Hammer them down or sandpaper lightly. Fill any large holes with fine chips of linoleum added to varnish; small spaces will be filled as linoleum spreads.

To freshen linoleum, first use alcohol and steel wool to scrub away old wax. Then apply two coats of floor enamel, any color you like. Make certain first coat is dry before applying the second. The job is now done, that is, if you want a solid color. To produce a stipple effect, use three brightly colored enamel shades that blend in with the base color on the floor. Pour some paint into paper plates; then dip crumpled paper into one color and dab on floor. Do same for other colors, making patterns.

For spatter painting, use three long-bristle brushes for the colors. Dip one into the first color and slap the heel of the brush (the metal band) against a stick held about a foot above the floor. Use the other colors next. Remember to protect walls from being spattered. When all the paint is thoroughly dry, apply a heavy coat of wax or clear plastic over the floor. A waxer will save time when doing this work. Keep floors well waxed to protect the paint finish, and your "new" linoleum will give many extra years of wear.

Freshening Linoleum. In addition to the solid color, stipple and spatter effects shown in the two photographs above, you can also obtain unusual effects on worn linoleum by using masking tape or stencils after first painting the floor a solid color. With the use of masking tape, you can paint stripes, boxes, borders and wide bands on the floor. Merely press strips of tape in place over the linoleum and paint between them. When the paint is thoroughly dry, lift the strips off.

PAINT OVER EDGE OF TAPE

1. Press masking tape, either ¾″ or 1″ width, on linoleum after the base paint coat is thoroughly dry. Paint border, stripe, or band in the color you want. The tape will prevent paint from going outside the border area; it serves also as a guide.

2. After border paint is dry, lift the masking tape slowly at an angle and you'll find a straight edge dividing base paint from border paint. By pulling the tape off at a right angle to the direction it was placed on the floor, you'll reduce the possibility of having an irregular edge.

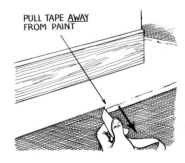

PULL TAPE AWAY FROM PAINT

STAIRS

Stairs should be designed for comfort in climbing and for economy of space. Below is a view of the portion of stairways which you do not ordinarily see —the supports and the manner in which they tie into the house framing. The flight broken by a half-way landing and the framing of the headroom above the steps are typical of a well-built house. The second-floor ceiling forms the top of the stairwell. The basement stairway, better known since it is usually visible in all its parts, is only partly shown at the right of the sketch. Headroom over these steps is provided by the incline of the upper stairway between the landing and the top floor. When you have occasion to re-model your stairway or build closets into its waste space, these are the details to consider when you begin to work.

Step Repairs. Battered stairs are easily made new again by the simple expedient of turning over the worn treads. There's good unworn lumber on that other side. (Unless, of course, someone before you has already done the job. If so, new treads are in order, or you might try the idea on page 89.) The only tools you will need are a pry bar, a hammer, a keyhole hack saw, nail-pulling nippers, and a nail set.

Some stairways vary in construction, however, as follows:

1. Balusters may be toenailed directly to the tread, in which case saw the nails off by slipping the hack saw under the baluster. Trying to hammer the baluster loose will only split the wood.

2. If the balusters are glued into bored holes, saw them off flush with the tread with the hack saw, leaving the end as a plug in the hole to be sanded smooth. Balusters may be toenailed back into place.

3. Some stairways have treads dadoed to fit over the risers and a rabbet at the back end to fit into a dado groove in the next riser. The turn-over system is difficult here, and you may have to buy a new tread. Saw off the tongue at the back of the tread, then use a chisel to remove the tongue from the riser's dado (see sketch). A similar cut removes the

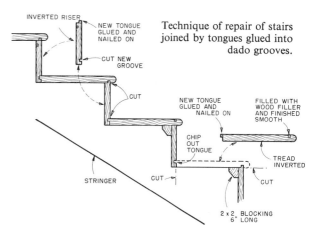

Technique of repair of stairs joined by tongues glued into dado grooves.

tongue from the riser below if it was glued instead of nailed. The new tread may be the type without grooves. Refit the old tread by following the sketch above.

4. In turning over a tread where the balusters fit into notches or holes, the turned step may end up with holes unmatched. Plug the holes with shaped blocks and make new cuts as needed for the balusters unless you cut them flush, in which case they may be toenailed into place.

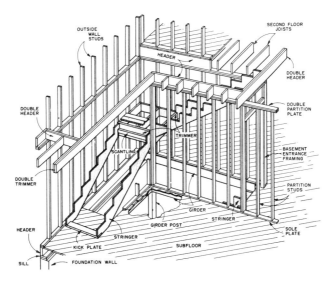

1. First step in tackling repairs is removal of balusters. For this type, remove end trim carefully with pry bar, then remove nails.

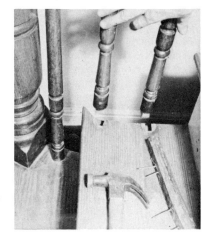

2. Sometimes toes of balusters are keyed in slots such as these; in others they are simply tocnailed into the stair treads.

3. With baluster ends freed, twist each baluster to break glued joint at top where hand railing is attached to balusters.

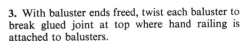

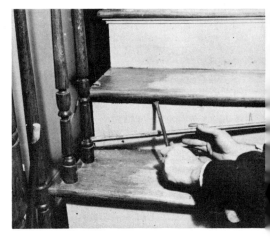

4. Remove trim under tread with pry bar, then pry tread up slightly from riser to allow entry of a keyhole hack-saw blade.

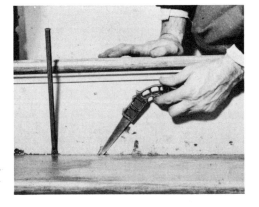

5. Since nails are set from various angles, cut all nails with keyhole hack saw rather than pry the tread loose all around.

6. With all nails cut but those where tread is set into stringer, simple leverage will free this last remaining end.

7. Underside of tread is good as new. Turn it over, remove any traces of old paint, and sand down rough spots on your new step.

8. Spread good grade of glue along all joint edges before replacing tread. This makes the joint stronger, prevents possible squeaks.

9. In nailing down tread, place nails at an angle so that they hold better and allow less chance for squeaks to develop in the future.

Remodeling a Stairway. For safety and convenience in use, step risers (the vertical pieces between steps) should be from 7½ to 8″ high, no more than that. The treads should be at least 10″ front to back. The stairway itself should be about 3½′ wide so that two people can pass and so that you can carry bundles up or down easily. Finally, and most important, there is the matter of headroom. Where the steps pass under the front header of the stairwell, there should be a minimum of 6′ 8″ between the header and the forward edge of the tread directly beneath it. With less clearance, someone will bump his forehead going down or the top of his head coming up.

Steep stairs are usually made that way to keep the stairwell (the opening in the floor) to a minimum and thus allow added floor space in the room. It isn't easy to enlarge this opening in most cases without pushing out walls and remodeling the whole floor.

Wherever possible, this is the best method since added length permits more, and less steep, steps. If the stairwell can be expanded to either side, then a platform can be installed near the center and the steps below that point run off at right angles to the existing flight. This is sometimes true of totally enclosed stairways where one wall is simply a partition.

If the stairwell cannot be enlarged in either way, it is frequently possible to install a turn-around,

using "winders" to turn the stairway at right angles below a given point. Winders are cut in triangle fashion with the pointed ends aimed at a central post. You turn the corner as you descend, and all the other steps can be made less steep.

As you remodel the stairway, so must the handrail be altered. This is a good time to improve its appearance as well. Of course, the open stair rail is a stock item at lumber yards and needs only to be assembled and mounted. Basement and attic stairways, however,

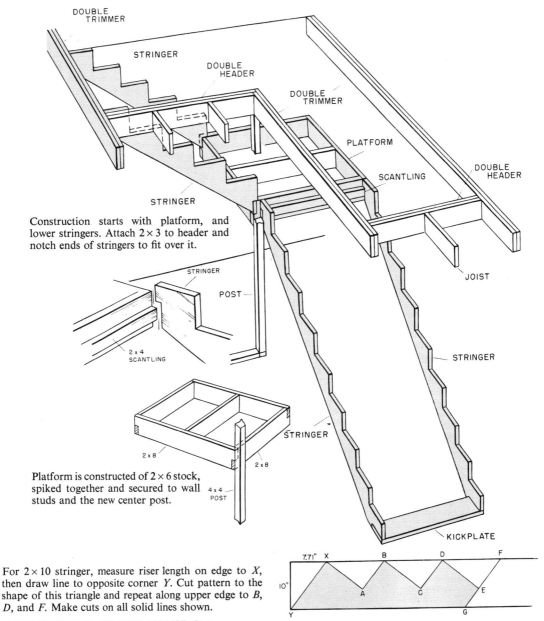

Construction starts with platform, and lower stringers. Attach 2 × 3 to header and notch ends of stringers to fit over it.

Platform is constructed of 2 × 6 stock, spiked together and secured to wall studs and the new center post.

For 2 × 10 stringer, measure riser length on edge to X, then draw line to opposite corner Y. Cut pattern to the shape of this triangle and repeat along upper edge to B, D, and F. Make cuts on all solid lines shown.

with only a length of pipe or a piece of 2-by-3 for a handrail, can be improved.

The totally enclosed stairway can be opened on one side (and sometimes both) without removal of the wall studs. By exposing these studs, finishing the rough wood, and then setting irregularly spaced shelves between them, interesting decorative effects may be achieved.

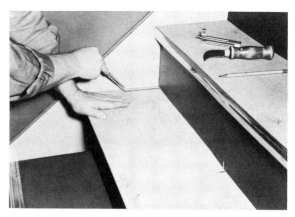

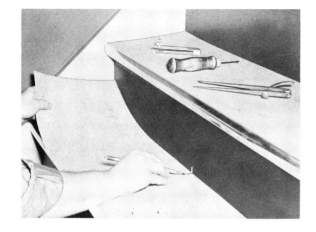

Steps can be further dressed up when wood is badly worn by covering them with linoleum. Level the treads with floor fill if they are too badly worn or corrugated. To protect the treads, a metal nosing should be installed along the front edge of each step.

To fit linoleum for length, mark the center of the linoleum strip and the center of the riser. Move the strip until it rests against the edge of the step. Distance between riser mark and linoleum mark is half the amount to be scribed and cut from the end of the strip.

WALLS AND CEILINGS How to build a wall · Finding a stud · How to fur a wall · Plaster walls · Finishes for walls · Refinishing dry walls · Wall anchors · How to install a new ceiling

Housing trends come and go with as much variability as fashions in dress and styles in automobiles. Often the very first to reflect changing tastes, the walls of a home are more than just protection against the elements. Basically, of course, they should always be sound and snug, but beyond that, their appearance, and often their location, is up to you. One family may prefer large open areas, using screens or dividers as semi-walls when needed, while another family may put more emphasis on privacy, with a wish for more rooms, although smaller.

In this section, you will find step-by-step directions for both building and removing walls and partitions, taking into consideration the often overlooked necessities of ventilation, adequate supports, electrical wiring and light from out-of-doors.

Styles in wall coverings come and go too, since decorating is a continuing process of renewal, but basically the successful application of materials is always predicated on their appropriate selection, accurate measurements, and careful, true workmanship. Wallpapers, fabric and plastic coverings, panels

of wood, inset tiles, each can bring years of added use and beauty to the seemingly most hopeless of rooms—provided the underneath wall is sound. This section shows you the basic steps toward sound walls—furring, stud location, plastering and dry-wall installation repair—to assure you of the results you want, no matter whether you're working with pine panels or glazed ceramic tiles.

HOW TO BUILD A WALL

Quite a few of your home improvement or remodeling projects are likely to include the building of an interior wall. While it sounds like a king-size job, it's really quite simple if you plan it thoroughly before you begin and consider what the new wall will do to your house. It is almost certain to alter the light and heat in the room, and it may make some wiring, plumbing and heating changes necessary. Plan these points first; then proceed, referring to the sketches beginning on page 92.

The wall will be only a partition and, therefore, bear no load other than its own weight. As a result,

AN X-RAY OF YOUR WALLS

1. **Wall Studs**—these support the floor above, the roof, and the covering of wall. They are usually 2 × 4's spaced 16" apart, center to center.

2. **Plaster Lath**—may be wood slats, rock lath, or wire-reinforced. Or your walls may be covered only with plasterboard, wood panels, or other sheet material.

3. **Thermostat**—from this little box, fine wires encased in armor lead through the walls to the furnace and control its operation.

4. **Plumbing Vent**—an open pipe running from sewer pipe up through the roof. It admits air into the sewer to permit even flow of water through the system.

5. **Hot Air Ducts**—these run from the furnace up through walls to individual rooms conveying hot air upward to registers and cold air back to the furnace.

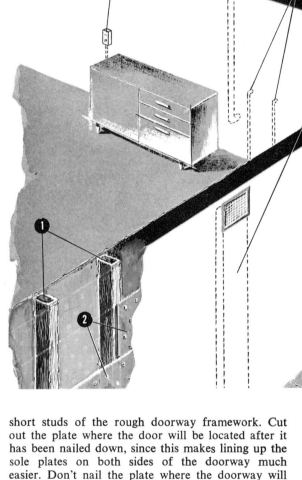

relatively light materials may be used. The framework of the wall consists of a sole plate on the floor, a top plate on the ceiling overhead and studs at regular intervals between them. Use 2-by-3 stock for plates and studs. These will support the "skin," the wall covering on both sides.

First secure the sole plate to the floor. If the floor is wood, nail down the plate with 10d nails at 2' intervals. If the floor is concrete, bore at least two or more holes through the plate every 3' and matching holes $\frac{9}{16}$" deep in the concrete. Fiber or metal plugs will hold screws put through the plate. If you plan a doorway, mark its location on the plate. Measure the door width, add 1" on each side for the frame (or jamb) of the door and $1\frac{5}{8}$" on each side for the

short studs of the rough doorway framework. Cut out the plate where the door will be located after it has been nailed down, since this makes lining up the sole plates on both sides of the doorway much easier. Don't nail the plate where the doorway will be located or it will be difficult to remove the section later.

Next, the top plate is cut and secured to the ceiling. Make use of either a plumb bob or a straight piece of wood, trued up with a level, to mark the location of the top plate. You can't use a nearby wall as a guide, since that wall itself may be out of alignment. Fastening the top plate depends on the ceiling material and the direction of the joists above it. If your plate is to run at right angles to the joists, it

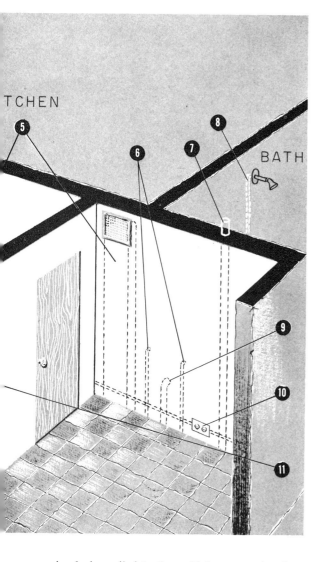

6. Hot and Cold Water Pipes—are always located in inner walls to avoid freezing; pipes might freeze if they were placed in outside walls of the house, despite insulation.

7. Sewer Pipe—this one starts at upper floor bath, picks up waste from first floor bath and continues to main sewer system in the basement, entirely unseen.

8. Shower Pipe—you see only the shower head, but behind the walls two pipes, hot and cold water lines, join to provided regulated flow and temperature.

9. Bathtub Drain—this is an overflow pipe which runs down through the wall to join the main drain, then to the sewer system; it is a short but essential pipe.

10. Wall Outlet—a maze of wires joins all these outlets to the main power source and fuse box. The insulated wires are encased in armor to prevent "shorts."

11. Wall Switch—another portion of the wiring. Wires lead from here to lights controlled by the switch, and to the power system, usually in the basement.

may simply be nailed to them. If, however, the plate is to run parallel to the joists and you have a plasterboard ceiling, it is necessary to plan the wall so that the top plate will be directly under a joist which will supply the required nailing surface. If your ceiling is good sound plaster, the plate may be fastened to it with Molly anchors.

Studs are cut to fit snugly between the two plates. While they are generally spaced at 16" intervals, they may also be spaced at 20" or 24" intervals, depending on the sheet size of the wall-covering material that will be used. Studs are toenailed on all four sides into the plates with 8d nails. It's practical to mark off the location of all the studs on the sole plate before any are nailed in. If you plan a doorway,

locate the two full-length studs on each side of it and then mark off the location of those to each side of the opening at the desired spacing. If your wall has an outside corner or a door, start at this point and mark off in each direction from it. Regardless of the final spacing, attach one stud to any wall your new wall contacts. Studs may be trued up with a level, their position marked on the top plate and then toenailed into place. You might find it easier to use spacers—strips cut from 1-by-3 stock to equal lengths (14¾" long where stud spacing is 16" on centers). Place these between studs, top and bottom, then nail into the plates. With these strips, no level is needed after the first stud is properly trued up.

Further bracing of the wall is made by horizontal

pieces of 2-by-3 nailed between studs. The location and number of these also depend somewhat on the wall covering to follow. For the average 8'-high wall, two cross braces equally spaced suffice. These will support all sheet materials (plywood, plasterboard, etc.), but if the covering is to be of full-length vertical boards, a single brace at the center will do. You may stagger these braces their own width so that nailing into their ends through the studs with 10d or 16d nails is possible. This eliminates a lot of toe-nailing. Use two nails into each end.

Framing a Doorway. The wall is now taking shape. Time to get on to the more intricate steps. Go back to the marked-off doorway and cut out the plate. You can use the two studs as a guide for the saw. Measure the height of the door you intend to use. Standard sizes are either 6' 8" or 7' high. Add 1" to this height to allow for the frame, and—if you plan to use a threshold—add 1" more. Cut two short studs to this combined length and nail them to the two full-length studs on each side of the opening. Be sure to put one nail through into the cut-off ends of the plate. Cut two pieces of 2-by-3 the width of the opening above these short studs, nail them together and insert. Keep the narrow dimension of these pieces vertical. Nail through the side studs into this lintel, or header, as the piece is called. A short stud, called a cripple, is then erected between the header and the top plate. Other openings in the wall are handled in

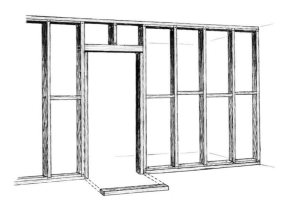

the same way. If the opening does not extend all the way to the sole plate, as in a pass-through, for example, fit a double 2-by-3 into the bottom of the opening. Short studs extend to the sole plate from the bottom one and from the upper one to the top plate.

Going Around a Corner. For the average short wall, an outside corner post consists of three pieces of 2-by-3 joined as sketched. If the inside surface of this wall is not going to be covered (as in a rough closet, for example), two pieces may be used, joined as an L and put in place on the sole plate. The three-piece post, however, is necessary where both sides of the wall are to be covered.

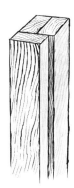

Inside the Wall. At this point, install any wiring that must pass through the wall, or position any outlet boxes, switch receptacles and light receptacles. If you have to extend heating pipes or ducts or plumbing facilities of any sort, get them in now. Also, if you plan on making use of any of the space between studs for built-ins, mark their location and set in supports for the future recessed items.

Covering Up. Gypsum wallboards are the odds-on favorite for covering walls in any area of the house. This material consists of gypsum plaster between two layers of cardboard, forming a plaster sandwich. Sheets range up to 4 by 12′. With the exception of wood-grained gypsum wallboard, which is pre-decorated, it lends itself to any decorative finish—paint, paper, fabric or texture. The decorative material may be applied as soon as the joints are thoroughly dry. Paint can be applied by brush, spray or roller. For all paints, be sure to apply the proper primer or sealer as first coat. The type of primer or sealer will vary with the sort of paint selected, so follow the paint manufacturer's directions.

The various types of gypsum wallboard are:

1. Regular or standard gypsum wallboard, available in $\frac{3}{8}$″ and $\frac{1}{2}$″ thicknesses. The $\frac{1}{2}$″ board is preferred in new construction. Generally, these boards are made with square, beveled and tapered edges. The square-edge board is used, as a rule, where no decorative treatment is required. The beveled edge is used where an accented joint is desired for architectural reasons. The tapered-edge board is to be used with the tape-and-cement joint concealment system.

2. Type X gypsum board, made in $\frac{1}{2}$″ and $\frac{5}{8}$″ thicknesses and with both square and tapered edges, has a specially formulated core designed to increase resistance to fire and sound transmission.

Wallboards are easy to cut; just score with a knife and break. Nailing is easy, too, but the paper face

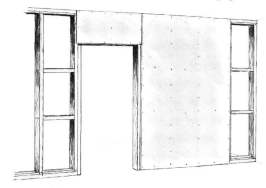

must not be broken. The big panels cover up to 48 square feet of ceiling or wall surface and go up quickly. However, it takes some patience in plastering and sanding to insure that the joints between the panels will be invisible under a finish coat of paint. Hammer dents or nail heads must be spotted with joint cement and perforated tape used at all joints plus inside and outside corners. All surfaces must be primed before painting unless you purchase wallboard with such faces as knotty pine, bleached and dark walnut. The following are some tips to make your wallboard installation easier:

1. Make sure that the framing members (the studs and joists) are straight and in alignment.

2. Start with the ceiling. If possible, span the entire width or length of the ceiling with one piece of gypsum board. This will reduce the footage of the joints that will require concealment later.

3. Nail the boards properly, using the annular-ringed, bright-finish nails specially recommended for the application of gypsum wallboard. Start nailing at the center of the board and work outward. Nails

APPLYING GYPSUM WALLBOARD

1. Apply long side at right angle to framing. Support in assistant's hand holds up ceiling board during nailing.

2. Assistant starts to support the ceiling board as it is carefully edged into place.

3. First nail is driven into center of sheet; then nail outward to opposite edge.

4. Left hand holds board against joists while nailing. Nails always "dimple" the surface.

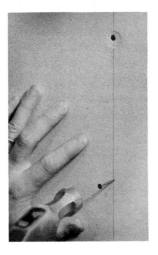

5. No saw is needed. Score both faces of the board with a hooked knife and snap off.

6. Scrap pieces can be used in small areas like the section around a window shown above.

7. Board is punctured with saw tip, then cut to provide opening for recessed light fixture.

8. Broad knife is used to spread joint cement. It is first step in joint-concealment procedure.

9. Reinforcing tape is applied over cement to entire length of joint and pressed into place.

10. After excess cement is removed, wait a day. Apply second coat wider than first.

11. Fine sandpaper, used with minimum of pressure, helps smooth the surface.

Wall Materials	Insulating Value	Resistance to Dampness	Resistance to Grease and Dirt	Durability	Ease in Application	Sound Deadening	Ease in Cleaning
Wood							
Solid hardwood— unfinished	G	G	P	G	F	F	P
Solid softwood— unfinished	G	F	P	G	F	F	P
Plywood—unfinished	F	F	P	G	E	F	P
Plywood—pre-finished	F	F	F	G	G	F	G
Stone and artificial stone	P	G	P	E	F	G	P
Brick	P	F	P	E	F	G	P
Plaster—bare	F	P	P	F	P	F	P
Wallboards & Plasterboards							
Fiberboard—unfinished	E	F	P	F	G	E	P
Plasterboard—unfinished	F	P	P	F	G	F	P
Insulating wallboards	E	F	P	F	G	E	P
Hardboards—pre-finished	F	E	E	E	E	F	E
Asbestos board	G	E	P	E	G	G	E
Perforated hardboard	P	G	G	E	E	P	G
Corrugated Plastic Sheeting	G	E	E	E	F	F	E
Plastic Blocks	G	E	E	G	F	F	E
Glass Blocks	G	E	E	E	F	F	E

Some of the materials listed above can be used to construct entire walls in themselves; others will make walls on wooden frames. In either case, they may be left in their original state—or finished to taste.

Insulating value—covers use on, or as outer walls.

Durability—is based on ability to withstand rough treatment without dents or damage.

Sound deadening—covers use on interior walls and the ability of the materials to soften sounds inside the room as well as resist sound transmission from beyond the particular walls.

E = Excellent   G = Good   F = Fair   P = Poor

should be spaced up to 6″ apart on the ceiling, up to 7″ apart on the sidewalls, and never less than 3/8″ from edges or ends of the board. The area of the board immediately surrounding each nail should be held tightly against the framing while the nail is being driven.

4. It is generally advisable to apply the long dimension of the wallboard at right angles to the studs or joists because it usually reduces the amount of joints to be concealed. In such horizontal application, start sidewalls at the ceiling. Fit lower boards snugly without wedging.

After you have applied the wallboard to the ceiling and all the walls, you are ready to proceed with "welding" and concealing all the joints and treating the nail heads. As the first step in joint treatment, use a 5″ broad putty knife to butter adhesive into the channel formed by the tapered edges of the board. The adhesive, recommended by the gypsum-wallboard manufacturer, should be mixed to a putty-like consistency. Apply moderate pressure, filling the channel evenly. Then lay the special reinforcing tape neatly into the adhesive, centering it over the joint. With the knife, press the tape firmly into the adhesive, removing all air pockets and excess cement. Next, cover the tape with a thin coating of adhesive. When the first coat of adhesive has dried, remove any remaining roughness by sanding the surface lightly and then apply a second coat, feathering it out on both sides of the recess, leaving it too as smooth as pos-

Coverings	Resistance to Dampness	Resistance to Grease and Dirt	Durability	Ease in Application	Ease in Cleaning
Paint					
Clear finishes (varnish, shellac, plastic paints, lacquer)	G	G	G	G	E
Paints with oil, rubber, alkyd, emulsion bases	F	G	G	E	E
Paints mixed with water	P	P	F	E	P
Linseed Oil	G	F	G	E	G
Wallpaper					
Non-washable	P	P	P	G	P
Washable	F	P	F	G	G
Scrubbable, fabric backed	E	E	G	G	E
Coated fabrics (oil pigment, vinyl, pyroxylin)	G	G	G	G	E
Uncoated fabrics (burlap, canvas)	F	F	P	G	P
Thermosetting plastic sheets (Micarta, Formica, etc.)	E	E	G	G	E
Tiles					
Glazed ceramic	E	E	E	F	E
Unglazed ceramic	E	G	E	F	G
Metal	E	E	E	G	E
Plastic	E	E	E	G	E
Asphalt, rubber	E	G	G	G	E
Vinyl	E	E	E	G	E
Glass sheets	E	E	F	F	E
Linoleum—inlaid	E	E	G	G	E
Enamel-on-felt	E	E	F	G	E
Leather	G	G	F	G	E
Cork	P	P	F	G	E

E = Excellent   G = Good   F = Fair   P = Poor

sible. After the second coat is dry, again remove any roughness by sanding and then apply a final smoothing coat of adhesive, feathering it out beyond the second coat. If any rough spots remain after the adhesive has thoroughly dried, sand very lightly with fine sandpaper. Nailheads are concealed with the same adhesive used to treat the joints. They should be spotted with adhesive at the same time that each of the three coats is applied to the joints. If the nailheads are not completely covered with the first layer of adhesive, they should immediately be driven further into the dimple with a crown-headed hammer.

Other Covering Materials. Aside from gypsum board, you might also use paper board, which is available in extra-large-sized sheets, up to 8 by 18′. While awkward to handle without assistance, they speed up wall construction. Fewer joints result, and nail-spacing may be greater. Thickness is about ½″,

and 1½″ nails are used, usually No. 9 flatheads, galvanized or cement-coated. Nails are placed 10 to 12″ apart along the edges and staggered on alternate studs through the center sections at similar intervals. For sheets this size, ⅛″ spaces are left between sheets to allow for expansion. Paper board may also be glued to studs and framing with special glue provided with the sheets. Cut with a knife or saw. Finishing can be done with wallpaper, paint or textures.

Another material is fiber board, usually made from wood pulp. It is light in weight, usually available in 4′ widths and lengths from 6 to 8′ up to 12′. They form a wall that is insulated by the material itself and, for the most part, provide sound-deadening qualities. Some are available in square tile form. Application is on furring strips except in the cases where, by means of adhesives, they may be attached directly to the wall as a flush surface. Others are beveled and the arrangement of panels will add eye appeal in lines or checkered squares. For attaching to furring, the usual nail is a 2d type, blued, or No. 17 flathead brad. Being soft, these fiber boards may be attached to furring with staples. Since fasteners should be spaced at 4″ intervals, staples are real time and labor savers. Where a thicker variety of fiber board is used, longer nails up to 1½″ are required. The material can be cut with a knife or saw. Where rough-edged fiber board is applied to walls and ceiling with butt joints, a crack filler is used, frequently with a paper strip to conceal crack and nail heads. Many types of fiber board are available ready-finished and require no more attention, once in place. Others can be papered, painted or finished with texture paint that will also fill in cracks and cover damage.

Hardboard is made by exploding wood chips into fiber form and, after processing, pressing the fibers together with heat and pressure. The result is an extremely dense, rigid, and durable material, capable of standing an enormous amount of wear and tear. Since these panels and squares are put up to form a finished wall without further covering, the completed finishes cover a wide range. Simulated wood grains in all colors, baked-on enamels and leather-textured surfaces are only a few of the choices available. When nailed up, furring is required under all edges. Nails should be 1¼″ long, lightly countersunk, and the heads concealed by hole fillers. Space nails at 4″ intervals on edges, 6″ on center studs and supports. Cut with a saw. These materials may also be affixed to walls with adhesives, with beveled joints left to form a pattern or filled as desired. They may

also be put up with special metal or wood strips used both as support and to conceal the actual joints. Owing to the strength of hardboards, they make an excellent covering for old broken plaster walls which they support and conceal. With their virtually water-proof finish, they are ideal for kitchen and bathroom and may be washed repeatedly.

Plywood is a firm base for the application of tile, linoleum, fabric, wallpaper or paint. There is little shrinkage or warping, cracking, or curling under normal household conditions. Plywoods may be obtained in literally hundreds of forms. Thickness varies from ¼″ to over 1″, with increasing sturdiness. As a rule, one side is rough, the surface side ready for the final coating. Unfinished plywood paneling is sold in sheets, usually 4-by-8′ and larger. They may be cut with a hand saw. Nailing, or screw fastening, should be made at 16″ on centers. Nail sizes depend on the thickness used, the nail being 3 times as long as the wood thickness. Butt joints can be made invisible with fillers in most applications. Striated plywood finishes help to conceal joints. In plywood, nails should be countersunk—in which case finishing nails and brads are more practical— and the holes then filled with plastic wood to be concealed later by the final finishing processes. Fabricated panels, including tongue-and-grooved sheets, are applied with special clips. While this leaves a slightly raised joint, the finished panels can be so arranged that the seams are invisible or else used to accent the paneled effects of the room.

Solid wood, of course, includes such paneling as knotty pine, clear pine and specially beveled and striated lumbers milled according to order for specific

TOP AND BOTTOM

As an alternate to cap molding, ceiling may be finished off with simple cove-molding cornice as shown.

Here is another ceiling treatment, using ¼-round, stocked by all lumber yards. More elaborate cornice and picture moldings may also be purchased.

Baseboard detail showing use of ¼-round, and plywood strip capped by ½-round. This can be simplified by omitting the molding and using the plywood strip alone. It makes a perfectly adequate base if the top is sanded to a bevel.

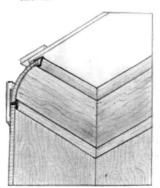
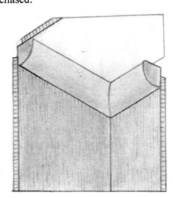
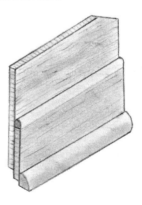

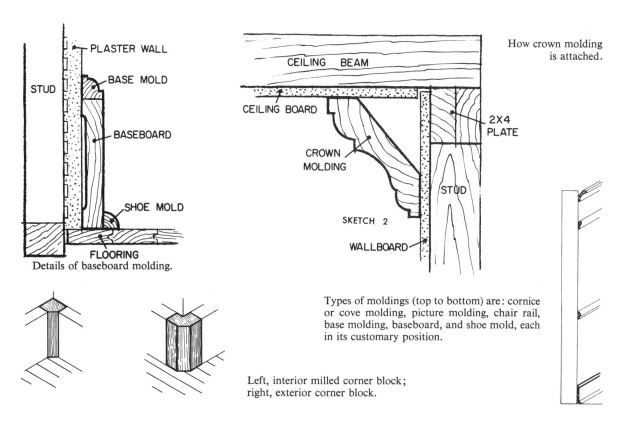

Details of baseboard molding.

How crown molding is attached.

SKETCH 2

Types of moldings (top to bottom) are: cornice or cove molding, picture molding, chair rail, base molding, baseboard, and shoe mold, each in its customary position.

Left, interior milled corner block; right, exterior corner block.

purposes. Random widths, special finishes and stains all combine to make paneled rooms as modern or as provincial as the decorator's fancy desires. Application to old walls or new should be on furring strips for adequate nailing surface.

The Finishing Touch. When the framing has been covered with the material of your choice, all that remains is the application of moldings to the top and bottom of the wall to conceal gaps between the wall and the floor and ceiling. Styles available at all lumber yards vary so widely that one can be found to match any decorating motif, but methods of application are standard. Sketches suggest application ideas. To apply baseboard and ceiling trim, cut to size, mitering at corners as needed (see Chapter 7). Use finishing nails driven through the trim into studs. Counterset nail heads and fill with wood putty.

FINDING A STUD

Whether you're making a major alteration or merely trying to hang a picture, hunting for a stud can sometimes be a baffling experience. A stud is one of those important, but invisible, parts of your house. It's usually a 2-by-4 that runs vertically between the floor and ceiling just behind the wall. And studs are generally spaced 16" apart, center to center.

To locate a stud, check the baseboard for any visible nail heads. Nails are usually driven in at stud intervals and, if you spot one, try tapping the wall at that location lightly with your knuckles or a hammer. A hollow, drumming sound means that there's no stud right there; a solid, thudding sound means that you've found it. If your walls are made of a paneling material such as plasterboard, you may be able to locate a joint in the wall, a spot where two panels meet. They're usually joined over the center of a stud; so, if you find a stud this way, measure along the wall at 16" to the next stud.

You might also measure from a corner of the room. From a corner formed by two exterior house walls, mark off 17". There should be a stud located there. If testing by sound indicates that there is, then there will be another at every 16" interval. If there is no corner formed by two outside walls, you won't be able to use this technique. Some inside walls are started against outside walls but there doesn't necessarily have to be a 16" centered stud at that point. In measuring along walls, do not include door and window studs. Here two studs are used, side by side, and they can be placed anywhere without regard to standard spacing.

Older houses frequently present another problem,

for the studs may be warped. If you find the location at the base near the floor, it might be off somewhat along the way. Another problem is sometimes met in newer homes where wallboards are used instead of plaster. The studs might be spaced 24" apart. If you can check with your builder, fine. Otherwise, tap the wall to test by sound for stud location.

One final method, sure to be successful, is that of making exploratory holes in the wall itself. Lift up the base molding with a floor chisel and drill small holes in the wall to locate the stud. If you are still drilling into wood after the drill is in to a depth of about 2½", you've hit the stud. The base molding, when replaced, will hide these small holes. Use a padded hammer (wrap a heavy layer of cloth around the head) when nailing the molding back so that the finish won't be marred.

HOW TO FUR A WALL

Almost every project which involves the finishing of walls—making your basement into a family room, for instance—requires the application of wood furring strips. These strips, usually 1-by-2's, serve as the surface to which the finish wall paneling can be attached. Usually strips 1" thick are used for this purpose.

Furring, on any type of wall, must furnish a flat, even surface. If it bends with irregularities which may be present in the wall, the finished panel installation will bend also and, in time, will probably work loose. On uneven walls, therefore, it may be necessary to whittle out sections of the furring to allow it to pass over high spots, or it may be necessary to insert shingle or other thin wood wedges to compensate for indentations. As you work use a plumb line to make sure that the surface of the furring is always flat and vertical.

To fur a plaster wall, first remove the baseboard and trim. Run the furring strips from center to center horizontally along the wall, spacing them 16" apart and nailing them to the wall studs with 8d common nails. Where vertical panel edges meet, it is best to nail a vertical furring strip to the wall, placed so that the edges of both panels may be nailed to it. Brick, concrete or other masonry walls should be furred with lengths of 1-by-2 lumber, nailed to the walls not horizontally, but vertically. Use steel-cut nails or other masonry anchors.

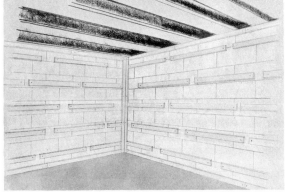

When it starts out in life, furring is just a pile of lumber— 1 × 2 or 1 × 3 or even larger widths of 1" scrap stock in assorted lengths. It doesn't become furring until you apply it to a wall or ceiling. As this sketch shows, the strips are applied for vertical panel stock, with the spaces between strips staggered. The floor line, the ceiling line, and the corners are fully stripped to give the panels a solid base. The wall is now ready for application of finish material.

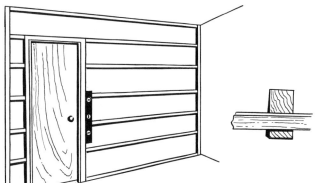

As indicated here, when an opening is reached it is completely surrounded with furring strips. All strips are checked with a level, and a straight-edged board long enough to reach from ceiling to floor is used to locate any variations in distance from the wall. Depressed sections are corrected with pieces of wood shingle used as wedges; high spots are planed down until furred wall is level. Any irregularities will make the finished wall uneven, whether panel or board stock.

Where furring is impossible owing to extreme wall irregularity, 2 × 2 stock may be used and the framework braced only at intervals with blocks.

To attach the furring to the wall, the easiest way, if the wall is concrete, or concrete block, is to nail it. Special masonry nails can be driven right through the furring and into the masonry. A heavy hammer or 4-pound sledge does it easily. Penetration of only ½″ to ¾″ of the nail is adequate. Use more nails rather than try for greater depth.

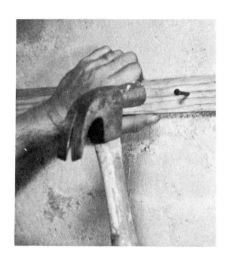

Assuming you have a battered ceiling, with plaster falling off in dangerous chunks, all is not lost. Furring will hold up what remains and give you a surface to which a new and firmer ceiling material can be applied. First, decide which material you wish to apply, and space the furring accordingly. If ceiling is especially poor, nail furring across and into every joist.

You can put a ceiling over your basement playroom quite easily. Here you'll be nailing the furring across the underside of the joists. Check them well before you start since some joists may be larger than others, some warped or sagging. Use bits of tapered wood shingle to bring the furring out level. If you select ceiling tiles that require fasteners along two *adjacent* edges, use 1 × 6 furring and space so there will be ample nailing surfaces.

How to Fur a Wall   101

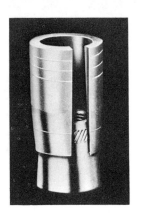  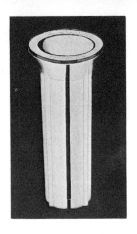 

If you encounter a mushy wall—old plaster or masonry—it isn't going to survive having nails driven into it. But you can use a screw, set into a device that can expand inside a hole drilled in the softer material. It takes a bit longer, but it will hold more securely. When you use screws this way, you need fewer of them than you would nails. In masonry, drill holes with a carbide bit or a star drill; in plaster, a wood-cutting drill bit will do. The anchors shown here are for: (left to right) heavy machine screws, lag screws, large wood screws, small wood screws.

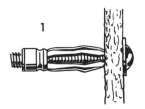 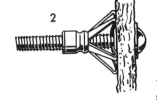

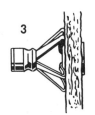 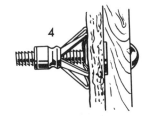

Where studs are irregularly spaced, some furring strips may be applied to the between-stud spaces of framed walls with Molly anchors. Simply drill a hole through the old wall covering and fit in the Molly. The screw is removable for addition of the furring strip. A useful idea, this, when furring might have to be placed vertically at a spot where no stud exists.

PLASTER WALLS

Preparing Walls for Plaster. Installing rock lath, the base to which wall plaster is applied, is not a difficult job and requires only a few tools. If you can swing a hammer or cut wire with tin snips or read a carpenter's level, you can do your own lathing. For speed and convenience, invest in a lathing hatchet. If you prefer to use your own hammer, you'll have to score and cut the lath with a knife, which takes longer.

First calculate the square yardage on all surfaces to be covered and order lath accordingly. Buy metal corner stripping by the linear foot for openings and corners. Ten pounds of lathing nails will be needed for each 100 square yards of rock lath.

The next step is to set up baseboard grounds— ¾" wood strips which allow for some foundation settling and prevent plaster cracks. Nail these along all walls to be plastered. Then proceed as outlined in the photographs. Remember to keep all lathing work neat and the corners square. The final job will be just as good—or bad—as this essential base job.

1. Keep printed surface visible, as this side is treated to hold finish plaster. Set center nail, then 4 nails to each stud. Set nails slightly below surface of lath.

2. Start at bottom on grounds, then work upward, staggering joints in each row to avoid weak spots which crack plaster. Leave no gaps larger than ⅛″ between boards.

3. When staggering joints, you will have to cut some boards. Hold lath in position, score with hatchet on stud center line. Avoid tight fits, which crack on expanding.

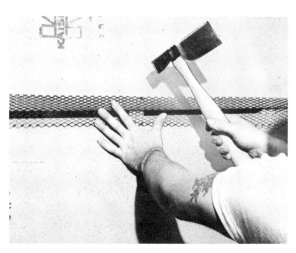

4. When cutting, score deeply in position, then snap sharply, turn board over, and cut paper on reverse side. Keep hatchet blade sharp so all cuts will be clean.

5. Where gaps wider than ⅛″ occur, cut strip of wire lath long enough to reach between studs and nail over the gap. Press metal lath flat, nail to studs securely.

→

6. Purchase metal lath corner stripping in pre-cut bundles, crimped at 90° (right) angles. Nail into corners over rock lath, overlapping ends of pieces at least 3″.

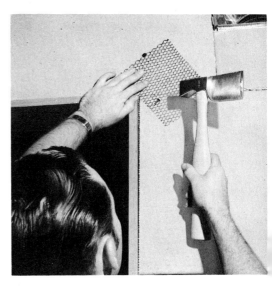

7. Points of stress, at corners, need extra strengthening. Place pieces of metal lath over these points, as shown, to provide needed reinforcement against cracks.

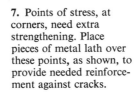

8. Where pipes protrude through walls for plumbing fixtures, rest lath against pipe ends and tap *lightly*. Remove lath and cut out with tip of hatchet. Keep holes small.

9. Slide lath over pipes, check to be sure pipes do not hold lath out of line, then nail up lath. Cover large holes with metal lath fitted around the pipe as needed.

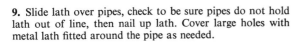

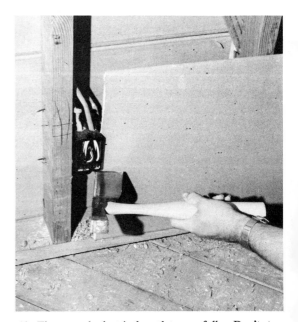

10. Fit around electrical outlets carefully. Don't tap lath against box, for you may dislodge the box. Score all sides of opening and tap out with hatchet, as for pipes.

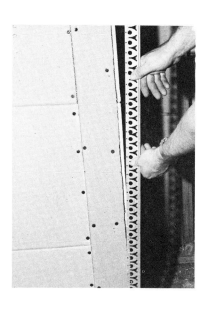

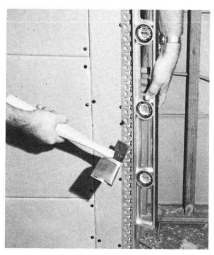

11. Outside corners are covered with metal corner bead over rock lath. Do not drive on too tightly, as ⅜" must protrude to allow for thickness of finish plaster.

12. Corner bead must be aligned with doors and windows with a level. Anchor top and bottom, then tap into place and test with level. Nail every 6" along both sides.

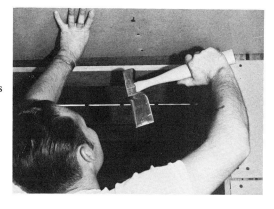

13. Rock-lath ceilings require staggered joints. Don't miss nails, for punctured paper deteriorates.

14. With wood windows, lath is butted against casings; with metal sash and frame, you nail lath to butt against sash frame. Allow gap of ⅜" between metal lath.

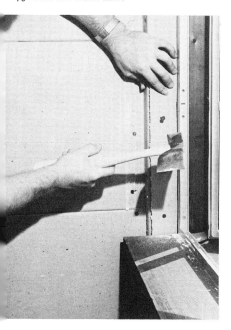

15. Finish metal sash with corner bead to produce plaster finish inside and outside beading. Plaster will conceal beading, butt against sash. True up beading.

How to Plaster a Wall. There's an art to making a good plaster wall, and the use of the proper tools is essential. These include a plasterer's trowel, a corner-shaping tool, a hawk, a darby, a screeding rod, a heavy brush and a bucket. To order the materials you will need, figure the square feet of the area to be covered. The undercoat is a mixture of sand, prepared gypsum plaster and water. You will need—for each 10 square feet of undercoat—90 pounds of plasterer's sand, cleaned and screeded, and 30 pounds of gypsum plaster.

TOOLS

1. **Trowel:** a plasterer's trowel is a *must*. This has a long brace bar on the top side in contrast with the shorter bar on a mason's steel float. It costs several dollars more and is worth the price.
2. **Hawk:** this is the classic mortarboard device. Use one made of aluminum and save wear and tear on yourself. The wooden type weighs a good deal more. Load with plaster and hold in the left hand while the right does the work.
3. **Darby:** a two-handled smoothing tool to level large flat areas. It is held flat against the wall as it is moved along and levels out raised spots.
4. **Screeding Rod:** a straight-edged wood or metal stick to level off rough plaster applications. One end is usually held against guides as the upper end scrapes excess plaster back onto board for reapplication.
5. **Water Brush:** this, and a bucket of clear water, must be kept on hand for finish plaster coating. The brush spreads as well as dashes water over the surface being troweled smooth.

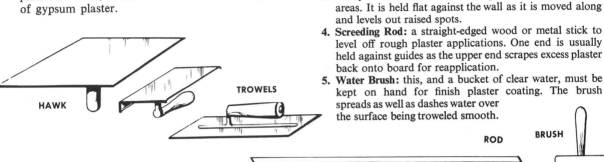

HAWK   TROWELS   DARBY   ROD   BRUSH

 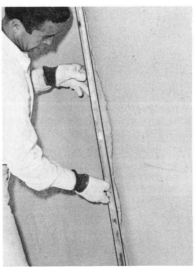 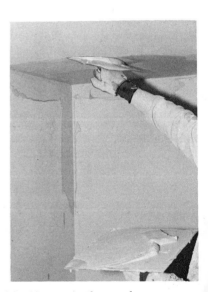

1. Mix 18 shovels sand and 100 pounds (1 sack) gypsum plaster as explained in text. Apply enough to cover lath, forcing into holes. Double back at once and cover with enough plaster to fill to level of grounds (guides set up along openings). Suction of paper on lath holds plaster fast.
2. After covering one section, use screeding rod to level off high spots, scraping off excess. Rest one end of rod on guides to avoid removing too much plaster. Set bar into corners, pull out gently to leave corners square.
3. Moisten wall with splashes from brush until wall is beaded with water, then rub darby over wall with even pressure to slick it for next coat. Keep darby flat to wall and avoid gouging corners with it. Press gently.

To mix, use either a wheelbarrow or shallow wood box and mix the sand and plaster, dry, in one end. Tilt the mixing box with the dry mixture in the upper end and put water in the low end. Then draw the mixed sand and plaster into the water a little at a time, mixing constantly. If water is added into the dry mix, or all of it is pulled into the water at once, lumps are formed which can't be easily broken up. Mix to a heavy creamlike consistency. Add more of the dry mix or water, as necessary.

Apply the base coat as shown in the photographs. The final coat of finishing plaster is mixed with water without sand and applied as illustrated. Troweling technique is quickly mastered. Plaster is applied from a full trowel on upward strokes, using light pressure only. The trowel, in finishing, is held at an angle of about 30° to the wall. If pressed flat against the wall, the trowel is held by suction and will pull the plaster off. If the angle is too great, the edge of the trowel will leave wavy lines in the surface.

4. After slicking walls with darby, smooth and cut corners with trowel. Trowel is worked squarely into corner, then pulled out and down. Repeat in both directions from corner.
5. Allow from 5 to 7 days between first coat and finish coat. Interior plaster finish is prepared according to bag instructions. Hose wall lightly to dampen. Using corner tool, apply finish coat to area about 4″ from corner in both directions. Coat is applied about ⅛″ thick.
6. Apply finish plaster to wall evenly, laying material on with a forward stroke, sealing by pressing out bubbles on back stroke. Finish all of ceiling first, then wall.

 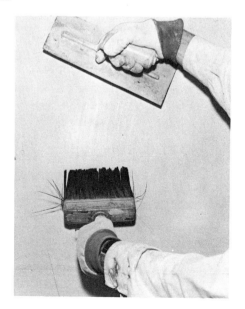

7. On walls, start at the base and apply finish coat upward, sealing with down stroke. Overlap strokes about 2″, working from left to right on all surfaces, with the toe of the trowel handling the overlap.
8. Final step in finish plastering is glazing. Run the wet brush over a section of wall and follow behind with trowel edge, stroking lightly from top to bottom. Overlap 6″. You will discover, and can remove, rough spots in this step. The more you trowel, the better the finish becomes.

Repair of Plaster Walls. Sooner or later, almost every plaster wall and ceiling develops cracks—if not in the broader expanses, then at least where flat surfaces join one another. Wind pressure on the house, structural expansion and shrinkage, traffic vibration, and household activities all contribute toward weakened plaster. Before any redecoration can take place, the inevitable patching must always be done.

First, clean away all material that appears loose in and around the crack. If it's a fair-sized crack, use a putty knife and a beer can opener and open the crack to its deepest part, then undercut it so that it's wider underneath than on the outer surface. Little cracks can simply be brushed clean. With a spray, a sponge or a wet rag, *thoroughly* dampen all surfaces of the crack. If this is overlooked, moisture from the new plaster will be absorbed into the wall, leaving the patch powdery and weak. Mix patching plaster to a thick paste and pack it into the crack with a putty knife, preferably a flexible one. (For thin, hairline cracks, use a paint brush.) Press the mix into the bottom of the crack, build up slightly more than necessary, smooth off the excess, and let it dry for 2 to 4 hours. Then use medium-grit sandpaper on a flat block to smooth off the excess. If you are going to paint later, a few strokes with fine-grit sandpaper will finish it off nicely. Before you paper or paint over this patchwork, brush on one coat or more of thinned shellac as a size coat. If there is no "glazed" look to the size coat when dry, apply a second coat.

One word of caution—when the job is finished, don't pour excess plaster down the sink, for it will solidly block the drain pipe. If you mixed the material in a china or plastic bowl, it's easy to clean out for the next batch. Each quantity mixed should be just what you can apply in 10 minutes. After that, it starts to harden and has little holding strength left.

The general procedure for patching holes where plaster has fallen from the wall is the same as for patching cracks: undercutting, cleaning, dampening and applying new plaster. Before applying the patch, however, make sure that the lath or other plaster base has not come loose from the framing members behind. If it has, nail it back into place.

In the case of wooden lath that is broken, you will have to enlarge the hole in the plaster until two adjacent studs or joists are exposed. Then remove the broken laths and replace them with short lengths of lath nailed to the studs. If the hole is more than an inch or so in diameter, apply the patching plaster in two coats. First put on a fairly thick undercoat and, before it has quite dried, score its surface with an old comb so that the next coat will bond to it. After the undercoat has dried and set, dampen the surface and apply the thin finish coat. If the area of the hole to be patched is larger than approximately one square foot, you will find difficulty in doing an adequate repair job with patching plaster alone. One way of repairing such large holes is to apply two coats of gypsum plaster as is done in ordinary plastering and then a third coat of finishing plaster. Another way, perhaps easier, is to cut a piece of plasterboard to fit the hole, nail it in place to the lath and apply a finish coat of patching plaster.

To repair a bulge, first create a hole where the bulge appears. Do this by rapping the bulge with a hammer until the loosened plaster falls out. Be sure to knock or pry away any loose plaster around the hole so as to have sound plaster at the edges of the patch.

FINISHES FOR WALLS

The walls of your home are never mere enclosures for your furniture or dividers between rooms. You and your family live with your walls every day of your life. They influence your selection of furniture and, frequently, your moods. The range of wall coverings is so wide that there's little reason why any family shouldn't have exactly what they like. Whether you choose the dignity of mahogany or walnut paneling, the color and easy maintenance of ceramic tile, the luxury of leather or the simplicity of paint, you will find it all easy to apply.

Wallpaper. Because of its variety, attractiveness and ease of application, many homeowners each year turn to wallpaper when redecorating. Washable papers, many already trimmed, offer a handsome finish with a long-lasting surface. Ceiling wallpapers

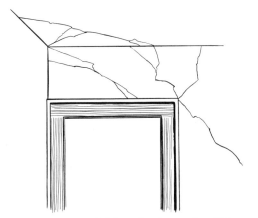

Most common type of failure is the crack which runs diagonally across a wall from a corner, or from a door or window opening. Cracks of this description are caused by slight settling of the house framework. They extend right through the coats of plaster down to the lath underneath. Because almost all houses settle somewhat as they grow older, structural cracks of this kind are fairly frequent.

create interesting decorative effects, and the fabric-supported type of paper not only hides imperfections in the ceiling but, as the house settles, the paper stretches and conceals minor cracks.

You can easily improvise a long table for pasting by putting a panel of plywood right over a table or laying it between two sawhorses. You will also need a 6' stepladder, seam roller, scissors, sponge, razor and handle. One particularly useful tool is a steel straightedge. A plasterer's mitering rod works best, but you can make one yourself from 14-gauge steel. It's about 4 by 10", with a beveled or mitered side. (See photos 8 and 9.) The long edge is slightly sharpened, assuring a snug grip on the paper to be cut and a much neater result.

All surfaces to be wallpapered should be dry, smooth and even. If the wall was previously papered, remove all loose paper and edges and sand along seams to avoid ridges later. Lapped seams should be stripped with a razor, then sanded. If the wall is of plaster, check carefully for holes, bulges and cracks, and mend any defects, remembering to apply wallpaper size to new spots of plaster and any unpainted, dry, porous plaster. If the wall was enameled or finished with a glossy paint, roughen it slightly with sandpaper before papering. (See "Refinishing dry walls," pages 117 and 118.)

If your paper is not pre-trimmed, mark matching guide lines with a light pencil at both ends of the roll. Then trim off the edges, using a straightedge and razor or scissors. To cut wallpaper to size, measure the distance from ceiling to baseboard molding and add 3 to 4", always watching pattern to make certain of matching edges. If a length of wallpaper does not fit properly, it can be removed easily by just lifting it off. The paste remains pliable and doesn't dry for a few hours.

1. Use scissors to cut paper to size—distance from ceiling to baseboard molding plus 3 to 4". Match pattern as you cut each piece. Cut all the pieces needed, plus one or two extra, before you paste.

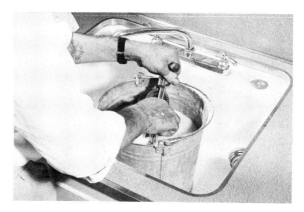

2. Pour paste slowly into water and use your hand to mix so you are certain to remove all lumps. An eggbeater afterwards will smooth thoroughly to a consistency of light cream. Don't make paste thick!

3. Apply paste to underside of paper with a wide brush, making certain to cover all the surface. Note string tied across ends of pail handle; this serves as brush rest and prevents brush from falling in.

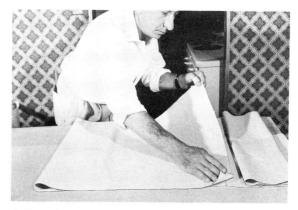

4. To make paper easier to handle, fold ends toward middle. Avoid sharp creases along folded edge. Fold paper over several times to a convenient size for handling. Paste all pieces before hanging. →

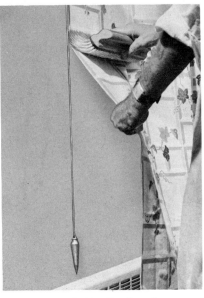

5. To align first piece on wall, hang plumb bob or chisel on end of cord the width of the paper from the corner. Let 1 or 2″ of the paper overlap ceiling molding and brush paper onto wall.

6. At a corner of the room, overlap one piece about $\frac{1}{16}″$ around the corner, and then add the next piece on the adjacent wall. Make certain to match pattern of paper as succeeding pieces are attached.

7. When setting additional pieces in place, leave a fraction of an inch, about $\frac{1}{64}″$ is enough, between the two sheets. A seam roller pressed on the seam will bring the edges together to form a butt seam.

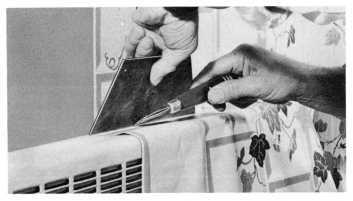
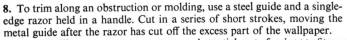
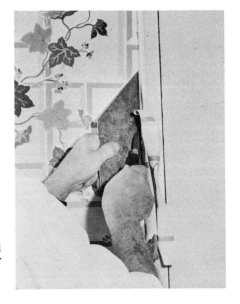

8. To trim along an obstruction or molding, use a steel guide and a single-edge razor held in a handle. Cut in a series of short strokes, moving the metal guide after the razor has cut off the excess part of the wallpaper.

9. When necessary to remove a substantial part of a sheet to fit around an obstruction, cut off most of the excess with a scissors. After rolling the seam, trim edge exactly for a perfect fit.

Don't throw away extra pieces of wallpaper which can be used later to cover switch and outlet plates. A screwdriver, scissors, some rubber cement and ten minutes are all that are needed. First, take out the fuse which controls the current to the light switch box at which you're working. Then remove the two small screws holding the plate. Line up a piece of wallpaper over the open switch box, match the paper pattern, and cut a piece 1″ larger all round than the opening. If the paper is not washable, spray it with clear plastic so that subsequent fingerprints can be easily removed.

Apply rubber cement to the back of this paper and lay it with pattern side down. Now place the plate over the back of the paper with the plate front turned down. With a sharp knife or razor, cut out an opening for the switch toggle. With an ice pick or the tip of a knife, puncture holes for the screws which hold the plate to the wall. Trim corners diagonally so that there will be a smooth surface when the ½″ fold of the wallpaper is pressed over the back of the plate. Apply rubber cement liberally to hold the side pieces in place. The plate is now covered and can be put back.

Plastic Wall Coverings. Extraordinarily resistant to household stains, particularly oils and greases, vinyl plastic is one of the most practical materials available as a wall covering. Upkeep for a wall of vinyl plastic is at a minimum. Made in the form of yard goods, tiles, simulated stone or brick and other designs, it easily conceals wall defects and irregularities.

If the walls were previously oil painted or enameled, they must be "pearlashed," that is, washed down with a potash solution. Your wallpaper or paint dealer can supply the compound. If the walls were previously water painted, calcimined or whitewashed, they should be gone over with a wire brush and a strong detergent. This will assure a good clinging surface for the new covering. If the walls were previously unpainted, scrape them with a wire brush to remove all loose particles and wash with a strong detergent to remove any grease and dirt. If walls were previously papered, make sure there are no loose edges or peeling paper, and apply a coat of glue size, allowing it to dry thoroughly before applying the vinyl.

Fabric Wall Coverings. Cracks in the plaster, uneven ceiling lines and spaces in the corners where the walls have settled, can all be brought under control with a fabric wall covering. It helps the plaster underneath to hold together. Available in pretrimmed 24″ widths, all you have to worry about is cutting it to the right length. The straight edge makes it easy to do a perfect butting job instead of overlapping the strips as is done with ordinary stock. The procedure for hanging fabric wall covering is exactly the same as that for any other wallpaper.

Wall Panels. Relatively little in the way of building materials can surpass the effect obtained by the use of vertical boards—knotty pine, golden oak, redwood, to name but a few. When you visit your lumber yard, be sure to buy no grade lower than No. 3 common boards. Below that standard, the boards will have loose knots, splits along the grain and bad ends, causing waste. Lower grades may also warp badly. If you are selecting knotty pine, be sure all knots are small and not protruding on either side. Reject boards with long knots which have been sawed off along their lengths. Boards should be free of warps and twists, as they will be if properly stacked in the yard.

After delivery, stack the lumber inside the house at the future room temperature, if possible. Do this at least one week before putting them up. While stacking, examine both sides and choose the side you want to use as the surface. Paint the other side with a colorless wood preservative to prevent undue absorption of moisture through the otherwise unfinished back after the wall is up. Then stack the lumber with small blocks between boards at 4′ intervals along their length. This permits air to reach all sides.

While the lumber is drying, put the walls in shape. If you plan to put the wall up vertically, you will need furring. If you plan setting up the boards horizontally, then no furring is needed, but mark the location of wall studs so you can find them to nail into later. Plywood panels and preassembled sections of board wall materials also require furring for secure anchorage.

Begin the job in one corner. Nail up the first board with the tongue edge out of the corner. Face-nail (through the outer surface of the board) 1″ from the corner edge into furring. Then drive finishing nails (preferably 8d or 10d) at an angle through the tongue where it joins the boards and into the furring. Set the nails just below the wood surface with a nail set. The second board is placed against the first, the groove pressed over the tongue of the first, and then tapped tightly into place with a block of wood held against the tongue as a pad to prevent hammer marks. Nail up through the tongue as before. No more face-nailing is needed.

Cut all boards at least ¼″ less than the distance from floor to ceiling so that, if dampness later causes them to swell, they will not bow in the centers and pull free. For an adjoining wall, the first piece is set into the corner, the groove end butted against the first board put up and face-nailed, then nailed through the tongue as on the first wall. In most cases, putting up a board wall raises the surface beyond its former limits, which means that some extra treatment around doors and windows is needed. Before applying boards to these areas, remove the original casings and put up 2-by-2's of the same material as that selected for the wall, setting them flush with the inner surface of the window or door frame. These, plus the furring, will provide a flush surface when the final wall boards are butted against the 2-by-2 strips. New casings of the same lumber as the wall can then be cut and applied over the 2-by-2's. You

INSTALLING PINE PANELS

1. Baseboard must be surface-nailed. For a job of genuine professional quality, drive the 6d finishing nails well into the wood with a nail set, then use filler to hide the holes.

2. Nail paneling to the furring strips at the tongued edge. In this way, the groove of the next panel will hide the nails. Hammer the grooved block as shown to obtain a tight fit.

3. Furring strips must be installed all around windows to give solid support for paneling. You must also cut panels to fit around windows.

4. For flat corners, a strip of paneling is beveled on both edges. It is laid right into the corner and then surface-nailed.

5. For a 90° corner, trim the pattern from a piece of paneling. Butt it into the corner against other end panel and nail.

6. A stair section of a basement recreation room finished in western pine paneling.

should treat the areas above doors and windows in a similar fashion.

Various treatments of the top and bottom of wood panel walls may be used. Some sort of trim is needed. A horizontal baseboard—3 to 4″ wide—is one form. Or a minimum of 1″ quarter-round to conceal board ends may be preferred. At the ceiling line, a narrow (2 to 2½″) crown molding may be suitable, or 1″ quarter-round to match a corresponding base. A

1-by-2 strip may also be used as a substitute where total absence of curved surfaces is wanted.

Plastic-surfaced hardboards make an extremely attractive, easy-to-clean finished wall surface. They consist of a hard, semi-luster plastic surface which has been baked onto a tempered hardboard base. They never require decorating and they can be cleaned with only a damp cloth. Follow the photographs on the next page for installation.

The ease with which a wall such as this may be put up would surprise most homeowners. Installing boards of the more expensive woods is no different a procedure than installing the more common varieties. The tongue-and-grooved boards— whether redwood, western pine, or any other clear wood with a pleasing grain—are blind-nailed to furring at intervals along their length. The base and crown moldings, and any intermediate moldings as necessary, conceal cut ends. And boards can be cut easily to fit around any obstructions or irregularities.

1. A level guide line for the top of a hardboard wainscot is marked around the room. Walls were plastered here, but plasterboard also serves as a good panel base.

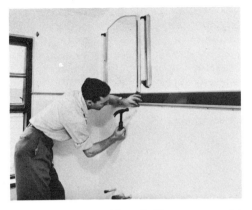

2. Nail-on moldings hold an ornamental strip of prefinished hardboard. The strip is red, to afford accent for gray planks. Color of moldings matches planks.

3. A plank of predecorated hardboard is cut to size with a regular crosscut saw. The paneling comes with tongue-and-groove edges for easy fitting of joints.

4. Wallboard adhesive is spread on back of each plank and on wall area it will cover. Metal clips, nailed along exposed edge, are hidden in completed joint.

5. Measure locations of pipes exactly so that panels fit over them neatly. Cut holes, finished side up, with a woodworking saw or bit.

6. If you have made your measurements accurately, the panel will slip neatly over the pipes and under edge of molding at top.

7. When the wall section is completed, the final step is to install base molding of predecorated hardwood. Drive nails through drilled holes, using a nail set.

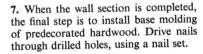

Peg-Board. Perforated hardboard, known as Peg-Board, is available in standard-size panels and may be cut with a hand or table saw to any size you need. A favorite of space-crowded homeowners, its interchangeable, self-locking metal hangers make it possible to hang up objects as heavy as a lawnmower or as light as a hat. You can use an entire wall in a room or a closet—or a small waste space—for storage or display. Perforated hardboard, finished on one side or both, can be painted with brush or roller, using any type of paint. Peg-Board $\frac{1}{8}''$ thick is adequate for most uses. The only precaution you need take in its installation is to use framing or furring strips thick enough to provide adequate hanger clearance in back of the board. For $\frac{1}{8}''$ Peg-Board, you need $\frac{3}{8}''$ hanger clearance. To attach the board to studs or walls, use nails, countersink holes and fill with putty—or use screws through existing holes.

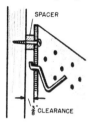

Peg-Board is a wonderful boon to children's rooms. Since it takes to paint, to bookshelves, to wall lamps, and, as shown here, to baseball mitts and caps, as well as countless other "in the way" articles, it's well worth every penny and nail you put into it.

Ceramic Tile. You can use either of two methods to secure ceramic tile to a wall:

1. Make a stiff paste out of standard cement, preferably white Portland cement, mixed 1 part to 2 or 2½ parts clean fine sand plus water. Thoroughly wet the wall surface and the back of the tile. Then apply the paste and set tile in place.

2. On the other hand, you can use a plastic adhesive. The black is waterproof while the white is not. Both types are available at the local hardware store. However, make certain that the wall and tile are perfectly dry before applying the adhesive.

Installation details and methods of replacing damaged tile are shown in the following series.

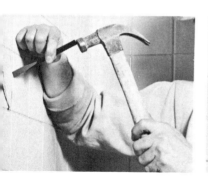  

1. Carefully cut around damaged tile with cold chisel to break the cement which holds it. Tap gently to avoid breaking adjoining tiles or chipping their edges.
2. Use chisel or old screwdriver to get behind tile and pry it out. Again use caution so that adjoining tiles are not dislodged. Break tile as needed to remove it.
3. Remove a portion of the cement on which tile was set to make room for new cement or adhesive. Otherwise new tile will protrude beyond others.

→

  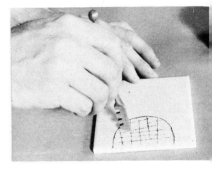

4. If you are using Portland cement, soak the interior of the hole thoroughly or the moisture will be drawn from the new cement and it will quickly crumble.
5. Soak the tiles meanwhile, preferably overnight, or they too will draw the moisture from the cement before it cures. Tiles would then fall out.
6. To cut a curve on the tile, cut the outline with a glass cutter, then score inside the curve to break the glaze up into small sections to avoid chipping later.

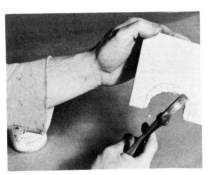  

7. Use pliers to break out the small scored sections, pressing downward. Do not try to remove all scrap inside a curve at one time or tile will break.
8. To smooth edges after breaking, if necessary, a sharp file, grindstone, or other tough abrasive does the job. Do not try to smooth glazed edges.
9. If tiles are set with adhesive, apply to back of tile generously. Press tile at once into opening, for adhesives dry rapidly. Excess is squeezed out and wiped off.

 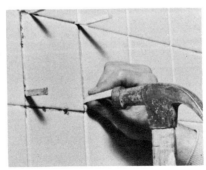 

10. If Portland cement is used, spread on dampened wall, then press tile into the cement, squeezing out any excess around the edges. Wipe off at once.
11. In both methods, once the tile is in place, set wedges into cracks to line tile up evenly with adjoining ones. Leave small space on all sides.
12. Use a flat board and tap tile down gently to level with adjoining tiles. If tile sinks too deeply, remove and add more cement. If too high, remove excess.

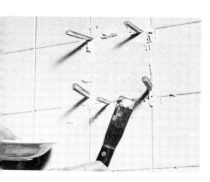  

13. Use white Portland cement and sand, or a white plastic tile calking to fill in cracks around the tile. Press into cracks with putty knife.
14. In about 5 minutes, remove wedges and smooth joint, filling evenly all around, especially holes left by the wedges. Indent filler slightly.
15. Wipe away all excess cement while still soft. Cleaning fluid will remove black adhesive; water will remove both Portland cement and white plastic.

REFINISHING DRY WALLS

Wallboards need special care when the time comes to redecorate. They can be easily damaged and dented, and their surface, which is usually paper-coated, does not stand up well under excessive scraping and steaming.

If the walls have been papered and you want to repaper them, first make sure that the original paper is glued down firmly at all points, leaving no loose corners or edges. If the paper was lap-joined—that is, one edge set over the other—remove the top layer with a sharp scraper or razor, slicing the upper layer off evenly. Don't press too hard. If the old paper was glazed or of waterproof stock rather than plain, washable paper, sand the entire surface lightly with fine sandpaper and apply a coat of glue size. After this dries, you can apply the new paper. However, if you want to paint over the original wallpaper, glue all loose edges and remove lapping sections as described above. Then test the paint on a small area and wait 24 hours to see if the paint has permitted the wallpaper colors to show through. If color does appear, brush a wash coat (half shellac and half alcohol) over the entire wall before painting or else use two coats of paint, allowing the first to dry thoroughly before applying the second. (You can use any type of paint—oil, rubber- or water-base—and in any degree of gloss.)

If the original paper is damaged, stained or full of oil spots, it should be completely removed before repapering or painting. A wallpaper steamer (rentable) will help "slip" the paper off. Steam softens glue, and you can lift the paper off without using a scraper, which might nick the wallboard. You can also use a sponge to soften the wallpaper paste, but be sparing. Use just enough water to loosen the paper so that it can be pulled and scraped off carefully with a putty knife. Excess water will soften the paper of the wallboard itself and harm its finish.

  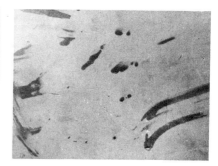

Before attempting to repaper your walls, check them for any loose corners or edges which will preclude the possibility of achieving first-class results.

Lap-joining—one edge set over the other—(as compared to butt-joining, shown) will not do under paint. Remove top layer by slicing vertically and lifting off.

Do not attempt to repaint oily spots, like these, caused by greasy fingers. Wash spots with warm water and detergent, or ammonia in warm water.

Before painting wallpapered walls, test the paint on a very small area. Wait 24 hours, then check to see if the dry paint permits the wallpaper colors to come through.

You can use a sponge to soften wallpaper paste but use only enough water to loosen the wallpaper. Excess water softens paper of wallboard, damaging finish.

When paste has been softened, scrape the wallpaper off carefully with a putty knife. After wallpaper has been removed, allow wallboard to dry thoroughly.

After the paper is removed, let the wallboard dry thoroughly and then apply a wash coat of shellac and, as a final step, sand lightly.

If the wallboards have been painted and you want to repaint them, first remove any peeling paint with a wire brush, but don't brush too hard. Wash oily spots with warm water and a detergent or 2 tablespoons of ammonia to each quart of warm water. Let the wall dry and then dust the entire surface before applying the fresh paint. If you want to paper a wall that was formerly painted, treat it as described above and then apply a coat of glue sizing; let it dry and then paper.

All nail heads should be countersunk and holes filled with plaster or spackling compound. Visible joint fillers and uneven strips at joint lines should be sanded smooth with fine sandpaper. Apply sizing over sanded areas. Fill any gaps between boards with spackling compound, sand smooth and size.

How to Repair a Dry Wall Puncture. Wallboards are rather easily dented. In fact, should the sharp edge of a table be pushed too hard against the wall, it's likely to cause a hole. One of three courses may be followed for repair. You can cut out and replace the entire panel. This means removing all trim and baseboard molding, making new joints between old and new panels, and repainting or papering the entire surface. Secondly, you can cut out a section between studs in which the dent appears and replace it, making only a small area where a

refinishing job is necessary. Draw a line about 3″ above and below the hole, extending to the center line of the adjoining studs, which may be located by probing by hand or with a wire through the empty wall space. Score the line with a sharp knife point to cut the hard surface of the panel, then cut along the mark with a keyhole saw. Cut down the center line of the studs with the knife point, take out the nails, if any, and then remove the section. Measure the opening and nail a new piece to the studs with a few shingle nails or 1½″ blued-steel nails. Sand lightly along new joints and cover with joint tape. Mix a thin paste of plaster-of-Paris and water, brush it over the tape, extending it outward from joints to conceal tape and joint. When dry, sand smooth. Then finish to match the adjacent walls.

The third method of repair is that of patching. This job involves making a backing for patching plaster. Cut out the area with the dent until the opening is rectangular or oval in shape. Cut a patch, preferably of the same wall material, that measures 1″ larger than the opening on all sides. Hold the patch over the hole and drill 4 or 5 holes of $\frac{3}{16}$″ diameter through the patch and the wall around the edges of the patch. Insert the patch inside the wall, center the holes, then insert fiber or plastic wall anchors through the holes. Insert flat-head screws in plugs; turn until they hold the patch in place. With the new backing as lath, proceed as outlined in the sub-section on plaster repairs, page 108.

WALL ANCHORS

Sooner or later every homeowner comes to the problem of how to attach something to a wall—a drapery or curtain rod, a cabinet or shelf, a flower box or mail box. The easiest way to attach any fixture to a wall is to use the correct fastener for the job. Ordinary nails and screws have their limitations, particularly when you encounter soft, crumbly materials such as plaster or very hard materials such as concrete.

The holding power of a fastener in a solid masonry or concrete wall depends to a great extent on the strength and tightness of the fastener used. In a hollow wall, the holding power depends primarily on the strength of the wall material; dry wall is weaker than plaster. In solid walls, fasteners are able to withstand up to a few thousand pounds' pull. In hollow wall construction, a few hundred pounds is usually the maximum.

Toggle bolts and expansion anchors, which expand to grip the back side of the wall material, can be used only on hollow wall construction. Machine-bolt anchors and shields, pin rivets and nail shields are designed to carry heavy loads in concrete or masonry walls. Fiber plugs, lead anchors and plastic anchors can be used satisfactorily on hollow or solid wall construction. Adhesive anchors are particularly useful for attaching furring strips to masonry or concrete walls.

PLASTIC ANCHORS

The most economical wall fasteners, these anchors come attached to stems and are broken off for use. When a wood screw is inserted into this device, it snaps apart behind hollow walls or expands in solid walls for a firm grip. A lip prevents the anchor from slipping through and covers the raw edges of the hole. The hole should be the same diameter as the shank of the fastener.

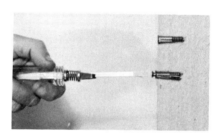

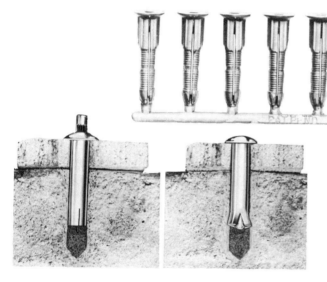

PIN RIVETS

Pin rivets are hammer-driven fasteners used on masonry or concrete walls. The hole should be made the same diameter as the shank of the rivet and about $\frac{1}{8}''$ deeper. The rivet is pushed into the hole all the way through the work piece. The rivet is then expanded and secured in the wall by hitting its head with a hammer.

FIBER PLUGS

Fiber plugs have a lead lining and are used with wood screws or lag screws on masonry, concrete, plaster, or dry wall construction. To prevent the plug from turning in the hole, drill the hole slightly smaller than the plug. If, by error, it turns out to be a loose fit, turn the screw into the plug a twist or two to expand it before inserting it into the hole. Sink the plug slightly below the surface of the wall and insert the screw through the fixture into the plug.

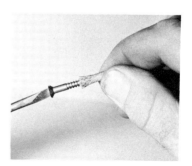

Wall Anchors 119

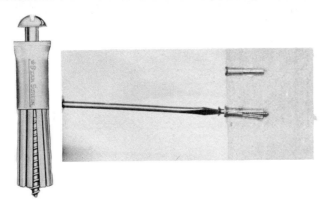

LEAD ANCHORS

Lead anchors are soft lead sleeves that can be used with a wood screw or lag screw for fastening to concrete, masonry, or plaster. They are installed the same way as the machine bolt anchors or shields. A wood screw or lag screw inserted through the work piece and driven into the anchor will cut its own thread and force the lead sleeve against the side of the hole.

NAIL SHIELDS

These nail shields are for use in solid masonry walls. A hole the same diameter as the shield must first be drilled in the wall. The shield is

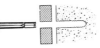 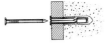 

then inserted and the nail is hammered through the work piece into the shield. This fastener gets its holding power from the shield rather than the nail, and it can support heavier loads than the pin rivet.

 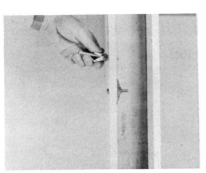

TOGGLE BOLTS

Toggle bolts are used in hollow walls and are particularly good on soft, crumbly materials such as acoustical plaster. They require an oversized hole to admit the wings, which spring open inside the wall. The fixture to be attached must be threaded on the bolt before it is inserted into the wall. Once in the wall, if bolt is withdrawn, the wings will drop into the wall.

MACHINE BOLT ANCHORS AND SHIELDS

The machine bolt anchor consists of a nut with a lead sleeve. The machine bolt shield is similar except that the nut is covered with a split, hard metal sleeve. Both are designed for carrying heavy loads in masonry or concrete walls. When a machine bolt is inserted and tightened, the nut is drawn up to expand the sleeve against the hole. The hole should be the same size as the anchor or shield so that it will fit snugly. Use a carbide-tipped star drill or

a carbide drill to make the hole. You can wrap a piece of tape around the drill so that you will know when you've made a hole of the proper depth, which is the length of the anchor or shield. A special setting punch is used to drive the anchor into place, but in a pinch you can do it with a block of wood.

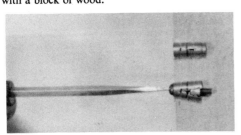

EXPANSION ANCHORS

This anchor expands inside a hollow wall and grips the back of the wall. Unlike the toggle bolt, it has a sleeve which remains in the wall and permits withdrawing and replacing the bolt. It has a lip which covers the edges of the hole. Unless this fastener is correctly sized for the wall thickness, it will not work. Insert a crochet hook or bent wire into the wall to determine thickness of the wall.

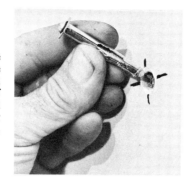
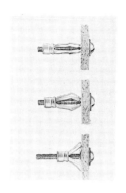

ADHESIVE ANCHORS

If you don't want to drill into the wall, you can use adhesive fasteners. They are flat perforated steel plates that have either a nail or a bolt projecting from the face. Simply spread the adhesive on the anchor and press it to any solid wall. After the adhesive has set you can attach lumber or a fixture to the anchor by hammering or bolting it on.

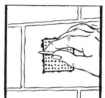

HOW TO INSTALL A NEW CEILING

You can add bright new life to any room by covering an existing worn and drab ceiling with easily installed tiles. They are available in many different colors, sizes and styles. No matter which type you choose, it is necessary first to level the ceiling in order to place the tiles evenly. Most rooms are slightly irregular; therefore, you must first plan and prepare. Start by marking off guide lines as shown in the drawings below; the second drawing assumes the use of furring strips.

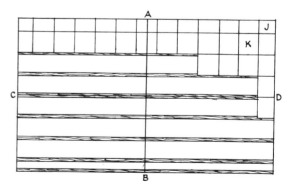

When you start applying tile, start at one corner of the room. Lines E–F and G–H, between the border tile and the first course of full tile, must always be parallel to lines A–B and C–D, which meet in the center of the room. This insures that the ceiling pattern will always be squared off attractively.

Cut the first tile, J, to size. Trim tongue edges to make grooves heading edges. Nail tile to furring strip close enough to wall so that rim will cover any opening. Next apply a complete border course in either direction. Return to corner, install the first full tile, K, and continue with full tiles.

Tiles may be applied directly to plaster or masonry walls or plaster ceilings with mastic. Wall must be clean, free of wallpaper or water-soluble paint. Mastic is applied in gobs, flattened as the tile is pressed evenly against the surface of the wall material.

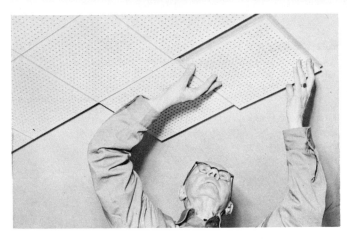

After applying adhesive, press tile against surface, using even pressure. Add or remove adhesive as needed to make the tile level.

Adhesives. If the existing ceiling is sound, not badly cracked or peeling, and if it's level without hills and valleys, the tiles can be applied with special adhesives. Work a thin priming layer of the adhesive into the four corners of the tile with a putty knife. Then apply several dabs over the primed areas, about 1½″ from the corners of the tile. Place the tile against the ceiling in approximate position, along the nearest guide line to a wall. Then slide the tile back and forth slightly. When good contact is made, the adhesive holding, slide the tile into position. If the ceiling is slightly uneven and the tile being installed is deeper than the one next to it, remove the tile. Dab more adhesive over it and again press it into position. Continue placing tiles along the guide line across the room. After one row is finished, start at the beginning corner and install another row of tiles. After all full tiles have been placed into position, measure and cut the remaining tiles needed to fill in at the end of the wall.

Furring Strips. If the ceiling is in poor condition, yet sound, you might have to use furring strips. Square off the ceiling as previously noted. Locate and mark all joists in the ceiling. The furring strips should be nailed at right angles to the joists. Use 2½″ coated box nails to hold furring strips to the existing ceiling. Place the strips 8″ apart, center to center, if you plan to use 16″ tiles. Nail the furring strips 12″, center to center, if you plan to use 12″ tile squares. Where the ceiling is uneven, you can make necessary adjustments when nailing the furring strips in place. Use shims—small pieces of wood of varying thicknesses—to adjust for the unevenness. Checking the strips with a level will assure accuracy and indicate the need for shims.

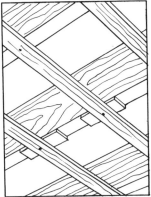

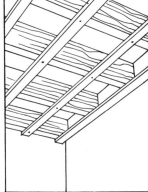

1. Use seasoned 1 × 3 wood for furring strips. Locate so that tile will join on center of strips.
2. Make sure the furring strips are level to avoid ceiling "waves." Shim with scraps where necessary.
3. Use the straight edge of an unwarped piece of lumber to check the level of the strips as you nail them.
4. Apply strips where ceiling joists meet bearing walls. Strips are a nailing base for border tile.

Fastening Tiles. Ceiling tiles can be attached to the furring strips by several different types of fasteners, none of which are visible after the job is completed. Most tiles have flanges along their sides so that they fit something like tongue-and-grooved wood stock. In this way, the tiles (aside from the first row, usually covered over one end with a cove molding) are fastened on two sides. The other two sides are held in position by the already-installed tiles.

Tiles can also be held in position with 3d blue lath nails about $1\frac{1}{8}''$ long with $\frac{5}{16}''$ heads or the type specifically recommended by the producer of the tiles. If you use staples, be sure to get the rust-resistant type with $\frac{9}{16}''$ legs. Some manufacturers provide special clips which are used to hold the tiles in position over furring strips. When these are used, a "starter strip" is often needed for the first row of tiles. After the starter strip is nailed into position, place the first row of tiles into position with one end held by the strip and the other by special clips. Then slide the next tile into place and position the clip held by a 2d common nail, one nail to a clip. Two clips are used for each $12''$ square tile. You can also apply the clips with a stapling gun.

Clips hold these tiles in place and are concealed by adjacent tiles. Note that in this case tile-laying starts in room center against guide board, works outwards from that area.

These tiles are stapled to furring through outer flange. Unstapled sides interlock, and the next tile will cover flange and staples of the first.

Practically all acoustical tiles are soft materials and can be easily cut on the exposed surface with a sharp knife. Such tiles are surface-nailed on the cut edge.

DOORS Cures for balky doors · How to hang a door · Solving lock difficulties · Converting an old-style mortise lockset · How to install a modern lock · Installing a combination door · Quick repairs to battered storm doors

Doors can and do get into trouble. They shrink from too little moisture in the air; they warp from too much; they stick from uneven alignment. Sometimes they won't close and stay closed when the latch becomes worn. Often a key won't budge a stubborn lock. And a broken door can create an immediate emergency. All of these problems can be handled quickly and efficiently with a minimum of skill and tools once the trouble is located and you know what to do about it.

CURES FOR BALKY DOORS

There are three main causes for stubborn and unruly doors. The first and most common is that of improperly adjusted hinges. The second possibility is distortion of the door so that it no longer fits the frame. And the third, more prevalent in older houses, is distortion of the frame so that it no longer fits the door.

To determine the cause, stand on the side away

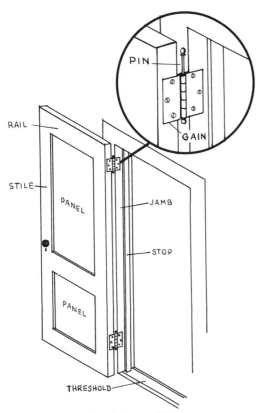

Details of door and frame.

from the door stop and close the door. Check all the way around and note the space between door and jamb. Where this space is reduced to a hairline crack, the door fits too tightly and sticks when opening or closing.

If such a tight spot is located on one side and a contrastingly large crack appears on the opposite side, the trouble is probably in the hinge setting. If the door fits too tightly all around, it has probably swelled from dampness. If there are telltale cracks in the plaster around the door frame, the house has probably settled from shrinkage in the framework, distorting the door frame until it presses upon the door at one or several points.

Hinge Adjustments. To correct the trouble, begin with the hinges. Remove the door. Most doors are hung on butt hinges consisting of two leaves held together with a pin. With the door closed, knock out the pin with a nail set and hammer, then lift the door from the frame. If the screws are loose in either half of the hinge, they must be tightened. If the holes have become enlarged, try longer screws or plug the holes with putty or plastic wood, and when this has dried, reset the screws. Tightening the screws in this manner will often correct the trouble. If it doesn't,

however, readjustment of the hinges is needed. If the sticking spot is located on the lock stile opposite the hinged side, set the hinges deeper by increasing the depth of the undercut, or mortise, in which the hinge leaf is recessed. (See Chapter One, "Chisels.") It may even be necessary to deepen the mortise on both door and jamb. However, when the sticking spot is found on the hinge stile, hinges set too deeply are the probable cause. Raise them by setting a sheet of cardboard under the leaves of the hinge.

Heavy doors, tending to sag at the lower outside corner, can be raised by deepening the mortise of the upper hinge and resetting it to pull the door up or by inserting a piece of cardboard under the leaves of the lower hinge to push the door upward from the bottom.

Distorted Doors. Occasionally a door will be so swelled by moisture that it no longer fits the frame. In such a case, remove the door and the hinges and plane down the hinge stile. Usually the length to be planed does not extend the full length of the door. Mark the sticking area while the door is in place, then plane to the mark. In planing, don't be over-zealous. A little may be enough. Frequently, a rub-down with No. 1 sandpaper will suffice, but take care not to bevel the edge of the door.

When a door sticks at the bottom, either the threshold has become warped or damaged or the door itself sags. If the sagging condition cannot be cured by hinge adjustment and the threshold is in good condition, the door itself must be trimmed to shape. Remove the door and plane the surface. Planing across the grain of the stiles will be difficult, and unless care is taken the wood may be splintered. Sandpaper is better on these surfaces. Occasionally the bottom rail alone is at fault, because of swelling. This can be remedied by levelling it with a plane. If the threshold is damaged, it must be replaced. (See "Replacing a Threshold," page 67.)

If a door is repeatedly exposed to moisture on one side and the other side is kept dry, the probability is that it will warp. One side swells, the other shrinks, and the door is pulled out of shape. Worse still, the top and bottom (too often left unpainted) soak up moisture and cause further warping. The pictures opposite show two ways to straighten out such a bowed door. To prevent recurrence of the trouble, be sure to give the top and bottom two coats of shellac and then prime and paint both sides of the door, covering every corner and joint. This will keep out the trouble-making moisture.

Misshapen Frames. A door that sticks at the top results from the settling of the house. Since the frame cannot be made "true" without dismantling it, the door must be made to fit. A plane does this job quickly. Frame distortion may also cause sticking at

Choice 1—If drying the door thoroughly in the sun won't straighten it, lay it across two supports with bulged side up. Then pile weights on until center is forced into a straight line. Let it stand for about 24 hours.

Choice 2—Heavy doors, or those warped unequally, can be pulled into shape with turnbuckles. Inset a screw eye in each end—top and bottom—and attach with wire and turnbuckle. Set in a temporary bridge or block and tighten buckle till door is true.

other points, and in such cases either adjustment of the hinges or planing the door to fit is necessary.

One more point—in curing the sticking door, the latch may have been thrown out of line. The door no longer sticks, but it won't stay closed. Note first the polished mark on the striker plate where the latch once fit. Partially close the door and mark the point where the latch must now fit. From this mark, re-locate the striker plate in outline. Then, with a chisel, cut a new mortise for the plate. With the plate reset, fill in the old mortise with plastic wood, sand smooth when dry, and touch up with a finish to match sur-roundings.

HOW TO HANG A DOOR

To work properly, a door must have a sound framework. Whether it is a brand new framework or the replacement of an old one, the procedure is similar. Select clear pine 1″ stock (actually ¾″ dressed) wide enough to cover the studs plus the covering on both sides of the wall. Two-by-three studs are actually 2⅝″ thick, most plasterboard ⅜″ for a total of 3⅜″. A 1-by-4 really measures 3⅝″ and may be planed down to the needed width. Check the rough frame first with a level. Assuming the lintel is level, cut one piece of the frame stock to fit snugly side to side and nail up with 10d finishing nails set ¾″ in from each edge.

If you plan to use a threshold, nail it in place now, setting nails through both shoulders only, not in the center or it will split.

Cut two pieces of the 1-by-4 for the sides and nail up the first one on the latch side of the door. Check with a level and, if need be, insert bits of wood shingle between the frame piece (jamb) and the rough framing. When plumb, nail tightly.

Measure the door width and check again the open-ing width with the second piece in position. There should be no more than ⅛″ clearance for the door. Since the material thickness has probably yielded more than this clearance, nail the last piece in place without driving nails in completely. Then insert pieces of shingle—at least four of them—to force the latch side piece out to the desired width, then nail it securely.

Install the casing next. Unless you buy casing stock selected at your lumber yard, the casing may be made of 1-by-4 stock like the frame, or—in the case of vertical board walls—from pieces ripped from this matching stock. First cut one piece to cover the width of the opening, plus twice the casing stock width, plus ¼″. Offset this piece ⅛″ back from the frame and nail into the frame and the lintel with 10d finish-ing nails. Cut two pieces to fit under this one end, offsetting ⅛″ to form a "bead," nail into place, setting nails into the frame and the studs.

HANGING A DOOR

1. Determine which side of door is to be hinged. Locate top of hinge 7″ from top jamb. Allow $\frac{3}{16}$″ clearance to door stop. Outline hinge on jamb, cut out mortise to depth of hinge-leaf thickness with a sharp chisel. By holding the chisel flat, the mortise will be cut smooth and level.

2. With hinge pin up, attach leaf of hinge to jamb with three screws. Insert door in opening and wedge upward. Allow ⅞″ clearance over a carpet, ½″ over a linoleum or tiled floor. If door fits, mark hinge location. Mark the areas to be trimmed away if the door does not fit.

3. Trim sides of door with jointer plane, working with grain. Latch side is beveled slightly inward to prevent binding.

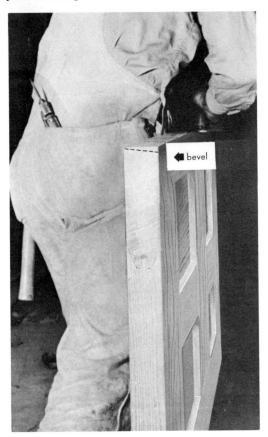

4. Place the trimmed door back in the frame, blocked up to the necessary clearance, and mark the exact location of top and bottom of hinge. Only a sharp pencil will do this job accurately. Locate bottom hinge 11″ above the floor.

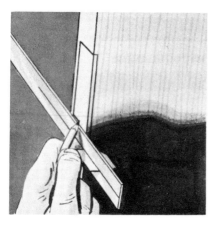 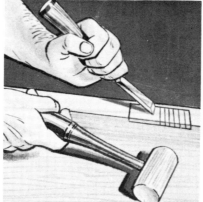 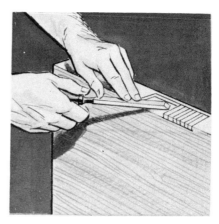

5. Remove the door again and cut out the mortises for the hinges. By making horizontal cuts across the grain, scrap can be removed with a sharp chisel without cutting below the marked line. All mortises are cut to the exact depth of the thickness of hinge leaves.

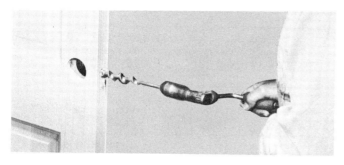 

6. Cut openings for insertion of door latch. Template for positioning is usually provided with latch. Knob is 36″ above floor. An expansion bit and standard auger bit are tools necessary for latch placement. After boring, insert and secure the latch.

7. Close door and note position where latch makes contact with door jamb. Mark top and bottom of latch on jamb, then position striker plate and cut out mortise for latch.

SOLVING LOCK DIFFICULTIES

Although there are many brands and types of locks, most of them work in the same manner. The most commonly used locking mechanism is the cylinder. Whether the lock is a mortise type, rim type or tubular, the cylinder works in the same way. It is not advisable for the average handyman to try to work on the inside of the cylinder, for in most cases this is a job requiring special knowledge and is better left to the locksmith.

TYPES OF LOCKS: Locks are classified by method of installation—mortise lock (top), rim type (center), and bore-in (bottom). Mortise is most difficult to install; rim type is easiest.

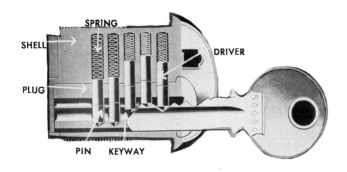

SPRING

SHELL

DRIVER

PLUG

PIN   KEYWAY

HOW THE CYLINDER WORKS: When the key is inserted, it passes under pins and raises them so that joining between pin and driver is at top of plug. When all are lined up, key can be turned.

COMMON LOCK DIFFICULTIES AND HOW TO SOLVE THEM

Problem	Cause	Cure	How to Prevent
Lock frozen—can't get key into the cylinder	Moisture in lock expands when frozen, thus binding free movement of cylinder	Warm key; insert in cylinder gradually; alcohol on key will speed process	Keep inside dry; best to spray with graphite; or use fine typewriter oil but not ordinary lubricating oil
Bolt stuck—key turns but bolt won't move open or closed	Door out of line puts pressure on bolt	Check door alignment; see pages 123–125 for details on how to cure faulty doors	Check door alignment regularly, especially when it shows signs of jamming
	Bolt blocked by paint over end	Scrape clean with knife; use paint remover to assure full removal of paint	Use extra care when painting edge of door to avoid going over bolt or plate
Key binds—goes into cylinder but won't turn	Improper mounting so that cylinder is out of line with lock housing	Remove lock; check all parts to see that they're aligned	Make certain to follow instructions when installing a new lock; use the templates or pattern included with lock by the manufacturer
	Cylinder in upside down; tumbler springs won't work properly	Remove cylinder; replace it in proper position	
	Poor duplicate key fails to line up tumblers inside of cylinder	Use original key to check if door works; have duplicate key checked at locksmith	Don't buy poor quality blanks for duplicate keys; stick to top names
	Outside elements affected metal inside of cylinder or housing	Remove cylinder; a new one undoubtedly will be needed	Make cover to fit over cylinder; use thin coated metal; cut to any decorative shape
Key breaks—part of key remains inside the cylinder	In 9 out of 10 cases, key not in all the way before it was turned	Remove cylinder; use long, fine pin to push key out from shaft end. Or slide long crochet hook along top of cylinder, lower hook over end of key and pull out. If no spare key available, tip of screwdriver can be used to open or close lock if cylinder is turned properly	Lubricate cylinder with graphite; insert key fully before turning
	Wrong key used; did not line up tumblers and therefore cracked when turned		Mark keys for easy identification; better yet, have one key to work all locks

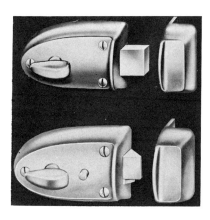

Bedroom and Bathroom Locks: To make a modern pushbutton lock inoperative, remove knob with button. Buy a glass knob in any hardware store and place it on knob spindle.

For Security Purposes: One technique used by thieves to break into a house is the prying of the latch bolt with a thin piece of metal. The best security against such prying is the use of a lock which has a deadbolt (top). There are modified springlatch locks (bottom) which, for convenience, can be opened with one hand.

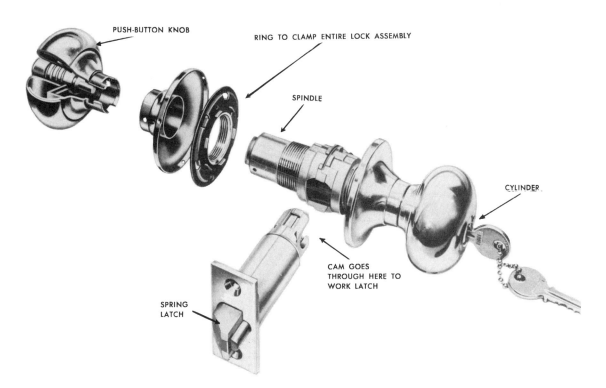

PUSH-BUTTON KNOB

RING TO CLAMP ENTIRE LOCK ASSEMBLY

SPINDLE

CYLINDER

CAM GOES THROUGH HERE TO WORK LATCH

SPRING LATCH

The Tubular Lock: The tubular lock, or bore-in type, is one of the most popular in today's homes. It is easily installed and many companies pack it in a "pre-installed" position—each part placed in its proper position for mounting in a door. Exposed view shows the major parts.

Solving Lock Difficulties 129

CONVERTING AN OLD-STYLE MORTISE LOCKSET

Since one of the focal points of any room is its doors—and, as a result, the ornamental hardware of the lock and knob—modernization of a room might well start here. An old door may be rejuvenated quickly and without scarring by the use of well-designed lockset pieces. For instance: (1) The new escutcheon plate which fits around the new streamlined knob completely covers all the holes left by removal of the old knob and lock plates. (2) Around the corner on the door edge, a two-piece lock-together latch plate conceals the gaping hole left by mortise-lock extraction. And the screws that hold it have new wood to grip and hold fast. (3) The

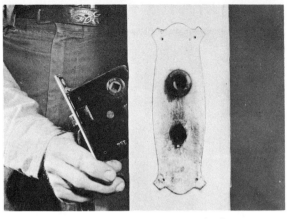

1. First remove the old mortise lock completely.

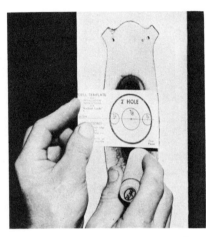

2. Then mark the new lock location with template.

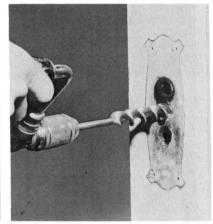

3. Drill the large center hole ⅞″ and smaller holes $\frac{7}{16}$″.

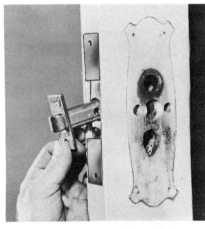

4. Drill through door edge and insert the latch.

5. Remove the old strike plate and replace with new.

6. Insert lock from outside to engage latch at side.

7. Secure lock with screwdriver inside the door.

strike plate for the new latch is long and broad enough to cover all the mashed door frame left by old strike plates. No new hole is needed for the latch, and there will be no trace left of the former damage.

A brace and two sizes of bits, plus one screwdriver, are all that is needed for new lock installation.

HOW TO INSTALL A MODERN LOCK

The tubular or bore-in lock is one of the easiest of all locks to install. It is far easier, in fact, than installing the usual mortise lock. Three standard tools are necessary—a screwdriver, a wood mallet and a $\frac{1}{2}$" wood chisel—in addition to a brace and an expansive bit. The latter has two blades, one of which can be adjusted to bore holes from $\frac{7}{8}$" to $1\frac{1}{2}$" and the other from $1\frac{1}{2}$" to 3".

With each lock there is a template, or pattern, for locating the position of the two necessary holes. While the standard backset (or position of the knob from the door edge) is $2\frac{3}{8}$", the new lock is apt to be located much farther from the edge. The template will serve for the length of the latch bolt of the lock.

Bore large enough hole with expansive bit until tip of bit shows through. Stop and remove bit. Reverse bit and complete hole by drilling from other side.

Insert latchboard into bored hole and mark outline for cutting seat for plate with chisel. Then cut out scrap.

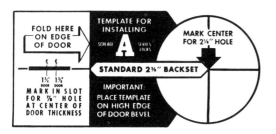

Template provided with lock is used to locate position of holes needed for installation of the lock.

Bore the larger hole with the expansive bit. To prevent marring the door, bore only until the tip of the bit emerges on the other side. Then remove the bit, place the point on the tiny hole and finish boring from the opposite side. This insures a clean hole with no broken edges on either side.

When the first hole is bored, reset the bit for $\frac{7}{8}$" and bore in from the edge of the door through to the larger hole. Care should be taken when boring that the bit is square with the edge and the face of the door. The latch bolt is then placed in the smaller hole and its plate marked on the edge. Remove the latch bolt and cut the outline with the chisel, then remove wood to the thickness of the plate. Next, install the door strike, the plate that is set on the jamb. The screws of this plate and those of the latch bolt should be exactly even. By holding the door partly shut, the

top and bottom of the latch plate can be marked on the jamb. Center the strike plate on these marks, outline its position with a pencil, and chisel out the seat for the plate and the hole for the latch bolt. Attach the strike plate with its screws.

Next, separate the knob mechanism. Depress the catch in its slot near the base of the knob and remove the knob, the escutcheon and the mounting plate.

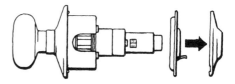

Lock is disassembled for insertion by removing knob, escutcheon plate, and the mounting plate.

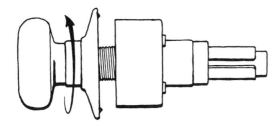

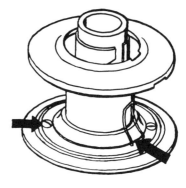

Adjust lock to door thickness by rotating escutcheon in necessary direction. Adjustment of ⅜″ is possible.

Insert the remaining portion of the mechanism and adjust it to fit the door thickness by rotating the escutcheon. The locks are adjustable from 1⅜″ to 1¾″. Insert the latch bolt and interlock with the knob mechanism through an opening in the side of the lock. Try the knob several times to be sure it operates the latch bolt. Then set in the screws on the latch plate.

Slip on the mounting plate and secure it with its machine screws. Slip on the escutcheon by depressing the spring clip which holds the knob in place. Then replace the knob, rotating it until the spring clip pops back into position to hold the knob securely.

INSTALLING A COMBINATION DOOR

The addition of a storm door always means more comfort in cold weather through more evenly heated rooms and a reduction in drafts. A combination door has another advantage in that the storm sash can be replaced with screens in warm weather. Combination storm doors are available in many different sizes

After latch bolt is positioned, unite sections by replacing plate, escutcheon and second knob.

and styles. Measure the height and width of the door frame, and buy a door that is an inch or two larger to assure a snug fit after the door has been cut to size.

1. On a new door, the stiles or vertical side pieces often project beyond the top and bottom of the door. Square off projecting ends and saw off excess stiles.

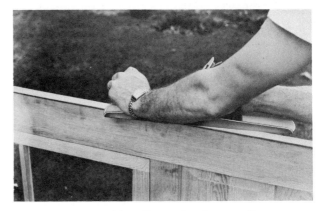

2. Measure width of frame at top, center, and bottom. Mark off measurement on door and plane off excess equally on each side. Allow $\frac{1}{16}$″ clearance on each side.

3. Measure height of door along frame by using a scrap piece of lumber as a guide. Measure each side separately just in case there is any variation in height.

4. Transfer measured mark to each side of outside face of door and connect. Measure bevel of threshold with bevel square; mark angle on bottom edge.

5. Allowing for a $\frac{3}{16}''$ clearance in height of door, set door on its side and cut along base line to the angle of bevel. Cut from sides towards center.

6. Slip door into frame and wedge base so it is $\frac{1}{16}''$ above threshold. If 3 hinges are used, top one is 7″ from top, bottom one 10″ from sill, center one between.

7. Use half-butt hinges—that is, only one leaf is set into a mortise cut in the frame. Mark outline of hinge and chisel frame out for it. Screw hinge to frame and door.

8. Test door to see if it swings freely. If it binds, mark off high areas, whether on sides, top, or base. Remove door from frame; use a plane to shave off excess.

9. Select type of lock you want and drill holes for handles and bolts. Template or pattern and instructions come with lock. Handle should be 36″ to 38″ above sill.

10. Door checks are used to prevent door from pulling out of hinges and to close by itself. There are many different types, complete with instructions for mounting.

11. With door in place, apply a sealer coat and then final paint coat; or stain and varnish door. Coat all edges—sides, top, and bottom—as protection from moisture.

Installing a Combination Door 133

QUICK REPAIRS TO BATTERED STORM DOORS

Storm doors undergo a great deal of wear and abuse. They are constantly exposed to harsh weather conditions and changing temperatures. It takes only one second's time, one big blast of wind, and your storm-door protection disappears in a shower of broken glass and splintered wood. Here are a number of ways you can set about putting a damaged door together and into service for the remainder of the rough-weather season.

1. If the weather is too foul to permit much work, you can repair a split stile with metal mending plates, inside and out.

2. If you have the wrist for the job and a countersinking bit handy, set a few long thin screws across the break.

3. You can use waterproof glue to mend a crack. Spread the cracked portion wide enough to coat both surfaces, then clamp.

4. Better method is to set glued dowels into holes drilled across the break. Use ⅜ or ½″ dowels.

5. Space dowels about 6″ apart. Coat with glue, drive into drilled holes. Dowel on hinge gain is set flush with mortise.

6. If you haven't time to replace broken glass, use a sheet of cord-reinforced plastic tacked over the opening.

7. Tack the plastic sheet at the top, unroll downward, tack loosely. Trim edges with scissors or razor blade.

8. Individual panes of glass broken from storm doors or sash may be temporarily replaced in a similar manner with plastic sheeting.

WINDOWS Cures for stuck windows · Sash cord repair · Replacing a broken window pane · Sweating windows · Metal window maintenance · Storm sash · Screens · Screen and sash storage · Venetian blind renewal

Sooner or later, almost every home is plagued by a window that refuses to budge. Even during winter, a window may absorb extra moisture in the air. It swells and sometimes the surrounding frames expand; the result is a hopelessly stuck window.

Occasionally, too, an accumulation of hardened paint or of dirt in the grooves will cause a window to operate stiffly and unevenly. Whatever the reason, there are a number of simple remedies, for although windows may seem complex, they are easy to understand and repair. This is especially so when you realize that the two sash (the upper and lower sections) of a double-hung window are set right into a frame, which in turn fits into an opening in the wall. The exterior casing and the interior trim or molding seal the joints, prevent drafts and leaks and conceal the working parts of the window.

You will rarely ever have to dismantle a window completely, but when and if you do, you can recognize its parts from the following diagrams and be familiar with their proper function.

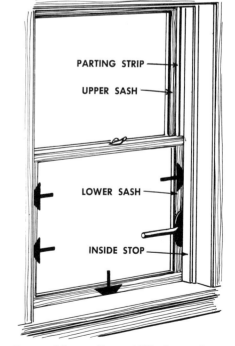

PARTING STRIP

UPPER SASH

LOWER SASH

INSIDE STOP

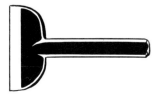

Floor chisel (left) has thin, strong edge, useful for window work. Note parts of window and frame (right).

WINDOWS

A—Siding
B—Builder's paper
C—Sheathing
D—Cripple stud
E—Double lintel
F—Double stud
G—Sashweight pulleys
H—Side jamb
I—Lower sashweight
J—Sash cord
K—Inside trim
L—Inside wall
M—Upper sashweight
N—Rough sill

O—Sash cord clot
P—Glazier's points
Q—Glazier's compound
R—Outside casing
S—Drip cap
T—Metal flashing
U—Inside stop
V—Parting strip
W—Blind stop
X—Pocket
Y—Pocket cover
Z—Sill
AA—Stool
BB—Apron

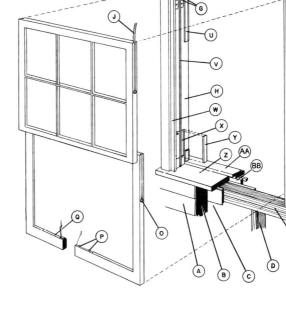

WOODEN BASEMENT WINDOW

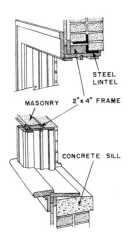

STEEL LINTEL

MASONRY 2"x 4" FRAME

CONCRETE SILL

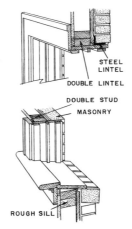

STEEL LINTEL

DOUBLE LINTEL

DOUBLE STUD

MASONRY

ROUGH SILL

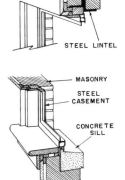

STEEL LINTEL

MASONRY

STEEL CASEMENT

CONCRETE SILL

CURES FOR STUCK WINDOWS

First, examine the sash, both upper and lower. The sash is the part of the window which holds the glass and slides up and down. The flat wooden molding on the inside of the window that holds the lower sash in place is called the "inside stop." The square-looking piece between upper and lower sash is called the "parting strip." Find the spot where the lower sash is jammed against the inside stop and hammer

a floor or glazier's chisel in about half an inch at this point. Then pull the chisel toward you and let it move back and forth several times. Be gentle; only a slight pull is needed. Repeat the chisel-inserting process in at least two places on each side of the sash or wherever it appears to be tightly jammed. This will pry the sash and stop apart and spring the window free of any paint bond.

When the lower sash feels free, slide it into its upper position. There may be more jamming here

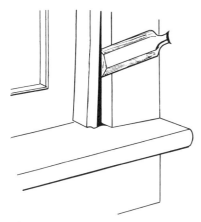

Use broad chisel or screwdriver to pry stop strip from window frame, starting at bottom.

or it may jam on the way up. If so, insert the chisel at tight spots and gently rock the sash as before. The upper sash can be made to move in the same manner. Never use a screwdriver instead of a chisel. You may get the window started, but you will also most certainly make ugly, gouged-out marks in the sash.

When you know that a window is paint-stuck because of a recent inside paint job, take your tool and go to the outside of the window. Insert the chisel under the bottom of the sash. The window will probably spring free and no tool marks will be made in the new paint job. It is also a good idea, especially if enamel has been used, to cut through any paint binding the sash to the stop. Use a sharp, pointed knife.

To expand the window frame itself, lay a small block of wood in the groove before or above the sash, then tap sharply with a hammer on the block. (See illustration.) Slide the block along the groove,

tapping as you go. Then repeat on the opposite side. The fractional amount of space gained by this method is often enough to free the sash. You may be able to jar the sash free by laying a block of wood against the sash itself and moving it slowly up and down while tapping the block lightly with a hammer.

If none of these methods works, it may be necessary to remove the sash from the window frame. Work from the bottom with your chisel. Pry out ½″ of the stop strip at one side, then move on to the next nail. These are long nails and you'll break the strip if you try to pry it all out at one point. With the strip gone, you can easily pull the sash toward you on that side and out of the opposite groove. Lift out the sash, remove the sash cord from both sides, and then plane the sash, a little at a time, putting it back into the groove occasionally to test it for fit. Push it to the desired position, then reset the strip slightly farther from the sash. Nails should be pulled through the back of the strip to avoid damaging the finish. Then treat the bare edges of the sash with a wood preservative or linseed oil. Sandpaper the interior of the groove and immediately apply a preservative, following with a treatment of floor wax or melted candle wax as a lubricant.

Occasionally a window fitted with metal weatherstripping will stick, although this is rare since the sash are deliberately trimmed to a looser fit. If it does, however, either the strip is damaged or it has come loose from the frame. To remove the sash, it is sometimes necessary to remove not only one stop strip but also one of the metal T strips on the groove of the frame. Handle the strip gently to avoid kinks. Pliers can straighten it, and relocated nails will hold it fast.

Remove T strips, working down from top with sash closed; slide sash to top, free lower end of T strip.

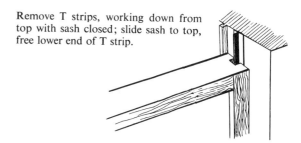

Block of wood, cut to window-groove width, is gently tapped along groove to expand frame.

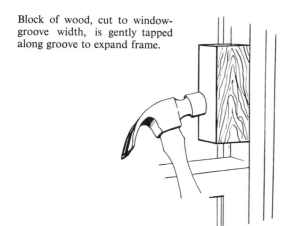

When removing a window from its frame, take firm hold of the sash cord, remove it from the slot into which it fits, and lay aside the sash. Then tie the cord around a stick of wood and let the rope gently slide into its socket over the pulley. Remember that the weight is equal to, or more than, half that of the sash and, if released suddenly, will snap the rope into the pulley socket beyond recovery.

Cures for Stuck Windows 137

SASH CORD REPAIR

Before any new cord—upper or lower—can be installed, the lower sash must be taken out of the window frame. Remove the pocket cover (see illustration) and cut off the old cord. The best way to pass the new cord over the pulley is with a guide

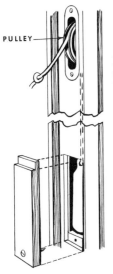

PULLEY

Removal of pocket cover is necessary to recover fallen sash-weight and tie on new cord.

Lower sash slips right out of frame after inside stop is pried off. To take out upper sash, remove the parting strip as well as the stop.

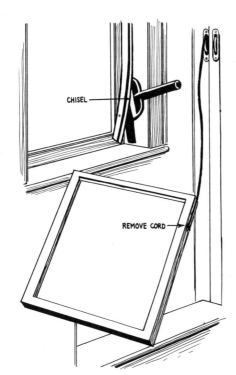

CHISEL

REMOVE CORD

line. Attach a small weight—a nail will do—to a thin string. Feed the weighted end over the pulley. When you can reach the nail through the pocket cover, attach the other end of the string to the sash cord, pull the sash cord through, and cut off the guide line. Tie the cord securely to the sash weight and put the weight back in the pocket. Next, place the sash on the window sill. Pull the new cord until the weight is at the top of the window against the pulley. Measuring the cord against the sash, cut the cord off 3″ below the socket in the sash. Tie a knot in the end of the cord and insert the knot in the socket, making sure that it fits well.

Attach the other cord in the same way and place the sash back in its grooves. Raise and lower it several times to be sure the new cord is the right length. The weight should not hit the pulley when the sash is closed or rest on the bottom of the pocket when the sash is up. If everything is correct, lift out the sash and replace the pocket cover. Replace the sash and the window stop, fastening the latter in place with new nails.

To replace an upper sash cord, remove the lower sash as outlined above. Then pry out the narrow molding and proceed as with the lower sash.

REPLACING A BROKEN WINDOW PANE

Sooner or later, any handyman is going to be faced with the problem of replacing a broken or cracked pane of glass, no matter what type of window. Putting in the new glass is relatively simple. The importance of a good glass cutter cannot be over-emphasized. Buy one that is individually packaged. Cutters stocked loosely in bins are likely to have nicks in the cutting wheel or they may be rusty. Test the cutter on a piece of glass before purchase. If the scored line shows a series of dots and dashes or skips, don't buy the cutter—it's worthless. Find one that makes a steady sound as it scores a line on the glass. Keep your cutter in good condition by storing it in a glass jar with a piece of cloth or felt in the bottom and about 1″ of kerosene over this pad. The pad protects the wheel from nicks and the kerosene prevents rust.

The glass to be cut should be clean, for dust or grit will interfere with the cutting wheel. Cover your working surface with a single layer of not too thick blanket, rug, or layers of newspaper. A China marking crayon or a piece of sharpened soapstone is ideal for marking the line on the *reverse* side of the glass where the cut is to be made. A good method to anchor your straight-edged cutting guide is to drive two brads into the table and set the guide against them. Metal makes the better guide. Hold the glass cutter firmly, in a more perpendicular position than you would hold a pencil. Keep the cutting wheel away from the body. The cutting line starts just inside the farther edge of the glass. Use an even pressure and draw the cutter toward your body and past the nearer edge. Only through experience and practice can you learn how much pressure is necessary. The slow, deliberate speed of the cutter will make an even sound which indicates the quality and depth of the cut. You will gradually learn to cut by "ear" as well as by hand.

After the line is scored, gently tap the underside of the cut near the edge of the glass with the reverse end of the cutter. This will start the cleavage, or split. The split will continue through the entire length of the glass if the break is forced by pressure. Another way to complete the break is to place a pencil or guide on the table under the scored line on the glass and press down on each side of the scored line. Cut only one line at a time. That is, don't score two lines crossing each other without breaking. (The cutting procedure is the same with heavier types of glass such as mirrors and plate glass—with this exception: apply a thin film of lubricating oil on the line to be cut. In the case of mirrors, do *not* apply oil to the backing side, as it may damage the mirror.)

The replacement of a broken window pane is similar for most styles of wood frames. The first step often proves to be the hardest, removal of the remaining shreds of glass and the old putty from the frame. The glass can usually be lifted out by hand (protected with heavy gloves), but only very old putty will come away easily. A soldering iron or electrical paint remover will often provide enough heat to soften the putty; and if you work fast, you can scrape it away before it cools and resets. Take out the old glazier's points along with the putty. The job then proceeds as shown on the next page.

When cutting heavy glass or mirrors, prepare path of cutter by painting on kerosene to cool glass at point of cut, increase life of cutter.

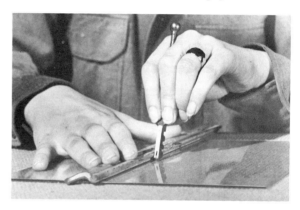

For scoring line, hold cutter at right angles to glass and slant in direction of cut. Use even pressure. A good cut makes a ripping sound.

Place glass over guide, or pencil, and snap with a gentle downward pressure. Long pieces of glass can best be separated over a straight edge. Press down firmly and confidently.

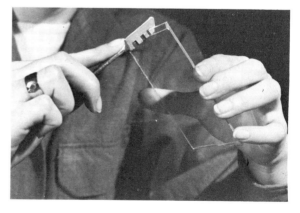

To remove narrow strips, score, then fit notched edge of cutter over glass and snap downward. Slivers too thin to be grasped are separated with chipping teeth after cutting.

Replacing a Broken Window Pane   139

1. Remove broken bits of glass with glove-protected hands. Remove old putty by softening with heat, then scraping off.

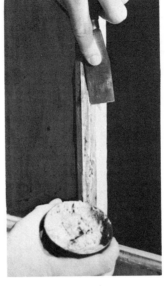

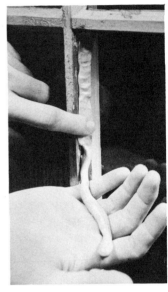

2. Paint groove of frame with linseed oil, then lay in a bed of putty or glazier's compound about ⅛″ thick all around. Layer of putty cushions glass and seals out air.

3. Putty should have consistency of thick, dry dough. To soften old putty, add linseed oil and knead on a piece of glass.

4. Run small ribbon of putty inside opening all around and press glass into putty. Insert two glazier's points at each side to hold glass in position and tap them halfway into wood.

5. Insert glazier's points about every 4″. Start points with finger pressure, then drive them in about halfway with chisel. Slide chisel along surface of pane.

6. Roll putty into a ½″-thick rope and lay it along all four sides. The easiest way to apply putty is with the fingers, pressing it against wood and glass.

7. Your putty knife now takes over and smooths out fingerprints, stripping off excess putty. Putty surface should be smooth, unbroken, and firmly sealed.

8. Any exterior grade, oil-base paint can be applied over the putty immediately.

stripping all around with tacks or adhesive. Condensation will not occur where metal weatherstripping has been installed on the windows unless the installation has been damaged or has become loose. Also, if the inner window sash fit loosely in the frames, they may be tightened if the stop strips are removed and reset closely against the sash. Where the two sash meet in the center, a strip of felt is

SWEATING WINDOWS

Moisture condensation on a window indicates one of two things—either the humidity inside the house is excessive or, since warm windows don't sweat, the panes of the sweating window are cold. It takes a flow of warm air over a cold pane to produce visible moisture. If condensation takes place on the windows, you either have no storm sash at all or they are not functioning properly and cold air is coming through or around them. If the condensation is on the glass of the storm sash, however, the *interior* sash are poorly fitted and are allowing warm air to escape into the space between the two. No matter where the condensation takes place, a sweaty window will cause rotted window sills.

Sweating Storm Sash. If the storm sash is doing the sweating, the inside window probably doesn't fit well. If it is double-hung, put up felt weather-

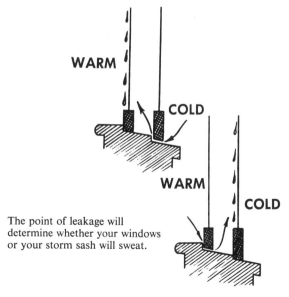

The point of leakage will determine whether your windows or your storm sash will sweat.

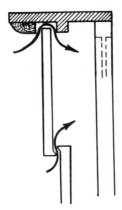

Felt weatherstrip will seal the joint between the sash, prevent air leakage.

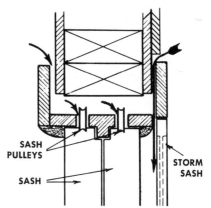

SASH
PULLEYS

SASH

STORM
SASH

Leaks may also develop around casings and through pulley slots in sides of frames.

often the only solution, since the gap cannot be reduced if the sash are warped or worn.

Occasionally it may be found that the storm sash sweats because of warm air rising into the walls from the basement and filtering through frame joints into the space between the sash. This can occur only when the walls are not insulated with wool batting or loose-fill insulation. Application of this material through basement openings will effect a cure.

It is also possible, of course, that the putty on the sash is defective. To repair this, the storm sash must be removed, the putty taken out and replaced. This is not an easy job in severe weather, so you'll save time and trouble by applying calking compound all around outside, and the refitting can come later. For easy application, be sure to warm the calking compound on a radiator or in a warm (not hot) oven, with the oven door open. You might also protect the window sills by covering them with a waterproof material such as linoleum, glass, laminated plastic, or ceramic tiles.

In the case of metal sash, casement windows that swing outward, and awning sash where storm sash are inside, the situations are reversed. With all of these types, sill protection is the first step to consider —otherwise rot will occur, making it necessary to replace the whole sill eventually.

Inside Sweating Windows. A storm sash is supposed to fit snugly between the exterior window casings and press tightly against the window frame. If it is not fitted tightly around all four sides, strips of rubber or felt, or both, can be added. If the sash still does not fit against the frame, calking the outer edges of the casing will prevent cold-air infiltration. Some storm sash are fitted with louvers, and if these cannot be tightly closed, in severe cold spells the

slight leakage is sufficient to cause the inside sash to become chilled. Louvers can be sealed temporarily with masking tape.

Occasionally, even though the storm sash fit tightly, the inner windows sweat in one or more spots, though not all over. Investigation may show that cold air is entering through pulley holes or the weight pocket cover. By removing the inner casing to expose the weight pocket, wads of insulation placed above and below the weight serve to reduce cold-air infiltration at these points.

The use of structural glass will end window sill maintenance worries forever; you'll find it entirely impervious to water, stains, etc. To install, follow the illustrated steps on the facing page.

1. As the first step, paint sill and surrounds with a sealing compound, a thin mastic coating which seals wood, provides more bond.

2. Give it a day to rest; then use a putty knife to dab mastic onto glass (reverse side). Dabs should be 2″ wide, 3–4″ apart.

3. Do not disturb mastic when positioning the sill. Support it until in approximate final position. Use level to make sure sill is right.

4. On this job, surrounds of Carrara were used. Mastics are made for cold temperatures, some for warm—get the right kind.

5. Set surrounds in place. Use bit of white pointing compound where bottom edge of surround meets sill. Be sure bond is tight.

6. After sill and surrounds are in position, use level to true them up. The completed installation requires no maintenance later.

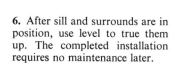

METAL WINDOW MAINTENANCE

All types of steel and aluminum windows are used in homes nowadays—and in a wider assortment of shapes than the original casement, including the familiar double-hung window, casements which swing out on side hinges, awning, vent, and jalousie styles as well as assorted picture windows.

Steel windows are made of a high-carbon steel with a baked enamel finish or they are bonderized or galvanized. The latter two are then usually painted to match house trim.

Aluminum windows are mill-finished, satin-finished (sanded, etched, or hand-buffed) or they may be bright-buffed (anodized by sulfuric acid). These treatments all produce an oxide coating which makes further protective coating unnecessary, at least for some time. When the finish or operation of either type of metal window deteriorates, however, repairs are quite unlike those provided for wood windows.

Where paint coats on steel windows have blistered, chalked, or chipped, rust will follow unless quickly treated. Removal of old paint is the first step. Use liquid or paste removers, as a torch is too apt to break the glass. With care, a scraper may be used with upward strokes on vertical surfaces. Where rust has already occurred, use a phosphoric rust remover just before repainting. Try to avoid damage to the factory base coat, for it is the ideal primer. After paint removal, wash down with alcohol, gasoline, or naptha, then wipe dry. Don't smoke! If a primer is needed, use a rust-inhibiting type or one of the old stand-bys such as zinc chromate or red oxide. Standard house paint is then applied or exterior enamels may be used. Avoid too many coats on metal windows. The paint just builds up in layers and inter-

Metal windows have moving parts which respond quickly to lubricating oils. Keep hinges, operating devices, and catches in good condition this way.

feres with the operation of movable parts. It should be remembered that some new paints won't be compatible with the old. Apply a daub of the new and let it dry overnight. If it wrinkles, the two won't blend. This is apt to happen with alkyd-base paint over zinc-base primer or with oil-base paint over plastic-base enamel. The alkyd-base paints are ideal in areas where paint may be attacked by industrial fumes or salt seacoast air.

While aluminum never really *has* to be painted, it often is for the sake of appearance. The same procedure in paint selection applies here as with steel. For first-time painting, brush off powdery oxidation

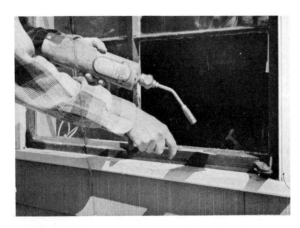

1. When glass in metal frame is smashed, break out remaining glass and soften the rock-hard putty with propane torch.

2. Brush up glass slivers and remaining putty to be sure that a smooth, clean seat is prepared to receive the new putty.

3. Materials needed for replacement are special metal-window putty and a few special clips which hold the glass in the frame.

4. First step is to spread a small bead of putty all the way around in the frame. A wide-blade putty knife spreads this evenly.

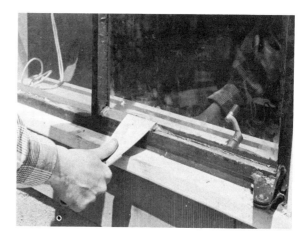

5. Press glass firmly into the first bead of putty, flattening it evenly all around. Then place and press special clips into their slots.

6. As with wood windows, spread the final layer of putty all around the glass edges, forming a cove between glass and frame.

with a fine wire brush and wash down with benzine or turpentine, then apply a one-coat alkyd resin enamel. When left bare, aluminum needs periodic cleaning. Use light household abrasive cleaners or mild detergents and apply paste wax (auto waxes are good). Mill-finish aluminum is more apt to discolor and stain than the other finishes. Here a heavy-duty cleaner is needed first. Scour with a sponge or stainless steel wool, size 00. Rinse off while damp with half alcohol and half water.

Replacing panes of glass in metal windows is quite different from that chore in a wooden sash. The photo series shows how it's done. Periodically, the hardware which operates metal windows can stand a bit of oiling and adjusting of working parts.

Homeowners are often alarmed when metal windows develop enormous quantities of condensed moisture on inside surfaces during cold weather. This condition indicates the house is well sealed but that interior humidity is excessive. Little harm will be done to the windows, although some paint finishes may suffer. The condition is corrected by a reduction in interior humidity and installation of inside storm sash to prevent contact of room air with the frames and sash, or outside storm sash to keep the metal windows sealed inside.

Metal Window Maintenance 145

STORM SASH

While permanently installed storm sash are desirable, readymade ones are very often costly. You can build your own for one-fifth the average purchase price.

The easiest method of making your own storm sash is through the use of aluminum channel for the framework, as demonstrated in the accompanying photographs.

1. Measure window between casings and reduce figure by ⅛″ for sash width. Measure height from sill to top casing and reduce by ⅛″. For 2-unit sash, required for openings over 9 square feet, reduce both measurements by ¼″ for both sash dimensions.

2. When installed, upper sash hangs on concealed brackets, half attached to sash, half to window frame. Bottom sash is hung on side brackets; it may be lifted off at will or swung out and propped open for room ventilation. To remove top sash, first remove lower one.

3. To cut frame pieces to size, first remove rubber glazing channel which is fitted inside frame stock. Lift at end, then pull out along full length of frame and lay aside.

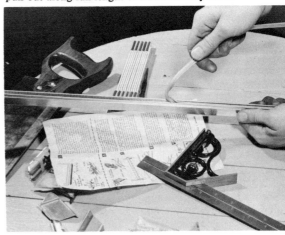

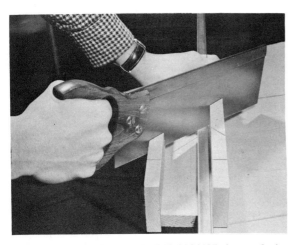

4. Metal frame is mitered at corners. Use a miter box for neat results. Metal can be cut with hack saw, back saw (as shown), or fine-tooth wood saw. Remove burrs from cuts with fine file on inside and outside of frame.

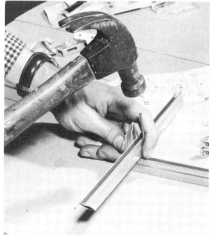

5. Insert corner locks in side frame pieces. These are friction-fit and can be pressed into place or tapped lightly into place with wood mallet. Do not use hammer, or frame may be marred or bent out of shape.

6. Corner lock is staked in place by punching inside of channel with nail or center punch, the resulting protrusion locking pieces together. Mark location by holding scrap stock against vertical leg of corner lock, as shown.

7. To make up 2-sash unit, attach aluminum channel to underside of top sash frame. Drill three $\frac{9}{64}$" holes through channel and frame and join with self-tapping sheet-metal screws. Do not tighten screws too much.

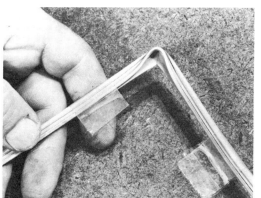

8. Order glass cut to size, measuring $\frac{3}{16}$" less than frame dimensions each way. Attach glazing channel by slipping over glass edge and holding in place with cellophane tape. Cut with razor blade and butt-joint ends.

9. Bevel corners of glazing channel with V-notch cuts on each side, then trim away protruding corners in mitered cut, which assures watertight fit of channel over glass edges.

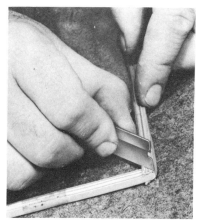

10. Attach top and bottom frames to glass by slipping over glass edges and pressing lightly into place. Insert corner locks of side pieces into top and bottom and tap into place alternately to make snug fit with glass.

11. Mark positions of hangers, clearing corner locks. Drill or punch holes and attach hangers with self-tapping sheet-metal screws. Do not tighten screws until sash is in place; the hangers adjust to fit irregular opening.

Storm Sash   147

The installation illustrated here has been designed for windows having one or more immovable sections. It remains in place all year round because it is placed on windows which cannot be opened. The secret lies in the use of a second pane of glass permanently installed over the one already there, separated from it by ⅜″ of air. The job is made easy by the use of a sponge-rubber strip with a self-adhesive back that not only acts as weatherstripping but also keeps the two pieces of glass apart. The layer of dead air between the panes is the insulating material.

STORM SASH FOR STATIONARY WINDOWS

1. Cut rubber stripping to proper lengths. Moisten self-adhesive back with solvent-dampened cloth. Pat, don't rub.
2. Press rubber stripping firmly into place on window frame next to original pane of glass. Hold until set.

3. Clean both panes carefully before setting new one in place against weatherstripping with glazier's points.
4. Cut and fit ½″ quarter-round molding. Fasten with 1″ finishing nails countersunk for neatness.
5. Seal all openings and fill nail holes with putty. Paint molding to match other window trim.

SCREENS

At some future date, this may be an insect-free world. Until then, screens are important and apt to be costly. As with window sash, you can make your own with either metal or wood frames at a considerable saving.

In almost any hardware store, you can buy the lengths of special channeled aluminum for the job, together with corner and center joining pieces. Measure the window opening accurately, cut the vertical and cross pieces (the corner joints are already mitered) with a hack saw and assemble as shown on the next page.

Wooden frames have one advantage—they can be cut and trimmed to fit an irregular window. Lap joints at corners make a durable joint, and they can be cut with a hand saw. The screen can be stretched across the frame and stapled down, the edges covered with half-round or with a flat trim strip made especially for the purpose and stocked by your lumber dealer. In another type, you can purchase a special frame stock which is rabbeted on its inner edges—or do this yourself if you have power tools—and insert the screen material in the rabbet. When covered with the trim strip, the outer screen surface is flush. For screens up to 30″, no center brace is needed. For larger sizes, the center brace will save the screen from damage.

All wood exposed to the weather requires protection.

ASSEMBLING SCREENS

1. First step in assembling metal screens is to cut metal channel with miter cut. Use a hack saw and miter box.

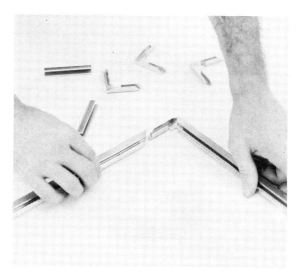

2. Metal frames are joined with locking devices inserted into hollow center of the channel stock.

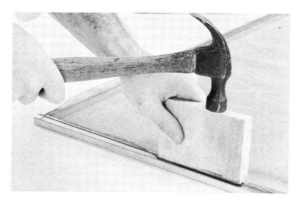

3. Screening is placed over recess in the channel; a locking rod is inserted and tapped into place with block.

4. Excess material can be quickly removed with a razor blade or a strong pair of household shears.

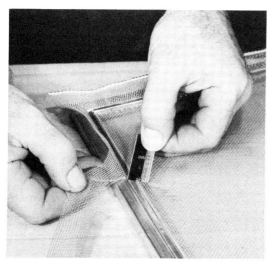

5. Whether metal or wood, screens are easily hung on standard brackets which also serve for storm sash. →

6. For wood screens, construct frames of 1 × 2″ or 1¼ × 2½″ stock. Lap joints at corner make a firm joint.

8. Frame is placed over two horses, the center bowed and screen applied at one end. When secured at the other end and bow is released, screen is taut.

9. Tacks or staples, ½″ apart, are used to fasten screen. Begin tacking at corners.

7. A useful jig for cutting lap joints can be made by nailing two scraps of ½″ lumber to a base and setting the frame pieces between them; the saw cut stops on top of scraps at correct depth.

10. Whether new or a replacement, the plastic type of cloth screening can be held in place with staples, the edges covered with half-round trim strips bradded into place.

Bare wood, treated with linseed oil, will endure all kinds of weather for years. Two to three coats of shellac or marine-type varnish will protect screen frames. And, of course, standard outside paints will do the same. On new wood, however, be sure to apply a base coat first to seal the pores and provide an adequate base for the final coat.

Screens and wood frames are likely to need repair after several years' use. They may even need replacement. The steps and suggestions shown on the next two pages will insure your screens a longer life.

SCREEN MAINTENANCE AND REPAIR

1. A small hole or break, large enough to admit insects, may be covered over with any quick-drying waterproof glue. It completely covers the hole with a film.
2. Larger holes may be patched by using a quick-drying waterproof glue to attach a new section of screen material to the old. Extend patch 2″ beyond torn spot.
3. Loose corner joints can be tightened by drilling ⅜″ hole, then driving in ⅜″ dowel coated with glue. The dowel extends 2″ into adjoining piece. Use slotted dowels.

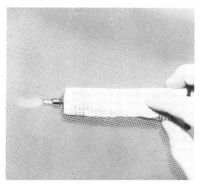
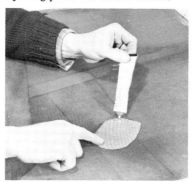
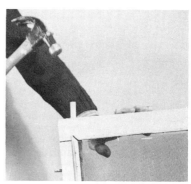

4. If ends of frame pieces are rotted but frame is otherwise sound, cut off bad part at angle and splice on new piece, joining with countersunk screws, and dowel at corner joint.
5. To replace screen with new material, first lift trim strips covering tacks or staples. Lift with putty knife and work gently. These strips are brittle.
6. If only half of screen is damaged, cut away bad portion at central brace, leaving good part intact. Screen can be cut away with heavy shears or tin snips.

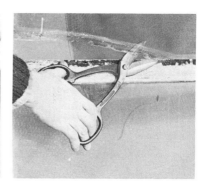

7. To provide necessary tension, tack screens down at center, then wrap end of roll around board, using board as lever to tighten screen for tacking.
8. If you don't have stapling machine, use regular staples, staggering points across screen mesh to provide maximum holding strength.
9. For full-length screen replacement, tack to one end, bow screen as shown, then tack at other end. This system provides proper tension. →

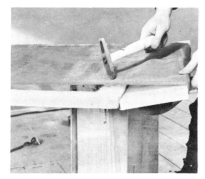

10. If screens are sound, go over them with wire brush to remove dirt and rust or corrosion. Brush both sides in all directions to do this job right.
11. After brush treatment, clean wire with vacuum cleaner to pick up dust in preparation for painting. This assures maximum vision through screens.
12. Apply shellac or varnish to wire screens (plastic screening requires no paint) and let flow through joints along edges to seal against rain penetration.

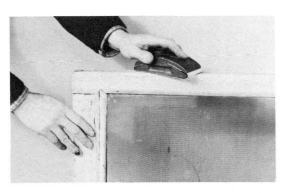 

13. Sand off old paint, particularly along edges, or new coat will make screen wider and produce tight fit in frame. Forcing damages paint.
14. Paint frames last. Use good-quality outside paint and be sure all wood is covered. If moisture gets under paint it swells wood, blisters paint off.

HOW TO PAINT SCREENS

You can make a handy screen painter by tacking a piece of carpet onto a wooden block. Dip the applicator in screen enamel (or trim-and-shutter paint thinned 25% with turpentine), then scrub the screen with it. Don't worry about any holes which clog up. After you complete one side, turn the screen around and scrub it with the applicator—*using no paint*. The clogged spots will then open up.

SCREEN AND SASH STORAGE

The semi-annual problem of storing screens and storm sash is easily solved by means of a convenient rack. The screens or sash are suspended on hinged supports which fold against the wall. Twelve screens or sash can be hung on the rack, yet all of them extend only 12″ into the basement. You can reach any one at any time by flipping the "pages" of the rack. And they may be painted as they hang and left to dry right there.

The base of the rack consists of a set of steps as seen in the sketch. Each step is 4″ deep, 4″ high. If you use undressed 2-by-4's, you will have this dimension out from the wall exactly. If dressed lumber is used, it should be built up with ½″ stock to the 4″ dimension. Join with 60d spikes or No. 19 4″ screws, countersunk. Drill pilot holes for screws or spikes to prevent splitting of the wood.

The base may be attached to a wooden wall with 8 spikes or screws or lag screws. To anchor it to a masonry wall, use a star drill and make four ⅜″ holes 3″ deep; insert lead or fiber anchors, then attach with lag screws set through the base unit into the anchors. In a basement, the upper ends of the base unit may be attached to the house sill if the sill is flush with the wall or to blocks nailed to the sill to make a flush mounting possible.

Scaffold-like supports for screens are made of 1-by-6 knot-free stock. Cut the upper arm to the width of the screen or sash and the vertical member to the same length. Cut the angled brace to fit 6 to 8″ from the outer ends of the other two pieces. Join with a good grade of glue and metal joint fasteners. Then add a metal angle as additional bracing for the extended arm.

On each side of these arms, place the pronged male screen hangers to match the distance between the hangers screwed on your screens. One of these screen supports is then hinged into each step of the base. Use 5″ "hospital" hinges, setting the strap of the hinge on the screen support, the butt on the base. Attach hinges with 1½″ screws.

It is best to place the larger screen supports to the rear, the smaller on the front or top step, as the weight will be less. Mark the support, the screen, and the sash with an identifying number and you'll never have trouble fitting the right screen to the proper window.

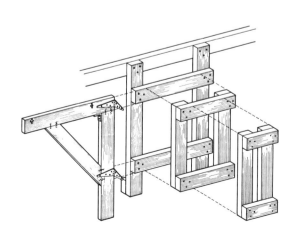

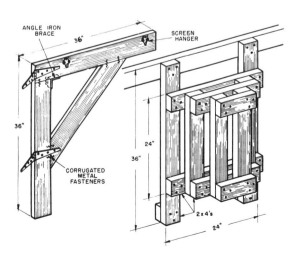

VENETIAN BLIND RENEWAL

Venetian blinds are indispensable for a combination of air, light, and privacy. Yet, as with everything else, time and use will make them dirty, worn, and shabby-looking, particularly those with woven cotton tapes. These tapes often break. Don't discard the blinds, however. By replacement of tapes and cords, available in hardware and dime stores, and by cleaning the slats, you can put them back into tiptop shape quickly and easily. Just follow the photographs.

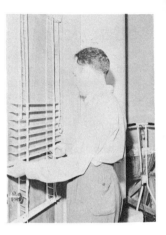

1. Clamp blind to top of door with C-clamps, remove old cords and bottom rail. Slide out slats and release tapes from fingers. Fingers are located inside headrail.

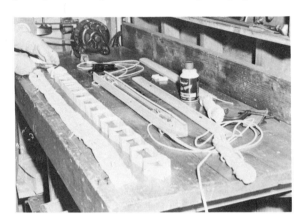

2. Stretch out old tape and cut new tape to same number of ladders and length. Cut 2 to 3 ladders from one end of tape to allow it to go into the headrail over the fingers.

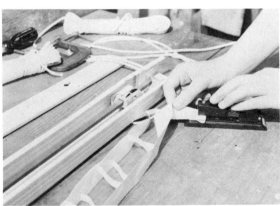

3. Turn back ends of tape with ladders cut-out and staple ends into a loop. Feed the loops through slot into headrail and slip over the fingers.

4. Wash the slats and, while they dry, cut new cords to length of old ones and feed through headrail. Clamp the headrail on door and fasten bottom rail to tapes.

5. If the dried slats are rusty or scratched, touch up with spray paint. When paint dries, replace slats with curved face down. Feed cords through slats, fasten to bottom rail.

CHAPTER 3

THE CLIMATE OF THE HOUSE

Fireplace, Chimney and Flue · The Central Heating System ·
Heating System Maintenance · Supplementary Heating
Methods · Insulation · Draft Control · Ventilation

No matter how beautiful, how well maintained, how new a home may be, *first* it should be a comfortable and healthy place for its occupants. Every cent spent on the heating of your home represents an investment toward good health—for chilly rooms, drafty corners and damp, humid air invariably lead to discomfort and possible doctor bills. Yet, there's no reason to over-invest—that is, to waste money on needlessly high fuel bills.

In this chapter, you will learn how to realistically estimate your fuel needs and how to fulfill them with minimum cost—all the way from the performance you can initially expect of your heating system to common-sense ways of stopping drafts. Proper methods of cleaning your heating system will help to keep it at top efficiency . . . and the right kind of insulation in the right place will go far toward conserving your fuel dollars. Often the addition of one supplementary heater alone may be all that's necessary to change an unpleasantly clammy atmosphere into a warm, comfortable one.

In the same way, installation of an attic fan or a kitchen exhaust will add much to summer comfort—at relatively little expense—replacing stale, hot or damp air with air that's cool and fresh. No matter in what part of the country your home is located, and no matter how old or how new it is, this chapter will guide you toward maximum temperature and humidity control at minimum cost.

FIREPLACE, CHIMNEY AND FLUE

Hot air rises and, in the properly functioning fireplace, creates the upward draft that carries off smoke through the chimney. When the smoke backs up from the fireplace into your house, some obstruction is preventing the draft from rising all the way to the top of the chimney—or else something is happening to keep the draft from forming in the first place.

To eliminate persistent smokiness, first check the damper (if any) to make sure that it's open and that it can stay open without falling shut. Next, place a small wad of newspaper in the damper opening and light it. If it burns readily and both the small flames and the smoke rise up the chimney, the flue is clear and the trouble lies with the fireplace construction itself. The following are a few of the most likely defects:

1. No damper at all.
2. No smoke chamber or one with unevenly sloping sides.
3. Damper at the back instead of the front.
4. Damper not all the way across the fireplace.
5. Fireplace opening too large for the flue size.
6. No smoke shelf.
7. Chimney top badly located or uncapped.

155

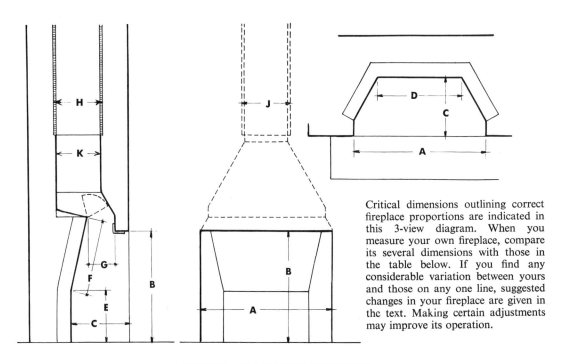

Critical dimensions outlining correct fireplace proportions are indicated in this 3-view diagram. When you measure your own fireplace, compare its several dimensions with those in the table below. If you find any considerable variation between yours and those on any one line, suggested changes in your fireplace are given in the text. Making certain adjustments may improve its operation.

FIREPLACE DIMENSIONS IN INCHES

	Finished Fireplace Opening						Rough Brickwork	
A Width	B Height	C Depth	D Back	E Vertical Back Wall	F Sloped Back	G Throat	H J Standard Rectangular —OD	K Flue Lining Round—ID
26	24	16	13	14	14	8¾	8½ × 8½	10
28	28	16	15	14	18	8¾	8½ × 13	10
30	30	16	17	14	20	8¾	8½ × 13	10
32	28	16	19	14	20	8¾	8½ × 13	10
34	30	16	21	14	20	8¾	8½ × 13	12
36	30	16	23	14	20	8¾	13 × 13	12
40	30	16	27	14	20	8¾	13 × 13	12
42	30	16	29	14	20	8¾	13 × 13	12
48	33	18	33	14	23	8¾	13 × 13	15
54	36	20	37	14	26	13	13 × 18	15
60	39	22	42	14	29	13	18 × 18	18
72	40	22	54	14	30	13	18 × 18	18

Start your checkup of the fireplace opening with a rule or measuring tape. Measure the width, the height and the depth. And, to be sure to have all the figures needed, measure the flue. (This will probably mean a trip to the roof.) Fireplaces should be made to definitely related proportions as indicated in the accompanying table. Compare your findings with these.

Dimension Adjustments. If you discover that the fireplace opening is out of proportion or too large for the flue size, correction is simple. Occasionally a fireplace will not draw simply because its height is too great. You can check this by holding a board across the top of the face of the fireplace. Slide the board up and down the face a bit to see if this improves the draft. Should it do so, you can make or have installed a metal hood which will have the effect of permanently lowering the top to the point you found advisable.

Often a fireplace doesn't draw properly because its cubic capacity is too large for its flue, that is, the flue is too small to handle all the hot air flowing into it. In such cases, experiment with loose brick to decrease the cubic capacity. For example, a layer of brick or concrete on the floor of the fire chamber will reduce the vertical dimension, and if you find this eliminates the smoke nuisance, install it permanently. Common brick or firebrick may be laid with standard mortar, or a concrete mix may be poured in to the desired level. If the fireplace is too wide, vertical courses of brick (preferably firebrick here) may be mortared to the side walls of the fire chamber. Point the joints between these bricks with fire clay. A fire-clay mix reinforced with asbestos fibers holds even better. A depth too great, less likely but possible, can be corrected with a course of firebrick mortared to the back wall and on up the slanting wall. (Note: whenever adding new courses to old, the old surface must always be soaked first.)

The Damper. As the sketch of a properly functioning fireplace indicates, the damper should be placed near the front of the fireplace and a smoke chamber above it. From the smoke chamber, the opening narrows abruptly to the flue, and a smoke

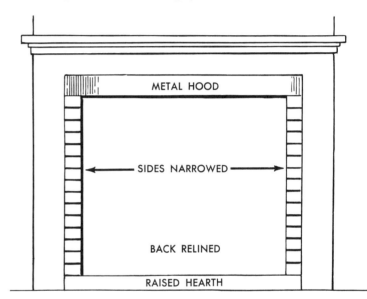

Fireplace dimensions may be adjusted by addition of a layer of brick over the hearth, or courses up sides as shown.

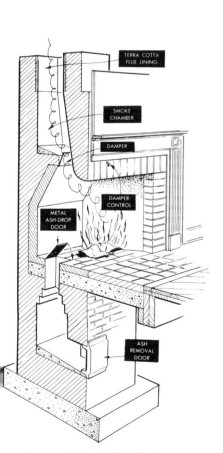

A properly functioning fireplace.

If damper is placed too low in opening, a metal hood lowering the actual opening by several inches offsets the oversight and restores proper distance between opening and damper location. The hood is attached to fireplace front, the joint completely sealed.

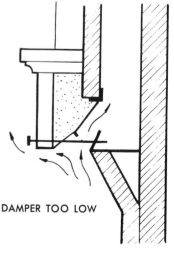

DAMPER TOO LOW

Fireplace, Chimney and Flue   157

shelf is usually located at the rear of the flue. This combination of angles and curves creates a good draft. The damper should extend all the way across the top of the fire chamber or smoke will curl out the corners and up toward the mantle. If the damper has been placed too low in the area above the fire chamber, it may be necessary to cover the top of the fireplace opening. Again, a metal hood that is secured to the masonry at each side and sealed across the top may be used. A more ornamental device, a glass screen across the entire front of the fireplace, will not only help solve the smoke problem but will dress up the fireplace as well.

Always make sure the damper is working properly. Sometimes it becomes loose in such a fashion that, when you turn the controlling handle to "wide open," the damper door is still partially closed. Scrape away any soot which may have collected at the seat of the damper or on the damper itself and which is thereby narrowing the escape passage. Some dampers are removable. Take yours off if you can; it will make the cleaning job much easier.

The Chimney. Your fireplace may be well designed and the flue properly proportioned, yet it may smoke owing to the shape or location of the chimney. Properly, a chimney should extend at least 2′ higher than the highest point on a pitched roof, 3′ higher than a flat roof. Insufficient altitude, or trees and buildings in the area around the house, may cause a pile-up of wind-driven air around the chimney top. This makes a high-pressure zone which tends to push air down the flue and force smoke back out through the fireplace. It can sometimes be remedied by removal of the tops of neighboring trees or, better still, by extending the chimney upward. You can also cap your chimney with brick and stone (see below and

Chimneys require careful maintenance for proper and safe functioning. Make certain there is no loose mortar between bricks. If there is, chip it out with old screwdriver; wet surface; fill with mix (1 part portland cement, 2 parts screened sand, enough water to make mix stiff). Use asphalt roofing compound along flashing.

facing page), or you can buy a ready-made metal chimney cap. These are available in several styles—a plain metal hood, or the weathervane type that swings with the wind, or the rotating kind that contains a bladed turbine activated by the wind. All effectively halt downdraft.

It's wise occasionally to examine the exterior of your chimney for weathering of the brick and mortar, resulting in chinks. These can be spotted by wisps of smoke emerging through them. Smoke from a normal fire should appear only coming out of the

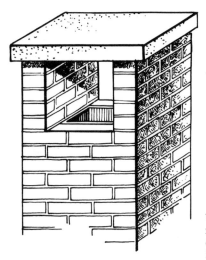

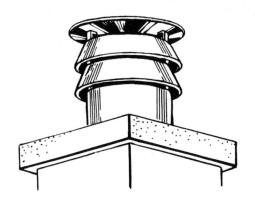

Where chimney draft is poor or downdrafts are common, a masonry cap (left and next page) is a big help; or a metal draft control can be set into the top of the chimney like that illustrated above.

One practical way to cap your chimney is to use common brick and a flat slab of stone at least 2″ thick (such as flagstone). You may have to hoist the stone up to your roof by rope and pulley.

To build the cap, first prepare a mortar of 1 part portland cement, 1 part hydrated lime, 6 parts clean sand. Mix with clean water until mortar is the consistency of bread dough. (The proper ready-mixed mortar, sold by building-supply dealers, may also be used—but *not* fire clay.)

Next, erect pillars of brick at each corner, as illustrated. Butter the top of each pillar with a generous ¼″ of mortar, then mount your stone.

Build the pillars high enough to make each opening under the cap at least as large as the flue opening. If your chimney has two or more flues (see photograph below), a brick wall must be erected on the separation between the flues, carrying this separation or "withe" upward until it meets the flat

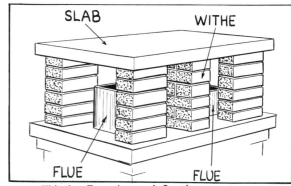

stone. This, in effect, gives each flue the separate cap necessary for proper functioning.

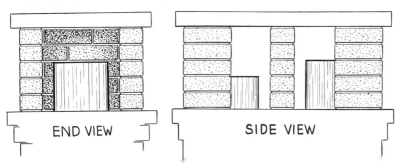

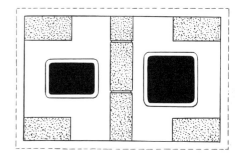

chimney above the roof, and *any leak elsewhere is a definite fire hazard!* It should be repaired immediately. Pick out the old, crumbling mortar, dampen the surface thoroughly and then apply a strong cement mixture—2 parts sand to 1 part portland cement. After this, the chimney exterior should be coated with a colorless masonry sealer paint which prevents further water absorption by the porous masonry. In this way, water cannot penetrate to plaster inside the house or flow downward to the flue outlets and clean-outs at the base.

It's wise, too, to go over your entire chimney occasionally, feeling for exterior hot spots with your hand. Any spot which is too hot for your hand is too hot for your house. Don't try to fix these hot places yourself. They may indicate a broken flue, and the whole lining may need rebuilding. Call in professional help. A loose brick in your fireplace, especially on the bottom, is also a definite fire hazard. Repair it with commercial fire clay, and if it is not available, use a strong cement mixture.

The Flue. Excessive use of pine or other kindred woods will cake a chimney flue with what is commonly called creosote. The gummy, smoke-borne residue of such fires clings to the inside of the flue and creates a rock-hard deposit that slowly cuts down

Sometimes stove or furnace opens into same flue as does the fireplace. This can cause draft troubles. Fireplace should have separate flue, as shown in this 2-flue chimney. Chimneys can contain up to 4 flues, which must be walled from each other by at least 8″ of brick unless lined with vitrified masonry.

Fireplace, Chimney and Flue 159

the draft and passage of smoke. To remove this residue, attach a length of tire skid chain to a wire or rope and dangle it down the flue from above (on the roof), pulling it up and down rapidly. This will break the deposit loose. The damper, of course, should be tightly closed while this process goes on. If you have no damper, be sure to block the fireplace front until the work is finished. You could use a dampened old blanket, sheeting or stretch of canvas for this. Another rapid and efficient method of ridding a chimney of soot is the use of common zinc dry cells. But this method is safe *only* if you are *absolutely certain* that there are no cracks in the flue or defects in the chimney's mortar joints. Chop up the dry cells with a hatchet and toss the particles on your fire. If batteries are not available, you can use a mixture

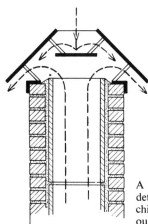

A simple baffle stops downdrafts by detouring them out the sides of the chimney cap. The smoke also pours out through openings in the cap.

of 9 parts rock salt and 1 part pulverized zinc. The fumes traveling up the chimney will settle on the exposed soot surfaces and burn the residue away in about two minutes.

The Fire Itself. To draw well, a fire must be built not too far forward in the fireplace. Otherwise, the rising hot air simply creates a vacuum in the room which sucks back the smoke. For this reason, when starting your fire, the opening of a door or window will often provide the necessary initial draft. Once the fire is burning well, it usually can draw in enough air through keyholes and cracks, for very few rooms are ever completely airtight.

Often an initial draft can be created by burning a piece of newspaper held up in the fireplace throat as the fire is starting. Andirons, or carefully placed bricks resting on edge, will permit the draft to get in under the fuel. Start the fire with crushed newspaper or fine, dry kindling, letting it spread to small logs. A large log should be placed in back of small logs, well toward the rear wall and with another small log or two burning behind it.

Sometimes a draft can be helped considerably when starting the fire by placing a crinkled sheet of newspaper on top of, as well as underneath, the firewood structure. The burning top paper, in effect, sucks up air and smoke from the bottom of the pile. And always bear in mind that tightly packed wood forms a mass which blocks the upward movement of the draft and cuts off the oxygen necessary to combustion. Pile your logs with plenty of air space around and between them; these spaces serve as little chimneys conducting the draft to the big chimney.

THINGS TO REMEMBER

1. Exercise every care in the repair and maintenance of fireplace and chimney. Remember, you are playing with fire.

2. If you clean the soot out of chimney and fireplace once each year, preferably in the fall before you start using them, you should have no soot difficulties. Flashlight cells or rock salt occasionally burned in the fire will help check soot formation.

3. Many fireplaces contain an ash dump and cleanout trap. Remember to empty the trap several times a season.

However, always leave enough ashes in the fireplace to form an inch-thick blanket under the fire. This helps it to burn more steadily and with less puffing.

4. When removing soot or ashes from a fireplace, first wet them down with a few cupsful of water. This prevents powdery particles from scattering through the air, holds down carbon dust.

5. Remember to test your fireplace on coolish days only. Many chimneys are not designed to draw well except at

outside temperatures of less than 50 degrees.

6. If your heating system is on but the fireplace is not in use, keep the damper tightly shut. Otherwise much of the room heat may escape up the chimney.

7. Occasionally a fireplace will be equipped with a damper of unsuitable size, shape or pivot arrangement. If your damper gives trouble or fails to provide full opening into the flue from the rear of the fireplace throat, consider installation of a different style of damper.

Modernizing a Fireplace. An old-fashioned, wooden mantle, handsome in itself, may be very much out of place in a modern interior; in fact, modernization of a room may well begin with a new fireplace face. Removal of an old wooden mantle may be accomplished in a very few minutes, and the homeowner is left with an exposed fireplace opening and free choice as to how he wants to modernize its appearance.

If an ornamental molding conceals the joint between the old mantle and the wall, pry it loose, using a screwdriver and a small pry bar. Then pry outward on the mantle shelf. You'll see where the nails are holding it to the wall studs. Pry all around and outward, and you'll be able to lift the mantle from the wall. Exposed will be the outer surface of the smoke chamber above the fire area, sloping back toward the flue. It is usually of brick or stone, corbeled in steps, and possibly the steps have been filled with mortar and made smooth. The row of face brick up the sides and resting on a lintel across the opening will now protrude into the room beyond the rest of the fireplace. The new fireplace front will be built around this opening.

A wood mantel is more easily taken apart, while stone or brick must be taken down piece by piece, using a cold chisel and pinch bar to free the stone from its mortar joint. You may encounter metal "ties" which hold the facing to the chimney, or "header" brick that must be cut in half with the chisel to leave the chimney intact. The facing usually will yield readily to prying by the pinch bar.

The first step in erecting a flush fireplace wall is to set up a frame upon which the new material may be applied. Outline on floor and ceiling the area to be included and nail 1-by-3 strips along these lines. Between the strips, run 2-by-3 or 2-by-4 lengths; toenail them in place on all four sides, spacing them 16″, center to center. If you intend to use tiles set in mortar or stucco later, it is necessary to add pieces of 2-by-4 or 2-by-3 between each vertical strip. Locate these at the center, between floor and ceiling. A stud, 2-by-3 or 2-by-4, nailed to the wall at either end, completes the basic frame.

The new flush wall will be somewhat back from the brick face around the fireplace opening, depending upon the thickness of the material selected. Where the wall surface is endangered by an occasional flame or by heat directly next to the fireplace opening, it is necessary to frame the fireplace opening with an incombustible material such as glazed tiles. The wall covering is brought up to the tiles and not to the fireplace opening. There is a wide variety of materials from which to choose:

1. Wood or hardboard paneling such as Philippine mahogany, various grained woods in natural finishes, hardboards in solid colors, wood finishes and leather grains. They are all applied in the same manner, that is, nailed across the studs with countersunk nails and/or with panel divider strips.

2. Tongue-and-grooved stock can be applied either horizontally or vertically and may be of knotty pine, clear pine, redwood or cedar. When set vertically, horizontal nailing strips are needed. When set horizontally, the panels are simply nailed into the studs with nails set into the tongues; if not tongue-and-

1. When removing fieldstone veneer from your old fireplace, do it piece by piece, without disturbing either the firebrick or chimney.
2. A cold chisel and a pry bar will be most effective in removing the stones. Be sure to protect the floors with cloth or paper covering.

grooved stock, set the pieces in place with counter-sunk finishing nails.

3. Stucco and simulated stone, both basically mortarlike mixes, require a more substantial backing. Use either ¼ or ⅜″ plywood covered with wire lath, firmly nailed down. Then trowel the first coat into the mesh; apply the final coating when the first has set.

4. Wall tiles such as glazed ceramic, mosaic, metal or even plastic can be used. Both ceramic and mosaic tiles can be set in mortar or bonded to plywood or wallboard with a special adhesive. Metal and plastic tiles can be applied with special mastic cement directly to a plywood or wallboard covering.

5. Panel mirrors may be used to cover the entire wall surrounding the fireplace. They are usually fastened to studs with special anchors set into drilled holes; or they can be held by metal strips between sections, each strip nailed or fastened with screws to the studs.

6. Imitation brick is nailed to the studs with blued-steel nails which, for concealment, must be carefully set into mortar lines and the heads touched with white paint. Lighter coverings, such as wallpaper, require a smooth surface on which to be applied. Plywood, with joints smoothed with crack filler, can be used. Nail the plywood at 6″ intervals to all studs to prevent warping and subsequent cracking of the paper.

It is important in any fireplace reconstruction that one vital element not be ignored: your fireplace may be fitted with a hot-air circulating device. This includes a metal jacket which acts as an air-warming chamber around the entire fireplace, fitted with a cold-air intake near the floor and warm-air ducts above the opening. If these are present, do the dis-mantling carefully, being sure not to damage the ducts. They will be incorporated into the new structure by adding necessary lengths of duct as needed to bring the open ends flush. You may use the same vent plates or devise new ones to match the material of the new fireplace. When surrounded with sheet asbestos, ducts may be carried through wood, but if they are conducted through masonry, no such shields are required.

THE CENTRAL HEATING SYSTEM

When the family complains that part of the house is hot, part of it cold, the furnace gets the blame. If fuel bills are too high, again the furnace is considered at fault. Actually, the furnace is seldom the real culprit.

Your heating system is a most important part of your home and requires certain attentions regularly. Like an automobile, it is a mechanical gadget and has to be treated as such. Try being your own heating engineer to find out just what your system is doing and what it *should* be doing. For major troubles and breakdowns, of course, turn to your heating contractor.

Determining Your Heating Needs. Start with the furnace itself. It is factory-rated to burn fuel and deliver heat at a definite rate. The measuring unit is the British Thermal Unit. One BTU is the amount of heat-energy necessary to raise the temperature of a pound of water one degree. The furnace output in BTU's is indicated either on the nameplate or in the manufacturer's catalog.

The manner in which heat is transferred from the furnace to the rest of the house will determine how much of the furnace's capacity you can utilize. If you have steam heat, or hot water with a circulating pump, or hot air with a forced feed delivered by blower, you can expect 80 per cent of your furnace's full heat output. If you have gravity-fed hot water or hot air, and no circulator, you can get only 75 per cent efficiency because, unless forced to circulate, both hot air and hot water rise at slower speeds and consequently lose more of their heat on the way to distant points. You might consider whether salvaging that extra 5 per cent by the addition of a circulating pump or a blower system to your heating plant is worth the cost.

Some of the heat delivered to the rooms by the furnace is lost through windows, doors, walls, ceilings and floors. The speed with which the heat is lost is determined by the construction of the house. The materials of the house and the way in which they are put together can mean the difference between an overworked furnace, high fuel bills and cold rooms, or an economical heating system with comfort for everyone.

Decorative ceramic tiles form frame around fireplace.

First of all, consider where your home is located. It's colder, as you well know, in Chicago, Illinois, than in Charleston, South Carolina. Heating engineers have worked out a table of temperatures in key sections of the country during a normal winter. Pick your location on Chart I and make a note of the temperature listed for your area.

Since you probably wish to maintain your home's heat at about 70°, where the numeral in Chart I is minus, *add* that figure to 70. Where the figure is above zero, *subtract* the figure from 70. This is the "Temperature Factor." In Chicago, for example, the Temperature Factor is 70 plus 10, or 80. Now, in order to determine the "Heat Loss Factor," measure your house—the outside length and width, basement height above and below the ground, and then the height of room walls. Use these figures to determine the ground area your house occupies and the area of all exterior walls less windows and doors. You'll also need the area of all flat roofs and attic floors, plus interior walls adjoining unheated porches.

As an example of how the several charts are used, imagine a house located in Chicago (where we have already determined the Temperature Factor to be 80), with a furnace rated at 100,000 BTU, forced-draft hot air and, therefore, delivering 80,000 BTU. The house is 24 by 36' with full basement, resting on an 8" concrete foundation of which 5' are below grade, 2' above grade, with a concrete floor. The walls are frame, asbestos shingles on tarpaper over wood sheathing with lath and plaster inside. The ceiling is plaster, over which there is a floored attic

without ventilation but with 2" of insulation between joists. There are two outside doors, each 6' 6" by 3'. There are three windows 2' 4" by 3' 10", and six windows 3' by 5' 2".

From these measurements, the various dimensions of the house can be determined. Referring to Chart II (all figures arrived at are starred), multiply the various area totals by the Heat Loss Factor found under the Temperature Factor column—in this case, all under the column marked 80. The completed calculations are as follows:

		Heat Loss Factor	
Ground area	864 sq. ft. ×	2	1,728
Foundation below grade	600 sq. ft. ×	5	3,000
Foundation above grade	240 sq. ft. ×	56	14,440
Ceiling with no heat above	864 sq. ft. ×	9	7,776
Exterior walls less openings	797 sq. ft. ×	24	19,128
Openings	163 sq. ft. ×	36	5,868
Total			50,940
And from Charts III and IV:			
Running feet door cracks	22 ft. ×	160	7,040
Running feet window cracks	119 ft. ×	34	4,046
Total			11,086
Grand Total			62,026

Since the heat loss is now determined to be 62,026 BTU, and the furnace provides 80,000 BTU, that furnace is not overloaded nor is it even working at its full capacity. (However, if the attic were unfloored and ventilated, and the windows and doors were without weatherstripping or storm sash, the picture would change considerably. The ceiling figure would become 42,336 instead of 7,776. The window and door figure from the crack chart would become 6,283 instead of 4,046. This would give a total heat loss of 98,823 BTU—more than the furnace could produce. The house would be cold and fuel bills high.) Since the furnace in the sample house has nearly 18,000 BTU to spare, more rooms may be added and heated by its present furnace. This may be done, for instance, by finishing the attic, enclosing and heating a porch or constructing an entirely new room. Properly insulated, the finished attic would have a lower heat loss than it has now, and actually less burden would be placed on the furnace. Since the house walls are not insulated, any addition of a properly insulated room against one of those walls would reduce the figure of 19,128, and an actual saving in heat could be made. Thus, we have been able to determine that a properly built addition would not only place no further burden on the furnace—it might even reduce the fuel bills!

Chart I. Expected Low Temperatures for Key Cities

	Degrees		Degrees
Atlanta	+10	Louisville	0
Baltimore	+10	Memphis	0
Birmingham	+10	Miami	+35
Boston	0	Milwaukee	−15
Buffalo	−5	Minneapolis	−20
Charleston	+15	New Orleans	+20
Cheyenne	−15	New York	0
Chicago	−10	Oklahoma City	0
Cleveland	0	Omaha	−10
Dallas	0	Philadelphia	0
Denver	−10	Pittsburgh	0
Detroit	0	Phoenix	+25
Fargo	−25	Portland, Me.	−5
Helena	−25	Portland, Ore.	+10
Houston	+20	Salt Lake City	−10
Indianapolis	−10	San Francisco	+35
Jacksonville	+25	Seattle	+15
Kansas City	−5	St. Louis	−5
Los Angeles	+35	Washington, D.C.	0

Chart II. Heat Loss Factor

Building Material	Temperature Factor								
	40	50	60	65	70	75	80	85	90
DOORS AND WINDOWS									
without storm sash or weatherstripping	45	57	68	73	79	85	90	102	113
with storm sash	30	38	45	49	53	56	60	64	68
with storm sash and weatherstripping	18	23	27	29	32	34	36*	38	41
WOOD SIDING									
tarpaper, wood sheathing, wood lath, plaster	10	13	15	16	18	19	20	21	23
tarpaper, wood sheathing, 1/2″ gypsum lath, plaster	8	10	11	12	13	14	15	16	17
tarpaper, wood sheathing, 3 1/2″ insulation, lath, plaster	4	5	5	6	6	7	7	8	8
no insulation, wood lath, plaster	40	50	60	65	70	75	80	85	90
composition siding on wood siding, tarpaper, wood sheathing, wood lath, plaster	8	11	13	14	15	16	17	18	19
tarpaper, wood sheathing, 1/2″ insulation board, fibre board or plasterboard	8	10	11	12	13	14	15	16	17
tarpaper, wood sheathing, 3/8″ gypsum board finish	10	13	16	17	18	20	21	22	23
tarpaper, wood sheathing, 3/8″ plywood interior finish	12	12	14	16	17	18	19	20	22
STUCCO SIDING									
wire lath, wood sheathing, tarpaper, wood lath, plaster	12	15	18	20	21	23	24	26	27
hollow tile, wood furring, lath, plaster	10	13	16	17	18	20	21	22	23
ASBESTOS SHINGLE SIDING									
over tarpaper, wood sheathing, lath, plaster	12	15	18	20	21	23	24*	26	27
8″ BRICK WALL									
bare wall	20	25	30	33	35	38	40	43	45
brick, furring, lath, plaster	12	15	18	20	21	23	24	26	27
brick, furring, 1/2″ insulation lath, plaster	9	11	13	14	16	17	18	19	20
12″ BRICK WALL									
bare wall	14	18	22	23	25	27	29	31	22
furring, lath, plaster	10	12	14	16	17	18	19	20	32
furring, 1/2″ insulation, lath, plaster	8	10	11	12	13	14	15	16	17
8″ CONCRETE BLOCK WALL									
furring, lath, plaster	13	16	19	21	22	24	26	27	29
furring, 1/2″ insulation, lath, plaster	10	12	14	16	17	18	19	20	22
CEILING BELOW ATTIC									
unfloored, ventilated	24	30	37	40	43	46	49	52	55
unfloored, unventilated	14	18	21	22	24	26	27	29	30
unfloored, unventilated, 2″ insulation between joists	5	7	8	8	9	10	10	11	12
unfloored, unventilated, 3 1/2″ insulation between joists	4	5	6	6	7	8	8	9	9
floored, ventilated, no insulation	11	14	17	18	20	21	22	24	25
floored, unventilated, no insulation	9	11	13	14	15	16	17	18	19
floored, unventilated, 2″ insulation between joists	5	6	7	8	8	9	9*	10	11
CEILING—NO ATTIC									
plaster, lath, sheathing, roofing	13	16	19	20	22	23	25	26	28
plaster, lath, 1/2″ insulation, sheathing, roofing	9	12	14	15	16	17	18	19	20
plaster, lath, 2″ insulation between joists, sheathing, roofing	5	7	8	8	9	10	10	11	12
plaster, lath, 3 1/2″ insulation between joists, sheathing, roofing	4	5	6	6	7	7	8	8	9

Chart II. Heat Loss Factor (continued)

Building Material	Temperature Factor								
	40	50	60	65	70	75	80	85	90
BASEMENT									
8″ concrete below grade	2	2	3	3	4	4	5*	5	5
8″ concrete above grade	28	35	42	46	49	53	56*	60	63
8″ concrete block above grade	22	28	34	36	39	42	45	48	50
8″ cinder block above grade	17	21	25	27	29	32	34	36	38
12″ concrete above grade	23	29	35	38	41	44	46	49	52
CONCRETE BASEMENT FLOOR	0	0	1	1	1	1	2	2	2
CONCRETE SLAB—NO BASEMENT									
slab unheated	2	2	3	5	7	8	10	12	13
ENCLOSED PORCH									
unheated, wood siding exterior wall, no insulation, plaster inside	12	16	19	20	22	23	25	26	28
same wall but with insulation	7	9	11	11	12	13	14	15	16

Chart III. To Determine Number of Running Feet of Cracks in Doors and Windows

Opening Height	Opening Widths									
	1′8″	2′	2′4″	2′8″	3′	3′4″	3′8″	4′	4′4″	4′8″
3′10″	12.7	13.7	14.7*	15.7	16.7	17.7	18.7	19.7	20.7	21.7
4′6″	14.0	15.0	16.0	17.0	18.0	19.0	20.0	21.0	22.0	23.0
5′2″	15.3	16.3	17.3	18.3	19.3*	20.3	21.3	22.3	23.3	24.3
5′10″	16.7	17.7	18.7	19.7	20.7	21.7	22.7	23.7	24.7	25.7
6′6″	18.0	19.0	20.0	21.0	22.0*	23.0	24.0	25.0	26.0	27.0
7′2″	19.3	20.3	21.3	22.3	23.3	24.3	25.3	26.3	27.3	28.3
7′10″	20.7	21.7	22.7	23.7	24.7	25.7	26.7	27.7	28.7	29.7

Example: if window is 3′10″ high and 2′4″ wide, result is 14.7 (starred) running feet of crack for one such window. Add up total of all cracks in all doors and windows, then multiply total by heat-loss factor from Chart IV.

Chart IV. Added Heat Loss Factor

WINDOWS									
double-hung wood sash, not weatherstripped or without storm sash	28	25	42	45	50	53	57	60	65
double-hung wood sash, weatherstripped or with storm sash	17	20	25	28	30	32	34*	36	38
double-hung metal sash, no weatherstripping or storm sash	52	65	75	85	90	95	105	110	120
double-hung metal sash, with weatherstripping or storm sash	25	30	35	37	40	45	50	55	60
casement windows, metal or wood	35	45	55	60	65	70	75	80	85
DOORS	80	100	120	130	140	150	160*	170	180

Multiply figures obtained from Chart III by these heat loss factors. Note that doors are not indicated as weatherstripped or otherwise. Frequency of door use upsets this calculation. Figures shown are average under all conditions.

Hot-Air Heat. Although your thermostat may read 70° (generally the most comfortable room temperature), the room may still *feel* cold. There are four factors in hot-air heating systems which may cause uncomfortable chilliness even though the heating system seems to be operating at highest efficiency:

1. *Air temperature* is controlled in most cases by a thermostat. Once you set the thermostat at a fixed figure, your furnace should deliver air warmed to that degree to the site of the thermostat. However, if the thermostat is located improperly, the corners of the room may become cold and uncomfortable.

2. *Air velocity* is as important to room comfort as air temperature. The human body tries to maintain its temperature at 98.6°, and with a room temperature of 70°, excess body heat is carried away by air in motion. When the surrounding air is too cold, the skin contracts its pores slightly in order to prevent rapid internal heat loss and, as a result, a chill is experienced. The speed of air around your body, therefore, has much to do with your comfort.

3. *Outer wall temperature*, if cold, actually takes heat from your body. Place your hand on the outer wall of your home some cold winter day. If your furnace hasn't warmed it, you can be sure that your own body will be trying to.

4. *Relative humidity* is as important to room comfort in the winter as in the summer. When the amount of moisture in the air drops below 40 per cent of saturation, body moisture is lost through the skin too rapidly and you become chilled even though the thermometer may read as high as 75° or 80°. At the same time, your home will suffer from excess drying —the floors develop cracks between boards as they shrink, the windows rattle in their frames and gaps appear between sections of wood trim. If the relative humidity figure exceeds 60 per cent, however, the moisture of your body can't evaporate readily and you will feel uncomfortably warm, even with the temperature at 70°. Your house will likewise suffer— from damp walls, sweating windows, swelled and warped woodwork. About halfway between these two extremes is the point at which to set your humidity controls.

Properly installed, the hot-air heating system should have the furnace centrally located in the basement or floor, which keeps the hot-air ducts at minimum length. The perimeter type of heating system, generally considered the most efficient arrangement, calls for locating the registers in series along walls near the baseboard. Air is delivered into the room from all angles, eliminating unwarmed areas. Cold-air return ducts are located on inner walls at ceiling height. Thus there is no return flow of cold air across the floors. From the standpoint of economy, this arrangement is expensive to install since the ducts are longer and, because these ducts are quite likely to pass through cold areas under the floor, they must be insulated to conserve hot air.

Older systems, with a centrally located furnace, provided ducts run through interior walls to near-ceiling level; the register's fins directed warm air to outer walls, down which the warmed air flowed, and back across the floor. As a rule, the area about 2' above the floor remained much cooler than the rest of the room. Where return ducts were placed at baseboard level on inner walls, this was inevitable. When the return-flow ducts were placed along outer wall baseboards, the cold air flowing down outer walls, and particularly walls with large window areas, was picked up before it could flow back across the floor, eliminating much of this discomfort.

Common complaints in hot-air heating systems and their cure are specified in the facing chart. The major flaws in warmed-air heating systems, and their elimination, include the following:

1. *Cold drafts down stairways.* Warm air from the lower floor travels up the stairs at eye level. Cold air flows down the steps at ankle level, and a chilly draft is felt near the foot of the stairs. At the top of the stairs you may provide an air break—modern folding doors or a screen—to overcome this discomfort. A better system is the installation of a return-flow duct at the top of the stairs, using a slot-type duct along the top step, with the duct itself suspended on the under-stair structure and going directly to the basement or furnace location. A wall-mounted return-flow duct is not as efficient.

2. *Lack of steady air flow.* When the furnace is set to fire infrequently, areas remote from the heat source may cool too much before newly warmed air is delivered. Such areas are alternately hot and cold. Use a thermostat which controls not only room temperature but the on-off cycles of the furnace as well. By setting the control at more frequent operating intervals, but at lower temperatures, your rooms will have a more even temperature and an increase in comfort. Also, fuel bills may drop appreciably.

3. *Hot upper floors, cold lower floors.* Ducts run to upper floors in straight lines from the furnace, warming upper floors first and providing more heat than for floors below. The homeowner's tendency is to close the upper registers in an attempt to force the heat through the lower ones. Instead, however, the ducts hold trapped hot air in the walls, which become heated in consequence and are, in effect, hot-air registers the full height of the walls. Proper control can be achieved in a damper at the first floor level, just above baseboard registers. When this damper shuts off the flow of air to upper floors at the right location, the lower floors are immediately heated. At the same time, the top-of-the-stair air

1. High Fuel Bills	**a.**	Oversize furnace for size of house.
	b.	Excessive fuel being fed to furnace. Reduce jet on oil burners, rate of feed on coal stokers; reduce jet size on gas burners; install furnace stack dampers.
	c.	Controls out of calibration. This requires factory check-up.
	d.	Blower belt slipping. Apply belt dressing.
	e.	Blades of blower dirty. Shut down system and clean.
	f.	Intake filters plugged. Shut down system and clean.
2. Rooms Too Hot	**a.**	Thermostat improperly located in relation to furnace. Relocate.
	b.	Furnace over-firing (see "b" above).
	c.	Registers poorly located, out of balance with each other. Relocate if possible.
	d.	Thermostat incorrectly set.
3. Noisy Operation	**a.**	Ducts of lightweight metal. Require stiffening to prevent vibration.
	b.	Inner casing of furnace loose. Shut down, investigate and tighten bolts.
	c.	Fan operating too fast. Reduce speed with control provided, or install one.
	d.	Blower troubles: belt too tight causing vibration, motor cable rubbing on fan or cabinet, blower not properly centered in cabinet opening, bearings in need of oil, pulley warped or bent, static electricity jumping from wheel to cabinet, end-play in shaft. Tape up loose cables, tighten cabinet nuts, replace defective parts, adjust thrust collars to take up the end play of shaft.
	e.	Motor trouble: motor not rubber mounted, base fasteners loose, pulley not tight on shaft, bearings worn, speed incorrect. Remount motor on rubber, tighten motor down, tighten pulley, replace poor bearings, adjust speed up or down slightly.
4. Insufficient Heat	**a.**	Controls improperly set.
	b.	Dirt on heating surfaces. Shut down system and clean.
	c.	Insufficient return air. Check baffles on all registers, remove dirt from ducts.
	d.	Filters plugged. Shut down and clean.
	e.	Check blower for: slipping belt, belt too tight causing overloaded motor to cut out, dirty blades, blower running backwards, defective motor, blower too small for house.
	f.	Check thermostat for: correct location, calibration, correct type for controls used.
	g.	Loose wires. Locate, tape joints, rewire as needed.

break, mentioned in Number 1, will slow down the flow of warmed air from lower floors to the upper ones, thus helping to keep the lower floors warm.

4. *Dirt streaks on ceilings.* These result from several causes—too much air speed, infrequent cleaning of ducts, dirt on blower fan blades and filters, and register leaks. Air speed can be reduced by manual manipulation of the controls. Periodic cleanout of ducts, fan blades and filters is sound economy as well as a cure for the dirt streaks. A clogged filter will even cause the blower to operate erratically. Change the filter, particularly if it has been in service for a few months. If you have no immediate replacement filter, vacuum the old one and use it temporarily. The fiberglass type is generally recommended, and it should be replaced at least once during each heating season. Registers or grilles should be vacuumed every six weeks during the heating season; failure to do so will result in a sizeable accumulation of dust. Air leaks from the base of the registers can be overcome by removal of the register, the gluing of a strip of felt around the base and then replacement of the register tightly in its mounting. (Foam rubber may be used in place of felt.) Diffusion-style registers also help to avoid this

unpleasant condition since the air is directed to all parts of the room and down rather than directly across the ceiling.

5. *Heat loss through ducts.* It is hardly necessary to state that much heat (as much as 25 per cent) will be lost through duct metal where the ducts pass through cold areas not intended to be heated by them. Even the longer ducts passing through a basement area should be insulated with asbestos to prevent undue heating of the basement at the cost of cold rooms upstairs. Sleeve asbestos insulation, with all joints sealed with tape and loose asbestos filler wet to a paste with water, will seal in the heat. Also, heat from uninsulated pipes discharged into basement air is a frequent cause of wet walls when the hot air, touching cold basement walls, loses its moisture by condensation. Where ducts pass though open crawl spaces, they definitely should be well insulated. Heat also travels up through outside walls to the attic unless these wall spaces are well sealed. In perimeter-type hot-air heating, all duct lengths between the furnace and outer walls should be insulated.

It is true that the gravity system is less efficient than the blower-type warmed-air system. If at all possible, conversion should be undertaken as an

HOT-AIR SYSTEMS

1. Hot-air systems require some special attention. Filters need periodic check-ups as they tend to become clogged with dust, lint, and sometimes soot. Surface can be brushed clean, but filter replacement is inexpensive.

2. After periods of furnace shutdown, be sure to vacuum registers before starting up blower system. Otherwise you may be unpleasantly surprised with a cloud of dust.

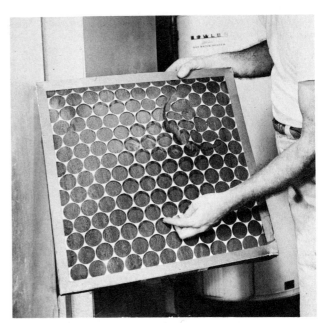

which type you have, check the following points of difference through which your own type can be determined. Then consider the advantages of one over the other with a view toward obtaining the most heat for the least cost and bother.

The gravity-fed system. 1. Water temperature: In this system, the maximum safe water temperature is about 180°. When heated, water expands, and to take care of the increased mass of water in a gravity-fed system, an expansion tank—open to the air—is provided at the system's top, usually in the attic.

economy measure as well as for comfort. Some gravity systems can be improved by relocation of ducts. Older installations placed the duct registers directly above the furnace floor or baseboard level. When registers are located higher on the wall, the rising air increases its speed as it mounts higher in the duct. This draws air into the furnace faster, and swifter circulation results. Also, the warmed duct distributes radiant heat into the walls and then into the rooms as supplementary heat. The improvement in heating efficiency is well worth the cost of the additional lengths of duct.

Hot-Water Heat. Hot-water heating is cleaner than warmed-air heating and can be better controlled to meet weather changes than can steam heat. With automatic gas, oil, or stoker-fed furnaces, the forced-feed type of hot-water system can be fitted with other automatic controls so that the entire heating system can be ignored for weeks at a time.

Basically, hot-water heating divides into two types of systems: gravity-fed, or the "open" type, and forced-feed, or the "closed" type. If you aren't sure

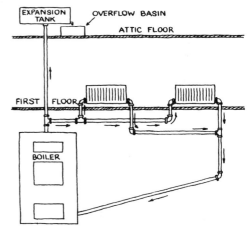

Gravity hot-water system has an open expansion tank which is located in the attic of the house.

2. Circulation: Since warmed water rises exactly as does warmed air, water in the gravity-fed system rises through pipes as it is heated by the furnace. When it reaches the radiators, it loses about 20° of its temperature and the cooled water then flows downward through return-flow pipes to the furnace for reheating.

3. Controls: Since the property of heated water to rise is the only means of getting hot water to rooms over the furnace, a sudden drop in outside temperatures means that the furnace must first heat a large mass of cold water before any of it can rise through the pipes. The delay could mean a well-chilled house before warmed water reaches the more distant rooms. Thermostats in rooms can be set manually to start the furnace operating at will, or "anticipatory" thermostats set outside the house to start it working when exterior temperatures drop below a predetermined figure. Even with these, there is the wait until the furnace has heated a sufficient mass of water to a degree where circulation begins.

4. Pipe sizes: Since the volume of heated water is important where the temperature of the water circulated is relatively low, gravity-fed systems usually start with a 3″ diameter main line, with 1″ riser pipes to radiators. Return pipes from radiators, where used, are of the same size and feed back into 3″ return mains.

The forced-feed system. 1. Water temperature: Since the forced-feed system is "closed," the water in the system may be put under pressure. The usual pressure of 20 pounds permits raising the water temperature above the usual boiling point (the boiling point being automatically raised along with the pressure). Water temperatures of 240° are not uncommon, yet no steam pressure is created by this method. Therefore, it is evident that the water delivered to

radiators takes more usable heat with it. Instead of an open tank at the top of the system to take care of water expansion—which would prevent putting the water in the system under pressure—a sealed tank is provided. This is first filled with air, which is compressed by expanding water, forcing water back out into the system as the water temperature drops.

2. Circulation: On the closed-type system, a small motor-driven pump forces heated water from the furnace through the system on demand of the thermostat, which controls the motor in most cases. Since the water can be heated to a much higher degree, it carries more heat. Whether or not all of its heat is lost, the water is forced through the radiator back to the furnace. In consequence, if sufficient heat has been delivered to the rooms, hot water returns to the furnace and needs little or no fuel consumption to keep it at a desirable temperature for heating purposes.

3. Controls: In the forced-feed system, since the thermostat normally controls the circulating pump, water temperature controls the firing of the furnace. This may be manually set (as explained later), but the general principle is that, as cold water returns to the furnace, an aquastat causes the furnace to fire to reheat the water. When the water is heated to the desired temperature, the aquastat shuts off the furnace. If the furnace itself becomes overheated, it will shut down in response to the stack switch on its smokepipe.

4. Pipe sizes: Since more heat is carried by the water under pressure, a smaller pipe is possible. Main line pipes of 1½″ diameter are usual, with ½″ riser pipes to radiators. Returns are the same size.

Where water is forced through the system, several methods of return are possible. The methods have come into existence as new forced hot-water systems have been developed. Therefore, yours may be any one of many, depending on how far the improvements had advanced when your system was installed. The various systems are known as the one-pipe return, two-pipe direct return and the two-pipe reverse return.

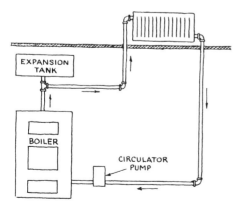

Forced-circulation hot-water system has a closed expansion tank with water under pressure.

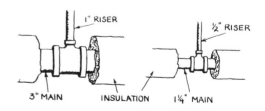

Pipe sizes—gravity and forced-circulation. Since more heat is carried by water under pressure, a smaller-sized pipe can be used with a forced-circulation system than with a gravity system.

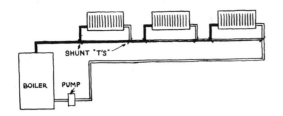

A. Early one-pipe systems with a single feed to each radiator were inefficient until special shunt T-connections were developed.

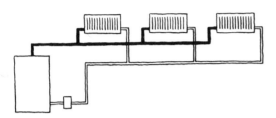

B. The two-pipe direct return system, while an improvement over the old one-pipe method, nevertheless resulted in high fuel consumption and uneven heating.

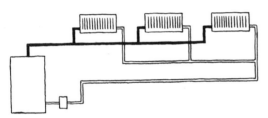

C. The two-pipe reversed return system permits the furnace to operate with an evenly balanced load at all times; all radiators are heated equally.

The first one-pipe systems had the main line and the radiators in a single line without risers or returns to each radiator. The first radiator—the one nearest the furnace—got the most heat, and those further along the line received progressively less. From the last radiator, water returned directly to the furnace for reheating. This one-pipe system has since been modified so that each radiator has its own riser and return connected to the main line. Baseboard radiators and in-line convector systems are adaptations of this improvement.

The two-pipe direct return system is shown in Figure B. Here water from the first radiator is the first returned, and this would be the hottest water with the least consumed heat, whereas the last radiator returns its cooled water last and thus places an added load on the furnace. Fuel consumption is higher, and the rooms are not evenly heated. To offset this problem, the reversed return system was intro-

duced. In this type of installation, water from the first radiator is sent to the return pipe but continues along the line of flow, picking up equally cooled water from each in turn, then returning all to the furnaces. All radiators are equally heated, and the furnace has an evenly balanced load at all times. Fuel bills are smaller.

The following lists some controls and control adjustments which can be used to increase the efficiency of hot-water systems. They result in even heat, low fuel consumption and more perfect control of the already well-managed heating plant:

1. In mild weather, set the water temperature control at 80 to 90° by means of the aquastat. To do this and to take advantage of the fuel saving, a separate hot-water heater (domestic use) is advisable. Otherwise, excess fuel is burned to heat hot domestic-use water, and the remaining heat goes up the flue.

2. Have the stack switch adjusted by your serviceman to provide brief but more frequent on-off cycles. This will provide a temperature better regulated to exterior temperatures in seasons of quick change.

3. Establish a two-pump system for two-story and ranch-style homes. Any part of the house you want heated above normal can be kept at a higher temperature without overheating the rest of the house. You can take full advantage of sun heat on protected sides of the house with this system. "Zone" your own home with this dual-pump system.

4. In extremely cold weather, increase pressure in the closed system. Pressure may be increased to 20 pounds. This raises water temperature; more heat is delivered to radiators.

5. Relocate the thermostat. If you find that the thermostat turns off the system when the room where it is now situated is warmed but the rest of the house is cold, place the thermostat in a more effective location.

Hot-water systems will not work properly unless the correct water level is maintained. To find the correct level, fill the system until the expansion tank is half full and all the radiators properly vented. Notice the black arrow on the boiler gauge. This arrow, which shows what the water level actually is, should rest over a red arrow which shows what the water level should be. Whenever the black arrow reading falls below the red arrow level, the reducing valve should automatically replenish the water supply. If it doesn't, check the valve. If you need to add water, do it slowly until the black arrow is returned to its correct position. Vent the radiators a week later to release air which will have been driven out of the new water.

When water is heated, the air is driven from it and, having no place to go in a closed system, it follows the flow to a point where, in

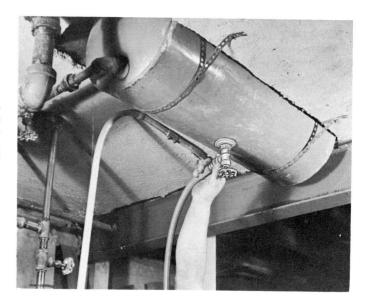

Closed hot-water systems are equipped with overhead pressure tanks which frequently become water-logged and thus are unable to develop pressure for higher temperatures. To remedy this, attach hose to tank, drain, close valve and remove hose.

bubble form, it can remain—in the tops of radiators, as a rule. The radiators remain cold because the air prevents them from filling with hot water. Check the pipes leading to the radiators. If the pipes do not run parallel to the joists and the risers are not perpendicular, air becomes trapped and efficiency is cut. Further, as water flows through pipe, it meets resistance from the rough interior pipe surface, rough fittings and the length of the pipe itself. Short-turn elbows, which present a two-thirds greater resistance to smooth water flow, can be replaced with long-bend elbows. The more resistance presented, the more time it takes hot water to reach radiators. As stated previously, hot-water pipes should be insulated between the furnace and the radiators to prevent needless heat loss along the way. The insulation will pay for itself in one season.

The regular venting of radiators is a routine job in the operation of a hot-water system. Use automatic vents which open to release air and close as water touches them. Otherwise, radiator valves that need manual attention must be checked and bled, if needed, every few weeks.

Steam Heat. Steam, a mixture of hot air and hot vapor, rises through pipes even more rapidly than does hot air or hot water. When water is heated enough to turn it into steam, pressure is created by expansion, and there is a limit to the pressure a home heating boiler can stand. To insure that this limit is never exceeded, every steam boiler is provided with a safety valve which is set to open and release excess steam when the safety limit is reached. Those on home heating systems are usually set to open, or blow off, at 15 pounds' pressure. Most are of the "pop" type. The valve pops completely open at 15 pounds'

pressure and remains completely open until a predetermined lower pressure is reached, when it pops closed again.

Many safety valves have a test lever by which the valve may be manually opened, and it is a good idea to check this at least once a month during the heating season. If the valve will not open and release steam or if it continually leaks steam, it is defective. How-

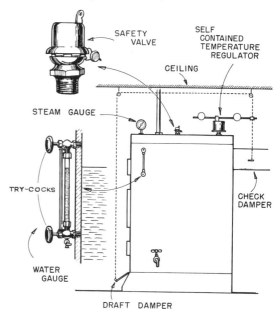

A steam heating system has different controls from a hot-water or hot-air system. If you aren't sure whether your system is steam or hot-water, check its controls.

STEAM SYSTEMS

1. Radiators may slant in wrong direction as floors settle. Prop them up on wood blocks so that slant is toward outflow; water-bound radiators will be noisy, will not heat.

2. Some radiator valves rust inside, cease to function. Remove defective valves and soak overnight in kerosene, then rinse out the scale. In emergencies, new valves are quick answers.

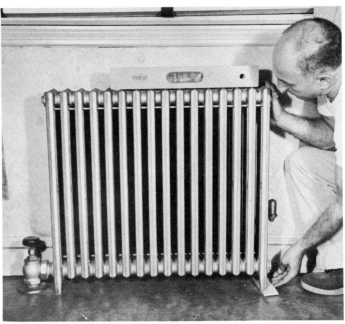

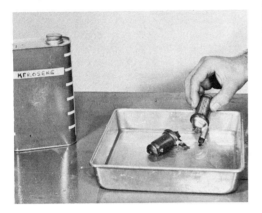

3. Sheet aluminum or foil makes a good reflector behind radiator. It stops heat loss through wall, increases radiator efficiency.

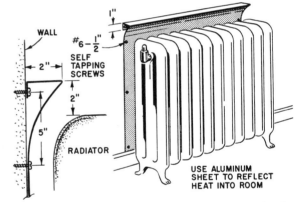

WALL

#6 - 1½ SELF TAPPING SCREWS

1"

2"

2"

5"

RADIATOR

USE ALUMINUM SHEET TO REFLECT HEAT INTO ROOM

ever, do not tamper with this valve. You can save yourself a repair bill by simply unscrewing the valve and replacing it with a factory-set new one, but don't tamper in any way with the inside mechanism or try to put it back in working order. Before removing, shut down the furnace and let it cool. Many safety valves, such as the one illustrated on the previous page, are fitted with a seal so that the setting cannot be changed.

Boiler try-cocks are used to determine the water level in the boiler. The proper water level is midway between upper and lower cocks, so you should get water out of the lower one, steam out of the top. These cocks become clogged with rust and water sediment, but they can easily be cleaned by unscrewing the handle all the way out, then inserting a narrow wire in the valve opening and into the boiler. Do this job, of course, when the boiler is cool.

The gauge glass is the most convenient way to check the water level. However, it is not as reliable as the try-cock method. If the gauge glass and try-cocks do not agree, the try-cocks, when known to be clear, are correct. The bottom connection between boiler and gauge glass may be stopped up when the gauge is half full, and thereafter it will remain half full—when there may not be a drop of water in the boiler! Clean the gauge glass cocks in the same manner as the try-cocks. The glass itself may be cleaned by removing it and washing with a strong ammonia solution. To remove the glass, turn off the gauge cocks, then remove the nuts at each end of the glass. Then raise or lower the glass to free one end. In replacing the glass, use regular glass-gauge washers. Lampwick packing is not as satisfactory.

The damper regulator, properly adjusted, automatically regulates the rate of burning. It either opens the bottom draft and simultaneously closes the check damper, causing the fire to burn rapidly, or closes the bottom draft and opens the check damper, shutting down the fire. The bottom door and check damper are connected by chains to the regulator arm, which is moved in response to the boiler temperature.

The chains should be set so that the draft door and check damper are both closed when the regulator arm is level and there is no steam in the boiler.

Thermostatic control, which transmits room temperature to the boiler and regulates it accordingly, will save you countless trips to the basement to regulate the furnace. Automatic firing, whether the fuel is coal, oil or gas, eliminates the job of adding fuel by hand. The combination of automatic firing and thermostatic control not only lessens work, but actually provides a much more even room temperature. And clock thermostats may be obtained which automatically reduce the temperature when you go to bed and turn up the heat at the time you like to get up in the morning.

Such automatic devices need more controls than just a thermostat to handle emergencies. Suppose, for instance, the thermostat called for more heat and there was no water in the boiler. For this emergency, you'd find, near the gauge glass, a low-water cut-out. This is float-operated and designed to stop burner or stoker operation at any time the water in the boiler drops below a safe level. This device is connected to an automatic water feeder which admits water as needed to the boiler. Except for a flushing once a month to remove sediment, it is best left alone.

Again, since no automatic firing device should be allowed to heat a boiler to the point where the safety valve can blow, a pressuretrol or pressurestat should be installed. These controls are operated by the steam or water pressure in the boiler and set to cut out at about 4 pounds' steam pressure. They should not be tampered with as they are generally factory-set. Replacement by a professional is necessary when these controls are out of order.

Suppose the thermostat calls for heat on an oil burner, the oil is sprayed into the fire box and fails to ignite. A dangerous amount of oil may be sprayed in, then ignited! Explosion would result. To prevent this hazardous series of events, a stack switch is mounted on the smokepipe or flue door. When the burner starts, the stack switch has from 15 to 45 seconds (depending on local regulations) in which to heat up. If it fails to heat, the burner operation is halted and will stay stopped until the cause of failure is located and corrected. This means calling in your heating serviceman.

Radiant Heat. Radiant heating systems eliminate registers, ducts, radiators and convectors. None of these heating facilities is visible in any room of the house. Instead, hot-water tubing (or, less frequently, electric heating cable) is concealed in the floor, in the walls or in the ceiling.

In the case of hot-water radiant heating systems, the tubing (almost invariably flexible copper tube) is run back and forth in rows from 6″ to 12″ apart.

Water from a standard hot-water furnace is reduced in temperature from 90° to 120° maximum and circulated continuously through the tubing. A mixing valve controlled by the thermostat regulates water temperature.

Where the tubing is placed in a concrete floor, the floor itself is warmed first and heat rises from it. Even though room temperatures may be as low as 65°, the degree of comfort is as great as in a room heated to 70° by any other system. Aside from the initial cost of installation, this type of system is economical in operation, since less fuel demand is made to keep water temperatures at the lower level.

Again, when tubing is placed in walls, these walls are warm to the touch and "cool" areas around any given room are eliminated.

Where electric cable is installed in place of hot-water tubing, thermostatic control turns the current off and on. Anticipatory outdoor thermostats will warm the room in advance of sudden cold spells, leaving the interior thermostat to take over and prevent excess heating.

Maintenance of both systems is virtually nil. The same care is required for the hot-water furnace as for any other system using one. In the case of embedding tubing in a concrete floor, the tubing is tested before the floor is finished, and only a major defect in the slab could bring about a leakage. Tubing suspended in walls and ceilings is protected by its own flexibility. With electric cable, the only likely difficulty would arise from a local power failure.

Conversion to Baseboard Radiation. The most obvious advantage of the baseboard radiator is that it's hardly noticeable, particularly when painted to match its surroundings in the room. No pipes or valves show, floor space is saved and the space under windows is available for any use you wish to make of it. This is a decided advantage where long, low picture windows have been installed. Floor-length drapes may be used, and there is more freedom in placing furniture.

Baseboard radiation is efficient from the technical point of view as well as the decorative. The old short, high radiator warmed a cold wall in a concentrated area only, and the walls to each side remained cold. Long, low radiators were an improvement, but the baseboard radiator covers the entire wall with a blanket of warm air.

Tests have shown that even when the outside temperature is at zero, baseboard radiation warms a cold wall from floor to ceiling with a variation of less than 3 degrees. To heating engineers, this means efficiency and low fuel cost, but to you as a homeowner it means comfort plus economy. The heat is not concentrated near the ceiling, and the floors are warm.

Starting at Figure A, with a cast-iron radiator designed primarily for hot water of either forced flow or gravity flow, the system may be used for steam heat as well. A two-pipe steam system needs a supply and a return line. If your present steam radiators have a two-pipe arrangement, you can use baseboard radiators, but if only one pipe it is better to forego the idea since furnace conversion is too costly to warrant the change. Not so with hot water. You may use a baseboard radiator with any hot-water system.

The so-called R type panel, illustrated in Figure A, delivers radiant heat primarily. Less than half the heat output is by convection, that is, by the circulation of hot air. The R panel becomes warm and sends out heat rays of the same type put out by electric heaters. The wall becomes heated to a height of about 5' and the wall itself becomes a radiant panel. In short, much the same type of heat is obtained as from pipes concealed in walls or floors.

The RC type of panel (Figure B) heats primarily

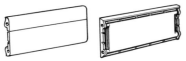

A. Two-pipe system, origin of baseboard heating, can be used with steam as well as a gravity hot-water heating system.

B. Units are built to be coupled closely. Standard close-nipples are concealed when sections are joined and covered.

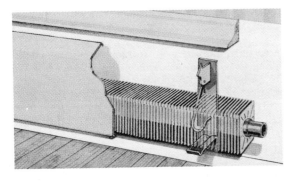

C. Single-pipe finned convector hangs on hooks. It requires forced-feed hot-water supply, delivers maximum heating.

by convection through the fins. This type delivers about 60 per cent more heat than does type R. Thus a 9' installation of type RC delivers as much heat as a 14' panel of type R. The latter thus not only costs more on initial installation, but frequently not enough footage can be installed to heat the room properly. This is particularly true of small rooms of limited baseboard area, such as bathrooms, or particularly cold rooms such as converted sun porches. The same applies to all rooms in colder climates—the New England states, for example. Type R is better suited to moderate climates.

The heating element shown in Figure C consists only of a finned copper pipe and not a radiator through which hot water or steam can circulate. This finned type of baseboard unit can be used only with a forced-flow hot-water heating system. In operation, hot water pumped from the boiler heats the finned pipe. Air enters around the pipe through concealed openings at the bottom of the baseboard, passes over the heating element and comes out warm at the top. Sizes range from 8 to 10" high and from 2 to 2½" thick. Lengths are in units of 6, 8 and 10'. The smaller units deliver less heat, of course, and thus it is important to calculate your heating needs accurately.

Depending on the manufacturer, the front baseboard panel is held in place by a type of snap device, either to a continuous back panel or to a series of small brackets. One firm combines in a single clip the holder for the heating element and a snap-on bracket. This is shown in Figure C. In all cases, the front panel is easily removable, allowing inspection and cleaning.

Normally, only the outside walls of a room are equipped with baseboard radiators. The panels may be cut on the job to fit the wall, and installation should begin in one corner. Matching baseboard fills walls not fitted with radiators. Also, bare pipe may be run around the outside walls and covered with a matching metal baseboard. In other words, instead of running the heated main line around the cellar and adding connections for radiator units, the main line is run around the room itself at baseboard level, thereby eliminating not only radiators but almost all of the cellar piping as well. A forced-flow hot-water system is, of course, necessary for this technique. As a supplement to this system, finned-type radiators may be added only where necessary, and the over-all cost is greatly reduced. Matching baseboards throughout conceal the system. Use of the matching extension pieces speeds up installation. Valves and fittings are concealed behind these "dummy" sections. Inverted and projecting types of corner plates make for a smooth, continuous installation.

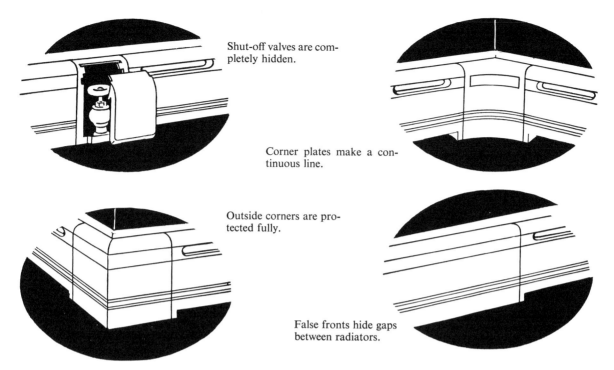

Shut-off valves are completely hidden.

Corner plates make a continuous line.

Outside corners are protected fully.

False fronts hide gaps between radiators.

The walls for all types of mountings are prepared in much the same manner. The old wooden baseboard is first removed entirely and the plaster, if any, patched and smoothed. Mark the location of studs. If the floor is not finished to the plaster line, fill the joint with molding strips. It is essential, of course, that a home be insulated for this type of heating, at least up the wall for a distance of 12″. While you are at work on this spot, it is a simple matter to add batt-type insulation to that height without tearing up the walls.

An air seal is necessary behind the radiator, otherwise warm air rising behind the unit would cause streaking of the wall. The air seal, of heavy asbestos or aluminum foil, is run from the floor to the top of the panel, then lapped over the heating panel $\frac{1}{2}″$. Hold the seal in place with quarter-round molding after the panel is set in place. Hang the panel by the method provided by the manufacturer.

Piping, valves and fittings are the same as for ordinary radiators. Long lengths of panel are assembled on the job by means of push nipples and assembly clamps provided by the manufacturer. Since the panels expand when hot about $\frac{1}{8}″$ for every 10′ of panel, make floor openings for pipe connections to the main line to accommodate this expansion (slots are better than holes). Steel or copper piping may be used interchangeably. Cast-iron panels may be fitted with adapters for copper pipe and, conversely, finned copper-tubing types may be fitted with adapters for steel pipe installation.

The final problem is the determination of how many feet of baseboard radiation will be needed. This figure is based on how much heat is lost from the room through windows and doors, lack of insulation, glass window area, thickness and nature of the walls, storm sash or none, and location of the room in relation to the rest of the house. The old radiator will help you in this calculation. Make a complete description of its size, number of sections and tubes, and consult your heating expert. He will know how much radiation area was received from the old radiator, which will tell how much is needed from the new installation. If the room has been altered, as by the addition of a picture window, this factor must also be taken into consideration in the new calculations.

HEATING SYSTEM MAINTENANCE

There is much the homeowner can do to ensure full value from each fuel dollar. Any heating system will lose as much as 20 per cent of its efficiency if it is forced to work below par. Rust, soot, lack of air and insufficient oil on moving parts will all contribute to a costly reduction in heat output. Maintenance may often be a task involving only a few moments' time. As simple a matter as vacuuming convectors and registers will step up efficiency immediately.

Radiators. With the coming of autumn and the starting up of the heating system, there are usually the problems of radiators which won't heat, radiators which knock and hammer, and radiator valves which spit and sputter steam. Fortunately, repairs are not difficult, nor are any special tools required—indeed, most of the repairs can be made without any tools at all. The skill involved consists almost entirely in knowing what to do.

For example, suppose you have a steam radiator that will not heat. Just in case you forgot, first make sure the radiator valve is turned on. If it is, the trouble is almost sure to be in the air valve. This valve does two things—it allows the cold air in the radiator to be pushed out by the steam coming up from the boiler; and when the steam hits the valve, the rise in temperature automatically closes the valve to keep steam from escaping into the room.

If the air valve is stuck because of rust, grit or corrosion, no air can escape, steam cannot enter and the radiator is air-bound. To remove rust and grit, first close the radiator shut-off valve, manually unscrew the air valve by turning it counterclockwise. Shake the valve vigorously—this may loosen rust—then try to blow through its threaded end. If air passes through, reinstall the valve; if not, boil it in a strong solution of washing soda and water for about 20 minutes. You can put the valve back on the same radiator to see if it works, but a much better test is to put the valve on a radiator that is heating well. If this radiator continues to heat, fine; if not, obviously the valve is defective and will have to be replaced.

You have, in the exchange, installed the good air valve in the radiator which formerly would not heat up. If this radiator still does not heat—and you know now that the air valve is all right—the radiator is probably waterbound. To remedy this, put small blocks of wood about an inch high under the radiator legs farthest away from the shut-off valve. With a

level, make sure the radiator is at least level, and preferably tilted slightly toward the shut-off valve. This will not only allow the radiator to heat but will cure the hammering noise which it probably has been making. If the hammering continues, put blocks under all four legs, but make sure the radiator is at least level.

Sometimes an air valve will sputter steam and water. Once again, try it on another radiator. If the valve still allows water to escape, the thermostatic device inside the valve is broken and the valve will have to be replaced.

If a radiator heats slowly, or only after all other radiators are hot, the air valve has too small an opening for the escape of air. You can buy an air valve with an adjustable opening and set the opening wide enough so that the radiator heats along with the others. The greater the distance between radiator and boiler, the wider the opening will have to be. With several of these adjustable valves, the system can be "balanced" so that all radiators heat equally, or for that matter, some radiators can be regulated so as to heat before any others.

Do not try to balance a steam system by partly closing the radiator shut-off valves, as this is likely to cause hammering. Keep steam radiator valves completely open or completely shut. Loosening of parts in the shut-off valve will also prevent a radiator from heating properly. Shut off the furnace and let it cool before taking a shut-off valve apart to see if it works.

Radiator valves sometimes leak around the packing nut. Tighten the nut a couple of turns. If it still leaks, shut the valve off and allow it to cool. Unscrew the packing nut and slide it up on the valve shaft. Wind some valve packing, which you can buy in any hardware store, around the shaft under the nut. Be sure to wind the packing in the same direction (clock-

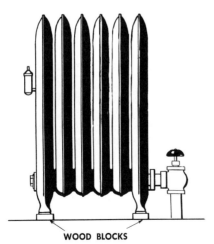

WOOD BLOCKS

Wood blocks under radiators aid return flow to boiler, cure knocks, and promote radiator efficiency.

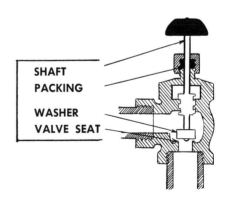

SHAFT
PACKING
WASHER
VALVE SEAT

Leaking radiator shut-off valves can easily be mended with a wrench and a length of valve packing.

wise) in which you are going to turn the nut when it is tightened. Then tighten the nut and turn on the valve. Hot-water radiator valves also leak around the packing nut and the repair is the same as for a steam valve, except that the water in the hot-water system must be drained out until its level is below the valve you want to fix. Unlike steam valves, hot-water shut-off valves may be set partly open or closed and used as throttling valves to regulate the amount of heat to each radiator. The entire system should be balanced in this manner to favor those radiators that do not heat enough and to cut down on those that are too hot.

Hammering in steam pipes is caused by water trapped in pipes no longer having enough slant back toward the boiler. This happens most often in old houses because of settling of the floors, sagging beams or the rotting away of pipe hangers and supports. The cure is to locate the low section where water can collect, then raise the pipe just enough to restore proper pitch. Since only a little movement of the pipe is needed to make a water "trap," by the same token only a little movement is needed to correct it.

Hot water radiators must be "bled" at intervals to remove air cushion which retards flow of hot water.

The Oil Burner. An oil burner is a carefully adjusted mechanism, and usually repairs must be made by a serviceman. However, there are a number of things a homeowner can do and should know about which might eliminate the necessity for calling in outside help. The photographs on pages 178 and 179 illustrate these.

A rumbling noise in the boiler itself, surging noises in the pipes or an unsteady water line in the glass are all signs that the boiler water is dirty. To drain the boiler, let the fire go out and the boiler cool so that rust and sediment in the water can settle to the bottom. Turn off the cold water feed valve to the

boiler. If you're not sure which valve it is, find where the cold water pipe enters your home and trace it to the boiler. Probably you'll find a shut-off valve just where the cold water pipe is attached to the boiler. Next, with the water in the boiler cooled, attach a garden hose to the drain cock at the bottom of the boiler. Open this drain cock and let the water out. When you're sure there's none left, open the cold water feed valve slightly. Let the water flush through the boiler. When the water coming out of the hose looks clean, you can shut the drain cock. This will start the filling of the boiler. Keep one eye on the water gauge on the side of the boiler. There is one with all systems except a closed hot-water heating system using an expansion tank. When water in the glass gauge shows the boiler is half full, shut off the feed valve. If you have a hot-water heating system with an expansion tank, close the valve from the system to the tank. Then open the drain valve on the bottom of the tank and let the water out. Leave this drain valve open about an hour or two and then close the drain valve and reopen the valve connecting the system with the tank. Remember, open this valve when you're finished draining the tank; it must be open before you start the system working.

While draining a rust-filled boiler is always recommended, excessive draining and refilling is not always the wisest policy. Heating water liberates minerals which then cling to the inside of boiler and pipes, clogging them. Where the water is known to be heavily mineralized, it is better to avoid draining and refilling and to use a rust-inhibitor chemical in the boiler water instead. Chemical treatment of household well water will either coat the entire system with a protective coating on inside surfaces of boiler and pipes or eliminate mineral content entirely.

Automatic Burners. Automatic heating equipment, owing to its complexity and the need for expert adjustment, is better tended by a professional. A homeowner can prolong the life of his heating equipment by cleaning dust, dirt and lint from fans and motor housings, and oiling motors periodically with S.A.E. 30 oil. Oil burner nozzles should be replaced once a year as the passage of fuel at high pressure widens the small jet orifices and eventually delivers a greater quantity of oil than required. This results in fuel loss and, furthermore, produces a poor flame. A smoking chimney is a sign of this trouble if you have an oil burner.

Gas burners require little attention as a rule. Gas alone will not burn until air is present. The gas burner merely mixes air with gas in proper proportion and passes it to the igniter. Observe the flame now and then. If it burns blue with a small yellow tip, the burner is functioning correctly. If there is no yellow tip, there is not sufficient air mixed with the gas. On the other hand, too much yellow indicates too much air. Adjust the air intake shutter—a simple process—until the flame is satisfactory. One more spot to check in gas burners is the ceramic flame spreader which most gas furnaces use. Replacing a broken or crumbled spreader is important as soon as detected, as an uneven flame wastes fuel.

SERVICING A FURNACE

1. Dirt, rust scale, and water sediment in the bottom of your boiler mean that it takes longer to warm up. Begin the tune-up by removing safety valve on boiler, loosening it with pipe wrench.

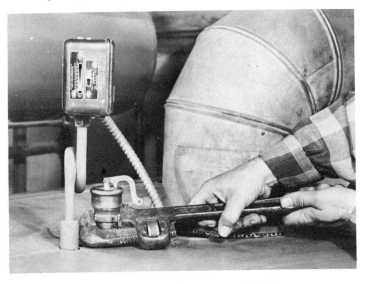

2. Next, catch water drained through clean-out faucet. Use a pail or run a hose to drain. Flush boiler by pouring more water into valve opening at top. Continue until water flows out of the boiler clear.

3. After shutting faucet, pour in water conditioner or a boiler-cleaning compound. Most of these compounds also inhibit rust. For best results, follow carefully instructions of the manufacturer of the brand you choose.

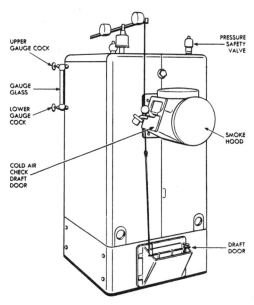

4. Safety valves protect against high pressures, prevent explosion. Do not adjust drafts and dampers, usually automatically controlled.

5. Water gauge glass may become rust-coated inside and conceal water-level line. To clean, remove top and bottom nuts and washers, pull glass up, then out at bottom. Clean with brush.

6. Boiler fins become caked with soot, which acts as insulation and causes heat loss. Remove door, scrape soot off fins with brush, then pick up dislodged soot with vacuum.

7. Hose-type vacuum attachment will serve to reach far corners. Soot also indicates poor burner adjustment, incomplete combustion.

8. Oil burner motors need periodic attention—a few drops of oil for bearings and removal of dust and fine ash from armature. Apply high-grade machine oil to cups.

9. Smoke pipes may fill with soot and fine ash or rust scale. This impairs draft, causes heat loss. A vacuum hose does the clean-up job without creating a messy basement.

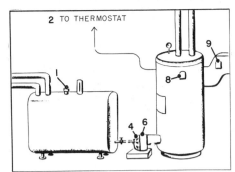

2 TO THERMOSTAT

OIL BURNER CHECKLIST

If an oil burner fails to operate or operates poorly, there are several trouble spots a homeowner can check. Numbers in sketch correspond with illustrated steps.

1. Check your fuel-oil tank. It might be empty. Even if the gauge shows oil in the tank, it might be stuck. Remove the cap and check quantity with a thin stick or dowel. There should be about 3″ or more to maintain the proper flow.

2. Left: Check your thermostat. The setting should equal the thermometer reading. Someone may have turned down the setting and forgotten to put it back. Of course, if the thermostat is on a warm inner wall, the temperature will be comfortable; outer areas of the house will always be cool by comparison.

3. Right: Shut off the electric current at the main fuse box. Then open the thermostat by removing the screws that hold on the cover. If you find dust like this, no doubt the thermostat has been prevented from working. Blow out or remove dust with a fine-bristle brush. No point in calling a serviceman.

4. Your furnace needs air to burn. Air is taken in through openings of this housing. A screw loosened by vibration may close the air intake. Adjust, while the furnace is burning, until the flame is clean, bright, and smokeless. Next time your serviceman calls he can make an accurate adjustment, but meanwhile the furnace will operate.

5. The large nut opposite the oil intake covers the fuel control valve. If the nut is tight, forget it. The trouble is elsewhere. If loose, remove by hand and adjust the set screw this nut covers—*while the furnace is operating*—until you have a large, clear flame. Have this adjusted and tightened correctly on the next call of your serviceman.

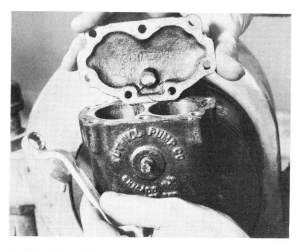

6. Check the oil flow. You may have plenty of oil, but it's not getting to the furnace. On top of the blower unit pump there's a cap firmly held down with a series of six or eight nuts. Shut off the burner switch first of all, then remove these nuts and lift off the cap. There's a gasket between the cap and the pump.

7. With the cap off, you can lift out the twin filters that screen dirt from your oil supply. There is usually grit from the oil, and rust scale from the inside of the tank. You'll see it coating the filter and preventing free flow of oil. Rinse the filter in clean oil or kerosene and replace filter, gasket, and cap.

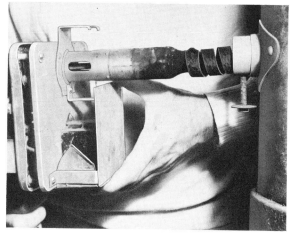

8. An aquastat controls water temperature of steam and water systems. You can look into this *with current off* by removing cover and blowing out dust. Check tilting lever to see that both mercury switches operate freely. If set too low, the aquastat may be preventing a supply of properly heated water from being delivered, even if furnace works well. Setting should be about 180°.

Shutdown for Summer. With a little care at the time you close down your heating system for the summer, the long life promised by the manufacturer when he built the equipment can be realized. The following applies to any centralized system, no matter whether gas, oil or coal is used as a fuel.

9. Inside view of stack switch. This keeps furnace shut down when smoke pipe is too hot for safety. Coil curls and uncurls as temperatures change, thus operating furnace. Smoky fires coat coil with soot and prevent proper action. Clean away soot with kerosene. Switch will not turn furnace on if stack is too hot—you'll have to wait from 5 to 30 minutes for stack to cool to see if switch is working correctly.

Not enough emphasis can be placed on the necessity for intensive cleaning. With a wire brush, scrape all heating surfaces exposed to the fire. They must be completely free of soot, ash, or residue. It is the combination of sulphur in soot and moisture in the air that seriously damages heating equipment

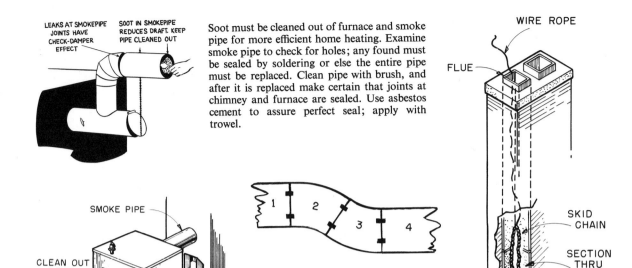

LEAKS AT SMOKEPIPE JOINTS HAVE CHECK-DAMPER EFFECT

SOOT IN SMOKEPIPE REDUCES DRAFT. KEEP PIPE CLEANED OUT

Soot must be cleaned out of furnace and smoke pipe for more efficient home heating. Examine smoke pipe to check for holes; any found must be sealed by soldering or else the entire pipe must be replaced. Clean pipe with brush, and after it is replaced make certain that joints at chimney and furnace are sealed. Use asbestos cement to assure perfect seal; apply with trowel.

WIRE ROPE

FLUE

SMOKE PIPE

CLEAN OUT DOOR

ASH CLEAN OUT

ASH PIT

Mark each section of smoke pipe so you can put it together afterward.

These are the main parts of a furnace from which soot must be removed.

SKID CHAIN

SECTION THRU BOILER FLUE

A tire skid chain can be used to remove soot.

during the shutdown period. Pick a time soon after a rain when the soot is still damp. Shut all the dampers and drafts to avoid a face full of soot. The dampers and drafts are marked on some heating units. Clean the chimney and the ash clean-out; then the smoke pipe. Before you begin to take apart the smoke pipe, mark the joint of one pipe on the other with a thin stripe of paint (automobile touch-up paint dries quickly). These stripes will be guide marks when the pipes are put together later. You might even number the sections if there are many elbows and varying lengths. Take the pipes out into the backyard on a windless day. Don't tap on them to free the soot; you might dent them. Use a stiff brush attached to a long handle and scrub them with soapy water or a detergent. This will prolong the life of the pipes, since removal of soot prevents damping during the summer, a process which quickly rusts holes from the inside out. Stand the pipes in the sun to dry. When they're reinstalled, open the stove damper to let the wind blow through to keep them dry, but only after soot has been removed from the furnace.

If your heating plant is made of steel instead of the more usual cast iron, coat the cleaned surfaces with lubricating oil. Make a thorough job of this, and don't skimp on oil.

Remove the grates from any coal-burning unit,

wire-brush carefully and store in a dry place. If you haven't a really dry spot for storage, oil them instead. The oil will burn off when the grates are restored to use. Thoroughly clean out the fire pit with a vacuum cleaner. Clean the inside with a wire brush, then leave the ashpit door slightly open for ventilation.

It is always a good idea to have the oil tank refilled after the furnace has been closed down for the summer. This reduces to a minimum the exposed areas of the tank walls, preventing formation of rust scale due to condensation of air moisture on the cold metal. At the same time, protect the tank bottom (where such accumulated moisture invariably settles) against pinhole leaks by introduction of a cartridge or dust type of rust-inhibitor coating. Tanks buried in the ground outside the house should be treated in this manner and coated on the outer surface with bituminous coatings before burial. Indoor oil tanks may be painted as a protection against rust. Should a pinhole leak be discovered in an oil tank, a small patch of chewing gum will stay the leak and, when the gum has hardened, a patch of plastic metal can be applied over it as a permanent seal.

When daily heat is no longer needed, pick a mild day to get the boiler drained.

The hot-water system should be left filled with water right up to the expansion tank. If, for any

TENDING THE BOILER

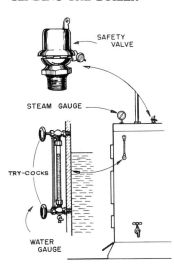

Water gauge on side shows height of water in boiler. Drain cock at bottom permits easy flushing of tank.

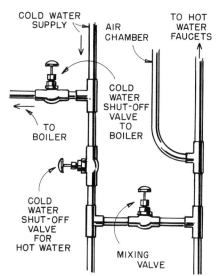

Here's a "map" of the valves in the usual closed hot-water heat system, showing what each valve controls.

reason, the system has been drained and refilled, the furnace should be fired long enough to raise the water temperature close to the boiling point (about 180° minimum) to eliminate gases found in fresh water. Such gases can start corrosive action very quickly. The steam boiler, which is usually filled with water only to the halfway mark on the gauge glass, should now be completely filled. Close all radiator valves and raise the water level to the very top of the system. Just be sure the water level is lowered in the fall when you fire up the boiler again! If you have a mixing valve to cool the very hot water you use at the faucet in the winter, see if it's still open. As your furnace will not be operating over extended periods of time for a while, you'll probably partially (or even completely) close this valve as warmer weather comes. Be sure to check this mixing valve or else you might have cool water instead of hot during the spring and summer.

All boiler accessories, regardless of the kind of fuel used, should be left in good working order. Oil the door hinges after brushing. Clean dampers the same way. Clean and replace the gauge glass on steam systems. Coat all polished surfaces with heavy grease which can be wiped up next heating season.

During the summer, it is best to cut off all electric power to the automatic heating systems. You can do this by either throwing the main control switch, if you have one, or by removing the fuse from its box on or near the furnace. If you plan to be away from the house for prolonged periods of time, it is the best possible insurance to shut off gas entirely, including the pilot light, so that a chance breakage and resumption of service won't leave your utility room gas-filled.

SUPPLEMENTARY HEATING METHODS

Many houses have one or two rooms that have always been hard to heat, and the central system which can reach into every single corner is rare indeed. Supplementary heat is the most reasonable and inexpensive solution. Even in brand-new homes, some areas may be bypassed by the normal circulation of warmth; and those houses wherein a room has been added, an attic or basement finished and put into use, or a porch enclosed, will almost certainly be in need of extra heating facilities. As a matter of fact, extra heat is often needed in just one room alone for a short period of time, and to heat the whole house to that degree would be wasteful, uncomfortable and expensive. Also, the usefulness of vacation houses can be extended later into the fall and earlier in the spring through the addition of spot heating equipment. Insulation and a heater in the garage make the garage workshop usable throughout the entire year; and in milder climates, one or two auxiliary heaters are often sufficient in themselves to heat the whole house.

The wide variety of auxiliary heating units makes it imperative that the potential buyer first knows just what they are and how they're used. Some are portable and some require installation. In some instances, outside help will be necessary for installation. Floor or wall space available must be considered as well as the decorative scheme of the room. Some units burn fuel, and some use electricity. Generally, the difference in operating costs is minimal because the area to be heated is relatively small. However, gas may not be readily available in your area, electricity rates may be unusually high or local building regulations may affect installation practices.

Built-in electric heaters come in many shapes and sizes, with and without fans, timers and other refinements. Individual units are often thermostatically controlled, or a series of units installed in a room may be controlled by one thermostat. Some heaters include a light for dual-purpose installations, many have a fan for better distribution of warmed air. There are types that recess between wall studs, others are surface-mounted. Some, which require no floor space, have add-on features for continuous baseboard installations. Safety is engineered into their design.

Quick, clean heat is available wherever electrical wiring can be run. In older houses, electrical units may be installed on existing walls or built in as part of a remodelling job. In a newly built wing, they might be used to eke out an overloaded central system. In existing houses, they can be strategically located to provide that extra heat needed to dispel morning chill or to warm the newly finished basement. Built-in units are generally designed for quick and simple installation. While wiring is within the range of some electrically minded handymen, some local codes prohibit them from doing it. Most manufacturers recommend installation by a professional electrician, regardless of the code requirements. Where 220-volt wiring is required, if not already present, it will have to be brought into the house by your utility company.

A console heater (also known as a "circulator" heater) is the successor to the old coal- or wood-burning stove. It is automatic and engineered to circulate as well as radiate heat. In oil-fired units, kerosene or No. 1 fuel oil can be piped from an outside storage tank or fed from one at the back of the unit. Installation is quite simple. The manufacturer's instructions cover the critical part of the job—provision of proper venting to insure complete combustion, correct operation of the controls and safe removal of combustion products.

Similar to the oil-fired models but often preferred in areas where natural or LP gas is available, vented gas room heaters are manufactured in many sizes and styles. Fully automatic and available with optional blower features, their prices vary. Installation is more likely to require professional help, at least for the gas line connection, which calls for an experienced pipe fitter. Certain venting rules must be followed to insure safety as well as observance of the guarantee provision. Ignoring the rules is dangerous. Failure to remove all the products of combustion is hazardous to the occupants.

Frequently thought of as a primary heat source, a floor furnace can provide excellent supplementary heat, though its use is limited to rooms over basements or crawl spaces because of the depth of the unit. Its chief advantage lies in the fact that it is space-saving, and it has a relatively low initial cost. Installation is quite simple, requiring an opening in the floor and framing to support the unit. By doing this part himself, the homeowner saves a substantial part of the installation cost. Automatic temperature controls and electric ignition are some useful accessories. Other units, floor furnaces in every sense, require baseboard space. They're especially useful in hall or partition locations, for they can be installed to provide heat at baseboard level to two rooms.

Recessed wall heaters also possess space-saving advantages over the typical space heater and are the most popular type of supplementary heating device. Versatile and comparatively easy to install, they fit standard 16" stud spacing and project only a little into the room. Gas of one type or another is the fuel used. Most units can be converted by the dealer from one to the other, should this become necessary.

Even on vented gas heaters, the installation procedure is not too complicated, thanks to prefabricated wall vents especially developed to remove combustion products safely. Venting and running of gas lines must comply with local codes and are jobs for the experienced gas-heating man. However, framing for the heater and the finish work may be done by the family handyman. Check with your dealer first.

INSULATION

Insulation will help keep your home warmer in the winter and cooler in the summer. Not only does it provide more comfortable living space, but it allows fewer drafts and more uniform heating throughout the entire house. The money saved on fuel bills alone will ultimately more than pay for the installation.

Without insulation, you may lose the use of one-third or more of your house, since the space up to three feet away from any uninsulated exterior wall is often too cold for comfort. Therefore, in an 11-by-18' living room with three exterior walls uninsulated, there might be only 96 square feet of comfortable living space. With insulation, you could make use of the full 198 square feet.

Types of Insulation. There are many different insulating materials, and some are more suited to a specific area and use than others.

1. Flexible insulation is usually in the form of blankets or batts, wide enough to slide in between joists and studs.

2. Reflective insulation, a metal foil or foil-coated surface material, depends upon the number of reflective surfaces for its heating value rather than upon its thickness.

3. Fill-type insulation, available in bags or bales,

GUIDE TO TYPES OF INSULATION AND MATERIALS

Material	Use	How Applied	Good Points	Bad Points
		LOOSE FILL		
Mineral wool (rock, glass fiber or slag)	Attic floors, between joists	Pour	Lowest cost, easy to use, fire resistant	Can irritate skin while applying
	Exterior walls of older homes	Blown in by special equipment		Provides no vapor barrier
Vermiculite (expanded mica)	Same as mineral wool	Same as mineral wool	Easy to use, good for filling in hollows of masonry walls, fire resistant	More costly; provides no vapor barrier
Wood fiber	Same as above	Same as above	Lightest insulation, fills in cracks and provides denser fill, no settling; fire resistant	Not always available; provides no vapor barrier
		BLANKET		
Mineral wool	Where framing is exposed, between studs, rafters, joists	Staple flanged edge to framing member, bowing blanket to form air space between it and wall	Inexpensive, widely available, continuous vapor barrier	Must be cut down to size; irritation caused by particles
Wood-fibre batt	Same as above	Same as above	Variety of widths for different stud spacing	Inconvenient where short lengths needed
Fibre blanket	Same as above	Pull to full length, then nail or staple	Compact, easily cut to any width desired	Lacks vapor barrier
Flame-proofed cotton insulation	Same as above	Same as above	Lighter weight, greater efficiency	More costly
		BATTS		
Mineral wool	Walls, ceilings, roofs, between framing members	Lay between floor joists, or nail to studs or rafters, ends butted tightly together	Inexpensive, cut to size, has vapor barrier, widely available	Air leakage between butted edges if batts not packed tightly together
		REFLECTIVE		
Aluminum foil single	Ceiling of attic	Tack to rafter faces, or between	Good for keeping out summer heat, good vapor barrier	Not as efficient at retaining house heat in winter
Aluminum-powdered building paper	Walls or roofs	Tack to face of rafter or stud	Low cost, tough, easily applied, good vapor barrier	Not adequate alone for insulation
Aluminum foil in layers	Where framing is exposed, good in warm climate	Staple to side of rafter, pull layers apart, then staple to rafter face	Ease of application, low bulk	Costly; can't be used with finished walls
Aluminum-covered insulation blanket	Where framing is exposed, between studs, joists or rafters	Staple or nail to face of framing members, bowing to provide air space	Combines insulation and reflectivity, and vapor barrier	Costly

is poured into position or it can be packed by hand into small places. When used by professionals, it is blown into place by special equipment.

4. Insulating boards, in a wide range of widths and lengths, are ½″ to 1″ thick and are often used as part of the house wall.

Amount of Insulation Needed. Although insulation is advised for most homes, the amounts needed and the type required vary throughout the nation. The Federal Housing Administration has divided the

country into three climate zones, as shown on the accompanying map. If you live in Zone 1, the coldest, and if you insulate your house, the savings on your fuel bill will pay for all the material used in 1½ to 2 years. Should you live in Zone 2, the moderate zone, it will take 2 to 3 years for fuel savings to pay for the installation. And in Zone 3,

the warmest, fuel savings will pay the cost in 5 to 6 years. The amount of insulation your house needs depends mainly upon where you live. As a general practice, partial insulation—that of the roof only, for instance—is not recommended. To gain the complete benefits of insulation, the walls as well as the roof should be protected.

Vapor Barriers. Insulation can do more harm than good if it is not properly applied. Most types are easy for the handyman to work with, but it is essential that he follow instructions carefully. The chief trouble with faulty insulation usually lies in condensation, the collecting of water, and a wet material is absolutely worthless as an insulator. Warm air, laden with moisture, seeps through the walls. (As a matter of fact, water vapor can pass through materials which air cannot.) In an uninsulated wall, the moisture will deposit on the inside of the outside wall. Since most insulations are porous— that is, filled with air pockets unless there is a vapor barrier, a surface through which water vapor cannot pass—the moisture will still deposit on the exterior wall. In order to be effective, the vapor barrier must be on the warm side; otherwise, it acts exactly like the cold window pane or the outside wall.

In cases where already existing construction prevents the addition of a vapor barrier—as in a completed house, for example—the next most effective method is to ventilate the outside wall. This can be done in several ways. One of the easiest is to use

It's important with all insulation that a vapor barrier be included. Barrier is placed next to warm side.

It's also important that every part be insulated. Don't overlook the spaces under windows.

Foil deflects heat to source; keeps rooms warm in winter, 15% cooler in summer.

small louvers spaced between the studs on the outside wall. Another method is to force small pieces of wood, even toothpicks, between clapboards outside the house. Also, attic vents play an important role. The size of the vents depends upon the type of material used for the vent. The basic type of vent opening is covered with ¼″ wire mesh, but if you use ⅛″ wire mesh, the opening must be 1¼ times greater than the basic vent. With 1 1/16″ insect mesh, the vent opening must be twice as large. If you use louvers in addition to the wire mesh, it is necessary to use even larger openings: with ¼″ wire mesh and a louver, the opening must be twice as large as the basic size; ⅛″ wire mesh calls for the opening to be 2½ times larger and 1/16″ insect mesh calls for a vent opening three times as large.

Exterior Walls. Exterior walls, already in place, can only be insulated with a loose-fill insulation. It can be blown in with special equipment by a professional, or the granular type can be poured in by the handyman after openings have been made through which to pour. Since an opening is needed in each space between wall studs, clapboards and shingles must be removed and holes bored in the sheathing. Make the holes as high as possible and drop a plumb bob in to detect any obstructions. If they are present, additional openings beneath them are needed. In many two-story houses, the same process must be undertaken for each story since the second-story plate would prevent insulation from filling the top-to-bottom

opening. After application of the insulation, the hole is covered and the siding replaced. In a stucco-covered frame house or a brick-veneer wall, this is not practical since the patching would be extensive and the appearance of the house would be permanently spoiled. It is also impractical to insulate any walls that are damp without first correcting the condition.

If you have the job done for you, as would be necessary with the blown type of fill, be sure that all spaces are completely filled from top to bottom, or the combination of hot and cold (between the insulated and uninsulated spaces) will create condensation in these spaces. If you do the job yourself, be sure to use only insulation which can be poured through 2″ or 2½″ holes.

If you intend to insulate only one wall, it may be more practical to cover the inside with tarpaper or roofing felt, furring strips and paneling. This would apply to an especially cold north wall, to those adjacent to an unheated garage, and to some masonry walls.

The Attic. The attic is the easiest part of the house to insulate, and since it represents about 25 per cent of all heat loss in the house, it is a highly worthwhile project. Attics may be described as unfloored and unfinished, floored but unfinished, or completely finished. These conditions determine the kind of insulation you will choose and how it is applied.

If the attic is unfinished and is not intended to be finished, the easiest way to insulate is with loose-fill

BATT INSULATION

Nail or staple batt through double layer of paper every 10 to 14″ along each edge. Batts are precut to right width to fit in between studs or joists which were originally placed with 16″ center to center.

Batts installed between joists in unfinished attic floor need not be nailed, but it is better to do so. Make certain that all batts lie flat and have no air spaces at sides.

GRANULAR INSULATION

Loose insulating material—used on floors in unfinished attics, in walls, and on concrete below basement floor—is poured directly from bag.

To spread it evenly to the same thickness throughout, make a spreader, as used by woman in picture, out of cardboard, cutting it to the required depth. Work this back and forth over fill until it's level.

materials between the floor joists. If it is floored but not to be finished, a board or two may be lifted and the same method employed. First, place a layer of building paper over the ceiling beneath the joists. When you reach the end of the roll, overlap the next sheet and tape the joint. (The paper must not have *any* rips or holes in it.) Then pour the insulation in to a 3″ level. The heat saved by a 3″ layer of insulation is 17½ per cent; 2″ gives 16 per cent; 1″ saves only 12½ per cent. If the attic is floored, lift a board or two at each end of the spaces between joists and draw the paper through before pouring in the insulation. In some cases, completely encased batts of insulation would be easier to manage in these spaces. But be sure to keep the vapor-barrier side of the batts toward the heated part of the house. If the attic is heated or apt to be finished and heated later, use blankets or batts between rafters. They are attached from the ridge on down, the vapor barrier facing the attic and lapped or sealed at the joints. When you come to the sharp angle where the roof

meets the wall, take the batt apart and stuff the material into the joint. Then tack a strip of vapor barrier over it.

There are two alternative methods that may be used: aluminum foil in layers, which insulates by reflection, and batts or blankets combined with foil. These are applied in the same manner as those without foil. If there are knee walls to consider, any of the insulation materials may be used between the studs, but vapor barriers should face the center of the attic.

Floors. Wherever a floor is over an open porch or over an unheated garage and both sides of the floor joists are covered, it would be best to have a professional do the job. Loose-fill insulation is used and blown into the space between joists. Floors over crawl areas, which are usually cold in severe weather, can easily be covered from below with foil that is stapled to the lower surfaces of the joists. Floors over porches, where access to the underside of joists is possible, can be handled in the same manner as those over crawl spaces.

 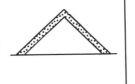 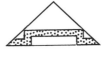

Left: In an unheated attic with no floor, place insulation between joists of attic floor.

Center: For a heated attic or one with a floor already in place, insulate between the roof rafters.

Right: If attic has finished room, insulate floor between roof edge and knee walls, along knee walls, and between collar beams overhead.

REFLECTIVE INSULATION

1. Accordion-folded aluminum insulation comes compactly folded in a single strip. Available in different weights, it is designed to fit between studs or joists spaced 16″ or 24″ apart.
2. Starting along one edge, staple the foil to the edge of the stud or joist along the entire length of the opening. Most hardware stores and lumber yards have staple guns for rent.

3. The aluminum insulation is cut to size after one side is stapled. Use tin snips; large household shears will also do the job. Now you're ready to continue the job of attaching the other edge of the aluminum insulation to the adjoining stud.
4. Using both hands, pull the accordion insulation out so that it extends to the adjoining stud or joist. Work from one end and avoid pulling too hard or tearing.
5. As soon as the free edge is extended fully at the end, staple it in place. Continue opening the accordion and staple the edge in place. Use a staple every 6 to 9″.

Filling Between Studs. The first step in filling between studs is to remove the crown molding along the ceiling (see Sketch 1). To do this, use a floor

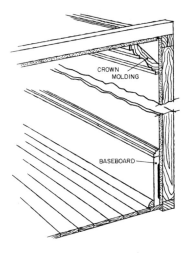

Sketch 1

chisel or pry bar and lift off the existing molding ½″ at a time along the length of the room. If you have plaster walls, you are likely to find a slight opening between the top of the wall and the ceiling edge. This was hidden by the crown molding. Use a cold chisel to chop an opening about 2″ deep and 8″ wide between each pair of studs (see Sketch 2). If any lath is in the way, remove it with a keyhole or utility saw. If you have plasterboard walls, score the seams over the studs to a depth of 2 to 3″ and then score

a line joining these points. Through a pre-drilled 1″ hole in a corner, cut the wallboard away (see Sketch 2).

Next, pour loose fill-type insulation into these openings until the cavity between each pair of studs is filled. With plaster walls, set a piece of screening into the opening as a base. Trowel on patching plaster and smooth it level with the existing wall. With plasterboard walls, cut a piece of identical wallboard to size and nail it along the edges to the studs. Cover the seam with perforated tape and apply spackle.

Adding Inside the Room. If you have the space to spare and do not wish to break into the existing wall, you can add furring strips, insulation and a new wall covering. Remove crown molding and baseboard molding with floor chisel or pry bar as noted above (see Sketch 1). Nail 1 × 3″ furring strips horizontally across the studs with 8d common nails (see Sketch 3).

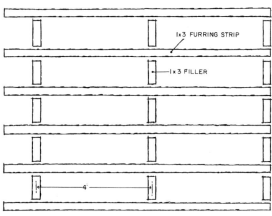

Sketch 3

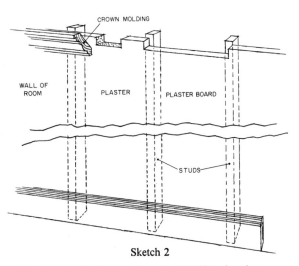

Sketch 2

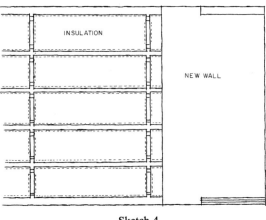

Sketch 4

If you add new walls of 4×8″ sheets, it is necessary to nail 1×3″ filler strips as a backing where edges of these sheets meet (see Sketch 3). With interlocking 16″ planks or random-width tongue-and-groove lumber, these 1×3″ fillers are not needed.

Attach batt-type insulation between furring strips with staples or nails (see Sketch 4). With filler strips, nail ends of insulation to these as well as to the 1×3″ furring strips.

After insulation has been added, install the new wall following the technique recommended by the producer of the wall material. With wall material installed, renail crown and baseboard moldings and the cold wall will now be well insulated.

DRAFT CONTROL

No house, old or new, can be made completely draft-free, but there is much you can do to reduce drafts to a minimum, as shown in the accompanying photographs. Heat lost through door and window cracks may account for 25 per cent of your fuel bill, which means, for instance, that $400 spent for fuel each winter can be reduced to about $300 if weatherstripping is applied to all openings. There are also other benefits. If your house is cooled artificially, weatherstripping saves that cooled air by preventing heat infiltration during the summer; it also shuts out dust and small insects such as ants, mosquitoes, and moths.

DRAFT STOPPERS

1. Settling of window sill often causes a gap—an entryway for drafts. Use 8d finishing nails to secure molding below sill; fill holes and cracks with wood filler.

2. Separation of shoe mold from floor forms another entryway for drafts. Use floor chisel or pry bar to remove mold; renail to baseboard so that shoe mold is flush with floor.

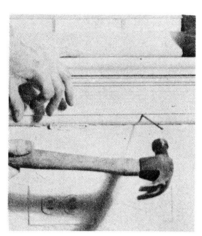
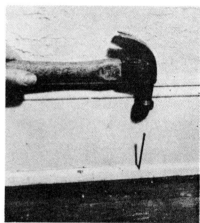

3. Holes surrounding pipes to radiators create drafts. Seal hole with paste of asbestos fiber and water. If hole is large, use wire screening as base for filler.
4. You may find cold winds seeping through under the threshold. Finishing nails on each side of its hollowed center will put it back securely. Countersink the finishing-nail heads. Then fill the hole with putty or plastic wood.
5. Old colonial-style flooring, particularly if it has shrunk with age, tends to leak cold breezes from below. Cracks can be plugged by sweeping in sawdust, then adding shellac. You can use paint, but shellac handles more easily.

→

6. Above: Check putty in all window sash. Any breaks here admit cold drafts, contribute to window sweating, speed up decay in wood sash or doors.

7. Above, right: Calking, in conveniently handled roll form, can be pressed into cracks with the fingers to seal around doors and windows.

8. Right: Before installing storm sashes, it's a good idea to weather-strip windows, quickly done with felt-plastic type.

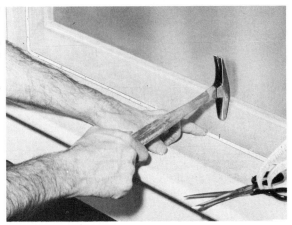

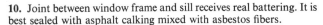

9. Be sure that the contact point between windows and masonry is sealed. Use calking gun.

10. Joint between window frame and sill receives real battering. It is best sealed with asphalt calking mixed with asbestos fibers.

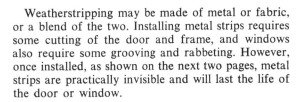

Weatherstripping may be made of metal or fabric, or a blend of the two. Installing metal strips requires some cutting of the door and frame, and windows also require some grooving and rabbeting. However, once installed, as shown on the next two pages, metal strips are practically invisible and will last the life of the door or window.

Application of fabric weatherstripping is very simple, as shown on page 195. An entire house may be protected with a single afternoon's work, and the efficiency of the material gives protection equal to that of the metal strips. Furthermore, the material may be repainted as often as desired whenever the house itself is redecorated.

METAL WEATHERSTRIPPING

1. With aluminum table edging, or J-strip, available in hardware stores, you can do a custom metal-weather-stripping job.

2. Check door for warping. If door is warped from true more than ¼", metal strips cannot be successfully installed.

3. Cut rabbet across inside top edge of door frame with rabbet plane, ½" deep, and as wide as the J-strip you purchased, about 1½".

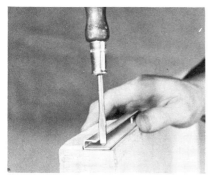
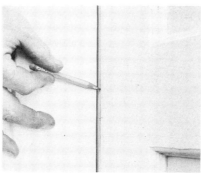

4. Cut identical rabbet along latch side of door frame. Be certain not to plane through position of door striker plate.

5. Connect two rabbet cuts in corner if your plane won't reach all the way. Use chisel to complete rabbet groove.

6. Fasten the J-strip in the groove with flathead screws spaced 12" apart. Be careful not to bend or kink the strips.

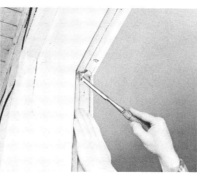

7. Remove wood saddle (or thresh-hold) and replace with aluminum one. Fasten down with long flathead screws.

8. Remove door and take off hard-ware, then cut rabbet identical to that on door frame across top and latch side of door.

9. Be careful not to extend rabbet past latch position. Clamp at this point stops plane from cutting this area. →

10. When cutting across top of door, use back saw on cross-grain sections; use plane for the remainder of the rabbet cut.

11. Attach J-strip as you did to the frame. Use flathead screws at ends of strip, drive-screws for remainder. Don't bend strip.

12. Cut two rabbets at bottom of door. One holds rubber-backed flat strip, the other provides clearance for saddle lip.

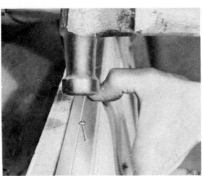
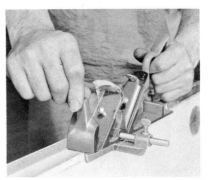

13. Attach rubber-backed strip to door in rabbet, using flathead screws. Keep outer edge of strip flush with door surface.

14. With back saw or rabbet plane, cut groove on hinge side of door frame to receive flat strip which is screwed to door.

15. Attach flat strip to door, with the edge of the strip inserted in the groove. Use round or flathead screws to attach the strip.

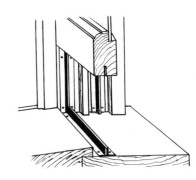

J-STRIPS AND T-STRIPS

Principle of interlocking J-strips.

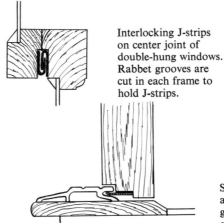

Interlocking J-strips on center joint of double-hung windows. Rabbet grooves are cut in each frame to hold J-strips.

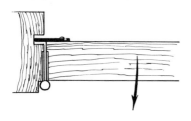

Position of flat strip on door set in groove to seal hinge side of doorway.

Position of closed door over metal threshold with rubber-backed strip in place.

Sliding door T-strips on top, sides, and sill of double-hung window. Dado groove is cut in sash with back saw and chisel or dado-cutting power-saw blade or dado plane. Strip is nailed to frame to match grooves cut in sash.

194 THE CLIMATE OF THE HOUSE : Draft Control

FABRIC WEATHERSTRIPPING

1. Tough wool pile of strips fits as snugly against any irregular surface as against smooth. Pile resists moisture.

2. To weatherstrip a door, insert tacks in strip as it comes in roll, spacing equally; then drive preset tacks in.

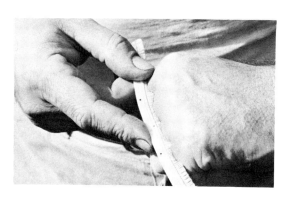

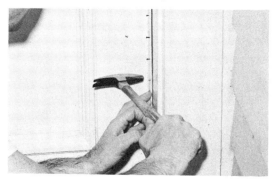

3. Cut the strip with ordinary household shears when you've finished each row. Tack as near to end as possible.

4. At door bottom, use metal-backed pile strip cut with household shears. Press pile against floor; space screws one foot apart.

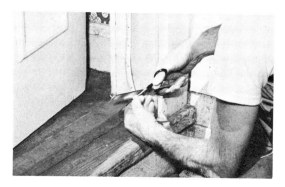

5. For windows, apply strips with pile pressed tightly against sash. Tack into frame every 4 to 5".

6. Instead of cutting strip at corners, bend so that it runs continuously around the entire window frame.

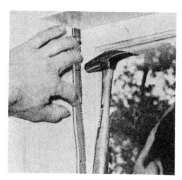

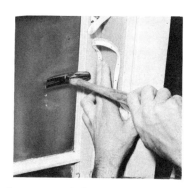

7. On wood casement windows, cut strips to bypass latch and tack just up to and away from the latch.

VENTILATION

Attic Fans. On a hot summer day, attic temperatures may easily run as high as 130° or more. With normal insulation, upstairs bedrooms would register around 100° with the downstairs at 90°. Walls and ceilings absorb the heat, with the result that even though outside night-time temperatures drop considerably, indoor temperatures remain uncomfortably high. Not until the early morning hours will the house become comfortable.

With a fan installed in the attic, conditions are quite different. It has been discovered that the 130° attic temperature can be lowered about 30°, resulting in a considerable cooling factor. In addition to lowered temperatures, an attic fan provides a constant flow of fresh air for easier breathing and greater body comfort, and is well worth its small initial cost and installation and operating costs.

First you need to decide what size fan is necessary for adequate cooling. This depends on two factors—the size of the house and the number of complete air changes desired each minute. Throughout most of the United States, one air change per minute is recommended. In the cooler Northeast and Northwest areas, satisfactory results may be obtained with one change every minute and a half. If the area to be

CHART FOR DETERMINING NEEDED FAN SIZE

Measure each room's floor area and multiply by ceiling height to determine cubic content of each room. Add all room figures together to arrive at total cubic feet of air in the house. Then select fan to handle this air volume.

Fan Diameter in Inches	Capacity of Fan in Cubic Feet of Air Moved	Fan speed in RPM
24	5,100	600
30	7,400	460
36	9,500	390
42	12,000	290
42	14,700	370
48	17,500	295
48	18,500	335
54	19,400	250
60	27,900	220

Example: 5-room house, living room 15 × 23, dining room 10 × 12, kitchen 9 × 12, bath 8 × 9, two bedrooms 11 × 13; ceiling height 8 feet. Total cubic feet of space in house is 7,448, and therefore a 30-inch fan with a capacity of 7,400 cubic feet will make a satisfactory installation.

cooled measures 24-by-32-by-8′ (length times width times height), for example, its volume is 6,144 cubic feet. Thus the fan must move at least 6,144 cubic feet of air per minute. If the change is to be every minute and a half, the total volume would be divided by 1.5. In this case, a fan with a capacity of about 4,100 cubic feet per minute would be needed.

If it is desired to cool only the upstairs rooms,

Attic fan centered under roof is the best arrangement for single-story ranch-style houses. Fan is directly above automatic shutters, and exhaust vents are in gables.

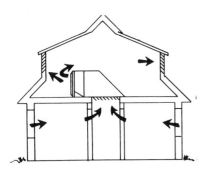

This location is suitable for one- and two-story houses. It affords an opportunity to direct fan discharge toward unobstructed attic area for ready exhaust.

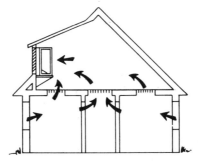

If fan is mounted on a wall the entire attic should be airtight, as all of it is used as a suction chamber. Louvers should be adjustable for shutting in cold weather.

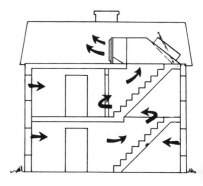

In houses having a stairway to the attic, the suction fan may be installed over the stairway opening. A tight-fitting door will provide easy access to the attic from below.

Sketches show possible locations for exhaust openings in attic fan installations. Select a location best suited to your home design.

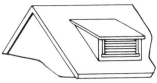

Dormer louvers

Gable end louvers

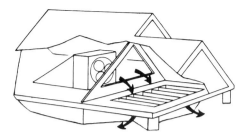

Exhaust grille in porch roof

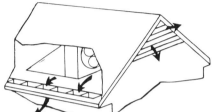

Screened opening in overhanging eaves

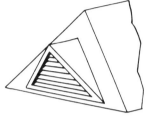

Dormer louvers

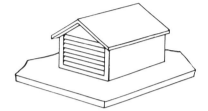

Flat roof penthouse

calculate their air volume only. However, since there will always be some air drawn from the living quarters below, the fan capacity should be 1.2 times the volume of the rooms to be cooled. For example, if you want to cool the finished attic area, which measures 24-by-20-by-8, the volume would be 3,840. This multiplied by 1.2 equals 4,608 cubic feet per minute.

The ideal spot to locate the fan is the center of the house, above the attic ceiling, to provide the easiest control of the air flow. It should be placed a distance at least equal to its own diameter below the rafters. A 24″ fan would be placed 2′ or more below the rafters. This will permit air to flow through the fan freely. A closer installation may partially "starve" the fan. If you set the fan next to a partition or bearing wall, the fan's weight will be carried easily and a quiet installation will result.

There should be no obstructions within 5′ of the fan outlet. Air discharges from a fan at high velocity, and obstructions add greatly to the load, reducing the air quantity. If the obstructions are serious, the fan

OUTSIDE WALL OPENINGS NEEDED FOR ATTIC FAN EXHAUSTS

The actual area necessary for an exhaust opening is governed by several factors, such as whether or not mesh screening or hardware cloth is used, whether the louvers are constructed of wood or metal, the thickness of the louvers or whether it is to be a completely unobstructed opening. The following table was compiled for a popular line of fans which range in size from 22″ to 48″ in diameter. Openings are noted in square feet.

Fan Size	22″	24″	30″	36″	42″	48″
Full opening (no screen or hardware cloth)	5.5	6	9	12	18	23
Full opening with 16 mesh screen	11	12	18	26	36	46
Full opening with ½″ hardware cloth	6.6	7.2	10.8	15.6	21	27
Wood louvers—no screen or cloth	8	9	13.5	19.5	27	34
Wood louvers with ½″ hardware cloth	9.6	10.8	16.2	23.4	32	41
Wood louvers with 16 mesh screen	16	18	27	39	54	69
Metal louvers—no screen or cloth	7.2	7.8	11.7	16.9	23	30
Metal louvers with ½″ hardware cloth	8.6	9.4	14	20.3	28	36
Metal louvers with 16 mesh screen	14	16	24	33	47	60

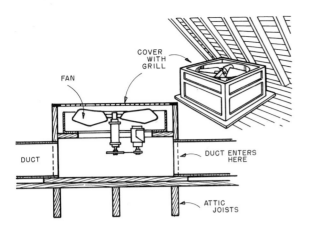

Horizontal-fan mounting box

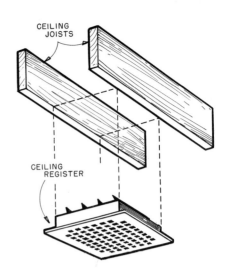

Standard metal louver

may become overloaded, causing the motor eventually to burn out.

An adequate exhaust area must be provided from the space into which the fan discharges. An exhaust grill in a porch roof is an excellent place, for it is protected from rain, snow and winds. Or, openings may be placed at the gable ends of the attic. If only one can be installed, it should be at the end away from the prevailing winds. Louvers also are built into dormers of various types. The sketches on the previous page may help you decide.

Engineers recommend the following safety precautions for the installation of any exhaust fan:

1. Adequate size of wire for the current required should be run in a separate circuit from the main electrical service entrance panel board to the control switch and fan motor.

2. Local codes and ordinances governing electrical installations must be followed. For this reason, it might be wise to have a licensed electrician do the wiring.

3. It is a good practice to install a thermostatic switch in the airstream on the suction side of the fan. This will shut off the fan, stopping dangerous drafts, if a fire in the home causes the temperature

to get too high. Only a "manual reset" type should be used.

4. If a suction box is used in the attic with a fixed grill opening in the ceiling, a fusible link should be inserted in the cord that raises and lowers the trap door. If automatic shutters are used in the ceiling opening, neither the fusible link nor the trap door would be required.

5. The fan motor should be equipped with automatic thermal cutouts to prevent the motor from overheating from any cause and protect it from burning. The motors of better fans are so equipped.

6. It is a good idea to locate the manual fan control switch where it won't be mistaken for a light switch. Inside a closet or high on the wall of a hallway, away from a door, are good locations.

Generally speaking, it costs proportionately less to install a fan that will ventilate the entire home than it costs to install one that will serve adequately for a few specific rooms. Installation costs change very little according to the size of the fan, and the cost of labor is the largest factor in a fan type of cooling system.

SUCTION BOX

Fan suction box is made of insulating board with a 1 × 2 framing on the outside. Make certain it rests on a floor and not directly on the joists. All edges of the box should be tightly sealed to prevent air leaks. Sketch and table detail dimensions.

Size of fan	A	B	C	D
		in inches		
24–inch	34	60	24	18
36–inch	42	72	36	21
42–inch	54	96	48	26
48–inch	60	120	48	26

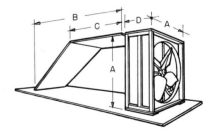

 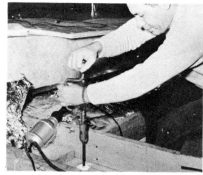 

1. Carefully select best spot for fan. Measure carefully for ceiling opening.
2. Drill "pilot hole" from which you can make exact measurements on both sides.
3. Using a square and pencil, mark out exact location of the automatic shutter.

4. Score plaster with chisel along lines. Cut with keyhole saw, wearing goggles.
5. Joists are now cut, headers installed. Make sure structure is not endangered.
6. Fan comes knocked down but with instructions which make its assembly easy.

 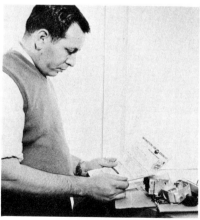 

7. Spring tension of automatic shutter is tested on workbench but must be adjusted in ceiling.
8. It pays to check all fan equipment against list included in kit before starting installation.
9. Headers are nailed to the cut ends of joists and to sides of joists which have not been cut.

10. Fan is placed over opening in attic. Shutter now is aligned and screwed into the joists above.
11. Canvas strip connects fan to frame. Fan is wired to junction box (right foreground).
12. Switch in hall can be set to run automatically for up to six hours, or until you shut it off.

Wall Fans for Kitchen and Bathroom. The easiest way to eliminate excessive moisture and heat in the kitchen and bathroom is through the use of ventilating fans, usually installed in either wall or ceiling. Kitchen fans should be as close to the range as possible, where most of the heat is generated.

The fan size needed depends upon the size of the room, again multiplying width times height times length to determine the number of cubic feet of air to be moved per minute.

All ducts from the fan to the outdoors should be as large as the fan opening. You can cut through the kitchen wall and install the fan within a few hours. The only tools needed are a drill, pliers, small saw, screwdriver, putty knife, and (if the exterior is stone or masonry) hammer and chisel. Before installing the fan, it is necessary to have electrical wiring brought to the point of the opening. Once this is done, follow the photographic steps beginning on this page.

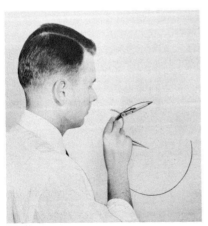

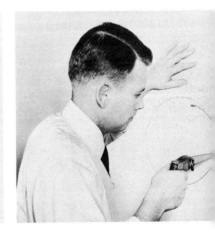

1. Locate fan in a wall space without obstructions and between studs. Draw circle ⅛″ larger than sleeve diameter, at least 1″ from either stud.
2. For plasterboard, plywood, and other sawable interiors, drill a series of holes within the circle for a saw starting point. For plaster walls, drill along the circle.
3. Saw the opening. If the wall is plaster, use ax, chisel, or hammer to break away the plaster. Work a small section at a time to avoid cracking the plaster.

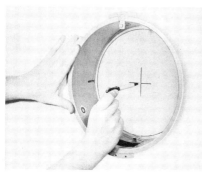
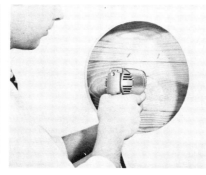
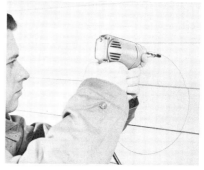

4. When sheathing is accessible, draw a circle slightly smaller than the inside sleeve on a piece of cardboard. Center the cardboard and mark the center point on sheathing.
5. Place a small drill upon the center point marked, and drill a hole straight through sheathing and exterior siding. If exterior is stone or stucco, use masonry drill.
6. Using the drill hole as a center point, scribe a circle on the exterior siding ¼″ larger than outside sleeve diameter. Drill small holes along circle.

7. Saw the opening. If exterior is brick or stone, use a hammer and chisel to break away the siding. With rough wiring in, you are now ready to install fan.
8. Depending on the wall thickness, remove as many sleeve knockouts from the outside sleeve as needed to make room for the outlet box. Be sure current is off!
9. First assemble the pull chain to the chain on the door. Then take door assembly outside and carefully mount it into the opening on the outside wall.

10. Here is how the assembly will look at this stage from inside the kitchen. Note how just enough insulation has been removed to make sheathing accessible.
11. Temporarily slide inside sleeve into place as a way of checking alignment with outer sleeve. With level, make sure outer door is plumb. Tighten corner screws.
12. Insert inside sleeve, pushing it tight against outside wall. Bring the cable through the outlet box opening. Tighten screws through openings in the sleeve. →

13. The cable is now inserted through the cable clamp and the threaded end of the clamp is inserted through a knockout hole in outlet box. This is an electrician's job.
14. When outlet is wired, it is inserted into opening in inside sleeve. Switch-plate receptacle is fastened down with two screws. Thread chain through guide.
15. Mount fan-motor assembly by setting the feet of motor-mount bar into slots. Slide to exact vertical position and tighten screws. Screw on cover. Pull chain to start fan.
16. When you release chain on fan, the door opens automatically and the fan starts. To turn off, pull the chain tight across the catch. Door closes and fan stops.

FOR REMOTE CONTROL OF YOUR FAN

1. In a convenient place inside the kitchen, mark off the location for a fan switch, using a switch box as a template. Cut the wall just as you did for cutting through for the fan opening.

2. Attach two 2-wire No. 14 BX cables to the switch box and secure box to the wall, preferably to a stud. Buy a double-pole, single-throw switch from your hardware store and connect it to the cables as shown in next diagram.

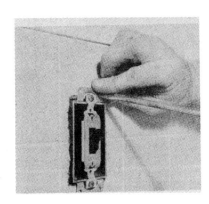

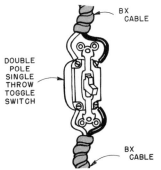

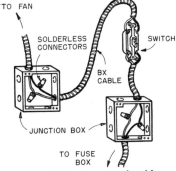

3. Attach white wire to one bottom terminal (screw) and the black wire from the same cable to the opposite side on the bottom. Now attach white wire from other cable to top and black wire to top on the other side.
4. Remove fuse controlling the line before you do any wiring! In the basement, connect one of these cables to the main power source from the fuse box and connect the other cable from the switch box to that coming from the fan. Use separate junction box for each.
5. Always connect black wire to black wire and white to white. One cable from switch is connected to line from fuse box; the other to the fan cable.

Condensation. Condensation and humidity can prove to be highly expensive. They will stain plaster, blister and peel outside paint, rot wood, rust metal. You can recognize their presence by any damp spots (if there is no leak) on ceilings and room-side surfaces of exterior walls, water and ice on inside surfaces of windows, moisture on basement walls and floors, frost on the underside of roof boards and frost or water on the nails in roof boards.

If yours is a new home, new plaster and new concrete may present large condensation problems within the first several months. In older houses, condensation is apt to be troublesome in very cold weather when interior humidity is very high.

The ordinary acts of breathing, cooking, bathing, washing, etc., may add 5 to 10 pounds of water a day to the air in your home. Washing and drying clothes may add another 30 pounds of water.

There are numerous cures for excessive moisture (which leads to condensation), and some of them require little more than common sense and a few seconds' time. For example, always open the window or leave the door ajar after bathing or showering, use the kitchen exhaust fan after cooking or washing in the kitchen, dry large amounts of laundry outdoors or in a well-ventilated area. If your home has become similar to an indoor greenhouse, cut down on the number of plants, for they add moisture to the air. These common-sense tips will do much toward eliminating condensation, but stronger measures are often needed. Moisture is usually a summertime problem in basements. Warm, damp air from outdoors enters a cool basement and condenses on walls, floors and cold water pipes. In warm, dry weather, keep the basement windows open; insulate cold water pipes with tapes sold in hardware stores for just this purpose; use silica gel or any other chemical moisture-absorbing material to cut down dampness; remove insulation from water heaters (if convenient) and use electrical dehumidifiers.

If you see paint blistering or peeling from the siding or suspect condensation inside the walls, attend to it as soon as possible. Fill all cracks and crevices around windows, doors and baseboards with crack filler or patching plaster inside; calk the outside. Use two or three coats of a high-gloss oil paint on inside surfaces of exterior walls; this acts as a vapor barrier. Do not use water-emulsion paint. If the appearance

---

CONDENSATION CHECKLIST

In the attic, water or ice collects in cold parts of uninsulated, unventilated areas. Cold metal surfaces (such as vent pipes) may have ice form on them. Icicles will also form on protruding nails in roof. Install adequate-sized louvers to solve this moisture problem.

In the bathroom, make sure you leave the window or door partly open after taking a bath or shower. Ordinary washing, bathing, etc., may add several pounds of moisture each day to the air in your house.

In the plumbing, you may find a source of trouble more difficult to locate and control. A leak may form lime salts which ruin interior wall paint. Also, water from the wet wall may find its way outward and cause exterior paint to blister and peel. Check for any leaks.

In the kitchen, the high humidity from cooking and washing may find its way through exterior walls to ruin exterior paint. Excess moisture in kitchens may be controlled by installing an exhaust fan.

In the basement, water may enter through poorly drained soil. Constant use of laundry equipment is another source of moisture vapor. Check automatic humidifiers in heating plants or unvented gas-burning water heaters for causes of high humidity. Installing a chemical dehumidifier will help; keep the basement windows open in dry weather.

Around the chimney and around vents, check for leaky flashings. Damaged brickwork may also allow water to enter the house from the outside. A periodic inspection of this area is a wise precaution.

On the roof, shingles and roofing must be kept in good repair at all times. Shingles should overlap generously or else they will be weak.

At gutters and downspouts, check for clogging by leaves. You will find peeling paint under eaves and around windows frosted on the inside. A poorly drained (or blocked) waterspout will also cause wall dampness and will mean costly repair bills.

Near the windows you may find paint failure, too. Rain draining downwards behind a poorly flashed window frame will cause damage to paint. Calk window frames; make sure they fit well. Seal butt ends of siding with paint. Install good flashings at tops of windows.

At the siding, blistering and staining may set in. Do not permit studs or siding to touch the ground. Siding joints must be tight.

On the porch, you may prevent peeling and cracking paint above and below a concrete floor by filling space between slab and siding with calking compound—and also by painting butt ends of studs and siding.

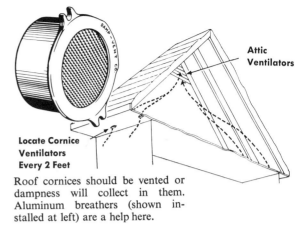

Locate Cornice Ventilators Every 2 Feet

Attic Ventilators

Roof cornices should be vented or dampness will collect in them. Aluminum breathers (shown installed at left) are a help here.

of a high-gloss finish is unattractive from a decorating point of view, you can use a semi-gloss or flat-finish paint over the high-gloss paint, after first sanding the surface slightly.

Moisture-coated windows will tip off the presence of water vapor when not visible on other interior surfaces. Install proper flashings at the top of windows and seal the butt ends of siding with paint. Install double windows or storm sash and make certain that they fit snugly.

Knobs of ice may form on nails protruding from the roof framing. These small icicles later melt and stain the ceilings below. To guard against this, clip off the nails close to the wood. Also, keep gutters clean and free from leaves so they don't overflow. A blocked downspout can cause dampness in a wall, too.

Attic ventilation is extremely important. Make sure you have two louvers at opposite ends of the attic. The total area of louvers should be at least 1/300 of the attic floor area. For example, in an attic 20-by-30, or 600 square feet, the total area of louvers should be at least 2 square feet. If the attic is used for living quarters, apply insulation between rafters and a vapor barrier on the lower surface of rafters. Also install vents (screened metal type or continuous screened slots) under the eaves.

Since one of the chief sources of dampness is apt to lie in the laundry, it is wise to provide a clothes-dryer vent through which the moisture may leave the house. Whether the dryer is located in the kitchen, in an upstairs laundry room, or in the basement, an exterior vent can be installed in just a few hours for very little money.

The most common method of venting a dryer is in the use of a smoke pipe from the dryer through the foundation wall. Smoke pipe is readily available in many sizes and in any length from your local tin-smith shop. Measure the over-all distance of the pipe

and have the pieces cut to size. See that the ends are crimped so that the pipes slip together easily.

If your foundation wall is made of concrete blocks, locate the vent outlet so that the pipe passes through one of the voids or hollows in the block; there's less chopping that way.

If you don't want to break through the foundation, you can run the vent through a basement window. First remove the putty around one of the panes of glass with a chisel, pry the glazier's points loose and remove the glass. Then cut a piece of ½″ exterior-grade plywood or tempered hardboard to fit the opening within the window frame, and drill a hole through the plywood to permit the passage of the smoke pipe. Nail the plywood in the window frame with quarter-round molding and nail the window shut so that it cannot be opened by accident. Set a layer of insulation between the metal pipe and the plywood. Insulation is also needed if the vent smoke pipe passes through the floor from upstairs to basement.

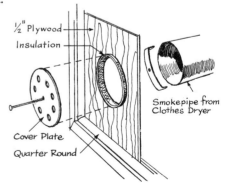

½″ Plywood

Insulation

Smokepipe from Clothes Dryer

Cover Plate

Quarter Round

To vent dryer through a basement window, replace the glass pane with a piece of ½″ plywood. Secure in place with quarter-round molding and insulate between metal pipe and plywood.

**VENT THROUGH
A FOUNDATION WALL**

1. Mark exact location of
   vent opening. Make a
   series of holes along circumference, using an electric drill and masonry bit or a hammer and star
   drill.
2. If you've used a masonry bit, it won't be long enough to go through the wall. Use a cold chisel and
   a hammer to remove the excess concrete as you deepen the hole.

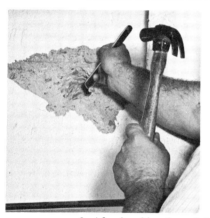

3. After breaking through to the inside wall, start chopping the concrete away from the inside out.
   A cold chisel and hammer do an effective job.
4. Measure distance from opening to clothes dryer and purchase necessary pipe and elbows from local
   tinsmith shop. Force-fit pipe together and set in place.
5. Wet concrete thoroughly and fill in with a mix of 1 part cement to $2\frac{1}{2}$ parts sand plus bonding
   agent. Smooth flush with wall.

Damp Closets. When you open the door of a closet
and the odor of mildew greets you, the closet needs
to be better ventilated. Ordinarily, a closet should
not be located on an outside wall, but if you have
one that is, try to provide it with more heat. You
can use a small spot-heating unit or, in a small closet,
hang a 100-watt bulb low and cover it with a wire
guard to avoid chance contact with clothing. For
added ventilation, a few round aluminum louvers
about $2\frac{1}{4}''$ in diameter, placed in drilled holes along
the top and bottom of exterior walls, will do wonders.
Also, louvered shutters may be used in the place of
panels in a paneled door.

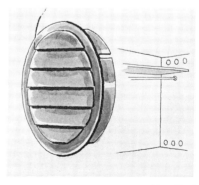

CHAPTER 4

ALL THROUGH THE HOUSE

Electricity · Plumbing

If you are an amateur home handyman, all the pipes and wires running through the house may at first glance seem like a maze, but they are easy to understand once you start dealing with them, tracing them to their sources, becoming familiar with their parts.

Electricity and plumbing are the very lifelines of your house. If a fuse blows, the lights go out, and all the appliances become immediately useless; your house is for the time being unlivable. And the same is true if your plumbing goes seriously awry—if a main drain backs up or the pipes freeze, for instance.

This chapter will help bring you to an easy understanding of the two great systems running through your house so you can keep it livable, comfortable and properly functioning at all times.

ELECTRICITY Definitions of household electrical terms · Adequate wiring · Grounding electrical appliances · Working with BX cable · Household wires · Simple appliance repairs · What to do when the fuse blows · Repairing and replacing a wall switch · Replacing a pull chain with a wall switch · Replacing a ceiling fixture · Adding an electric outlet · Electric surface ducts · Cures for a balky doorbell · Fluorescent lighting · Outdoor wiring

Electricity can be your home's friend or foe—friend when all lights and appliances are working at tiptop efficiency, foe when fuses blow, the house is in darkness and even the doorbell won't ring. Sometimes repair is a simple, quick matter—a mere replacing of a fuse, for instance—but sometimes a complete overhaul of the whole electrical system is indicated. Perhaps the house just isn't adequately wired to cope with ever-increasing demands made by new appliances.

How much electrical work a homeowner may undertake is usually governed by community codes, which vary greatly from one locale to another. Some communities require that all electrical installation be made by a licensed electrician; some require that all

electrical repairs be similarly made; and some (usually smaller) communities have no codes at all other than the National Electric Code which sets minimum standards for the nation as a whole. Before beginning any electrical work, the home handyman should check with his local authorities to see just which work he is allowed to do himself and which must be done by a licensed professional.

However—and this is true no matter what the local code—every homeowner will benefit immeasurably by understanding the wiring system of his own house. He may wisely postpone, for instance, the purchase of an expensive freezer if he knows in advance that it will mean additional expense in bringing more power to the house. He will know when outlets have

The modern kitchen, adequately wired and provided with sufficient current for all appliances, is a great consumer of current. No modernizing program can get far without adequate outlets.

become overloaded and dangerous and whether or not his outdoor wiring is properly weatherproofed. He can save many times over the cost of outside help by being able to trace a blown fuse, by the simple repair of a frayed cord, or the easy replacement of an old-fashioned fixture.

In this chapter, the things a homeowner should *know* about his home's electrical system, as well as those things which he can *do* toward its greater efficiency, are detailed.

DEFINITIONS OF HOUSEHOLD ELECTRICAL TERMS

Currents DC (Direct Current)—flows from the source (generator or battery, etc.) to the point of use and back to the source in a *continuous flow in one direction.*

AC (Alternating Current)—reverses the direction of its flow at measured intervals or "cycles," usually 60 times per second.

Voltage A unit of measure of the pressure of electric current. The normal household voltage is 115 (plus or minus 5 volts). Voltage force causes amperes to flow along the wires.

Ampere A unit of measure of the *size* of electric current passing a point on a wire at a given moment. Amperage (AMP or A) is indicated along with voltage on appliances, fuses and other electrical devices.

Watt A unit for measuring the delivery of electric power. One thousand watts equal 1 kilowatt. You pay for the power you use in terms of kilowatt

hours. An appliance consuming 2 amperes on a line voltage of 115 uses 230 watts (2 times 115) per hour, or less than one-quarter of a kilowatt.

Fuse A protective device in which is located a short length of soft metal that melts as soon as the heat generated by the passage of excess current through it exceeds its melting point. Once this strip of metal melts, the flow of current is interrupted. Thus the fuse "blows" and a new one is needed.

Circuit breaker A device used in place of a fuse. The flow of excess current operates a device which flips a spring and the circuit is mechanically broken as though a switch had been turned off. When the cause of the excess current is established and corrected, the circuit breaker may be reset and used again.

ADEQUATE WIRING

Very few homeowners are completely aware of what their home's electrical wiring system actually does. The available power supply is revealed only by pushing the button of a switch or plugging an appliance into an outlet. For the most part, the complex wiring is hidden inside the walls. The "brains" of the system—the master switch and fuse box—are located out of sight, perhaps in the basement, the garage or behind a tree outdoors.

When a new electrical appliance is brought home, it's usually plugged right into the nearest convenient outlet. If that one is already full of push-plugs, a double-outlet device is added to make room for more —and then the fuses blow. The lights go out and that particular circuit is dead. This is because only a fixed amount of electric current (amperes) can flow along a wire of a given size. If too many amperes are sent into the wire, they "pile up" and the wire gets hot. The same thing happens with a garden hose too full of water. When the pressure is too great, the hose bursts. When a wire gets too much pressure from the current trying to get through, it gets too hot and the insulation around it (or even the wire itself) melts. To prevent this, the line is protected with a fuse. The fuse contains a special bit of soft metal inside it through which the current must pass. Instead of the entire length of wire becoming too hot from the overload and starting a fire, this little bit of metal in the fuse gets hot and melts first. The fuse blows, halting the flow of current. No more current can pass through that line until the condition is corrected and the fuse replaced—but the wires are safe. In replacing a fuse, always be sure to use one of the proper size, i.e., one that will blow before the current consumption becomes high enough to overheat the line. To substitute a larger fuse in place of one which keeps blowing is to invite serious trouble.

What Electric Current Does. Electric current produces light, heat or power. In the case of light, the current is passed through a very fine wire inside the bulb—too fine, in fact. It gets hot, just as other wires do when overloaded, but the fine wire in a light bulb is made of tougher stuff. It gets hot and glows, but it doesn't melt. It produces light.

In producing heat, the same principle is used. The current is fed, at a controlled rate, into a wire (called the heating element) too small for it. Depending upon what this wire is made of, the passage of the current may or may not be seen as a red glow. In some cases, the heating element is shaped to spread the heat over a wide area.

To produce power, the current activates magnets inside a motor. The shaft to which one of the magnets is attached rotates, and from the spin of that shaft comes motive power. Practically all uses of electrical power in the home start with a rotating shaft, called an armature, inside a motor.

By understanding that some devices require very little current and other far more, you will begin to understand the complexity of household wiring. Lamp bulbs require from 25 watts to 300 watts; the brighter the bulb, the higher the rating. A small portable electric fan motor needs 100 watts. On the other hand, a heat-producing appliance such as an electric clothes drier demands 4,500 watts. Obviously, the wires used to convey current to your lights and to the small fan motor need not carry as much wattage as the drier.

The amount of current each electrical device requires is indicated clearly on it somewhere. It's shown on the large end of light bulbs, on the manufacturer's plates of all motors, and on the plates of practically all heating units. It's a wise homeowner who knows how much wattage is being consumed by each of his appliances. Through being familiar with this information, he can spread the total load used by his appliances over several circuits without overloading any one of them; and he will also know if his home's wiring has the capacity to handle other appliances which he intends to add at a later date.

Checking Your Home's Electrical System. In investigating the source of your electrical power, the first step is to cut off the power by pulling the lever of the main switch. This step precedes *any* electrical work in the house. The fuse box can then be opened safely. Touching any set of two wires, or the "hot" power line and a grounded object, can result in a severe shock or worse. Large current supplies, such

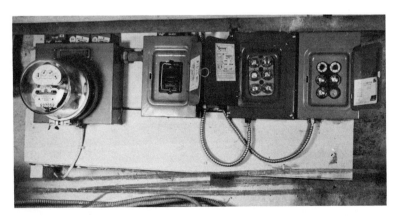

Typical "power course" installation—the meter at the left, cartridge fuse box, and two branch-line fuse boxes make up the complete service panel.

Cartridge fuse container is pulled out by its handle, exposing the fuses on the back. They can be safely removed for replacement when the container is out.

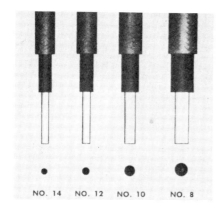

Wiring sizes as used in the home. No. 14 gauge wire is about $\frac{1}{16}''$ (64/1000) diameter. Beware of using No. 16 and No. 18 lamp cord to wire heating-type appliances! Never use a smaller size wire than No. 14.

NO. 14   NO. 12   NO. 10   NO. 8

as the main line bringing electricity into the house, usually pass through closed boxes containing cartridge fuses. Smaller demands pass through the familiar screw-in fuses, or circuit breakers. The wires leading to various parts of the house start just in back of the fuses or breakers. All those controlled by one fuse or one circuit breaker are considered to be on "one circuit." To know where the various circuits lead, remove one fuse, throw the main switch on again, then check the house to discover which lights and outlets are not working. Indicate *all* these units on a chart near the fuse box. Add up the current requirements of all the electrical equipment that takes its current from this one fuse. Repeat the step with each of the other circuits.

An expert can tell at a glance the size of the wires behind each of your fuses. In case you aren't an expert yet, check the equivalents below. They indicate wire sizes and the amperages they can handle at the usual 115 volts.

No. 14 wire—15 AMP fuse, 1750 watt capacity
No. 12 wire—20 AMP fuse, 2300 watt capacity
No. 10 wire—30 AMP fuse, 3500 watt capacity

Older houses may have only one or two 20 AMP fuses and thus they are limited to relatively few lights and appliances. As soon as the 20 AMP-per-line capacity is reached, those lines have reached their maximum. No more appliances can be purchased and plugged in. Electrically, the house is outmoded.

In recent years it has become commonplace to find in new houses a 220/240-volt supply entering the house over three-wire, instead of the usual two-wire, lines. Two of the three are "hot" wires. The third is called the "return" or "ground." In effect, this means that there are two separate 115/120-volt lines, each

consisting of the ground wire and one hot wire. The current enters the house through a box containing cartridge-style fuses and is then connected in such a way as to provide a number of 120-volt circuits and usually one 240-volt line to operate such appliances as electric stoves, driers and heaters specifically designed for this higher voltage. Each circuit is then fed through circuit breakers or fuses.

To obtain a larger supply of current, start with your power company. Consult them first of all as to power available. They will advise further as to what equipment is needed at your power-supply depot, the so-called "service entrance." From that point on, distribution to the various parts of the house must be made over wires of adequate size, capable of handling the loads listed here and protected with the correct AMP-size fuses shown in connection with each wire size.

To summarize, the steps toward adequate household wiring include:

1. Bringing enough current to the house.
2. Correct protection for that current with the right type and size of fuse or breaker.
3. Sufficient branch lines with the proper size of wires leading from them, each protected with the right size of fuse.
4. No overloading of the branch lines.

GROUNDING ELECTRICAL APPLIANCES

You can be seriously injured by an appliance that is not grounded. Every time you open a refrigerator door, you are taking a chance—unless you have provided the safety insurance of a ground. Grounding, simply put, is an electrical connection to the earth from the appliance. It usually means attaching one end of a wire to the appliance's frame and clamping the wire's other end to a water pipe.

Grounding provides many safeguards. If the insulation covering an appliance's wire should wear so that bare wire makes a contact with the frame, having the frame grounded will immediately cause a fuse to blow, warning that something is wrong. There is no danger of shock to you. However, if a worn wire makes contact with the frame of an appliance that has no ground, no fuse will blow. The machine will continue to function as before. There will be no warning to you that the machine has become "hot," "alive," its entire frame charged with electric current. If you were to touch it under average circumstances, you would get a shock, though perhaps not a serious one. However, if you were to touch it while standing on a damp floor or while your other hand was simultaneously in contact with a water faucet, your life would be seriously endangered. The current would surge through you into the ground contact you were making with the wet floor or water faucet.

Fortunately, in most cases, there is no such hazard.

1. (Right) Purpose of grounding is to blow fuse if electric current enters appliance frame. The machine otherwise will give you a severe shock if you touch it while in contact with an electrical conductor. Be particularly careful to ground appliances in a bathroom.

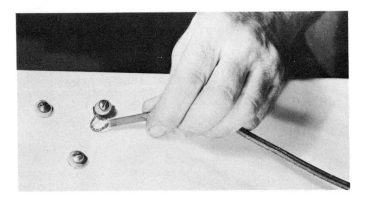

2. (Left) Ground wire can go on bolt at back of refrigerator, washing machine, dishwasher, air conditioner, etc. Be sure to scrape off enamel under bolt and remove rust. Use 14 or 16 gauge wire.

3. Clamp is fastened over pipe; then ground wire is attached by tightening the crimping screws. Clean pipe with emery cloth or sandpaper before attaching clamp.

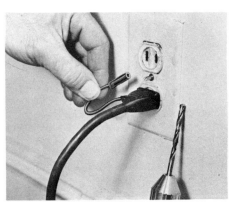

4. Portable electric tools like this drill have a three-wire outlet. Third wire is called a "pigtail," has plug-in jack which is attached to nipple on electric receptacle cover.

Electric irons, mixers, clocks and heating blankets are used under conditions which do not involve simultaneous contact with pipes or other conductors. But larger appliances, particularly washing machines, dishwashers, refrigerators, broilers, air conditioners and clothes driers, are used under circumstances that make grounding extremely advisable.

Grounding is easy to do. One end of an ordinary single electrical wire is connected to the frame of the appliance in question. Make the connection by loosening a bolt on the appliance, turning the bare end of the wire around it and retightening, but first make sure that the bolt and metal surface are clean and free of rust. The other end of the wire is then connected to a water pipe by means of a grounding clamp which has a bolt or other device for tightening around the pipe and a screw for securing the wire. If no pipe is nearby, a ground connection can be made by fastening your grounding wire to a screw on the plate of the electrical outlet where your appliance is plugged in. This is feasible *only* if your home is wired with BX cable; all armored cable and conduits, as well as their outlets, are already grounded.

Non-armored cable is provided with a separate grounding wire which, if attached to each fixture or outlet box by a screw and to the main ground line of the master fuse box, will ground these fixtures and outlet boxes just as armored cable does.

WORKING WITH BX CABLE

When doing electrical wiring work about your home, you'll undoubtedly use BX, or armored cable. In some sections of the country, BX is the only type of electrical cable permitted by the local code.

BX is composed of two or three copper wires, each protected by a thick covering of rubber and a layer of moisture-and-fire-resistant cotton fabric. A waterproofed kraft paper binds the wires together just inside the shell of steel armor. There is also a small uninsulated wire inside the cable. This is a ground wire that requires no attention whatever from the handyman. Snip it off if it gets in the way.

Most ordinary household circuits use No. 14 cable, often referred to as 14/2, the second figure indicating that there are two separate wires in the cable. You'll find a 15-ampere fuse in the fuse box protecting this circuit. To safeguard against overloads, it is important that no fuse rated higher than 15 amperes is used on average household circuits wired with No. 14 cable. To determine the number of outlets already on a circuit, remove the fuses from every circuit except the one you're testing. Then, with a test light or a table lamp you can carry about, insert the plug into the outlets. Whenever the light goes on, you have found an outlet. Try the wall switches; if the room light goes on, that light is on the line. If there are twelve outlets on the line, safety demands that you do not add any more.

Kitchen ranges are on separate circuits and usually need a 3-wire No. 6 cable and a 50-ampere fuse.

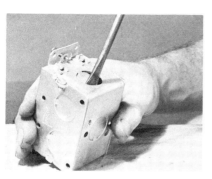  

1. Punch outlet box knock-out (partially precut circular openings) through by pushing down with screwdriver. Then push backward and, if necessary, pry off with pliers.
2. Cut diagonally across cable with hack saw; don't cut wires inside. After cutting halfway around cable, twist it in your hands and it will snap loose. If not, saw a bit more.
3. Make second cut about 8" from the end of the cable to bare ample wire for making connections. Slip fiber bushing over wires and press into the cable.

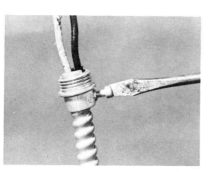 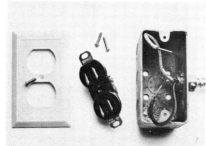 

4. Slip connectors over wires and onto cable. Tighten screw in connector to hold cable fast. Remove the slotted nut before inserting connector in outlet box.
5. Insert wires and connector into an outlet box (pictured), switch, or junction box as needed. Attach slotted or cogged nut on connector. Tighten by pushing screwdriver against cog.
6. To join wires in box, bare about ¾" off ends and twist in a clockwise direction. Screw solderless connector on in same direction. Shown is a 3-wire joining for stoves.

HOUSEHOLD WIRES

When the time comes to rewire a toaster or iron or to replace a worn-out lamp cord, the job will be easier if you know which wires are designed for what work. The wires found attached to appliances or lamps and connected to outlets are called flexible cords by technicians. Each cord consists of two separated groups of fine copper strands. Around each bundle of strands is a wrapping first of cotton and then of rubber insulation. The main types are:

Rubber or Plastic Covered Parallel Lamp Cord. This is Type POSJ in the Code of the Underwriter's Laboratory. The copper wires are set in solid rubber or plastic. The wearing qualities of this wire are good, although the rubber does dry out, becomes brittle and cracks after many years of service; the plastic covered variety stands up better. Excellent for wiring lamps because it slips through narrow tubing easily.

Rayon Covered Lamp Cord. Type PO. This is the shiny, colorful variety found in most boudoir lamps. It looks pretty but does not wear well. As soon as the rayon frays, the thinly insulated conductors are exposed and replacement becomes necessary. Most appliance manufacturers don't use this type any more because they have found that Type POSJ parallel cord stands up better.

Heavy Duty Cord. Type SJ. This is the kind found attached to vacuum cleaners, washing machines and other hard-working appliances. It stands up well against crushing, knotting and moisture. Like the others, it consists of rubber-insulated stranded conductors. However, it has greater strength because the pair of conductors has been wrapped in paper twine until round, then imbedded in high-grade rubber.

Green and Yellow Twisted Lamp Cord. Type C is the code name. The copper strands are imbedded in heavy rubber, then each conductor is encased in strong green and yellow cotton braid and twisted. This type of wire is really tough; it stands up long after other lamp cords wear out. When possible, use this type for replacements.

Heater Cord. Type HPD. Used for toasters, flatirons, electric heaters and broilers. Again we find stranded conductors for flexibility. This time a layer of asbestos surrounds each rubber-covered bundle of strands. Finally the two asbestos-covered conductors are twisted round each other and the whole assembly is then covered with rayon or cotton.

SIMPLE APPLIANCE REPAIRS

Electrical appliances play a most important role in today's homes, and when something goes wrong with one of them, the whole family is liable to be inconvenienced. Usually the trouble may be simple enough to correct by yourself in only a few minutes.

Most appliance troubles are due to a defective power cord or plug, since these are exposed and receive the most wear. Pictured here are the steps needed to fix a toaster. Use this information also to repair waffle irons, heaters, percolators and even small motor-driven appliances such as vacuum cleaners, for the same techniques apply to them as well.

The electrical tester pictured in the first photograph can also be used to determine quickly whether or not the break is hidden in the appliance's power cord, somewhere along its length. To test the entire cord as a unit, disconnect it from the appliance, first making sure that the plug is removed from the socket. Twist each bare end of the cord around one of the tester's wires, being careful to keep the exposed ends from making contact with each other. When this has been done, place a heavy book over the wire to make sure it will not fall off the work table. Now you are ready to test. Plug in the cord just as if it were still connected to the appliance. If the tester glows, the cord is good. If it does not, and the steps illustrated in the photos don't help either, then the cord is faulty and must be replaced. As soon as the test is ended, disconnect the plug. Care must be used throughout. Do not allow your hands or any part of your body to come in contact with the exposed wire ends while the plug is connected.

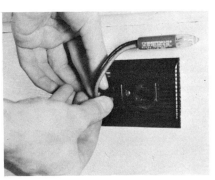

1. Electrical tester indicates whether current is present. Lamp known to work will do, too. If no indication, check house fuse.

2. If plug slips in and out too easily, bend prongs out slightly. If the prongs are corroded, brighten them up with sandpaper.

3. Inspect cord and plug closely for worn insulation and broken wires. If cord is badly frayed, disconnect and cut off worn area.

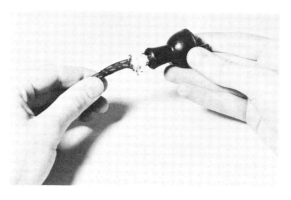

5. If insulation is asbestos, wrap with thread to protect. Tie knot in leads and bend ends around plug terminals. Tighten.

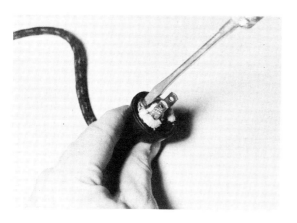

7. Disassemble appliance, remove cut-off end from terminals, and attach new wire. Make joints stronger by wrapping with strands.

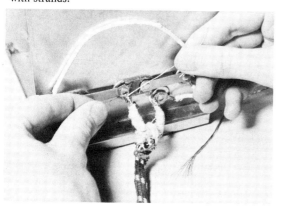

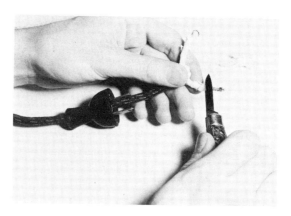

4. Slip plug over wire, then cut away 3″ of braid. Clean ½″ of each lead and twist the strands of each wire together.

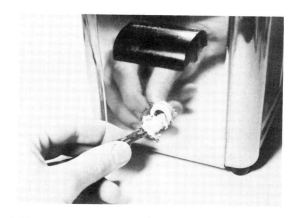

6. If cord is damaged near point where it enters appliance, cut cord just below damaged portion. (Unplug before cutting!)

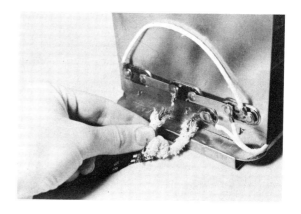

8. If no frayed areas show on power cord, disassemble the appliance and look inside for any loose or broken connections.

Simple Appliance Repairs   213

SPECIAL ELECTRICAL DEVICES FOR SAFETY AND CONVENIENCE

All-plastic pliers are designed for safe removal of plug and cartridge fuses. Accidental contact of hand with live units is avoided. Knurled handles aid firm grip.

Same pliers, reversed, make a line tester (below, center). Hinged prongs at base of handles serve as probes, lighting neon bulb in hollow handles of translucent plastic, assuring safety.

Assure safety for children by plugging wall outlets with plastic inserts (below, right). Curious children can't push metal objects into sockets, and danger of any serious injury is averted.

Silent switch, using mercury, eliminates noisy click of standard types. Throw main switch, disconnect wires, then attach them in identical location on the new device.

Flat plug, in contrast to standard types, keeps wires close to wall. The cords are out of the way and plug cannot easily be dislodged by anyone walking by.

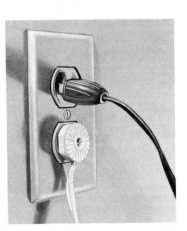

Pocket-sized tester will tell you, by means of its neon glow, whether current is being provided in outlets, sockets, fuse boxes, or appliances. Two plastic-coated wires end in small terminals which fit sockets and make a sure contact with the bare wires.

WHAT TO DO WHEN THE FUSE BLOWS

Do not try to replace a fuse in the dark. Use a flashlight. On the side of some fuse boxes is a switch handle. Pull this handle to the OFF position before you open the box or touch any fuses.

If there's no handle, when you open the door you may find one or two cartridge-fuse holders at the top of the box. Pull both of them out. This turns the current off. Don't worry if there's a small spark when you do this.

It's easy to recognize a "blown" plug-type fuse. Either the *window* in the fuse is blackened or the wire is parted. A blown fuse should be replaced with one of the same ampere size.

If none of the plug fuses is blown and all are firmly screwed in their sockets, insert new cartridge fuses. It is usually difficult to spot a defective cartridge fuse by eye examination alone. Cartridge fuses snap into clamps.

If you find a blown plug-type fuse, remove it by turning counterclockwise. Insert a 25-watt bulb and put the current back on. If the light bulb shines dimly, there's an overload. Turn off the current, disconnect an appliance or two to eliminate the overload and replace the fuse. But if the bulb shines brightly, there's a short circuit. One by one, disconnect appliances, lamps and switch off lights. When the test bulb goes out, you've located the trouble maker. Turn off the current and replace the fuse. If the fuse blows again, the trouble may be inside the wires and that's a job only for an expert.

There should be a wiring diagram of the entire house pasted inside or near the fuse box cover. This diagram is easy to prepare. To determine which outlets and switches are controlled by each plug-type fuse, remove one fuse at a time and see which lights don't go on. Use a test light to check each outlet. List next to the fuse the fixtures and outlets that fuse serves.

In some areas, circuit breakers may be used in place of fuses. They work like switches—pop off automatically when a short occurs. A small plug-type circuit breaker is available for use on individual branch lines as a screw-in replacement for a fuse. When a short occurs, a button in the center pops out. Remove the source of the short, push the button in and current is restored.

REPAIRING AND REPLACING A WALL SWITCH

The next time you flip a wall switch and the light that it controls doesn't go on, follow these steps to find the remedy:

1. First, check the bulb itself. It might be defective or burned out.

2. Check for a short circuit on the line. See if the other lights on the line go on. If you're not sure which ones belong on the line, turn them all on and unscrew the fuses separately, as described above. This tells you exactly which lights each fuse controls. If none of the fuses are burned out and all the lights but the one go on, then:

3. Remove the fuse for that light and switch, cutting off the power, and then check the switch.

To check the switch, remove and keep the two screws that hold the face plate to the switch against the wall; then remove the two screws that hold the switch in the box. Pull the switch out as far as the wires will permit (see Sketch A). *Do not tamper with any other wires in the box but those connected with the switch.* Check for loose wires. If there are any, reconnect as shown in Sketch A. Push the switch back into the box, screw it into place and put the face plate back on. Turn on the power and test the circuit; you'll find it working perfectly.

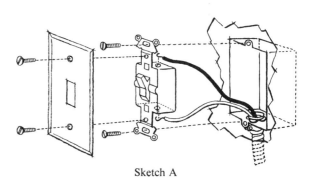

Sketch A

If, however, there are no loose wires, the switch is faulty and must be replaced. Disconnect the 2 wires connected to the old switch (see Sketch A) and connect them to the terminals of the new switch. If the new one is of the mercury type, be sure the side marked "Top" *is* at the top. In making the connections, twist the wires around the terminal in a clockwise direction, as in Sketch B (in the same direction as you turn a screw to tighten it). This will prevent the wire from loosening. If one wire connected to the switch is white, follow the recommended pro-

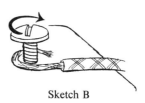

Sketch B

cedure of the electrical code and paint the last 2 to 4″ of the insulation black since it is carrying current and is "hot." In this way, anyone else who works with the wire at a later date won't mistake it for a ground wire, which is usually the white one in the electrical circuit.

Then push the new switch back into the box and screw it into place. Do not tighten the screws too much because they might crack or bend the switch frame. Finally, replace the face plate and turn on the current. Your job is done.

REPLACING A PULL CHAIN WITH A WALL SWITCH

A wall switch to replace a pull chain on a light fixture can be installed in any room and on virtually any wall. It is merely a matter of moving the electrical switch from the fixture itself to the wall. First, the main switch at the fuse box must be shut off or else the fuse controlling the line must be removed. When installing a wall switch, you are putting it in somewhere along the hot lead—the one that carries the power—and this is usually the black wire. The other wire—the white one—is usually the ground (see Sketch 1).

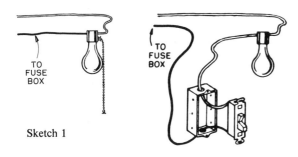

Sketch 1

There is no single technique for doing the job. It depends upon the accessibility of the wires in the ceiling. In the following examples, four possible methods are detailed, and one of them should work no matter how difficult the problem.

1. If the attic is open and if you're able to get to the fixture box from above, proceed along the following steps:

a. Shut off the power; remove the fixture to get at the wires; disconnect the two wires going to the socket.

b. Directly above the position in the wall where you plan to install the wall switch, drill a ¾″ hole with a brace and bit. You'll usually have to drill through two 2-by-4's which run along the top of the wall (see Sketch 2).

c. Cut a hole for the switch box between two

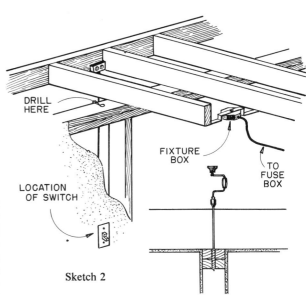

Sketch 2

studs, the same two between which the hole in step 2 was drilled.

d. Connect a 2-wire BX cable through the fixture box at the ceiling. Join the black wire from the fuse box to the black wire of the new BX cable. Tape twisted wires or use a solderless connector to join. Attach one white wire to one terminal of the socket; attach the other white wire to the other terminal (see Sketch 3).

e. Bring the new BX cable along the attic floor, anchoring every 3′ with a BX staple, and run down through the hole to the wall switch box.

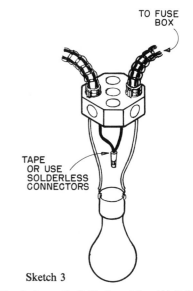

Sketch 3

f. Pull the wire through the hole in the wall and anchor it to the switch box. Leave about 6″ of wire without cable inside of the box.

g. Secure the switch box to the wall by anchoring to a stud or box holder.

h. Strip clean about 1½″ of each wire. Connect black wire to one terminal, the white wire to the other of a single-pole, single-throw toggle switch (see Sketch 4). This is an everyday type of switch used throughout the house.

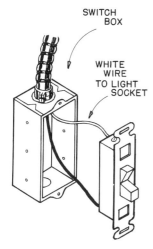

SWITCH
BOX

WHITE
WIRE
TO LIGHT
SOCKET

Sketch 4

i. Screw the toggle in place, attach the cover plate, and the job is finished.

2. There are times when you cannot easily reach the ceiling fixture and to do so would involve considerable work. Then follow the first step as noted above (*a*) and:

b. Cut a hole about 3″ square between ceiling joists right next to the wall on which the switch is to be placed (see Sketch 5).

c. Cut another hole, the same size, on the wall right next to the one just cut in step (*b*).

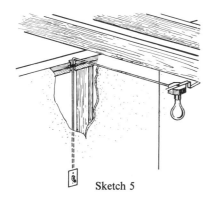

Sketch 5

d. If the switch is to be just below this cut, there is no problem. But often the switch is to be placed elsewhere along the wall. This can be done by coming up in the wall through the basement to the desired location. If you cannot do this, use one of the alternative methods given here.

3. If you can come up through the basement to get into the wall, then from the basement:

a. Drill a 1″ hole upward into the wall in between two 2-by-4 studs just where the box is to be placed.

b. Cut the hole for the box in the wall and drop a line with a hook attached through this hole and get the line to go through the 1″ hole drilled in step *a* (see Sketch 6).

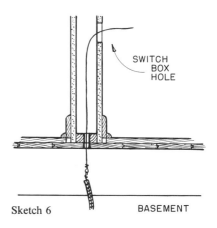

SWITCH
BOX
HOLE

Sketch 6   BASEMENT

c. Bring 2-wire BX cable up on cord; anchor it to the switch box and wire in the toggle switch, as noted previously.

d. Drill another 1″ hole in the same wall just below the 3″ square hole cut in wall in line with the ceiling fixture.

e. Drop cord and hook through this wall hole and bring BX cable up to this position.

f. Push wire into the 3″ square ceiling hole and force it over to the fixture box.

g. Remove the fixture box and grab the cable in the ceiling. Bring the new cable through the box and replace the box in the ceiling.

h. Join the black wire from the new cable to black wire from the fuse box. Connect one white wire to one terminal of the socket, the other white wire to the other terminal. The switch will now control the light fixture.

4. On the other hand, there are times when it is not possible to go through the basement to reach the wall. In those cases:

a. Cut about a 1"-wide path along the wall just where wall and ceiling join. Make certain there is room to slip the wire in the wall; if any timber is in the wall, cut down until there is a clear opening (see Sketch 6).

b. It is often necessary to cut away part of the 2-by-4 studs so that cable can go into the wall. Do this by using a keyhole saw to make the cuts; then chop out with chisel and mallet.

c. Next, cut a hole in the wall for the switch box. This should be directly in line with the last cutting out of the wall near the ceiling level.

d. Remove the fixture box; add new BX cable and push it through the ceiling until it reaches the hole near the wall.

e. Connect the black wire of the new cable to the black lead from the fuse box and the white wires to the terminals of the socket.

f. Run cable from the ceiling hole into the wall hole and then through the opening cut along the wall near the ceiling until it is directly over the switch box. Anchor the cable with BX staples.

g. Drop the cable down inside the wall and pull out the loose end through the hole for the switch box.

h. Now cut the cable; secure it to the box and place the box in position as noted previously. Attach wires to the toggle switch. The job is complete except for the repairing of the holes in the wall and ceiling.

REPLACING A CEILING FIXTURE

Before touching the existing fixture, be sure to turn off the power to the line upon which you'll be working. It isn't safe just to place the wall switch in the "off" position, since the current may come to the fixture before it goes to the switch. As with all electrical work, you must first remove the fuse controlling the line or shut off the current to the whole house.

After the current is off, start removal of the old fixture by loosening the screws or nuts that hold it in place. (The accompanying sketches show the more common methods of fixture mounting.) Then lower the old fixture to expose the wiring and the ceiling box. For easy identification later on, wrap two small pieces of adhesive tape around the two wires in the box that are connected to the fixture. Then cut the fixture wires or, if solderless connectors have been used, unscrew them and disconnect the wires. (Do not touch any other wires in the box!) The fixture can now be removed.

If the new fixture is identical with the old, there's no problem in reattachment. However, if you are changing to a different type of fixture, the way in which it will be attached to the ceiling box depends not only upon the box itself but also upon the design and weight of the fixture. Light-weight fixtures, such as those used on stairway landings or entrance halls, may be attached directly to the ceiling box with long

Sketch 1—Standard box with side screw holes

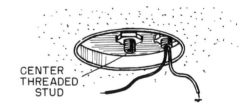

Sketch 2—Shallow box with center threaded stud

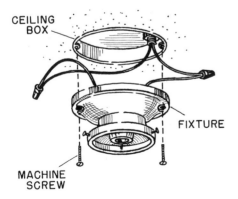

Sketch 3—Direct mounting to box with machine screws

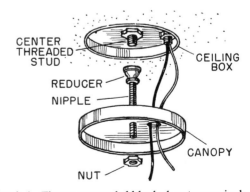

Sketch 4—Fixture canopy held by lock nut over nipple

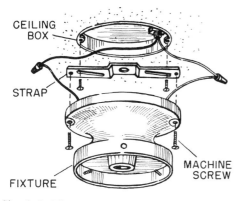

Sketch 5—Fixture screwed to strap attached to box

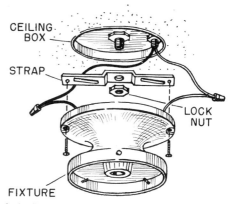

Sketch 6—Strap secured to center stud with fixture attached to strap

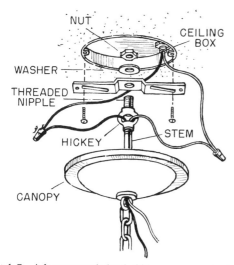

Sketch 7—Adapters needed to hold heavy canopy to standard box

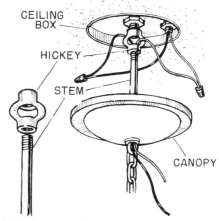

Sketch 8—Stem and hickey used on shallow box with center stud

machine screws. However, if the holes in the ceiling box and the fixture do not align, a strap is necessary (see Sketch 5). Medium-weight fixtures require a metal strap for mounting, regardless of the type of ceiling box (see Sketches 5 and 6). This method of attaching is more secure. Heavy fixtures, such as chandeliers, are usually held in place by a stem which is attached to the center stud in the ceiling box. The fixture wires run through the stem and out through a hickey (see Sketch 8). A fluorescent fixture is attached in the same way as an incandescent fixture of the same weight.

To wire in the new fixture, connect the two wires from it to the two wires in the box previously marked with adhesive tape for easy identification. (Remember that you must always connect white to white and black to black.)

Usually, the cable wire in the ceiling box is solid, while the wire from the fixture is stranded. Twist the two together—one from the cable and the other from the fixture—in a clockwise direction. It is not enough just to wind the stranded wire around the solid one. To finish the wire connection, it is necessary to screw a solderless connector over each pair of wires in a clockwise direction so that all exposed ends are completely covered. As an alternative, you can solder the wires and tape each pair separately. Finally, secure the fixture and turn on the current.

ADDING AN ELECTRIC OUTLET

Long extension cords can be dangerous. Trailing from lamps, appliances and TV sets, they may be tripped over, a lamp may be pulled off a table, a wire may be snapped and a fire hazard created. If you live in an area where non-metallic cable can be used for wiring (and aside from a very few big cities, this type of cable is permitted under local building codes), you can add a new outlet in less than an hour.

In most homes, a new line can be brought to the outlet by drilling a hole in the wall from the basement (see Sketch A). First, however, you must decide upon the location of the outlet and make the necessary opening in the wall (see Photograph 1). After the hole is made for the outlet and the hole from the basement drilled, fish the cable up from the basement through the outlet hole with a stiff metal wire. Only after the outlet is wired and the cover plate screwed in place (Photograph 6) should you connect the wire to a junction box in the basement. Merely shut off the current leading to the box by removing the proper fuse and remove the cover plate.

With the wires inside exposed, strip about 1″ of insulation off both the black and white wires coming from the wall outlet. Attach the white wire to the white wires in the box and the black one to the black wires. Use solderless connectors, or solder and tape to join (Sketch B). Replace the cover and turn on the current.

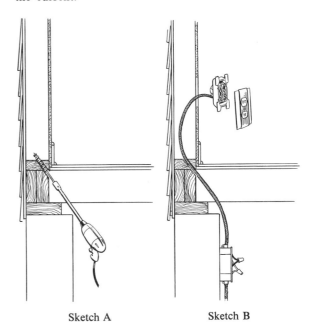

Sketch A   Sketch B

 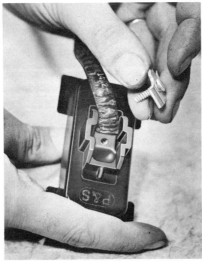 

1. Trace outline of outlet on wall. If wall is plaster, cut along outline with cold chisel and hammer. Otherwise, drill holes in two corners and cut with keyhole or utility saw.
2. Strip cable to expose about 2″ of both wires and thread cable through knock-out holes in back of unit. Replace the metal clamp to cover the opening and tighten clamp against cable.
3. Strip about ½″ off the ends of both wires. Form end of one wire in shape of a hook and insert under screw. Tighten screw so as to anchor wire. Now repeat for the other wire on other side of unit.

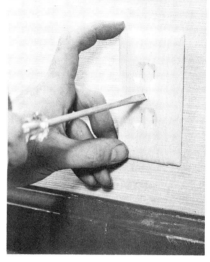

4. Fasten metal strap clips to top and bottom edges of the opening by placing the teeth of the clip in the back and bending the strap outward. Two clips come with each unit.

5. Keeping clip straps outward, press outlet into the wall recess. Then force the extended straps into the two end pockets of the outlet. Straps are out of the way and not near the wires.

6. Slip the plastic cover plate over the outlet and secure it by turning the small center screw in a clockwise direction. Connect the other end of the cable to the house current.

ELECTRIC SURFACE DUCTS

Installation of concealed wiring may sometimes involve damage to walls. The plaster may be chipped, paint spoiled and wallpaper torn. A more simple and easier alternative is found in the use of a metal surface duct, consisting of a flat metal base which is attached to the wall surface and covered with a snap-on molding. Two wires or, if necessary, three, can be slipped between retaining clips on the base. Special fittings simplify joining ducts to wall switches, outlets or power-junction boxes.

If concealment of wiring is important, you can very nearly hide the molding on horizontal runs by locating it on or adjacent to the baseboard molding strips and painting it to match. When finished, it's difficult to distinguish them from the molding.

Metal surface ducts are also especially useful when

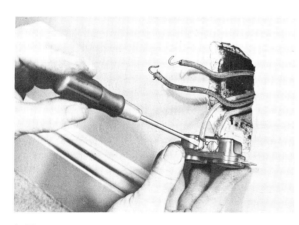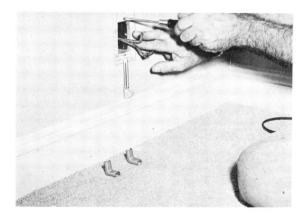

1. To tap power source, throw main switch, then remove wall outlet plate and socket and disconnect wires from screw terminals.

2. Attach notched plate to receptacle, connect duct to plate. Note right-angle turn fitting just above the baseboard molding. →

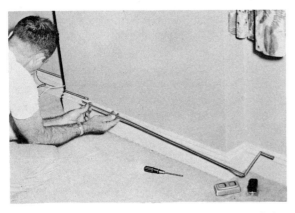

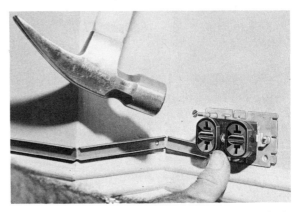

3. For a new outlet, run surface duct from receptacle just above baseboard or remove the molding and substitute surface ducts.

4. Attach new receptacle plate to wall where new outlet is desired. The surface ducts can be keyed into edge of plate on any side.

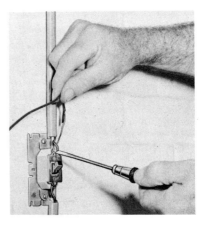

5. After wires are inserted in ducts, snap duct covers into plate over wires. Right-angle units cover inside or outside corners.

6. A box extension adaptor is connected so that it is flush with upper part of surface ducts. Wires are reconnected to screws.

7. With a masonry wall, attach switch plate with screws set into plugs in drilled holes. Switch-box cover goes over the entire unit.

8. Lamp canopy is attached to ceiling with screws. Fixture, with wires attached, is joined to canopy with mounting screws.

you have to run wiring across masonry walls and basement foundations where it's impossible to conceal conduit or armored cable inside the wall.

Any handyman can easily install these additional outlets, but he must not overlook the usual precautions when working with electrical lines: (*a*) make wiring connections after removal of the fuse governing the lines worked on, or make them after pulling the main switch of the house; (*b*) do not connect additional outlets to a power source already heavily loaded with appliances; and (*c*) be sure to use wire that is heavy enough for the anticipated load.

CURES FOR A BALKY DOORBELL

Since doorbells work on low voltage, repairs can be made without fear of shock or fire. There's only one place to exercise caution, and that is at the transformer. Here two heavy wires connect the bell system with the house's electrical system. *Do not touch these wires.* If you must, as described below, by all means shut off the master switch or remove the fuse controlling the bells. If you're uncertain, remove all the fuses so that there's no guesswork as to which fuse controls this circuit.

Sometimes, when you replace an old bell or chime with a new one, you might find that it just doesn't work. Before checking the system to find the probable cause, check the transformer. Many new chimes and bells will require a higher voltage than older ones—12 to 24 volts as compared with 6 to 8. Only after you're certain the transformer is the right one for the job should you check the system.

1. The first step in curing a balky doorbell is to trace all the wires from the push button to the bell and back to the transformer. These wires usually are exposed along the beams in the basement ceiling. But in finished basements they may be more difficult to find. When tracing the wires, make certain that all connections—at the push button, bell, and transformer—are tight and clean. Tighten any loose screw or bolt as you go along and sand wire ends clean.

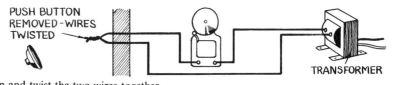

2. The second step, if the bell still doesn't work, is to have someone push the door button while you listen to the transformer in the basement. If you have no assistance, remove the push button and twist the two wires together.

a. If the bell rings when the wires are touched together, your job is almost over. You have a defective push button. See Step 4 for details on how to fix it.

b. If the bell doesn't ring but you hear a hum in the transformer, then the trouble is between the transformer and bell or in the bell itself.

c. If the bell doesn't ring and you don't hear any hum in the transformer, then there's a break in the wiring or a burned-out transformer.

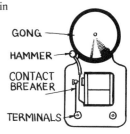

3. The third step, if the trouble is in the bell itself, is to remove the cover from the bell. Do this only after you are certain there are no wire breaks. Even if you can't get at the wires, do this anyway. Use some emery or fine sandpaper to clean the contact-breaker points. Remove paint or dirt around the mechanism. Also check to see if the hammer touches the gong when the contacts are closed. If not, just twist the hammer slightly; it's pliable and easily adjusted.

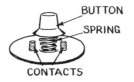
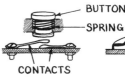

4. Step 4 is the push button itself. It is exposed to the elements and sometimes dirt covers the contacts so they won't work or something causes a malfunctioning of the spring. Here, again, use emery or sandpaper to clean the contacts. Check to see that the contacts touch when the button is pushed in. Also scrape clean the ends of the two wires that connect to the bell; they may be corroded. Tighten screws or nuts when putting wires back in place.

→

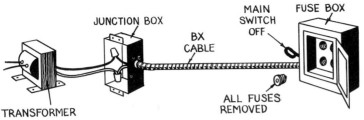

JUNCTION BOX   BX CABLE   MAIN SWITCH OFF   FUSE BOX

TRANSFORMER   ALL FUSES REMOVED

5. Step 5 is at the transformer again. If it's burned out, it must be replaced with a new one. Throw master switch and remove the fuses before you touch any of the wires. Then unscrew the connections to the bell and push button. Disconnect the heavy wires from the house current. Place the new heavy wires in the same manner as the old. Use solderless connectors, or solder and tape, to join this end of the transformer.

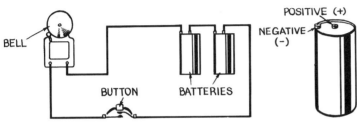

BELL   BUTTON   BATTERIES   NEGATIVE (−)   POSITIVE (+)

6. The sixth step applies only to bells that are battery-operated. Check batteries to see if they're fresh—just touch a wire across the terminals. If there's a blue spark, the batteries are working, and therefore you must check for wire breaks. Also check the push button and the bell.

FLUORESCENT LIGHTING

Most people, unaccustomed to the clear shadowless light given off by fluorescent lamps, believe that their best use is in kitchens and workrooms. Actually, there isn't a room in the house which can't be improved by a fluorescent installation. Fluorescent lights provide three times the illumination of filament bulbs for the same current consumption (wattage), and they are cooler.

The efficiency of fluorescent lighting is dependent to a great extent upon your local power supply. Occasionally, a fluorescent lamp will flash before settling down to produce a steady light. This happens when the house current falls below its usual level of 110/120 volts, sometimes occasioned when line loads are heavy. If the tube ends darken before 200 hours of service, it is probably because your current delivery is too far above the 110/120 volt limit. Reverse the bulb in the fixture when one end darkens much more rapidly than the other. If local power-station output is consistently too irregular, it is best to do without fluorescent lights until it is stabilized.

If lights burn out prematurely, the cause may lie with too frequent on-and-off operation or incorrect starter capacity. Check the starter's rating, printed on its case, against that shown on the bulb you are using. Starters are rated to match different lamp sizes.

If the light is in a cool or cold place, it would be best to install a thermal-type starter which helps the lamp to light quickly and lessens tube damage from on-and-off flashing.

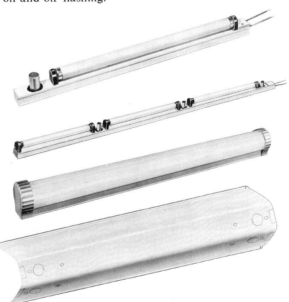

Top to bottom: single wired channel, triple channel, channel with translucent shield, clip-on reflector.

When house current is DC and fluorescent lighting is desired, special fixtures must be purchased. Their internal wiring, as well as their components, are completely different from the ordinary AC type. Because of their voltage requirements, nothing larger than 20-watt fluorescent tubes will operate on 110/120 volts DC.

Fluorescent fixtures can be purchased in many types and sizes. Probably the most familiar is the ornamental type designed for installation on or in ceilings and walls. But the most adaptable type of fixture is the simple "wiring channel." It consists of an enclosed white-enameled metal box containing the necessary wiring, ballast, starter and lampholders. Electrically speaking, the channel is installed in the same way as the ornamental fixtures. Just connect the leads to any electric outlet box. But since the channel itself is not very handsome and leaves the lamp exposed, you will probably want to use some means to conceal it. What follows are several ways to use the wiring channel fixture attractively and effectively.

Fluorescent-Lighted Valances. Most fluorescent-lighted valances are designed to increase the general light level of the entire room as well as to enhance the decorative value of windows and draperies. Several points, therefore, must be considered in building such a valance:

1. To give wide distribution of light on the ceiling, the top edge of the valance should be at least 12" from the ceiling.

2. To light the entire vertical length of the draperies and throw light evenly on ceiling and upper wall, the center of the end of the lamp should be at least 4" from the wall. It is necessary in many cases to put a strip of wood in back of the channel to bring the lamp out this far.

3. The inner surface of the valance should be at least 6" from the wall and 2" from the lamp.

4. The valance itself should be 5½ to 7" high.

5. The lamp used should be about as long as the draperies are wide. The inside length of the valance can be exactly equal to the length of the wired channel or can extend several inches on each side.

6. Ends of the valance should be blocked by wood baffles of the same height as the valance and extending from the valance to the wall. This prevents light leaks at the sides.

7. Drapery material must be hung so that it is at least 1" closer to the wall than the fluorescent bulb.

VALANCE LIGHTING

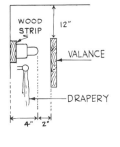

End view of valance

Valance with end light-baffles in place. Note use of angle irons.

To block light from ceiling, fasten board across top of valance.

UNDER-CABINET LIGHTING

Channel behind overhanging doors requires apron to conceal light when doors are open.

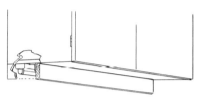

Channel set at rear sheds softer light. Hang channel and apron to metal cabinet with bolts, to wood cabinet with screws.

Cabinets and Shelves. For brilliant kitchen-counter lighting, you can install wired channels under the bottom front edges of wall cabinets over the counter. An apron must be added to the cabinets to shield the lamps, unless lower edges of the doors overhang the cabinet enough to hide the light. Such aprons can be hung by angle irons screwed to the apron's inner side. When the cabinet is wood, the angle irons as well as the wired unit itself can be hung to the cabinet bottom with screws. When the cabinet is metal, you will first have to drill holes through the cabinet

bottom to take bolts for fixing the angle irons and the fluorescent unit in place. If you prefer softer, glare-free lighting, install the channels not along the cabinet's front edge but under the back edge against the wall. Under-the-shelf lighting is handled the same way. Screw or bolt the channel to the underside of the shelf, then hide it with an apron hung by angle irons. Some metal shelves, as shown in the illustration, come with downward-bent flanges which serve to hide the channel and make building an apron unnecessary.

SHELF LIGHTING

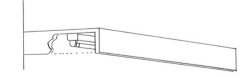

Flange hides channel, making apron unnecessary.

Unflanged shelf requires apron to conceal light. To hang apron, use angle irons.

WALL BRACKET

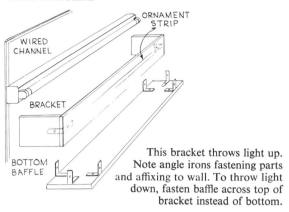

This bracket throws light up. Note angle irons fastening parts and affixing to wall. To throw light down, fasten baffle across top of bracket instead of bottom.

Wall Brackets. Fluorescent wall brackets increase the general light level of a room and also provide local lighting over the heads of beds, dressing tables, etc. They are particularly useful in low-ceilinged rooms which are difficult to light with ceiling fixtures. And when used on inner walls, they balance window-valance lighting on outer walls. You can set them vertically on both sides of a dressing table or bathroom mirror. You can run them horizontally, and you can build them to extend the length of a single wired channel or the length of an entire room. Brackets look and function like valances, differing chiefly in the fact that they are not hung on top of windows. Build a wall bracket just as you would the valance previously described, bearing in mind these points:

1. The top edge of the horizontal bracket should be at least 12″ from the ceiling. But you can install it, if you wish, in a much lower position, with the bottom edge as low as 68″ from the floor. If the bracket is for general lighting, install it high; if for local lighting, install it in the lower position.

2. The center of the lamp end should be at least 3½″ from the wall. The inner surface of the bracket should be at least 6¾″ from the wall. The bracket should be about 6″ high and as long as the installation requires (two, three or more lamps in a row).

3. Like valances, brackets can have a reflecting board underneath to throw light upward or one across the top to throw light downward. In the latter case, the naked fluorescent bulb may be visible to the eye if you look up at the bracket, and you probably will want to mask it. If so, nail a strip of translucent plastic across the bottom of the bracket. Or you can use a wired channel which comes with a plastic housing for the bulb.

CLOSET LIGHTING

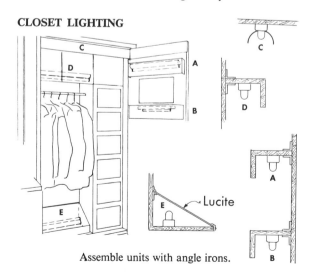

Assemble units with angle irons.

Workroom Lighting. Wired channels may be screwed directly to the bottom of exposed joists in a basement ceiling, but some of the light is lost among the joists and bridging. Better illumination can be had by nailing a 4' square piece of white painted wallboard to the joists and mounting the channels on it. To shield the bright lamps, suspend a louver about a foot beneath them. The louver is made of ¼-by-1" scrap-wood strips glued 2" apart on a frame, then sanded and painted white.

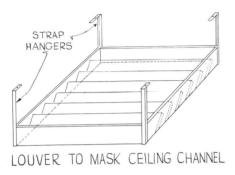

LOUVER TO MASK CEILING CHANNEL

The same lighting is effective in a basement playroom. Paint the joists, bridging, pipes and bottom of the subfloor black. Then mount the white wall boards, wired units and louvers below the joists (as above). The fixtures cast all the down-light needed,

yet the unsightly ceiling construction is hardly noticeable.

Another method of workroom lighting is first to fix the wired unit to the ceiling, then shield it with a fabricated metal reflector. Such reflectors, made to snap fast easily to wired channels, are available at electric-supply dealers. This type of lighting is preferable when the workroom has finished walls, of plaster, for example.

Wiring Connections. If you connect a wired channel to a convenient outlet with a heavy extension cord, it will work perfectly well. However, such wiring of a built-in (permanent) channel is considered illegal. It should be wired permanently into an outlet box. Use BX (armored) electric cable to make the connection between channel and outlet box. Fasten the black lead in the cable to the black lead in the box and the white lead in the cable to the white lead in the box. Similarly, the black and white leads on the channel fasten to the cable's black and white leads. Use solderless connectors or electrician's tape to join the wires.

If your apron or valance does not hide the cable, you may be able to run it through your wall to an outlet box. Or you can buy surface ducts—attractive hollow moldings built to be fastened easily to the wall. These conduct the wires from channel to outlet box, and they come with elbows to turn corners if necessary. See pages 221 and 222 for more about surface ducts.

HOW TO REPAIR FLUORESCENT LIGHTS

1. After checking fuse to be sure current is reaching lamp, test bulb. It may be loose, or—if blackened—burned out. Try a new lamp. If there is still no light, try a new starter button. Be sure replacement is of the same wattage and size as the one removed or called for by type of unit.

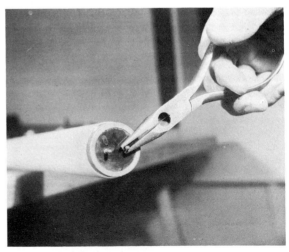

2. Lamp prongs may be bent and making poor contact. On straight lamps, these may be corrected with needle-nose pliers. Sand any corroded spots.

3. Shut off power, then check contacts in sockets. They too may be bent. If so, straighten with needle-nose pliers. Sand points to remove corrosion.

4. If there is still no light, shut off power again and remove fixture by loosening knurled nut which holds it to outlet. Hold fixture firmly while removing nut.

5. With nut removed, fixture is held only by wires. If fixture is heavy, a helping hand to hold it is advisable while you detach wires.

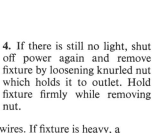

6. Place fixture on table and run temporary power line to it, connecting to fixture wires. Tape joints well or use solderless connectors.

7. Junction box in fixture comes apart, exposing wire ends joined with solderless connectors. Before opening this box, be sure current is off!

8. Remove solderless connectors from each group of wires to see if any connections have pulled loose. If so, retwist wires and replace connectors. →

Fluorescent Lighting 229

9. Switch may be at fault. Check wire connections and tighten. If still no light, remove wires from switch poles and join them. If this lights the lamp, the switch is defective. Replace it.

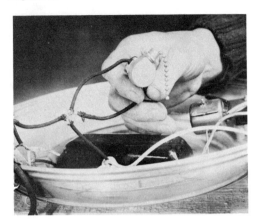

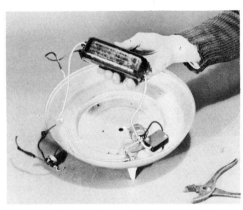

10. Final trouble point may be the ballast or transformer. Mark wires as to location with tags, then remove them from the ballast and replace it with a new one, making sure make, type, and mounting poles for wires are identical with the one removed. Then reassemble fixture and replace.

OUTDOOR WIRING

There are three good reasons for installing outdoor wiring facilities on the grounds around your home—safety, convenience and beauty. A fourth reason is that, as with any home improvement, it increases the value of your property.

When you move out of the house to patio and lawn, there is no reason to leave push-button electrical conveniences behind. You can provide light and power at every corner of your property. You can propel the lawnmower and hedge clipper, plug in portable cooking equipment, provide added safety to dark stairways and driveways.

The advantages of outdoor outlets have been antici-

Well-lighted patio is illuminated by outdoor-type standing lamp and other units below eye level. Spotlight is used to accent tree.

pated by manufacturers who have made available the various items of equipment necessary for you to make these installations yourself. To determine your needs, first walk about your property and mark the places where you want to install outlets. Measure the distance from the farthest, back through the closer ones, right up to the house. Add 10 to 20′ to this figure to obtain the number of feet of cable to purchase.

If your property is small and you need only a single outdoor outlet, it may be most convenient to locate it just outside and on the wall of the house nearest the scene of greatest use. Select a spot where, by a hole drilled through the wall, the wiring will come out in the basement or crawl space, or—if that is impossible—drill between two wall studs where a wire can be dropped into the basement over the house sill. (If yours is a brick or stone house, it may be more convenient to go through the lower part of a door frame or window frame and drop a line through to the basement from behind through the door jamb.)

After you've purchased the necessary fixture, mark out its size on the chosen spot and, with a keyhole saw, cut out the shape of the box in the outer wall. Here you can use standard BX cable run from the new box to the nearest junction box in your household wiring set-up. Connect the wires, wrap the entire connection with electrician's tape, and coat the entire taped area with shellac or varnish as an added precaution against moisture. Press the socket into place in its box, add the face plate, and, once you've completed the junction box hook-up, your first outdoor outlet is in working order.

To install more distant plugs on different surfaces, a trench is required from the house entry point to the

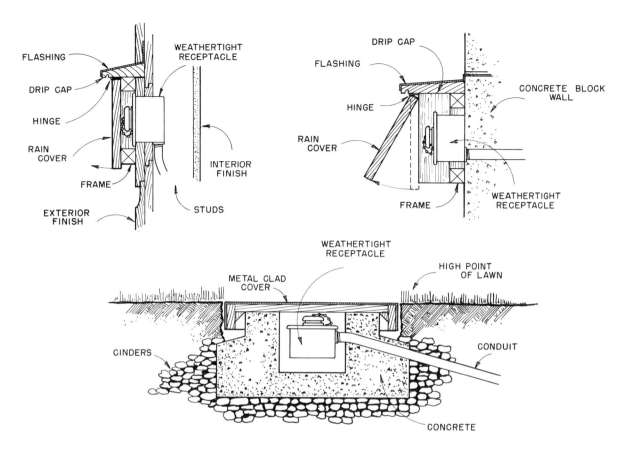

new site. In this trench you will bury trench wire or leaded cable, the latter containing the two conductors necessary. Rubber-coated cable can be used, but it will not stand up well under earth-corroding chemicals and will eventually short out and have to be dug up and replaced. Do not use wire lighter than No. 14, and if you have really heavy-duty equipment for the far end, use No. 12 or heavier wire.

If you have a raised terrace or patio, mount a weatherproof box on a length of conduit pipe set in cement, resting the box against the edge of the terrace where it will remain inconspicuous. Connections in these boxes are the same as the one described above.

For a remote spot, you have two choices. A box set on an upright length of conduit pipe will be safe from all but severe flood conditions. The weatherproof box won't mind a rain storm but cannot survive total submersion. Here the cable is run in its trench to the site of the installation, then run through the conduit which is set in concrete. The box is ready to be screwed to the top of the conduit pole with special connectors which are part of the equipment.

Since the upright type of outlet is quite visible, you may prefer a subsurface type. Here the box is installed inside a concrete chamber in the ground (see center sketch), the wiring being brought through the side of the chamber concealed in its conduit. It is best to waterproof the chamber, and the conduit should be plugged around the wires with calking compound at both ends.

Another style of mounting, using a tree as a mounting block, will make the box less conspicuous, but you'll find that digging the trench up to the tree is difficult because of roots. The same is true of trying to conceal an upright-style pipe in a hedge or shrubbery.

In connection with the trenching operation, location below frost line is not important. It is only necessary to put the line deep enough so that it will not be disturbed by gardening operations. One foot of depth is recommended, but just below the sod (about 6″) will serve most purposes. Cut out the sod in blocks and lay it aside on burlap; in this way, you can then cover the work neatly and without damage to the lawn.

OUTDOOR WIRING CIRCUITS

1. Outdoor Outlet Mounted Flush on the Wall—Drill hole for pipe through foundation wall. Outdoor-type box is mounted on exterior wall and junction box in the basement or inside a garage. Mount outlet at least 18″ above ground level. Special covered outdoor receptacle is used inside exterior box.

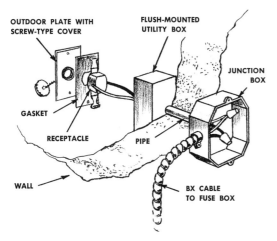

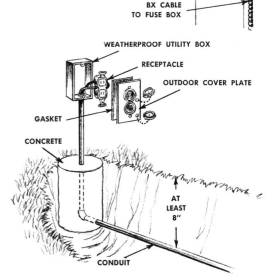

2. Outdoor Spotlight with Exterior Switch—Regular interior cable, BX or Romex, is run through the exterior wall of the house. Outdoor-type boxes are used for mounting light fixture and outdoor-style switch. Switch must be placed so that it's at least 18″ above ground level.

3. Outdoor Switch to Control Distant Lights—Here's the wiring diagram for a wall switch to control lights which have been set away from the house. The basic work is the same as adding an outdoor outlet. However, in place of the outlet, you have an outdoor-style switch and a continuation of the wire in a conduit to the exterior fixtures.

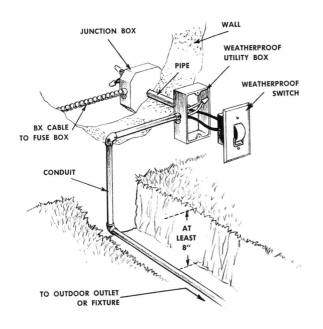

4. Outlet Box Mounted in the Garden—Extra outlets away from the house are extremely handy, particularly if you have an electric power mower. Run conduit up to desired location, add fittings and outdoor-type box. Base is held firm by setting lower section in concrete. Set box so that top is at least 18″ above ground level.

12 BASIC RULES FOR OUTDOOR WIRING

1. Use only weatherproof cable—Type UF, neoprene covered—for any outdoor wiring project.

2. If the wire is to be strung along a wall or any place where there is danger of its being frayed or cut, use metal conduit.

3. Metal conduit is also recommended in place of Type UF weatherproof cable if it is run underground and there are sharp rocks present.

4. Always complete all the wiring hook-ups, including the securing of box covers, before you join an outdoor wire circuit to the house line.

5. Never lead any wires through windows or door openings where they're subject to damage from closing doors or windows.

6. If it's necessary to use an electric drill or any other power tool outdoors, make certain you ground the tool before using it. (See pages 43–45.)

7. Use waterproof boxes for all exterior switches and receptacles. Also use only approved exterior-type switches, outlets and sockets.

8. Where possible, avoid running any light fixtures under water. If you must run under water, it can be done, but only with special underwater fixtures designed for this use.

9. When running conduit along a wall, a rafter or any house surface outdoors, make certain it is securely anchored to that surface with special cable or pipe clamps.

10. Even after the wiring job is finished, always shut off the power whenever it's necessary to replace an electric bulb.

11. While it is permissible in many locales to use solderless connectors to join wires in outdoor-type boxes, it is best to solder, tape and shellac all connections where there is any danger of movement of the cable.

12. Check your local building and electrical code before undertaking any outdoor wiring job on a do-it-yourself basis.

Route of new circuit from distant junction box inside the house, via an octagonal gem box and conduit through the foundation is shown here. Outlet box is weatherproof. In addition to plug-ins, UF (underground feeder) cable can be run from this box underground through conduit, and then in trench to site of outlets away from the house. Connection between exterior wiring and new circuit is shown in upper right diagram.

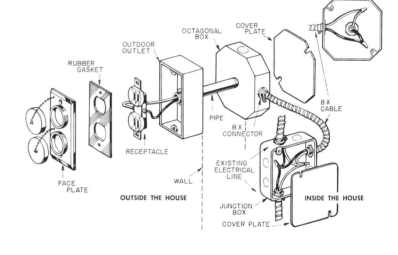

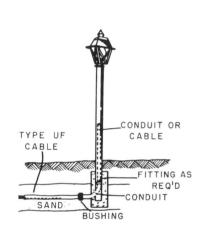

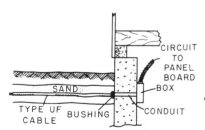
Wires can be brought from underground trench up through lamppost for lighting of remote areas.

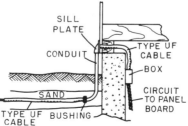
Power conducted underground through house foundations.

Power line through conduit and sill of house.

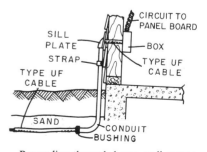
Power line through house wall passes wire through conduit.

USING PIPE FOR OUTDOOR CIRCUITS

Current for a few lights can be brought from any conveniently located junction box inside the house or basement. From the box to the foundation, armored BX cable is used. But to conduct it through the foundation and to the site of the light itself, use the more rigid and waterproof conduit. This can be bought in measured lengths with ends already threaded to add on switches and light fixtures.

Fit the pipe together first, then erect it against a wall and anchor it with special clamps. Add the switch, the fixture, then a diffuser bulb, and the job is completed. These photos show how it's done.

1. Diffuser bulb spreads soft light over a large area. Located well above the patio, it reduces insect annoyance to a minimum.

2. Assemble pipe (conduit) first. Outdoor junction box has waterproof cover; shorter length extends through foundation to interior junction box.

3. Pipe union, with waterproofing gasket, unites lengths easily. Wire has been brought from basement to junction box.

4. Thread wires, previously attached to fixture terminals, through the upper conduit length before putting up the pipe.

5. Lift completed pipe system into place after switchbox is properly located. Brace it, then get ready to anchor it by drilling hole for bolt.

6. Insert lead plug into drilled hole. Hole should be at least 9/16″ deep. Lag screw expands anchor in hole and holds bolt.

7. Final step is connecting wires to switch which, with cover plate attached, is protected from moisture with gasket.

234 ALL THROUGH THE HOUSE : Outdoor wiring

PLUMBING

How to unclog balky drains · The right valve in the right place · A quiet plumbing system · Cure for dripping faucets · Adding a faucet · Working with plastic pipe · Replacing leaking pipe · Pipe patching · Prevention and repair of frozen pipes · Cure for sweating pipes and tanks · Plumbing vents · Sump pump outlet · The hot water system · The septic system · Water conditioning · Detergents

The plumbing work you undertake will most likely be that of repairs to, and maintenance of, already existing facilities rather than the addition of new installations—unless, of course, you are adding another room to your house. However, as with electrical work, local building codes often determine the extent of work homeowners may or may not do, so be sure to check with your local authorities before initiating plumbing repairs or installations.

While the plumbing system may seem like a complicated maze to the amateur home handyman, actually it is a logical series of connected pipes, parts and valves, easily handled once understood. And it pays to understand it, for you will save both time and money each time you clear the stopped-up kitchen sink or bathroom basin, for instance. A dripping faucet quickly runs up the water bill, yet its repair is only a matter of minutes. Repairs to frozen and burst pipes may hurt the family budget, yet had a little forethought and attention been applied, the pipes could still be intact.

Last, but not least, every homeowner owes it to his family to know all about the water supply, drainage and sewage systems of his home. Health and comfort depend on their purity and efficiency.

HOW TO UNCLOG BALKY DRAINS

While single drain fixtures can and do stop up, *all* fixtures flow into one large pipe called the house drain, which discharges into the sewage system. If the house drain itself is clogged, no one fixture can flow off. Knowing where the stoppage is, whether in a local drain or the major house drain, determines what needs to be done and which tools are needed. You know that there is a stoppage in the sink drain, for instance, if all other fixtures run off, thereby showing that the house drain is clear.

Kitchen Sink Drain. A plugged kitchen sink drain is one of the most common problems of the homeowner, and one of the most annoying. It may be a periodic stoppage that is easy to break free chemically or with a snake or cable, or it may be one so constantly troublesome that a plumber has to be called. In either case, if your sink stops up at regular intervals, it's probably due to faulty drain line installation. The following lists a number of errors in drain installation that contribute to frequent stop-ups:

1. Horizontal length of drain pipe with insufficient slope. This permits water to trickle through, but grease and particles of garbage remain behind to harden as they cool and then gradually pile up.

2. Too great a slope to the longer runs of pipe. Here water gushes away but leaves solids to adhere to the pipe.

3. Drain pipe too small.

4. Drain pipe too large. Here water flows along the lower surface only and the pipe is not self-scouring.

5. Too many changes in direction of the flow; too many bends in the pipe.

6. Right angle bends in the pipe.

7. Wrong kinds of fittings at the bends.

If it is at all possible to reach the sink drain pipes, it would pay to change over to a correct installation and put a permanent end to the nuisance.

Your local code specifies what a sink drain should be. With a few minor exceptions, here is what is called for:

1. Horizontal pipe slope should be at least 1/4″ per foot.

2. Pipe size should be at least 1 1/2″ inside diameter, preferably but not more than 2″.

3. Elimination of as many bends as possible.

4. The use of two 45° elbows with a short length of pipe (called a nipple) between them in place of one right angle, 90° elbow.

5. The use of fittings *designed* for drain lines. Such fittings have an inside ledge against which the ends of inserted pipe can rest. Where threaded ends jut into the fitting and are exposed, sludge gathers and starts a blockade. Improper fittings also make the use of clean-out cable more difficult.

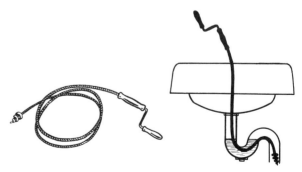

Snake is designed to pass through curved pipes, remove obstructions.

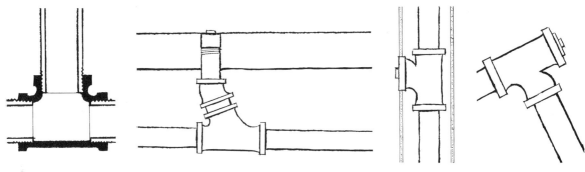

At far left is a standard galvanized pipe T lacking a smooth turn; the pipe-end threads are exposed and catch waste. Replace with one of the unions shown above. Where drain extends under floor, install a clean-out, properly capped, flush with cellar floor (left). A clean-out may also be installed in vertical lengths (center). Every right-angle turn should definitely include a clean-out (right); use T instead of elbow for turns.

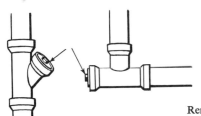

Removal of clean-out plugs (arrows) permits easy access to obstructions.

6. The use of clean-out plugs at intervals along the drain in such places as right-angle bends and vertical lengths, as shown in the sketches.

However, if the drain installation itself is not at fault, there are several methods to use to break the stoppage. The first tool to try is the plunger. Run enough water into the sink to cover the rubber cup of the plunger and place the cup over the drain. Then work the plunger up and down vigorously for 10 to 20 strokes. Remove the plunger and allow the waste to run off. If the drain is still clogged, try again. Waste water will be sucked back into the sink; pick out any matches, paper, hair or other solid matter that may be in it. Keep the strainer clear. Don't give up too easily. Repeat the whole plunger operation 8 to 10 times, if necessary. Often it takes some time for the plunger to be effective.

Once the stoppage has started to break and the water to run off, then—and *only* then—can you use a chemical solvent, such as caustic potash. Chemical solvents made especially for drain stoppages will, in most cases, dissolve grease, a common culprit in balky drains. Do *not* use solvents if the sink is completely stopped up. First, solvents take a long time to work their way down to the stoppage, from two hours to overnight. Second, the solvent may *not* work, and then you will have an entire waste line filled with a caustic solution dangerous to your skin and eyes as the actual work of cleaning out the stoppage continues. *Do* use chemical solvents to keep clear the "sluggish" drain of any fixture that has a tendency to stop up. But play safe; make sure the drain is only sluggish, not completely clogged.

If the plunger will not start even a slow run-off of the waste, the next step is to remove the plug from the trap beneath the sink. Remember that all the waste water above the plug will run out when the plug is removed. Put a pail under the trap to catch this waste; if the sink contains a large amount of water, you'd better bail it out first. If any caustic chemicals have been added to the waste, wear rubber gloves and be careful of splashes.

You may find that the stoppage is within the trap itself. If so, make a small cleaning hook out of wire and clean the trap thoroughly.

If the stoppage is further on in the drain, the only way to get at it is with a flexible wire snake. Insert about a foot of the snake into the trap, heading it away from the sink. Then slide the movable handle along the snake to a point just under the trap, tighten the handle and turn the snake. Keep working the snake on into the drain in this manner, turning it so as to work it into or through the stoppage. Once you feel that it has gone through, or if all the snake is in the drain, remove it, always turning it in the same direction as when you worked it in. If the sharp tip of the snake works into and pierces the cause of the stoppage—a dish cloth, for instance—while being turned in one direction, it will hold on better if turned in the same direction when withdrawn.

After the snake is withdrawn, replace the sink trap plug and pour boiling water into the sink. If the run-off is slow, add a chemical solvent. If the water backs up and there is no run-off at all, remove the trap plug and try again.

If you're on the second floor or above, you've done

1. Drain runs from sink (left) and turns down to sewer below. Elbow is broken off with cold chisel in order to open line.

2. Short length of pipe between elbow and sink is removed but stoppage has not yet been located, so probing follows.

3. Snake enters pipe between elbow and sink, and stoppage is discovered. Waste must be caught in container under pipe.

4. Pipe from elbow to sewer line is then cleared of possible stoppage. Vertical lengths are rarely plugged up, however.

5. Vertical pipe is fitted with T into which plug is fitted on top. A close nipple is added to connect T to line.

6. Distance from T to drain is measured and allowance made for collar union which permits opening line easily later. →

7. Short length of pipe is cut and threaded, attached to union, and inserted in drain line, then joined to nipple.

8. Collar joint is sealed with oakum and lead wool tapped in with yarning iron. Use pipe compound for all other joints.

about all that you can do. All upper-floor fixtures are connected to the stack by horizontal, relatively short drains. If on the first floor, you can trace the sink drain in the basement to the place where it joins the large, cast-iron house drain into which *all* fixtures flow. Somewhere along the sink drain there should be a clean-out plug. Remove this plug and work with the snake from there. If there is no plug—or you can't get out the one that is there—hacksaw a V-shaped cut in the top of the drain at some convenient spot and insert the snake through the opening. The cut is easily repaired by putting a ring of putty around it, squeezing down the putty with half a tin can that has been cut in two lengthwise, and wiring the can in place. If you have a hole-boring hacksaw bit for your electric drill, you can cut a standard-size hole and later tap it and close it with a threaded plug. This is neat but not necessary.

It may be that the stoppage is too solidly packed for the flexible snake to go through. If so, use a stiff, flat, steel snake, sometimes called a sewer rod. It will pay you to buy one rather than to call a plumber. If there is enough room behind the clean-out plug and its position enables you to do so, you may be able to use something solid, such as a piece of pipe, to break up the stoppage. If there's not enough room for this, try a garden hose, nozzle and all. When the nozzle reaches the stoppage, pack some rags around the hose where it enters the drain and then have someone turn on the water and stand by to shut it off again. If the stoppage is due to sand, as is often the case in seashore homes, there's no better way to clear a line than by flushing it out in this manner with a hose.

Basins and Bathtubs. Should a bathroom basin or bathtub be stopped up, the same plunger and snake methods of clearing the stoppage are used. When the plunger is worked on these, a sucking noise will be heard at the overflow; hold a sopping wet rag tightly over the overflow to direct the full suction into the drain. Some basins have a "pop-up" waste in which the basin stopper is raised and lowered by means of a handle on the basin. Disconnect the ball joint underneath the basin at its back and remove the joint and short horizontal lever. The stopper may then be lifted out. On other "pop-up" models, all you do to remove the stopper is to turn it slightly and lift. Often the stoppage will be found and cleared by this method alone as these stoppers tend to clog up with hair and lint. If necessary, the trap plug may be removed and a snake used as described above.

Some bathtubs have a "drum" trap which has an access cover set even with the bathroom floor. Unscrew the cover and clean out the trap. The snake can also be worked into a drum trap. If there is no drum trap and the strainer cannot be removed, the snake will have to be worked directly through the strainer holes, since bath traps are generally inaccessible and usually do not have trap plugs.

The Toilet Auger. If the toilet is stopped up, first use the plunger. If this does not work, the next tool to use is a toilet auger, a stiff wire snake especially designed to go completely through a toilet trap. Before using the auger, fill the bowl with water to a point just below the rim. This additional weight of water will help to flush any object which may be loosened down into the drain and will also indicate when the stoppage has been cleared. In use, the end of the snake is drawn up against the curved end of the auger, and this curved end is placed in the curved trap of the bowl. The snake is then forced through by pushing and turning the steel rod; it is withdrawn in the same manner, always turning in the same direction. If the auger pulls out the stoppage, fine; if not, work it through three or four times. If the waste runs out, pour a pail of water into the bowl. If this

Mechanism operating drain closure. The stopper base is released by first removing large nut.

Nut slides off, pulling out interlocking device. Be sure basin is empty before removing.

With base rod free, closure may be withdrawn for removal of lint and other clogging debris.

runs off readily, flush the toilet. Next, put about 5 or 6 feet of toilet paper in the bowl, let it get wet, then flush it down with a pail of water. If the toilet backs up now, you know that some solid object—toothbrush, comb, medicine bottle—is caught in the bowl. It allows plain water to pass but not water and paper. Try again with the augur, and if the stoppage then continues, call your plumber. He can remove the bowl, which you cannot do. By doing this, turning it upside down and shaking it, a jammed object may be loosened; sometimes, flushing backwards through the bowl will work; and once in a while nothing will succeed and the bowl must be replaced.

Main House Drain. Suppose, when first trying to locate a stoppage, you find the washtub or some other basement fixture backing up and the waste of upstairs fixtures backing into the basement fixture. This means that the stoppage is in the main house drain. Follow the drain to the point where it leaves the house. Near the wall there is usually a U-shaped house trap. Unscrew the trap cover on the street or septic-tank side of the trap. If the drain leading outside seems clear, the stoppage may be in the bottom of the trap. This can be probed with a stick, but there's no better way of clearing a house-trap stoppage than with your hand, wearing a rubber glove. If the bottom of the trap is clear, unscrew the other trap cover. If no stoppage is visible, screw both covers back on; when you do clear the stoppage, a lot of waste will suddenly gush to the trap and overflow if the covers are not on.

Next, locate the clean-out plug in the house drain. A flat steel snake will be needed as for the sink drain—preferably a heavier one. If you can't reach the stoppage from the clean-out, unscrew the inside trap cover and work to the stoppage. You can also cut an access hole in the cast iron. Mark off an oval shape on the top of the pipe and then, with a sharp cold chisel, make a continuous cut along the mark. Keep going around the cut, increasing the force of the hammer blow, and the piece will fall out. Or, with a hacksaw, make two vertical cuts 3 to 4″ apart. Join the cuts horizontally with a cold chisel, then chip out the piece. The hole is repaired with putty in the same manner as the sink drain.

Remember that all this work is likely to be dirty and wet, so wear old clothes. Wash the snakes when you've finished with them and wipe them with oil before putting them away. This will prevent rust.

THE RIGHT VALVE IN THE RIGHT PLACE

All valves are used to control the flow of water within a pipe. Similarly, it can be said that all trucks are used to carry goods. But just as there are different types of trucks, each designed to do one carrying job the best, so there are different types of valves, and for the same reason. Using the wrong valve for a job is just as illogical as using a trailer truck to carry a single bottle of soda pop.

The homeowner encounters many valves within his home. If one of these goes bad, it may have to be replaced. Here, for example, are some ordinary valve problems you might face, together with the recommended valve for each situation.

1. For an underground sprinkling system where water pressure is low, use a gate valve because it offers the least resistance to the flow of water. However, in many communities, depending upon local codes, you may have to add a vacuum-breaker valve to prevent backflow from the sprinkler system into the main water line.

2. If you are adding an outdoor water connection, install a drainage valve inside. This permits draining the outdoor part of the line to prevent winter freezes from bursting the pipe. However, if you wish to use that connection all year long, use an anti-freeze valve.

3. If you need a sump pump in your basement, it's best to add a check valve immediately after the pump on the exhaust line. This prevents the water from backing up through the pump after it has been shut off.

4. Should you be installing connections for a new washing machine, use globe valves if the water will be turned on and off frequently.

These are but a few examples of how the handyman encounters valves in his home. If a valve has been giving considerable trouble, it may be that the builder used the wrong kind for the job, and replacing it with the right one will eliminate the difficulty.

Globe Valve. The globe valve is probably the most familiar type of valve to the homeowner because it is so widely used and because it operates like the average kitchen faucet. It is used in cases where a valve must be opened and closed frequently—for example, between a washing machine and the hot and cold water pipes—and where a positive shut-off is essential, such as the supply line to a steam boiler or hot water tank. Globe valves are made in several styles. The two most commonly used are the standard model (inlet and outlet water pipes are in a straight line as shown in Sketch 1) and the angle type (inlet pipe is at right angles to the outlet pipe as in Sketch 2; the valve also serves as an elbow).

Generally, globe valves can be installed with the

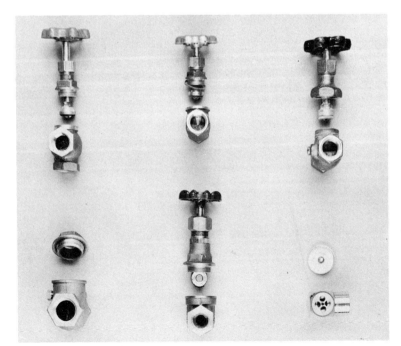

Valves control the flow of water in different ways. In some, like a globe valve, a washer presses against a seat (or an opening) to stop the flow of water. In a gate valve, a metal disc blocks the diameter opening of the pipe. In a check valve, a small flap pushes up against a rim to stop the backflow of water.

Across the top are three types of globe valves: (1) angle valve, (2) standard globe, and (3) drainable valve. In each, the direction of the flow of water is changed; this causes water resistance and decreases the water pressure.

Across the bottom are (4) a check valve with a metal flap that is forced against a rim to stop water backflow, (5) a gate valve in which the opening is of the same diameter as the pipe and therefore offers very little resistance, and (6) a vacuum-breaker valve which permits air to enter through the holes in the top to break a siphon action.

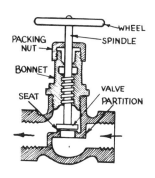

Sketch 1—Cross-section view of a globe valve. Note changes in direction of water flow and the reduction in the size of the opening through which the water passes. This type of valve markedly reduces the flow of water as well as the water pressure.

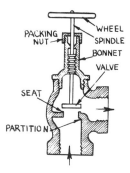

Sketch 2—Cross-section view of an angle valve. It not only acts as a water cut-off to control the flow of water, but also takes the place of an elbow.

spindle in any position. However, if the valve is in a line that is drained for the winter, the spindle of the standard type should be horizontal. There is less chance of water freezing within the valve and making it inoperative. Furthermore, it is essential, when installing any type of globe valve, that the water pushes up against the valve or washer. Some of the better globe valves have an arrow indicating the direction of flow. The advantages of globe valves are that (1) they will remain watertight longer than a gate valve when opened and closed frequently, (2) it is easy for the handyman to replace a faulty washer and (3) it is also easy to regrind the valve seat. All you need for the last is a regular valve-seat grinder

VALVES AND WATER RESISTANCE. The flow of water through a valve is affected by:

(a) The size of the opening within the valve, especially through the seat.

(b) The change of direction within the valve and the number of changes in some types of valves.

If maintaining adequate water pressure is a major problem in your home, here is a guide to water resistance of different valves.

Water Resistance Comparison

Type of Valve	Elbow	Gate	Angle Valve	Standard Globe
Standard globe	8	16	2	—
Angle valve	4	8	—	$\frac{1}{2}$
Gate valve	$\frac{1}{2}$	—	$\frac{1}{8}$	$\frac{1}{16}$

NOTE ON USING THIS TABLE: A standard globe valve offers 8 times more resistance to the flow of water than a 90-degree elbow; it offers 16 times as much resistance as a gate valve. On the other hand, an angle valve offers only 4 times the resistance of an elbow and only $\frac{1}{2}$ the resistance of a standard globe. The gate valve, for example, offers only $\frac{1}{2}$ the resistance of an elbow and $\frac{1}{16}$ the resistance of a standard globe valve.

used on the average household faucet. The chief disadvantage of globe valves is that, because of the reduced opening through the seat, they offer considerable resistance to the flow of water (see Water Resistance table). Also, foreign matter in the water line may result in frequent changing of washers as well as the need to regrind the seat.

Angle Valve. An angle valve is a globe valve with a right-angle bend. It not only acts as a valve but also as an elbow. The homeowner is most familiar with this valve as the shut-off valve for his radiators. It is also used, because of its lower flow resistance as compared with a standard globe valve, as the branch line control valve for vertical pipes going up from the basement. The angle valve is often favored where there is a bend in the water line and need for a valve. Its use here will eliminate the need for an elbow.

An angle valve will work with the stem or handle in any position. On water lines, use a valve with a replaceable composition washer. However, on steam lines, a ground metal disc is used in place of the washer. If the valve is installed in a line where the water will be drained for the winter, have the handle and stem pointing downward. In this way, any water remaining in the valve after the line is drained can be removed by unscrewing the bonnet. The advantages of an angle valve are that it eliminates the need for an elbow, often saves time in joining pipes, and its resistance to water flow is only half as great as a standard globe valve. Because of the last, it is better suited to areas with low water pressure. The disadvantages of an angle valve are the same as for the globe valve.

Gate Valve. Most homes have a gate valve as the main water shut-off in the house. It is located immediately after the main water line enters through the foundation wall. Gate valves are used primarily where full flow of water is of vital importance, since they offer practically no resistance. These valves can be installed in any position, and it makes no difference which end is connected to the inlet and which to the outlet pipes. In cold climates, however, the valve

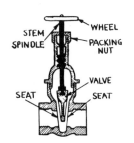

Sketch 3—Cross-section view of a gate valve. Note that the opening in the valve is of the same diameter as the pipe when the valve is opened fully.

Sketch 4—View of a drainable valve in use, connecting a water supply line to a hose cock outside the house wall. Note that the drainage screw cap is located on the side toward the outside faucet.

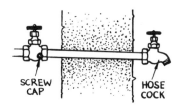

should be set so that its stem is upright, or at least at an angle slightly above the horizontal. Otherwise, the valve bonnet will remain full of water even when the line is drained, and a freeze-up could split the valve bonnet.

The gate valve is the only valve which opens to the same size as the pipe with which it is used. Therefore, it does not cut down on the water pressure at all and permits the greatest flow of water through a valve. Since it can also be connected with either end toward the inlet or supply pipe, it presents no problem to the handyman when he installs it himself. One disadvantage of the gate valve is that it is closed by wedging metal against metal, which causes it to wear quickly and eventually lose its watertight quality. Furthermore, the disc or movable section is easily damaged if closed on particles of sand or grit. If the disc wears out, the handyman cannot make the repairs; it is necessary to replace the entire valve.

Drainable Valves. Both globe and gate valves are made with special side openings to permit the draining of the water in a branch line without disconnecting any pipe or fittings. These drainable valves are used primarily inside the home as a shut-off for outside water cocks. In winter, this valve is shut and the water beyond it to the outside hose connection is emptied from the line by opening the small cap on the side of the valve (see Sketch 4).

When connecting this type of valve in a line, be sure that the drain opening is on the non-pressure side, that is, on the side toward the outside hose connection. A gate valve should be set so that its stem is upright, or at the very lowest, slightly above horizontal.

However, a globe valve spindle should be set so that it is horizontal. When the drainage valve is closed for the winter, open the outside hose cock as well as the drain cap to remove all the water. Leave both open during freezing weather. The advantage of this valve is that the water in a line can be drained and freeze damage prevented without disturbing any pipe or fittings. The disadvantages are the same as for a globe or gate valve, depending on the type used.

Anti-freeze Valves. If you live in a cold climate and need running water outside your home during the winter, you should use either an anti-freeze valve or a non-freeze hydrant. The former is used to connect a hose cock through the house wall (see Sketch 5); the latter is connected to a pipe underground and can be located anywhere on your property (see Sketch 6).

Actually, these valves are more like a pipe in appearance. They are 30″ or more in length, with the handle on one end and the actual valve closure at the opposite end. When installing an anti-freeze valve through a house wall, pitch the valve downward toward the outlet. This will permit any water to drain out of the pipe when the valve is closed. Otherwise, it might freeze and burst the pipe. The non-freeze hydrant should be placed so that the movable valve end is at least 2 to 3 inches below the frost line. Furthermore, the pipe leading to the hydrant should also be set below the frost line. The advantage of both valves lies in the fact that you can have running water outdoors during the freezing weather without danger of a water freeze or a bursting pipe. The disadvantage of the anti-freeze valves lies in the fact that it is not possible to resurface the seat of the valve if

Sketch 5—Installation view of an anti-freeze valve which is used when you want running water outside the home during the entire year. Note that pipe is pitched downward toward the outside to permit adequate drainage.

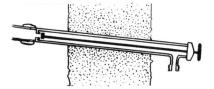

Sketch 6—Installation view of a non-freeze hydrant. The base of the hydrant as well as the supply line should be below frost line to prevent the freezing of the water.

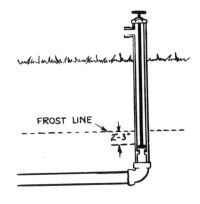

it becomes rough or uneven. Unlike the seat of the ordinary globe valve, the seat of an anti-freeze valve is too far away from the handle to permit use of a resurfacing tool.

Check Valve. The primary purpose of a check valve is to prevent a backflow of water in a pipe. There are two types of check valves, one used with vertical pipes only and the other with horizontal pipes only.

If you have a sump pump, the discharge line should be connected to the pump through a check valve. In this way, when the pump is shut off, the excess water in the discharge pipe will not flow back through the pump. A check valve is a must if the sump pump empties into a sewer. A flow-direction arrow on the valve indicates the correct installation position. The arrow should point in the direction from which you want no backflow (see Sketch 7).

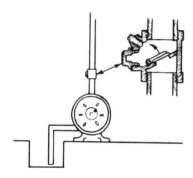

Sketch 7—Check valve in use with a sump pump. Note that hinged lid lifts upward in direction of the water flow.

The advantage of this valve lies in the fact that it prevents water from flowing back through the valve and acts as a safety measure for controlling the flow of water. However, check valves are seldom completely tight. They should not be used to prevent the backflow of sewage into a water line. Here a vacuum-breaker valve should be used instead. Also, check valves easily become inoperative. Particles of sand or dirt lodging on the seat will prevent full closing, and repairs are difficult.

Vacuum-Breaker Valve. The vacuum-breaker valve is used to prevent siphoning of polluted water into the drinking water supply line. Operating automatically, it allows air to enter the line whenever a "negative pressure" or vacuum occurs. Thus, it breaks the siphon action immediately and prevents any polluted water from siphoning back.

This "negative pressure" develops only under rare circumstances; yet a vacuum-breaker valve must be used as a safety measure. If there is a fire and the water from the mains is exhausted faster than the mains can be filled by the water company, a "negative pressure" may develop. Thus, if you are filling your washing machine at the time, this vacuum in the main water line can cause all the water in the washer to be siphoned back into the drinking water line. A vacuum-breaker valve, however, lets air in instantly and the water remains in the washing machine.

The valve must be installed so that it is at least 6" above the overflow level of the fixture it controls. Most vacuum-breaker valves have to be installed so that the valve itself is perfectly vertical, although there are some models which will operate in any position. Some types are installed in the traditional plumbing technique—added in the line—but there are others available that can be screwed directly onto a hose cock in the same manner in which a hose coupling is attached. The latter type can be used for washing machines or underground sprinkling systems.

Most vacuum-breaker valves drastically reduce the flow of water. If you live in an area with low water pressure, make certain you use the type which does not constrict the water flow.

A QUIET PLUMBING SYSTEM

Most of your home's plumbing system is supposed to be unseen—all of it should be unheard. Chattering and whistling noises are two of the most common (and annoying) plumbing faults and, fortunately, the most easily corrected. If, when you turn on a faucet, you hear a chattering noise and feel a vibration, the faucet washer or its spindle is defective. The loose parts vibrate up and down because of water pressure. Perhaps the faucet washer has become loose, and merely tightening it will effect a cure. If not, its replacement will be necessary. The spindle may also need to be replaced, or you may use a faucet insert which has the effect of renewing the working parts of the faucet.

A whistle results from a poorly closed valve where the washer is worn out. Replacement of the washer, or grinding down the old seat, will remedy it. A whistle in a toilet tank, accompanied by splashing and dripping sounds, is also due to a faulty valve. Remove the tank cover and observe the water level. If water runs down the overflow pipe, the float is improperly adjusted, it leaks, or its rod is bent. In some cases, the valve in the ball cock (the tall rod on which the float arm hangs) is damaged and needs replacement. If you can raise the float manually and you find that this shuts off the water, bend the rod to set the float lower. If this doesn't work, replace the damaged ball cock, first shutting off the water and draining the tank.

If there is a steady splashing and flow from the tank into the bowl, the rubber valve at the center on the bottom of the tank is defective, hardened or resting on an uneven outlet seat. With steel wool, you can rub down the seat after the tank has been drained, or you can replace the valve at relatively little expense.

If there is a splashing sound in the tank as it refills, direct the filler tube (which is movable) against the sidewall of the tank. If this tube leaks at its base, it's best to replace the ball cock completely.

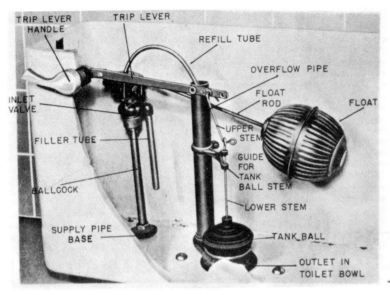

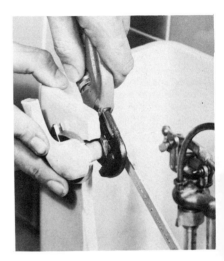

1. Cutaway view of the inside of a toilet tank. Always shut off water supply and flush toilet before starting any repairs. Work carefully, for the tank is made of porcelain.
2. The trip lever and handle are removed by holding nuts on both sides with wrenches. First disconnect upper stem from lever, then turn inside nut *clockwise* to loosen.

3. A new float is easy to install. Hold float rod and turn old float counterclockwise to remove. New type of plastic float won't rust or corrode, and should last a lifetime.
4. To replace tank ball with newer type of ball, unscrew old unit and remove both stems. Guide is removed by loosening side screw and slipping unit over overflow pipe.
5. Unit pictured here is slipped over the overflow pipe and rests at the bottom. A bead chain replaces stems. Pendants over chain at trip lever hold unit.

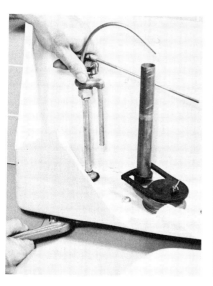

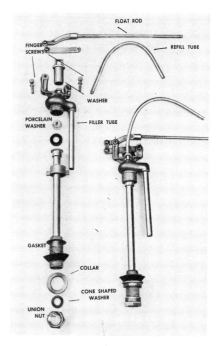

6. To replace ball cock, hold top of unit in one hand and turn nut on underside of tank with wrench (see 8). Sponge excess water out of tank before removing.

7. New quiet type of ball cock is installed. Screw in new refill tube. Hold base in one hand; bend tube into overflow with other.

8. The ball cock—disassembled and assembled. Note washer, at top of the unit on left, controlling intake of water.

TOILET TANK TROUBLE

Symptom	Check Action	Cause and Cure
Water flowing into toilet bowl through overflow pipe *from refill tube* (gently lift out tube from overflow pipe to check source of water)	Lift up on float arm—if flow of water stops	Float does not shut off valve in ball cock—bend float arm downward so it will cause float to rise higher to close valve. If this does not stop water flow, then float has a leak—replace it with a new one.
	Lift up on float arm—if flow of water does not stop	Washer in ball cock is worn—remove ball cock from tank and replace worn washer.
Water flowing into toilet bowl through overflow pipe *from seat below tank ball*	Press down on lower stem to force tank ball into seat of outlet pipe—if water stops	Trip lever may be stuck and does not allow stems to return to normal "closed" position—jiggle lever to see if it is working freely—lubricate bushing next to handle or replace lever. Lower stem might be bent out of shape—remove it and see if there are any bends—straighten with a pliers or replace. Tank ball may have gone "soft"—remove and replace it with a new one or one of the newer types that does not require a stem.
	Press down on lower stem to force tank ball into seat of outlet pipe—if water does not stop	Guide for tank stem might be out of alignment with seat of outlet pipe—loosen screw and readjust this guide. Seat in which tank ball rests might be dirty and gritty and prevent the proper closure—remove tank ball and smooth seat with sandpaper.

A slamming, banging hammer in the water pipes is called water hammer. It's caused by sudden halting of the forward flow of water when a faucet is closed. The water piles up, bounces backward and forward, and this motion creates a tremendous vibration, causing the pipes to sound as if hit with a hammer. It's not only annoying—it's damaging to the pipes and fittings. Leaks can develop at elbows, pipe hangers come loose (increasing the vibration), and some fittings may even break.

To discover which valve is causing the trouble, close each faucet in turn rapidly, listen, then close it again slowly. If you have the spring-type of faucets which close automatically when released, hammering can be reduced by replacing them with faucets which close manually, slowly. The best cure, however, is to install a shock absorber to take up the vibration. It should be installed as close as possible to the faucet causing the trouble, or at least on the main line to the area where the trouble exists. The most common type of shock absorber (often installed during the initial construction of a home) is a vertical pipe about 2' long and capped at the top (see A and B below). Adding such a device to existing lines may mean a lot of work, especially if the pipes are enclosed in walls and run along the underside of joists in the basement. For sinks, an easier solution is that shown in C below, where clearance may be possible. An alternative arrangement consists of a coiled length of copper tube, ½" in diameter, closed at the upper end and installed on a line of pipe where minimum clearance is possible.

There are two drawbacks to these types of shock absorbers—they can become filled with water as the water flowing by gradually picks up air (particularly true of hot-water lines), or they may become slowly

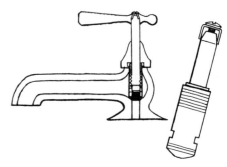

New stem of duplicate make often serves to quiet a noisy faucet.

caked and finally closed if the water is heavily alkaline or full of rust. One method of overcoming this trouble, particularly the tendency to become filled with water, is to install an automobile tire valve on the top of the shock absorber tubing or pipe. When the tubing becomes filled with water, replace the air by forcing it in with a bicycle pump. The only other way to restore air in such a chamber with a sealed top is to drain the water lines and refill, trapping air automatically in the vertical length.

Commercial shock absorbers have been developed which require little clearance or space. One of them employs an expandable tube encased in foam rubber, the whole enclosed in metal. It picks up the back surge of water without losing the air which remains in it. Since this type neither fills with water nor is damaged by foreign elements in the water, it seems to have solved the problem. Another successful type, employing a metal bellows technique, expands as the shock hits it, preventing air loss. It requires more space for the expansion and tends to corrode under the deteriorating elements contained in some water.

A few sections of the country are supplied with water under unusually heavy pressures, a condition which may contribute to water hammer throughout the house. Sometimes this can be checked by partially closing the main valve near the intake or meter, to reduce pressure; if you find such pressures in your home, install a permanent pressure-control valve. You can't leave the main valve half-open as a check, since it will very soon wear out. It wasn't designed to work in that position.

Pounding and rumbling noises are usually found in hot-water lines only. They accompany a surging sound in the hot-water heater. One cause may be that the water temperature is too high and steam is active inside the system. Water for domestic use should not be heated above 140°. If any hotter, it's dangerous and may blow the tank apart. Another cause of noises in hot-water lines may be poor circulation between the heater and the storage tank.

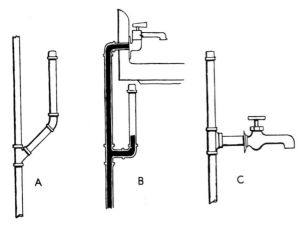

Air cushion of capped pipe may be located on vertical run (A), under sink (B), or just above faucet on inside of wall (C).

Often the passage of water through pipes produces a faint humming noise. It's hardly noticeable *unless* the pipe is tightly anchored to a floor or wall, and then the sound is magnified out of all proportion. A hum can be entirely eliminated and the pipes quieted by insertion of bits of felt between the pipe and its hangers or anchors. This is a good method anyway to reduce vibration caused by water hammer. Search along all visible pipe lines, locate the hangers, loosen screws or nails on one side and insert felt strips. (An old cut-up felt hat will do well, as will lengths of felt weather-stripping.) If the noise persists, installation of larger-diameter pipes to the service area is called for.

CURE FOR DRIPPING FAUCETS

No matter how complex or concealed it may seem, *any* faucet can be taken apart. To find out how yours is put together, remove each piece step-by-step and lay them all out in a row in the order of removal. Then you will have no trouble in putting the faucet back together again. The usual order of removal is: the cap screw, the handle screw, the handle, the large nut holding down the spindle housing, then the housing and finally the spindle. At the base, you'll find the washer. Remove the brass screw, replace it and the washer. Be sure the washer is just a trifle smaller than the recess into which it fits. Most washers can be trimmed down with a rasp if they happen to be too large. Then a few turns of packing (or a sleeve) around the stem before replacement will stop all leakage for a while, but frequent replacement of washers to stop faucets from dripping is usually a sign of a worn faucet seat. The rough metal chews

1. To open faucet for washer replacement, unscrew cap-cover over handle screw, then remove the screw.

2. Handle is then lifted off. If stuck tightly, tap underside all around with a block of wood.

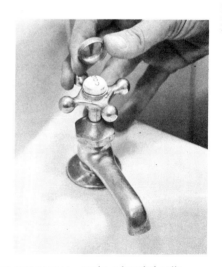

3. It is sometimes necessary to untwist a knurled collar on the top of the handle. This comes off by turning in a counterclockwise direction. →

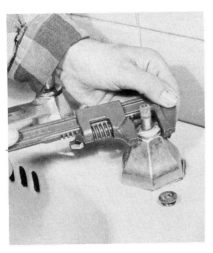

4. Use smooth-jawed wrench to remove large nut holding down the spindle housing. Don't scar chrome.

5. Spindle housing lifts off, exposing nut which holds spindle in position. Remove it with a wrench.

6. With bearing nut gone, spindle can be twisted out. Use handle to turn spindle if it sticks.

7. Holding spindle in vise makes removal of brass washer screw easier. Replace washer and screw.

8. With a clean cloth, wipe out the inside of the faucet and then insert the new spindle or stem. Remove old stem from bonnet but don't touch packing inside the bonnet.

9. Slip bonnet over new stem to see if it fits. If bonnet cannot be hand-screwed onto first two threads, remove some of the washers. Then tighten and replace handle.

10. If you don't wish to use a new stem, try a combination seat washer. It comes in various sizes to fit any faucet. Force in place with nail set or awl.

away the washers, and there are several techniques to solve this problem. You can reseat or smooth the faucet seat, or you can either add a new seat or a self-contained seat and stem. The latter technique has several advantages. A new faucet insert (the replacement for the existing stem and seat) not only provides a trouble-free seat but also reduces chatter or water hammer and eliminates the need of further washer replacement. This faucet insert is made to fit virtually all types of sink and tub units. It is available in long or short stems, in chrome plate or brass finish and for hot- or cold-water faucets. The only difference between the hot- and cold-water units is the direction in which they turn to open and shut. The cold turns clockwise to open and counterclockwise to shut, while the hot is just the opposite. The only tools needed are a screwdriver and an adjustable open-end or pipe wrench.

ADDING A FAUCET

This is a quick and convenient way to add a faucet for a washing machine, for example, without disconnecting any pipe. All you need is an open-end adjustable wrench, a drill, and ¼″ bit. The saddle-type faucets fit over ½″ iron pipe or copper tubing. Follow the photographic steps for easy installation.

1. Select a convenient location for the faucet and sand the pipe surface lightly to remove any scale and dirt. Remove bolts from strap and slip unit over pipe. Draw straps together, insert bolts, and tighten.

2. Shut off water supply and then remove the valve bonnet and stem. Insert the drilling guide that comes with the faucet kit. It screws into place so that it aligns at right angles to the pipe as a guide for drilling.

4. After the drilling guide is removed, blow out any metal chips. Replace the stem and bonnet and tighten with wrench. Turn on water and flush out unit.

3. Use a ¼″ drill bit through the guide and drill through one wall of the pipe. If water pressure is low, enlarge hole to $\frac{7}{16}$″ with a reamer or drill bit.

WORKING WITH PLASTIC PIPE

Armed with only a sharp pocketknife or a saw, plus a screwdriver, a homeowner can add a cold-water line anywhere around his house and grounds, indoors or out—if he uses plastic pipe.

Plastic pipe has some unusual qualities. It will never rust or rot; it can be bent and curved around corners and does not require fittings or threading as metal pipe does. It can be filled with water and frozen solid without injury, splits or leaks. It can be used as an electrical conduit through which normally insulated wire can be run underground or underwater. Its only limitation is that it cannot be used to conduct water over 140°.

As to the necessary skill required to work with

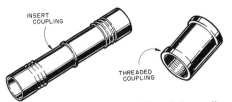

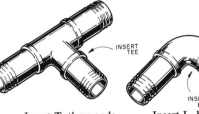

Insert adaptor, male
end threaded

Insert coupling,
both ends serrated

Threaded coupling,
inside threads at
both ends

Insert T, three ends
serrated

Insert L, both
ends serrated

plastic pipe, you need only follow the illustrations which show the various steps to complete installation of a water line. In the first photograph, the pipe is cut to the desired length with a sharp pocketknife or a hand saw. The second photograph shows the standard joint between lengths of pipe. The coupling —in this case an insert—is serrated at each end. A stainless-steel clamp is slipped over the cut ends of pipe, and these ends are then slipped over the serrated end of the coupling, after which the clamps are tightened with a screwdriver. The connection is finished.

To make a branch line from the first, use a T fitting with its three ends serrated and clamped tight in the same way. For compactness and rounding corners sharply, an elbow is provided to be attached in the same manner. Should you later decide to make changes in the pipe arrangement, the clamp may be loosened, the joint pulled apart by hand and a different fitting inserted. To change from the regular coupling to a T, all you need is a screwdriver.

Plastic pipe may be connected to your present pipe by the addition of a plastic adaptor, a fitting which has one serrated end and one threaded end. The threaded end may be screwed into any female joint (one with the threads on the inner pipe surface) of metal pipe of an inside diameter corresponding to the outside diameter of the plastic pipe. Once this

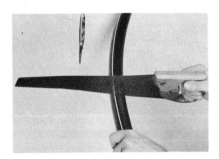

1. Flexible plastic pipe can be cut with sharp pocketknife or saw.
2. Lengths are joined with insert coupling and stainless-steel clamp.
3. Branch lines can be added by using T coupling in place of regular insert.

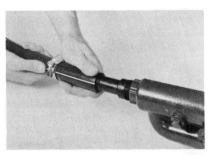

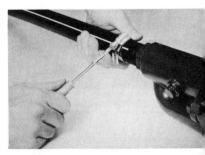

4. Attach to metal pipe with threaded adaptor, and dope on threads.
5. Plastic pipe is attached to the adaptor by hand pressure and metal clamps.
6. Screwdriver tightens clamps. This is only tool needed once pipe is cut.

fitting is put in place—and here pipe-joint compound should be applied to the male threads before insertion—the plastic fitting is coupled to the pipe in the usual clamped-joint way.

Once you've added joint compound, you'll need a wrench to tighten this joint. Any adjustable or pipe wrench will do. Such a connection may be made to a basement faucet or any other faucet that is equipped with standard threads.

Plastic pipe can be used to conduct water to any area around the house and grounds. Suppose you need a more convenient spot to hook up a hose to wash the car. Look over your water supply system and select an easily accessible spot to cut into the line. With a hacksaw, cut through a long, straight length of the cold-water line along an outside wall. Shut off the water supply first, of course. Remove both pieces from their adjacent fittings by turning them with a pipe wrench while holding the fittings rigid with a second wrench. Have the cut ends threaded, fitted with a union and a T of a size to fit the plastic pipe. Before threading the cut ends, a short length equal to the new union and T must be cut off so that when the new assembly is put into place, its over-all length will match that of the original pipe. When replaced, one piece at a time, you'll have a place to add a branch from the main water line through the T.

Another way to do this is to cut a length of plastic pipe 1″ longer than the face-to-face distance between the metal pipe fittings. Insert a threaded adaptor in each fitting of the metal pipe. Cut into the length of plastic pipe and insert a T. In either case, you can then run plastic pipe from the T to the outdoors where it can be fitted with a faucet or other usable connection.

To bring water to the outdoors from inside the house, first a passageway must be made through the foundation. Drill a hole through the masonry with a star drill and enlarge it with a cold chisel until the pipe can be pushed through. Anchor the pipe with clamps to the wall or adjacent fixed timber inside and extend one end through the foundation far enough so that a connection can be made outside. If you plan to have the pipe come through the foundation below grade, you'll need an excavation outside large enough to work around the pipe end comfortably. Pack the hole in the foundation with a stiff mixture of cement after coating the pipe with asphalt or tar.

Using plastic pipe outside the foundation is a simple matter. Since plastic pipe does not deteriorate if frozen, it may be used outside wherever it will not be too conspicuous. (Metal pipe should be placed below frost line.) With a spade, turn sod up slightly and push the pipe just below the surface, replacing

the sod and tamping it flat with your foot as you go along. No trench digging is necessary.

Where the lawn area is extensive, you may need several outlets; cut the pipe at intervals and insert T's for faucet connections or to add sprinkler system heads. Wherever you want a faucet, add an elbow on the plastic pipe so that a vertical length may be added. On this, a standard faucet is mounted with an adaptor in the same way a metal-plastic joint was made in the basement.

An outdoor faucet can be handled in two ways—conveniently up in the air about 2′, or concealed in the ground so that a mower can pass over without damage. Owing to its flexibility, the pipe may be run alongside a tree and fastened with a clamp or concealed in shrubbery where it is supported by a post. For an underground faucet, a wooden box is embedded 2″ below ground level, the pipe brought through the open lower end and supported on a cross brace where the faucet is attached. This necessitates a wooden cover set just below ground level, strong enough to support the weight of a man or a mower passing above it. Treat all wood pieces with preservative to prevent rot.

REPLACING LEAKING PIPE

Imagine that water pipe C in the illustration below has been split by a freeze-up and needs to be replaced. First of all, turn off the water and then follow the line back toward the house supply system. At the first valve you come to, turn the handle clockwise. While it's not necessary to drain the line, it does make for cleaner and easier working conditions if you do. Open any faucet or drain lower in the line than the split pipe C.

With a hack saw, cut pipe C at any easy-to-get-at point. Put one wrench on the raised part—called the "bead"—of elbow B where pipe C is screwed into it. If you are facing the job as you are now facing the sketch, the jaws of the wrench will be open away from you. At a point about 1″ away from elbow B, put the other wrench on pipe C, this time with the

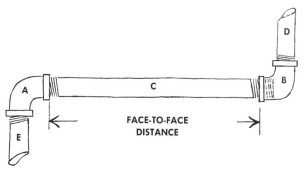

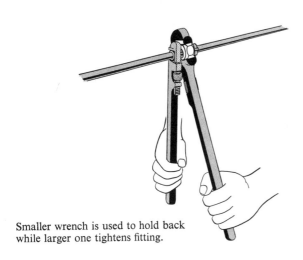

Smaller wrench is used to hold back while larger one tightens fitting.

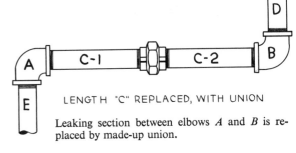

LENGTH "C" REPLACED, WITH UNION

Leaking section between elbows *A* and *B* is replaced by made-up union.

jaws open toward you and the handle down. Maintaining an almost equal pressure on the wrench holding the elbow, pull the other wrench toward you with enough pressure to unscrew this section of pipe *C*. The use of two wrenches in this manner is known as "holding back" and should be employed, whenever possible, when working on pipe. If you were to use only the wrench on pipe *C*, elbow *B* might turn or swing on pipe *D* and cause a leak, or it might even twist elbow *B* right off pipe *D*. The older the pipe, the more care is needed.

As you begin to unscrew the first section of pipe *C*, you will notice that it seems to grow longer and tends to jam up against the other section. There will be ½" of extra length since *C* is made up ½" into elbow *B*. Usually, this extra length causes no trouble, for if either section of pipe *C* is long enough, it will also be flexible enough to pull aside. There may also be enough play in lines *E* or *D* to take care of the increased length. But if *C* is short, and lines *E* and *D* rigid (one may be against a beam and the other coming up through a floor, for instance), either *A* or *B* will have to be moved slightly in order to get the pipe sections out. Move or swing the elbow that is easiest to get at, using the "hold back" method with your wrenches. If you turn elbow *A*, hold back on pipe *E*; if you turn elbow *B*, hold back on pipe *D*. And always back off, or unscrew, an elbow so that when it is returned to its former position it will be as tight as it was originally. This backing-off process lessens the possibility of a leak.

To replace pipe *C*, you will need two pieces of pipe joined by a union (the over-all length equal to pipe *C*). The union can be placed anywhere between elbows *A* and *B*, depending on wherever it is easiest for you to reach. Water pipe usually measures ½" or ¾". The outside diameter of ½" pipe is $\frac{13}{16}$", that of ¾" inch pipe is exactly 1".

Make up sections as shown in the illustration above, holding back as you screw each section into place. When making up section *C-1*, hold back on elbow *A*; and for section *C-2*, hold back on elbow *B*. With both sections of pipe in place, the ground joint face on each part of the union should fit evenly and snugly together. If some lining up is needed—that is, if you must turn one of the elbows to get the parts of the union to face each other squarely—be sure to hold back as you turn the elbow.

When the union is properly lined up, the big ring which joins the two sections can be turned up almost all the way by hand, with only the final turn or two made with the wrenches. It takes two wrenches to tighten a union. Put one wrench on the section of the union onto which the big ring will be made up and the other wrench on the ring itself. Hold the union section to keep it from turning, then tighten the ring. Turn on the water, and you've done the job.

Once the first principles of pipe fitting have been mastered, improvements in technique can be added with ease. For example, you can measure the pipe and have it on hand for immediate installation before you remove the old pipe, thus reducing the time the water must be shut off.

Suppose you measure pipe *C* before cutting and removing it. Return to Illustration 1 and note the face-to-face measurement, that is, the distance from the face of elbow *A* to the face of elbow *B*. Since pipe *C* is made up ½" into each elbow, pipe *C* is actually 1" longer than the face-to-face measurement. Supposing the face-to-face measurement is 4', then the over-all measurement is 4' 1". You can tell your dealer you want a piece "4' 1" long, end-to-end, over [meaning including] a union."

If pipe *C* is sound pipe, but you want to put in a T fitting and from the T run a pipe through the cellar wall for an outside hose connection, first determine where in *C* you want the center of the T. Say it should be 10" from the face of elbow *A*. Tell your dealer to make up a piece "4' 1" long end-to-end, over a T and a union with center of the T 10½" from the end." The extra ½" is the length *C* will make up into elbow *A*.

Not all pipe sizes screw into a fitting exactly ½".

The table shows the length the different sizes of pipe will make up into fittings. Actually, in any repair work, if there is a union nearby, another one need not be put in. But if you must take apart three or four fittings, or take out a length of pipe to get at the union, you'll find it easier to install another union.

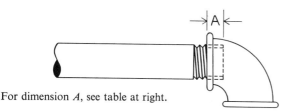

For dimension *A*, see table at right.

PIPE PATCHING

Pipe leaks are usually quite simple to repair. The first step is to turn off the water at the nearest shut-off valve between leak and water supply and open the nearest outlet to drain the pipe.

For the easiest repair of leaks at joints or fittings, use commercial iron cement and a special pipe clamp, both available at hardware stores. Fit the clamp around the pipe and bolt it in place against the fitting. The cement, which comes in powder form, should then be mixed with water to the consistency of stiff putty and tamped into a groove in the clamp. As soon as the cement hardens, turn on the water.

Small holes in pipe, such as those made by accidental puncture, can often be sealed with self-threading screws. These require a gasket cut from an old inner tube or other piece of rubber. The gasket should be about twice the size of the screw head. Punch a hole in the center of the rubber, insert the screw, coat both sides of the rubber with iron cement, then drive the screw into the hole by turning its

Distance a Pipe Should be Screwed into Valves or Fittings

Size of Pipe	Distance Inserted into Fitting
$\frac{1}{8}''$	$\frac{1}{4}''$
$\frac{1}{4}''$	$\frac{3}{8}''$
$\frac{3}{8}''$	$\frac{3}{8}''$
$\frac{1}{2}''$	$\frac{1}{2}''$
$\frac{3}{4}''$	$\frac{1}{2}''$
$1''$	$\frac{9}{16}''$
$1\frac{1}{4}''$	$\frac{3}{8}''$
$1\frac{1}{2}''$	$\frac{5}{8}''$
$2''$	$\frac{11}{16}''$

head with a monkey wrench. This method is not recommended for pipe under $1\frac{1}{2}''$ in diameter, since the plug impedes the water flow, nor is it recommended for pipe too thin to form a thread as the screw is driven in. In $1\frac{1}{2}''$ pipe or larger, you may prefer to use a utility plug that has its own neoprene gasket and requires no thread to hold it in place. Instead, it carries a metal "spider" that expands into the pipe as the plug is tightened, clamping it firmly in place. Install by drilling a $\frac{3}{8}''$ hole in the center of the leak. Insert the utility plug. Hold the plug cap with one wrench, and with another turn the screw head until tight.

For holes in smaller pipes, and for corrosion or cracks in all pipes, the most practical remedy is the use of an ordinary pipe clamp. Apply by cutting a rubber or leather gasket large enough to cover the break amply. Coat both pipe and gasket with iron cement. If the pipe is cracked, force iron cement into the crack with a hammer. Then place the clamp around pipe and gasket and tighten bolts. If the crack is too long for the width of a single clamp, use two

A small-hole leak can develop at any time anywhere along the pipe. First thing to do is shut off water valve that feeds the line.

Remove nuts and bolts from clamp. Spread it open and slip it over the hole. Place rubber patch directly over hole in pipe.

Squeeze ends together; then insert bolts and start nuts by hand. Tighten bolts with screwdriver until tight. Reopen water valve.

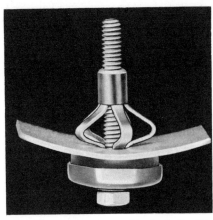

Utility plug for stopping pipe and boiler leaks. Note metal "spider" which draws up as screw is turned and locks plug in position.

or more clamps spaced an inch or two apart over the gasket. These patches will stand up for a considerable time if water pressure is not too high.

Punctures in tanks and boiler sections can be repaired with a self-threading screw or utility plug in the manner described above. It is not recommended, however, that you try repairs on cracks or corroded spots. These require reinforcing patches difficult for the amateur to install. Call in an expert. In general, corrosion repairs of any sort are, at best, only a temporary expedient. If a pipe or tank is corroded through at one point, it is sure to go, sooner or later, at another.

PREVENTION AND REPAIR OF FROZEN PIPES

When temperatures drop below freezing, the pipes in your home are subject to freeze-up unless preventive measures are taken. If water left standing in them freezes, the pipes will split and you will have the resulting expense of replacement. This waste of money can be avoided if you take some of the following precautions.

1. Dig out your stored-away fan, set it on your furnace. The pre-warmed air of your furnace, even when well jacketed, will serve to keep pipes in remote corners safe. The agitated air stops frost even if the thermometer says it's below freezing.

2. If commercial wrappings aren't at hand when the weatherman says "beware," you may resort to that old stand-by, newsprint, as a pipe wrapper. Several layers are necessary to provide insulation, and should be loosely wrapped around the pipe and tied with string.

3. If no other method is available, in case of emergency you can protect water pipe from freezing by slightly turning on a faucet. The steady flow will also keep the drain from freezing. However, in sub-zero weather this method cannot be relied upon.

4. An old-fashioned kerosene lantern hung under a U-bend or clean-out point along a main drain will prevent freeze-up in these critical points where water stands. Heat will be carried by the metal to some distance from the lantern.

5. Shut off water at an interior point on those faucets outside. Then open the faucet and drain the pipe, leaving the faucet open until the weather warms up. Some exterior faucets are shut off inside by turning the outside handle.

6. If you leave the house unattended for several days during winter months, and a complete loss of heat due to storm-downed power lines is possible, drain the entire water system. You'll find a shut-off valve near the intake. Many systems have a drain-valve near this point through which the system may be emptied.

7. If you've drained your system, there may be water standing in valves which, on freezing, would wreck them. Drain these by way of the valve tap, which requires but a few turns of a wrench or pair of pliers to open.

8. Don't open a window directly above a radiator which you have turned off for the night. A sharp drop in temperature (which you may not notice until morning) can freeze the water standing in the radiator, splitting it.

9. The thin metal of sink traps can be split readily if the water in the trap freezes. Isolated sinks in unheated areas are apt to be victims. Drain the tap by opening the bottom end of the U with a wrench or extended pliers.

10. In unheated bathrooms, the toilet bowl is subject to freeze-up in severe weather. The porcelain can be cracked, and replacement is costly. Protect it with the same anti-freeze you use in your car. This will not injure the bowl.

11. In sub-zero weather, even the last remaining inch of water in a drained toilet tank can freeze and damage the mechanism. If you are closing up a house and there is any chance of such extreme cold temperatures, remove this bit of water with a sponge. Damage here is costly.

12. The pump of your washing machine or dishwasher is always filled with water. If this freezes, you'll need a new pump. Drain out the water by opening the snap-catch which holds the cover. Drain into a shallow pan.

If you forget to take necessary precautions, and a quick freeze leaves your plumbing solid with ice, you still may manage to prevent further damage if you go about defrosting correctly. But be wary. It's possible to make a bad matter worse if you make an error here. A quick thaw or too much heat may produce steam in a confined area and blow the pipe to bits.

Since it's the long cold spell which freezes pipes, the first job is to restore some heat to the room where the frozen pipe is located. If this is impossible, let it remain frozen until you can, or you'll have the job to do over again. Then follow these steps:

1. Locate a frozen pipe by feel after a test of the faucet shows the line blocked. Your hand alone may tell you, but a thermometer held against the pipe helps considerably.

2. Start all defrosting at a faucet so that steam generated by your efforts can escape. Leave the faucet open! A small propane torch is a handy, not-too-hot defrosting tool. Play it over several inches of pipe at once. Beware of anything combustible nearby.

3. If you have no torch, but do have a soldering iron, wire it to the pipe at the freeze-up point and turn it on. Heat from the iron will travel along the metal for quite a distance and thaw out the ice inside slowly enough for safety.

4. A hair-dryer is an ideal defroster. It works slowly but safely in melting all interior ice and thus prevents explosion and subsequent pipe cracks. Once you notice a slight drip of water from the open faucet after this treatment, turn off the blower.

5. If you have neither torch nor dryer, you may have a heating lamp. This works as well as the other methods on exposed pipe. In addition, it will melt out ice from pipes behind walls of moderate thickness such as plasterboard and similar panel-type walls. It takes a bit longer but is just as effective. Keep the lamp at least 6″ away from the wall.

6. If none of these systems is at hand, you can wrap a thick towel around the frozen pipe and continually pour small streams of hot or even boiling water over the towel. This transfers heat from water to towel to pipe and to the ice inside, and pipes cannot burst from too-rapid defrosting.

7. The most serious problem is a frozen boiler. Thaw the intake pipe first. Next, open the drain and thaw the pipe and its fittings. Finally, apply warmth to the boiler. If completely filled and frozen, the probability is that the tank has split. This will become evident as the ice is melted. Do not attempt to start a fire in your furnace until all ice is melted from the boiler.

CURE FOR SWEATING PIPES AND TANKS

Dripping water from sweating cold-water pipes during hot, humid days can cause serious damage. While ventilation will help, a more positive cure is the use of a special waterproofing tape. It can be applied over any size of pipe and will prevent water from accumulating on the floor or dripping on items stored below. The tape is available in roll form and you merely wrap it around the pipes, as shown. Additional protection is necessary around pipe fittings—T's, unions, valves, etc.—where an extra layer should be taped for a waterproofing seal.

Toilet tanks sweat because the water in them is cold. It chills the porcelain, and the warm, moist air of the bathroom quickly condenses on the cold tank's surface. Result: a persistent puddle on the floor. Here are a few methods which have proved useful in combating this annoyance:

1. Since air circulation around the tank is partly stopped by the fixed position of the tank against the wall, try inserting two wood wedges about ¼″ thick

1. After cutting the edge of the tape at a diagonal to fit the necessary diameter of the pipe, wrap the tape loosely around the pipe. Unwind the entire roll before closing the gaps.

2. Starting at the beginning, work your way over the tape and press the waterproofing material together by hand to seal the gaps. The tape is sticky and will adhere to itself.   →

3. Special care is necessary over pipe fittings such as the T shown in these photos. Cut a short piece and wrap it around the T so that it joins the other already on the pipes.

4. Cut a piece of four rows of tape sufficient to go around the top of the T. Wrap this around to form a perfect seal of the waterproofing tape over the pipe fitting.

between tank and wall at the base of the tank. This must be done carefully so as not to dislodge the tank from its moorings. Circulation of air completely around the tank often serves to stop condensation.

2. Shake thoroughly ½ ounce of glycerine (from your druggist) and ½ pint of alcohol. Spread several layers of newspaper beneath the tank to protect the floor from possible spotting. Dry the outside of the tank, apply the liquid mixture with a paint brush or soft cloth. The coating lasts from 3 to 6 months and may be renewed after washing the old solution off with warm water to which a spoonful of ammonia has been added.

3. Add warm water to the cold by running a line from one of the hot-water pipes of the bathroom to the underside of the tank and joining it to the tank intake pipe with a mixing valve. This method costs several dollars but makes a permanent cure.

4. Drain the tank, dry the inside thoroughly. Line the inside walls with ½" foam rubber such as is used for chair-seat padding. Attach it to the tank walls with waterproof resin glue but do not apply it to the tank bottom. Let it dry 24 hours before refilling the tank. This method is also a permanent cure and needs no further attention.

PLUMBING VENTS

A properly designed house drainage system does two jobs: (1) it conveys waste matter from house to sewer or, in country areas, to a cesspool or septic tank; and (2) it prevents offensive odors and explosive gas, produced by decomposition of waste matter, from rising through the drain pipes and re-entering the home.

Everyone is familiar with job number 1. You pull out a sink plug and the waste water disappears down the drain, to be carried away by pipes flowing continuously downhill to sewer or septic tank. Job number 2 is not so familiar, but it stands to reason that if the waste matter is offensive in the house, it will become more so in the sewer as decomposition progresses. It also stands to reason that since the waste matter disappeared down open pipes, the gases could return by the same route. The question is, how is this prevented?

One of the ways is shown in Figure 1. Any pipe that carries the discharge of water closets is known

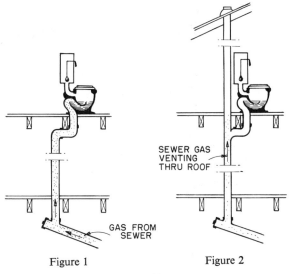

Figure 1   Figure 2

as a soil line; those pipes receiving a discharge from other fixtures are known as waste lines. In Figure 1—an old-time installation—the soil pipe was brought up only as high as the water closet. Sewer gas could and did rise this high but no higher, being prevented from going further by the water-filled trap of the toilet. But consequently the entire drainage system always contained trapped sewer gas which could escape through pipe leaks. In Figure 2, the soil pipe was brought through the roof and the sewer gas escaped into the air. The soil pipe in this installation was used as a vent.

Vent Variations. Unfortunately, extending the soil pipe through the roof is not all that must be done to be safely rid of sewer gas, for while the water closet in this case is now vented, there are other fixtures to be considered.

Suppose, for instance, that a sink were added on the first floor as in Figure 3. The sink drain must be connected to the soil pipe, and if waste can flow from the fixture to the soil pipe, gas can rise from the soil pipe to the fixture and from there into the house. To prevent this, the line is fitted with a device known as a trap, a piece of pipe looped so as to trap a column of water, hence the name.

Many people believe that plumbing traps are used to prevent objects such as pencils, toothbrushes, pins and diamond rings from getting into the sewer and blocking it. Actually, the main function of a trap is to keep gas out of the home. Correctly considered, then, a trap is a valve which allows liquid waste to pass through to the sewer but does not allow gas to pass back through to the fixture. The column of water which performs this function is known as a trap seal (Figure 6). When water in the trap falls

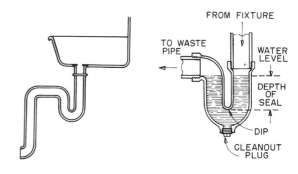

Figure 5   Figure 6

below the dip, it is obvious that gas can return through the trap and the seal of the trap is broken.

Trap Siphonage. Since sewer gas will rise to all fixtures, every fixture connected to a house drain should be trapped. An exception may be made in the case of a combination sink and tub on one drain, or where three-section laundry tubs are hooked up. One trap will serve the combination fixture when located between the soil pipe and the set of fixtures.

Now let us assume a drainage system in which the soil pipe is carried through the roof and each fixture has its individual trap, as in Figure 3. Sewer gas cannot enter the house provided the traps retain their water seals. That seal *can* be broken in the following way. Assume that the upper floor toilet is flushed. There is at first likely to be a slight pressure (called back pressure) from the soil pipe to the basin trap on the floor below. Trap water rises toward X (Figure 3). As water spirals down the soil pipe past the basin drain connection, it creates a suction, forming a vacuum in the soil pipe at this point. Atmospheric pressure at X pushes the trap water into the soil line from the basin trap and, while not all water will leave the trap, enough will have left to break the water seal. The remaining water will not reach the dip of the trap, and the trap is left open so that sewer gas may flow upward through the trap. Until water runs into the basin drain to renew the seal, the trap stays open. This is known as loss of seal by siphonage, or more technically, indirect siphonage.

Trap siphonage is prevented by permitting air to enter the system. One way of doing this is shown in Figure 4. Water flowing down the soil pipe still creates a suction, but it merely sucks air through the vent instead of drawing water from the tap.

Vent Installation. Now let's look at the main vent installation shown in Figure 4, a very handy way of venting a house of two or more stories. The main vent is connected to the soil line at least 3' above the inlet of the highest fixture.

The vent pipe could also go through the roof, but

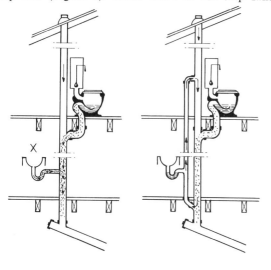

Figure 3   Figure 4

this is generally not done in small homes because the return to the soil line is easier and cheaper. The main vent arrangement is handy in that, as additional fixtures are added, the fixture drain is connected to the soil pipe and the vent for the new fixture connected to the main vent. Each drain and vent can be made to serve more than one fixture.

For instance, in Figure 9, a drain and vent arrangement is shown for a bathroom on one of the lower floors. All three fixtures—lavatory, bath and water closet—share a common connection to the soil pipe. Notice that as waste comes down the drain from the upper floor, creating a suction, air is sucked through the vent rather than water being drawn from any of the traps. A similar hook-up could be used on any floor, merely continuing the main vent and joining it at the soil pipe before the soil pipe goes through the roof. If a kitchen sink were added to the left of the soil pipe, the sink drain would connect to the soil line, the sink vent would cross the soil line and hook into the main vent. This venting must be done if any fixture empties into the soil pipe higher up on the line.

How about the top floor? Here the homeowner is lucky. If all the fixtures on the top floor are within 5' or less of the vertical soil pipe, they will be sufficiently vented by the soil pipe itself. This is known as stack venting, but it is permissible *only* when the fixtures are set close to the stack on the top floor or on a lower floor where no fixtures empty into the soil stack at a higher level. It is a good practice, when stack venting, to have the water closet connect to the soil pipe below any other fixture.

From the homeowner's point of view, venting is a fine thing when a new house is being built. For new installations and additions to existing homes, where installing a venting system means tearing up walls and floors, such installations would be expensive and involve repairs. Strictly speaking, to be absolutely safe from sewer gas, it is necessary. Most plumbing codes, disregarding expense, rule that venting must be done. There is one thing, however, the homeowner under such circumstances can still do. It has been pointed out that as long as a trap retains its water

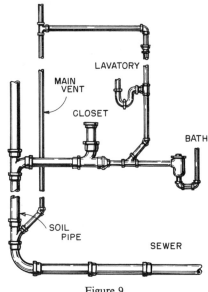

Figure 9

seal, no gas can enter the house. In addition, every plumbing code outlines certain conditions under which, because the expense of venting would be prohibitive, permission is given to use a trap that requires no venting. Such special traps are called non-siphon traps, resealing traps, anti-siphon traps and similar names. A homeowner faced with the problem of expensive venting work can go to his local plumbing supply dealer, find out which non-siphon trap is allowed and use it. Not all of those available are equally good, and the inexperienced homeowner can assure himself of getting a good one by accepting only a code-approved type.

Two of these, known as drum traps, are shown in Figures 7 and 8. The S-trap (Figure 5) is out, of course. In fact, if there are any in the house, they should be replaced. The drum trap will not siphon out but will collect sediment at the bottom and should not be used for kitchen drains where there is a lot of solid matter in the water; but it is fine for bathtubs or showers. Another weakness of the drum trap is that, unless the screw cover is tightly closed, sewer gas can come right through the trap lid itself.

Most non-siphon traps are, at best, a compromise. While all operate well when new, they require periodic cleaning. Traps designed with movable parts or flaps are always objectionable, as are those with interior partitions or baffles which cannot be taken out and cleaned.

When a non-siphon trap is used in place of a venting job, check for bad odors. If none arise, fine. If odors persist, there is only one solution—vent the traps. On new installations, do not try to improvise a system of non-siphon traps and no vents. Plain

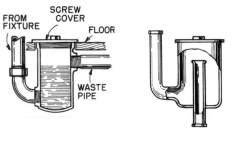

Figure 7   Figure 8

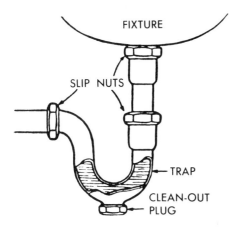

Cross section of drain trap—use monkey wrench to open clean-out plug or slip nuts.

traps and a vent system are far better and can be easily installed on a new structure.

To summarize what you should know about vents:

1. No trap should be more than 5′ horizontally from its vent.

2. Vent pipes must have no sag and must be connected so that condensation inside them will flow either into the soil pipe or drain.

3. Bring each individual vent up vertically at least 6″ above the overflow point of its fixture before turning off horizontally to the main vent.

4. Vent pipes should be at least as large in diameter as the trap being vented, and any pipe venting a water closet should be 2″ in diameter.

SUMP PUMP OUTLET

Frequently a sump pump is called upon to lift waste water from basement wash tubs to the house drain, which in turn flows to the septic system. In another arrangement, it discharges the laundry waste water to dry wells. These systems work well until the

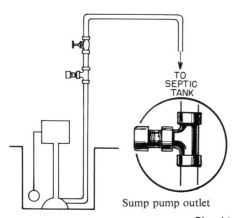

Sump pump outlet

sump pump has to remove water from a flooded basement during heavy rain seasons. At such times, sending this flood of water into a septic system or dry well results in the water soaking through the ground and back into the basement, only to be pumped out again.

To overcome this perpetual motion of water, the arrangement sketched is a great improvement. In the discharge pipe from the sump pump, two breaks are made. The first is fitted with a T, a short nipple inserted in the T, and a hose connection added at the end with an alternate cap when the hose is not connected. The second break in the line is fitted with a shut-off valve.

At flood season, the cap is removed from the nipple and the hose connected, then the shut-off valve closed, preventing the waste water from being pumped into the drain. As a result, the waste is pumped through the hose. The hose is led through a basement window to a point far from the house where the flood waters cannot re-enter the ground at the foundation to flood the basement a second time.

While not a permanent cure for a flooded basement, this method does prevent flooding the septic system and keeps the basement dry.

THE HOT-WATER SYSTEM

If at present your hot-water system is connected to your home heating plant and a supply of hot water all summer means keeping the furnace operating, you can benefit by installing an "independent" hot-water system, one which will run only in the summer. This takes the strain off the furnace and reduces fuel consumption.

Or, maybe, you have a summer place and would like hot water there just as you have in your home all winter long. You can have it by installing the system yourself. It's not a difficult job, but you need four things: (1) cold water under pressure, (2) a heater, (3) a storage tank, and (4) pipe to conduct hot water from the storage tank to the faucets.

If your water is drawn from a well by hand pump or bucket, you'll have to put off this idea until a pressure system is installed.

The heater you select depends upon your preference and needs. The heat to warm the water as it passes through the coils of the heater can come from burning wood, coal, gas or oil, or electricity.

The more you know about how the system operates, the better job you'll do in installing it. Note in Figure 1 in the first system that the water flows from the source into the storage tank through the top and down a pipe inside the tank. It goes out through the lower side pipe into the coils of the heater and re-enters the tank from the heater near the upper end. When the heater is on, the water in the coil becomes

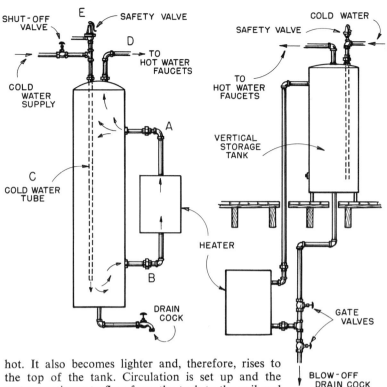

SHUT-OFF VALVE

E

SAFETY VALVE

D

TO HOT WATER FAUCETS

COLD WATER SUPPLY

A

C

COLD WATER TUBE

HEATER

B

DRAIN COCK

COLD WATER

SAFETY VALVE

TO HOT WATER FAUCETS

VERTICAL STORAGE TANK

GATE VALVES

BLOW-OFF DRAIN COCK

Figure 1. Traditional water-heater hook-up with heater beside tank is shown at far left. While this system is efficient, the hookup shown next to it is better. Placing heater well below storage tank level increases amount of hot water stored, saves on fuel bill.

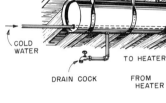

TO HOT WATER FAUCETS

COLD WATER

DRAIN COCK

TO HEATER

FROM HEATER

Figure 2. How to hang storage tank from joist.

hot. It also becomes lighter and, therefore, rises to the top of the tank. Circulation is set up and the water continues to flow from the tank to the coil and back to the tank.

When the faucet in the house is turned on, it draws the water from the top of the tank where its temperature is highest. Cold water will flow into the lower part of the tank to replace the hot water drawn out. If the cold water entered at the *top* of the tank, it would mix with the hot water—a condition called "shorting"—and at best you'd get lukewarm water.

There's a safety valve at the top of the tank. If the heater runs a long time and no water is drawn off, steam develops under pressure. This valve, often required by law, but a must for safety whether legally required or not, allows steam to escape without causing damage. Finally, you'll note a short pipe and a drain cock at the bottom of the tank to permit getting rid of rust and sediment that collect at the bottom.

The second system in Figure 1 is ideally located. The heater is in the basement or even in a shed outside the house. The higher the heater is placed alongside the tank, the more difficult it is to heat all the water. Sometimes, to keep the heater lower than the tank, the tank is placed horizontally. It is suspended from the floor beams exposed in the basement by means of perforated metal straps (see Figure 2). Although common practice, this is not the best. The water in the lower half of the tank is lukewarm, as a rule. And the sediment is distributed over a larger area.

No matter where you locate the heater and tank, installation is about the same. Sketches 3 to 8 show the progressive steps. After the system is completely connected, (1) open the faucet at the sink or tub, (2) turn on the water at the cold water supply, and (3) wait for the tank to fill and the water to come out of the sink faucet. The system is now full, so shut off the sink faucet and then start the heater. Never turn on a heater unless it has water in it.

In making the pipe connections to hook up the hot-water heater, you can use either $\frac{1}{2}$ or $\frac{3}{4}$" pipe, depending upon the amount of water you need. When joining two pipes, coat the threaded joint with pipe joint compound, wrap it several times with pipe joint cord (a loose cotton thread in multiple strands), and screw into the other pipe by hand; then tighten with a wrench. The rule-of-thumb is that each threaded end extends into the fitting as deep as its own diameter. Furthermore, use unions where indicated for they make possible disconnecting sections of pipe or even the entire tank or heater without disturbing the system. When connecting any sections of pipe where unions are used at each end, it's best to assemble that pipe completely and then insert it between unions.

Where pipe is run along walls or floors or open beams in the basement, use metal pipe clamps to hold it firmly.

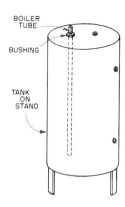

BOILER TUBE

BUSHING

TANK ON STAND

Figure 3. To install system, insert boiler tube, as the cold-water intake pipe is called. There is a bushing that fits into tank opening through which this tube passes. Brass pipe is better than iron, for it won't rust. Copper can be used, but it requires a special flared end at the bushing so that it can be connected to the cold water supply.

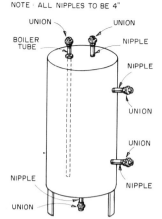

NOTE: ALL NIPPLES TO BE 4"

UNION   UNION

BOILER TUBE   NIPPLE

NIPPLE

UNION

UNION

NIPPLE   NIPPLE

UNION

Figure 4. Next, attach 4" nipples—short lengths of pipe with both ends threaded—to each of the other tank openings: one on top, two on the side, and one on the bottom. Add a union to the end of each and also to the boiler tube you installed in the preceding step. This permits you to take the tank out without disturbing the entire system.

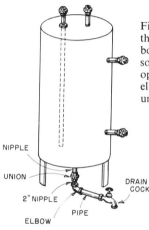

NIPPLE

UNION

2" NIPPLE

PIPE

ELBOW

DRAIN COCK

Figure 5. Install a drain cock, a valve with its end threaded so you can connect a garden hose to tank bottom. First, connect a length of pipe to drain cock so it extends beyond tank legs. Add an elbow to opposite end of pipe and insert a short 2" nipple into elbow. Connect nipple and entire pipe assembly to union at bottom of tank.

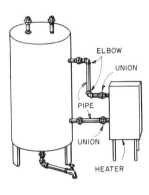

ELBOW

UNION

PIPE

UNION

HEATER

Figure 6. Before you connect heater to tank, add a union to each of the threaded openings of the heater. The lower opening of heater goes to lower opening of tank and the two upper ones are also connected. See Figure 1 on what to avoid; other sketches indicate correct way of making this connection without unusual angles in the connecting pipe.

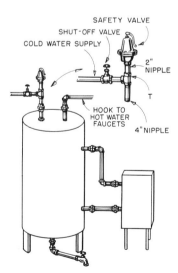

SAFETY VALVE

SHUT-OFF VALVE

COLD WATER SUPPLY

2" NIPPLE

T

HOOK TO HOT WATER FAUCETS

4" NIPPLE

Figure 7. Connect necessary pipe from hot water take-off (upper right on boiler) to sink or tub faucet. Next, add a short nipple to boiler tube (upper left on boiler), then a T. To top of T add 4" nipple with safety valve on other end. In center of T insert a short nipple, then a shut-off valve. Then connect to cold water supply line.

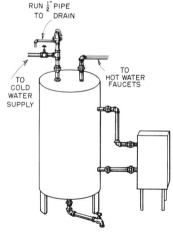

RUN ½" PIPE TO DRAIN

TO COLD WATER SUPPLY

TO HOT WATER FAUCETS

Figure 8. To prevent water from splashing all over if safety valve blows, insert a short ½" pipe nipple into side opening of valve. Connect additional pipe to carry this run-off to a drain or dry well in the basement. Keep this pipe end free and open; it should be lower than the top of the tank, preferably near the floor level

THE SEPTIC SYSTEM

To homeowners with a septic tank, spring and early summer often bring a dismal reminder that all is not well in this hidden system of pipes and tanks. Everything is out of sight. No one can readily determine if there's trouble until it shows itself. That trouble is there is unmistakably revealed by one or more of the following signs:

1. The house drain backs up, and sewage fails to flow by gravity, or even force, into the system. It's a sure sign that the system is clogged to capacity—barring, of course, the unlikely possibility of a clogged drain between the house and the tank. Or the drainfields might be flooded; possibly spring rains have been heavy and the ground cannot absorb any more water.

2. Low-placed drain vents suddenly boil over with sewage. In this case, it's certain that bacteriological action in the overfilled tank has forced waste material to back up in the drain pipe.

3. The ground along the drainfields or near the tank erupts with gas or bubbles. The chances are that the tank is inadequate, thereby forcing untreated sewage into the drainfield where further bacterial action is taking place. Flooded fields may cause similar symptoms.

4. Grass and other growing plants along the drainfields take on a darker hue and grow more vigorously than elsewhere. This is a sign that non-sterile sewage has been forced upward through the gravel surrounding the drain tiles.

To understand the septic system is part of the battle of getting it to work properly. The main part of the system is the septic tank (see sketch below). It is the discharge point for the house sewage line. Since the flow into the tank is rapid, a baffle is provided to prevent the flow of sewage from immediately being discharged from the opposite side into the drainfield. Heavier contents in the sewage are deposited in the bottom of the tank. Only the liquids enter the drainfield at once. It should be noted at this point that the tank is always filled with liquid right up to the lower level of the discharge pipe.

Bacterial action takes place at the bottom of the tank. Heavier materials are reduced to liquid for subsequent discharge into the drainfields. The drainfields consist of drain tiles, usually 4″ in diameter, spaced from $\frac{1}{2}$ to 1″ apart in a gravel trench which is about 24″ deep. The tiles are placed on 6″ of gravel and the joints are covered with a strip of tarpaper. Then they are buried in more gravel to within 4 to 6″ from the ground surface. Soil and sod cover the gravel.

Liquids seep either through the gravel into the ground below or upward to be consumed by plantings, or else they are discharged into the air by evaporation.

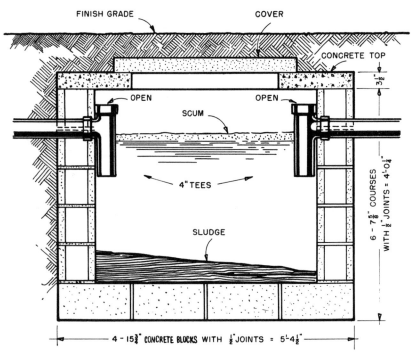

Typical cross-section of septic tank. Pipe with T serves the purpose of a wood baffle; it must not be closed at ends. Sod over cover is removed for sludge removal periodically.

When the telltale signs of septic tank trouble appear, it's time for immediate action. Trouble can usually be traced to the following causes: inadequate tank, inadequate drainfields, clogged drainfields, sluggish bacterial action or a dirty tank.

The first step is to clean the tank. This is a job you'll have someone else do. Call in a professional septic tank cleaning service and have your tank pumped out. After it has been emptied and thoroughly cleaned, you might want to check its size or inspect the drainfield, but more about that later. Next, the tank must be treated by adding a bacteriological agent, a chemical which reduces solids to liquids. Make it a regular practice to flush stimulants into the system four times a year down any drain or directly into the tank after it has been cleaned.

The Tank. While the tank is empty, you can take the opportunity to determine if it is large enough to meet the demands of your household. Tank capacity should be figured roughly to hold about 75 gallons per person per day. For example, for a family of four, the tank capacity would be 300 gallons. It should be pointed out again here that the tank is never filled to the top. It is filled only to the level of the discharge pipe. Therefore, for this family of four requiring a 300-gallon capacity, the tank must hold about 500 gallons. It is always best to add about another two-thirds to the family's requirement to determine the size of the tank needed. Another point to remember in computing the family's tank needs is the possibility of additional members in the family and the use of water-consuming laundry equipment. Both mean an increase in tank size. Determining the size by the number of rooms in the house is another method you can use. If you have a guest room, then you sometimes have additional people in the house and, therefore, need a larger tank.

The Drainfield. The most common cause of a clogged drainfield is root growth. After the tank has

been cleaned and the bacterial chemical agents added, clean the drainfield. Since it is constantly moist, roots seek it in dry weather and penetrate between the loosely laid tiles. This root action dislodges or plugs the tiles. Furthermore, where the tank is small, sediment may be forced into the drain tiles and gradually close them. At one time, boring out the tiles with an electrically-operated reamer was the only solution. However, chemicals are available now which reduce all deposits to a liquid state so that they are disposed of by seepage into the gravel. Add these chemicals at the point where the drain tiles leave the tank. Since this treatment should be periodic—once every three months—a capped vertical drain is built between the ground surface and the

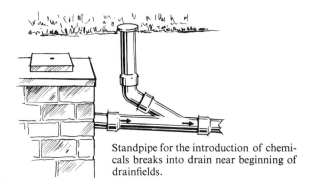

Standpipe for the introduction of chemicals breaks into drain near beginning of drainfields.

T tile with cover is another effective means for the introduction of chemicals.

A distribution box makes it a simple matter to introduce chemicals safely into several drainfields.

SEPTIC TANK SIZES

Number of persons in house	Tank size should be
4	500 gallons
6	600 gallons
8	750 gallons
10	900 gallons
12	1100 gallons

Number of feet of drainfield (18″ wide, 18″ to 30″ deep) required per person in the following soil types:

Coarse sand and gravel	40′
Sandy clay	80′
Clay with little sand or gravel	150′
Fine sand	60′

end of the tile line through which the chemical can be poured.

After the tank has been cleaned, the chemicals added and the drain tiles unclogged, there may still be trouble. It's possible that the size of the drainfield is inadequate. To check its size, climb down into the tank (or have it done for you) and, with a plumber's snake or any long, strong wire inserted into the drain tiles, measure the length of the various lines. The drainfield size is based on the size of the tank and the absorption qualities of the soil in which the fields are laid. In general, the drainfield gallon capacity should be one-half the capacity of the tank. Since this is a difficult measurement to make, try the easier method of digging a 1' square hole about 18" deep and pouring 6" of water into it. Then check the time required for the water level to drop 1". To do this, set a wooden ruler into the bottom of the hole; if the water falls 1" in less than 5 minutes, the drainfield capacity needed is about 25' of tile per person in the household. If the water takes over 10 minutes, figure on 50' of tile per person. For example, if the water drops 1" in less than 5 minutes and there are four people living in the house, you need about 100' of tile in the drainfield. But if the water drop takes over 10 minutes with four people in the house, you need about 200' of tile in the field.

Soil quality is important in a drainfield. Porous soil is good; you'll need only a short drainfield. Heavy clay, rocky ground or near-surface hardpan will absorb water slowly and may mean trouble in the future. In the event that the ground is poor for proper drainage, or the area is not large enough for an adequate field, leaching pools may be substituted for drainfields. These are small, cistern-shaped underground reservoirs into which the septic tank flow is directed through sealed pipelines. The bottom is bare earth; the sides are fieldstone or concrete blocks with occasional holes providing space for seepage. The

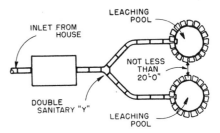

Typical plan view of septic system with leaching pools supplementing drainfields. Ideal for properties of limited area.

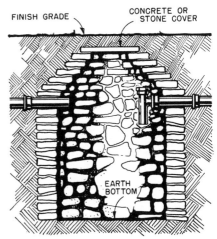

Cross-section of leaching pool made of field stone. As a supplement to drainfields, it should not need cleaning for years.

pools require a concrete cover over which plantings can be made in the 4 to 6" of soil above the cover. The cover must be strong enough to support the earth and ordinary traffic around the house grounds. The combined capacity of the leaching pools should be 50 per cent of the tank capacity.

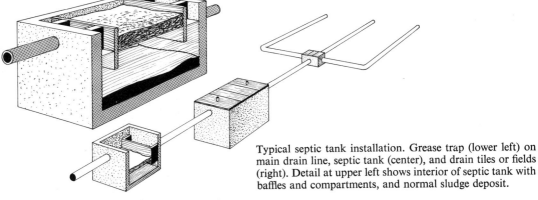

Typical septic tank installation. Grease trap (lower left) on main drain line, septic tank (center), and drain tiles or fields (right). Detail at upper left shows interior of septic tank with baffles and compartments, and normal sludge deposit.

WATER CONDITIONING

Few homes have *pure* water. Although drinkable and reasonably clear, most home water supplies are loaded with chemicals and minerals, gases, unpleasant tastes and smells, dirt, and decayed vegetable matter. Such water can be vastly improved with inexpensive filtering and conditioning devices which you can easily install yourself.

Rain water is considered "soft," free of minerals, but owing to stagnant storage, it is apt to be loaded with vegetable substances. Some of these produce corroding gases and unpleasant tastes and odors. Water from other sources almost invariably has tiny, usually invisible, particles of mineral and chemical matter. These substances are deposited on the inside of pipes, storage tanks and boilers. When such water is heated, the rate of deposit is increased so that hot-water systems suffer more.

The greatest water problem in practically all parts of the country is that of "hard" water. This is mineral-loaded water. It gradually clogs water pipes to the point where flow is stopped (see photograph below). It defies soap, forming curds which cling to clothing, hair, skin and dishes. Detergents place most minerals in suspension, but these are still deposited on all touched surfaces and are difficult to rinse away.

Another frequent cause of trouble is "red" water, which is water loaded with iron or one of iron's many chemical variants. Other minerals, too, are often found in combination with iron. Water that contains these elements and drips from a faucet quickly stains porcelain fixtures. The minerals and gases with them etch through iron and brass pipe, particularly at joints. The joints leak and grow blooms of corrosion, and pipes develop pinhole leaks. Boilers and storage tanks suffer the same fate.

You can make several tests of your water supply. It's important to your home economy that you know what you have to contend with.

1. If your source of supply hasn't been tested for bacterial count, ask your druggist where such a test can be made. While water supplied by municipal systems is usually treated to destroy all harmful bacteria, the treated water often has an unpleasant odor, which can be removed.

2. Take a sample of hot and cold water in corked bottles and let stand for several days, then note the sediment at the bottom of the bottles. Any visible sediment is removable by filtering.

3. Buy an ounce of tincture of green soap. Half fill a 1-ounce bottle with water, add a drop of the soap, cork and shake the bottle. Continue adding a drop of soap at a time until the shaken bottle fills with rich suds. Count the drops you have used, then multiply by 2.5 to get a measurable rating of the mineral content of the water. Treatment devices are scaled to handle water of varying degrees of hardness measured in this manner.

Some communities are treating water to make it mineral-free as well as safe to drink. For the most part, however, this water treatment is a matter that the homeowner must attend to himself.

Hard water can be made soft by passing it through a special sand known as zeolite. Zeolite removes the calcium and magnesium compounds which make water hard. The cost of operation is practically nothing since the zeolite's useful properties can be restored by treatment with common salt.

While you can install a filtering device capable of handling *all* the water your home uses, it is not necessary. Filter only the water used for drinking, cooking, laundry and bath. Your lawn, for example, does not need filtered water. A re-piping arrangement to split the water supply between filtered and unfiltered water is shown in Sketch A on the next page. You can install a water-treating unit yourself with little effort. The type you select will determine somewhat how and where it is installed. Conditioners, as contrasted with water softeners, are used to remove objectionable matter from water, but they do not soften water in all cases. They do remove odors and gases and corrosive elements. In some areas, it would be a good plan to install both a softener and a conditioner.

Opened section of pipe, showing mineral deposit. Heaters and boilers become clogged the same way and 'will eventually burn out.

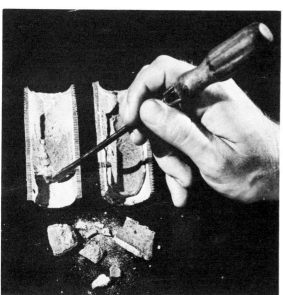

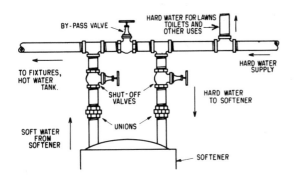

A. It isn't necessary to filter all your water. To split your supply, an arrangement like this can be used, with some water by-passing the softener and conditioner.

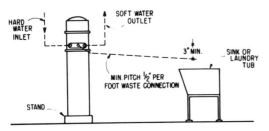

B. Pipe and drain connections for one type of unit. An open sink is necessary for process of regenerating zeolite in softener. Drain line must pitch minimum of ½″ per foot.

After making your own tests and deciding that you need water softening or conditioning equipment, take a water sample to a dealer who will help you select the necessary equipment.

In the average home, an installation will pay for itself in a year or two in lowered soap and plumbing bills.

DETERGENTS

Suds are fine in a washing machine, but they have no business bubbling up out of sinks, bathtubs or floor drains. There are only two likely reasons for the sudden appearance of suds where they aren't wanted —an overproduction of suds in the first place or a stoppage (or partial stoppage) of the drain itself. More often, the cause is the first, since a backwash of suds alone isn't apt to occur with a drain stoppage. The stoppage in a drain would back up suds, water and anything else.

If too much suds is the cause, prevention lies in using a detergent that doesn't produce as many—or none at all. The quick cure, if you happen to catch the backwash of suds in time, lies in salt. Common table salt sprinkled on the suds will quickly dissolve them. More used in the drain will clear it shortly. If you aren't apt to be around, you can install a drain-

closer for floor drains, which are often flooded owing to their position. But you can't stopper a sink or a tub with any success since the overflow openings near the top rim of sink and tub can't be sealed. Needed here is a backflow valve, a type of check valve which can also be installed instead of a closer on the floor drain. The backflow valve (see sketch) allows waste

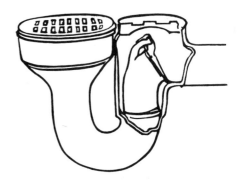

water to flow into the drain because the brass flap is pushed up and away from the opening by the pressure of water. The flap then falls of its own weight, and no water or suds can push it up from the opposite side. Installation of the valve shown here is simple; the old drain trap can be removed and this type substituted. There's a clean-out on this type of valve so it can be inspected and cleaned now and then, if needed.

These solutions are all right if you have a one-story house. But if you happen to live in a multi-storied building, or on the lower floor of a duplex structure, the situation can get complicated. You don't know when your neighbors are going to use their washing machines, nor can you control their choice of detergents. *Your* drains can be clogged with *their* excess suds. The problem of too much suds is fairly common in multi-family dwellings. Wash water containing high-sudsing detergents flows down vertical drains or "stacks" with a spiral motion. This agitates the suds water even more, and an excess is created inside the drain. The same thing occurs in a single-family home where the washing machine is on the first floor and there is an open floor drain (or laundry tubs) on the floor or basement below. The column of suds builds up inside the vertical drain—it can build up as high as four stories!—and eventually the pressure forces the suds out of all open drains.

The word "detergent" is very widely misused. Actually the word describes any cleansing agent. This includes soap as well as the synthetic, or non-soap, detergents. To avoid confusion, people in the trade have coined the word "syndet" to distinguish *syn*thetic *de*tergents from soap, which is a combination of fat and potash or soda.

In hard water, soap combines with minerals in the water and forms a curd or film which will not dissolve. It gets on clothes and produces what has been called "tattletale gray" on white clothes and discolors or dulls colors of other kinds of cloth. It also makes the ring in a bathtub—an indication of hard water. Perspiration, or any other mildly acid material, neutralizes the effectiveness of soaps and more must be used. Suds increase as a result. Syndets, on the other hand, do not combine with the minerals in hard water and form no curd, no film, no bathtub ring. If the question arises, then, as to which is better—soap or detergent—the answer depends on the hardness of the water being used. In soft water, soap and syndet are equally effective. In hard water, the syndet is better. But with the use of a syndet, you have a choice as to non-sudsing or full-sudsing types. Here,

then, lies the answer to prevention of the suds-clogged drains. Choose a syndet that will be non-sudsing when released from the machine into a drain. The high-sudsing type of syndet was the first placed on the market. Housewives were accustomed to seeing suds in wash water and wanted to continue doing so. Besides, a 2″ layer of suds on wash water was a good way to determine whether enough was being used. Since this quick guide to adequate cleanser isn't possible with the non-sudsing syndet, measuring is needed—but troublesome excess suds are eliminated.

Both types of syndets should be used as directed. Too much of the high-sudsing type will flood the washing machine with suds and will certainly overflow the drain. In general, low-sudsing syndets do as good a job as the high-suds type. In rotating washers they are probably superior.

CHAPTER 5

THE EXTERIOR OF THE HOUSE

The Roof · The Outer Walls · The Foundation

This chapter deals with the outside of your house, from top to bottom. The old adage that "you can't tell a book by its cover" doesn't hold true as an analogy when it comes to judging a house, for you *can* tell a good deal about a house from its cover—its roof, outer walls and foundation.

You can tell whether the house has been well taken care of or whether it's been allowed to deteriorate, whether it's watertight or damp, whether its foundation is good and sturdy or apt to crack and let the house sag.

Aside from the problems of, and the answers to, year-round maintenance and repair, you'll find much in this chapter aimed at *prevention* of damage and deterioration, the many little things which, tended to immediately, go far toward eliminating major repairs and high, needless bills.

THE ROOF Remedies for a leaky roof · Gutters and downspouts · Snow and ice · Flashing care and repair · Retread your roof for a sun deck

While the greater part of the roof over your head is hidden from view, it's important that you know just how it's put together, for you may have to locate a sudden leak; you will need to know what *not* to touch if you plan any remodeling and, when budgeting winter fuel bills, you will certainly need to know whether or not your roof is insulated and to what extent. The diagram on pages 270 and 271 will serve as a preliminary guide to your roof and its maintenance.

The proper care of gutters and downspouts prevents water damage to walls and saves what may later become serious expense. Snow and ice on the roof don't have to be hazardous; safety measures are simple if they're taken in time. Effective, water-repellent flashing will add years, not only to the life of the roof, but to the entire house. Generally speaking, a good sturdy roof depends upon *prevention* of damage as much as it does on immediate repairs. Before doing any work on the roof, be sure to study the rules and photographs on the next page. You'll appreciate the confidence that comes with sure footing and ladder security.

REMEDIES FOR A LEAKY ROOF

A leaky roof can cause serious damage to your home and its furnishings. Even a damp and discolored ceiling spells trouble. Joists will rot, and in due time a plastered ceiling is quite likely to fall. The first step toward a cure is to locate the leak, which is not always obvious. Careful examination should be made of the underside of the roof over the wet ceiling area. If the house has an open attic, you can easily trace trickling water to its source by the marks it makes on the underside of the roof. It may run along a strip of roof sheathing or a rafter and then along a joist, or it may originate in the flashing on a chimney, a dormer, the plumbing system's vent pipe, an adjoining wall or a valley formed by the junction of two roof sections. Upon locating the leak, drive a thin finishing nail up through the roof (except slate or tile) to mark the spot on the outside. On the inside, put a chalk mark around the nail, but nothing more for the moment.

Should the space between the joists and the roof be closed, an examination must be made of the outer roofing itself. (Use the ladder safety practices as illustrated.) Look for cracked, rotted or missing wood shingles, cracked tile or slate, curled or torn composition shingles, for rust and crevices in a metal roof and for openings and defects in flashing. A loose or cracked board high under a gable may be the source of trouble. Often a leak can be located by pouring water on the suspect spot on the roof top and having someone watch for the results inside the house.

Methods of stopping leaks vary with the type of roofing material used, but all are relatively simple. A broken tile should be mended with asphalt cement or one of the name-brand cements manufactured for that purpose. On roll roofing, a patch of asphalt cement or tar mixed with fine sand will do the trick. Where the composition is particularly bad, a new piece of roll roofing should be cemented and nailed (use only galvanized or other rust-resisting nails for roofing) in place. Curled composition shingles can be cemented and nailed down again. Any holes should be filled with asphalt cement.

10 RULES FOR LADDER SAFETY

1. If your ladder is wood, lay it flat and walk along the rungs. You'll find the weak ones—safely—this way.
2. Don't use a wood ladder that has been painted. You can't see weak spots through a coat of paint.
3. Don't try to put up a ladder where there are power-line wires overhead.
4. Select a level, solid resting place for the feet of the ladder.
5. Place the feet of the ladder one-fourth its length away from the wall. At this angle you can't overbalance and fall backward.
6. Before you start carrying materials up the ladder, be sure you have a place to put them when you get to the top.
7. Cans of liquid materials should be fitted with hooks on handles so they can be hung from the ladder.
8. If there's a strong wind blowing, stay on the ground.
9. Don't carry tools loosely in your pocket. They may fall on someone down below.
10. Don't try to reach from the ladder. Take the time to move over.

To raise a ladder safely, prop the base against a wall, raise the upper end over your head, and walk in hand over hand until the ladder is upright.

When raising an extension ladder, brace the base against your foot, lift ladder away from house and pull rope to extend the ladder to the desired height.

Use both hands when climbing a ladder. Make certain bottom is secure on the ground and that the ladder is at the proper angle against the wall.

Remedies for a Leaky Roof   269

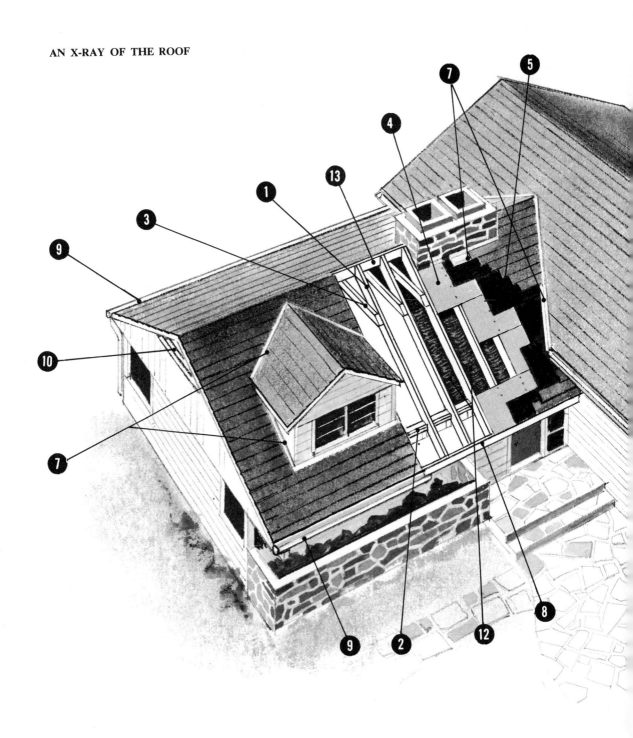

1. **Rafters**—main roof supports.

2. **Top Plate of Walls**—on which rafters rest.

3. **Collar Beam**—prevents outward thrust of rafters, which would push walls apart.

4. **Sheathing**—covers rafters, joins them rigidly, provides support for roofing material.

5. **Felt**—waterproof barrier to any rain penetrating through shingles.

6. **Shingles**—the outer roof covering.

7. **Flashing**—metal lining for joints around chimney, at junctions of walls and roof, and at junction of two sections of the roof.

8. **Fascia**—trim strip at eaves covering rafter ends.

9. **Gutters**—to conduct rain from the roof to rainspouts.

10. **Louvers**—used to provide ventilation to the underside of the roof, and to spaces directly under the roof.

11. **Roll-Type Roofing Material**—used on flat roofs and those where pitch is less than 23°, where shingles would admit rain.

12. **Insulation**—placed between rafters and over collar beams to keep artificial heat inside, and in some cases to exclude radiant sun rays.

13. **Ridge**—thin board between upper rafter ends, joining sets to each other.

TYPES OF ROOFS

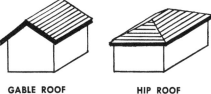

GABLE ROOF   HIP ROOF

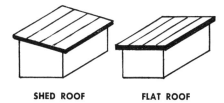

SHED ROOF   FLAT ROOF

Where whole shingles are torn or gone, you'll need replacements, but first remove the old shreds. Carefully raise the next good shingle above and draw out all the nails you can reach. Those out of range can be driven flat by resting an iron strip or long screwdriver on the nailhead and hitting the strip or blade with a hammer. Slip the new shingle into place and insert nails under the overhanging good shingle and drive them down. Along hip joints, where pieces of shingles have been angled over the ridge, breaks occur often in winter. Remove the broken pieces and replace them in the same manner as the first were laid (see illustrations). Cover the hip with roofing asphalt first; then cut the necessary number of pieces from whole shingles and start at the lower end of the patch. Continue on up to the sound rows of pieces and insert the final new piece under this. Tack all down at two exposed corners and set nails to go through the two concealed corners of the last one laid. Finally, return to the attic, find the chalk mark you made earlier and coat the interior surface with roofing asphalt; spread a large section of tarpaper over the patch and hold it in place with a piece of wood jammed and toenailed between rafters.

SHINGLE REPAIRS

1. Small breaks in shingles can be patched with a spread of roofing asphalt.
2. To remove broken shingle, pry up next one to get at shingle nails.

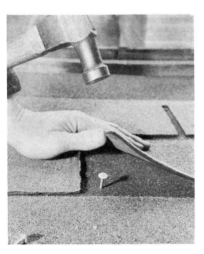

3. Nail down new shingle by carefully raising edges of the shingle above.
4. If old shingles are brittle, press nail in with thumb, then drive it as shown.
5. To repair hip covering, apply asphalt liberally as a base under new shingles.

6. Overlap the new shingle pieces at least two inches, nailing down all four corners.
7. Where leaks are discovered, coat the underside of the roof with asphalt.
8. Spread tarpaper over asphalt, then hold patch in place with a 1 × 3 strip.

If a slate shingle is broken, remove it by inserting a hacksaw blade under the shingle and cutting off the nails which hold it in place. Slip a sheet of galvanized iron or copper into the slot occupied by the shingle and nail it into place as close as possible to the bottom of the shingle in the next course above. Cut the sheet metal long enough so the bottom end can be bent up and curled around the exposed end of the new shingle slipped into place.

Slate shingles can be held down with asphalt under lower edges and joints painted with asphalt. Knock out broken shingles with hammer.

SLATE ROOF REPAIRS

1. Seal cracks that have widened into possible sources of leaks with a plastic roof cement.

2. Necessary tool is a slate puller—a piece of strap iron bent and notched as shown. You may have to make one, or have it made for you.

→

3. Insert puller under slate, hook notches over nails, then drive puller back with hammer to draw out nails. There are two nails per slate.

4. If a slate must be cut to fit, first score each side deeply with a screwdriver or a cold chisel. Scored lines should be matched up evenly.

5. Hold scored slate on some solid base and tap lightly along scored lines with hammer. This deepens the scored mark.

6. Lay slate flat after tapping the mark. Slate will break evenly but with a ragged edge.

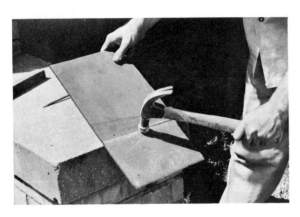

7. By holding slate at an angle on a masonry surface, then tapping along edge, the raggedness is smoothed.

8. Slip the new slate into position temporarily and mark its surface with a nail or awl where nail holes are to be drilled.

9. Heavy nail or center punch can be used to make holes in slate. Use one sharp blow of hammer to make holes while propping slate up on a block.

10. Final step is to cover roof area under new slate with roofing cement. Insert drilled slate and drive nails through holes.

A flat roof covered with heavy felt is subject to leaks just as is any shingle roof. Potential trouble is indicated by blisters in the roofing material which ultimately crack, and a leak is in the making. See the illustrations below for repair methods.

Holes in flashing can be repaired with asphalt cement. Fine sand should be worked into the cement if it is too thin. Eroded flashing should be mended with a new piece of metal. Cut it to size with snips or an old pair of scissors and crimp it to the necessary shape. Cement it in place with asphalt. Tin roofs and valley flashing are repaired with patches of asphalt cement and repainted at intervals to protect them from the weather.

FLAT ROOF REPAIRS

1. Here a bulge has burst, a chunk of the roofing material has blown away, and the roofing asphalt is exposed, allowing a leak.

2. With a linoleum knife, cut back from the break to remove all loose roofing that has lifted away from the protective layers below it.

3. Using a trowel, spread a liberal coat of roofing asphalt over the uncovered edges. This asphalt spreads best above 70°.

4. Cut a section of new roofing felt so that it extends about 2″ all around to provide an overlap. This will help prevent leaks. →

Remedies for a Leaky Roof 275

5. Set the patch on the roofing asphalt spread over the hole and press it down heavily. Stamp on it—but take care of your shoes!

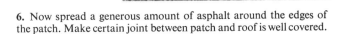

6. Now spread a generous amount of asphalt around the edges of the patch. Make certain joint between patch and roof is well covered.

7. If your roof is exposed to high winds, better anchor the patch with roofing nails. Then cover all nailheads with asphalt.

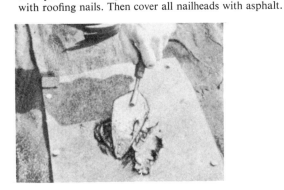

8. When you've finished patching, spread dry sand over the new asphalt. It helps to protect the roof from the elements.

SOME TROUBLE SPOTS

1. Where roofing ends at roof edge, it may curl upward. Nail this section flat; then coat edge and nail-heads with roofing asphalt.
2. Dirt often collects in depressions on the roof. Sweep area carefully, for new application of asphalt won't stick if there are loose particles.
3. Roofing asphalt sometimes softens and runs down slopes to form a crust over hollows. Then it cracks. Therefore cover these areas well.

276   THE EXTERIOR OF THE HOUSE : Remedies for a Leaky Roof

GUTTERS AND DOWNSPOUTS

Architects plan to keep gutters inconspicuous. They are tucked up under or into the eaves so they appear as little more than another line or two of trim. As a result, many homeowners do not know what material has been used in the construction of their gutters, and sometimes not even if there are any on the roof at all. But the gutters are important. Thousands of gallons of water may fall onto the roof of an average house each year, and weakened and imperfect gutters and downspouts are easy prey for heavy spring rains. The weight of snow and ice may pull gutters away from the house or loosen the downspout straps. Rust and wear may result in holes in the gutter. Clogged and frozen downspouts may develop seam cracks, and rain flowing off the roof may go down the house wall, wetting it sufficiently to cause interior wall damage. Also, water rushing down a cracked downspout will create a greater opening and result in a flood instead of the water draining into a dry well or sewer pipe. Armed with only a few tools and patching materials, you can easily forestall any serious damage.

Clogged Gutters and Downspouts. Leaves, twigs and other miscellaneous debris often choke gutters and spouts, causing roof water to back up. Make it a point to clean out your gutters with a stiff brush regularly. Check the gutter slope so you always maintain a $\frac{1}{4}$" per foot drop to downspouts. You can check on a clogged downspout by seeing whether the water backs up into the gutter during a heavy rain. In a dry spell, turn the garden hose into the gutter to see if a back-up occurs. Should the spout appear clogged, the easiest way to clean it is to feed a plumber's sewer auger into it from the top, turning it until you have loosened the obstruction. The water

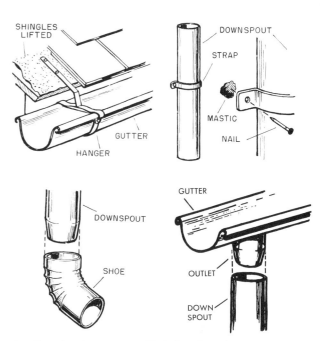

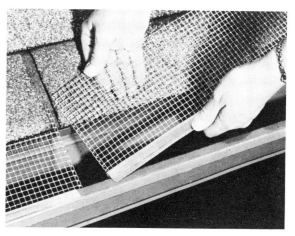

standing in the gutter will help clean it out as it washes down after the obstruction has been broken.

You can prevent clogging or blocking of downspouts by using a $\frac{1}{4}$" mesh screen over the top of the downspout opening. Built cone-shaped and inserted in the downspout opening, it permits a free water flow but holds back leaves, sticks and other debris. The lower ends of downspouts may be handled in either of two ways: left open with a splash block (a channeled shelf of concrete 2" thick and gutter-shaped) to conduct the water at least 4' away from the house foundation; or else closed, in which case

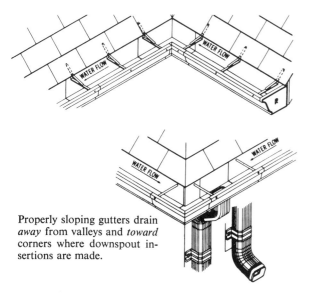

Properly sloping gutters drain *away* from valleys and *toward* corners where downspout insertions are made.

Keep gutters free of blocking debris by covering with gutter screens; these slip under shingles, over gutter, diverting debris over edge.

the water flows through a drain from the downspout to a distant dry well or storm drain. Each has advantages. Ice and debris carried from the gutters are more easily removed from the open type. The closed type, however, can be set below the frost line so that freeze-ups never occur. A guard above prevents the entry of debris.

Sagging Gutters and Loose Downspouts. If a gutter sags, water or melted snow will accumulate in the sagging portion and freeze, and the weight of the ice may prove great enough to pull the gutter entirely away from the house. You can usually check for sags by simply sighting along the gutter. Or pour a pitcherful of water into the gutter at the end away from the downspout. All the water should run out promptly. If any pools or puddles remain, they indicate sags at those points. Correction of a sagging gutter will depend on the type of hanger used. Hangers are commonly of two kinds, cast or strap. The cast hanger has two parts: a shank fastened to the wall or roof, and a bracket which holds the gutter trough. Shank and bracket are held together with a nut and bolt, and additional bolt holes are provided so the height of the bracket can be adjusted. If the gutter is sagging, unbolt one or two of the hangers nearest to the sag, lift the brackets (and the gutter),

Left, a cast hanger. Right, a typical strap hanger.

and rebolt. Strap hangers, being flexible, can sometimes be bent sufficiently to correct a small sag. If bending doesn't do the job, you will have to reset the hanger or hangers. To add a new hanger, all you have to do is lift the shingle along the roof edge, taking care not to break it, and secure the hanger to the gutter, setting the hanger bar flat on the roof. (Use large-head, coated nails.) Then spread asphalt or calking compound over the nail heads to seal the entire area and replace the shingle. The technique used for tightening an existing hanger is similar.

Straps holding downspouts should be securely attached to the wall. If any nails have worked loose, remove them and replace with new ones. To prevent water seepage through the nail hole, apply asphalt or calking between the strap and the wall. Then press the strap into place and nail securely. The mastic forms a seal around the nail.

Patching. Rust is the greatest enemy of galvanized gutters. Painting the outside is not sufficient to prevent rust holes. Clean the gutters thoroughly with a steel

Left, above: Metal gutter has become corroded, metal is eaten away, and repair is badly needed.

Left, below: Glass-fiber cloth is cut to fit, saturated with resin, and smoothed over hole.

Below: After 20 minutes of full sunshine or sun-ray lamp, patch is complete. Paint to match.

wire brush. Badly pitted spots may have to be sanded, since a corrosion-free surface is necessary for repairs. At any corroded spots, apply a coating of asphalt on the inside of the gutter, extending about 6″ on either side of the hole. Then lay a piece of asphalt-impregnated glass membrane or a piece of burlap or aluminum sheeting over the area. Apply another coat of asphalt over the entire area. If the damage is extensive, cut a length of identical gutter material, cement it down with asphalt and crimp the outer edge to hold fast and, finally, seal the joints with asphalt.

Narrow, short cracks in downspouts can be mended by filling the hole with asphalt mastic. When dry, it's hard enough to withstand normal water pressure. On the other hand, if there's a large crack, it's necessary to replace the section. If the cracked part is a separate section, such as an elbow, disconnect by pulling it apart and set a new unit in place. But if the crack is located in the major section of the downspout, its replacement is advised. Remove the straps, and the spout can be lowered and pulled away from the gutter. A new one is pushed up into position and held by straps.

MAKING SIMPLE REPAIRS

Coat gutter inside with asphalt, using a paintbrush and smoothing as much as possible.

Cover with burlap, pressing smoothly with a brush. Add second coat of asphalt.

REPAIRING EXTENSIVE DAMAGE

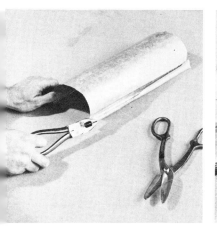

Cut length of identically shaped gutter and flare beaded outer edges with pliers.

Coat area with asphalt, fit metal patch over coated area and press down firmly.

Crimp outer beaded edge over lip of old gutter with pliers. Calk edges with asphalt.

Gutters and Downspouts 279

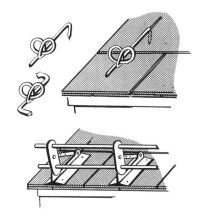

Electric cable, plugged into outdoor convenience outlet, cuts drainage channels through snow. Note zigzag pattern.

Two common types of metal snow guards.

SNOW AND ICE

On gently pitched roofs, drainage of ice or snow is often overly sluggish in particularly cold areas of the country, and ice may build up on the edge of the roof, blocking draining water from ever reaching the gutter. This occurs because under a blanket of snow there may be considerable melting, whereupon water trickles down toward the roof edge. Refreezing takes place as soon as it creeps out from under the snow blanket along the edge and receives the full effect of wind and cold air. The result is a solid barrier of ice that prevents the roof from draining at all. Water backs up under the shingles, where it may do damage. It may gradually undermine the ice barrier, causing the latter to let go in chunks, threatening even greater damage.

To thwart these ice dams and keep water evenly draining off the roof, the best recourse is an electric heating cable. Covering the entire roof would be prohibitively expensive and, as it happens, wholly unnecessary. Simply plug into an electric outlet sufficient length of the special cable to form a zigzag line along the roof edge. This won't melt the whole wall of ice, but it will cut through it to form a sufficient number of drainage channels. The cable, which consists of an insulated wire enclosed in a lead sheath, comes in any length.

On steeply sloping roofs, especially those of slate, tile, asbestos, cement or metal, the homeowner runs into an entirely different situation. Here the chief danger is that of avalanche. Snow and ice may start sliding down in big chunks which can actually rip out the roofing, tear away gutters, and damage shrubs on the ground. To prevent such slides, install snow guards, small metal fingers which protrude from the roof surface. Installation is easy and depends on the type of roof. For instance, guards meant for new roofs have a sharp hook to be driven into the sheathing before the shingles are laid; those for use on old roofs have a tongue which hooks around nails under the shingles; those for metal roofs come with lugs for soldering.

For adequate protection, first figure your roof pitch. The steeper the roof, the more guards needed. For each hundred square feet of roof, you will need 125 guards on 12/12 pitch (1' rise per foot); 75 guards on 8/12 pitch (2' rise in 3'); and 50 guards on 6/12 pitch (1' rise in 2'). On flatter roofs, use two rows of guards staggered, placed a few feet above the eaves. On the steeper ones, space the rows about 10' apart and stagger units in the rows.

FLASHING CARE AND REPAIR

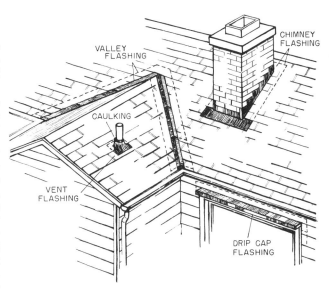

Flashing is the metal stripping which covers the joints and seams on the outside of your house—for example, the junction points between the roof and house wall, chimney and roof, dormer and roof. These strips, made of copper, galvanized sheet metal, or plastic materials, divert the flow of water and prevent leaks into the house. Application is made by nailing and sealing with roofing compound.

For flashing to be effective, the water must flow down *over* it from higher areas; and to avoid the uphill flow of water often caused by wind pressures, the flashing is carried *under* uphill slopes at least 6″ and down *over* lower slopes the same distance. The more gradual the slope, the larger these figures. Since water tends to creep uphill through narrow cracks by capillary action, the edges of all pieces of flashing must be thoroughly sealed with some sort of calking material. On roofs, asphalt cement is commonly used since it won't be seen anyway, while on visible surfaces a gray or white mastic compound is used. The latter can be painted, if desired.

Valley flashing should extend 6″ under each of the two rows of shingles which meet at the valley. If it doesn't, a strip of this width should be inserted and cemented down with a roofing compound. Nail edges securely except in certain instances where the compound is also a mastic. Start at the eaves and work up. At joints between material, overlap 3″. Flashing around chimneys is particularly important. The sides and lower edge are fitted with flashing which extends up the chimney at least 6″. The top edge of the

material is curled to fit into a mortar joint and sealed to the masonry. The lower edges are carried out over the shingles and nailed down, and the edges sealed with compound. Most doors and windows are protected on the top by a piece of metal flashing which extends over the top of the frame. This is called the "drip cap."

It should be remembered that, owing to industrial fumes and the exhaust gases from chimneys which burn oil, metals can be attacked by corrosion. This, plus possible damage by electrolytic action—owing to a combination of unlike metals, such as galvanized nails in copper flashing—can cause the metal flashing to deteriorate. Holes and leaks develop. It is a wise move, therefore, to inspect all the flashing of your house periodically and replace or patch defective portions at once.

Plastic flashing molds itself to curves of vent stacks and is handy for other flashing purposes.

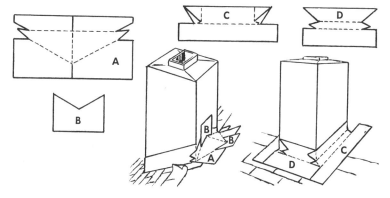

Patterns for cutting flashing pieces to fit around chimneys. To apply, follow letter key. Note that on the uphill side, a cricket is installed and flashing pieces cut to fit over it. This part comes last.

Flashing Care and Repair 281

PROTECTING ROOF FLASHING

1. Examine the flashing edges, especially along the chimney. Apply a coat of roofing asphalt, extending it about 2″ on either side.

2. While on the roof, apply new coat of asphalt along all flashing as a safeguard.

3. Don't neglect the joint between porch roofs and higher walls. Cover flashing here.

RETREAD YOUR ROOF FOR A SUN DECK

Any flat roof not put to practical use is just a waste of space. On the basis of square footage, a roof is one of the most expensive parts of the house. It's good economy to make the most of it, and transforming it into a sun deck does just that.

You'll find flat-roofed areas above porches, garages and many rooms of split-level homes. Some are exposed to full sun all day, others are divided between full sun and full shade. Being away from ground-level traffic and intrusion, each can be put to good use. Furthermore, many flat roofs are high enough to be out of mosquito range, a valuable asset in summer.

Before a roof can be put to this use, it has to be made traffic-proof so that wear will not cause leaks. Most flat roofs are covered with a webbing of impregnated felt, tar, or asphalt and gravel, or simply a layer of 90-pound felt rolled roofing. None of these can withstand much traffic, and all can be easily punctured by the legs of outdoor furniture. Then, too, not every "flat" roof is sufficiently level for comfort when converted to a sun deck. The preliminaries, then, must include an adjustment of roof pitch (if needed) and a stronger covering.

If the slope exceeds the ¼″ per foot needed for drainage, it can be adjusted by the addition of "sleepers" which become, in effect, new floor joists. Anything from 2-by-2's blocked up at intervals, to 2-by-8's or 2-by-10's cut on a diagonal across the face to form long wedges, will serve the purpose. These are nailed into the roof sheathing through its present covering and new flooring is nailed over them. The "sleepers" are spaced at 16″ intervals, the usual spacing for floor joists. The outer end is then closed with a fascia of the same material as the flooring boards, and the surface is ready for its traffic-proof covering.

A variation of the "duckboard" protection system, outlined below, can also be used to correct the roof pitch.

Your choice of new deck floor covering can be made from the following:

1. Duckboards, for a boardwalk effect.
2. Plywood, with or without canvas over it.
3. Tempered hardboard.
4. Asphalt paving.
5. Fiberglass-reinforced plastic on plywood.
6. Paint-on coatings applied over the present roof.

The choice should be governed in part by the present roof. For example, many garage roofs are flat, particularly those over masonry-wall garages. A low parapet often surrounds the roof and the felt roofing is carried up over the parapet walls. Such a roof lends itself readily to the duckboard type of decking, or asphalt paving. Certain types of paint may also be used.

Where roof pitch must be corrected, the sleepers are first covered with ⅝″ exterior-grade plywood over which canvas, plastic film or hardboard may be applied.

Duckboards are easily made in 3′ square platforms. Two 2-by-2 sleepers 3′ long are cut, then joined with strips 1¼-by-2 or 1¼-by-3 (sometimes referred to as ¾-by-3) nailed across the 2-by-2's, spaced with ⅜″ gaps between them for drainage. The 2-by-2 sleepers are tucked under, 6″ in from the ends of the strips.

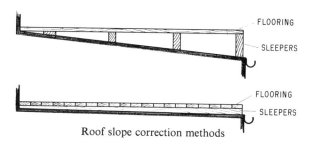

Roof slope correction methods

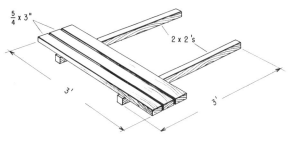

Duckboard construction

Make enough of these platforms just to cover the roof when they are laid side by side. By cutting the sleepers in a wedge, duckboards can also accomplish slight changes in roof slope. They may be lifted up at will for roof repairs underneath or for recovery of lost items that may have fallen through.

More permanent, but lacking the easily movable feature, is the use of full-length boards similarly separated for drainage. These are nailed to sleepers of 2-by-2 stock (or larger if needed to change a slope), spaced 16″ apart. Redwood may be used for deck covering without finish of any kind, but other woods should be treated with preservatives before construction and then painted.

Asphalt paving may be applied directly to an existing roof, but the outer edges of the asphalt need support, so a roof with a parapet is ideally suited. A webbed double layer of heavy impregnated felt is nailed down, then 2″ of asphalt (cold mix) paving is applied and tamped flat. After four days it is hard enough to resist traffic.

Exterior or marine-grade plywood is good for covering roofs. If the surface is even, sheets not less than ¼″ thick may be screwed right into joists in the roof below. If sleepers have been used, ⅝″ or ¾″ thickness is necessary for rigidity. The panels are butted, and calking compound is forced into cracks and spaces. Finish with two coats of deck enamel or, for a longer-lasting surface, the panels can be canvas-

covered. You'll need a sheet about 18″ larger than the deck. If you cannot obtain a large enough piece, yard goods can be sewn together. The plywood is covered with white lead paste applied with a toothed trowel. Canvas is drawn tight over it and nailed around the ends. After rolling with a rolling pin, a second application of lead paste is worked into the surface with a smooth trowel. When it has dried, apply spar varnish or paint with oil-base deck enamel.

An extremely tough and totally waterproof material is a strong sheet of plastic film reinforced with fiberglass. This is applied over plywood with a "dope" which acts as adhesive. Warmer weather— about 70°—is desirable for ease in handling. Tempered hardboard, available in 4-by-8′ sheets, is a weather-proof material which can be applied over existing roof coverings with non-rusting screws. Joints must be calked against leakage. The sheets are kept ⅛″ apart to allow for expansion. The surface may be painted or not, as you prefer.

If your roof is covered with roll roofing, a smooth coating may be applied easily by painting with compounds made especially for the surface. However, for heavy service, one of the other methods would serve better. In any event, the original roof drainage must not be blocked. Do not interrupt the flow of water over or through your new decking to gutters and downspouts.

THE OUTER WALLS   Resurfacing old walls · Clapboard repairs · Stucco repairs

Often time and weather seem to combine their efforts to batter your house, and eventually, in spite of the best maintenance efforts, you sometimes cannot help concluding that your exterior walls need a new covering. When this point is finally reached, you will find there are many materials and methods of application from which to choose. While determining which is best for your home, keep in mind the fact that you can effect considerable saving of money— immediately and in the future—by your choice. For example:

1. With many materials you can add wall insulation, which will not only add to your comfort, but immediately cut fuel bills.

2. With some materials, painting and touch-up chores are eliminated, and you pocket that expense right away.

3. With many old materials handled in a new way, you can achieve both the points mentioned above.

Wood siding includes clapboard, dropsiding, shingle or shake, vertical board, plywood. Some of these are pre-finished so that they'll need no further

EXTERIOR WALLS

While framing styles vary considerably, these sectional views —with the component parts labeled with their technical names—are a guide to what you'll find in your own walls.

Siding on frame wall

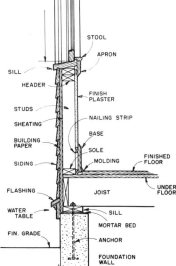

Brick veneer

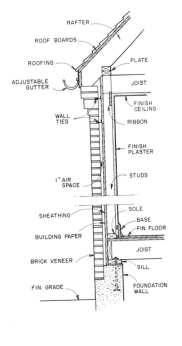

Stucco on frame walls

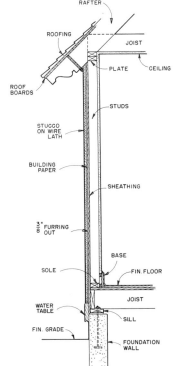

Brick wall

painting. Pre-dipped shingles and shakes may last as long as twenty years without a renewal of the finish. A single sealer coat on redwood or cypress can protect these woods indefinitely in their natural state. They are virtually immune to rot or insects. Plywood is also available pre-finished.

Take a long, slow look at the varied types of siding available—and along with this, the manner in which they may be applied to your present home.

RESURFACING OLD WALLS

Shingles and Shakes. Shingles are one of the most attractive, economical and easy-to-work-with materials of all exterior wall coverings. There are asbestos and asphalt shingles in many shades and

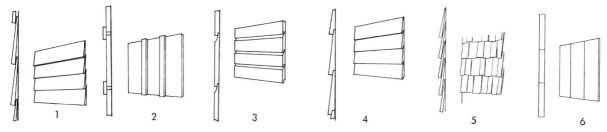

Types of Wood Siding. 1—bevel siding or clapboards. 2—board-and-batten. 3—drop siding. 4—rabbeted bevel siding. 5—shakes. 6—vertical board siding.

colors as well as the old stand-by wood shingles which can be laid in a variety of patterns. More rugged, and often considered even more attractive, wood shakes are frequently used in place of shingles. They are also more costly. Shakes are irregularly shaped lengths of wood applied like shingles to overlap but exposed from 12 to 24″ to the weather. Their upper ends are tapered to permit the successive courses to lie flat.

Shingles and shakes may be applied over defective siding, or you may start over and apply them directly to the sheathing. If the old siding and sheathing are removed, loose or rotted boards should first be repaired and new sheathing paper applied. If the old covering is not removed, the surface should be as true, level and smooth as possible.

Since shingles are a series of small pieces, they can be used to cover misshapen walls which have changed shape as the framework settled. They fit around obstructions easily. The only guides needed are a piece of string and a level. Above windows and doors, shingles extend outward and over the upper edge of the drip cap. To fill the space behind, nail cut-off ends of shingles across this surface, with the lower edges resting on top of the cap and the following full-shingle courses covering the upper edge of the

cap. Shingles are butted tightly against the sides of window and door casings.

Under the eaves of most houses there is a trim board concealing rafter ends and the roof wall joint. Shingles should extend up under this board, so it must either be loosened or removed entirely. The full-length shingle courses are thrust under the board, the second higher course likewise, then the board fastened down tightly. A third course of wood shingles, cut short, can be butted against the lower edge of this board if you prefer its appearance.

One method of applying shingles, known as double coursing, provides an interesting texture and a deeper shadow line than does single coursing. In double coursing, a double layer of shingles is used, one on top of the other, with the outer shingles extending about ½″ lower than the shingles underneath. Use of a cheaper grade of shingles for the undercourse will save money, and the siding will be just as strong as if you used top grade.

Wood shingles and shakes should be nailed with at least 2 nails, each placed about ⅓ the shingle length from its top edge and ¾″ from the side edge. Nails should be driven flush, but the heads should not damage the shingle.

It's a good idea to wet wood shingles by soaking a

1. Cover old walls with tarpaper or foil insulating sheets as first step in reshingling.

2. Apply metal flashing over doors and windows with tarpaper or foil carried over the flashing.   →

3. Use metal strip at corners and around door and window casings; butt shingles to casings.

4. Level asbestos shingles at corners where metal corner strip is used to assure a neat pattern.

5. Cut shingles to allow indentation in groove under window sill for watertight joint.

6. Cut asbestos shingles with special knife, use an abrasive disc, or score and break.

bundle of them several hours before use. Then butt them tightly on side edges. In this way, you'll avoid any popping off from swelling in the first rain. If they are to be painted later, paint the rough under edges in the bundle before soaking. It will save a lot of extra work.

Asphalt shingles may be cut by scoring with a linoleum knife and breaking, but it's a hard job. They may also be cut with an abrasive disc in a portable power saw, but be careful to avoid splintered bits reaching your eyes. The simplest and quickest cutting method is by rental (purchase is not worth while on a single job) of a cutter such as that illustrated above. It knifes through a single shingle on hand pressure. Turpentine or kerosene keeps the blade clean.

It is not necessary to adhere to the standard patterns in shingle application. Many people deliberately apply them off the straight line to simulate aged and falling shingled surfaces. Sometimes, regular shingles are permitted to drop off line to imitate the more rugged lines of shakes. In contrast, the slapdash appearance of irregularly edged shakes may be laid to form a neatness-from-disorder pattern.

Asphalt shingles need no paint, since they are finished with a durable surface, and they need no treatment for many years other than cleaning. They may be painted with ordinary exterior house paints when it is finally necessary. Wood shingles and shakes may be stained as soon as dry or painted with exterior paint.

7. Rugged shakes or smooth shingles are applied the same way. Wall is covered with tarpaper, chalk lines drawn with a level, courses with even exposure calculated. Nail each piece twice.

8. First course is double, following courses are single. If corner trim is not used, a staggered overlap provides a neat and finished appearance.

9. Butt shingles at corner trim at inner and outer corners.

PLYWOOD SIDING

Plywood pattern, Texture 1–11, designed for interior or exterior use, makes an interesting pattern under a wide roof overhang. Plywood has the advantage of rapid installation, fewer joints, and is totally water-proofed. It may be pre-finished before installation.

Aluminum siding with a built-in plastic foam insulation is applied over old. Corner trim locks the two siding pieces together in a rigid, weathertight joint.

Metal. Clapboard shapes in aluminum and stainless steel are sold both with and without a baked-on finish in a wide range of colors. These materials are impervious to weather and, once either one is on your house, your maintenance worries are ended. Both forms are available, too, with insulation already attached so that your walls are insulated at the same time. Shapes and forms other than clapboard are also on the market.

Masonry. This group includes a great variety of man-made materials. Stucco (a form of cement), thin bricks that can be nailed on over old wood siding, and simulated stone less than 1″ thick are the most widely used in this group. Underneath all of these, additional wall insulation can be put up as a base coating or blown in as fill between studs.

An easy way to cover a wall is to nail special thin bricks up with metal clips, right over the old wood siding.

Corner and straight pieces of real brick with clips are nailed up, joints mortared as usual.

Composition Materials. These are pre-finished materials made to order for the job, such as hardboards, cement-asbestos shingles, and boards pre-finished and in no need of paint. They are weather-defeating in themselves, and insulation may also be applied beneath them, making further maintenance unnecessary.

Application Techniques. For the most part, all of these materials can be applied right over the present siding. The principal obstacle to this is that it makes the walls thicker and you may end up with recessed windows. The thinner the new material, the easier the job.

If the chosen material will cause your windows to be recessed, remove the original window casing and extend the exterior portion of the frame outward as far as needed by the addition of narrow wood strips of 1″ stock. The sill is often sufficiently deep to accommodate the new siding beneath it but, if not, it too can be made bigger. All added pieces are first

glued, then nailed, the waterproof glue concealing the joint. An extension of the drip cap over the window is also sometimes necessary.

For insulation, there is an extensive choice of materials, determined to a degree by the siding selected. (See Chapter Two for a thorough discussion of insulation.) Where the new siding is put up over furring, there is room for batt insulation between strips. If the new siding is set right over the old, you may need only foil backed with strong waterproof paper or a fiberboard covering laid flat and used as a base for the new siding, or a combination of both.

CLAPBOARD REPAIRS

A battered and unpainted clapboard wall may appear hopeless at first glance, but often the mere patching of a few single boards will make the whole as good as new. Of course, clapboards are overlapped and nailed together and it may appear at first that disturbing one means removing the next above and so on up the wall to the top. But, with a little care, you can remove not only one board at a time but even parts of one board for replacement. Others can be mended on the spot without removal.

Take the case of a split board, one cracked along its grain. You can nail down individual sections, but not without first drilling pilot holes for the nails, or the ends will only split further. The best way is to gently pry the lower split end outward, just far enough to spread glue along the edges of the split; then push the board back together. To hold the glued

Mending a Split Board—If not mended immediately, a split board allows water to penetrate and induce rot. Pry up loose portion and spread waterproof glue along the split with a putty knife. Slip board back into place and drive finishing nails beneath, directing them upward to force the split edges tightly together. Let glue set hard before removing nails and plugging nail holes. If necessary, plane thin inserts to size; glue in place.

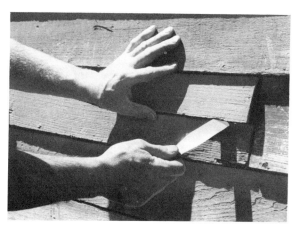

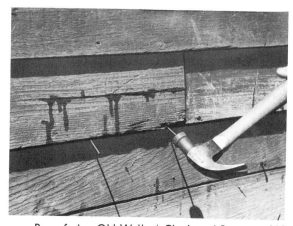

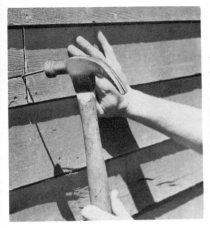

Warped Board Treatment—Warping widens joints between boards, causing wall leaks. Nailing dry board will often split it. As a precaution, drill pilot holes for nails and drive them in until heads are slightly countersunk. Warpage may be overcome by nailing. Fill end joints between boards with wood putty.

joint firmly, drive a few finishing nails closely under the bottom edge and bend them upward. This will force the glued joint tightly together. Use waterproof glue and remove the nails when it has dried. Then plug the nail holes with putty.

If a wide board has curled or bulged outward without splitting, it may be drawn back flat by boring a few small holes in the center of the bulge for screws and pulling it back by tightening the screws. Once they've taken hold, soak the board before tightening down completely. This is to avoid cracks. Countersink the screws and fill the holes with putty.

When you discover a clapboard that is beyond hope of repair, remove the damaged section, as illustrated in the photographs. Make vertical cuts as high as possible in several places along the damaged area with a back saw. Then try to reach under the next

board above without disturbing it, using a chisel to chip off the rest of the cut. If you can't manage this way, use a hacksaw blade to cut the nails holding down the upper board, then carefully insert a wedge under the edge of this board. A chisel will finish the removal of damaged sections. When this is completed, patch any holes in the tarpaper covering of the sheathing. Use roofing asphalt or apply patches of tarpaper over large gaps with the same material used as adhesive.

Finally, cut a length of matching clapboard to fit tightly in the opening and push it into place under the upper board. Nail it into place and nail down any loose ends of adjoining pieces. Replace the cut nails in the strip above the replacement. For all nails in old wood, be sure to drill pilot holes or you'll have more patchwork to do as the nails split the wood.

REPLACING DAMAGED CLAPBOARD

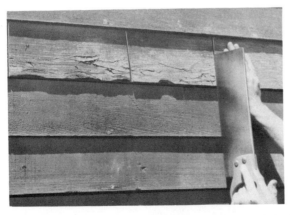

1. Cut bad section vertically with back saw as close as possible to overlap.
2. Cut out chunks of cut lengths with a sharp chisel. Do not cut into tarpaper.

3. Where possible, remove nails from edge of upper board to free the cut length.
4. If need be, insert wedge under upper board and cut nails with keyhole hack saw.

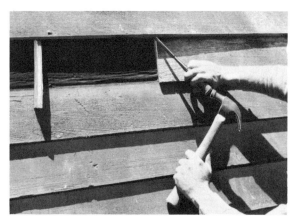

5. With upper board wedged, chisel out ends of cut length even with saw mark.
6. To avoid splitting good section, hold chisel at angle and cut short pieces.

7. If upper board can be wedged outward far enough, cut with hack saw.
8. Patch nicks in tarpaper, cut new length, and nail in place top and bottom.

STUCCO REPAIRS

The most common damage to stucco walls is the development of fine cracks near doors and windows. Settling foundations, water seepage and subsequent freezing are only a few of the causes of these cracks. All are easy to repair and should be taken care of before cold weather sets in. First remove all loose stucco in order to form a proper base for patching. Ready-mixed concrete is convenient to use for small patches but, if you prefer, you can mix your own. A mixture of 1 part portland cement to 2½ parts fine sand is best for patching. Add a waterproofing compound at the same time; it will make the mix easier to work with and will assure a more certain bond. On the other hand, should large areas of stucco become damaged, it may be necessary to remove the old stucco completely and apply new. Simple repairs are illustrated below; major repairs are shown in the photographs on the facing page.

FILLING HAIRLINE CRACKS IN STUCCO

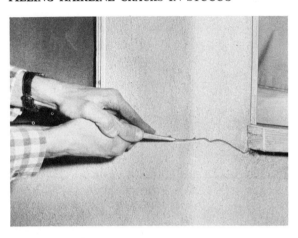

1. Use a cold chisel to dig out all the loose cement; open the crack to about double its existing depth. Undercut the crack to provide a key or slot for the new cement to hold.
2. Wet the crack thoroughly with a brush or cloth, or use a hose. Fill crack, using a putty knife, and overlap each side about 1″, smoothing cement into the existing surface.

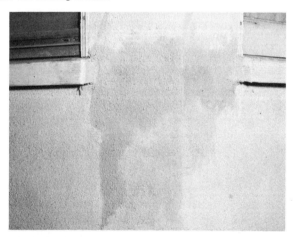

3. If your stucco is colored, buy matching colored stucco, called sand-finish, and dab a wet sponge in the material. Dab the material over crack filler, applying in circular motion.
4. This is the way the repaired crack should look. In 3 or 4 days the sand-finish will dry—it fades as much as 70% and should nearly match the old stucco finish.

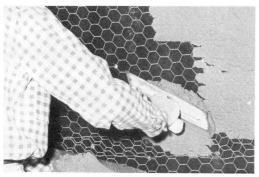 

1. Remove damaged stucco down to the wood underneath. Cover area with tarpaper, then nail securely 1″ mesh wire or wire lath. Mix plastic cement (1 shovelful) with sand (3 shovels) and spread on upward to cover the wire.
2. You can make your own scratching tool from a piece of heavy-gauge scrap metal, or buy the professional type shown at the right.

3. Scratching is done while the first coat is still soft and workable. Hold scratching tool lightly; press just hard enough to score, but not hard enough to take off stucco.
4. Allow first coat to dry 7 days, then spray area with fine mistlike spray to soak it, then apply a second coat, using same mix.

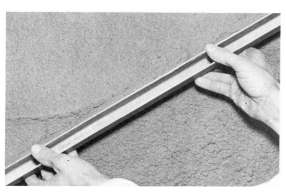 

5. This second coat must be smoothed off level. Use a tested straightedge. A metal bar is best, since it won't warp and bend.
6. It's a good idea to work this second coat with a trowel while still damp. You can make a trowel from a wood shingle by putting on a handle. Float surface until sand grains show.   →

7. Colored stucco is last coat applied. The second coat should set 2 weeks. Spray to dampen it, then trowel on colored finish. This coat is thin, just enough to cover the undercoat completely.

8. Texture the finish coat with a rubber float. Keep a wet brush working just ahead of the float to prevent it from sticking and pulling off this finish coat. This must be completed within one half hour after application of stucco.

THE FOUNDATION   Cures for a damp basement · Crawl spaces · Termites and dry rot

The foundation is the very basis of your house and should always be kept sound and secure, for once it becomes weakened or undermined, the whole structure of the house is threatened.

Few homes have a really dry basement, particularly in the early spring. Concrete and masonry foundations are porous and water seeps through steadily unless halted by a waterproof barrier inside or outside. However, dampness, seepage, even downright flooding, can be corrected. Except for serious problems, such as periodic floods, improper sewer systems, or uncontrollable drainage in the area, the great majority of home waterproofing problems are usually solved simply and at little cost.

Crawl spaces, properly vented and insulated, mean greater protection for your house, with warmer ground floors and lessened dampness; control of termites and dry rot means less depreciation and much longer life for your house.

In this section, the homeowner can come to a thorough understanding of the foundation of his house.

The construction illustrated is recommended by the Housing and Home Finance Agency to control condensation on basement walls. It calls for a good coat of asphalt paint on the inside of the masonry wall and furring strips made from the heartwood of a durable wood such as redwood or southern cypress, or one which is treated with a good wood preservative. The lowest furring strip and ornamental finish should be kept about ½″ above the concrete floor. The Agency says that while the insulation is not highly essential, it will keep the finish paneling at a higher temperature and lower moisture content, and it will also help to keep the basement warm in winter. In extremely wet soils, it may be necessary to place a drain on the outside near the footing and to waterproof the outside wall.

FINISH

VAPOR BARRIER

THERMAL INSULATION

FURRING STRIP

WATER-PROOFING

ASPHALT PAINT

AIR SPACE

DRAIN TILE

½″

WATERPROOFING

CURES FOR A DAMP BASEMENT

If water seeps into your basement, it is usually an indication of one of three basic conditions:

1. Settling of the foundation. Some parts of the footing, which rests on the soil and bears the entire weight of the house, are weaker than others. The result is an uneven distribution of the weight, with a sag in the footing and a crack in the wall, through which moisture can enter.

2. Poor workmanship in the construction of the foundation. Sometimes a mason laying a concrete block foundation uses a poor grade of mortar or fails to make a solid bond between the blocks, and water from the ground outside is permitted to penetrate. Or, if the foundation is of solid concrete, it may have been poured in layers and there was an imperfect bond between the layers.

3. Heavy ground moisture. In ordinary soils, a reasonably well-built foundation will resist the normal water pressures. But in some areas, especially those with clay subsoils, high water tables or other poor drainage conditions, the tremendous force exerted by water in the ground will drive through the pores of the foundation. Naturally, if such conditions exist in your neighborhood, you should know about them before beginning to put in basement walls or floors.

Musty odors and mildew are simple to solve. First, make certain that there is no water penetration. After a heavy rainstorm, inspect the understructure for signs of water. If there are none, by merely finishing

Filling around pipe openings will keep out water. Trowel in a mix of 1 part cement to 3 parts sand.

the basement with stud framing (see photo) and walls and covering the floor with tiles, you may completely cure the dampness. You can also cover sweating pipes, which create moisture in the basement, with felt tape and pipe wrap-around material. Cover all exposed surfaces except actual control wheels and the stems of valves.

Increase basement ventilation. Either keep a window open, add louvers, or use a ventilating fan. If the air is extremely humid and condensation cannot be controlled by the above methods, reduce moisture with special moisture-absorbent chemicals or with an electric dehumidifier.

If water seeps into the basement, watch for cracks in poured concrete, loose or crumbling mortar between cement block and brick walls, openings around pipes and electrical conduits, window openings and floor cracks.

Small openings around pipes and electrical conduits coming into the cellar should be stuffed with oakum, then filled with calking compound. Fill larger holes with a concrete mix.

The joint between the window frame and concrete foundation should be filled with concrete. If there's water seepage at the wall-floor joint, chop the concrete away at this joint, forming an opening about 1″ to 2″ wide and about 4″ deep. Fill with asphalt and extend this waterproofing material about 2″ above the floor level. Add a cove of concrete to seal this wall-floor joint.

If a wall is free of visible cracks or other defects, but actual moisture is present, you can solve the problem by use of a waterproofing compound. Apply only to clean, unpainted masonry walls, never to painted or whitewashed walls. Use a stiff-bristle brush and work the compound into the pores of the wall.

Before studs went up, the inside of this foundation was treated with mastic and asphalt paper.

Cures for a Damp Basement 295

All cracks outside around windows should be filled in. Pitch sill away from the frame.

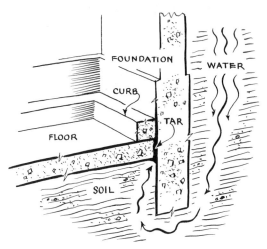

Water seepage through the wall-floor joint is a frequent cause of dampness. Here the joint is filled with asphalt and a curb, made of concrete, is added above the joint.

It is always wise to prevent water accumulation along the outside of the foundation wall. Channel it away from the house. Downspouts or leaders from gutters should not dump the water next to the foundation. Place a splash block under the leader to direct the flow of water away—or, if the ground is spongy and absorbs water readily, connect the leader through clay tiles to a sewer or dry well.

In waterproofing from the exterior, the most effective and permanent cure is to dig a trench along the outside walls so that the foundation can be waterproofed all the way down to the footing. Remove shrubs and walks and dig a trench wide enough to work in, without danger of the dirt wall falling in on you. Next, put clay drain tiles into the bottom of the trench just below the footing, allowing a gap

of 1″ with a tarpaper covering. Run the tiles to a sewer or drywell. Apply a waterproofing mastic to the (clean) foundation wall, followed by one or two coats of asphalt paint. Line the wall with asphalt paper, overlapped 6″ at the edges. Finally, apply another coat of asphalt paint. Backfill the trench but make certain not to tear the protective paper coating on the wall. Fill the upper 4″ of this trench with cinders or gravel, sloping it away from the house.

If there is a high water table or subterranean springs under your home, or if the sewer periodically back-flows, a sump pump may be needed. The pump

Waterproofing the outside is effective. Note the shoring (heavy timbers) used to prevent cave-in. Waterproofing mastic is applied to exterior wall with a brush and covered with asphalt paper.

Drain tiles will carry the water coming from the roof down the leader away from the foundation. Set tiles in trench with a slope of 1" to a foot.

Tiles are easily cut with a cold chisel and hammer. Mark outline around tile, scoring with a chisel. Tap cold chisel lightly with hammer all around scored line until pieces separate.

and motor should have a capacity equal to the greatest possible flow of water you may encounter.

Check the pitch of the cellar floor. You will find that it slopes toward one end. Dig a pit to the depth of 4 to 6' in the lowest part. Line the sides of the hole with concrete, making a plywood form to hold the mix until it sets. Install a sump pump so that the water flowing into the pit can be removed out through the wall into the sewer. (To install a special sump pump outlet, see page 259.)

PATCHING CHIPPED CORNERS OF FOUNDATIONS

1. Right: A chip or a knock-out at a corner is easy to repair, and with a straight corner when the job's complete. With a stiff wire brush, remove all the loose particles.

2. Below, left: Prop a 2 × 4 against the corner and wet the area thoroughly. Fill the crack with patching cement, smoothing it off with a trowel so that patch is flush with the wall.

3. Below, right: Now prop the 2 × 4 against the outer side of the corner. Use the edge of the trowel to slice off any excess cement sticking out of the corner. Leave 2 × 4 in place for at least 4 hours.

CRAWL SPACES

Homes with partial basements and those with additions over unexcavated areas are apt to face special problems during winter months. The floors over such areas are cold, damp, sometimes warped and occasionally beset with dank odors. These problem areas can be eliminated and the rooms above such areas made livable by understanding the causes of the trouble and applying suitable remedies.

When the space under the floor and the floor itself seem to be damp, look first of all for inadequate cross ventilation. Foundation vents may be needed. With these, the crawl space itself is rarely damp but it may be cold, with resultant cold floors overhead. Vents should be covered in severe weather—or, to make the job easier, install louver vents which are adjustable to open-close positions and leave them closed during cold spells.

Also, to prevent cold floors, add 4″ batt-type insulation between floor joists. Insulation is stapled between joists flush with the lower edges, forming a dead air space between insulation and subfloor. A second form of insulation, which can be relied upon to seal out dampness as well, is heavy felt applied across joists. By using 50- to 90-pound felt, lapping it at joints, and attaching it to sills on all sides, a perfect seal results. Lapped joints should be asphalt-sealed and sagging of the strips prevented by adequate stapling or tacking.

Not infrequently, a house may have been erected on swampy ground, sandy or heavy loam soil. Dampness and dank odors may be a continuing nuisance. Here the remedy consists of covering the ground of

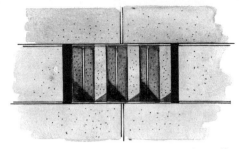

Simple vent to exclude rain yet permit ventilation can be constructed by removing one block or series of bricks and inserting bricks as shown.

the crawl space with tarpaper, lapped 4″ and sealed to foundations all around. A 2″ layer of *dry* sand is then spread over the tarpaper. Moisture from below cannot penetrate the crawl area and the floors are dry and warmer.

TERMITES AND DRY ROT

Any homeowner, when confronted with the possibility that dry rot has a foothold in his home or termites have invaded the premises, should take immediate action. The first step lies in understanding the problem and its true dangers or lack of them.

Termites build shelter tubes such as these to maintain contact between moist earth below and food supply in the wood sills above. These tubes may extend for many feet across concrete foundations. Break them open.

The wood of the first floor of your home, if moist and untreated, is ready to receive these destructive pests. Both will thrive and spread where the moisture content of wood is generally high. Termites are visible and the paths they leave are apparent. Dry rot, on the other hand, is invisible. It's a microscopic, plantlike fungus growth. It is air-borne until it finds moist wood—and there it settles down, grows and multiplies with amazing speed. Its food is the cellulose fibers of moist, cured lumber. This is attacked and eaten away, leaving a mass of weakened cells that gradually loses its power to hold the piece of wood together. It collapses. The wood is then able to absorb more moisture, stays wet and breaks down under the stress placed on it by the house structure. The alternate wetting and drying of wood leads to the rapid growth and spreading of dry rot. On the other hand, where ventilation is good and moisture absent, wood will remain intact for literally hundreds of years. A board infected with dry rot may even appear normal to the uneducated eye, but if it is pine, for example, and cuts like cheese and feels as light as balsa wood, the chances are very high that dry rot is present.

Looking somewhat like ants, termites live in similar colonies. They consist of three groups—the reproductive adult males and females, the soldiers that defend the colony against intruders, and the soft-bodied wingless workers that digest cellulose in wood and convert it into food for themselves and other members of the colony. Only the sexed adults have wings, and these are shed when a new home is found. If you find a little pile of such wings, they were left by termites (ants do not shed theirs) and somewhere nearby is the point they have tried to enter your home. If living conditions are good, they will set up housekeeping. If not, they will die.

The typical invitation to dry rot and termites is a home with one or more of these situations:

1. Sloppily cleared land full of stumps and large roots near the house, and scrap lumber from construction tossed into crawl spaces, under porches, into back fill.

2. Wood siding low to the ground or covered with earth during the leveling and landscaping.

3. Open downspouts splashing water back up onto and under low siding boards.

4. Concrete slabs and block foundations full of cracks and damaged mortar points.

5. Paint on clapboards badly peeled or blistered.

6. Damp crawl space poorly vented, with moisture rising to sills and joists above it.

7. Wood steps outdoors with their stringers touching the ground, and wood fences nailed to the corners of the house.

8. Excessive moisture inside the house with windows sweating all winter and paper about to peel from walls.

9. Basement windows in contact with masonry and often dampened by rain.

10. Joists adjacent to sill that are open to attack.

If your house has even one of these defects, it's time to check up for signs of dry rot or termites.

Dry rot or termites can be located by much the same methods, probing suspected wood with a sharp tool or a slender ice pick. If hand pressure can force the tool into the wood over 1″, that wood is so badly deteriorated that it requires replacement. Saw out a length of the suspected wood. If the center is badly tunneled, it is probably the result of termites. If the wood appears sound but is spongy, and close examination shows countless tiny open cells, dry rot has been at work. Split down the grain, the wood

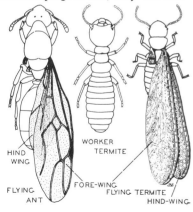

Harmless flying ant (left) is often confused with termites (right). Note waistlines.

Probe sills with icepick. If pick can be thrust deeply into timbers, either termites or dry rot are present.

Removal of lowest siding board reveals damage done to house sill. Close contact with masonry stoop kept wood damp—an ideal invitation to termites or dry rot.

sometimes shows visible indication of the plantlike growth's destructive habits.

In either event, replacement of the damaged wood is necessary. Removal of infested wood will indicate the extent of the damage. Termites sometimes leave cellulose-and-mud tubes running from wood to earth along foundations. Break these up and examine carefully the wood from which they start, for it has probably been infested.

The same measures taken to eliminate infestation with either dry rot or termites also serve to offset further invasion. Obviously, the sanitation measures taken to avoid termites—moisture elimination—will automatically avoid dry rot development.

Development of dry rot is prevented by wood treatment before construction. Preparations forced into wood under pressure prove most effective; dipping does very well, and paint-on coatings are fairly effective, particularly when introduced into end grain. Since your house is already built, access to a good deal of the wood is impossible, but the paint-on method is at least partly effective. In planning any new construction, make use of treated materials. The pressure treatment, while it does increase the cost of materials, is assurance against both dry rot and termite infestation.

If termites have already invaded the house, poisons placed in the soil will exterminate them. Those isolated in the timbers of the house by poisons in the soil will die. The poisons most frequently used today are chlordane and dieldrin, although the formerly standard treatment with DDT is still effective. The former two are nontoxic to plants, and both are odorless. They may be mixed with water, whereas DDT was mixed with fuel oil. The oil-mixed poison is effective for as long as 20 years, the water mixes about 5 years.

Termite poisons are sold as concentrates. Chlordane, mixed with water, is applied as a 2 per cent solution. Dieldrin is applied at 0.5 per cent solution. Estimate the number of gallons needed for your trenching. Check the concentration percentage on the container you purchase, then divide that by the above percentage. For example, you buy chlordane in a 50 per cent solution, and it is applied at 2 per cent, so divide 50 by 2. If you find you need 150 gallons, divide this by the 25 obtained through the dilution figures. The answer, 6, is the number of gallons of the concentrate you must buy. If it were dieldrin, which is diluted to a 0.5 per cent solution, you would need only one-fourth as much, or 1½ gallons.

To apply the poison, a trench is dug along the foundation outside as well as in crawl spaces. If the basement is involved, the trench should be 24″ deep, and holes spaced 12″ apart are made from the trench bottom to the footing. Where there is no basement, the trench is 12″ deep. Mix the selected poison and apply to the bottom of the shallow trenches, then refill with 6″ of earth, treat again and refill the trench. With the 24″ trenches, fill the holes, then soak the bottom of the trench, replace half of the earth and apply more poison. Continue to the surface. You'll need about 1 gallon for each 5′ of shallow trench and at least 2 gallons for the deeper ones, depending upon depth of the footing.

On new construction, making use of pretreated

1. Dig a trench 1′ to 2′ deep around the foundation to be treated. Do not dig beneath footings. Usually, foundation plantings can remain.

2. Selected termite poison in concentrate form is carefully measured for mixing with water. It's a good idea to wear protective gloves.

3. Pour mixture over soil at bottom of trench at prescribed rate. Replace half of the excavated earth and treat it at the same rate of application.

4. Trench is then refilled. You get double protection if this last replacement of earth is also saturated with poison before replacing.

lumber is of primary importance both as a preventive of dry rot and a deterrent to termites. In addition, observe the following rules:

1. Make use of termite shields (metal) on all sills. This measure also prevents moisture penetration of the sill from masonry on which it rests.

2. Clean up all scrap lumber left over from construction.

3. Soil should be at least 6″ below siding, preferably more, and drained away from the foundation.

4. In crawl spaces, provide 18″ or more space between earth and floor joists, and vent this area with at least one vent for each 25′ of foundation.

5. No wood should be left in direct contact with the ground.

6. Foundations and slabs should be free of cracks and all mortar joints should be sound.

Metal apron method of termite-proofing a house at the sill when a slab abuts the structure. This serves to exclude termite entry and also acts as flashing in that it prevents water penetration, which can easily create dry rot. 18″ is minimum termite-safe distance between earth and unprotected wood.

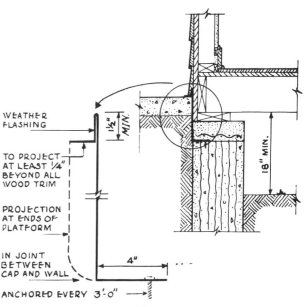

WEATHER FLASHING

TO PROJECT AT LEAST ¼″ BEYOND ALL WOOD TRIM

PROJECTION AT ENDS OF PLATFORM

IN JOINT BETWEEN CAP AND WALL

ANCHORED EVERY 3′-0″

1½″ MIN.

18″ MIN.

4″

CHAPTER 6

OUTDOOR MAINTENANCE

Driveway and Sidewalk Repairs · Outdoor Stairs · Fence Building and Mending · Sturdy Gates · Patching Piers and Posts · Retaining Walls · Cure for a Flooded Yard · Using the Garage for Storage · Renew and Brighten Your Garden Furniture · Care of Garden Tools and Equipment

No home is more attractive than its surroundings. Just as a fine painting can be enhanced or spoiled by the nature of its frame, so does the appearance of your home depend upon its setting and its measure of upkeep.

Spring is usually the season which finds the home handyman outdoors once again. Winter's freezing temperatures, rain and snow always leave telltale marks, and much usually needs to be done as the weather turns warm. Piers and posts must be inspected carefully for signs of rot and weakness—cracked, crumbling pavements need immediate mending; driveway ruts must be smoothed out, sagging fences repaired or replaced, outdoor steps checked for safety, and retaining walls built for water drainage and terracing. Garden tools and hose must be readied for use, as well as the lawn mower and patio furniture.

Most families accumulate more equipment year by year, but storage facilities needn't become a problem when the garage has useful space going to waste.

Most handymen find that the outdoor care and repair of their property is one of the most rewarding things about owning a home. The work is relaxing and enjoyable, the results extremely satisfying.

DRIVEWAY AND SIDEWALK REPAIRS

The following are some of the most common outdoor maintenance projects requiring work with masonry materials. Before you set to work on any of them, you might want to refer ahead to Section 3 of the next chapter, which covers masonry work in general.

Cracked Sidewalks. When grass and weeds begin to grow up through a sidewalk, it's high time for action. Rain entering the crack will wash away the fill under the slab, and eventually at least one side of the walk will sink. Then the repair is twice as difficult. By using the following method, there will be no broken concrete to haul away, no new concrete to mix or pour. The only cost is the price of a chisel and a little cement.

First, cut out the crack with a cold chisel to a width of about 2″. Scrape out all loose earth and broken masonry and remove any other loose material with a wire brush. Wet the inside thoroughly with water or, for an even better patch, with a bonding

1. Widen crack with cold chisel to about 2″ width and clean out broken masonry and dirt down to the bottom of the crack.
2. Wet the interior of the crack with water, or, better still, paint with a bonding chemical which will assure adherence.

3. Mix prepared cement and water thoroughly until batch is uniformly plastic. Then trowel into crack and press down.
4. Level off and let stand 30 minutes until surface is watery, then smooth with steel float. To roughen, use wood float.

chemical such as may be purchased at any building supply yard. Mix cement to a rather stiff consistency and, with a trowel, pack it tightly into the crack, forcing it down to the very bottom of the joint. Then level with the walk on each side. Keep the patch moist for two or three days to help it cure properly.

If you started this job too late and the two sections adjoining the crack are no longer level with each other, you have two choices: either pry up the sunken side with a crowbar and block it there while you pack crushed stone under it, and then mend the crack, or break up the sunken section, excavate the area to a depth of about 4 to 6″ and use the broken pieces of walk as fill, and then cover with new concrete. This requires a form board on each side, and

the surface is made level with adjacent sections of the walk.

Most concrete walks are poured in one piece, with a fiber separator about every fifteen feet. Obviously, you cannot hope to lift an entire fifteen-foot length. If the sunken section has not already cracked free at a score or cross line, you can crack it there. Raising a single square can then be readily and safely done by one man.

Tree-lifted Sidewalks. Often a tree growing close by a sidewalk may lift a portion of the walk with its expanding roots. Usually the cement slabs crack evenly along the expansion lines. These slabs can be raised with a heavy crowbar or an auto jack fitted with a lift hook at the bottom. Raise each piece of slab until it clears the ground at one side, block it there, and then lift the other side and block it up. Next, use a mason's broad chisel and a heavy hammer to score straight lines each way across the center, dividing the slab into four parts. Make successively heavier blows with the hammer and chisel along the lines until the slab suddenly breaks at the scored mark. These easier-to-handle pieces can then be moved aside while the roots, which caused the trouble, are cut down to size with an ax. Level the ground, then replace the four sections, chipping off the edges, if necessary, to provide an even crack between them. Then, with a mortar mix of 1 part cement and 2½ parts sand, cement the slabs to each other, to the adjoining walk, and to the curb or building, if necessary.

1. Assemble the tools and material you'll need. Measure how far the section of walk has sunk, so you'll know how far you'll have to raise it.

2. Check the level of the adjoining walk. If its slope is too great, you may have to raise it, too, for a satisfactory appearance.

3. Use a cold chisel and follow the score mark, chipping carefully and slowly until you have cracked the concrete all the way across at this point.

4. Using a pick or shovel, loosen the soil along the edges of the sunken slab. Clear a strip a few inches wide, to a depth below the concrete.

5. Using a pick, crowbar, or other lever, carefully and slowly pry up the edges of the concrete square. Make certain it is free all the way around.

6. With a crowbar or other lever, raise one edge of the slab on blocks, working it up higher and higher until you have it raised about a foot in the air.

7. With your rake, spread enough cinders underneath the slab to raise it to level. Gravel or crushed rock may be substituted for cinders.

8. Use your rake to make certain the supporting layer of cinders conforms to the uneven bottom of the slab. One high point may cause the slab to crack.

9. Lower the slab and go to the other edge. Raise this edge as in Step 6. A longer length of lever would have made this handyman's work even easier.

10. Shovel in some more cinders and rubble. Note the rough bottom of the slab and make sure supporting bed you prepare conforms to these irregularities.

11. Use the rake to get in under the slab. Make absolutely certain no single clod of cinders or rubble is raised above the rest.
→

12. When bed is properly spread, lower the slab and sweep it clean. Use edge of broom to sweep all loose dirt from the crack between the squares.

13. Spread asphalt into the crack. It will permit the slab to shift slightly without cracking. Sand on the asphalt prevents its sticking to shoes.

Cold-mix for Sidewalks. For building new walks or driveways or for mending old, the cold-mix method is highly efficient. Cold-mix can be purchased in 60-pound bags, but it is more economical to buy it in bulk and haul it yourself. Store it on a double layer of tarpaper to protect the ground under it. By all means, buy in bulk for large jobs such as patios, tennis courts and playground areas.

For heavy traffic areas, a 2"-deep ballast of rock is best, topped with 2" of cold-mix. Drives should have more ballast, depending on the weight of the cars or trucks using them, but for garden paths 1" of each (rock and cold-mix) will do on firm soil.

Redwood is best for the headerboards since it doesn't rot and is very attractive. Locust also will not rot and is as hard as iron when thoroughly dried out. Or you can use impregnated lumber of other types, but the harder the better.

Before beginning the job, cover all tool surfaces with a film of motor oil to prevent adhesion of the cold-mix.

For cold-mix patchwork on old blacktop surfaces, clean out all holes deep enough to allow the addition of 2" of crushed rock and 2" of cold-mix. Then follow the same procedure as for new work, as detailed in the photographs.

1. Remove weeds, grass, old roots, not only from the site of the new path but alongside it, too; such growths can crack the walk.
2. Sprinkle a weed killer at the rate of about 10 pounds to each 100 square feet over the site to kill off sprouted seeds and roots.

3. Rake in the weed killer, wet down, and then roll the area thoroughly (about 30 minutes) to compact soil. This is good insurance against cracks.
4. Set corner stakes and lay off path with heavy twine. One stake every 3′ is good. Inner edge of stakes should just touch line.
5. Set headerboards against stakes and nail them there. A concrete block against the stake makes the nailing easier. Use rustproof nails.

6. Make frequent use of your level and measuring tape. Keep sides level unless you plan to slope the whole walk to one side for drainage.
7. Bank the outside with earth and tamp it down to add more strength to headerboards. They have to support the ballast and the cold-mix.
8. Use ¾″ crushed rock for ballast. This should come to within 2″ of the top of headerboards; the remaining space will be filled with cold-mix.

→

9. Level off ballast and then roll both lengthwise and crosswise to compact and force into the earth beneath. Don't dislodge headerboards.
10. Apply the cold-mix at the rate of 22 pounds per square foot. Pour into piles at short intervals and then rake out, adding more as needed.
11. Use the back of a rake to level off. Cold-mix should be piled on until it is ½″ above the tops of the headerboards, enough to allow compacting.

12. A lawn roller filled with water is used to compact the cold-mix. Roll for at least 30 minutes to 1 hour. Your footprints can be rolled out later. Keep at it!
13. Dry cement, of a selected color, can be spread over the top at the rate of 10 pounds per 100 square feet, then broomed into pores of the cold-mix.
14. Final rolling lasts 15 minutes. Afterwards, take a wet brush and dust off the tops of the header-boards. Conceal stakes at sides with earth fill or sod.

Black-top Driveways. Drives which are composed of heavy rock and black-top frequently come apart during sub-freezing weather. Water penetrates through the cracks, freezes, expands, and finally breaks the black-top surface into pieces. Then, on thawing, the water works into the fill beneath and washes it away. Continued use of the drive further enlarges the damage.

Repairs are remarkably simple, and they can be made with several types of material. Best of the lot is cold-mix asphalt mixed with fine, sharp gravel. This is simply poured into depressions and cracks, tamped tightly, and built up to a point ¼″ above roadbed level. Traffic will level it off slowly.

Lacking this material, you can use roofing asphalt impregnated with asbestos-fiber binder and a bucket or two of coarse sand. Apply in alternate layers, starting with the asphalt mixture. Sprinkle sand over the surface to prevent tracking into the house, for these materials remain sticky for a day or two.

Black-top drive, when it begins to disintegrate, shows depressions, loose rock, moist areas—sure signs that real damage is going on below.

After a time, puddles remain in the broken areas. Seepage from puddles makes further trouble. Edges of cracked areas break off in chunks. Repair is essential.

REPAIRING BLACK-TOP DRIVEWAYS

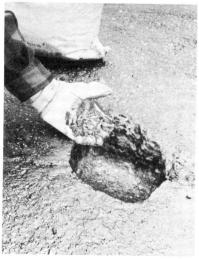

1. If necessary, warm patching material against radiator or furnace; but put several sheets of paper beneath to protect the floor.

2. Remove loose material from bottom of hole, particularly sand and dirt. Get down to a solid section of the driveway.

3. If easily available, place a few large rocks in the base of deep holes. It will save you some money, for you'll use less patching material. →

4. Fill in around large stones with cinders, smaller crushed rock, or clean gravel. Don't use vegetable matter, such as grass, or any earth with seeds in it.

5. Use a length of 2 × 4 and tamp this fill firmly so that the base is as compact as possible. Work fill into spaces between large rocks.

6. Fill hole to within 1″ of the top with patching mix, making certain mix is loose and crumbly. Avoid mixing in surrounding dirt.

7. "Cut and stir"—that is, drive shovel in and push mix about—to remove air pockets. Then press material against the sides of the hole.

8. Tamp firmly; then fill hole so that mix is about ½″ above surrounding surface. Driving your car over surface will compact it further.

9. To prevent asphalt patch from sticking to shoes or car tires, spread sand over the patch and work it into the surface by hand.

OUTDOOR STAIRS

By making use of durable materials—concrete, flagstone, and stone, for instance—you can make outdoor steps which will last indefinitely. Such masonry work can be done by almost any amateur. It's simple and inexpensive, and the results remain attractive over a period of many years.

There is actually only one "rule" to follow. That is, first make a sound footing for the stairs you intend to build. Otherwise, they might be undermined later by heavy rains or unsettled by frost upheaval.

When building steps, the first thought is for the ease with which they can be climbed. The two parts —the treads on which you step and the risers (the vertical distance between steps)—must be of correct dimensions. Treads should have a minimum width of 10"; 12" is even better; and 16" will make a particularly wide and attractive stairway. Risers should never exceed 8", and they may be trimmed down to 6 or 7" for added comfort. Steps leading to a door should be at least 4' wide to allow space on either side of the door.

In calculating the riser-tread figures, measure first the distance from ground level to door sill (or other point of arrival). Divide by units of 6, 7, or 8 to decide how many equal risers will be needed. Then count the number of treads needed (calling the ground level one tread and the sill another) and lay out the plan of the whole stairs.

One-step Rise. Suppose you have a simple one-step rise from the ground to a door sill, patio, or stoop. It's best to provide a footing of about 6" of crushed rock below grade, for which you'll need an excavation. Then lay out the outline of the step with brick-on-edge mortared together. The center is then filled with cement (or waste mortar) and a capping of brick or flagstone applied on top. Coat the tops of flagstones (but *only* the tops) with floor wax before setting in place and before pointing up the joints between them. This prevents mortar staining and keeps them clean and bright. After an hour, brush away any excess mortar with a stiff, dry brush.

Concrete Steps. The simplest form of concrete step construction is that of making one step at a time. Box in the lowest step to size with heavy lumber (2" stock), braced by stakes driven securely into the ground. Fill with a concrete mix of 1 part portland cement, 2½ parts sand and 5 parts gravel or crushed stone, and compact with a float, then level off the forward portion, which will become the lowest finished step, leaving the back section rough. When this has set, repeat the process for the next step, pouring directly over the rough part of the first. Repeat again for each higher step. For higher sets of steps (more than three or four), cut out two stringers to tread-riser size and use these as a form for the sides, nailing on wood riser boards to contain the concrete. Then pour all the steps at once, smoothing off after compacting across each tread. After 48 hours, remove the forms. Don't be discouraged when you first see the results. The sides will be rough, the tops of the treads will be flaky. In some cases, rock from the concrete mix will be exposed. All this is natural. The next step is to cover this concrete base with cement, at the same time waterproofing the steps and adding color if you wish.

Mix cement of 1:2½ mix, adding a waterproofing chemical to the water used in making the cement. Color may be added by including an additional ingredient in the mortar mixture. Prepared dry color in powder form can be added to a maximum of

How to construct progressive form for pouring one step at a time with concrete. Attach each added form to the one below with securely anchored cleats.

10 per cent of the volume of the portland cement used. The use of smaller quantities results in lighter shades. Dry color may also be sprinkled on the surface of the mortar immediately after it has been applied. It is then scrubbed into the mortar's surface with a stiff bristle brush (not wire), after which the surface must be troweled smooth.

Wet down the concrete steps thoroughly with a hose. Then trowel on ½" of the cement mix, starting at the base and working up the sides, up the risers, then over the treads. The use of a steel float glazes the surface and also cuts the angles sharply for neatness. But if safety is an important factor (concrete or cement may become slick when wet), use a wood float.

Concrete Block Steps. Concrete blocks can be stacked up and used for steps. However, since the average block is approximately 8-by-8-by-16", the 8" tread is not wide enough for comfort. On the other hand, if blocks are laid with the square 8-by-8 end toward the riser end, the extended 16" surface makes a good tread. Lay a series of blocks side by side, cement them together, and the steps are easily and quickly made. To bind sections together for greater stability, scrap pipe can be run through the voids of adjoining blocks and a flange can be screwed to each end before the voids are filled with cement.

Stone Steps. Cutting stone is an art quickly learned. Don't try to break a large stone by hitting it dead-center with a sledge. Dangerous splinters may fly, and if you do succeed in breaking it, the fragments will probably be useless. Wrist work, rather than arm-and-back muscle, will reduce even the toughest stones to the size you want. A length of twine tied to stakes may be of help in laying out your steps, but you may also go by eye. If you wish, set in a few double-length steps to vary the effect. Your stone stairway need not

Stone mason's double-edged ax will cut virtually all types of stone to shape.

be a straight drop but may be curved gradually down the slope. However, the straight drop uses the fewest stones.

Stone steps on earth are best laid from the top down. Make a smooth spot for the top step and set it in place. With a shovel, cut straight down to the position where the next step will be, adding the thickness of the stone to your cut. By scraping the removed earth forward and tamping it into place, another shelf is created for the next stone. The process is repeated down the grade until the stair is finished.

The beginning and ending of the stair may be given a touch of grandeur by adding larger border stones, by rounding off the last step or by flaring the borders apart toward the lower end. On extremely loose soil,

it may be a better plan to support the forward ends of each step with smaller upright stones to prevent undercutting by rain rather than to leave this riser area bare. Just remember that in placing these supporting stones, they should not tilt the step upward. This would cause rain to collect and seep into the soil, loosening it further and eventually causing the stones to settle deeply into the earth. Tilting them slightly downward allows the rain to run off. Eventually all stones will settle somewhat, but rarely will any have to be dug up and earth replaced beneath them.

Above: Massive borders, with flat edges toward the steps make a formal though rustic stair.

Left: Where earth is inclined to crumble, use small stones to support front edges.

Below: Large slabs on smaller stones make cutting into the hillside unnecessary.

Above, left: Alternate wide and narrow steps create a pleasant pattern, make climbing easy.

Above, right: Cut into the hillside to form a shelf on which to rest the next step down.

Right: Tamp down the new shelf evenly and smoothly to serve as seat for the next rock.

Flagstone and Brick Steps. Often a facing of flagstone, particularly on treads, is needed to match an adjoining patio. In this case, allow for the thickness of flagstone in making the concrete steps (usually about $1\frac{1}{2}''$), and when the concrete forms have been removed, wet the concrete and set the flags in a $\frac{1}{2}''$ bed of cement. To make brick steps, make allowance for the brick thickness on both the risers and treads and then set the bricks with mortar flat against the two surfaces, using the technique required for flagstones.

KEEPING BRICK STAIRWAYS IN CONDITION

1. Cracks in mortar need immediate attention to prevent water penetration which would widen crack and rot mortar.

2. Cut out all mortar from damaged area, exposing bare brick; use cold chisel and hammer.

$\rightarrow$

3. Clear away all loose material and scrub the surfaces with wire brush. Don't settle for half measures on this part of job.

4. Rinse out cracks with hose and soak brick thoroughly to prevent absorption of moisture from new mortar before it sets.

5. Mix only small quantities of mortar (1 part cement, 2½ parts sand) at one time so that mix will not harden as you work.

6. Lift mortar into cracks carefully to avoid staining bricks. Wipe up spills at once, as mortar stains are hard to remove. Pack mortar tightly into every crack with your trowel, then smooth off level with adjoining brick surfaces.

7. Use trowel tip to indent mortar in joints to shed water rapidly. After mortar is cured, apply masonry sealer paint.

Repairs for Outdoor Wooden Stairs. Outdoor wooden steps take a beating during the winter. They should be checked over carefully for any signs of weakness or decay.

First inspect the stringers—they're those side pieces that hold up the steps. In some cases, they're saw-toothed with the steps nailed across. In other cases, they're merely straight with a step support nailed to them and the steps nailed in between.

If there are any cracks along the grain, these sides can be strengthened by bolting a 2-by-4 along the full length. Use bolts, as nails in old wood only split it further. Use ¼" carriage bolts spaced at 1' intervals.

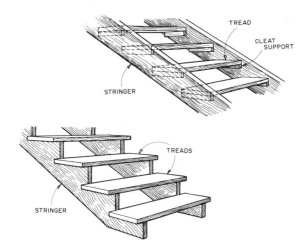

It's best to drill a $\frac{5}{16}''$ hole through the side support and the 2-by-4. Then insert the bolt with washers around the bolt head and under the nut.

With those saw-toothed stringers, if the step support shows signs of weakness, remove the step first. Do this by tapping up lightly a little at a time on each end of the step. Next, cut 2 pieces of wood to match the shape of the saw tooth out of 2″ stock or stock as thick as the original stringer.

If the stringer is still in good shape, cut off any weakened saw tooth. Replace it by bolting the new piece as noted in the sketch. But if the stringer is

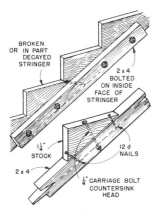

supported by a 2-by-4, just add a new supporting angled piece to it in the same way. Then renail the step in position.

Maybe the steps need attention. Some may be worn uneven in the center; if so, they can be turned over. With others it may be necessary to visit the lumber yard to buy replacements.

If your steps are the saw-tooth stringer type, it's easy to remove a step. Simply tap upward on each end as noted before.

With the other type of step construction, where the steps are nailed in between the side supports, the job is somewhat more exacting. The step, despite the side nails, is removed by tapping upward at each end. You have to hit a little harder but the step will come out. After the step is removed, hammer the exposed nails back through the supports.

If the step supports attached to the stringers are worn, replace them. They pry up easily. Attach new ones with $\frac{1}{4}''$ carriage bolts the same way as for the saw-tooth stringer supports.

Nail new steps first to these step supports. Then drive nails through the stringers into the step.

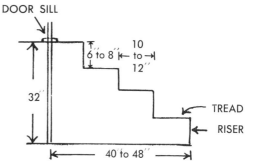

Calculate size of risers by measuring distance from ground to doorstep sill and dividing it into units of 6″, 7″, or 8″ plus fractions necessary to make the total. Then measure from house outward in units of 10″, 11″ or 12″ for treads.

FENCE BUILDING AND MENDING

You'll find fencing easy-to-do, rewarding work. Privacy, rather than security or boundary definition, is often the chief function of fencing. Fences can be used as walls to enclose outdoor living areas, isolate a service yard or cut off an undesirable view. Before building a fence, check with your local building department as to possible restrictions and permit requirements. The top height allowed for a home fence in most coded communities is 6′.

The materials used and the way they are put together determine how long your fence will resist the forces of the elements. Some types of lumber, such as redwood and cedar, resist exposure very well in their natural state. Others, among which are Engelmann spruce, the Western pines, and Douglas and white fir, are easy to work, straight-grained, and accept finishing readily. With proper treatment, these too will last for years.

Poorly-built fences just don't stay built for long. Wind and weather wreak their havoc. Undersized lumber soon sags. Flimsy gate hardware gives way and out-of-plumb posts lean even further. Damage

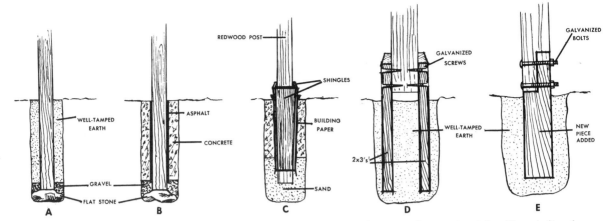

Treat repair materials to prevent deterioration. Use wood preservatives, coat metals with asphalt and use galvanized screws. (A) Post in tamped earth and (B) with concrete collar. (C) Surround redwood post with shingles and building paper before pouring concrete. Remove when concrete sets and fill gap with sand. (D) Replace damaged pieces with splints, or (E) make lap cut and bolt on extension.

can sometimes be patched, but faulty basic construction and the deterioration which follows mean more work. In the long run, it's better to do the original job correctly.

Low, light fences don't blow over easily, but the posts can be lifted by frost. High, solid fences offer areas large enough for wind to work against. If posts are too short or are loosely set, they may not be able to resist pressure. Examine a tottering or loose post by excavating around its base. If the post is set in the earth, it may be rotted or the soil so loosened around it that there is inadequate support. If set in concrete, the entire mass of concrete may have shifted, taking the post with it; the post may have rotted in its concrete jacket if water seeped in between it and the masonry.

Probably the most common disease of fences is rot, which may result when no preservative is used or when rusting nails provide water pockets. Rot can also stem from poor painting techniques and end-grain absorption of water. There is just one thing to do when rot is discovered. Remove the rotten pieces and take steps to prevent recurrence. The sketches suggest patchwork steps to take at the various points where rot starts. As a rule, it is the end of a rail that rots first. Nails rust out and rain is carried into the end grain through these openings. If not more than an inch or two of the rail ends are damaged, you may make an attempt at salvage and repair. Cut off the rotted end of upper and lower rails equally and

Woven wire fencing is good protection for animals or children, but it's not the most attractive material on the market. To dress it up, use strips of tempered hardboard run through the wire mesh. Cutting ⅛″ hardboard into 1″ strips is no job at all on a power saw. The slats permit air circulation, more sunlight than a solid fence would allow, and still hide the view enough to make an effective screen.

nail a length of 2-by-4 to them, then nail the 2-by-4 to the post.

Before planting any posts or, for that matter, any other parts of a fence, they should be treated with preservative to retard decay. Even those woods listed above as being weather-resistant will benefit from this treatment. One of the best liquid preservatives is pentachlorophenol. To apply, soak post ends for 2 to 8 hours. Other surfaces may be painted with a generous coat. Do this before assembly of the fence so that surfaces which may be hidden inside joints are adequately protected.

The length of the below-ground portion of a post should equal half the height of the fence above the ground. And length alone won't help if the post is improperly set. In such cases, new holes must be made and a flat rock or brick dropped into the bottom of the hole on which to reset the post. Tamp the dirt solidly around the post. In firm soil or clay, it's not generally necessary to use concrete,

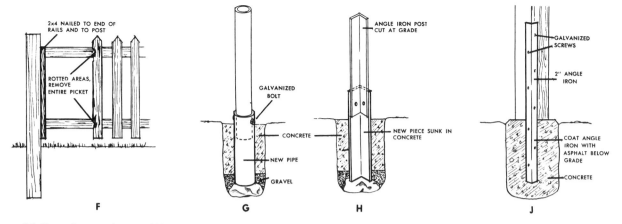

(F) Cures for rotted areas. (G) When metal rusts, set old post inside larger piece, bolt together. (H) Replace rusted angle iron with new piece bolted on. (J) Bolt wood post to angle set in concrete. Leave gap between to prevent rot.

HOW TO ANCHOR A FENCE POST TO CONCRETE

1. Pour concrete posts at least 8″ deep on a rock fill and insert upended bolt in wet concrete. Let base set 48 hours before erecting posts.

3. Before putting posts in place, coat the grain end with asphalt paint as a seal against water penetration. This will check possible rot and insect invasion.

2. Drill holes in ends of posts to fit over anchor bolts. If patio concrete is already in place, drill hole in masonry and insert lag screw in post end to fit into the hole drilled in the concrete.

4. Slip post over anchor bolt in concrete. This type of anchorage resists side pressures, heavy winds.

Fence Building and Mending   317

1. If your fence posts have been pushed over or have pulled up, reset them, using a posthole digger to make holes as small as possible.
2. A good wood preservative is of greatest importance when mending fences. Treatment with this chemical insures a long life for the posts.
3. When it comes to replacing pickets, a good spacer is quickly found in a spare picket placed between the others for uniformity.

but in looser soil use 1 part portland cement to 3 parts sand and 5 parts gravel or crushed rock. The concrete should form a collar around the post. With rock and gravel in the hole, brace the post in position (see Sketch B, page 316). Compact the concrete well and bring it 1″ above grade. Trowel off the top so that it slopes away from the post for drainage. When the concrete sets, seal the space between post and concrete with asphalt.

Rusted steel or cast-iron posts may be salvaged by cutting a piece from a spare and splicing it to the old piece with carriage bolts. Pipe-style posts can be mended by slipping the old post into a pipe of larger diameter. Apply protective coatings to metals, using red lead for above ground and asphalt compounds for below grade.

Broken or rotted pickets are best replaced individually, using an old one as a model for forming new ones. They can be cut quickly from standard stock obtainable in your lumber yard.

STURDY GATES

The simplest gate of all is one built of boards using only lap joints, a process of nailing one board to another. The first sketch shows the Z-shaped frame of 2-by-4's which joins the boards and adds strength. The boards are ¾-by-6″ stock.

Gate No. 2 is a combination of a picket fence with the pickets increased in length to form an upward curve at the hinge end. The strength of this gate lies in a solid footing for the post, plus the extra-long strap hinges on which it swings.

Gate No. 3 requires only one complex joint, a cross lap joint in the center which can be completed with a hand saw and chisel, but which adds greatly to the strength of the gate. All the joints are nailed; strength can be gained by the use of angle irons screwed to the inner surfaces of the points.

For rustic fencing, a simple gate is shown in Photograph 4. Here, of course, the homeowner can let his own talent have free rein, since there are no hard and fast design rules to follow.

Gate No. 5 is a major project. It will look solid from all angles and—properly built—*be* solid. The body of this structure is tongue-and-grooved stock, which adds rigidity. Bracing is all of 1″ stock, the

Board fence offers a maximum of privacy. Open bottom helps air circulation, allows shielding where it counts most, and makes a third rail unnecessary. A third rail is usually required for any fence over 5′ high.

1. Wide board gate, 2 × 4 supports on back, top curve made with straight-line cuts.

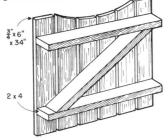

2. Picket fence gate, supported on long strap hinges, makes a graceful picture anywhere.

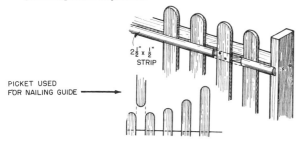

3. Simple but substantial gate of heavy material requires but one cross lap joint.

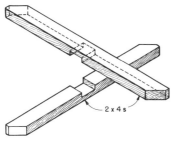

4. Rustic fence, with beveled ends in slots for added strength, cannot be moved unless both hinge supports are turned at once.

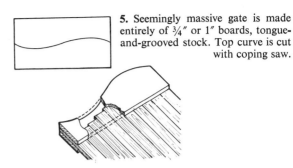

5. Seemingly massive gate is made entirely of ¾″ or 1″ boards, tongue-and-grooved stock. Top curve is cut with coping saw.

6. Three-rail gate with seemingly mortised joints is easily constructed of overlapped boards, which add strength as well as beauty.

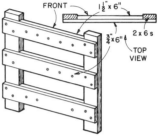

same as is the body part, and the bracing is duplicated for both sides. The monotony of the pattern is relieved by the upper curve which requires a band or sabre saw (power), or coping or keyhole saw (hand). Cutting a curve can be accomplished for all needed pieces in a single cut, using the system shown. Nail two wide boards together, mark the curve, and cut an identical curve matching both sides and right and left gates. After the cutting, you'll have four pieces, each with the same curve. Assemble as shown.

The sixth gate, although plainer in appearance, is more complicated to construct but has added rigidity. The two uprights are 2-by-6 timbers; the cross members—visible from the front side only—are 1½-by-6's set flush on the rear side and covered over by ¾-by-6″ boards. The latter, in overlapping the uprights, give the appearance to the visible cross members of having been set in mortises.

PATCHING PIERS AND POSTS

Out of sight and frequently concealed by shrubbery, therefore likely to be overlooked during periodic house check-ups, are those piers which support porches, girders and parts of the house foundation. In the case illustrated at right, a brick pier under a porch corner was the culprit. Once cemented over, cracks developed in the cement and water penetrated to the brick, which in turn crumbled. Many bricks were defective and replacement of the entire pier was the only economical and safe procedure.

First clear a space for a temporary footing for a house jack, which may be borrowed or rented. Broad boards and heavy timbers are necessary for ground supports under the jack. Proceed carefully with the jack, raising the building only $\frac{1}{32}$″ above the pier; this should be just enough to remove the defective material.

Since the new pier will not be ready to receive the weight of the building for at least 24 hours, provide additional props as a safeguard. Your jack may not be able to hold the weight that long, particularly if it has a slight leak or if your temporary base under the jack is on soft ground.

After removal of the defective pier, the all-important footing should be checked. Frost action, roots and animals may have undermined it. Concrete is the best material to use here. With a mix of 4 parts gravel, 2½ parts sand and 1 part cement, rebuild the pier as illustrated. The core of a brick pier may be filled with rubble or concrete to form a solid masonry unit.

If, as will probably happen, the new pier does not exactly fit under the sill, the space between should be filled either with mortar, forced into the space to fill it completely, or with wood wedges (preferably hardwood) inserted all around and the protruding ends sawed off.

Cement must be allowed to set 24 hours before the jack is removed and the building's weight placed on the new masonry. Whether the brick pier is left

1. Investigation reveals a badly worn and weathered pier, stucco peeled away, and bricks no longer sound and safe.

2. Both eye and level show the house has not dropped and rebuilding the pier to the same size is possible and practical.

3. A building jack needs a firm footing before it can hold the house load. Long planks and large blocks are pyramided as a base.

4. A borrowed screw-type jack is tried for size and the block footing adjusted to dimensions of the jack.

5. Jack bar is turned until the load rests on jack instead of footing. One more half turn is enough to lift house from pier.

6. Paper slips between house sill and pier. Jack now carries the load and the pier may be removed with safety.

→

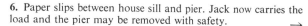

7. Pier comes apart easily, as most of the mortar has decayed and turned to sand.

8. A new footing for a new pier is the first step undertaken. Cement square is ready to receive brick at ground level.

9. New pier doesn't fit, so a concrete filler between pier and house is constructed to fill gap. No form is necessary.

10. Final touch is new stucco coat over the new brick pier. Stucco is brushed smooth, then troweled over.

bare or cemented over, it's best to protect it against water penetration by means of a masonry-sealer paint after the cement has cured for a week or two.

The proper way to set a post in the soil is to use a concrete form around the base (see sketch). If you have this type of post, chances are that you will not encounter rot . . . as long as you maintain a protective coating over the exposed section of the wood.

If this type of post does develop rot, it is best to remove the entire post and concrete block base. Set a new post into the ground, cover the under-surface section with asphalt and then add a concrete mix of 1 part cement, 2 parts sand and 4 parts gravel together with enough water to make it a slow-flowing mass.

Methods of setting other types of posts are detailed on the next two pages.

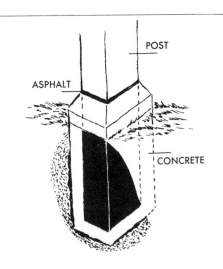

POSTS ON A WOOD-FLOOR PORCH

1. If the outside edges of the post have rotted, rabbet-cut the post with a saw and remove the excess with a chisel. The center part *A* must be at least half the thickness of the post.

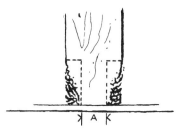

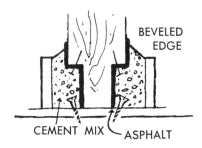

2. Drive several coated nails into this center base and into the underside of the exposed part of the post. Also set several large screws into floor within cutout area.

3. Make a form of ½″ plywood to fit around the four sides of the post. This form should be about 2″ wider and longer than the size of the post. Coat the inside of the form with oil or grease.

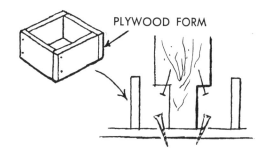

PLYWOOD FORM

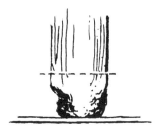

BEVELED EDGE

4. Coat the exposed wood with asphalt. Then mix 1 part cement, 2 parts sand and water, and compact into form. Bevel the upper edge of the cement mix. Let cement harden, then remove form.

CEMENT MIX — ASPHALT

5. If, however, most of the base has rotted through, it is necessary to cut across the post about 2″ above the rotted area. Hold post securely while sawing so as not to disturb the upper part.

6. Make a base out of several pieces of wood, beveling the edges so that it sheds water easily. Nail pieces together with aluminum or coated nails that won't rust.

7. Slip base between bottom of post and wood floor of porch. Nail in position with coated finishing nails. Use calking compound or asphalt around base to keep out water.

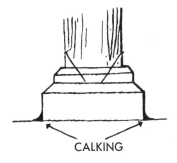

CALKING

Patching Piers and Posts   323

POSTS SET IN A CONCRETE PORCH

1. When a wood post set in a concrete porch rots at the base, remove the rotted portion with a saw. Cut as sketched to form two rabbets for new base.

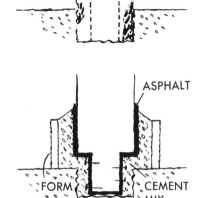

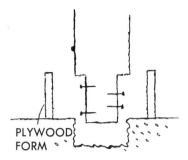

2. Drive several nails into lower part of the post where new base is to be added. These nails will hold post securely in the cement which is to be poured into the form.

3. Coat exposed underpart of post with asphalt, and compact 1 part cement to 2 parts sand plus bonding agent and water into form. Bevel top to shed rain quickly.

RETAINING WALLS

A retaining wall is a masonry fence that holds back earth. While it may be ornamental to enhance the landscape, its primary purpose is one of utility. Its construction differs considerably from that of a simple fence. Retaining walls permit drastic changes in your present landscape. For instance, a steep, unusable slope where not even grass can gain a foothold may be divided into a series of terraces with low retaining walls. The terraces may then be planted to grass or flowers.

Erosion, which covers graded walks and drives with silt during each rainfall, can be stopped by setting up retaining walls. Then, too, outdoor living requires flat areas for patios and playgrounds. The sloping lot, naturally adapted to such pastimes, may be leveled by means of a retaining wall of the necessary height behind which the flat area may be constructed.

All retaining walls begin at a point below frost level. Since water in the ground expands on freezing, it will lift anything upward, including a masonry wall. With thawing, the heavy wall sinks deeply and irregularly into the soft ground. Cracks will develop, or the wall may even tumble. To avoid any of this, build the wall on a footing below maximum frost depth, generally no more than 24″ in most areas.

The base is the widest part of a retaining wall. The footing it rests on is at least 6″ wider than the base, and the wall may taper toward its top. This is possible since the greatest pressure of earth on the uphill side of the wall is at its base. The exposed face of a retaining wall should be slightly inclined toward the uphill side. If it were truly vertical, it would appear to be toppling forward. The slant is approximately 1″ for each foot of height. Before backfilling behind a retaining wall, lay a row of field tiles along the footing, sloping ¼″ per foot toward either end. Then fill to at least half the wall height with loose gravel and scrap masonry to provide quick drainage. At 6′ intervals along the wall's base, leave weep holes 2″ in diameter to prevent water from accumulating behind the wall.

Masonry materials for wall construction include irregularly shaped fieldstone, cut stone for more formal effects, concrete and cinder blocks which may be faced with cut stone or brick, concrete blocks cast in decorative patterns, and common and face brick. Common brick and concrete blocks may also be faced with simulated stone. It is wise to choose a material suited to the architectural style of the home as well as to the general appearance of the planned landscape. Formal gardens deserve cut stone or formal brick patterns. Rustic scenes and backgrounds are enhanced with retaining walls of fieldstone, laid up dry or mortared together. In contrast, an informal gathering place, such as a patio with a grill, might

Selected flat fieldstone joined with mortar, with larger stone keyed in, supports earth base of this terrace, encloses stairs.

Low cut-stone wall, laid up dry, creates a formal effect. Similar stone, also laid up dry, is retaining wall for broad stone-capped step. Flags and wall cap are similarly cut.

Large blocks of stone, laid up dry, make level spot around the house, divide the playground area from wooded slope.

appear to best advantage against a wall of common brick.

In planning to control a slope with a wall or with a series of walls, first consider the soil characteristics. Heavy clay slopes with slow water penetration should not exceed a rise of 1' for each 3' horizontally. A greater slope will result in erosion, and the surface will deteriorate into a series of gullies. Grade accordingly uphill of the wall. Sandy soil or deep loam, where water penetrates quickly, may be graded for a 1' rise in each 1½'. Start the excavation on a slope so as to follow land contours if at all possible. This will keep the footing of the wall reasonably level and will produce the maximum amount of usable land when the wall is finished and the ground graded behind it.

For walls up to 2' high, where the ground levels off at the wall-top point, an 8"-thick wall may serve the purpose. For higher walls, and those where the ground rises above wall level, the base is made thicker in proportion. General wall proportions are indicated in Sketch 3. For stone walls, consult Sketches 1 and 2, which show forward slope and other proportions.

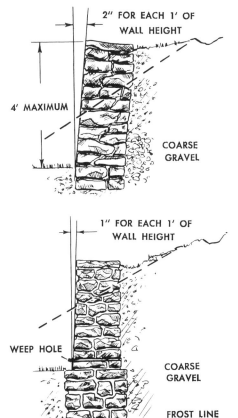

Sketch 1 (left). Where stone is laid up dry, entire wall is inclined toward retained-earth. Fill is the same as for mortared wall.

Sketch 2 (below, left). Proportion of cut-stone retaining wall laid up with mortar. Face inclines at less of an angle than with dry wall. Footing begins at frost line. Note gravel fill behind wall.

Sketch 3. Measurements indicated in inches.

Wall Height	Depth to Footing	Footing		Wall	
		Thickness	Width	Top	Bottom
A	B	C	D	E	F
12	12	6	14	6	8
24	18	8	24	8	16
36	24	10	36	10	24
48	30	12	48	12	32

So-called dry-wall construction means that stone is gathered and selected by shape—preferably flat—and stacked up, keyed together without any mortar at all. In a wet wall, masonry is joined with mortar. The mortared wall is obviously stronger since the masonry is combined into a solid mass and individual stones or blocks cannot be pushed out. Where earth is level at the top of the wall, dry construction may be followed, but if the hillside continues upward above the wall, mortar the materials together for greater strength.

Pointing (shaping) of masonry joints on a retaining wall has much to do with the wall's appearance. With stone in particular, interesting effects may be produced. Where mortar is raked out to a depth of an inch or more, a deep shadow pattern results. Brick is usually pointed in a manner similar to that on house walls and chimneys. Concrete blocks may be pointed with concave or convex mortar joints, or you can allow the mortar squeezed out to harden without pointing.

1. In laying a block or stone wall, the footing below grade is most easily made with poured concrete onto which block or stone is cemented.

2. When laying concrete or cinder block, or cut stone, check work frequently with level to insure strength and even appearance.

3. Where a slope is to be established, use a level and a rule to form the triangle indicated in Sketches No. 1 and 2 on the previous page.
4. Rear of block wall is not finished with pointed joints. All should be tight, however, and scrap masonry used as fill.
5. This block wall is built up with scrap brick and mortar on "fill" side. Inclined brick discourages juvenile wall-walkers.

6. Visible mortar joints are carefully pointed with concave stone beader, excess mortar being brushed away when partly dry.
7. Filled in behind wall and planted to lawn and shrubs, the new terrace, created by means of the wall, adds new attractiveness to property.

CURE FOR A FLOODED YARD

If your rainspouts periodically flood your yard, or if you're the recipient of downwash from your neighbor's property, a dry well or catch basin will solve the problem of excess water. A dry well alone will handle most ordinary situations. However, if the soil is of clay, hardpan, ledge, or otherwise very poorly drained, a dry well alone may not suffice. A drain-tile line may be needed in addition to carry the water from the well to your sewer line, storm drain, or a slope where run-off is possible.

A small grille can be used to cover the well or basin if the volume of drain water is never too great. If the problem is that of an occasional flash flood, a large grate is a wiser choice.

In the well illustrated below and on the next page, 6″ wide cement blocks were used in two courses, laid directly atop a 2″ floor of cement. A 6″ vitrified tile line carries the water from the well into the regular city sewer. The large, barred cover was made with lengths of 1″ pipe butt-welded to two lengths of ⅜″ by 1½″ strap iron. The grille was painted thoroughly to prevent rust. Many hardware stores or building supply dealers carry a variety of stock-size grilles, if you would rather not make one.

1. Dig a hole 38″ square and 28″ deep. From it, dig a foot-wide trench for a run-off pipeline, if desired. Make certain pitch of trench is away from well by pouring water into it.
2. For a small well, a depth of two blocks is sufficient. If there is no run-off line, you should make it at least three blocks deep. You may have to cut a block or two for staggered joints. →

3. Run the bell end of your drainpipe line into the well, as close to the bottom as possible. Use cement and rubble to fill in to level of other blocks.

4. Drain line is made of 6″ vitreous tile, and joints are filled with mortar. Connect into regular city storm drain line, using a "Y" fitting.

5. This is the way the well looks before the cover is added. You do not have to worry about packing joints with a lot of mortar. There is little or no strain on them.

6. The cover, in this case, is made of 1″ pipe welded to two bars of heavy strap iron. You can buy any of a variety of covers at your local building-supply house.

7. A wood frame is nailed around the edge of the well. This frame serves as a guide for the pouring and molding of a cement border around the cover. Trowel cement smooth.

8. The cover is removed carefully, and the supporting surface is troweled smooth with cement. Finally, the cover is replaced and the cement border is given a last touch-up.

USING THE GARAGE FOR STORAGE

Most garages are either square or rectangular in shape, and since cars don't match such shapes, there are vacant corners, spaces overhead and room all around the car that can be used for extra storage.

The Overhead Area. By far the largest space available is found in the gable-roof garage, with a hip-roof structure second in line. Except for large multi-car structures where a small apartment may be built overhead, this space is often entirely wasted. With a two-car garage, the entire space may be utilized. A

second floor may be built and, except for an entrance into it, the whole floor can be used for storage. The sketch on the next page, top left, indicates the manner in which such a floor is supported. Where possible, the new floor joists, which are run across the shortest dimension, can rest on the top plate of the walls. Where there is no room because of the construction of the roof, the joists can be set below the plate and rested on blocks attached to the wall studs. For average lightweight storage, 2-by-6 joists spaced 16″ apart will do. If heavier materials are to be stored, use 2-by-8's. Just be sure to pro-

For small 1-car garage, overhead space is at a premium; good use is made by means of short, shelf-like areas supported in part by the roof rafters. Reach these from a short ladder.

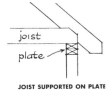

JOIST SUPPORTED ON PLATE

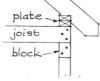

JOIST SUPPORTS ON BLOCKS

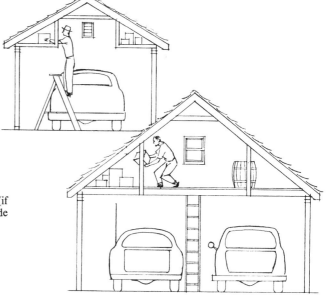

When whole floor is built, support joists either on top plate (if roof structure permits), or on blocks attached to studs of side walls, again gaining added support with rafter ties.

vide clearance for the car. Partial flooring over the area is also a very good idea—in fact, it may even be preferred in order to provide easy entrance from below by way of a folding stairway. With a one-car garage of limited width—and, consequently, limited headroom above—a partial floor along both walls, leaving a triangle-shaped storage area on each side of an open center section, is a good alternative. Small items can be stored this way and access easily made by removable ladder.

Along-the-wall Storage. A storage wall in the home is a popular feature, and the same idea, but with a fraction of the cost, can be adapted to the garage. The shelves are the easiest part—regular sheathing or shelving supported on 3″ strips along the wall and cross pieces connecting the two vertical 2-by-3's in front (one in the middle, the other set out ½″ to serve as a stop for the panels; a 2″ furring strip the length of the opening is nailed to the floor to serve as an anchor for the vertical 2-by-3's and also as a guide for the bottom edge of the panels). The sliding panels are two standard 4-by-8′ pieces of hardboard, cut down slightly to fit the space exactly and to provide an inch overlap at the center. One of the pieces

cut from the hardboard serves as a valance to hide the edges of the hanger rails.

Inside-the-wall Storage. Where the walls of the garage are open and the studs visible, innumerable small articles can be stored on small shelves between studs. Set a ¼-by-1½″ strip along the outer shelf edge to keep articles from sliding off. The variety of such shelves is almost endless, with spacing between them determined by the items to be stored.

In some parts of the country, this "open" storage might well be objectionable owing to dust accumulation or insect invasion. A cover of transparent plastic in the form of a weighted drop curtain will, in the majority of cases, handle this problem.

Shelves between wall studs can be supported on cleats attached to adjacent studs, spaced to meet storage needs, from floor to plate.

RENEW AND BRIGHTEN YOUR GARDEN FURNITURE

Here is a quick and easy method to give outdoor metal furniture a finish equal to a factory spray job —a finish that will last through any kind of weather.

1. Assemble all materials and tools and spread a protective cover over the working area.

2. Replace rusted bolts and screws with new ones, tighten any that are loose. Use one size larger where holes have rusted wide.
3. Sandpaper and a wire brush remove rust. Steel wool gets into tight corners. Use varnish remover to take off old finish.
4. Next, brush on a metal undercoat or primer.

5. Sand the prime coat smooth. Ridges and brush marks here will show up sharply in the final finish.
6. For a two-color job, enamel arms first. Wrap when dry to prevent spotting when painting finish coat on seat and back.

CARE OF GARDEN TOOLS AND EQUIPMENT

Hoses. Sooner or later almost every garden hose springs a leak. An unseen kink causes a break when the water is turned on, or the constant rubbing of the hose against a rough wall wears it thin. Hose-mending is a simple process and requires only a few minutes, particularly if you keep a garden hose first-aid kit handy. This should include several splicers or mender tubes and pipe clamps, one or two male and female coupling-splicers, some hose washers and, if you have a rubber hose, a tube of black rubber-base cement (not the ordinary household rubber cement) and a roll of friction tape. When you buy the splicers or mender tubes, make certain to get the right size for your hose.

When you use a splicer, insert one end flush into the garden hose. Tap the prongs gently and gradually, working your way around all the prongs until they are firmly set into the hose. Make certain the prongs grip the hose tightly; then insert the splicer into the other end of the hose and repeat.

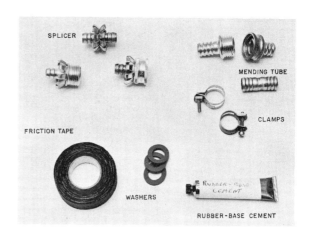

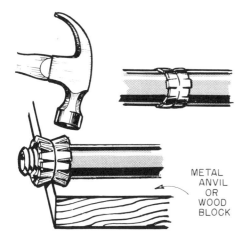

METAL ANVIL OR WOOD BLOCK

If you use a mender tube, insert one end of the tube into the hose. Slip a pipe clamp over so that it's about ½" away from the edge of the hose and tighten the nut and bolt with a screwdriver. Then slip on another pipe clamp and slide the mender tube into the other section of garden hose so that the two hose ends are touching. Push the second clamp so

that it's about 1" from the first and tighten the nut and bolt.

The same method is used to add a new coupling to your hose. Couplings are available in brass, rubber or plastic.

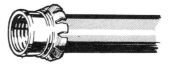

It is easier to repair a rubber hose that has sprung a small leak than a plastic hose. To fix a rubber hose, clean the damaged area thoroughly and dry with a clean cloth. Apply a thick coat of the rubber-base cement and let it dry from 5 to 10 minutes. Then apply a second thin coat and wrap a single layer of friction tape around the hose. Hold the tape securely for a minute or so and then let it dry. To fix a small leak in a plastic hose, add a splicer in the same way as you would if there were a large leak.

To repair a large leak, cut out the defective section of the hose with a sharp knife, making certain the ends are square or straight up and down. If you're repairing plastic hose, dip the ends in hot water to soften the plastic, thus making it easier to work.

In the fall, before you store your hose for the winter months, separate each length of hose and drain any water out of each. Lay them flat or on a slight slope to dry out. Remove all old washers and disconnect any automatic coupling attachments. Roll each length of hose separately without kinks or twists and store them in a bushel basket or on a hose reel. Use a brush with detergent or soap and water to clean the nozzles and couplings, then rinse several times and wipe dry.

1. Special force-fit fittings for plastic garden hose come with locking key used for assembly. Both male and female units are available.
2. Insert threaded bushing into the plastic hose; it's tapered for an easy fit. Slip male or female coupling over outside of hose.
3. Special key fits into slots inside the bushing. Turn clockwise to tighten until top edge of bushing is flush with edge of hose.

Lawn Mowers. The power lawn mower is not complex and its maintenance is relatively simple. There are three major types of power mowers—rotary, traditional reel, and hammer-knife. Most of these are powered with either a 2-cycle or a 4-cycle small, rugged, air-cooled engine. Horsepowers range from 1 to 3, and prices are based on brand name, size, and horsepower. Size versus price is determined by the cutting width. If you have a small lawn under 5,000 square feet, a 16″ to 18″ cut is good. Up to 12,000 square feet calls for a 20″ to 22″ mower. For larger areas, try a 24″ to 26″ or smaller units ganged together to cut a single wide swath.

Rotary mowers have one or more blades mounted parallel with the ground and they spin like a fan. In most models, this spinning blade extends in front

Rotary power motor

Reel power mower

of the wheels, which makes possible cutting within ½" of trees, walls or shrubs. The blade is adjustable for depth cuts ranging from ⅝" to 3" simply by raising or lowering the wheels. The blade can be removed for sharpening, a job which can be done in a bench vise with a fine-cutting file.

Reel mowers cut more evenly and keenly than rotaries but are less maneuverable, which means that edging with other tools is necessary. Setting adjustments are simple to make with a wrench, and the cut can be lowered to ½" and raised to about 2½". The blades do not usually require a sharpening more than once a season.

The hammer-knife mower has a number of loosely hung T-shaped knives attached to a horizontal shaft between the wheels, and they rotate at high speed. The knives cut with a scythe action, fold back when they strike a hard object, and return to cutting position automatically. Large wheels and lightweight construction provide easy maneuverability. The knives can be removed for sharpening.

Power mowers use either a gas engine or an electric motor. The gas engines are almost invariably 1-cylinder. Both the 2-cycle and 4-cycle use regular gas and a high-grade motor oil. The 2-cycle is lighter in weight and has fewer parts but is apt to create a smoky exhaust because oil must be mixed with the gasoline (½ pint oil to 1 gallon gas). The 4-cycle type has its oil added separately, and this must be checked periodically. The relationship of horsepower to the job is important. An 18" mower, for instance, can use 1½ HP, while a 20" or 22" requires 2 to 2½ HP. Extra power is also needed to cut St. Augustine, Bermuda, or crab grass.

1. After every 4 to 5 hours of operation, check oil level by removing the crankcase oil plug. Add oil to plug base. After 20 to 25 hours, drain oil by opening drain plug, pour a cup of clean oil through and then refill crankcase with fresh oil.

2. Add oil to the air filter every 4 to 5 hours; there's a gauge mark to show proper level. A small wing nut is all that holds filter in place. After every 20 to 25 hours, clean old oil out of filter, wipe clean with dry cloth, and refill with fresh oil.

3. Keep mower clean for proper, efficient functioning. After mowing the lawn, brush away grass clippings, leaves, and other debris from the cylinder fins, blower housing, and flywheel. An old whiskbroom or brush will do a perfect job of mower cleaning.

4. Check tension of drive belt periodically. A loose-fitting belt will impair the operation of the blades. Apply belt dressing every 20 to 25 hours to keep it in shape. Also make certain the drive wheels are free of grease and dirt. Wipe these wheels clean with a cloth.

5. At the same time that you change the crankcase oil, inspect the spark plug. Remove it by turning counterclockwise with an adjustable open-end wrench. Brush points at bottom clean; do this gently. Pour a teaspoonful of gasoline in cylinder and replace plug.

Electrically powered motors can be had in both reel and rotary types. They are quite silent compared to gas engines. Original cost, maintenance and operating costs are lower. They use 110-volt house current and are best on a small, well-kept lawn that is flat and has few trees and shrubs to interfere with the cable.

Dirt causes most of the trouble in power mowers. The best weapons to offset dirt are a whiskbroom and a screwdriver with a cloth wrapped around the end. With these, keep the air filter, the blower screen and the motor cooling fins cleaned after each use. Kerosene will keep the steel wool of the air filter cleansed inside. Rule No. 1 on repairing: disconnect the wire to the spark plug on gas engines, unplug the electric types. You can do 90 per cent of the repairs needed by checking the ignition, the fuel system and the compression.

POWER MOWER TROUBLE-SHOOTING CHECKLIST

4-cycle engine smokes while running
> CURE: Fuel mixture is too rich; turn needle valve in a clockwise direction, using a screwdriver.

Motor won't run unless choke is pulled all the way out
> CURE: Fuel mixture too lean; needle valve should be turned in a counter-clockwise direction.

Engine sputters and misfires—there's a kickback while you hold the mower
> CURE: Spark plug might be dirty or cracked; check it and replace if necessary. The condenser might be faulty; have a serviceman check it.

Engine missing while in operation—motor doesn't hum evenly and mower runs jerkily
> CURE: Spark plug not functioning properly; clean it, or replace it if necessary. Wire connected to top of plug might be loose or dirty; disconnect, clean with emery paper and assemble tightly. The magneto might be defective; this is not a job for the average homeowner.

Run-away engine—mower keeps moving ahead even when handle is in stop position
> CURE: Check idle speed adjustment screw and spring near it to see if either is blocked by grass clippings. Turn this screw clockwise one turn; if this does not correct difficulty, try several half-turns, checking the motor in between each turn.

THE UNPOWERED MOWER

 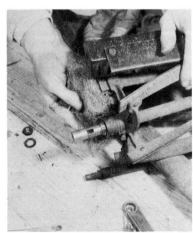 

1. If you forgot to remove last year's dirt and scale, take the wheels off—it'll be easier. Remove all parts carefully; remember how they were placed.
2. After cleaning wheels, end housing and gears, get to work on the axle. Hard rubbing and steel wool will get it shining and ready for work.
3. Reassemble end housing with all parts in position. Put the "dog"—that gear with grease over it—in reverse. Smear all gear and bearing surfaces with a coat of light grease.

4. Don't try to sharpen the cutting edges of the reel. Go over sides of each blade with a mill file to remove burrs but do not try to file cutting edges. Confine your sharpening to the bed knife or strike bar as in Photograph 5.
5. With wheel on again, remove and clean strike bar. To replace, use thin metal sheet as gauge. Every part of each blade must touch it evenly. Smear strike bar and blades with valve-grinding compound used on cars; this polishes and sharpens the cutting edges.

 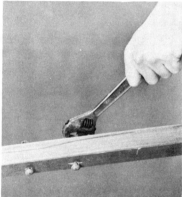 

6. With dogs reversed, run blades backward; adjust strike bar so that it just barely touches the blades. Now, put dogs in the right way. Make final adjustment between blades and strike bar. A good distance is one where blades just cut a triple thickness of newspaper.
7. Now the cutting surfaces are ready to roll. But how about the rest? Maybe the handle shaft is split—if so, drill holes for ¼″ carriage bolts and anchor bolts with a nut flush with wood surfaces. Cut off excess of bolt with a hack saw; file smooth.
8. Or maybe the handle is broken. If you have one of the "T-shaped" units pictured above, you'll find a broom stick end makes a good hardwood replacement for the two grip handles.

Garden Tools. Garden tool handles usually break because of dry rot, caused by being left out in all kinds of weather alternately to soak and dry. Repairs are seldom effective for a long period of time. However, a split handle can be temporarily mended by spreading waterproof glue the length of the split, bringing the two sides together and taping the handle tightly. Then drill one or several holes through the handle at right angles to the split and insert round-headed carriage bolts, adding a washer and nut on the opposite side.

Shovels and spades often turn up corners by banging into unyielding rock. These can be hammered flat, then a new edge filed on the dull surface. Use

To remove unusable handle, file off rivet head on one side, then pull remainder through with nail puller or pry.

Some socket-type handles have a hole where wedge can be used to loosen them.

Sharpen to original bevel. Long bevel gives sharper edge, but is easily nicked.

Follow original bevel in sharpening cutting tools and clippers. Thirty degrees is right.

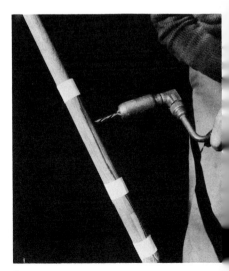

Split handles can still be used if taped and glued, then bolted through split.

Above, left: Bamboo or wood-slat rakes with broken teeth can be put back into service easily.

Above, right: Teeth are held by wire over metal tongues. Depress tongue to remove wire.

Right: Broken teeth overlapped reduce width of rake, but it's still a usable tool.

a mill file or a grinding stone. Sharpen spades from both sides. Hoes, on the other hand, are sharpened only from the outside face—that is, the edge toward the ground is filed toward the user. A long, thin edge will work more easily. A blunt edge lasts longer but doubles your work on weeds. It's a good idea in sharpening tools of this sort to follow the lines of the original edge. This applies particularly to assorted grass and pruning clippers. Those joined by pins can readily be dismantled for sharpening and oiled for reassembly.

Steel rakes with missing teeth are best replaced. Wood and bamboo rakes, however, can be given new life with little effort. An expediency for broken teeth is shown in the illustrations above; replacements can be made from sawed strips of hardwood, shaped with pliers after soaking in boiling water.

Before storing tools away for the winter, clean all working edges. Use steel wool or a wire brush on shovels, rakes and hoes. Use kerosene to remove dirt. Paint linseed oil on all wood handles to help preserve the wood. Apply a protective coating of grease or oil over metal parts. For grass shears and pruners, wash in kerosene and use sandpaper on

tough spots. Sharpen cutting edges on whetstone; loosen tension on all springs; replace worn or rusted nuts and bolts and coat with grease or oil.

Any sprinkler needs a complete post-summer check-up. Remove and clean all nozzle tips. Then clean the sprinkler itself, discarding old washers. After drying all the parts, lubricate bushings and bearings with a waterproof grease and coat all metal surfaces with a thin layer of oil.

Care of Garden Tools and Equipment   337

3. If you prefer, use steel wool instead of the brush. This does as good a job unless the metal is pitted by long wear and rust.

1. The items you need are few—paintbrush, wire brush, linseed oil, machine oil, steel wool, a metal file, a handful of rags.

2. First step for tools—scrape off all caked dirt. The wire brush takes the last of it away, leaves the metal bright.

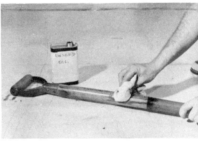

4. File cutting edges sharp *now*. Spring may come fast, giving you no time later for putting the lawn equipment in good shape.

5. Clean all wood handles and parts thoroughly and, unless they are protected with a coat of paint, apply coating of linseed oil.

6. Spray cleaned metal surfaces with a good grade of penetrating oil, or, if you prefer to distinguish your tools by color, paint the metal.

CHAPTER 7

THE USE OF MATERIALS

Painting · Working with Wood · Masonry

Any home is as fine as the workmanship that goes into it . . . and often the work of the home handyman surpasses by far that of the professional painter, carpenter or mason. Maybe this is the result of his special interest, care and pride—whatever the reason, the fact remains that home handymen can quickly become experts if they have the proper directions and follow them carefully, the right tools and use them properly, and the appropriate materials for the job and understand them thoroughly.

This chapter explains the latter—how to choose and use the materials you will most frequently handle in the work around your home—wood, paint and masonry. From one end of the house to the other, from one property line to another, you will use these materials for most of your repairs and home improvement projects.

It's important, therefore, that you know how to choose the right paint for each specific surface, how to buy lumber economically, how to mix the ingredients for sidewalk crack repairs, to mention but a few situations. In other words, just as important as the right tools and methods, selection and use of the proper materials mean all the difference between slipshod results and an efficient and lasting job.

PAINTING Safety in painting · Choosing the right paint · Painting tools · Paint failures · How to paint interiors · Painting exteriors

Paint can transform your home far more quickly—and inexpensively—than any other material available. A new coat of paint on the walls can bring with it a sparkle and a beauty which will affect every member of the household and enhance all your furnishings.

But paint is more than beauty alone—it is protection, too. Paint will add years to the life of your home. Applied correctly, it may have to be renewed only at long intervals, depending upon your own requirements and tastes.

The proper preparation of surfaces is a vital factor in successful painting. But paints must be matched to surfaces or to requirements just as carefully. A paint for wood is quite different from a paint for masonry. Wood swells and shrinks with weather changes; it requires a full-bodied paint which can expand and contract with the wood without flaking or cracking. Metal and masonry surfaces require paints which dry hard and contain waterproofing substances.

You'll want one type of paint for your living room walls, another for the outside of the house and still another for masonry. Use each wisely—to add to the enjoyment and protection of your home.

SAFETY IN PAINTING

The paints which you use to protect your home and to enhance its appearance may also be harmful; actually, many paints, varnishes, lacquers and

339

When pouring thinners, hold metal container so that spout is at top (right) to avoid dribbling (left).

enamels contain both fire and poison hazards. Certain components—such as lead, mercury and chromates—are definitely poisonous. While a good deal of lead is necessary for acute poisoning, even small quantities ingested into the body or in contact with the skin may cause illness.

Make sure that you have adequate ventilation when mixing or applying paints. Many solvents—such as alcohol, turpentine, ethyl acetate, benzol and naphtha—are combustible and toxic, both on skin contact and by inhalation. Parents should always be certain to use only *lead-free* paint on children's furniture or toys.

The following lists a few general precautions for the painting handyman:

1. Take special care with all quick-drying lacquers. They contain highly inflammable solvents. Keep them away from heaters and the pilot lights of gas stoves.

2. Wear gloves when handling paint removers, thinners and any other materials which may irritate the skin. Plastic gloves are best, since the solvents of rubber-base paints may adversely affect rubber gloves.

3. When using rags for wiping up paints, dispose of them or store them in tightly sealed metal containers.

4. When pouring thinners such as turpentine, hold the metal container so that the spout is at the top. This will prevent splashing and dribbling.

5. Use nonflammable solvents for removing wax from floors.

6. If you use a blowtorch or a wire brush (instead of a chemical paint remover) to remove lead-pigment paints, remember that enough lead may be discharged into the air to be dangerous. Use a respirator, if possible.

CHOOSING THE RIGHT PAINT

A good deal of confusion often results from terms such as "rubber-base" paint, "rubberized," "latex," "water-thinned," or "water base." Since each surface to be painted has its own special requirements, the success or failure of the job depends upon the correct choice of paint.

Paint Formulas. Paint is made of two major components—the pigment and the vehicle. Pigment, as the name implies, gives the paint its color, although sometimes it merely serves as an extender and leaves a transparent film through which the painted surface underneath is still visible. Pigments seal against wear and moisture penetration. The vehicle carries the pigment. Since dry pigment could not flow by itself, the vehicle keeps the paint fluid for spreading, often with the aid of thinners and driers. Some vehicles render a paint usable on one type of surface only; to attempt its use on any other would result in a painting failure. Three of the most common vehicles, from which many paints take their name, are alkyd, latex, and oil. Occasionally, as with white lead, the pigment gives the paint its name.

Types of Pigment. As a rule, pigments are mineral or metallic in origin, particularly those used in outdoor paints. Originally, white lead was the most common form of house-paint pigment, but it has been supplanted to a great extent by titanium oxide, which has about sixteen times the "hiding" power of lead. Because this element is quite costly, it is eked out with other elements. One in particular, calcium carbonate, "chalks" readily. This means that it powders and drops off or is washed off the surface by rain. To a degree, this is desirable because dirt is removed along with it. However, if the process is too rapid, the surface is soon unprotected and the house wall and the ground below are stained. The relative percentages of titanium oxide and calcium carbonate must be regulated to insure proper chalking (see "Paint Failures" for more on chalking).

Special-Purpose Paints. As new building materials are introduced, paint manufacturers are keeping pace. While many well-known house paints have been used for years to cover clapboards and shingles, later houses with newer materials—vertical siding and pre-dipped shingles, for instance—require special protection. Among such special paints are those described below.

Anti-moisture paints are used to offset excessive moisture so common in modern housing. With asphalt roofs, moisture cannot go up and out as it does through wood shingles. As a result, it slowly penetrates through the walls from the inside and appears under the house paint, which promptly blisters and peels off. Alkyd-base paints (see below) have a definite quality of resisting such action. While the moisture condition should be corrected speedily, an alkyd-base paint with a high percentage of titanium oxide will endure far longer in spite of adverse conditions.

Clear-finish pigmented paints are particularly desirable for vertical siding of high-quality woods. Gable ends and portions of the full-length walls of modern homes are often fitted with vertical boards for contrast. To preserve and protect these and yet leave the grain of the wood visible, varnish has been considered standard. However, varnish has a limited length of life. It weathers and needs frequent renewal. On sunny exposures, it shrinks, cracks and bares the wood, which then turns dark or black. Recommended here is a preservative, zinc-naphthenate, which hardens the wood surface. When followed by varnish, protection is assured for a longer time. In addition, a periodic treatment with a good paste wax offsets the damaging effects of weather.

Redwood finishes are used where vertical boards and other parts of the structure are made of redwood. Here the finish must be clear, the color preserved in spite of the strong sunlight. A treatment of water-thinned polyvinyl acrylite has been developed which combines a sealer and a natural redwood color. It is applied to the bare wood in two coats, one right after the other.

Shake paints are used to cover pre-dipped shingles with another color. The initial dip preserves the shingles, but it will not accept paint without bleeding through. Special shingle and shake paints have been developed which partially offset this difficulty. It is suggested that at least six months' weathering be allowed on the dipped shingles before painting. You can test their readiness for paint by brushing an area with a stiff brush and water. If the water collects in small droplets as it does on a newly-waxed surface, withhold painting for a longer period. Once sufficient weathering has taken place, shake paints will adhere without the previous color bleeding through, a thing standard house paints cannot do. Shake paints may also be used on asbestos shingles.

Alkyd paints, available in both enamels and flats, derive their name from the synthetic resins from which they are made. Alkyd-type finishes produce tough, durable and quick-drying coatings that are much harder than ordinary paint films. They have good gloss retention and produce strong, tight paint films for use in areas where surface moisture (caused by high humidity conditions) is common. They are excellent for kitchens and bathrooms, have very good leveling properties and exceptional resistance to yellowing. They need no primer, leave no lap or

Oil-base paints that seal wood, protect against elements, are best for painting wood siding.

If colored finish is desired on masonry, use penetrating paint that leaves weatherproof coating on surface.

Iron rusts on exposure to air. Rust retarder weatherproofing paint assures longer life.

Choosing the Right Paint 341

Type of Paint Vehicle	Type of Exterior Surface	Application	Sq. Ft. Coverage Per Gallon	Drying Time	Type of Thinner	Weather Resistance
Oil	Wood	Brush, spray, roller	500–600	48–72 hrs.	Turpentine	Good
	Masonry		150–200			
Alkyd Resin	Wood (flat finish)	Brush, spray, roller	275–300	24 hrs.	Mineral spirits or naphtha	Good
	Masonry		275–300			
Rubber	Masonry	Brush, spray	300–400	1 hr.	Special	Excellent
Vinyl (polyvinyl acetate emulsion paints)	New masonry	Brush, spray, roller	300–400	1 hr.	Special	Excellent

brush marks, and may be applied by brush, roller or spray. Their washability and resistance to marring is excellent. These are oil-base paints which may be thinned with turpentine or a similar solvent. Read the labels on the cans for directions.

Enamels are special paints which use a varnish vehicle rather than raw oil and produce a smooth, hard film. There are various types of enamels, each having different properties. With all of them, the use of a smooth undercoat is necessary in order to obtain a first-class enamel finish. This undercoat is a flat paint especially formulated to flow out smoothly and leave no brush marks. Interior enamels are termed "high gloss," "semi-gloss," and "flat," and their finish lustres are as their names would indicate. The difference between high gloss and semi-gloss lies in the relative proportions of pigment and binder. The higher the proportions of binder, the higher the gloss. The flat enamel paint produces a dull, soft finish. It is sometimes used as an undercoat for high gloss enamel. Exterior enamel is of much higher durability than interior enamel and is used for porch floors, decks, boats, outdoor furniture, and other outdoor projects. Exterior enamel used for implements or farm machinery is known as implement paint or enamel.

Rubber-base paints are thinned with solvent naphtha, toluene or turpentine. They have a high alkali resistance. Since they usually dry too fast to be applied with a roller, a brush or spray gun must be used for application. Rubber-base paints are very effective on concrete and stucco surfaces.

Latex paints are favorites with millions of homeowners, for they're tough, durable, easy to apply, and cleaning up is a simple matter, requiring only soap and warm water. Some are specially formulated for exterior use, others for interiors. Latex paints are invariably water-thinned emulsions with a synthetic base and are probably the easiest to apply of any paints. You may use a brush, roller or spray. Latex paints adhere to plaster, old paint, wallpaper, wallboard, brick, concrete, cinder block, wood or primed metal. They dry very quickly and may be given a second coat within a few hours. These rubberized emulsion finishes provide a tight, impervious film that will not permit dirt to become imbedded. Ink, crayon, lipstick, mercurochrome, etc., may be easily removed without noticeably changing the sheen of the surface. You may remove spots without leaving a shiny surface on the paint. Latex paints, incidentally, may be applied over fresh plaster (don't attempt this with oil-base paints); you can touch up any areas which may have been missed, and lap marks won't show. Some manufacturers make a line of matching colors in both latex and alkyd finishes so that you may use a latex paint for walls and the same hue for woodwork in an alkyd finish.

Other water-thinned paints are used primarily because they are inexpensive. These paints include calcimine, whitewash, and casein paints. Water-thinned paints are more washable now than they were years ago and they dry very quickly, but they should not be used if the surface must be cleaned or washed frequently. Calcimine is essentially chalk and glue and is sold only in powdered form, ready to be mixed with water. Its principal use is for temporary or inexpensive decoration of interior plaster walls and ceilings. Be sure to remove old calcimine if you are applying a new coat or a coat of any other paint. Casein paint is a derivative of skim milk and may be purchased as a dry powder or a paste. Use it for walls where an extremely dull finish is required. Like latex emulsion paints, casein may be applied over new plaster walls. Whitewash is a mixture of lime and water and is used primarily on farms and in industry where a quick, inexpensive coating that can be easily renewed is needed. For general purposes, prepare any surface for water-thinned paints as you would for oil paints. Don't neglect a primer for new work and be sure to clean and mend old surfaces before beginning to paint.

P.V.A. (*polyvinyl acetate emulsions*) are used chiefly for exterior masonry painting and, for normal exterior exposure, provide a waterproof film. They're as easy to use over brick, concrete, or stucco as latex paints are over interior walls. They are resistant to alkali in masonry, to fading under sunlight, and to fumes and acids. Use brush, roller, or spray to apply them. They're fast-drying and may be cleaned, like latex, with warm, soapy water.

Aluminum paints contain varnish as a vehicle and are unrivaled for some purposes. They give coatings that are durable, light and attractive. They reflect light and heat and have superb hiding power. Just as with oil paints, surfaces must be prepared carefully and all rust, grease, and dust removed. Ready-mixed aluminum paints must be suited to the surface to be coated, as follows: (1) aluminum paint for wood, or aluminum house paint, rich in oil and useful as a primer or finish coat; (2) aluminum metal and masonry paint for metal, brick and concrete surfaces; (3) aluminum enamel (heat-resistant) for interior use, a fast-drying, satin-smooth finish which will protect hot surfaces (600°–800° F).

PAINTING TOOLS

Paintbrushes. Choosing and using the right brush correctly is fully as important as the correct choice of paint for a specific project. A poor brush will cause delay and adversely affect the appearance of the paint coat. The greatest difference between one brush and another lies in the bristle stock. Good hog-bristle brushes have a large number of "flags," or split-bristle ends; the more flags, the better the brush, for they help to hold paint and to spread it in an even film. A brush should not be too coarse or fanned out at the painting end, and it should be springy and elastic.

You'll always save time if you use the widest brush practical for the job. For large flat surfaces such as walls, ceilings, and floors, use a brush 3 to 6″ wide, a 4″ brush being about average. For woodwork, paneling, and trim, use a trim or sash brush 1 to 3″ wide. Use a flat or oval brush 1 to 3″ wide for sash and trellises; choose a flat varnish or enameling brush 1 to 3″ wide for furniture and small, flat

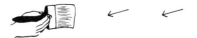

Daub paint on in spots before stroking with the brush.

Use long and level brush strokes. Spread the paint smoothly over surface.

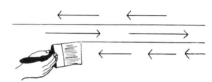

Alternate direction of brush strokes. You'll find finish will be uniform and attractive.

surfaces. For narrow table legs, use the narrowest size of sash brush. If you are painting with enamel, varnish, or lacquer, use a flat varnish brush of a fine finishing type. Such a brush has softer bristles that are "chiseled" to permit easier flowing of the paint onto the surface and to permit the brush to "cut in" better on various surfaces.

Proper brushing is important. Paint, applied properly with a good brush, is bonded well to the surface, lasts long, and looks well. A poor paint job means that the paint is not bonded properly and becomes a short-lived surface film. Proper brushing will overcome surface tension, break moisture film, and dispel the air in surface cells, actually forcing the paint into intimate contact with the surface. Wrinkling of paint is eliminated, in most cases, by sufficient brushing.

Always try to paint an entire surface at one time; lap marks will be less likely. The way you wield the brush is important, too. Keep the bristles at a downward angle, never upward, lest paint run down into areas that are already wet; this will blend your strokes for a more uniform finish. Follow the grain of the wood with your brush, particularly if the wood is new. Paint brushed on crosswise may ripple when it is dry. It's a good idea to keep an old brush handy to work into corners, for the shape of a good brush will be distorted if used for this purpose. Always use the flat side of a brush, even if you're painting a narrow strip or angling into a corner. Painting with the edge of a brush will cause it to divide into clumps, and if these are left in the brush overnight, the bristles will be set permanently.

CHOOSING A PAINTBRUSH

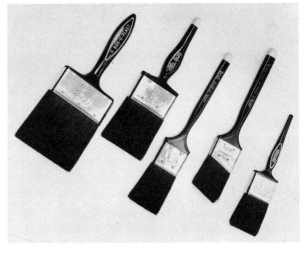

1. These brushes will cover anything: (left to right) 4″ wall brush, 3″ enameling brush, 2″ flat sash brush, 2″ trim brush for paneling, and 2″ "chiseled" varnish brush.

2. Test for "bounce" by brushing bristles against the back of your hand. Bristles should feel springy and elastic in a good brush, should not fan out excessively.

3. Separate the bristles at center of brush with pencil or stick and note the "strip" in heel of brush which improves bristle shape, makes brush easier to clean.

4. Note the "flags" (splits at bristle end) which indicate a quality brush. The more "flags," the better; they aid in holding paint and in spreading it smoothly.

When applying finishes, use a new or absolutely clean soft-bristle brush. Dip your brush about half the length of the bristles into the can. Lightly wipe off excess paint against the side of the container. When carrying the brush from the pail to your work, keep the loaded bristles down. This prevents paint from running down into the metal ferrule, where it may harden. If you're using rubberized wall paint, you can dip the brush a bit more deeply and just touch the ends of the bristles on the container to remove excess drops. Flow paint onto the surface and work it out in easy, regular strokes to a uniform film. To apply enamel or varnish, use short, light strokes, letting the finish flow together with as little brushing as possible. Check the enamel during the first half-hour after application to remedy runs or sags before they dry. If they appear, brush them out with light strokes. It's best to do this with a filled brush. Don't try to fix any uneven areas with a dry brush.

CONDITION BRUSHES BEFORE USE

1. Remove loose bristles, dust, and dirt to insure best results. Simply knead the bristles; then twirl brush rapidly against palm of hand and tap bristles across fingers. You'll find your brush will paint much better.
2. To keep bristles flexible and to assure faster, smoother spreading of paint, always try to precondition a new brush by suspending it in linseed oil for at least 12 to 24 hours before use; brush will hold more paint.
3. Any linseed oil which is not absorbed should be pressed out with a stick, screwdriver, or similar article—or by squeezing the bristles between two dowels. Next, dip into turpentine to remove any excess remaining.

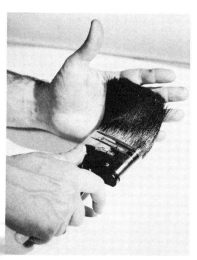  

HOW TO CLEAN YOUR PAINTBRUSHES

1. Solvents used for thinning paints are recommended for cleaning brushes. After brush is soaked in thinner for a few minutes, work bristles against side. Soap and water are used for all water-mixed paints. Neglected brushes full of hardened paint can be salvaged sometimes by soaking them in turpentine or brush cleaner for a day or two.

2. Repeat with fresh solvent until liquid remains clear. Squeeze bristles with fingers to work paint out of heel. Use plenty of thinner at all times. A putty knife is sometimes necessary if bristles are gummed. →

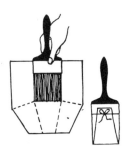

3. If the brush is stored longer than overnight, wash it with an alkali-free soap and warm water. Rinse well and shake out excess water in jar by spinning dry between palms. If bristles are synthetic, do not use alcohol for cleaning.

4. When you have removed as much of the thinner as you can, comb bristles thoroughly with a metal comb. This straightens interior bristles and is important in preserving the shape of your brush for future jobs.

5. Wrap for storing in oilcloth or heavy paper and be certain that the bristles lie straight. When a brush is to be stored for months, saturate wrapped brush with linseed oil, hang with bristles pointing down.

Rollers. The popularity of rollers is due primarily to the fact that they can be used to coat a surface very quickly. If the surface is free of wood trim, windows and doors, progress will be much more rapid. But the roller is not a tool that can be used to the exclusion of brushes. You still need a good brush to "cut in" around woodwork, leaving all the large areas for the roller.

The pan type of roller is the most widely used and ranges in size from 1 to 13½″. With the magazine type of roller, paint is stored inside the hollow cylinder. Up to a pint of paint may be poured in, and it oozes through the cover as it is rolled on the wall. There are also pressure-type rollers (used principally by professionals) in which the paint is forced through a hose into the inside of the roller. Some rollers have a cover permanently glued to a cylinder; others have slip-on covers.

Don't try to roll on finishes that dry too rapidly, such as shellac, lacquer, fast-drying enamels and some primers. And don't thin your material beyond good brushing consistency. When selecting a roller, be sure to get one with the correct kind of cover: mohair (short nap) for latex and rubber-base paints, oil paints and texture paints; wool (long nap) for rough stucco and concrete and fences where a heavier

texture of paint is desired. Follow the manufacturer's directions on how to use a specific roller.

For the pan or dip type of roller, you need a special pan which can be safely anchored to the top of a step ladder when you're painting a ceiling or upper wall. For lower areas, it's easier if you have your dip pan at least 30″ from the floor. Before beginning work with a new roller, wash its cover in warm soapsuds and rinse it well to remove any lint or dust. If you're going to use an oil-base paint, allow the cover to dry thoroughly before you start. If you're going to use a water-mix paint, however, your roller should be wet when you begin.

Pour the paint into the pan until half of the sloping bottom is covered. Roll the paint roller into the paint until it is uniformly filled. Roll back once or twice and shake the excess paint gently back into the tray. Then roll the paint onto the surface with a light, even stroke. Roll it up and down, then back and forth. This will help distribute the paint smoothly. A proper job of roller coating will leave a pleasant, light-stippled effect that often covers small blemishes better than brushing.

With a newly loaded roller, always begin by rolling upward. Start each new load of paint somewhat away from the already painted surface and roll toward the completed work. To obtain even coverage and avoid laps, roll the paint vertically, overlapping each stroke 50 per cent, and finish by rolling all strokes in one direction. If you can fit an extension handle to your roller, you can paint floors or ceilings with ease, thus eliminating bending or tedious kneeling.

When you're finished with your roller, it is very important to clean it thoroughly. Place it in a container of the solvent for the paint you are using. This should be done immediately after completion of your project. Shake the solvent through the roller, then roll it out on newspapers to remove the liquid. After all the paint has been worked out, wash the roller in warm suds, rinse and then dry.

USING A ROLLER

1. A roller will speed painting time considerably, but you will still need a brush to "cut in" around woodwork.
2. For roller painting, use measured amount of thinner. Unthinned paints may wrinkle and crack later. Choice of thinner depends on paint type.

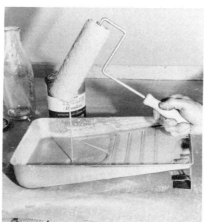

3. Water paints settle quickly. Rubber-base paints dry rapidly. Both leave hard lumps on roller, spots on surface painted. Thinner prevents this trouble.
4. Fluffy roller holds a lot of paint. Don't overload it. Roll out excess on upper part of pan, which is kept free of paint for just this purpose.
5. When using a roller, begin with several crisscross strokes and always start painting by rolling upward.   →

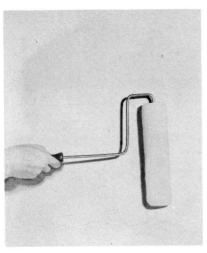

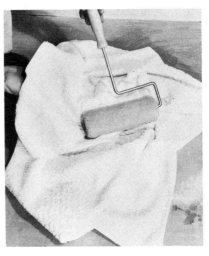

6. Don't rush the job. If roller is moved too rapidly, it throws paint up ahead. These spots dry quickly, will show under final coating. Work slowly.

7. Keep roller and pan clean. Dip roller frequently into thinner, whether water or turpentine or alcohol. Shake lightly to remove excess thinner.

8. Wash and rinse roller as soon as all painting is finished. Several rinses in thinner, then drying, will put it back in shape for next job.

Spray Guns and Cans. There are two general types of spray guns—those with the paint cup or container an actual part of the gun and those with the paint tank separate from the gun. These two types are further divided into (a) external or internal mix, (b) pressure, gravity, or suction feed types, and

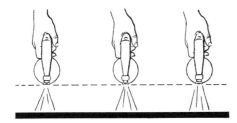

Right Way—Keep the gun moving back and forth with even strokes, at right angles to the surface.

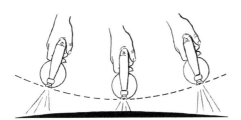

Wrong Way—Never use a circular or "arcing" motion with wrist; this leaves too much paint at the center.

(c) bleeder or nonbleeder types. There is a good deal to be said for the self-contained, light-duty sprayers which operate on a vibration principle. The best of these are ready to use as soon as they're plugged in, are equipped with their own filters, and can be easily cleaned by simply spraying clean solvent for a few seconds. A light-duty sprayer, working on a super-jet principle, is ideal for all household jobs. It will spray paint, enamel, shellac, varnish, lacquer and other materials. Its built-in filter strains materials automatically and it may be cleaned in seconds.

Virtually every type of coating and every type of surface can be sprayed with guns or cans, including wood, metal, plastic, paper and cloth. Just as with any other kind of painting, make sure the surface is cleared of dust, grease, and dirt. Spray painting of portable items should be done in the garage rather than in the house. Every effort should be made to keep the area well ventilated to reduce fire hazard. Be extremely careful not to spray where an open flame, or even a cigarette, may be reached by the paint fog. If spraying out of doors, work only on windless days.

Anyone who has had difficulty in applying lacquers will appreciate the spray-gun method. The thickness of each coat is easily controlled. Brush marking is done away with. The same applies to application of several varnish coats to fine pieces of furniture. Bubbles and brush marks can be eliminated. Also, colorless plastic can be easily applied to newly

USING A SPRAY GUN

Right: Painting a picket fence can be one of the most slow and tiresome tasks imaginable, but a spray outfit makes short shrift of it. Avoid spraying on very windy days.

Below: An efficient spray gun will cut down working time on any job. It is a particular boon with difficult projects like clapboard; be sure to protect grass.

polished copper and brass, forming an invisible coat that ends tarnish. Doorknobs, brass fireplace fixtures, copperware, and anything made of brass on a boat will benefit from this spray application.

The paint flow is regulated by the fluid adjusting screw on the gun. Start with the adjusting screw nearly closed, then gradually open it until the spray seems right. A distorted spray usually indicates a dirty air cap. To remedy this, take the cap off and wash it carefully in clean solvent. If it is necessary to ream the air cap holes, use a matchstick or a broom bristle—never a hard or sharp instrument, which may enlarge the tiny hole. It is a proven fact that 90 per cent of spraying ailments can be traced to lack of cleanliness. Clean your gun thoroughly immediately after use. If the paint dries in the gun, it will be almost impossible to get it out later.

Many pigmented stains and synthetic enamels can be diluted with lacquer thinner to obtain a quick-drying material for use in suction guns. Always test before you mix a full can; if the linseed-oil content is too high, the addition of lacquer thinner will curdle the material.

When spraying, hold the gun 6 to 10″ from the object, and with steady, even strokes made with a free-arm motion, move it across the surface. Keep the gun perpendicular to, and at a constant distance from, the surface. It's important, until you are familiar with the gun, to practice on cardboard until you get the feel of it.

Always be sure to overlap your strokes. Even a perfect spray pattern will deposit more material at the center than at the edges. For this reason, always overlap adjoining strokes between one-fourth and one-third the width of each sprayed stroke. Paint that is applied too thickly may "sag" before drying, or it may be so long in drying that it becomes dirt- and moisture-laden, so don't try to cover in one coat with slow-drying materials. Apply coats thin enough to dry properly (even if this makes two or more coats necessary), and wait for the first coat to dry thoroughly before finishing.

Do not tilt the gun excessively. If it is tilted so that material from the cup flows into the cup cover, the nozzle and air passages in the cover will become clogged, causing the gun to "sputter." Straining all lumpy or dirty finishing material is always smart spray practice. A good strainer is a fine-mesh tea strainer; one popular size fits a quart cup exactly. Old nylon stockings are even better.

When aiming at an angle, "shoot" the nearest part first. If you're spraying a horizontal surface with a regular nozzle, keep the container only partially full so that you can tilt the gun 30° to 45°. Spray the near edge first and work across (laterally) in successive strokes toward the far side. The denser, near side of the pattern will be the portion that overlaps as you make each stroke, and thus you can control the coverage better.

If you are painting cabinets with drawers, open the

SPRAY CAN TECHNIQUES

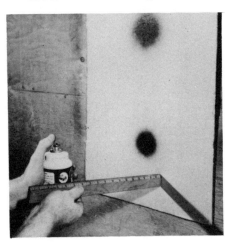

Test spray pattern against cardboard before starting work. Measure distance from target, and note the spread of the sprayed pattern.

Start coverage of surface at left and work to right evenly. Carry spray on past end of work, and then release button to stop it.

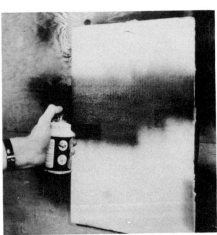

Second stroke overlaps the first by about one-third. Maintain equal distance from work at all times for uniform application.

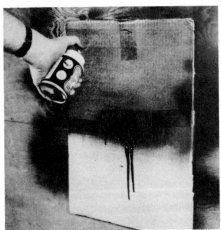

If spray is tilted at an angle while spraying, paint "piles up" and runs badly. Right-angle position is best for flat work.

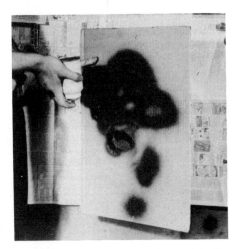

After spraying, turn can *upside down* and press button once or twice. This frees feeder tube and valve, prevents clogging of orifice.

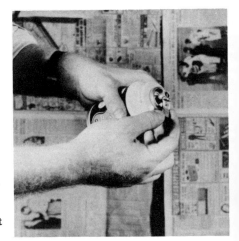

Removable trigger on some cans insures non-clogging since trigger can be cleaned after use. Thinner or solvent will clean it.

MATERIAL GUIDE FOR SPRAY-GUN PAINTING. Most finishing materials formulated for brush applications can be sprayed at can consistency with a pressure feed gun. Always follow can label directions. Strain all doubtful materials. Keep the gun clean.

LACQUER — Reduce clear lacquers about 25% and pigmented lacquers 100 to 150%, depending on type. Suction feed, external mix gives cleanest pattern, least clogging, and is the preferred gun for all lacquer work. Material can be thinned to any extent since almost instant drying eliminates sags and runs which would occur with other thinned materials. Must be sprayed wet to retain gloss. Use a fairly small pattern of 5–6″, holding gun about 6″ from work.

OIL-MIX WALL PAINT — Pressure feed only. Spray at can consistency; avoid thinning unless specified. Some types formulated especially for spraying are exceptionally free from misting.

VARNISH — Most clear varnishes can be sprayed at pressure of 70 pounds or higher. Satins and flats are usually heavier and may require thinning. Gun distance is 6–8″. Avoid heavy coats.

RUBBER BASE — Pressure feed, external mix only. This material tends to clog internal mix guns; it is too heavy to spray suction feed. Use maximum fluid flow. Rubber base is exceptionally free from misting.

ENAMEL — Usual 4-hr. dry product is an excellent spraying material with pressure feed gun. Use at can consistency; do not thin. Apply medium wet coats. Complete or touch-up second coat can be applied as soon as first coat has set up slightly.

---

drawers ¼″ so that the spray will cover the sides, top, and bottom to that distance. Spray chairs upside down first, working along legs and rungs, then reverse to spray the top. Only when spraying open work, such as wicker chair seats, screens or radiators, do you turn the spray can at an angle. Here, tilt it to 45° to prevent too much paint from passing through the openings. Spray the first coat left to right, the second top to bottom, to make sure all surfaces are covered.

When spraying inside corners, spray the adjoining walls instead of the corner. Have the spray pattern horizontal and use a vertical stroke, placing the dense center portion of the pattern close to (but not directly in) the corner. When both walls are done in this manner, the overlapped thinner deposits formed at the edges of the patterns sprayed on the walls will cover the corner. Spray important parts last. The most clean and even coverage is obtained from end to end of any one single stroke. For this reason, always finish important parts of a project with a single stroke, if possible.

In spraying a chest of drawers, open drawers about ¼″ so that all the edges are completely painted.

Turn chairs upside down to spray inner surfaces of legs and rungs, then outer edges. Then spray upper portion.

Painting Tools   351

Try not to jiggle the trigger. When the trigger is closed and reopened, a small excess amount of material, collected in the nozzle during the interval when the gun was stopped, is blown out in a dense, coarse blast. Jiggling the trigger will produce a series of these blasts and result in "spattered" coverage. And never stop the movement of the gun with the trigger open. Even though your eye may not see the accumulating deposit on the work surface (some paints when first sprayed look much lighter and thinner than they actually are), the deposit is being "piled" up just the same.

Stenciling with a spray can is simple. Make a stencil cutout and paste it to the wall or other surface with a paste made of soap flakes and water. Spray through and, when the paint is thoroughly dry, remove the stencil. It picks off easily, and the wall can be wiped down to remove the paste.

In spraying a finish on wicker work, spray is held at a 45° angle so that paint is not forced through the crease opening.

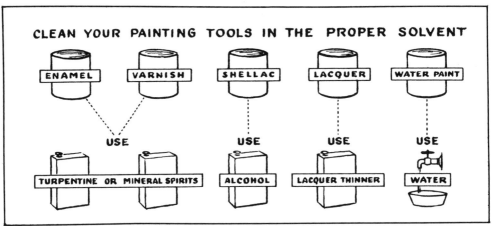

Proper cleaning of painting tools will keep them in shape for the next job.

PAINT FAILURES

Common Causes. No paint lasts forever. At some time or other, you may find that the paint on your house has "failed" in a matter of months, or in a year or two. The most convenient scapegoat is, of course, the paint—but it's a most unlikely culprit. Inevitably, the cause will turn out to be something far different from what you had imagined. The following are the most common causes:

1. The surfaces were not prepared properly. Knots should be sealed with shellac or aluminum paint. Resin must be scraped and sanded away. Lime is harmful to oil paints; you must allow for aging before you can successfully paint over concrete and plaster.

2. Incompatible paints were applied. It's best to repaint with the same type of paint unless you've experimented and found that the new type you plan to use is compatible. Strong solvents used in a rubber-base paint may "lift" the surface of an old paint. Paint or enamel applied over varnish will result in an alligatoring pattern. Alligatoring has also been known to result after a few months when one paint has been used over an earlier paint with which it is not compatible.

3. The surfaces were not completely dry. Damp walls are a guarantee of paint failure. No paint, no matter how expensive, will stand up to this condition for very long. Check for leaks and excessive condensation. These cause paint films to blister, peel, curl, or flake.

4. The technique of paint application was at fault. You may have thinned the paint too much, added too much oil, painted when it was too hot or too cold.

Experts suggest you paint in the fall to get the most from your paint job. If, however, you suspect a sharp drop in temperature within a few hours after you finish, it's best to hold off for another day. Remember, too, that woods differ in their paint-holding qualities, a factor which will account in part for the success or failure of your paint job.

Types of Paint Failures. *Alligatoring* consists of interlacing lines over large areas of the paint film. This condition may begin as small checks, but the breaks will become wider as the top coat contracts and exposes the undercoat, and the resultant appearance is similar to an alligator's skin. The causes are (1) the use of incompatible paints, (2) the use of paint or enamel over a resinous surface, (3) the use of too much oil, or impure oil, as a thinner, (4) not allowing sufficient time for the undercoat to dry, and (5) painting over a greasy surface. Remove alligatored paint before repainting or else the new paint will also fail.

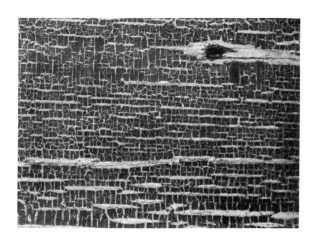

Alligatoring is an advanced form of checking, which causes the film to take on the appearance of alligator skin. It is often due to deteriorating of improperly built-up paint.

Bleeding can be caused by action of the solvents in paints on the resin in some wood. White paint will turn yellow or the paint film will break up. Painting over creosote or some stains may cause some of these ingredients to dissolve and stain the finish coat. If the resin has already exuded from the wood and is clotted on the surface, scrape and sand the area down to bare wood and seal it with orange shellac, clear sealer, or aluminum paint. Knots should always be treated with sealer before painting.

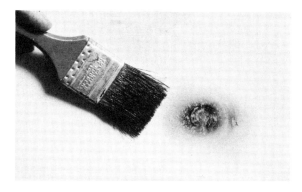

Bleeding cannot always be prevented, but a good primer coat will often check this cause of paint failure. Aluminum paint rates high as an effective sealer.

Blistering is an indication of the pressure of moisture behind the paint film. Blistering is not linked to excessive rainfall on the finish, or even to painting on wood which is not perfectly dry. (Sometimes it is considered better to paint on wood which contains normal moisture than on wood which is "bone dry.") Special primers or paints are of little value when blistering occurs regularly. To remedy this condition,

Blistering always indicates dampness *behind* and not *on* the paint film. This will continue until the cause of excessive dampness is discovered and stopped.

first determine what causes the excessive dampness. Check for leaks in walls and any factor contributing to constant dampness behind the paint film. If your insulation (exterior walls) has no vapor barrier, moisture will work its way through the walls and right behind your paint, trying to find its way through to the surface. This will, of course, result in heavy blistering. Remove blistered paint before repainting.

Moisture from the crawl space under this home rotted sheathing and actually forced paint to scale off.

Chalking after two or three years is usual, even desirable. It's an aid in keeping the surface of the paint clean and, in wearing away, it reduces the thickness of the film. This can be quite important, as studies have shown that paint which is built up year after year will eventually form a coat so thick that it will crack or scale. As a rule, chalking will start soon after your paint has lost its gloss. The titanium dioxide paints will tend to chalk more than those containing white lead or zinc oxide. Chalking that

Paints of inferior quality containing the "controlled chalking" or "self-cleaning" feature may wash down, staining walls below.

occurs too soon is usually the result of (1) the use of too thin a coat or (2) rain, fog or dew affecting the paint before it has dried. Before repainting, remove all chalk by scrubbing with water or by brushing with a stiff brush.

Checking can be ignored if it is slight. However, do not let it deteriorate to the point where paint begins to flake off. Usually, checking is caused by the undercoat's not being perfectly hard and dry before the finish coat is applied. Rub down with No. 1 sandpaper before repainting.

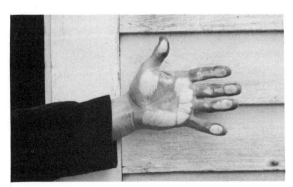

Chalking, normally, is desirable, and manufacturers try to incorporate this feature in paint formulas. Excessive chalking may be due to improper application.

Checking is usually a minor fault and may often be prevented by allowing sufficient drying time between coats (3 to 7 days), and using proper prime and finish coats.

Cracking is an advanced stage of checking. It differs from that condition and from alligatoring in that the cracks extend through the coatings all the way down to the bare wood. The paint films will eventually scale off, exposing the surface beneath. The causes may be (1) insufficient oil in the paint, giving it poor elasticity, or (2) too much oil or other solids in the paint which cannot be brushed out well. When cracking occurs, you must remove all the cracked or scaling paint down to the bare wood, then repaint.

Cracking is often due to improperly made paints which dry too hard. Undercoats and finish coats must be of equal elasticity, and expand or contract equally.

Crawling is the term used when paint draws itself up in drops or globules soon after it's applied. It is due to (1) application of paint over a cold or greasy surface, (2) application of one glossy paint over another new glossy coat, (3) too much oil in the finish coat, (4) the mixing of different brands, (5) painting in foggy or cold weather, or (6) the application of paint to a surface containing wax left from the use of paint removers. Crawling can be eliminated if painting is done under ideal conditions (clear, dry days, not under 50° F), and if the undercoat is hard and dry. Sandpaper glossy undercoats, rub the surface with turpentine and steel wool before painting, and add turpentine to the paint being used for the finish coat.

Fading is usually due to excessive chalking, failure to seal or prime surfaces properly, exposure of paints to weather, or a chemical change in the pigment. Paints containing white lead will develop a grayish or brownish film if there is any hydrogen sulfide in the air. Wipe with a sponge soaked in hydrogen peroxide to bleach this out. A paint which contains too much oil will hold much more dirt than one in which the oil content is kept at the minimum. Paints containing alkyd resins are less likely to fade.

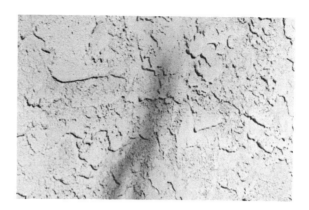

Fading may be due to a variety of causes. In this case, too much thinner was added to an oil-base stucco paint and fading was serious in less than four months.

(In interior work, a "hot spot," a heavy concentration of lime in plaster, with a shiny look, must be primed before applying any paint if fading is to be prevented.)

Mildew is a fungus that is often mistaken for dirt on paint films. Some paint dealers have testing kits that will help you to determine whether an area is disfigured by dirt or mildew. Mildew thrives under conditions of warmth, moisture and shade, particularly near heavy shrubbery. Its growth on paint is more common than on any other material and is a problem in almost all areas of the country with the possible exception of dry desert areas in the West. It grows more readily on soft paints (exterior house paints) than on enamels. It is particularly prevalent on woods where linseed oil has been rubbed in for a natural finish. Dirt will wash off readily, but mildew is considerably more difficult to remove.

Mildew is most often mistaken for ordinary dirt on paint films. A mildewcide must be used in paints against this fungus and any dampness eliminated.

On new work or on a slightly mildewed surface, prepare the surface as usual and apply paint with a mildewcide in it. Bichloride of mercury (a dangerous poison which should be safely stored out of reach of children) may be used, or pentachlorophenol, which is relatively nontoxic to human beings. On a medium-mildewed surface, wash the surface clean with a solution of three heaping tablespoonfuls of trisodium phosphate per gallon of water, rinse with clean water and allow to dry. When thoroughly dry, use a mildew-resistant paint. On a heavily mildewed surface, wash the surface clean with a solution of 3 heaping tablespoonfuls of trisodium phosphate, 1½ cups of household bleach and 1 gallon of water. Rinse with clean water and allow to dry. When thoroughly dry, use a mildew-resistant paint.

Running, or sagging as it is sometimes called, happens when paint is applied over a glossy surface without first sandpapering and when paint is applied in too heavy a coat or contains too much oil. Good technique calls for paint to be applied by spreading it out all over the surface, using long, straight strokes, without brushing too thin. It should be brushed out *with* the grain in even strokes.

Slow drying, or tackiness, is another one of those problems which may be caused by any one of a number of factors, including (1) too much or too thick paint, (2) painting during cold, foggy, wet weather, (3) not enough drier in the paint, (4) painting over an undercoat that isn't quite dry, (5) finger marks, grease or wax on the surface. Tackiness can be prevented by seeing to it that you paint at the proper time and that the condition of the surface is as it should be.

Spotting is caused by unequal absorption of the oil in paint. Adequate sealing of surfaces before painting reduces the likelihood of spotting.

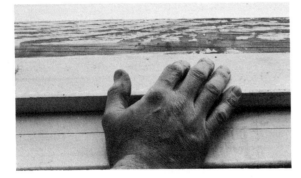

Spotting is due to unequal oil absorption and will often show up when poor paints are used. Adequate sealing of the surface is the secret of a good paint job.

This unusual form of spotting was caused by an electrical storm and occurred on a fresh film of paint. The effect vanished gradually over a period of 3 months.

Staining can result from a variety of causes, including water dripping from metal (copper or iron pipe or gutters, nails, etc.). The cure for this is to paint the metal properly. Also, when damp wood is painted, water will work its way into the paint film, carrying with it substances which cause brown stains. The cure here lies in the use of properly seasoned wood and the prevention of moisture accumulation behind the wood.

Left: These iron nails were not set or puttied, and they show through primer and three coats. After a while, they will rust, stain the surface, necessitate repainting.

Right: Staining may be due to other causes, too. Wood must be seasoned so that excess moisture is gone before the wood is painted; structural defects must be eliminated.

Wrinkling occurs when the surface of the paint film dries first, leaving soft paint beneath this skin. Usually it is due to an excessively heavy application of paint during damp, cold weather. Guard against this by painting only under ideal conditions—if you must paint during cold weather, do it between 10 A.M. and 3 P.M. Add a little turpentine to the paint and brush out paint fully.

HOW TO PAINT INTERIORS

Choosing Colors. The colors you choose for your home play an important role. Wisely used, colors can conceal defects, emphasize important points, make rooms seem larger or smaller, as cool or as warm as you wish. Correctly chosen, colors will do just about anything you'd like them to do.

The light in your rooms is tremendously important. If your room does not receive much natural light and is used throughout the day, it's better not to choose a very dark wall tone—it may seem gloomy on a rainy morning. If you really want dark walls, however, use a white ceiling to bring more light into the room. You can also gain dramatic effects by painting one or two walls in a dark color and the others in a lighter shade. This will help to lighten the room as a whole. If you use the room very little during daylight hours, of course use as dark a color as you wish, with enough artificial illumination for entertaining or reading.

Before you start, it might be well to consider the idea of one noted architect who feels that you should not have unrelated color schemes for individual rooms. His idea is that you should use a color palette for your entire home, then use these shades from room to room. This gives your furniture added flexi-bility, since it may then be used in any section of your home.

When choosing colors, remember that they must be to your liking by both daylight and artificial light. Some people find blue difficult to deal with as far as lighting is concerned. Daylight bulbs, with no yellow in them, will keep the color true but will give the room a cold look. Yellow is another problem at times. It may seem to disappear at night, to take on a dull beige aspect or turn cream. A touch of green added to the paint will counteract this strange behavior. Too much blue is depressing. Yellow, on the other hand, is stimulating. Blue and yellow, mixed to make a blue-green, yield an excellent neutral background. To tone down, or gray, any color, mix it with its complement. Generally, adding white cools color tones; black warms them.

If your bedroom receives light from the south and west, use cool colors such as green, white, light ivory, Wedgwood blue, or blue-green. If your bedroom receives cooler light from north or east, choose a warm paint color—pale yellow, rose-beige, coral or buff.

You can have the exact color you want. With some paints, the color is mixed right before your eyes in the store. With others, you buy pigment, sometimes in color-in-oil form, and add it to a basic quantity of white, gray or cream paint. With still other paint systems, you may readily intermix paint colors, in various quantities, to get the exact hue you want.

Paint always appears darker or lighter when dry than it does in the can. Do the actual mixing a day before the room is to be painted, brush on a sample and allow it to dry thoroughly. Then decide how well it meets your requirements. Inspect the sample by

---

HOW TO CHOOSE COLORS

LIGHT COLORS reflect more light; seem lighter in weight; make things seem farther away; make you feel cheerful.

DARK COLORS absorb light; seem heavy; make things seem smaller; make things seem closer; depress you if used on surfaces too large.

BRIGHT COLORS seem larger in area than they actually are; attract the eye—are sometimes used to draw attention away from unattractive features; are distracting.

WARM COLORS (reds, oranges, yellows, yellow-greens) seem to advance toward you; convey the feeling of warmth; are stimulating.

COOL COLORS (blues, violets, blue-greens, blue-grays) make things seem cooler; seem to retreat from you; are subduing.

THE LIGHT REFLECTANCE
OF VARIOUS COLORS.

Do you wish to make the most of the natural and artificial light within a room? Or do you wish to soften the skyglare that sometimes enters through large glass areas? Remember, dark colors absorb light while light ones reflect it. This chart will help determine the colors that reflect the most light.

White	80%	Salmon	53%
Ivory (light)	71%	Pale apple green	51%
Apricot-beige	66%	Medium gray	43%
Lemon yellow	65%	Light green	41%
Ivory	59%	Pale blue	41%
Light buff	56%	Deep rose	12%
Peach	53%	Dark green	9%

Darker color on walls pulls them together, creating feeling of intimacy. Large rooms can be made smaller, in effect, with this simple treatment.

Spaciousness is created by light background along side wall, dark end wall. Note dark background for display pieces on shelves.

night light as well as by sunlight. If the paint being mixed is for the walls of a room, the selected tint should be a little lighter than the actual color you desire. The reason for this is that walls reflect each other and intensify color. Also, be sure to have *enough* if you're mixing a special tint. It may be very difficult to make the same shade again should it run short.

While a coat of paint will not change the physical dimensions of a room, you can make a room or a wall seem larger or smaller by a correct color choice. Long, narrow rooms, for example, may be made to look wider by placing a dark color on the wall at each of the narrow ends and a lighter color on the remaining walls and the ceiling. Rooms which are square and uninteresting in shape can be improved by making one wall a focal point of interest. If there's a fireplace, put the decorative interest on the fireplace wall. If there's an alcove, try dramatizing that. A ceiling which seems too high can be made to seem lower by painting it in a color darker than the side walls. A darker ceiling, it has been found, has a soothing, eye-resting effect and is particularly recommended for bedrooms. You might try repeating the ceiling color on one wall, with the other walls in a lighter tone.

Painting the walls and woodwork of a room in the same color gives an air of spaciousness and a seeming lack of clutter. If the room is large and well lighted, you can make it seem more friendly, and smaller, by painting the walls in a darker tone. A wise color choice will also affect your feelings concerning the weather, particularly as far as the temperature is concerned. Dark walls will retain heat and affect you subconsciously. Use the "reced-

ing" colors of the spectrum for cooler effects—blues, greens and grays. They'll give the illusion of more space and make you feel cooler. Ivory, light cream and oyster white are useful for this purpose, too.

What to Do Before Painting. You can paint indoors at any time of the year, but most homeowners prefer spring or fall. Both are ideal seasons for painting. The weather is neither too warm nor too cold, and you can open the windows wide for ventilation.

Estimate how much paint you will need. Paint estimates are governed by several factors: (1) the area in square feet to be covered; (2) the condition of the surface (whether smooth, rough or porous); (3) the number of coats of paint required. Although paints vary in coverage, most paints cover about 500 square feet per gallon. To determine how much paint you will need, measure the area to be painted in square feet. Divide the total square feet by 500 (coverage per gallon). The result will give you the number of gallons of paint required. If the surface is unusually rough or heavily textured, 20 per cent more paint may be required.

But, before you even open a paint can, make a checklist of repairs or preparations to be made before painting and then follow your list scrupulously.

Woodwork must be intact. Loose or warped wood trim must be nailed down securely. Use finishing nails of proper size; set heads of nails below the surface of wood and cover with a wood filler. If a gap exists between the baseboard molding and the floor or between the shoe molding and the baseboard, relocate them for a better fit. To attach the shoe molding securely, drive nails diagonally into the subfloor, not into the baseboard or finish flooring. Any cracks between pieces of trim (mitered joints above doors and windows) should be filled properly. The filler, which may be plastic wood, patching plaster, etc., should be heaped up slightly above the adjacent surface and then sanded down flush when dry. Seal before painting.

Any loose, peeling paint should be completely removed before attempting to repaint (see "Paint Removers," pages 406–408).

New plaster is not ready for paint until it has completely cured, or dried. Exactly how long this may take is a question which provokes a wide variety of answers, ranging from two months to two years. Allow as long a period as possible, then protect yourself further by using a primer, a "first coat" which is applied to the pores of a surface and prevents the uneven absorption of final coatings. Allow this to dry

thoroughly and then use two coats of a regular flat paint. If you're using a dark color, tint the first coat slightly with a small quantity of it. This will prevent the final coat from appearing lighter.

Previously painted walls are likely to need some preparation before redecorating. Holes and cracks must be filled. Loose plaster should be scraped away before the area is filled with spackling compound or prepared crack filler (see Chapter 2). Spackle can be applied quite simply with your finger, particularly in corners. You can also use a putty knife, forcing the material into the cracks and smoothing it level with the knife edge. While the filler is hardening, clean the rest of the wall by washing it with mild soap and water or any commercial wall cleaner, and then rinse well. Since it is impossible to paint satisfactorily over grease and since any dust and dirt will

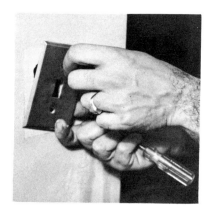

Before painting, remove switch covers and any other fixtures which are likely to become splattered.

Nails in wood should be set and holes filled with putty. With sheetrock, avoid breaking protective paper.

As the final preparation step, clean walls thoroughly with detergent and water, allow to dry before painting.

A few extra moments spent in preparation for painting make for a neat job and, later, a happier painter.

How to Paint Interiors   359

be picked up by the brush or roller and spread into the paint, get the walls as clean as possible; always dust well after sandpapering.

When the wall is clean, mended (and the filler is sanded level with the wall) and dry, apply your paint. It's a good idea to seal any spackled spots by dabbing a bit of the finish paint over the sanded spackle and allowing it to dry. This will eliminate shiny spots. Whether one or two coats are needed will depend upon the paint you are using and the colors of the wall and the new finish coat. A sealer is unnecessary when painting previously painted walls, but if you're changing from a dark to a light color, it is usually recommended.

Similarly, special treatments may be necessary under certain conditions. If water-thinned paint was used previously, seal it with an oil-base primer or remove it before applying new water-thinned paints that may dissolve the old coat. A solution of starch and strong soap will be useful in removing the old water-thinned finish. Calcimine should be removed from walls before repainting with any type of paint. An inexpensive calcimine scraper is the best tool for this job.

If the previous paint was glossy, it should be dulled by washing with a mild solution of sal soda or a prepared surface conditioner; you can also use sandpaper or steel wool.

With latex-emulsion paints, primers are not necessary. Before using any latex paint, make sure there is no glue on the walls. If there is, remove it with steel wool and warm water. Test for the presence of size by wetting a section. If little flakes show up when it dries, your wall is sized.

Mixing Paint. Thorough mixing of the paints you will use is essential. The durability of a paint is directly affected by the proper balance of pigments in relationship to the other contents. Unless the paint is thoroughly mixed, its protective properties will not be fully attained and, further, the painted surface will vary slightly in color and an imperfect job will result. Oil paints can be agitated on a mechanical shaker in your dealer's store at the time of purchase. This is all that is usually needed when the paint is used within a short period of time. Latex paints, when agitated mechanically, should be allowed to set at least one hour before using.

Be sure to mix enough paint to do the complete job, especially if you are intermixing colors. It is important that the total amount of paint required for a room, plus a little extra, be mixed at the beginning.

Always try to finish at least one entire wall, or panel, from the same mixture because even the same color from various paint cans may sometimes vary a bit in hue. The best results can be obtained by starting a new can of paint only at corners or intersections—never in the middle of a wall or ceiling, if you can at all help it.

Be careful with thinners. All paints are formulated according to exact specifications. A paint can be ruined by adding the wrong thinner or oil. Read the label directions and use only the exact quantity of thinner recommended.

To be sure of getting full value from your paint, follow these simple mixing steps:

1. Pour surface oil into an empty, clean container.

2. Stir up pigment thoroughly from the bottom.

3. Pour oil back gradually, while stirring. Stir vigorously and pour from can to can.

Saving Paint. The easiest way to do any paint job is the correct way, and that implies adequate preparation so that you don't spend more time in "cleaning up" than you do in painting. These photographic suggestions illustrate a few methods of saving time and paint.

When you've finished painting for the day, wipe the rim of the can and cover it tightly to keep out dust and dirt. To close the can, place it on newspaper on the floor and press the lid down firmly with the foot. If a skin should form on a partially used can of paint, remove it carefully before stirring. *Don't stir it in.*

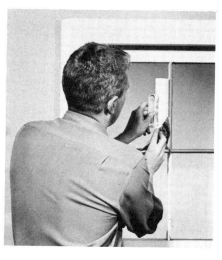

1. Shields of metal, wood, or cardboard are useful in keeping paint where it belongs when you are painting windows, woodwork or trim, and save tedious clean-up.

2. With old paint that has become lumpy, this is a real boon. Cut a piece of wire screen to fit can. Mix paint, drop in screen. It sinks, carries lumps with it.

3. To avoid splattering when you hammer back the lid on a paint can, drape a cloth over the lid. You'll save yourself, and clothes, from a dosage of paint.

4. A series of holes punched around the bottom of the lid groove will enable paint to drip back into the can. Paint will not splatter or run over when lid is replaced.

5. Cheesecloth is good for straining paint, but an old nylon stocking makes the best strainer. It is lintless and ideal for this job and may be used for varnish, too.

6. Here is another use for old nylons. Slip one over your hand to detect any roughness (which will snag the hose) so that you may sand it down for a glasslike finish.

7. You'll find that drilling a few large holes in a paddle used for mixing paints helps to stir them thoroughly. Enamels, particularly, must be very well mixed.

8. Glue a paper plate to the bottom of a paint can to catch drippings. You can then move the can anywhere while on the job without clean-up after you're through working.

9. To prevent "skin" forming on paint, pour a little turpentine over the paint, making sure it floats on the surface. Stir turps in when you're ready to paint.

Interior Painting Methods. Flat paint used on walls will give rooms a soft, pleasing appearance. It has no shine or gloss and is by far the most popular finish for bedroom, living-room and dining-room walls. Semi-gloss and eggshell enamels have a slight sheen and are popular for woodwork and walls that are frequently washed. Since semi-gloss is its own best primer, two coats will provide an excellent finish if one coat doesn't do the job. Kitchens and bathrooms, which receive a lot of scrubbing, are usually painted with high-gloss paint or enamel for a hard, washable finish. If you use enamel, you might encounter difficulty with a roller; most handymen will find it easier to use a 4-to-6″ brush on ceilings and walls. However, flat and semi-gloss paints are adaptable to either brush or roller.

Left: Dip paintbrush about half the length of the bristles. If paint is allowed to run back into the heel of the brush, it will harden and be difficult to remove.
Center: Lightly wipe off excess paint against the side of the can. Deeper dipping is a waste of paint, leads to splattering; hold brush so loaded bristles are down.
Right: Keep all painting strips on the wall narrow so that you are always working with a wet edge. Failure to observe this rule will result in unsightly lap marks on wall.

Lay on paint with short, slightly curved strokes, lifting the brush gradually at the end of each stroke. Do not apply paint by using brush in just one direction.

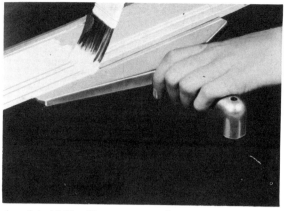

A paint shield will protect your floors when painting the baseboard or the bottom of a door. If any paint splatters on floor, wipe off immediately with a rag.

If you're painting with a brush, begin in an upper corner and paint a strip about 3' wide from there to the baseboard. Cross-brush horizontally and finish with vertical brush strokes toward the ceiling. Do the whole wall this way. When you have completed several strips, go back and remove any brush marks by brushing lightly over the finished area with the tip of your brush, using a semicircular motion. Paint rapidly so that the edges of the strip don't have a chance to dry, or there will be shiny lines where your strips meet. You'll find that many of the brush marks will disappear after the final coat has dried. Allow ample drying time between coats.

If you're using a roller, first "cut in" around the ceiling corners and woodwork with a 2" brush. Begin with the roller in the upper corner and paint a strip down to the baseboard. Then go back over the painted area at right angles to the previous strokes. This will pick up any bare spots the roller may have missed the first time and will also remove roller marks. Always finish by rolling all strokes in one direction. Before you put on another coat, check the first one. Even if the proper number of hours have gone by, it may still be a bit damp. Press your thumb firmly into the paint. If it doesn't leave a mark, go ahead with the next coat.

When putting enamel on walls, you must work as quickly as possible because enamel sets rapidly. Do not try to paint the whole surface at once. Work in small sections and remove the brush marks as you go along. Keep the edge of your sections wet so that you are not applying wet enamel next to dry. Work from the top of the wall to the bottom and from corner to corner. If the wall is a new one, use a

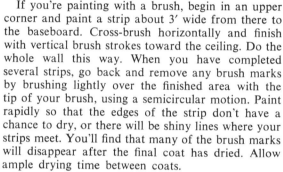

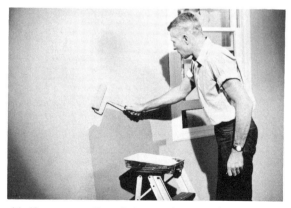

The task of painting a room is speeded up considerably if one person "cuts in" around woodwork, etc. with a brush and a second uses a roller for large wall areas. Rubber-base paints are self-sealing and usually require no prime coat. With other paints, new plaster may absorb oil from top coat and leave an uneven appearance.

How to Paint Interiors   363

primer as the first coat, enamel undercoater as the second coat, and then one or two coats of enamel to finish the job.

On woodwork that is new and that is to be given an opaque coating, an undercoater is required. For a finishing coat, use semi-gloss enamel or flat oil paint. Keep in mind, however, that flat oil paints are easily fingermarked and are unsatisfactory for window sills. You can use emulsion and rubber-base paints for woodwork, too. All of these coatings can also be used to refinish woods that have previously been painted, varnished or shellacked. Just be sure there is no wax or polish on the old finish and then sandpaper it lightly, making sure to level chips, scratches and mars such as cigarette burns. To do

this well, it may be necessary to sandpaper some spots clear down to the bare wood. Touch these places up with enamel to seal them before you repaint.

Never use aluminum or any metallic paint on a radiator—it cuts heat! Instead, use a flat alkyd-base paint, the paler the better. If you can, use pale yellow. It won't fade or change color. Paint only the visible portions, leaving the rest bare metal for greater efficiency.

The quickest and easiest way to remove old paint from a radiator is to spread newspaper under it after it has been turned off and cooled, and apply paste-type paint remover; it won't drip, but if it does, the paper's there. When paint starts to lift off, use medium steel wool to gather up softened paint. Remember to wear gloves and work the steel wool into all

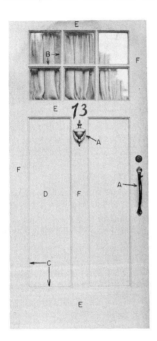

TO PAINT A DOOR

1. Remove as much of the door hardware (A) as possible.
2. After window panes have been masked for protection, paint the muntin bars (B). These are the small wood trim pieces holding the glass in place. Paint the horizontal ones first.
3. The molding edges (C) around any inset wood panels in the door are painted next. If any paint overlaps the edges, wipe it off with turpentine-dampened cloth.
4. The inset panels (D) are painted by using long vertical brush strokes over the entire panel.
5. The wide horizontal parts of the door (E), called the rails, are now painted, working the brush across the door.
6. You complete the job of door painting after you have applied the paint to the vertical end pieces (F), the door stiles.

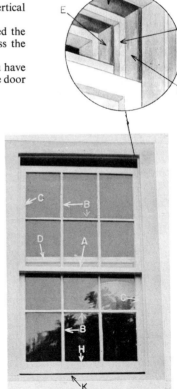

TO PAINT A WINDOW

1. Move the bottom section of the window all the way up and pull the top sash part of the way down. Paint the check rail (A), that is, the bottom horizontal piece of the top sash.
2. Protect the window panes and paint the muntin bars (B), using the same technique as for the door. That is, cover the horizontal pieces first.
3. The stiles (C), the vertical sides of each sash, are painted next.
4. The top rail (D) of the upper sash is painted and so is the top rail of the bottom sash.
5. The side jamb (E) and the parting strip (F) are now painted and so is the head jamb (G).
6. Raise the bottom sash until the bottom rail (H) just clears the apron (K). Paint the bottom rail and apron.

grooves and spaces. Wash the radiator clean with water (adding a few drops of vinegar if remover requires a neutralizer). If you can detach the radiator and move it outdoors, use a washable remover and rinse it off with a hose.

When painting a door and doorway, paint the casing first, then the door edge that swings toward the room being painted. When painting paneled doors, do the edges, then each individual panel. Then do all the horizontal panel separations and finish by doing the vertical sides. Do not close the door completely until it is thoroughly dry. It's best to paint windows after the ceiling and walls have been painted. Paint the window sash first. Start with the horizontal members, then paint the vertical ones and follow by painting the sash frame. Slide the sash so that you can paint all surfaces. Next, paint the sash tracks; then the casing, starting with the top section. Paint the edges first and finish the face surfaces last.

Finally, paint the sill. Let the windows remain partially open until the paint has dried. Baseboards are painted last. First paint the top edge and bottom of the board, then the face area between. Paint short sections at a time. A piece of cardboard used as a guard will be helpful to prevent paint from being brushed onto the floor.

Ceilings must be properly prepared to obtain first-class results. Before beginning work, protect the floor with a drop cloth. All cracks should be filled with spackling compound or patching plaster. Recurrent ceiling cracks are a construction problem. Get the advice of an expert and remedy the cause *before* doing any painting. First, determine whether the ceiling is plasterboard, plaster, or wood, and paint it just as you would any wall of that type. If the ceiling is a new one, prime before you paint it. If you're repainting your ceiling, find out what kind of paint was last used. If it was calcimined, you'll have to

1. To prepare for painting a ceiling, first cover furniture and floors with dropcloths and newspapers. It will spare you a good deal of tedious cleaning up when painting is done.

2. Patch cracks in dry-wall materials with joint tape over crack. Then coat tape with a film of patching plaster or spackle; cover nail holes the same way.

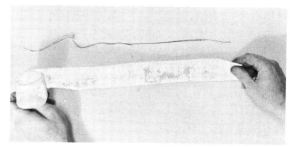

3. At ceiling-wall joints, fill with patching plaster. Or, if crack is wide, cover with tape, then plaster. Finger work, followed by putty knife, speeds the job.

4. To protect walls from paint, run masking tape along wall at ceiling line. Or, for a "dropped ceiling" effect, run tape along level lines around room.

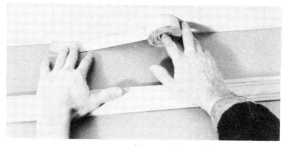

How to Paint Interiors 365

HOW TO PAINT
A CEILING

If the ceiling is a new one, prime it before finishing. Outline corner of the ceiling first. Angle into corners, keeping bristles flat against surface.

Whether you use a roller or not, work in strips across the shorter dimension of the room. Adjust ladder so you paint to the front instead of directly overhead.

"Cutting in" at the edges of ceilings is still a task for a brush even if you are using a roller for the bulk of the job. A 2" brush is ample for a small area.

Always brush paint towards a previously painted area, not away from it. If you are right-handed, it is more convenient to work left to right.

Work as rapidly as possible, using long, twirling strokes. Try to complete the entire ceiling before paint sets. Clean brushes promptly.

painting any ceiling, avoid overloading the brush or roller with paint. Do not flip the brush, spin the roller or over-thin the paint; splattering may result. Allow the first coat to dry overnight or longer before applying the second coat.

Calcimine, because of its low cost, is a favorite for finishing ceilings. Water takes a good deal out of bristles and so it is advisible to use the special brushes made for calcimining. Have two brushes ready before you begin any calcimining work; each brush will work best for only an hour or so. It will be found difficult to fan out the calcimine to feather edges after that period, the flag ends of the bristles being the worse for wear. All holes and cracks in the ceiling, as for walls, must be patched. Plaster must be sized well with glue or thin, bleached shellac in order for the calcimine to flow on well. Mix the calcimine to a heavy paste with boiling water the day before using and pour on a little cold water to prevent crusting. The next day, put the container of hard, jellied calcimine in a bath of hot water to make it thin enough to brush. Strain the calcimine through a double cheesecloth strainer when first mixed and again before brushing. Apply calcimine heavily but not so thick as to be ropy and show laps. Take narrow stretches across the narrow dimension of the ceiling. Use half strokes of crisscross direction and fan out the edges of each brushful to allow the good flag ends of bristles to do their work. Start brushing against the light, beginning at the window wall and working away from it. If the calcimine crawls or beads because some greasy substance was in the pail or on the surface, add a little alcohol or vinegar. Dark shellac or dirt discolorations may be given a thin wash coat of calcimine before the whole ceiling is coated.

wash or scrape it off. Scrubbing off calcimine by hand is a tedious job; it's far easier to simply soak the ceiling with a sponge and warm water, then scrape the coating off with a calcimine scraper. After you've removed the calcimine, paint the ceiling as though it were new, using a primer coat first.

Plan to paint an entire ceiling in one session, using a 3½ or 4" brush or a roller. Arrange the work platform or ladder so you can paint comfortably and safely. You may have to get by with one stepladder, but, if possible, borrow another one and use a plank between the two. You'll find it lots easier than getting on and off one ladder constantly.

Work in strips across the shorter dimension of the rooms. Adjust the ladders so that you can paint before you instead of directly overhead. Paint a strip 2 to 3 feet wide. Work as rapidly as you can to avoid lap marks, particularly with oil paints and enamels. When you have finished a strip across the ceiling, begin a second strip abutting it. Continue in this manner until the entire ceiling is painted. When

INTERIOR PAINTING SUMMARY

1. Determine color scheme, amount and type of paints to be used.
2. Remove all lightweight furniture.
3. Cover floor and remaining furniture with drop cloths.
4. Prepare surfaces:
   a. Patch plaster.
   b. Sandpaper woodwork and trim, wash with ammonia to remove gloss.
   c. Remove hardware from doors and windows, curtain rods and other removable obstructions not to be painted.
   d. Clean walls and ceilings of calcimine and dirt with detergent and water.
   e. Remove wallpaper. If wallpaper is to be painted over, test first to see if paper color bleeds.
5. Dust thoroughly, taking special care of top edge of doors and door frames.
6. Apply wall primer and sealer to unpainted plaster surfaces. Start on the ceiling and at the window end. Start walls at left side of main window frame or left-hand corner of window sill.
7. Apply enamel undercoater to woodwork. Start by painting inside of closet door. This "works in" the brushes. Finishing brush stroke always runs with the grain of the wood.
8. After 24 hours, apply finish coat to ceiling and walls if first coat is completely dry.
9. Lightly sand enamel undercoater on woodwork and trim. Then apply finish. Avoid overlapping where woodwork contacts wall and floor.

WHAT PAINT TO USE ... AND WHERE

Black dot indicates that a primer or sealer may be necessary before the finishing coat (unless the surface has been previously finished).

	Flat Paint	Semi-Gloss Paint	Enamel	Rubber Base Paint	Emulsion Paint	Casein	Interior Varnish	Shellac	Wax (Liquid or Paste)	Wax (Emulsion)	Stain	Wood Sealer	Floor Varnish	Floor Paint or Enamel	Cement Base Paint	Aluminum Paint	Sealer or Undercoater	Metal Primer
Plaster Walls and Ceiling	✓			✓	✓	✓											✓	
Wall Board	✓			✓	✓	✓											✓	
Wood Paneling	✓		✓				✓	✓	✓		✓	✓	✓				✓	
Kitchen and Bathroom Walls	✓	✓•	✓•	✓					✓								✓	
Wood Floors							✓	✓	✓	✓	✓	✓	✓	✓•			✓	
Concrete Floors														✓•			✓	
Rubber Tile Floors									✓	✓		✓						
Asphalt Tile Floors									✓	✓			✓	✓				
Linoleum									✓	✓			✓	✓				
Stair Treads							✓	✓	✓	✓	✓	✓	✓	✓•			✓	
Stair Risers	✓	✓•		✓			✓	✓	✓		✓	✓	✓				✓	
Wood Trim		✓•	✓•	✓			✓	✓	✓		✓	✓	✓				✓	
Steel Windows			✓•															✓
Aluminum Windows						✓												✓
Window Sills		✓•	✓•	✓			✓	✓	✓	✓	✓	✓	✓				✓	
Steel Cabinets		✓•	✓•	✓														✓
Heating Ducts	✓															✓		✓
Radiators and Heating Pipes	✓															✓		
Old Masonry															✓		✓	
New Masonry															✓		✓	

PAINTING EXTERIORS

A good paint will do much more than restore the beauty of your home. It will preserve and weatherproof it as well as protect it from possible rot, decay and expensive repairs. While you may want to use paint on metal and masonry surfaces, you will be concerned primarily with painting wood, which expands under hard rains and contracts when a blazing sun dries it out. To allow for this shrinking and swelling, house paint has a built-in elasticity which endures for the normal lifetime of the coating, an average of 4 to 6 years.

Preparation. The vast majority of paint failures are the result of failure to prepare the surface properly. *This is the most important phase of your painting.* First and foremost, make a minute inspection of your home in order to list (and correct) all structural defects. Joints, copings and siding must be sound and secure to prevent the entrance and trapping of moisture.

Calking is easy to do and pays big returns for the modest investment involved. It seals out fuel-stealing drafts and moisture, both arch enemies of wood and paint alike. Calk cracks around window and door frames, balustrades, butt joints of wood and stone on porches, and butt joints of siding and corner boards.

Nail heads that haven't been properly set and puttied are another potential source of trouble. In

time, such nail heads may rust out entirely and allow a clapboard to loosen and admit moisture. Make sure that all exposed nails are counterset, then primed with paint and filled level with putty.

Check the foundation of the house. Any hair lines in concrete or cement blocks should be covered with paint. A year or so of frost and weather will convert hairlines to gaps and cause the concrete to crumble like cake. Use one of the special cement paints available for a durable, frost-resistant film. It's wise to paint the entire foundation when cracks and crumbling first develop, as this preserves the masonry.

Leaking roof gutters and downspouts are always dangerous. They provide a means for water to get under paint, thereby starting a process which destroys the film of paint and leads to rot and large repair bills.

Before painting, calk open cracks. Don't count on paint to do it for you. Calking compounds can be painted over.

Fill nail holes, loose knots, depressions and cracks with putty or a good wood filler. Let dry, shellac one or two coats, then paint.

Replace loose and rusted nails. Tighten down boards which have warped and pulled loose to leave cracks between clapboards.

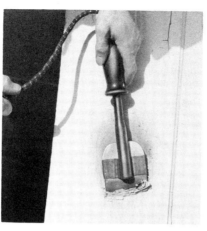

Where considerable paint must be removed, soften paint with a reliable blowtorch; follow immediately with scraping and sanding.

If a blowtorch is not to your liking, try an electric paint softener, which requires no flame and scrapes as it softens.

Coarse sandpaper held on a block to protect the fingers will make quick work of removing loose paint scale and smoothing rough surfaces.

When paint has a tendency to peel in the area surrounding windows, the source of trouble can often be traced to leaks resulting from improperly applied flashing which has deteriorated—or to failure of the builder to provide any flashing at all. Poorly fitted boards around the window are another major cause. Flashings (preferably of copper) should be included at the tops of windows and doors and at the bottoms of windows. The overhead flashing should extend from the sheathing under the building paper out to, and over, the drip cap of the window or door.

A careful inspection of all sash, both steel and wood, is imperative. Sash deteriorates quickly, particularly where condensation is a frequent problem. The many joints and cross-members, unless well calked, offer easy access for moisture and disintegration.

If previous painting was done properly, the surface will be marked with a uniform, dull, chalklike film. In chalking, the film of the paint is wearing away evenly and has no openings where moisture can seep through. If this has happened, the surfaces often can be prepared for repainting simply by proper sanding and wiping.

Dirt itself is no indication that repainting is necessary. There may be, underneath the dirt, a coat of paint in fine condition. You may be able to "bring

A wire brush will remove dirt, scaling paint, and any other loose material which might foul a paintbrush and make it impossible to do a good paint job.

A chemical paint remover may be used to soften several layers of paint. Use the semi-paste type for vertical surfaces, then scrape away loosened layers.

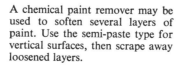

it back alive" by using a wide scrub brush with fiber bristles and any good detergent. Remember that unpainted or unvarnished copper and galvanized iron surfaces, drain pipes, gutters and screens may stain your paint badly. Coat these surfaces with a recommended paint or spar varnish to obviate staining.

A good paint job will make it much easier to prepare the surface for the next painting. When a house is painted with the same paint year after year, and no defects develop, many coats can be built up. However, some paints will not perform properly on a base coat of another type. Some paints *must* be applied only to new wood or masonry, while with others the two vehicles will not blend. In such cases, and also when the base coat is unknown, removal of the present paint is best. Professionals burn off old paint, but it's a risky job even in the hands of experts. A sparkless, flameless electrical heating device can be used to soften paint for removal with a scraper. The current needed is considerable in some cases and a long extension cord is essential. The cost of using a chemical remover may be considerably higher, but the job is done safely. The chemical is applied and allowed to work for as long as the manufacturer recommends, softening the paint coats for scraping off. Some chemical removers and the paint they've softened are washed off with a hose rather than taken off with a scraper. While this is fast and easy, surrounding shrubbery must be shielded.

After all paint has been removed, all cracks filled, nail holes puttied, loose boards nailed down tightly and all structural defects remedied, the surface to be painted should be wire-brushed. All uneven spots, humps and jagged edges must be sanded. When the surface is uniformly smooth, dry and clean, you may apply the paint—but only at that time and not before. Only by such painstaking preparation can the right kind of job be done.

Weather Is Important. Check the weather before you begin painting. Paint will not dry properly when the weather is too hot or too cold, so try to choose days when the temperature is between 55 and 90°. A hot sun will blister new paint; if you're working during the summer months, paint in the shade. Don't paint if you expect a sudden drop in the temperature several hours later, and avoid painting on humid, dusty and windy days. Because of the early morning dew, begin painting only after the sun has had a chance to dry out moisture, and never paint during foggy or damp weather. After a heavy rainstorm, give the house a few days to dry out and, if possible, paint only after a week of sunny, dry weather.

Protect Before You Paint. Take a good look around your house for the things you don't want to paint. Mask the windows with tape or use a paint shield to protect them while you paint. Tie your

---

---

shrubbery away from the house; a strip of cloth attached to stakes will hold it back and protect it from being spattered. Spread drop cloths over anything else that might be splashed.

Primers and Paints. A coat of priming paint will substantially increase the durability of the finish coat. In fact, even those woods that do not hold paint well, if primed properly, will retain a coating of paint almost as long as cedar and redwood. Aluminum house paint, which is specially made for exterior woodwork, is excellent as a primer. *Do not use aluminum paints or enamels designed for other purposes.* Next best are those house paint primers which are free of zinc oxide and which have "controlled penetration."

After paint removal, apply a penetrating sealer, particularly at grain ends. This assures longer paint life.

The amount of paint needed to paint the exterior of your home depends, primarily, upon the size of your house. Take into consideration, too, the number of coats of paint required. Certain conditions and surfaces necessitate extra amounts of paint. These include:

Very rough or heavily-textured surfaces—20 per cent more paint.

Narrow lap siding—10 per cent more paint than wide siding.

Corrugated metal surfaces—33⅓ per cent more paint than smooth metal.

Concrete block—the first coat requires 50 per cent more paint.

In estimating trim paint, allow one gallon for each five gallons of body paint. Paints vary in coverage, but you can estimate about 500 square feet per gallon. To determine the number of gallons needed, measure in square feet the area to be painted and divide the total by 500 or by the coverage-per-gallon listed on the label of the paint can.

For a three-coat house-paint job, thin the primer with a small amount of turpentine or mineral spirits and apply so that one gallon of the mixture covers about 600 square feet of surface; apply two coats of house paint in white or any light color, each gallon of paint spread over 700 square feet.

For a two-coat house painting, do not thin the primer, but apply a thicker coating so that a gallon covers no more than 450 square feet of surface; apply one coat of good house paint (over the primer coat) thickly so that it covers no more than 550 square feet of surface.

Use a 3½ or 4″ brush for siding, a 2½ or 3″ brush for trim, and a 1 to 2″ angular sash brush for work around windows. In repainting, apply just one coat of top-grade house paint.

Sealers will penetrate wood fibers and seal the pores against moisture. This type of finish is especially useful on screens and storm doors.

USE THE RIGHT PAINT

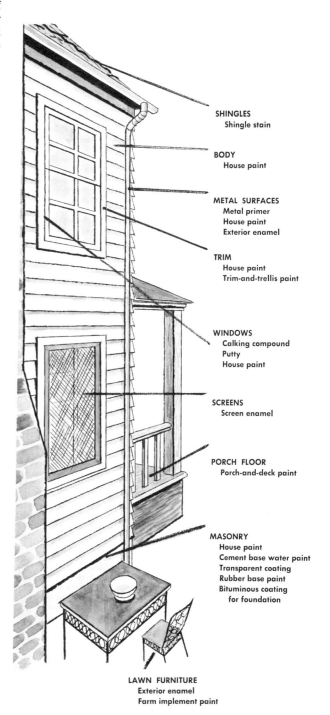

SHINGLES
Shingle stain

BODY
House paint

METAL SURFACES
Metal primer
House paint
Exterior enamel

TRIM
House paint
Trim-and-trellis paint

WINDOWS
Calking compound
Putty
House paint

SCREENS
Screen enamel

PORCH FLOOR
Porch-and-deck paint

MASONRY
House paint
Cement base water paint
Transparent coating
Rubber base paint
Bituminous coating
    for foundation

LAWN FURNITURE
Exterior enamel
Farm implement paint

When painting the side of a house, begin at the highest point and apply paint in horizontal strips about 3″ wide. Paint above the top of the ladder, when possible, as you can reach a wider area. Do not stop in the middle of a strip for any length of time. The distance between the house and base of ladder should be about ¼ to ⅓ of the ladder's length.

Begin at the Top. The best place to begin painting is at the top, so set up your ladders and plank (it might be a good idea to check back to the ladder safety pointers in Chapter 5) and, starting with the highest point, paint a strip about 3′ wide across the building. If you paint the lower part of the house first, there is the danger of dropping wet paint from above onto finished surfaces below. Cover this entire area, then move down and begin again right below it with another 3′ strip. Paint the edges of the wood first, then the flat area in between. Always paint with the flat of the brush to avoid streaks and to keep the brush from wearing down at the edges. Never use the brush edgewise. Brush the paint out well, covering as large an area as possible with a brushful. Finish the stroke by brushing the paint out very thin around the edges to prevent lap marks. If painting stops at the middle of an unbroken surface, the next day's painting that begins there will leave a streak.

Wait at least three days before putting a second coat over the first, or the paint may crack or wrinkle later. If the weather is damp or cold, allow several days' more time between coats.

Trim. Many quality paints are made with "controlled chalking" or "self-cleaning" features, an enormous advantage when painting clapboard homes. However, these paints should not be used on white trim or shutters of brick or masonry homes. The reason is that the white pigment may wash down over the surfaces below, resulting in streaks. Use a paint which does not "chalk" (white lead or zinc oxide) for white trim on such houses.

The trim and shutters of your home should be painted last. Clean and prime any new wood or metal trim before starting to paint. Trim paints come in many bright and attractive colors and have a glossy finish similar to enamel. For ease of painting, take shutters down, place them across sawhorses or boxes, and paint them horizontally.

Suit the brush to the job. Here a 2-inch brush is wide enough; a wider brush would be wasteful.

1. Above, left: Load your brush, then apply two or three dabs of paint along the joint of the siding. You will find this will help to distribute the paint quickly and easily.
2. Above, right: Brush the paint out well and be careful to coat the underedge of the clapboard. If possible, paint only after a week of dry weather.
3. Left: "Feather" the ends of your brush strokes so that the coat will be smooth where one section joins another. A 4″ or 5″ brush is most often used for this job.

Roofs. New wood shingles should be primed before they are applied by thoroughly dipping them in finishing products such as shingle stain, house paint (thinned to shingle-paint consistency), thinned boiled linseed oil or creosote. The finish coat should be brushed or sprayed on after they are laid. Shingle stains, to be effective, should penetrate. Do not apply over painted shingles. Coat tile roofs with exterior enamel or rubberized exterior masonry finishes.

Ordinary paints should not be used on composition roofs or shingles. Use special coating materials such as liquid asphalt, fibrous roof cement or aluminum asphalt paints. Liquid asphalt roof coatings may be applied on either damp or dry surfaces but should never be used on dusty or hot surfaces. Apply with a roof brush. Soak the brush in kerosene and rinse out before using. Apply aluminum roof paint with a clean paint brush. *Never paint asphalt shingles in a hot sun, when the shingles are likely to be soft.*

Porches, Floors, Steps, Railings. Some homeowners prefer varnish ceilings on porches; others prefer paint or enamel for better light reflection and durability. Either is satisfactory. For floors, railings and steps—for both priming and finishing coats—use only porch or floor enamel. This finish is specially designed to withstand constant wear, the destructive effects of weather and regular scrubbing. It can also be used on concrete floors. Be sure to paint the underside of wood steps.

Metal Surfaces. In preparing any metal surface for painting or repainting, make absolutely certain that all traces of oil, rust or grease are removed. Failure to observe this precaution will automatically ensure that the paint job will fail. Oil and grease may be removed by the use of common dry-cleaning solvents

THE BEST EQUIPMENT FOR DIFFERENT EXTERIOR SURFACES

Surface	First Choice	Second Choice	Third Choice
Clapboards	Brush	Roller	Sprayer
Wood shingles			
New, unpainted	Sprayer	Brush	
Old, painted	Brush	Sprayer	
Asbestos shingles			
Plain-type	Brush	Sprayer	
Serrated-type	Sprayer	Brush	
Brick			
First coat, unpainted	Roller	Sprayer	Brush
Second coat, painted	Roller	Brush	
Stone, rough masonry	Sprayer	Brush	
Vertical siding	Brush	Roller	Sprayer
Windows, doors, irregular trim	Brush	Sprayer	

or by such thinners as turpentine or naphtha. Remove rust with a wire brush, steel wool, a scraper, sandpaper or emery cloth. Paint applied over rust will not hold.

After the surface has been thoroughly cleaned, it's a good idea to use a prime coat immediately so that oil or grease has no chance to settle again. The primer must, of course, be thoroughly dry before the finish coat is applied. If the metal has been previously painted and the finish is not cracked and no rust has formed, simply apply a fresh coat of paint. If there are signs of wear, sand all chips and cracks smooth, remove rust before touching up spots with the appropriate primer, then paint.

Galvanized iron, tin and steel will eventually rust and disintegrate without adequate protection against moisture. Copper will not rust but will give off a corrosive wash which will stain adjacent surfaces. Aluminum will neither rust nor corrode.

Masonry. Just as with any other surface, masonry must be clean before it is painted. No matter what type of paint you expect to use, remove any dirt and loose paint with a wire brush. Then wash thoroughly with clean water. If you used cement water paint previously and it adhered firmly, brush it vigorously with a stiff-bristle brush. If you used an oil-base paint previously and you intend to use it again, just clean the surface and repaint. If you wish to use any other type of paint, first remove the oil-base paint by scrubbing with a caustic soda solution and rinsing with water. (Use every care when working with caustic soda.) If you used whitewash or a similar water-base paint, brush every bit of it off before repainting.

Efflorescence is caused by a salt found to some degree in all concrete and masonry products. Mois-

ture affecting the masonry will cause the salts to move to the surface and dry, leaving a white, powdery film. *Never attempt to paint over efflorescence; if you do, the paint film will fail.* With a solution of 1 part muriatic acid (very dangerous to skin on contact—wear rubber gloves and protective goggles) to 5 parts water, scrub the masonry and then rinse thoroughly. This should remove any efflorescence. Allow the wall to dry out completely before repainting.

Masonry paints are available in six different types —cement water paint, resin-emulsion paint, oil paint, rubber-base paint, polyvinyl acetate emulsions and silicon sealers. These paints may be used on such masonry surfaces as foundations, gate posts and fences or enclosures. For masonry floors, however, only rubber-base paints specially formulated for this purpose should be used.

Cement water paints are mixed with water and are specially suited for concrete walls that are damp at the time of painting or are subject to dampness. This type is hard, strong and relatively brittle. Use commercial brands of already tinted cement water paints if color is wanted because it is difficult to obtain even tones in the types to which color must be added. Apply it, preferably, in two coats. Less than 24 hours' drying time should elapse between coats, for they adhere best when not completely dry. The addition of fine sand to the first coat will help conceal defects. Use a short, stiff-bristled brush and scrub into the surface. Keep the sealer coat moist with a fine fog spray for at least 12 hours; keep the final coat moist for 48 hours to cure it.

Resin emulsion paints are applied by brush or spray and dry in a few hours to a smooth, opaque, flat finish. Do not wet down walls before or after

Masonry surfaces also require treatment before painting. Wire brush knocks off old paint, loose scale, dirt.

Stucco surfaces should be carefully checked before painting, and all cracks and breaks patched with fresh stucco.

It's easy to apply silicon masonry water repellents with just a brush. Simply apply one full flooding coat. These sealers give good protection, can be used over cement-base paints and will retain texture and color of the masonry.

painting. Two coats are generally recommended and brush or spray may be used. If you're working with open-textured masonry, use a cement water paint with sand in it to fill the voids before finishing with resin-emulsion paint. Wash brushes and spray guns thoroughly with warm, soapy water immediately after use.

Oil-base paints should be applied to dry, sound walls. A week of clear, dry weather should precede painting, which must not be done in damp or humid weather. The first coat of oil-base paint will usually seal the surface sufficiently to avoid "spotting" of the second coat. Two coats are recommended for good hiding durability.

Rubber-base paints are divided into two types, rubber-solution and rubber-emulsion. The rubber-solution types use solvents like toluene and have high resistance to moisture, soaps, alkalies and acids. The rubber-emulsion types may be thinned with water.

Polyvinyl acetate paints must be used on masonry never before painted or on masonry that has been painted with the same type of paint. Easy to apply, they will usually cover well in one coat, resist alkali, and provide a waterproof film. They release interior vapors that cause paint-peeling blisters to form.

Silicon sealers provide an excellent water-repellent seal that gives good protection and yet retains the original color and texture of the masonry wall. These sealers should not be applied over oil- or resin-base

coats but can be used over cement-base paints. They do not permit the formation of blisters or efflorescence.

Natural Finishes for Exteriors. The use of such woods as redwood and cedar (and exterior grades of hardwood plywood) for the exteriors of homes has resulted in a large demand for "natural finishes." These are finishes so transparent that the grain of the wood will show through. However, some prejudice has developed against the "natural finish" because (1) such finishes are less durable than house paints, (2) there have been cases of transparent or natural finishes deteriorating so badly that they had to be renewed each year, and (3) the finish has been used inadvertently or incorrectly.

Natural finishes come in three main types—varnish, sealer and drying oil. Linseed oil, relatively inexpensive, is sometimes used but is a poor selection because it darkens redwood excessively, mildews more rapidly than other finishes, dries slowly and is not a good moisture sealer. If linseed oil is used, however, add a little color-in-oil for a pigmented oil finish. This will not otherwise affect the qualities of linseed oil but will appreciably lengthen the life of the finish. Make sure the unabsorbed oil is wiped off before it dries (usually about 30 minutes).

A marine spar varnish is used for a maximum of gloss in a natural finish. Most often, varnish is chosen for small areas—doors and trim—rather than for expanses of siding. However, varnish has some drawbacks in that it may craze, develop milky spots or become opaque in some areas. After several renewals, you will have to strip the accumulated varnish from the wood with a remover (a tedious job) before refinishing. Do not—if you are using varnish in spite of these drawbacks—use shellac as an undercoat. It will ruin the finish.

The most promising note in the natural finish field is struck by the pigmented sealers. These are combinations of pigments, solvents and mildewcides (with or without resins) that have shown remarkably favorable results in many tests. Homeowners have found it gratifyingly simple to brush on two coats of sealer and to renew the finish a few years later by brushing on an additional coat or two. Color choice is good and may be varied by intermixing several shades, including redwood, mahogany, gray, green, etc. The use of pigments in these compounds is far more important than is generally realized. They repel the destructive ultraviolet and infrared rays of the sun. Without pigments, the organic matter contained in a clear coating deteriorates fairly rapidly under the effects of sunlight.

Some of them add to the durability of the finish, tone down variations in natural color of the wood and obscure slight grayness or bleaching from weathering of the wood if the renewal of the finish is postponed. Some sealers are pigmented gray or brown to give the appearance of bleached or weathered wood where such finishes are desired.

Other types of finishes include different kinds of oils, waxes and combinations of stains and clear-gloss or clear-flat compounds.

Whichever finish you choose, it is always best to (1) apply a penetrating, water-repellent preservative to the wood, (2) make sure that the finish contains a mildewcide (although some mildewcides can be added separately) and (3) make certain that your choice seals in tannic acid or any other poisons contained in the wood. If it doesn't, these impurities will later come to the surface, staining the finish.

EXTERIOR PAINTING SUMMARY

1. Examine present conditions.
2. Estimate needs.
3. Preparatory work before painting is started:
   a. Scaffolding
   b. Removal of shutters and screens
   c. Carpentry repairs
   d. Replace broken glass
   e. Clean out gutters
   f. Remove loose and scaling paint
   g. Remove rust from metal
   h. General cleaning and sandpapering
4. Primer undercoater to all surfaces.
5. Preparatory work before finish coat:
   a. Puttying
   b. Sandpapering
   c. Touching up any defects in first coat
6. Finish coat to dormers and cornices and roof metal work.
7. Finish coat to body of house.
8. Finish coat to windows and porches.
9. Finish coat to doors and shutters.
10. Finish coat to porch floor and steps

WORKING WITH WOOD   Buying lumber · Lazy man's lumber · Working with plywood · Primer for built-ins · Tricks with moldings · Wood finishes · Wood fillers · Linseed oil

In almost every chapter in this book, you will find yourself reading about wood, no matter whether you want to drive a nail or change a lock on a door. Probably no other material is used in the home to the extent of wood, and with good reason. Economical, durable, versatile and attractive, wood has a thousand and one uses, ranging from the fencing that may surround your house to the floors you walk on and the furniture you live with.

It follows that throughout the large majority of your home repairs and maintenance, you will be concerned with wood. You may need to put together a rough sawhorse or erect some temporary scaffolding, or you may want to build in highly finished bookcases along a living-room wall or make extra kitchen cabinets. Before beginning any woodworking job, first familiarize yourself with the varying grades of wood. Living-room built-ins made of Grade No. 4, for instance, will be woefully disappointing, for no amount of sanding and polishing will ever result in a high-gloss, smooth finish.

This section provides information on grades of

wood, types of wood, and how to gain finished and professional effects using wood. Correct joinery often means all the difference between success and failure. Should you use a dado joint or would a butt joint be better, for instance? And even the most accurate and sturdily built job will not be attractive unless the finish is even, smooth and thoroughly dry. With careful treatment and application, less expensive woods can be brought to a glowing satin finish or made to take a coat of enamel that's as smooth as glass. With wood in so much evidence all about your home, this section is a sure guide to better home maintenance and beauty.

BUYING LUMBER

Buying the right type of wood and the proper grade for the job you plan to do will not only save money but will also help you to do better work. All lumber is arbitrarily divided into two categories—hardwoods and softwoods. Any broad-leaf tree—maple, oak, walnut—is classed as hardwood. All trees with needle or scalelike leaves—pine, fir, cedar, spruce—are softwoods. Most softwoods are used for general construction, and most hardwoods are used for trim, molding, cabinets and furniture. Furthermore, all lumber is graded. While there are some variations within grades, they are slight inasmuch as all grading follows standards set up by an industry-government group. There are two sets of grade classifications. One is for building and is called structural lumber; the other is for household carpentry and is called yard lumber.

Nos. 1 and 2 Clear (or Grades A and B of yard lumber) are almost free of all blemishes and are good for natural finishes.

C Select Grade may have some blemishes but can be used for high-quality painting.

D Select Grade is the lowest of the finishing grades but still is suitable for a paint finish.

No. 1 Common is sound and suitable for use without waste.

No. 2 Common is for all-round utility and is only slightly inferior to No. 1; it too can be used without waste.

No. 3 Grade may have large knots and other defects and is not as strong as either Nos. 1 or 2. There is always some waste.

No. 4 is the lowest grade which homeowners should buy. It will decay quickly and is used mainly for temporary structural work.

Lumber is usually sold by the "board foot". A board foot is equal to a square foot of lumber one inch thick, all dimensions being nominal rather than actual (see table on page 383 for differences between dressed and asked-for lumber sizes).

The table below will guide you to the right selection of the type of wood for the job you intend to do. You might refer also to page 368 for paint durability of various woods.

WHAT WOOD TO USE

	Easy to Work	Resists Shrinking, Warping, Swelling	Unusually Strong	Resistance to Decay
SOFTWOODS				
Cedar	×	×		×
Cypress	×	×		×
Douglas Fir	×		×	
Redwood	×	×		×
Spruce	×	×		
Western Larch			×	
White Pine	×	×	×	
Yellow Pine	×		×	
HARDWOODS				
Ash			×	×
Basswood	×			
Birch			×	
Cherry		×	×	
Gumwood	×			
Mahogany		×	×	×
Maple		×		×
Oak		×	×	×
Poplar	×			
Walnut		×		×

LAZY MAN'S LUMBER

If you're short of spare time, tools or ambition, let some of the ready-made items in your local lumber yard help out. They can give your do-it-yourself projects a highly professional look at very low cost, and all you need for the job are a few simple hand tools.

Some of the outstanding time-savers are shown in the photographs on the next two pages, but the variety available is too great to include all of them. Familiarize yourself with the molding racks in your lumber yard before beginning your next project. (How to work with molding is detailed later in this section.) Look at ready-made sash, too. You can plan a glass-doored cabinet around a standard size. If you have qualms about your ability to do a good finishing job on built-ins, look at prefinished plywood or hardboard. To build a project with material of this type, you simply cut the pieces to size, fasten them together and the job is done.

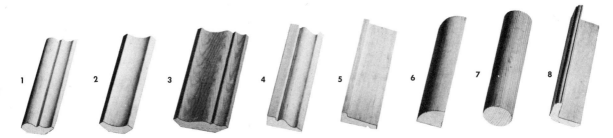

Samples of molding shapes. Your lumber dealer has a wide assortment. They sell by the foot. Cove moldings (*1, 2,* and *3*) trim inside corners. Outside corner molding (*8*) is fine for cabinet work. Closet pole (*7*) makes a shelf support. Quarter-round (*6*) also is good trim. *4* and *5* lend themselves well as cabinet trim.

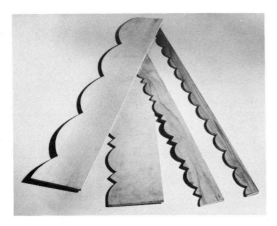

Valance strips like these are available in more than a dozen patterns. Buy them in 6′ to 8′ lengths for valances, and also for shelf edging, cabinet trim, cove lights.

Shelves shown are No. 2 common pine and the posts are 1½″ closet pole cut to length. Where shelves are not braced against wall, run them through holes cut into the shelves, with metal pins run through to anchor shelves.

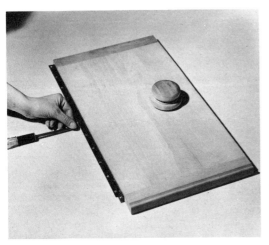

Solid birch breadboard like this makes a warp-free cabinet door. The massive knob is a cap for a stairway newel post. It's a standard item and inexpensive.

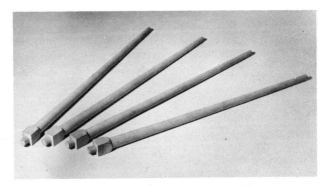

Stair balusters, used in hand railings, make graceful table legs. They come in 30″ lengths, may be cut to table height of 28″. Use pine for shorter legs, birch (which is sturdier) for high tables.

Left: To make legs removable for storage, and to avoid boring into underside of table top, use plywood squares like this with leg fitted into ¾" hole and glued there. Screws at corners hold leg to top.

Center: Using balusters, you can make a table like this in an hour or two. Allow ample time for glue to dry before putting table to use. Edging shown is ready-made inlay border strip found in cabinet-maker's supplies.

Right: Ornamented picture-frame stock is sold in lengths up to 4'. Cut in a miter box as shown to make picture frames, trays, shelves. Use also as a trim. Join corners with glue and brads.

WORKING WITH PLYWOOD

Cutting Plywood. Beginners often run into one serious problem in cutting plywood. Whether a hand saw or power saw is used, the cut—on one side at least—is apt to be ragged. Chunks, splinters and chips of wood are torn loose, necessitating extensive patchwork to conceal the damage. One basic rule should always be followed: the point of each saw tooth must enter the wood on the surface to be exposed. This rule may be observed in each photograph shown here.

In planing end grain, the blade of the plane meets the finished side of the material first and is slanted slightly toward the central core of the plywood. Use short strokes only.

HOW TO CUT PLYWOOD WITHOUT DAMAGE

1. In cutting plywood with a hand saw, hold the saw nearly flat to the surface and score the first ply (or laminate) with forward strokes only. Then cut through with saw at normal angle. Cut until end of scored line is reached, then repeat the operation.

2. Table-saw teeth rotate in direction of operator, enter top surface first. Therefore, place wood with *finished* side upward. This applies to plain plywood, veneers, or any form of plywood with laminates attached.   →

3. Cutting with a portable power saw (circular type) finds teeth entering wood on the underside. Place the finished side *down*. If using a sabre saw, note direction of teeth points and have these enter wood on underside.

4. Where *both* sides of wood are finished, use fine-tooth blade without any set at all, or use a cabinetmaker's hollow-ground saw blade with teeth widely spaced and without set. Saw blade can then enter either side.

5. To make a smooth bevel cut or a miter cut, first set blade at the desired angle and retract saw until teeth points are just flush with the wood surface. This applies to both table and portable circular saws.

6. On a table saw, the fence is fitted with a wood runner strip for bevels and miters. Teeth, pointing toward the fence, barely protrude above the cut. Either side of wood may be up, damage is very slight.

7. To smooth a rough-cut edge with a plane, press blade against finish side first and angle plane toward centerline of wood. Use short strokes and avoid forcing blade out to opposite side or grain will be shattered.

Finishing Plywood Edges. It is not necessary to use special moldings to cover the edge grain of plywood, nor is it necessary to fill the grain, sand it, and hope to get a near-matching finish. You can use a special edging, in the form of tape, which conceals the unfinished edges neatly. The tape is actual wood, about $\frac{1}{32}$" thick, with a pressure-sensitive adhesive back. It comes in $\frac{3}{4}$"-wide strips made of birch, fir,

oak, walnut, and red or white Philippine mahogany, and can be cut with scissors to fit $\frac{1}{4}$" or $\frac{1}{2}$" plywood. Here are some rules to follow:

1. Before you use the tape, remove it from the sealed cellophane package and let it stand overnight in the same room with the plywood to equalize the moisture content of both tape and plywood.

2. Secure the tape to the plywood edge with

moderate heat. You can use an ordinary household iron (make certain that the bottom is clean) or a special bonding iron which is sold with the tape or which may be rented from some dealers.

3. A higher heat is needed for some woods than for others. A temperature of 300° should be used to bond birch, oak and walnut, and only 250° for fir and mahogany.

4. Heat alone will do the job. There is no additional gluing, clamping or nailing.

5. When applying the tape to curved surfaces or inside-circle cutouts in a sheet of plywood, the special bonding iron will do a better job than the conventional household iron. Because it's so small, it can fit into tight spaces and be used around curves with more ease.

6. All necessary sanding should be done with fine sandpaper, preferably 000 grade.

7. To prevent the lifting off or chipping of the tape edges, feather the edge of the tape slightly where it joins the plywood.

8. Do not use a water-base stain on the tape.

1. Strip the protective paper backing off the pressure-sensitive adhesive side of the tape, using your thumb as a guide to prevent the accidental tearing of the protective paper.

2. Set the tape in place so that it slightly overlaps the edge grain of the plywood. Press tape into place by applying light finger pressure and keeping the adhesive side toward the wood.

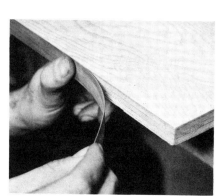

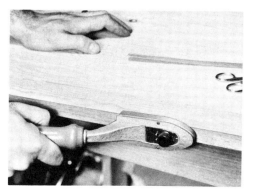

3. Light heat is necessary to bond the tape to the plywood. An ordinary household iron will do, or you can use a special bonding iron for just this purpose. Keep iron moving at all times.

4. With the tape firmly adhered to the plywood edge, sand off the excess which protrudes above and below the plywood surface. Fine sandpaper on a block will do a neat job.

5. When bonding two adjoining edges, cut the second strip of wood tape somewhat longer than the side. Leave about $\frac{1}{16}''$ to $\frac{1}{8}''$ overhang at each corner. This will make for a perfect joint.

6. Using fine sandpaper and a sanding block, remove the excess of the second piece of wood-edging for a perfectly square corner. Bevel the edge at the corner slightly. →

7. To prevent any disturbance because of moisture in the air, seal the tape by applying a coat of shellac, varnish, or any other finish. This should be done within 8 hours after applying the tape.

8. Where an individual length of tape is not long enough to cover the entire edge, butt two pieces together. However, do not use a right-angle butt. Cut the pieces at an angle of 45°.

PRIMER FOR BUILT-INS

Hand Tools. Ever since the art of cabinet working began, hand tools have been used; and they will never be completely replaced, for every project starts with the rule and the square. Until a true measure is taken and an accurate line is drawn, the actual cutting cannot begin. Provide yourself, then, with an accurate rule. Both the folding rule and steel tape have their advantages. At the same time, a combination square and level is highly useful for smaller projects. For larger ones, a framing square and a longer level will prove most accurate.

Then comes the cutting of the wood. The crosscut saw and the rip saw make the major combination for cutting. An all-purpose saw for both operations—across and along the grain—may be used, but the two for separate operations are best. The back saw with its fine teeth for accurate cutting, the pointed keyhole saw for cutouts, and the coping or scroll saws for scallops and curves complete the list.

For notching and various jointing operations, the chisel is often used. A set of various widths is important, and all should be kept sharp. A hammer may be used to force the chisel, though a mallet is the better weapon. A mallet does not burr the handle of the chisel as quickly, and with the narrower hammer it's easier to miss your target entirely.

Once cut to shape, the wood must be fitted into place. Rough edges and surfaces can be smoothed best with planes—the smoothing and jack planes are the most commonly used. Important, too, is the wood rasp, a coarse file which removes wood rapidly, shapes curves and rounds edges before sandpaper does the final polishing.

Assembly of the pieces involves the boring of holes for dowels, for screws, and for starting mortises completed with the chisel. There are many devices for boring holes. They are the hand auger (rare these days), the brace and its assortment of bits, the drill that imparts a twist to the bit by forward motion

of the handle, and the drill that is revolved by turning a crank (the smaller size has a handle; larger models have a curved rest held against the chest for added pressure).

When all wood has been prepared for joining, fastening devices come into play. There is, of course, the simple hammer-and-nail method. For most cabinet and built-in work, two types of nails suffice. These are the common and box nails with broad, flat heads, and the casing and finishing nails—and the shorter tapered brads—with heads so small they can be set beneath the surface and concealed with wood putty.

To join heavier pieces where nails will not be visible, use common nails or, better still, coated box nails. These are thinner, and the resinous coating grips hard and fast. The thicker, common nails might split the wood where box nails will not. Bear in mind when nailing that about two-thirds of the nail should extend into the second piece of wood for the greatest holding ability; when joining two pieces of equal thickness, this does not apply and a greater number of nails, closely spaced, are necessary.

You will certainly need a nail set, a tapered length of steel with a truncated point at the working end which fits the head of finishing nails and drives them beneath the surface when tapped with a hammer. Finally comes the screwdriver to set screws. Since screws are threaded, they hold better than smooth nails. Being shorter, they are more adaptable to thinner pieces of wood. And, because screws are thicker than nails, more steel is present to withstand shear pressures. Except for ornamental purposes, use flathead wood screws. And the screwdriver? Buy several of assorted bit widths. You will be using screws of various sizes. In addition to these, your tool chest should include assorted sandpapers with some appropriate holding devices. You'll find the following also useful: a cold chisel for cutting masonry and plaster, a countersinking bit for your drill or brace, a screwdriving bit where many screws must be set. Use of all these tools is detailed in Chapter 1.

Methods of Attachment. There will be cases where the use of nails or screws will not serve for attaching your built-in unit to walls, floors, or ceilings. In such instances, special devices are required. For example, in attaching to masonry or concrete surfaces, either of two methods may serve. You can sometimes attach wood to cement or mortar (between bricks, stone, or cement blocks) with steel-cut nails, driving them like regular nails. In harder materials, drill holes from $\frac{7}{16}''$ to $\frac{9}{16}''$ diameter, insert fiber or lead plugs, or split devices called expansion bolts, then run screws through the wood into these anchors. These devices expand as the screw enters, and the sides of the hole are securely gripped. You cannot attach a built-in directly to a plaster wall (except with adhesives for very light support). A hole must be drilled through such a wall and a hinged-style butterfly bolt or a Molly anchor inserted, which opens out behind the plaster and distributes the weight over a large area inside the wall. (See "Wall Fasteners," Chapter 2.)

Caution: Do not attempt to fasten heavy loads to a wall unless screws can be driven *through* the wall covering into the studs.

Wood Joints. There are many types of wood joints. The most commonly used—the butt joint—simply butts the end of one piece of wood against the other at right angles. When secured with nails, it is strong; but with screws it is even stronger. The rabbeted joint is stronger still and prevents side sway. The miter is used for neatness on trim and the dado for setting horizontal members, whether supports or shelves, into vertical pieces for greater strength. In all joining work, be sure to use a high-quality glue. It will double joint strength.

The dovetail joint, used principally for finely-fitted

LUMBER SIZES. When you purchase lumber, check its actual size against what you asked for. The dressed lumber is smaller in actual dimension than its nominal (asked-for) size due to loss in planing. In general, dimensions under 8″ will be ⅜″ less than nominal, and dimensions over 8″ will be ½″ less than ordered. There may be slight variations between different lumber yards.

What you ask for	What you get
1 × 3	25/32 × 2⅝
1 × 4	25/32 × 3⅝
1 × 6	25/32 × 5⅝
1 × 8	25/32 × 7½
1 × 10	25/32 × 9½
1 × 12	25/32 × 11½
2 × 3	1⅝ × 2⅝
2 × 4	1⅝ × 3⅝
2 × 6	1⅝ × 5⅝
2 × 8	1⅝ × 7½
2 × 10	1⅝ × 9½
4 × 4	3⅝ × 3⅝

Plywoods are actual size in thickness and usually available in sheets up to 4′ × 8′. Hardwoods are usually asked-for size.

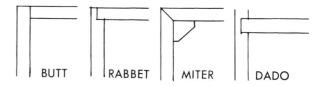

BUTT   RABBET   MITER   DADO

drawers, may be made with a hand saw and the scrap removed with a chisel, as shown in the first photo series, or it may be made with the sabre saw, as shown in the second series.

DOVETAIL JOINT WITH HAND SAW AND CHISEL

1. Below: Make a cardboard pattern for corner dovetail joints to insure the accurate cuts required for a neat job.
2. Right: Trace pattern on matching ends of sides, invert pattern for opposite ends. Number matching pieces. →

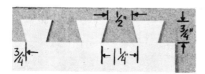

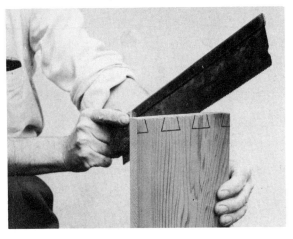

3. Cut on vertical marks with back saw. Follow line with care, stop even with base line of dovetail.

4. With sides of dovetail cut made first with saw, the scrap can be removed easily with a sharp wood chisel.

5. Use cutout ends of side pieces as a pattern to mark matching cuts on end pieces, and number corners.

6. Apply weatherproof casein glue liberally to all the surfaces of the dovetail cuts that will be in contact.

7. Align the parts to be joined and tap each joint together, using a block under the hammer for leveling.

DOVETAIL JOINT WITH SABRE SAW

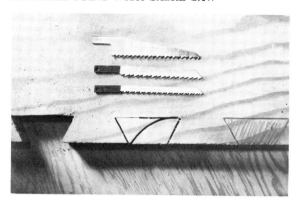

1. Draw dovetail outlines and mark cutouts to avoid error. Cut as shown in center to remove scrap. Set blade full depth for this.

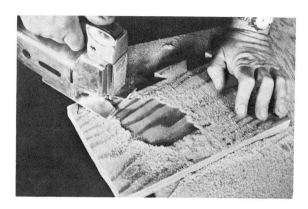

2. Guide lines are easy to follow since fan inside case blows sawdust out of its path. Hold saw firmly against stock at all times.

3. Hold cutout on edge of piece it is to mesh with and mark outlines. Even if the first cuts were poor, this method will match them.

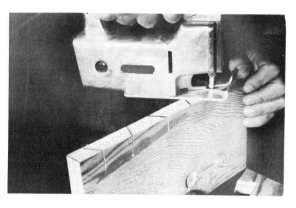

4. Clamp stock and set saw blade to exact depth of cut. Then follow marked lines exactly, removing lines with the saw cuts.

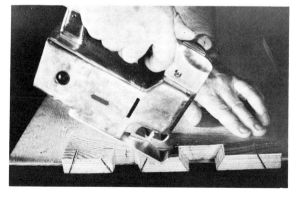

5. Remove center stock as before, then hold saw nose at angle to cut out corner stock, setting saw blade at full depth for job.

6. Assembled joint is firm, interlocked. This joint has been power-sawed with plywood to show the fit possible with sabre saw when finished.

The mortise and tenon joint is exceedingly useful when making storm windows and screen frames, your own doors or furniture. Although a professional joint, it's easily made with simple hand tools. The tenon should be one-third or one-half the thickness of the board, the first width preferred for hardwoods and the second for softwoods. Cut and sand all pieces carefully and test the fit before final joining.

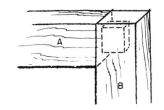

TWO MORTISE AND TENON JOINTS

Blind Mortise and Tenon—Tenon of piece *A* extends part of the way through piece *B*. Secure with glue; if stronger joint is needed, dowel or finishing nail is set through *B* into the tenon.

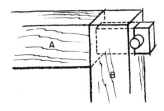

Key Mortise and Tenon—Mortise or square hole in *B* goes all the way through. Tenon of piece *A* extends beyond outside edge of piece *B*. Hold tenon as with blind mortise or with dowel peg set through tenon.

MORTISE AND TENON JOINT WITH HAND TOOLS

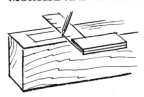

1. Measure and mark location of mortise, using a square to make certain of perfect alignment.

2. With brace and bit, drill series of holes in area. For blind mortise, use a depth gauge set for proper depth.

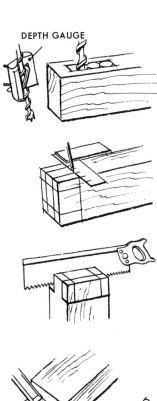

DEPTH GAUGE

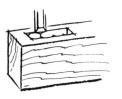

3. Clean excess wood out of mortise with a sharp chisel. Make sure corners are cut square and even.

4. Mark tenon, drawing all lines square with edge of board. Mark on all sides to avoid error.

5. Use back saw to cut "shoulder" of tenon. Cut across board first to exact depth, keeping saw perfectly aligned.

6. Turn board in vise and cut down edge to the two points cut in previous step to form a square corner.

7. The other parts, called "cheeks," are cut in the same manner as the wide sections. Add guide lines down sides before cutting.

8. With sharp chisel and rasp, smooth surfaces of the tenon and check fit in mortise. Sandpaper smooth afterward.

MITER JOINT WITH SABRE SAW

Right: Fastest way to make a miter joint is to overlap the two pieces at right angles, hold with brad, and run saw down miter line as shown.

Below, left: This is the actual miter shown right. Actual cutting time: 15 seconds. It's perfectly square and *has* to fit, even if saw cut is crooked.

Below right: As no other saw can, the sabre saw easily makes this curved miter joint. Handled the same way as above, saw follows wavy line.

Mitering is usually accomplished with a hand or back saw in a miter box, or by setting a table saw fence at the desired angle before making the cut. In both cases, each piece is cut separately. A wavy-line miter is impossible with any tool other than the sabre saw, with the possible exception of the coping saw. On heavy stock it could not be done with any but the sabre.

Gluing. When preparing wood for gluing, remember that shrinkage and a tendency to warp are greatest at the ends of the pieces. To join long pieces, plane an extra shaving from the middle section so that greater pressure will be applied at the ends by the clamps. Flat boards should be glued together with the sap sides back to back to equalize the strain of this warpage tendency. Boards glued side to side to form wider boards should have heart and sap sides turned up alternately so warpage will be held to a wavy pattern rather than bowing from outer edges.

Engineers will tell you that two surfaces can be made so smooth that they will cling together more tightly than any adhesive can bind them. Such perfection cannot be expected in the home workshop, but you should come as close to it as possible. It takes but a few seconds to turn a poor fit into a good one. When glue is added, the material will then be so well joined, the joint will be stronger than the materials themselves.

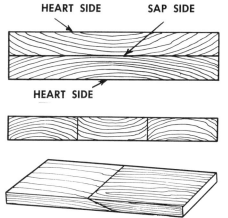

By alternating heart sides, warping is cut to a minimum.

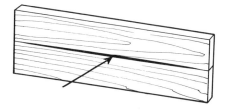

Extra shaving from middle section increases end pressure.

Installing Shelves. Few built-ins are constructed without shelves of some sort. Installation may be completed in various ways; which to use should be indicated by the nature of the project. The permanently fixed shelf is usually supported on a wood cleat, a narrow strip of wood attached to vertical pieces with nails or screws on opposite sides of the space. With this type of shelf, it is only necessary to cut matching cleats and check their placement with a level so the installed shelf won't tilt. The shelf may be rested on the cleats or anchored to them with brads. When installing cleats for shelves, bear in mind the fact that the weight to be carried on the shelf is the governing factor, both in the size of the cleat and the way in which it is attached. Small shelves to hold light weights, as in decks, may be supported on stock as light as ¼" quarter-round or cove molding. For heavier weights and broader shelves, cleats may be made of stock as heavy as ¾-by-¾", or even up to 1-by-2" stock.

If supporting materials are ¾" thick, as is usual in cabinetmaking, 1¼" screws are best for holding cleats because they will reach almost through the supporting stock. The more delicate type of cleats may be attached with 1" brads spaced about 2 to 3" apart. A quick substitute for cleats is the metal U-channel, preferably of easily cut aluminum. These channels are attached on the shelf line instead of below, and the shelf—of ¼" plywood or hardboard—slipped into the channels. Attach channels with short, flathead screws.

Also, in installing certain types of shelves, it must be remembered that even the heaviest timbers cannot

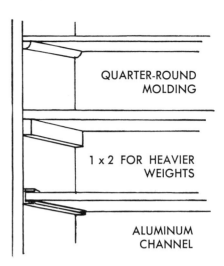

QUARTER-ROUND MOLDING

1 x 2 FOR HEAVIER WEIGHTS

ALUMINUM CHANNEL

hold a weight unless they are braced to stand the load.

A post set under the outer end will prevent the shelf from dropping. However, since the post may be in the way, it may be shortened and its lower end bent back and attached to the wall below the shelf (see third sketch below). It will still support a heavy weight, and the shelf will not fall. If a wider board is used for the shelf, it carries its own concealed brace, as indicated in Sketch 4.

Methods of holding shelves between supports are illustrated on the next page.

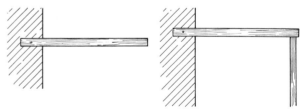

1. Cross arm nailed or screwed to wall won't stay when weight is added.
2. A post under free end of the shelf increases its loadbearing capacity many times.

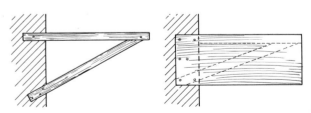

3. Another way to support shelf is to set base of support against the wall.
4. Wide board contains cross braces in itself; strong edge withstands the weight.

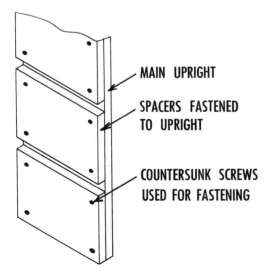

MAIN UPRIGHT

SPACERS FASTENED TO UPRIGHT

COUNTERSUNK SCREWS USED FOR FASTENING

Lacking dado-cutting tools, the handyman may use this substitute method for sturdy shelf supports.

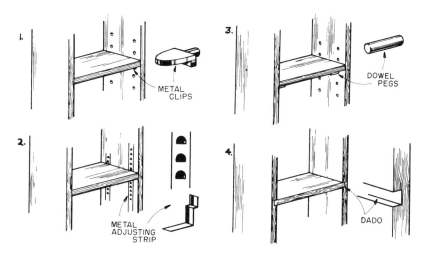

There are several different techniques which can be used to hold shelves to upright supports. In addition to cleats (either 1 × 1's or ¾″ cove molding or quarter-round), the shelves can be nailed through the supports. This latter method is not particularly strong when used with long shelves that carry a heavy load.

Other methods include: metal clips (1), which can be shifted so that the shelves are adjustable. However, here again, the shelves cannot carry any great weight. A stronger method for adjustable shelves is metal strips with clips (2).

You can make your own adjustable shelf bracket by drilling ½″ holes, evenly spaced, through the uprights (3). A dowel forced through the hole and extending about 1″ to 2″ under the shelf can hold medium-weight loads.

Most secure, but permanent shelves, are those held by a dado cut in the upright (4). You can cut the dado the thickness of the shelf with a dado blade on a power saw or else use a dado plane. The shelf is force-fitted into place and held by glue and nails.

Table Legs. The problems of bracing for adequate support discussed for shelves also hold true for table legs. When legs are braced in a vertical position, the table they support becomes capable of carrying relatively great loads. Therefore, some means must be devised to keep the legs in their proper attitude. This can be accomplished easily by certain principles, as illustrated below.

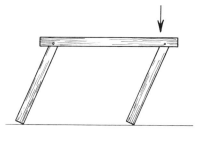

Legs of table will support great weight if held vertically.

Side pressure on table will simply twist nails holding legs.

Bracing each leg like the cross arm makes table strong.

Wide cross board is in itself a brace and holds legs upright.

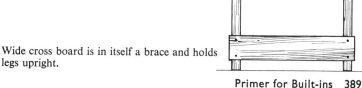

Doors and Hinges. Except for built-ins with specific types of wood exterior where doors must match (as with random-width pines), doors for all built-ins may be made of plywood. To avoid warping, use ¾" stock for doors up to 2' widths and 3 to 4' heights. For larger openings, doors should have supports attached on inner surfaces. The selected plywood may be fir or have a hardwood-veneer finish. As an alternative, a ¾-by-1¼" frame may be constructed with mitered corner joints and a ¼" ply or hardboard surface attached. Since the hardboards have many types of finishes, from wood grain to marble, the selection is almost unlimited.

The variety of hinges is great. There are invisible hinges with both leaves embedded in door and frame material; butt hinges with only a narrow pin showing—either butt style requiring a gain or mortise, or the no-mortise type that are flush-mounted with one leaf folding into the other. Then there is the ornamental style of H/L or strap-hinge style in brass, wrought iron, or antique metal.

Door handles and pulls should be selected to match hinges, if the latter are visible. But it is also important that the hardware match the spirit of the built-in and the decor of the room. Door latches on cabinets and built-ins are a personal matter. You have the choice of magnetic, friction, or touch latches, the latter opening from a slight inward pressure on the door which releases the spring to thrust the door outward. Latches are attached to the cabinet base or to a shelf, preferably on the underside.

The Uses of Dowels. In almost every woodworking project it becomes necessary to make a firm joint between two pieces of wood where their narrow edges meet. Frequently the bulk of the pieces prohibits the use of nails or countersunk screws. The answer lies in the use of dowels, small hardwood pins which tie the pieces together. Anyone, using everyday hand tools, can make good use of dowels. If you have a well-equipped workshop, you will discover that using dowels is as simple a process as nailing.

Dowels come in 3' lengths and in an assortment of diameters. It's good practice to have a stock on hand

at all times. When inserted in the drilled holes of a joint, they add considerably to the strength of that joint.

There are two methods used in doweling, the "open" method and the "blind" method. In the first, a hole is drilled completely through one piece of wood and deeply into or through the one to be joined. The dowel is coated with glue and pushed completely through the drilled holes, joining the pieces, and the remainder is sawed off flush with the outer surface. In the blind method, holes are drilled part way into each piece from the joined faces, and a dowel cut to the combined length of both holes. The dowel is then glue-coated and inserted in one hole and the second piece is pressed onto the protruding dowel end.

To insure adequate glue on a snug-fitting dowel, some dowels are spiral grooved and others provided with a lengthwise slot. When filled with glue, these indentations assure a firm grip. In most joints, two or more dowels are used in place of one to prevent the

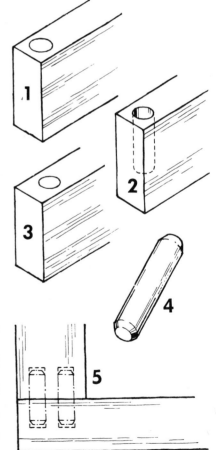

FIVE BASIC RULES FOR BLIND DOWELING

1. The diameter of the dowel used should not be less than ⅓ nor more than ½ the thickness of the boards to be joined.
2. The depth of the hole should be not less than ¼ nor more than ⅔ of the width of the narrower board. A maximum depth of 4" is sufficient for 1" lumber and 8" for 2" lumber.
3. When drilling a hole near the end of a board, the hole should be the thickness of the board away from the end.
4. Always chamfer the ends of the dowels to prevent them from splitting when being inserted.
5. The total length of the dowel should be the combined depth of the two holes less ⅛".

pieces from twisting on the dowel. When using the open method of doweling, the problem of aligning the drilled holes does not occur. Even when poorly centered, the holes match and the dowel can be driven through both holes. In the blind system, however, two separate holes must be drilled—and here trouble can develop unless a jig is used. A jig is any type of device which holds several successive pieces of wood in position so that holes can be drilled equally distant from one or more edges of the several pieces. In some instances, the drilling device is clamped into position and the wood guided to it along measured channels to insure proper centering of the holes. In others, the wood is clamped and the drilling device guided along

identical channels for all holes drilled. In either case, the guide is actually a jig. Furthermore, it is also possible to arrange the jig so that the depth of the hole is controlled.

For further insurance against the dowel's turning or becoming loose and permitting the joint to crack or spread as the surrounding wood shrinks, set small finishing nails or brads through the wood surfaces into the dowels.

Should it ever become necessary to remove the dowels and reinforce the joint, there is but one possible method: drill out the old dowel, enlarging the hole by $\frac{1}{8}''$, and replace with a new dowel of larger diameter, adequately glued.

1. Mark exact position of each hole to be drilled with scriber and square. This enables you to center the dowel in the piece of lumber.

2. Use doweling jig, where possible, to obtain a perfectly aligned hole. Different-sized tubes are used to match different drill sizes.

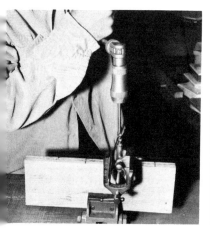

3. Hold piece to be drilled rigidly. Use auger or drill through jig, and resultant hole will match with companion piece to take dowel.

4. Place dowel pins in drilled holes to align two narrow boards when making a wide one out of them. Pins mark centers of holes.

5. Mark center of hole accurately and let the drill press do the rest of the job. If board is held properly, the hole will be perfectly vertical. →

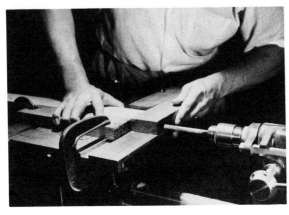

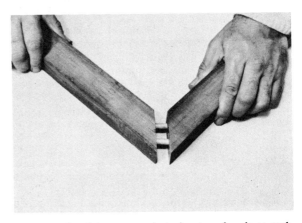

6. If you own a lathe, you can convert it into a drill press handy for doweling. Use a built-up wood-block jig to assure positioning.

7. Make miter joints strong by using two dowels at each corner. Use blind method as shown in Photo 4; dowels fit inside miter.

8. Open doweling method requires a hole drilled completely through one piece into the next; the glued dowel is then driven into both holes.

9. Eliminate drilling through wood surface by using blind dowel method. It protects the surface of the wood and assures a good finish.

10. Force dowel and glue into drilled hole. Some dowels have grooves to hold glue for tight joining. Wipe excess glue off after dowel is in.

How to Make a Drawer. The type of drawer you make depends to a large extent upon its use. If appearance is not a factor, a drawer is simple to make and takes only a little time. On the other hand, if a particularly good finished job is needed, the drawer should be somewhat more detailed. Any handyman can make either type with only a few simple hand tools: a crosscut or back saw, a keyhole saw, ruler, try square, hammer or screwdriver, chisel and mallet. The size of lumber used depends upon the height, width and depth of the drawer. But the thickness of the lumber is more uniform; it should be about ½″ to ¾″ thick for the front end, about ⅜″ or ⅝″ for the two sides and the back, and at least ¼″ for the bottom.

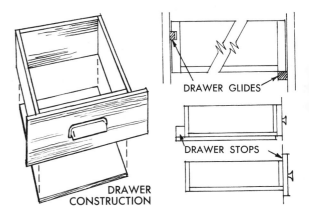

DRAWER GLIDES

DRAWER STOPS

DRAWER CONSTRUCTION

The front end and sides can be put together in several different ways. The four most usual, illustrated below, cover virtually any type of drawer. Each has certain advantages and limitations. (Top left across to bottom right.)

1. Butt corner—simple to make and used where appearance is unimportant; a general all-purpose utility drawer corner.

2. Rabbet corner—most commonly used about the house; easily made with only a few hand tools; fairly strong.

3. Dado corner—used mostly for small drawers which are not subject to strain or heavy use.

4. Dovetail corner—strongest of all corners; used primarily in furniture and fine joinery; requires the most care for good results.

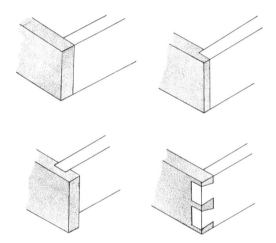

There are several ways to hold the front end to the sides. Aside from the dovetail corner, all the rest can be held together with finishing nails, screws or dowels. (See sketches below.) Where the finished drawer front is to be painted, nails or screws should be countersunk and holes filled with wood putty.

But where a natural wood finish is desired, another technique must be used if the front surface is to remain unmarred. There are three ways to do this.

First, nails, screws or dowels can be used, as in the case of painted drawers, but they should be countersunk ¼″. The holes are then closed by means of

wood plugs. These can be cut out of the same type wood.

Secondly, a "face," an extra front end, can be added. This is held to the original front end by means of screws which pass through the front end into (but not through) the face piece. (For additional details, see next page.)

Thirdly, blind doweling can be used. That is, the front end is attached to the sides by dowels that do not emerge through the front surface.

When placing the bottom of a drawer in place, it is best to leave some room for shrinking and swelling. This usually is not necessary when either pressed wood or plywood is used. Yet even in these cases, it is best to allow for some freedom of movement.

In general, when attaching the bottom to the fronts and sides:

1. Make certain that the grain of the lumber used for the bottom runs parallel to that of the front.

2. If the bottom is held by dado, glue it to front only.

3. The back of the drawer should rest on the bottom; or

4. The dado cut in the back should be wide enough to permit free movement of the bottom if it swells or shrinks.

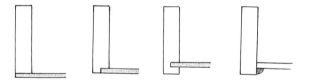

Left to right: drawer bottom attached flush with side; inserted in rabbet cut in side; dado to hold drawer bottom; quarter-round added to bottom and side.

The drawers thus far discussed are for general purpose, but they are not dust-free. To make the front end dust-free—that is, make the front end cover the opening provided for the drawer—you can:

1. Make the front end wider and higher than the side so that it is close up, in fact flush, against the drawer opening frame; or

2. Add 4 pieces of quarter-round around all four sides of the front end; these corners should be

Left: nails or screws (A) hold corner; head countersunk (B); hole filled (C).

Center: dowel with glue (A) to hold corner; dowel flush with drawer front (B).

Right: Blind dowel method; dowel from side goes halfway through front end.

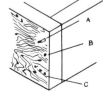
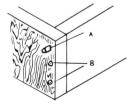
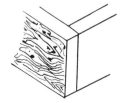

mitered. (See sketch.) The molding should be the same thickness as the front end.

3. Add an extra-large piece of lumber as a face over the front end. (See sketch.) This is often used to conceal home-made dovetail joints. It can also be used when decorative drawer fronts are desired. The face is attached to the front end by screws from the inside of the drawer, through the front end and into the face. The screws do not come through the face.

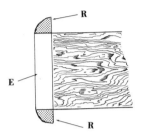

Quarter-round (R) cut and mitered to fit around all four sides of front end (E).

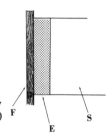

Decorative face (F) held by screws through front end (E) after sides (S) are attached.

To hold a drawer together with blind dowels, first mark off the center of the edge of the side piece. Next, mark off the location of dowels along this line. Use at least 3 dowels if the drawer is 4" high; at least 4 dowels if the drawer is 6" high.

Next, with a hand drill (and try square to make certain that the drilled holes are straight), drill holes for dowels in the edge of the side piece. These holes should be about 1" deep.

Insert dowel centers (these can be bought in many hardware stores) in the holes just drilled. Take the front end and lay it back side up on the work bench. Take a side piece with dowel centers in place and place it in position over the front end. When all edges are aligned, tap the side piece gently with a hammer and the dowel center points will mark the positions for drilling into the front.

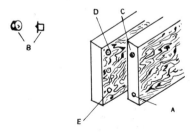

Hole in end (A); dowel center (B) inserted in hole (C); marked position (D); front drilled (E).

Use the same size of drill as dowel size and drill holes in the front end; make certain that you do not go through the entire thickness of the piece.

Remove dowel centers, cut dowels to size (the depth of the hole in the side piece plus the depth of the hole in the front end minus $\frac{1}{8}$"). Apply glue liberally to the dowel and force into the side piece. It is best to hold the wood in a vise and hammer the dowels in. Then position the front end and force the dowels into the already drilled holes.

Sticking drawers are probably the commonest complaint about the home. In any drawer, the sides generally ride on pieces of wood anchored to the frame. Warping, shrinking, swelling, all make for trouble. There are many ways to make drawers slide more easily and some are shown here.

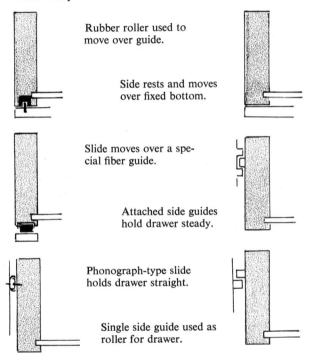

Rubber roller used to move over guide.

Side rests and moves over fixed bottom.

Slide moves over a special fiber guide.

Attached side guides hold drawer steady.

Phonograph-type slide holds drawer straight.

Single side guide used as roller for drawer.

If you plan to have the sides ride along wood supports, you must:

1. Leave about $\frac{2}{32}$" clearance around all four sides of the front end if the drawer is to be varnished or lacquered.

2. Leave about $\frac{3}{32}$" if the drawer is to be painted.

You can easily check if you have left sufficient space. In the first case, with drawers to be varnished or lacquered, take a dime and see if you can insert it in the space left free. In the second instance, try a nickel to test for clearance space.

TRICKS WITH MOLDINGS

One of the earliest materials used in dressing up the home—wood molding—is still one of the best. Drab areas may be rid of monotony, windows converted into attractive frames enhancing the view of your garden, or the boxiness of a high ceiling subdued with this easy-to-use material. Wood moldings can add length, height or grace to any wall, door or cabinet. The list of applications is nearly infinite, using time-tried stand-bys as well as new patterns. There are tricks to measuring, marking and applying molding that will make the job more fun than work.

Long lengths of molding to go *between* parallel surfaces, such as from a door or window casing to a wall, should be cut slightly longer—as much as $\frac{1}{16}$"—than the surface measures. To install, bow the strip and place the ends in position first. When the center of the strip is nailed, you have a very snug fit indeed. To measure lengths of molding to go around an object against a flat surface, such as a door casing, you must mark exact dimensions in order to obtain well-mitered joints at the corners. A carpenter's old trick works perfectly here. Hold the strip to be measured in place and mark it at the corner with a sharp blade held flat against the intersecting surface. A very hard pencil, well sharpened, will work nearly as well. The mark represents the *short* side of the miter. Your saw cut should just graze it. To measure the correct length of long pieces where it is hard to use a tape, use two overlapped pieces of straight, stiff molding or other thin lumber. A pencil mark on one stick where the end of the other stops gives you an exact gauge to mark the molding. When two or more pieces are required to fill a given space, do not join ends with a butt or square joint. In time, the best of wood will shrink and an open butt joint is very noticeable. Make a simple scarfed

CROWN   BED   COVE

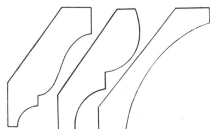

Crown, bed, and cove moldings in many traditional and modern styles and sizes are designed to be used at the break between ceiling and walls indoors, or the similar break outdoors at the roof overhang, to make painting easier and soften angle lines.

BASEBOARD

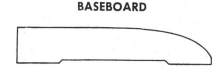

A baseboard serves the practical purpose of keeping floor-cleaning preparations off walls and also hides the edge of wall-surfacing materials. Often base and casing (used around doors, windows) are identical.

SHOE

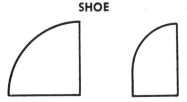

Shoe moldings finish off the baseboard at the floor and are flexible enough to compensate for slight deviations in level of finish floor surfacing as they hide its edge and also protect the baseboard from scuffing.

CASING

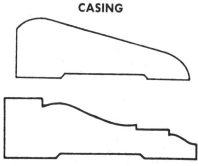

Casings come in a number of designs, both modern and traditional, with a wide variation in size. When casing and base are the same in cross section, you know they match. When they differ in size, select something similar in shape, using either a modern or traditional style but not both.

Shrinkage on a slant is less noticeable than a butt joint that opens. Use your miter box to cut the meeting ends at 45°. Use it, too, to point high-contour molding that is to join another piece at right angles. With 45° cuts as guides, remove stock.

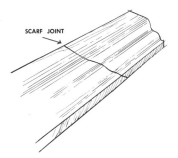

SCARF JOINT

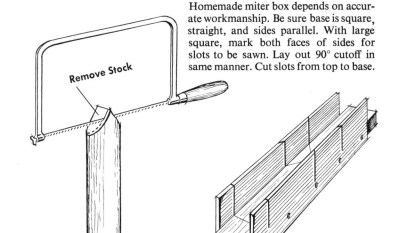

Remove Stock

Homemade miter box depends on accurate workmanship. Be sure base is square, straight, and sides parallel. With large square, mark both faces of sides for slots to be sawn. Lay out 90° cutoff in same manner. Cut slots from top to base.

joint (see sketch) by cutting each piece at 45° to match, as shown. Shrinkage then is unnoticeable.

The most important cut in joining moldings at corners is the miter, best done in a miter box. Manufactured boxes may be purchased with or without a saw. The best ones may be set for any angle. You can also build your own miter box, as shown in the drawing. If possible, always cut *into* the molding, since saw teeth tear wood more where they emerge than where they enter. A very fine-toothed saw, such as a cabinet saw, is preferred for cutting molding—even a hacksaw with a fine-toothed blade cuts well. An important cut for joining inside corners is the "cope," since it may be made to fit even when the corner is slightly out of square. The photographs

show you how to cut a cope. Use it to put moldings around a room at the ceiling line for decoration, lower down the wall as a picture mold, or below for baseboard trim.

To go around a room, square both ends of the first piece of molding. One end of the second strip is coped to fit the first strip and squared into the opposite corner, and so around the room to the fourth piece of molding, which must be coped to both the first and third strip. If the wall is so far out of square at any corner that an open crack

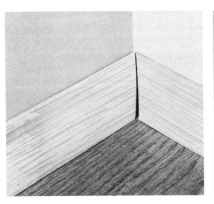
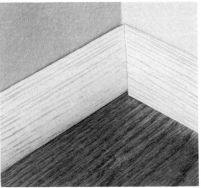

1. Irregular wall and floor surfaces cause perfectly cut 45° miter to gap. Crack, being deep, is hard to fill.
2. Irregularity in purchased stock, not exactly true to measure, shows up when ends are miter-joined.
3. For turned, or coped joint, cut one strip flush and butt against wall, nailing it into place.

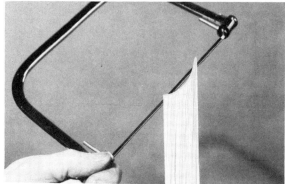

4. Mark outline of free end of butted piece on back of piece to be cut with coping saw.
5. Holding saw at 45° angle, cut along marked line. Resulting crescent-shaped surface fits against butted strip.

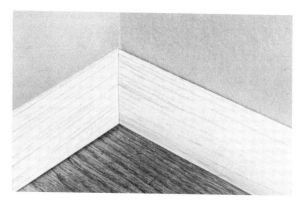

6. Turned corner, even though separated by ⅛″ gap, still does not show as unsightly crack, and gap is easily filled.
7. On more intricately shaped moldings follow same procedure, marking pattern on back of piece before coping.

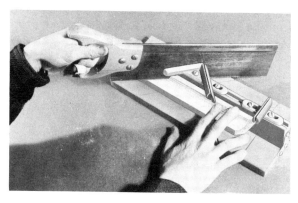

8. On crown moldings, where back is not flat, cut molding in miter box to 45° angle as first step.
9. Start cut with coping saw along edge of miter cut, using this line as pattern, holding saw at 45° angle.
→

Tricks with Moldings   397

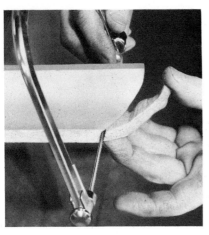  

10. This is the finish of the coping cut, with section removed showing beveled shape of the actual molding pattern.

11. Result of coping cut. Molding fits exactly over surface pattern of piece which is butted against wall.

12. Finished joint will remain neat in spite of wood shrinkage or wall irregularity.

shows, undercut back of the finish surface of the cope with a sharp knife or half-round wood rasp.

At times, one molding must be "blended" or joined to the middle of another. The way to do this with flat, simple moldings is shown in the photographs. Moldings higher and narrower in cross section are almost impossible to mark for such a cut. They may be blended by a modification of the coping method. First, the point of the intersecting member is cut to a 45° mitered point as above, then stock is cut out with a coping saw using *both* edges of the bevel as guide lines. The other strip is not cut at all.

Below: To blend, symmetrical moldings, point the first molding 45° each side of center.

Right, above: Trace cut onto molding to be intersected, carefully make two saw cuts to remove vee.

Right, below: First molding will now fit easily into second if you've worked accurately enough.

 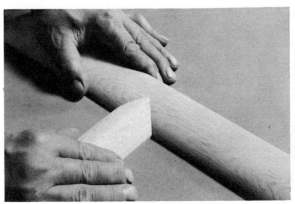

Decorative moldings can be used to make attractive picture frames. Joints are miter-cut and glued, then secured by any of the following three methods.

1. Blind doweling is exceedingly strong and is recommended for very large frames. See page 391 for how to install blind dowels.

2. For added strength, you can use small brads to hold the corners together. Counterset nail heads and fill holes with wood filler. Sand when dry.

3. Corner fasteners are another way to make picture frame corners more secure. Special countersink attachment with these fasteners can be used for a concealed joint.

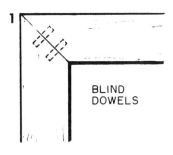

1

BLIND DOWELS

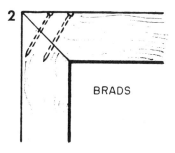

2

BRADS

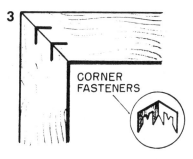

3

CORNER FASTENERS

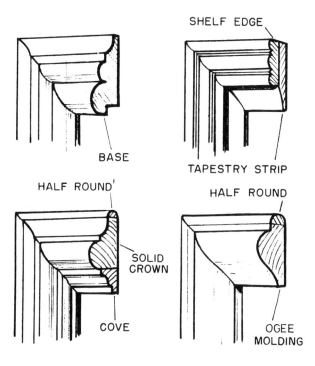

SHELF EDGE

BASE

HALF ROUND

TAPESTRY STRIP

HALF ROUND

SOLID CROWN

COVE

OGEE MOLDING

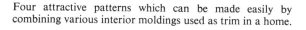

Four attractive patterns which can be made easily by combining various interior moldings used as trim in a home.

There are forms of molding for every purpose. Many can be used for purposes other than those for which they were originally intended. Picture molding makes excellent drawer or door pulls with the rounded extension intended to hold picture hooks used instead for finger grips.

WOOD FINISHES

A can of paint, a little brush, and almost *any* old piece of furniture. These are the items which started the do-it-yourself trend. Close on the heels of those who prefer resurrecting relics is that host of home handymen who start with newly built, unfinished furniture and built-in units of their own creation. For the first group, there's the all-important step of removing every bit of the former finish. The rest of the steps apply to all: the preparation of wood to receive a finish, the choice of the right ingredients, and the fateful application. A successful job of finishing calls for care with all these steps. On the next six pages various finishes and their application are described and illustrated.

Much can be done with finishes to enrich the looks of inexpensive pieces of furniture.

Concealing Defects in Wood. Prebuilt furniture, unfinished built-ins as well as reclaimed pieces of furniture may, on close examination, prove to have some grain blemishes which will detract from their beauty when a transparent finish is applied. But there is a way out of the dilemma. The defects may be partly obscured, yet the grain may still be visible. The trick is done with a stain you make for yourself, adding a pigment which adds enough color to hide such blemishes.

Let's assume you have just purchased an inexpensive pine chest of drawers or removed the finish from an old unit. You discover the surfaces are built up of joined boards which do not match in grain line or wood color. Obviously, a clear finish will not do. Stain will not appear the same on each section. Obtain some turpentine, linseed oil, ground-in-oil pigments and a wide-mouthed jar. Mix an equal amount of oil and turpentine and squeeze in a few drops of color. Stir well and try it on a sample of wood to check the shade. Add more color if needed, and apply the stain along the grain. If an extra amount of stain is applied, wipe it off with a clean cloth and apply more until the stain is spread evenly over the entire surface. After thorough drying (usually overnight), sand with 3/0 garnet paper to remove brush marks and air bubbles. Then a coat of shellac, thinned 50 per cent with alcohol, is applied and allowed to dry overnight. Repeat until three coats of shellac have been given to the piece. Next, mix powdered pumice in blooming oil to a thick paste. The oil is a special acid-free type usually sold in paint stores and art supply shops. With fine steel wool, rub this mixture onto the wood until a high gloss is produced. A light touch is necessary for good results. Oil residue is removed with a cloth, and a coat of paste wax follows. The blemishes are now concealed, but the wood grain has been brought out to resemble a far more expensive piece of furniture.

1. Prepare your own stains with equal parts turpentine and linseed oil, plus ground-in-oil pigment.

2. Apply prepared stain heavily but evenly along the grain to hide defects such as board joints.

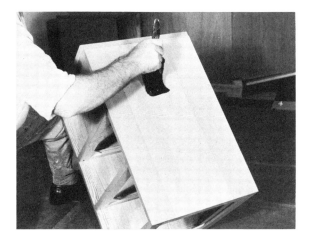

3. Apply three coats of shellac after stain has dried, thinning shellac 50% for each application.

4. Next, prepare a paste of powdered pumice and blooming oil, a special acid-free variety of finish oil.

5. Saturate a wad of steel wool in the paste and work over the surface with a light touch to glaze.

6. After removal of oil residue, apply a coat of clear paste wax rubbed briskly with a wad of clean cloth.

Bleaches. If you examine various types of wood closely, you will note that some—notably unfinished oak and mahogany—have tiny pores between darker, harder grain lines. Other woods, such as pine and maple, have much smaller pores or none visibly open. The open pores resemble pinpoint indentations.

A two-tone wood finish requires an application of colored filler to these holes, one which will contrast with the stain applied to the rest of the wood or with the naturally darker grain lines. Another method consists of filling the pores with one shade, then painting or staining the harder grain lines in a non-wood color. To have complete control of both color tones, it is often necessary to bleach darker woods. There are many bleaches from which to choose. Com-mercial bleaches are powerful chemicals requiring a neutralizer. These are sold in two separate bottles and can be purchased together as a set. Follow the manufacturer's directions carefully. Usually, the first preparation remains on the wood from 5 to 15 minutes before the second preparation is used. The wood is allowed to dry for 24 hours and then lightly sanded because the treatment raises soft fuzz on the grain. If you can't easily obtain a commercial bleach, you can make a solution of oxalic acid—about 8 to 12 ounces per gallon of warm water—and use that instead. Oxalic acid is somewhat weaker than the commercial peroxide type of bleach. Allow it to remain on the wood for 15 minutes, then rinse with a lot of clear water or a solution of borax and

Modern "blonde" finishes start with bleach to remove wood grain color.

1. After the paint remover has had enough time to work on the old finish, it is picked up with a broad-bladed scraper.

2. Bleach is applied according to directions for the particular brand. Be sure to wear gloves to protect your hands.

3. When bleach has remained on the surface for required time, usually 5 to 15 minutes, apply neutralizer as directed.

4. Allow wood surface to dry for at least 24 hours. A light sanding with a block will be necessary, for bleaching raises grain.

water. (A saturated solution—all the borax that can be dissolved—will do.) Let dry. With any type of bleach, wear gloves and avoid inhaling the dust from sanding just in case you didn't neutralize the chemicals completely.

Two-toned Finishes. Apply an oil-base stain to the wood as discussed previously, wiping it off quickly as you work, using a clean cloth. Let it dry thoroughly. Next, apply the "filler" contrasting color, lead or zinc paste in pure white or colored form, or a commercially prepared filler. This is applied with a brush or cloth along the grain and immediately wiped off *across* the grain with a clean cloth. Use a touch light enough to allow the filler to settle in the pores and soft areas but none on the raised, hard grain lines. Let dry. A gentle rubdown with steel wool then prepares the piece for a protective shellac, varnish or lacquer treatment.

An alternative method is to *first* apply the filler just as directed above. Then rub down lightly with steel wool, dust off, and apply the stain. The stain will lightly color the filler but will not penetrate as readily as it will into the hardwood grain. There will be a contrast, but more subdued than with the first method.

Examples of the first method are "pickled" wood, "liming," "seafoam," and "wheat" (pale brown background with brilliant yellow in the pores). Any sharp contrast between background and filler is produced by this method. Examples of the second method are "driftwood" (which may use a pale green background with white), "antique" (an off-white filler with brown stain) and many other subdued finishes.

Textured Wood Treatments. Many woods, particularly plywoods, are finished with a three-dimensional surface. This material gives the ambitious wood finisher a whole new field to conquer. The bleaching process is not necessary except when the natural wood color is to be subdued. The whole piece may be stained first, then the second color applied with a short-nap paint roller. This leaves the second color only on the raised portion, the stain in the depths. To reverse the process, stain and then apply the color with a paint brush and wipe off across the grain with a cloth, leaving the stain on the raised portion.

The use of various shades of red, bright green, yellow, jet black and orange with assorted backgrounds can produce eye-catching panels of plywood, and here is how a "zebra" finish is achieved—a flat black stain is applied and wiped off across the grain to leave as little on the raised portion as possible; then white, tinted slightly with a drop or two of Van Dyke brown, is applied to the raised portion with a roller. If you prefer stripes running the other way, apply the stain and let it dry without wiping it off. Then apply the white with a brush and wipe across the grain, leaving the residue in the recessed portion.

Pine. Pine, the handyman's favorite, can be converted to almost any purpose by the methods described here. Bleaching opens the soft-grain portion by etching it and you obtain a fair imitation of the open-pore texture of oak and mahogany. The pickling of pine is one of the original two-tone wood treatments, but all the sharp contrasts and subdued two-tone effects may be used also.

Stain Finishes. To allow the natural beauty of wood to show, stain is used as a finish because it is transparent. Color may be applied with it and yet still leave the wood grain visible. Selection of the shade of stain is important. For soft pine, a golden tint is best. Use it sparingly, for the wood itself will darken in time. For mahogany, which varies considerably from light brown to deep red, stains ranging from Korina yellow to dark Bismark brown may

be used. Mahogany with considerable red in it will show up best if a darker shade of stain is used. Always make walnut somewhat darker, using a walnut stain, as it will improve the grain appearance. For maple, use a golden tone with a dash of red if an Early American effect is desired.

The beginner should use a ready-mixed penetrating oil stain, available in a wealth of colors. They may be altered with ground-in-oil colors thinned with turpentine and stirred in. One may also create his own stains by using ground-in-oil colors, turpentine and boiled linseed oil. Try to have a small sample of the same type of wood as the piece on which you are working and test the stain on the sample, allowing it to dry at least several hours.

No skill is needed to apply stain with a brush, since it can be spread in all directions. However, for best results, apply along the grain with an even stroke and in an even quantity. At the end of each stretch, wipe up the excess with a dry, lint-free cloth. This controls color depth and overlaps will not show. On softer woods, such as pine, it is sound practice to apply a single coat of thinned shellac to end grain before applying any stain. This partially seals the wood and will prevent the stain from soaking into the grain too heavily, making the end much darker

Salvaged from oblivion, this chest is now a handsome piece under its stain-lacquer finish. Wood grain is softly visible.

1. First step after preparing the surface is application of the desired color stain. Apply along grain and wipe off the excess with a cloth.

2. After the stain has dried, apply the first coat of lacquer. A large brush is best, as lacquer dries rapidly. Apply along grain.

3. Each lacquer coat is rubbed *lightly* with fine steel wool wadded into a ball and frequently turned inside out. Use even pressure.

4. Final coat of lacquer (and there may be from 3 to 5 coats) is rubbed with blooming oil and fine-grit waterproof sandpaper.

than the rest. As soon as the entire piece is stained, rub every surface briskly with a clean cloth. With it, use the finest grade of steel wool. Between the two, any lap marks and bits of dust clinging to the damp stain will be removed.

Lacquering. Once you are satisfied with the stain, preserve it under lacquer, a clear, hard finish which completely seals and protects both wood and stain coloring. It dries very fast. Keep that in mind!

To apply lacquer, start with a very clean, or new, brush. Lacquer solvent will soften any paint residue in a used brush and color the lacquer. Since drying is rapid, apply with as much speed as possible. There is no time for going back over an area already

covered. Make the strokes long, straight, with the grain, and lift the brush at the end of the strokes. Make each new line slightly overlap the last. You won't see the lacquer you apply—it's too clear. Not until it has dried will you detect skipped spots, or "holidays."

After each coat, rub the piece well with fine steel wool, wadded into a ball. Use a light touch and dust the surfaces thoroughly after use. At least 3 to 5 coats of lacquer are necessary for a perfect job.

The satin finish—not quite as glossy as pure lacquer left untouched, but much prized by those who value fine furniture—is produced with the final coat of lacquer. Instead of steel wool, use waterproof sandpaper 400A (an extremely fine-grit paper) and first soak it in water. With hand pressure only, not a sanding block, rub the surface gently along the grain. With this, use blooming oil to keep the paper lubricated and produce the broken-line finish known as satin. The oil is poured on, rubbed with the sandpaper, and with a very light touch the entire surface is gently rubbed. When the paper dries, wipe up the oil, resoak the paper and start over. The final step is cleansing the surface with white vinegar diluted with an equal amount of clear water. Use a pad of cheese cloth and wipe the surface along the grain. Do not wipe dry. Let nature dry it. Another technique calls for powdered pumice, blooming oil and a cloth in place of sandpaper. This is used in the same manner and the result is a somewhat higher gloss than that of a satin finish.

Paint as a Wood Finish. For the person who has never attempted the job of finishing furniture—new built-ins or reclaimed pieces—the use of enamel is best. This tough finish flows on easily without streaks, blisters or brush marks. It hides everything, blemishes in the wood, incomplete removal of older finishes, even lack of experience on the part of the painter.

Enamel should not be used on an expensive wood where the grain enhances the beauty of the piece. But for inexpensive utility articles to be put to use in a child's room or the kitchen or bathroom, enamel is the best choice. It can take hard usage, withstand washing, resist moisture, and can be touched up as needed when marred.

First select the color you want and obtain a white enamel undercoat at the same time. The finish coat

The bright enamel finish of this combination cabinet and chest of drawers results from the careful paint job shown below and on the next page.

1. All finishing work starts with sanding—first with coarse (2/0) and then with fine (4/0) sandpaper—either by hand or power.

2. Apply both undercoat and enamel from the inside out, starting with hard-to-reach points, then sides, then top, edges last.

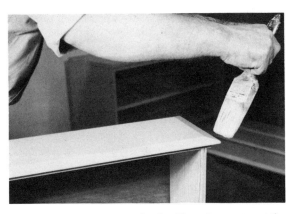

3. The wide brush is held at an angle, enamel being flowed on with even strokes. Always follow along the grain lines of the wood.

4. Most important—the stroke should continue out past the end of the surface. Hold brush at near right angle, move in steady strokes.

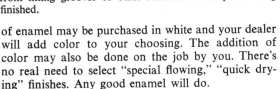

5. Excess enamel should be picked up by brush to keep it from filling grooves or other recesses in the piece being finished.

6. Removable trim, knobs and hardware, are removed and enameled separately. Scrap lumber with drill holes provides a simple drying rack.

of enamel may be purchased in white and your dealer will add color to your choosing. The addition of color may also be done on the job by you. There's no real need to select "special flowing," "quick drying" finishes. Any good enamel will do.

Clean the surfaces to be enameled with coarse sandpaper, 2/0 garnet, for example. Use a sanding block of some sort or a flat vibrating-type of sander. Then switch to a finer paper such as 4/0, and after this, remove dust with a dry brush. Finally, wipe all surfaces with a lint-free cloth.

Tint the undercoat to match as nearly as possible the finish coat, either by adding ground-in-oil color from tubes or a small portion of the colored finish coat. Use at the consistency in which it comes from the can.

Plan the work. On a cabinet, for example, start with the inside of the shelves, then do the sides, then the top and finally the narrow front edges. Here you

may find a narrow sash brush best to use. Let the freshly painted piece dry overnight in a room with closed windows in order to avoid dust. In humid weather, allow at least 24 hours' drying time. The undercoat is then sanded thoroughly, first with coarse 2/0, then with finer 4/0 sandpaper, until the surface is perfectly smooth.

Dust carefully and apply the final coat as you did the undercoat. The removable parts are handled separately and replaced only after all pieces are thoroughly dry. Contrasting colors may be applied then. Do *not* sand after the final coat.

Paint Removers. Paint removing *sounds* simple, the chemical way, but it can become complicated. Old finishes are tough and stubborn, and care is required to avoid damaging the wood under the finish. The first obstacle you may encounter is a coat or two of wax or oily furniture polish. These successfully resist most chemical paint removers and will clog up close-

Liquid and semi-paste paint removers may be poured onto flat surfaces, then spread with the edge of a piece of fairly stiff cardboard. This provides even distribution.

After chemical remover has had ample time to work, paint strips off with dull knife.

Paste removers, being somewhat thicker, spread over flat or vertical surfaces. Remover starts work at once.

With most chemical removers, paint wrinkles and pulls off wood surface. If given sufficient time, many layers come off at one application of remover.

If remover used includes a waxy retarder, follow scraping operation with a rinse of paint thinner—alcohol, solvent, or turpentine.

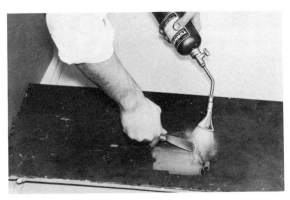

Above, left: A quick rubdown with fine-grit sandpaper on a rubber-backed disc removes shreds left after scraping and any paint missed.

Above, right: A sanding block is indispensable on paint-removal work. It goes into recesses, cleans curves, smooths work as nothing else can.

Left: When correctly handled—the flame spread with a nozzle to cover a wide area—a propane torch is a quick means to paint removal.

grit sandpapers. A household wax remover, such as that used on floors, is the best remedy.

Chemical paint removers are applied with a clean paint brush. Apply a thick coat with a single stroke of the brush, using the side rather than the tip. Avoid brushing back and forth as this breaks the surface seal that prevents evaporation. You can also apply the remover by pouring it on a flat surface and spreading it with the edge of a piece of cardboard. Both methods work well. Allow plenty of time for the remover to work. Some chemical removers—notably the pastes—will stay soft and work for several hours. With some finishes, the remover makes the paint "pop up" in heavy flakes. These should be removed with a broad scraper and a second application made if further coats remain under the first. With the water-wash removers, the softened paint wipes off with a cloth. With all chemical removers, clean the surface afterwards with steel wool to remove flakes of loose paint. If a wax-type remover was used, moisten the steel wool with turpentine or denatured alcohol. When this part of the job is done, allow the piece to dry thoroughly. If the grain of the wood was raised by the removal operation, it will appear fuzzy

and must be smoothed with fine-grit sandpaper. Rub lightly and work along the grain only.

Sandpaper alone will sometimes remove an old finish, but it is a tedious method. If the finish is thick, start with an open-grit paper. This variety will not clog as readily from waxy materials. Finish with medium and then fine-grit paper. Naturally, power sanding will eliminate a lot of hard work. If a disc sander is used and leaves semicircular marks on the work, they can be removed with an orbital type or a hand sanding block.

It is possible, too, on flat surfaces to remove old finishes with a small propane torch and a scraper. The torch, fitted with a spreader nozzle, directs the flame over a fairly large area, "popping" the finish up in flakes which are immediately scraped away with a broad knife or scraper blade. Care must be taken to keep the flame moving for, if left to heat one area too long, the wood may be scorched. On curved surfaces and intricately carved surfaces, the chemical removers are by far the best.

Wood Finish Renovation. No matter how careful the family may be, scratches and other annoying marks manage to appear on wood surfaces. How they get there is often a mystery, and how to get rid of them is another unless you know just how to go about it. The suggested remedies pictured on the next two pages will take care of most of these blemishes very neatly and easily.

CHIPS

If veneer corners are chipped, salvage pieces if possible, or try to match wood with scrap. Glue into place with good furniture glue. Cover with cloth and press under heavy weight for two or three days. Touch up joint between old and new with shellac. If bare wood is still exposed, touch up with oil stain before application of the shellac.

SCRATCHES AND NICKS

Light scratches vanish when rubbed with a cloth dampened with furniture polish to which a few drops of alcohol are added. Rubbing alcohol will do the trick.

Scratches on mahogany show up in white streaks. Wrap a matchstick with surgical cotton, dip in iodine, and touch scratches lightly. When dry, polish gently.

If scratches are deep enough to expose bare wood, apply stick shellac rubbed back and forth across scratch, then stroke on matching oil stain with a soft brush.

After the oil stain has dried (several hours), apply clear shellac thinned 50%. This should be brushed along grain, feathered to the edges, using a soft camel's-hair brush.

If furniture has been dented with blunt objects, wipe with gum turpentine. Apply damp cloths several hours to swell wood fibers, then apply warm iron over the cloth.

To fix holes, scrape with knife. Fill partly with matching plastic wood, let dry, fill rest with shellac stick. Clear varnish, covered with oil and rubbed in circles, completes the repair.

STAINS

If an alcohol stain has not penetrated to wood, remove with a paste made of cigar ash and castor oil. Rub with the grain, then polish with a clean cloth and wax.

Perfume splash spots can *sometimes* be removed with a mixture of powdered pumice and linseed oil in a thin paste. Rub gently, then wipe dry and apply furniture polish.

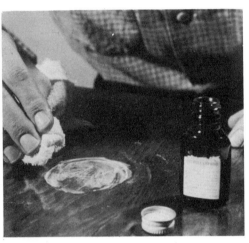

When hot objects are laid on a varnished surface, the area becomes milky or cloudy. It can be cleared up by gently rubbing with spirits of camphor. Polish when dry.

Stubborn white rings from wet glasses (water or alcohol) respond to rubbing with a mix of equal parts olive oil and white vinegar. Rub with the grain, then polish.

BURNS

To treat table-top burns, first apply silver polish, keeping clear of unmarred finish. Wipe dry, then apply your regular furniture polish or a coat of paste wax.

STICKING PAPER

Paper under a hot object will stick to furniture. So will damp newsprint. To remove, cover with olive oil, let soak, then rub off paper and stain with a clean cloth.

WOOD FILLERS

Fillers help conceal many faults in wood. Defects, knots and cracks, joints, nail or screw holes, all can be hidden by fillers. Furthermore, poor craftsmanship can also be hidden to some extent.

There is no one filler that will do all the jobs. Some cannot be stained, others must be mixed with paint before applying; some dry quickly, while others take a long time to harden. While it is possible to use glue mixed with sawdust for some purposes, there are commercial fillers designed for specific jobs. In some instances, more than one filler is necessary. Here are some of the more general fillers useful about the home.

Linseed Oil Putty. Commonly called "putty," this is used to hold window glass in sash. It is pliable but won't shrink. Although it has little strength, it won't fall out of depressions. It dries hard and waterproof in two days. Furthermore, it can be colored in advance with dry or oil colors.

To use—Compress into holes or cracks with a putty knife or fingers. Smooth off or sand when dry. Apply a coat of shellac before painting over it. If the putty is hard, knead it and add linseed oil to soften.

Plastic Wood. This filler comes in wood grain colors or clear. Since it does not take stain evenly or readily, it is best to color it in advance with powdered pigments. It dries quickly and must be sanded to make smooth. Plastic wood has a tendency to shrink slightly but it will hold on rough surfaces.

To use—Apply with a putty knife, old chisel or fingers but clean applicator before it dries. Build up in successive layers of about ¼″ thickness, letting one dry before a new one is added.

Wood Putty. Mixed with water and applied, wood putty dries in 2 hours without shrinking. Since it dries white, it is best to stain it with water-soluble powder colors before applying or while still wet. Sand smooth after drying.

To use—Shellac the surface to which putty will be applied to prevent the staining of adjoining wood. Apply with a putty knife or fingers, building up slightly more than needed to fill. When dry, sand smooth and level with the wood surface.

White Lead. This filler comes in paste form. It dries slowly but doesn't shrink. Avoid physical contact as it is a slow poison. It can be painted over with oil paints or colored with oil-base colors, and it is very good as a waterproofer under and over canvas on deck roofs.

To use—Soften with linseed oil so it may be spread with a putty knife or trowel over uneven surfaces or cracks. It may be used in place of linseed oil putty on large areas. Smooth the surface with a putty knife.

Calking Compound. This is preferable to white lead since it is not poisonous. It will stick to anything. Its surface hardens but remains flexible underneath. It is an excellent waterproofer which can be painted over at once, and it is particularly useful outdoors for exterior joints or in the house to seal joints between tub or sink and walls.

To use—Apply with a calking gun, putty knife or directly from the tube. Do not sand; use a putty knife to smooth the surface. Wipe the surrounding surface clean to prevent staining.

Urea Resin Glue. A tough-surface filler as well as an adhesive, this can be used for end grains on window sills and doors or on areas requiring hard wear. It cannot be painted or varnished without first rough-sanding the surface.

To use—Spread with a putty knife or a flat stick, smooth and let dry. Then sand lightly or with medium-fine paper if the surface is to be painted. Build up gradually with ¼″ coats, making certain to sand between each coat before a new one is applied.

Glues. In general, glues make good fillers; they're brittle but adhere well. By mixing plastic resin glue and plastic wood in equal parts, you can create a tough, non-shrinking filler that will stick on any surface.

WHICH FILLER FOR THE JOB?

Job to Be Done	If Painted	If Stained
Nail or screw holes	Any of the fillers	Glue-and-sawdust or wood putty*
Rebuild an edge	Plastic wood or plastic resin glue mixed with plastic wood or urea resin glue	Glue-and-sawdust or wood putty*
Cracks in a floor	Plastic wood, white lead, wood putty, calking compound	Glue, or shellac mixed with sawdust
Knot hole	White lead, plastic wood or wood putty	Plastic wood† or wood putty*
End grain of wood	Any of the fillers	Wood putty*
Joint between two boards	Any of the fillers	Wood putty*

*Wood putty should be stained to match before applying for best results.
†Use pre-stained plastic wood or mix with stain before applying.

1. Before applying fillers to surface, open the wood pores by rubbing water over surface with a sponge. It's best to test the finish on sample piece.

2. In place of wetting the wood, you can rub the surface down with a stiff wire brush. This can also be used in combination with wetting.

3. Above, left: If you don't want filler to darken the wood, apply wash coat of shellac after opening pores. Use 50% shellac and 50% alcohol.

4. Above, right: Work filler into grain with stiff brush, squeegee, or heavy cardboard. Wipe excess off across grain. Filler here is plaster, varnish, and oil color.

5. Left: When filler has dried—about 24 hours—sand smooth in direction of grain. If filler was not stained, stain now. Finally, varnish or shellac.

Plastic resin glue and wood putty are also a good combination. Glue mixed with sawdust is often used when the surface is to be stained.

To use—Unless mixed with plastic wood, wood putty or sawdust, apply straight from the can or tube. Otherwise, use a stick or a putty knife.

LINSEED OIL

Linseed oil, an extract of flax seed, is the oldest wood preservative known to man. Its name comes from Anglo-Saxon times and means, simply enough, "linen seed." Most homeowners associate linseed oil with paint. It's true that linseed is without peer as a mixer, but this versatile household aid has many other uses. There are two types of linseed oil, boiled and raw. The raw oil is very heavy and takes up to four days to dry after application. Boiled down, and with alcohol or turpentine added as a dryer, it penetrates wood surfaces more deeply and readily and will dry in six to eight hours. The thinners evaporate quickly, leaving the oil inside and outside in protective coatings. Diluted still further with turpentine, linseed oil becomes a first-rate polish and household oil, a substitute for wax and an all-round friend of the home.

First and foremost among its functions are the time-tried uses as a wood preservative against moisture, rot, decay and excessive heat from the sun. Wooden fence posts, garden marker stakes, tool handles and garden furniture will all acquire added years if painted over with, and thoroughly soaked in, raw linseed oil. Let them stand for several hours and then wipe dry. Paint will be unnecessary and a natural wood finish, slightly darkened, will be the result.

MASONRY Cement, mortar and concrete · Working with brick and flagstone · Stone cutting · Patio bases

Webster defines a mason, simply enough, as "a person whose work is building with stone, brick, etc." And masonry itself is simple enough for the home handyman who learns the rules and then *follows* them. No shortcuts here—for the ingredients of concrete, mortar and cement must be mixed in the proper proportion; otherwise the results will be dusty, crumbly or leaky, and the job will have to be done all over again. In the same way, every brick wall needs a strong footing below the frost line, and hurried construction without the proper footing will only lead to quick collapse of the wall.

Masonry materials are particularly enduring. Stone, brick, flagstone, fieldstone, each has been used through many centuries by homeowners. As these materials weather, they mellow, giving an air of charm and dignity with minimum upkeep. This section tells you where and how to use them and then how to protect them to preserve their function and beauty.

Use these pages as a basic reference for all the major masonry around your home, from sturdy brick walls and new patio bases to chimney-chink repairs. Special outdoor maintenance is covered in Chapter 6.

CEMENT, MORTAR AND CONCRETE

Frequently the home handyman is exposed to the terms "cement," "mortar" and "concrete." In fact, he often uses them himself without knowing the actual differences among them. The homeowner who has never mended broken masonry or poured his own driveway or walk often wonders what goes into each and is puzzled over which to use. Part of the confusion results from the fact that portland cement, the prime ingredient of all of them, and the finished mixture of portland cement and sand are loosely termed "cement." To clear up the confusion once and for all, here are the differences:

1. Portland cement is a manufactured product. It

THE RIGHT MIX FOR THE RIGHT JOB

CEMENT

Use	Portland cement (bags)	Sand (cubic feet)
Setting flagstones	1	2½
Masonry surfacing	1	2½
Stucco	1	2½
Filling tree cavities	1	2

MORTAR

Use	Mortar cement (or add 10% lime to portland cement)	Sand (cubic feet)
Brick and block laying	1	2½
Repointing brick	1	2
Stucco (in place of cement)	1	2½
General masonry patching	1	2 to 2½

CONCRETE

Use	Portland cement (bags)	Sand (cubic feet)	Gravel
Foundation footing	1	2	4
Floors	1	2	3
Foundation walls	1	2½	4
Walks (heavy traffic)	1	1½	3
Walks (light traffic)	1	2	4
Stairs	1	2	4
Cast posts, lintels and other forms	1	1½	3
Setting posts	1	2½	4

consists of limestone, chalk, clay and other natural products finely ground or fired in kilns to a clinker state, after which it is pulverized and bagged. The usual bag contains one cubic foot and is sold by hardware stores and building supply and lumber dealers.

2. Cement, as used on sidewalks, stucco and masonry patching, is a mixture of portland cement and sand added to water.

3. Concrete is the same as 2—portland cement and sand—with gravel added for extra bulk and strength.

4. Mortar, in the general sense, is a mixture of portland cement and sand with the addition of about 10 per cent by bulk or volume of hydrated lime. This keeps the mix fluid longer and makes it easier to handle. It also adds to the hardness of the mix when dried.

5. Grout is the same as 2 or 3—cement or concrete —with enough water added to make it a flowing mass. It is used to fill holes or poured into confined spots or, on occasion, utilized to bind two masonry pieces together.

Whatever you use, be it cement, concrete or mortar, it is necessary to mix the parts dry. Always measure the amounts used. If you have no measuring box—merely 4 boards to form a 12″ square 12″ deep —then use a shovel. As a guide, remember that one shovelful of portland cement is equal to (a) one shovelful of damp sand, (b) two shovelsful of dry sand, (c) two shovelsful of gravel. After all the parts have been mixed in the right proportion for the job (see table above right), add the water until the mix is

WATER-CEMENT RATIO. Under average conditions, you should use the specified number of gallons of water per sack of portland cement for the following concrete work about the home:

Basement floor	5½	Patio floor	5
Cast posts, forms	5	Sidewalk (light traffic)	5
Driveway	5	Sidewalk (heavy traffic)	4½
Footing	5½	Stairs	5
Foundation wall	5	Topping for house floor	4½

Because sand is seldom thoroughly dry, you must make an allowance for its moisture content. Deduct the following from the amount of water to be used, depending upon the condition of the sand:

- if the sand is slightly damp to the touch but leaves only a slight amount of moisture on your hand   ¼ gallon per bag
- if the sand is damp and leaves your hand wet and covered with some grains of sand   ½ gallon per bag
- if the sand is very wet and drips water   1 gallon per bag

uniformly damp. When the entire mix assumes the same consistency, it's ready to use.

Working with Concrete. The gravel used in concrete may be either screened riverbed gravel (round) or crushed stone. It is ordered by diameter, as it is sifted through a screen in order to size it correctly. When ordering or using gravel, its diameter should never be less than one-fourth or more than one-third the thickness of the poured mass. For example, in a

1. All concrete and cement patching starts the same way. Clean out loose material, dirt, plant life. Use a wire brush where possible, an old screwdriver for getting into deeper crevices.
2. Next step is thorough soaking of old masonry. Every part to be repaired must be wet. If you can't manage it with a hose, use a sponge. Just be sure the full depth of a crack is sopping wet.
3. Fill crack with cement—a mixture of mortar cement (1 part) and sand (2 to 2½ parts) and water. Add waterproofing agent for a better bond. For vertical cracks, make mix stiff so it won't run out.

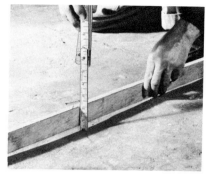

4. Where covering to avoid rapid drying isn't possible, soak new work with a hose. Using a fine spray, wet it twice a day, if necessary, to keep surface damp. This cures cement.
5. After cement has partly set and appears sandy on the surface, take a wire brush and remove excess cement. If you don't do this now, you'll have trouble doing so when the cement is hard.
6. To fill depressions where water collects, first check depth of hollow. Figure the area (length times width) and multiply by half of depth for an average. This determines quantity of filler needed.

7. Important on this type of patch is roughening surface. Light sledge does a good job, but don't crack the slab! Remove debris, then soak surface. Sweep away any excess water in hole.
8. Mix material on the spot. Two shovels sand, 1 shovel portland cement, ½ pail water make only 2 shovels of mix—since both cement and water disappear in mix without adding to its bulk.
9. Mix until the whole mass is one color and one consistency. There should be no dry portions, no streaks of clean sand through the mixture. Adding a waterproofing agent makes cement stick better.

10. Use straightedge to level off patch even with surrounding area. Remove all excess cement from the surface now. Later, when it sets, you won't be able to remove it at all.
11. Smooth new surface with pointing trowel or steel float. Because of sand in mix, you won't be able to feather edges, so mix cement and water to a paste and apply to edges to smooth off evenly.

Cement, Mortar and Concrete   415

4″ concrete slab, use gravel screened to 1½″—the nearest to the required size.

Concrete which is to be used as a walk, driveway or floor must be "floated." This means to press a wooden or metal trowel heavily into the concrete before it has set and while it is still surrounded by a "form," i.e., boards which outline the final shape desired. Always grease or oil these form boards so that they can be easily separated from the concrete after it has set. Floating accomplishes three things at one time. The concrete is compacted and pressed together, thereby eliminating hollow pockets or air bubbles. The heavier gravel is forced downward, allowing the sand and portland cement to come to the surface. Thirdly, the surface is made smooth and more nearly resembles cement than a concrete finish. To make the surface even more resistant to heavy traffic, you can add a top sprinkling of crushed stone before floating. When this is pressed into the wet concrete, it leaves a rugged surface which is not easily worn away. If extremely heavy wear is expected, particularly along curbs and aprons to garages, make the concrete into a stiff mix, compact with a heavy flat tool, and then float it smooth.

HOW TO ANCHOR TO CONCRETE

1. Setting a lead anchor in a concrete wall or floor is accomplished by first drilling a hole in the concrete. Use a masonry bit with an electric drill or a hammer and star drill to make this hole in the concrete.

2. After drilling the hole so that it's slightly larger than the diameter of the anchor and about ⅛″ deeper, slip the lead anchor into the hole. Some anchors require a setting punch (see Photo 1) to secure them in place in the concrete.

    3. Line the wood to be attached over the hole and mark its position. Lift wood and drill a hole through it. Then replace and line up holes, using a pencil as a probe. A lag bolt through the hole into the anchor secures the wood to the concrete.

    4. Furring strips, 1″ or less in thickness, can be anchored in the same manner as a stud or plate. However, steel-cut nails will do the job faster. Hold wood firmly and drive nail through wood into concrete.

    5. If you do not wish to break into the concrete, you can use adhesive fasteners. Spread adhesive on concrete and set anchor in adhesive. When dry, hammer the board onto the nail and then bend the tip over.

Adding Color to Cement. Color can be added to cement and concrete in either of two ways: by mixing it into the cement beforehand, or by "dusting" it on afterward. There are two types of pigments, natural and synthetic. The synthetic type gives more color brilliance and is also less apt to bleach out or fade into blotchy areas. Pigments are added by weight, not by volume. Figure that a bag of cement weighs 94 pounds net. That would mean about 9 pounds of pigment per bag, since the pigment should never exceed 10 per cent of the mixture. It is better to use a white portland cement since it does not reduce the color brilliance and less pigment need be used. Lighter shades of the same color are created with less pigment. If you have to use other than white portland cement, plan to use a greater amount of pigment—but do not exceed the 10 per cent limit by weight. Weigh the cement, then the pigment, mix them thoroughly, and put the mixture through a sieve for even blending. Then add 2½ parts sand for the cement mixture. When adding water, do so sparingly. Too much will cause the pigment to wash out or else it will create a blotchy effect. Pour enough of the colored cement onto the concrete slab to add 1″ to its height. Level with a straight board and trowel smooth with a wood float for a rough finish. If you prefer a glossy surface, glaze with a steel trowel while the cement is still wet. Avoid overtroweling with either tool lest the surface develop hairline cracks or turn "dusty."

The dust-on method may be used with a concrete slab after floating the concrete (if the surface isn't so large that it will set before you are finished), or you may dust the pigment into a cement mix added to the concrete slab. Mix the pigment with dry portland cement, then add 1 part of this mix to 1 or 1½ parts mortar sand (not the coarse concrete sand) and spread over the wet cement surface at the rate of 1¼ pounds per square foot. Scrub into the wet cement with a stiff bristle brush and trowel smooth at once. In dry weather the slab may appear to lose color; and yet after a rain it may appear fresh again. Liquid wax or linseed oil will help to maintain an even color through all kinds of weather. When soiled, apply liquid soap, leave it on overnight, then scrub and rinse thoroughly the next day.

Using Mortar. Mortar, because of the addition of lime, remains workable longer than either cement or concrete. To check the proper consistency of a mortar mix, make a ball and hold it in your hand. It should not fall apart—and it should be able to hold a brick or block in place without compacting. You can use cement in place of mortar and it will also do the job if you maintain the correct proportion of portland cement and sand.

Causes of Failure. Failures in a cement, concrete or mortar job are usually due to any one or a combination of the following:

1. Too much sand in the mixture; it crumbles, pits, dusts and falls apart. The beginner is better off measuring very carefully until he learns to tell a "good mix" when he sees it.

2. Too much water in the mixture; it flows away from the surface, carrying with it the cement and leaving only the sand.

3. Freezing of the concrete or cement, causing it to crumble. This can be overcome by adding to the mix any one of various bonding chemicals made specifically to prevent such failures.

4. Inadequate curing. It's best to keep the surface damp for several days. Either spray lightly at intervals or cover with a waterproof covering such as tarpaper or damp burlap.

5. Mix too old. Don't let any mixture of cement, concrete or mortar stand for more than half an hour. Anything unused after that time should be discarded and a fresh batch prepared.

6. Using color to judge the mix. Color is not a good guide. Since portland cement is made in many parts of the country, using locally obtained ingredients, you can never be certain just what color your particular mix will be when it dries. Colors range from almost pure white to a dark slate blue-gray.

Removing Stains from Concrete. Metal furniture or a child's bike standing out in the rain on a concrete patio may leave rust stains, and oil dripping from a car onto a concrete driveway will leave dark spots which won't just wash away. One of the easiest and quickest ways to remove such stains is to combine lemon juice with salt and brush it over the stain. Several applications may be necessary before the surface is actually clean again. If the lemon juice and salt technique does not work because of unusually deep penetration of the stain, there are several other things you can try. Benzine or a grease solvent rubbed over the stain with a brush may remove stubborn oil and grease stains. Be careful not to smoke when using inflammable benzine. Really stubborn oil and grease stains, as well as bad rust stains, can be removed as follows:

1. Dissolve one part sodium citrate in six parts of water and add six parts of commercial glycerin. These can be purchased in most drugstores.

2. Combine this mixture with powdered whiting to form a thick paste. The whiting is available in paint and hardware stores.

3. Spread paste over the stain; apply a thick coat.

4. When the paste dries, moisten it with the remaining liquid or replace it with fresh paste.

5. Keep the moist paste over the stain for about a week or so and then wash it off with clear water.

1. Most rust, oil, and grease stains on concrete can be removed with salt and lemon juice. The only "tool" you need is a stiff scrubbing brush, one with natural and not plastic bristles.

2. Make a thick, soggy paste out of the lemon juice and salt and let it stay over the stain for several minutes. Then scrub vigorously with the brush. Several applications might be necessary before you wash off the surface.

WORKING WITH BRICK AND FLAGSTONE

Common brick—a baked clay slab that measures approximately 2-by-4-by-8", usually colored red in various shades and often faced on the exposed side with a variety of patterns—is one of man's most beautiful and durable building materials. It is found all over the world, and any handyman can successfully work with brick if he keeps in mind the following basic requirements:

1. A strong footing below the frost line.
2. Sound brick, new or second-hand.
3. Well-mixed mortar in proper proportion.
4. Well-filled mortar joints between bricks, able to resist water penetration.
5. Careful placing of each brick.
6. Proper pointing of mortar joints.
7. Curing and protection of the masonry.

Footings. Bricks, when cemented together, weigh about 120 pounds per cubic foot. For an 8" brick wall, this is about 90 pounds per square foot of wall area. In the average small home, the following additional loads must be taken into consideration: 35 pounds for each square foot of roof and 60 pounds for each square foot of floor area. These loads, when placed on a brick wall, are carried by it to the footing. It is not unusual for a load of 1,000 pounds per running foot to be placed on the footing. Add to this the weight of the footing itself, 140 pounds per cubic foot (for concrete), and you have the total load to be carried by the base. To support this load, the footing must be started below ground level at such depth that it will not be disturbed by frost heaving, undermined by water seepage, or shifted in soft ground. A footing should be started 36 to 48" below ground level, be made 20 to 24" in width, and consist of poured concrete or stone and rubble cemented

together to form a single solid mass. Concrete should be 1 part cement, 2½ parts sand and 4 parts crushed stone or irregular gravel. Add enough water to make a workable mixture. Stone and brick footings are rarely used, owing to the price of the materials, but where this is not a factor, their use is satisfactory.

Choosing Brick. The common brick, without center holes, is usually 2¼-by-3¾-by-8" in size. Smooth-faced brick will measure 2¼-by-3⅞-by-8". Fire brick is 2½-by-4½-by-9". In various parts of the country and among manufacturers, brick will be found to vary somewhat from these figures. The important point in selection is that the brick be clean, uncracked and free of surfaces weathered from exposure to moisture.

Before beginning any job, measure the brick you have chosen so that you can accurately figure how many courses, or layers, will bring you up flush with sills, the tops of proposed openings, and against the frames of doors and windows. Measure so that no piece smaller than a half brick need be used at the end of a row to finish any given distance.

You can buy larger brick, which makes possible a single width of brick wall. The resultant wall is still of sufficient strength to stand alone without any backing material or ties to a frame wall. This type of brick measures 2 1/16-by-5½-by-11½". It weighs only 8 pounds, owing to two rows of holes down its length and a ¾" slot cut vertically across each end. The holes lighten the weight of the brick, make it easy to handle and improve the bond between bricks. The vertical slot not only adds strength to the joints but makes window and door framing much easier, as it provides a groove for insertion of the framing members. This brick speeds construction many times over other methods and permits walls to be built to a height of 9' without additional bracing or departure from standard construction.

Mortar. Since you are going to hold the bricks together with mortar and that mortar must be expected to last as long as the bricks, its ingredients and consistency are particularly important. In most cases, you can get mortar cement in which lime has been included in the correct proportions. Use 1 part of this cement, from 2 to 3 parts clean, sharp sand, and enough water added slowly to the ingredients to make a mass which will slide readily from the trowel. First mix the dry cement and sand together, then add the water. If you have both sand and gravel on the job, keep them separated, for one pebble in the mortar mix can be very annoying. When working with mortar, mix one-sixth to one-fourth parts of lime to one part of water, and add a little of this liquid occasionally in order to keep the mortar moist and workable for a longer period of time.

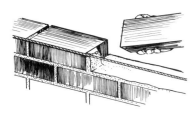

1. Mortar forced into joint from side cannot properly join bricks.

Joints. Successful bricklaying, which means an attractive and durable wall, is the result of care and attention to seemingly minor details. Since it is porous, a dry brick wall is apt to draw moisture from the mortar before it sets, leaving a sandy, crumbling bond. Therefore, the bricks themselves should be damp, or even wet, when the time comes to bond them together. Fill every joint completely with mortar. Since bricks are closely set together, it is impossible to squeeze mortar between them after they are once placed. For this reason, a system of "buttering" is used. Mortar is spread on the brick *before* it is placed, to make certain that every joint is completely filled. In a single-brick wall (such as a veneer), the ends are buttered. In a two-brick wall 8″ thick, one end and one side are buttered and the brick pushed into place. Once placed, leave the brick alone. Trying to squeeze mortar into a crack will invariably leave a hollow space somewhere else and dislodge the brick. Heavy tapping to get a brick into line will produce similar trouble and may also dislodge other bricks where the mortar has begun to set.

Brick Placement. The first, or starter, course placed on the footing must be level and square at each corner. It must not bulge outward or curve inward. Constant use of level and steel square will be necessary, and a white guide cord strung from corner to corner should be followed. After the starter course is laid, the square can be put aside and a plumb line put to use, for a third dimension must

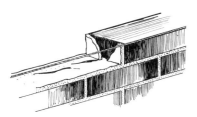

2. Mortar forced into space from both sides cannot reach centerline.

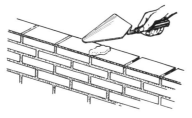

3. Spread on top, mortar still cannot penetrate to mortar line below.

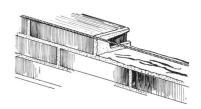

4. Removed brick reveals partially filled joint of poor bricklaying.

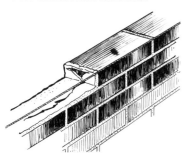

5. Forced into space from sides and top, joint is poor, will not hold.

6. Buttering end of brick is quicker, guarantees a mortar-filled joint.

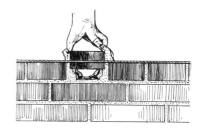

7. Closing header course with brick buttered in both sides is correct.

Working with Brick and Flagstone   419

now be observed—the wall must be plumb at every point. These measuring devices should be kept handy and a constant check made as work progresses.

If you find you've laid a brick or two incorrectly, remove them. They cannot be pushed into place after the mortar has been spread for as little as five minutes. Moving the brick will result in hairline cracks in the joints, through which water will ultimately filter and destroy the wall. If this means removing an entire course or two, do it. Better a little extra work now than much regret later.

Pointing. There are several types of mortar joints which may be used on a brick wall. Study the illustrations of these and the values of each. A metal rod, bent to form a handle at one end, will make a good joint-finishing, or pointing, tool. Whatever style you prefer, start finishing the joints as soon as you've laid two or three courses. Later, the mortar will begin to set and you will cause cracks. By finishing each joint while the mortar is still workable, you will seal every crack against penetration by rain. Once water penetrates in cold weather, freezing results and the expansion rips the mortar loose in small chunks. Repointing (see next page) will then be necessary if the wall is to stand.

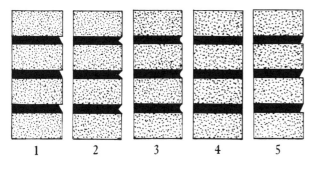

Types of mortar pointing joints: 1—weathered, 2—V-joint, 3—concave, 4—flush, and 5—struck. All but *5* will shed water. *1, 2,* and *4* are done with pointing trowel, *3* with rod.

Masonry Protection. Once the wall is up and the mortar has set and cured, it is sound economy to coat the wall with a masonry sealer. This penetrates the porous brick and mortar and fills the spaces with a colorless liquid which hardens into a water-repelling surface that remains weathertight for years. Instead of gradually crumbling and weathering, with loose mortar that needs repointing at intervals, the wall will remain the same in appearance as the day you finished the job.

Wall Construction. Except for veneer and cavity walls where metal ties are used, walls of double thickness are standard for house construction. At least

Laying wall with large brick is speeded by 12″ brick length and by laying single course to 9′ heights without necessity of header coursing.

every seventh course in this type should be laid endwise. The small end of the brick is exposed to the exterior in a style called bonding. Primarily employed to strengthen the wall, bonding also adds an interesting pattern. By varying the location of bonding courses, different patterns are produced, such as herringbone, basket weave and diagonal. These are also used in laying walks and terraces, but their beauty in walls is something the handyman can exhibit with particular pride.

Another phase of bricklaying which must inevitably be given consideration is the lintel. Every opening in a brick wall will require a lintel—unless an archway is substituted, a difficult business. Neither door nor window frames can support the load of bricks above. Therefore, steel is generally used. The standard lintel in average openings is an L-shaped piece of steel, 3½-by-3-by-¼″. The slightly longer leg is set vertically inside the wall. On the other leg, bricks are laid across the opening, the forward edge

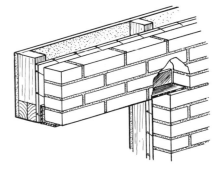

Lintel in 4″ wall consists of L-shaped steel member with brick set on extended leg. Bearing on each end must be 4″.

of the steel being set back $\frac{1}{2}''$ and virtually concealed by the brick width. The lintel does not bear the entire load from the opening upward, but rather only that portion contained in a triangle formed by the top of the opening and a 45-degree angle, extending upward from each side of the opening. If another opening is built above the first and within this triangular area, then the lintel carries the load entirely up to the next opening's lintel. The weight is normally carried to each side of the opening by the manner in which the bricks are laid.

To distribute the lintel's load to either side, it should have a bearing of at least 4″ on each side. In a single brick or veneer wall, one lintel of $3\frac{1}{2}$-by-3-by-$\frac{1}{4}''$ will carry a safe load. In a two-brick or header-course wall, two such L-shaped lintels back-to-back are used.

Care of Brick and Flagstone. Since brick is composed of clay scooped from the ground, it contains the impurities of the basic clay. As a result, durable brick is sometimes less enduring than promised when it was first put in place. After years of exposure to weather, brick faces allow water to seep in deeper and deeper. And when the moisture in a brick freezes, the expansion chips off the face of the brick in small flakes and efflorescence results. This is a white substance which forms on the outer surface of bricks, caused by the release of soluble salts in the bricks or the mortar when water penetrates the masonry. It is a sign that the brickwork has absorbed water. In many cases, it can be removed with a wire brush and water. A really stubborn case may require a solution of 5 parts water to 1 part muriatic acid. Apply it with a wire brush and wash it off with ammonia and water as quickly as possible or it will etch the brick and soften the mortar.

When mortar in the joints of brickwork crumbles and disintegrates or cracks, it must be removed and new mortar applied, a process known as repointing. First, clean away all loose or cracked mortar by chipping with a cold chisel and hammer or by raking out with some other sharp tool. A nail through a 2-by-4 can often be used for such raking. Then thoroughly moisten all the brick on the sides of the cracks and, with a pointing trowel, force a new mortar mix (fairly stiff) into the spaces between the bricks. Finish the joint to match the rest of the masonry. During this operation, you may come across bricks which are loose or broken. Remove them by carefully clearing the mortar around them with a chisel or pick. Soak the replacement brick in water for a short time before placing it in the opening with new mortar.

Cleaning Brick. Exterior or fireplace brick blackened by smoke deposits can be restored to virtually the original appearance. If smooth brick, simply rub it down with an ordinary carborundum rod or block such as is used for sharpening knives. If common brick, rub it with coarse steel wool dipped in water and a grit-containing mechanic's hand-cleaning compound. After cleaning off the soot, bring back the color of the brickwork by painting it with raw linseed oil. Even the most persistent paint smears on brick will usually prove no match for a pound of common caustic soda dissolved in three or four quarts of hot water. Keep applying this potent fluid to the paint spots, washing them off each time with clean water until they disappear. *Remember that caustic soda is dangerous.* Wear waterproof gloves when working with it, and it's also a good idea to use goggles to protect your eyes.

Flagstones. With the constant passage of feet, time and weather, the cheerful colors of flagstones are often reduced to a monotonous drabness. Restoration of color to stone is not a difficult process. It consists largely of scrubbing the surface to remove dirt which has been ground into the somewhat porous face of the stone. While you can use water, a strong soap and a good stiff brush, a quicker way is to use an acid or an alkaline agent to dissolve the dirt. Among the many preparations are muriatic acid, oxalic acid, caustic soda, lye, ammonia, trisodium phosphate and household chlorine. Dilute acids about 8 to 1 with clear water. Ammonia and chlorine preparations may be used straight. Lye and caustic soda are put into water solutions. Use a long-handled brush and scrub an area of 10 to 20 square feet, then rinse off immediately with a hose, making certain that none of the waste is washed down around plant roots nearby. In the case of acids, rinse after about 10 feet have been scrubbed. The action of acids on mortar usually tends to soften it; and if the stones are set in cement, the mortar will crumble if the solution is allowed to stand. After the cleaned stones have dried, their normal color will be found restored. To preserve the fresh appearance, apply a coat of liquid floor wax to the stones. Dirt can't penetrate as easily, and the firm surface helps prevent scuffing. Boiled linseed oil is also used for this purpose, applied with a cloth. After standing for 30 minutes, the excess is carefully wiped off.

Repointing Flagstone. Use a cold chisel and hammer to chop away any loose cement between flagstones. Then brush all debris and chips out of the grooves. To prevent fresh cement from staining, apply several thin layers of paste wax over the flagstones where repointing is necessary. Wet the grooves between stones thoroughly. Then mix 1 part portland cement with 2 parts fine sand and water and trowel into space between tiles. Let the cement cure for several days, sprinkling the area lightly once or twice a day during this period.

STONE CUTTING

No phase of the mason's art has been so exclusively, and so willingly, left entirely to professional workmen as the art of stone cutting. The materials are heavy, moving them is apt to be difficult, and cutting them is considered a complete mystery. Actually, however, stone cutting is a simple business and easy to learn. The photographs on the next page illustrate how it is done.

Rocks have a grain similar to that of wood. That is, there is a flat plane along which the rock can be split. In sandstone, slate, bluestone, porphyry and marble, the grain is readily detected. Granite and particularly weathered and rounded boulders have a grain too, but it is often difficult to locate. Sometimes it's evident as a lighter streak through the rock once the dirt and oxidized surface have been knocked loose. When working with large rocks, the first job is to split them along the grain. Remember to keep the cutting tools—star drills and chisels—sharp at all times.

If you are doing considerable drilling in a confined space, such as your basement, you will want to keep the dust down to a minimum. Pour a bit of water into the holes as you drill. This makes a sort of mud out of the dust, and it is necessary to wash the drill occasionally to keep it from becoming clogged. Whether you use cut stone as a veneer facing, for a solid wall, or as an outdoor floor, keep the visible surface neat and even. A light blow of the hammer will remove any flakes or chips. The edges are not too important, for they are concealed by mortar or packed sand.

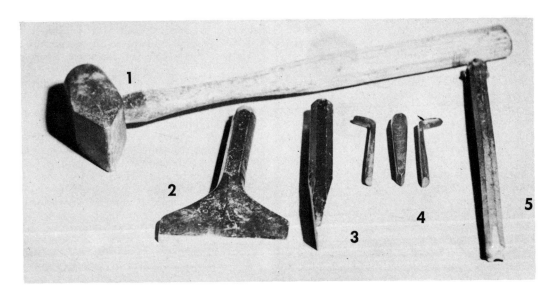

Stone cutting tools: 1. A mason's or heavy 4-pound hammer; 2. Broad-blade cold chisel; 3. Heavy cold chisel; 4. Set of plug-and-feathers; 5. A ¾″ or 1″ star drill.

USING CUT STONE

Where used	How thick
Veneer facing on house walls, chimney, outdoor grill, fireplace, inside basement.	Stones must be about 4 inches thick.
Solid walls for house foundation or any other structure.	Use cut stone 8 inches thick.
Flagstone for porch, patio, terrace or walk.	Outside perimeter stone should be about 1 to 1½ inches thick; inside stones about ¾ to 1 inch thick.

To cut a moderate-sized rock, groove deeply around all sides with a broad-blade chisel. This will work on large rocks too, but it's faster to do the job with drilled holes instead.

To split along the grain, lay broad-blade chisel along grain and tap with hammer several times. Follow grain around, each time making groove deeper until rock splits.

To cut across the grain, groove around all sides with a broad-blade chisel. After grooving deeply, tap lightly on the outer end of the cut-off until it breaks free. Any remaining small points can be knocked off with a hammer by a light blow directed outward from the center of the stone. This flaking can be used to make straight-line cuts or curves.

To cut a large rock, drill one or more holes in the center with a star drill. Rotate drill after each hammer blow and periodically remove rock dust from hole. When hole, or holes, are one-third the rock depth, use set of plug-and-feathers or three chisels, as shown in center photo. Strike plug or center chisel, and rock will split as shown in photo on right.

PATIO BASES

No home is truly complete unless it includes a place outdoors where family and friends may gather to relax and enjoy summer's pleasures. The basis for this is your patio or terrace, and the choices of material are many, from easiest-to-build brick in a bed of sand to formal flagstone in concrete.

A patio grows, like a plant, with its roots underground. How far below depends to a great extent on the ground's characteristics, its slope, and the materials you plan to use for the final surface. Basic materials are brick and stone, concrete and cement, asphalt, and wood. But no matter which you use, singly or in combination, your first step is digging. There is a layer of topsoil filled with humus, decayed

vegetation and moisture-retaining matter which must go. It ruins the strength of the concrete, leads to undermining and later cracking, and induces insects and small animals to burrow beneath it, all of which weaken the structure. That topsoil is prized in gardening, so don't discard it. Save it or sell it for landscaping.

The Underground Work. If the spot chosen for the patio is flat, remove the topsoil and compact the ground beneath with a lawn roller. If the ground has a slight slope, you will need some form of retaining wall along the lower end of the slope. Practically all patio materials will require a border wall to keep the basic materials from spreading out. Various methods of handling this problem are indicated in the sketches. Beware of trying to build in a swampy

SIDE SUPPORTS FOR PATIO BASES

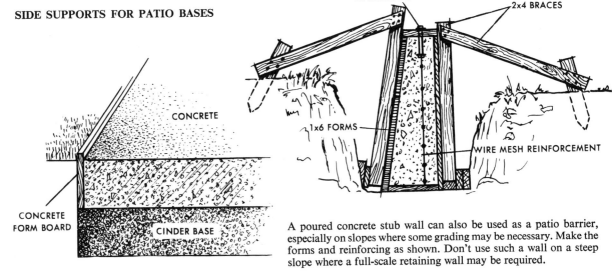

A poured concrete stub wall can also be used as a patio barrier, especially on slopes where some grading may be necessary. Make the forms and reinforcing as shown. Don't use such a wall on a steep slope where a full-scale retaining wall may be required.

Cross section of typical concrete slab. Excavate 10″. Make forms of rough lumber nailed to 2 × 4 stakes. Pour 5″ of concrete over 5″ cinder base.

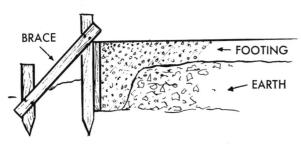

Concrete patios need adequate footings on edges to support any wall or patio structure that may be added later.

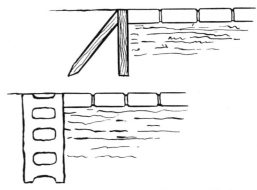

Patios of brick-in-sand need edge walls, too. Blocks or braced planks keep edges from shifting.

spot where water stands after every rain. Unless this spot can be drained to a downhill point, avoid it. Drainage by 4″-diameter field tiles through a sloping trench will often make the area usable, but keep such areas as the last choice. A "ballast" of gravel or crushed stone is the next step. This is tamped down as compactly as possible and is used under concrete or just plain sand and, in some softer soils, is practical under asphalt.

Concrete and Cement. Concrete will form the basis for all materials set in mortar: brick, stone of all kinds and quarry tiles. A mix of 1 part portland cement, 2½ to 3 parts sand, and 4 to 5 parts gravel (not to exceed one-third the final slab thickness in diameter) will usually serve well here.

For endurance, wire reinforcement is suggested. This is variously handled. In one case, it is spread over the ballast and, after the concrete is poured, the wire is pulled up with a rake as close to the center of the 5″ mass as possible. In other cases,

about 2″ of concrete is poured, the wire spread over it, and the final 3″ poured. Just bear in mind that concrete must be poured, tamped or "floated," and leveled off quickly. Use the method most suited to the patio size, your ability, and the number of friends you can call in to help.

The concrete base, on being floated, brings sand and cement to the surface above the gravel and this, when smoothed off, may be used as the final surface. It may be stained, if desired, after curing. The better method—one which gives you more time for neater work—is a cement topping. When cement is applied over concrete, the latter surface should be wet. The thickness of the cement should be ½ to ¾″. You can "work" the cement smooth and glaze it only one half-hour after mixing, so it is best to divide a large patio into sections and treat each separately. The worst error committed by beginners is over-troweling. This results in a "sandy" or "dusty" surface which will have to be done over.

After you have done the necessary underground work, you are ready for the patio base. To make one of concrete, follow the text above and the photographs below.

Right: Area for proposed patio is leveled, rolled flat. Forms are level to act as guides for the concrete mix when poured.

Below, left: Lay down fabric reinforcing, overlapped at joints. Wet ground thoroughly so concrete cures slowly. Wire adds to strength.

Below, right: As pour begins, lift wire with rake halfway through concrete thickness. With help, surface can be both leveled and smoothed.

Simple asphalt construction calls for leveling of area and erection of wooden border. Pour mix from bags, break lumps with pitch fork.

Spread lumps around with a steel rake. Warm weather is needed, for cold makes the material very difficult to work.

Stone on Sod. For an informal effect—and if you wish to avoid work—an attractive patio may be constructed on a good sod bed where grass will be permitted to grow between stones. The process of making the patio is simple. Lay down a stone, trace its edge pattern on the sod with cutter, lift the stone, then lift the sod. It can be used elsewhere, incidentally, to patch bare spots in the lawn. Remove about 2″ of soil and fill with sand to bring the stone up to within ½″ of the surface. Drop in the stone and tamp it level. At this depth, a lawn mower can be run over it when cutting the grass.

Asphalt. Asphalt is well worth considering as a patio-surfacing material. It is blended with finely crushed gravel which it cements together when compacted. The surface is smooth and waterproof. It is possible to sprinkle sharp, colored crushed stone on an asphalt surface and roll it in if your roller is heavy enough and the job is done on a warm summer day. This relieves the flat black appearance—when contrast in color is not provided—and reduces the heat-absorbing quality of the material.

Brick and Stone in Mortar. These basic materials are secured to the concrete base with mortar, a mixture of 1 part portland cement which includes lime (and purchased as mortar cement at 70 pounds per bag as contrasted to the 94-pound bag of straight cement) plus 2½ to 3 parts of sand. After wetting the concrete, the mortar is spread over a small area ½″ thick and the stone or brick pressed into it.

Brick may be laid flat—and usually is—in mortar. It may be laid on edge, if desired. Work out the

desired pattern in advance and follow it closely, keeping spaces even. Stone is laid in the same manner, the precut stone requiring a pattern to work from and an identifying mark on each piece of stone. Random sizes in slate should be prefitted, laid out in advance, cut as needed, and matched for color. Number all pieces to keep track of them as you work along. Quarry tile is handled like precut stone, the

1. When using random-sized stone, chip edges with mason's hammer for better fit. Beveling underside leaves room for sufficient mortar.

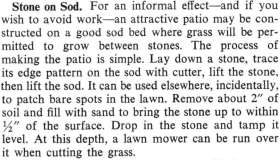

2. Check surface frequently with level. Keep stone flush with edging. Expansion strip against house wall keeps this joint sealed tight.

3. Fill joints between stones with mortar applied with pointing trowel. Strike joints with slight concavity to aid water to run off.

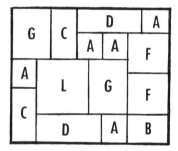

4. Formal design in precut stone requires a pattern laid out in advance. Drawing shows one of infinite number of combinations possible.

pattern worked out in advance, the spacing kept even. Informal patterns in mixtures of these materials are laid along the same basic lines.

Pointing is the second step in this masonry work. The pointing mortar is the same as that used to set brick or stone. It's practical to coat the stone, and even most brick, with floor wax in advance of pointing since it prevents adhesion of mortar to the porous surfaces. Mortar stains are hard to remove entirely, once set. In pointing, force the mortar to the bottom of every joint with the trowel tip (a small, pointing trowel is best) and then "strike" the joint, forming the mortar surface between bricks or stones. A

slightly rounded indentation on a patio is the best method since it promotes drainage.

Brick or Stone in Sand. There is no need to slope a patio of brick and sand for drainage. Rain is quickly absorbed into the sand between the bricks. If your proposed patio is already on a slope, however, it is necessary to build a slight retaining wall along the circumference, if it is to be circular, or on the downward side, if rectangular.

Equip yourself with a long string and stake. Drive the stake into the proposed center of the patio and use the string as a compass to outline its shape or mark its corners. To prevent grass and weeds from

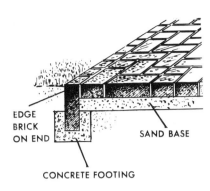

EDGE
BRICK
ON END   SAND BASE

CONCRETE FOOTING

Brick or stone in sand must be kept from shifting. Upright brick in footing provides side support.

Premixed sand-cement may be used instead. Fill all spaces and spray carefully.

later growing between the bricks, it's best to remove about 2″ of the topsoil with a spade. Break up the subgrade with a hoe and rake and level the surface. Use a roller to compact the ground within the patio area. Finally, add a 2″ layer of sand and tamp it so that it, too, is compact.

How to lay an attractive circular patio of brick is shown in the photographic series. To lay a rectangular patio of brick or stone, set a single row of bricks on edge at the perimeter of the patio area; then spread the sand evenly with a rake or broom and lay the remaining bricks or stones within this

1. With sand smoothed and compacted, use a board, with 2 nails driven through, as a compass, to draw inner circle of terrace. Circle shown has a 15″ radius.
2. Lay the first row of bricks, either used or new, fan-shape, with the wide side face up. Line the ends up with the inner circle just drawn in the sand and space bricks evenly.

3. Fill in this 30″ diameter circle with bricks. Start along any segment of the circle and fill in the gaps with cut pieces of brick so that openings are at a minimum.
4. It's easy to cut the bricks to size or shape needed. If you're handy with a mason's hammer, use it. Otherwise, use a wide cold chisel and a hammer, setting the brick on a board.

5. After the inner circle has been filled, lay the outer circles around it. Try to maintain even spacing when adding the additional circular rows of brick.
6. To check over-all appearance, stop after you have two outer circles of brick. Dump sand over this area and, with a broom, brush it into the joints between the bricks. →

7. With a fine spray, water the sand down to compact it. When dry, add more sand, sweep into place and wet again until sand is fully compacted. Continue adding bricks and sand.

8. Outer row of brick is cemented in place with a mix of 1 part cement to 2 parts sand. If you need a retaining wall, build it first of single bricks set one upon the other.

area. When the pattern of the material is arranged to your satisfaction, spread sand on top and sweep it into the cracks between the bricks or stones. With a fine hose spray, wash the sand down into the cracks. The job can be speeded up by poking the sand down into larger cracks with a broad-edged tool. Add more sand as necessary until the joints are level full. It may be a few weeks (with plentiful rain) before the sand is tightly compacted, but use of the patio speeds up the process considerably.

THE HOME WORKSHOP

Chapter One describes the various hand and portable power tools available to the home handyman. Almost any type of home repair, maintenance or improvement can be managed with these tools alone. Ingenuity and patience make up for a great deal. But there is no denying that the larger stationary power tools are invaluable as time savers and in giving shop work a finished, professional appearance.

The quality of work turned out by your power tools will depend in large measure upon the type of workshop you have. Often a home workshop has sprung into being from lowly origins—a shaky table set in an off-corner and piled high with an assortment of tools, scraps, nails, screws and junk. As the home handyman becomes more adept and skillful, his tool collection increases and, finally, he must make order from the chaos. With a sense of direction and a guide, even the simplest shop can take on new proportions of efficiency and neatness.

Obviously, no two shops will be alike. Locations may vary from attic to cellar, garage to tool shed, but each will have in common such factors as good lighting, proper ventilation, adequate electrical power and compact storage areas. Without these, power tools cannot give their best performance, nor can you do your best work.

This appendix details various shop layouts adaptable to your own space and facilities and then describes the wonder-working power equipment which raises the home handyman to professional ranks.

PLANNING YOUR WORKSHOP

In planning a workshop, ten major factors should be taken into consideration. These are:

1. *Adequate Space.* You can't do much with a room less than 8 × 12 feet or one with less than 7-foot headroom. In a smaller space, you'll be crowded and cramped and will have to move outside the shop for all major projects.

2. *Location.* The shop should be close to heat and electrical power—heat because you will want to work on cold winter nights—electrical power because, as your shop grows, you will probably need to run in heavy lines to power the big equipment you acquire . . . and long runs of 220-volt cable can be costly. You will also want the shop to be away from the first floor stairs so that persons going up and down will not disturb you while you're working. It

should be accessible to the outdoor basement entrance so that you can bring big pieces of plywood, lumber, etc., in and out without lugging them through the rest of the house. If you find that existing heating ducts or pipes are difficult to hook into, include a space heater in your plans. Buy one which will produce a great deal of heat in a hurry so that you will not have to wait an inordinate period of time on a cold day before you can begin to work. Also, get one with a thermostat which will maintain the heat at a steady, desirable temperature.

3. *Adequate Wiring.* An average shop requires two circuits—one for tools and the other for lighting. If ordinary power tools are used, both circuits may be of 15 ampere capacity. For tools running on motors of ¾ HP or more, a 20-amp or even a 30-amp circuit may be called for. If it is likely that several tools will be used at the same time, even heavier

lines may be required. Double-check your workshop wiring. If a fire should start in that area, and if the insurance claims representative finds that it was caused by a poor electrical installation which was not approved by the local inspector, you may have trouble collecting for damages. As to lighting, your workshop should have a shielded lamp of 100 watts or 150 watts over each power tool. It should be possible to move this light about so that it will shine on the precise spot where the work and the tool come together. You should also have overhead fluorescent lights of the "cool" type which do not generate intense glare or heat, with one or two double-tube fluorescent fixtures over the workbench.

4. *Sufficient Ventilation.* In working about your shop, you'll manufacture a lot of dust. You'll also load the air with fumes of paints and stains, thinners and removers of paint. In an unventilated room, such fumes can be highly dangerous. By all means, provide an exhaust fan. If you can't cut directly through a wall to the outside in mounting a fan, set it into a stove-pipe duct leading outward. Whichever method you use, it's a good practice to set the fan before a frame covered with cheese-cloth or glass fibers which act as a filter. Electric dust collectors can be bought for most sanders (the tool which produces the most dust). Some ingenious craftsmen have used old vacuum cleaners or blowers to collect waste from other power tools.

5. *Noise Control.* Some heavy pieces of workshop equipment sound like a jet bomber roaring down the runway. For the peace of mind of the other members of the family, use acoustic materials on the ceilings and walls of the workshop. These not only prevent sound from penetrating into other parts of the house but also absorb some from the workshop itself,

making it a quieter place in which to work. Make certain, too, that your tools are properly noise-cushioned. It is usually possible to mount machines on rubber or fiber mats which help absorb vibration.

6. *Conventional Tool Placement.* Don't place your power tools along walls or wall-anchored benches and rests. Place them in the center of the room so that you can walk completely around them to handle large stock. This arrangement will also make it easier to clean up afterwards. The best system is to have each powered unit mounted on small wheels or casters so that it may be rolled away from the shop center when not in use.

7. *Enough Tools.* Don't skimp on tools—buy enough to do good work. They may be mounted in cabinets on hooks and fasteners, the cabinet to be closed and locked at will. Compile a list of tools you will want at once and those to be added later. Arrange a place for all tools whether you have them or not. When you do get them, the place will be waiting.

8. *Adequate Material Storage.* There is always plenty of wood and hardware lying about in the typical workshop. You should provide space for lumber because some economy may be practiced in buying stock lengths and saving scrap for future use. V-shaped pipe racks suspended from ceiling joists are good "storage bins." They can be constructed of $\frac{3}{4}''$ pipe (even plumber's scrap pipe) and held in place on wall flanges.

9. *Ease of Cleaning.* Since unfinished concrete is not only hard to keep clean but also tends to create a dust of its own, put some coating over it to maintain a presentable appearance for the workshop. A grease-resistant asphalt tile is particularly good.

10. *Safety.* This is the most important factor of

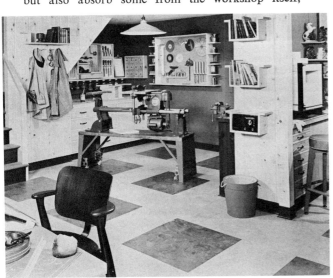

Safety is the most important requirement of a home workshop, and plenty of floor space is desirable so that you can move around your work sure-footedly.

432   APPENDIX A: The Home Workshop

all. If you have youngsters, always keep the workshop locked. This precaution will not only avoid the possibility of their getting hurt, but it will also reduce their temptation to experiment with your equipment. Provide a master switch in a location which the youngsters cannot reach. Then you will be able to cut off power in the workshop whenever you are not using it.

How to Place Your Power Tools. Placement of power tools for their most efficient use is based upon several basic principles of workshop layout. Here are a few simple shop layouts to consider.

For a Minimum Space. When your shop area is limited—about 8′×10′—it is unwise to crowd it with a multitude of single-purpose power tools. Instead, you should have one of the compact multi-purpose, single-unit power tools.

Floor plan #1 indicates the best placement of a multi-purpose power unit. It should be located near the center of the shop. In this way, you can work on long boards or 4′×8′ panels without running your work into the wall midway through the operation.

Two of the side walls can be used for a workbench with storage above for hand and portable power tools, storage below for lumber.

For the Medium-Size Shop. If you have a moderate amount of space—between 10′×10′ and 10′×12′—and desire single-purpose units, you can plan a shop to accommodate the most needed units—circular saw, band saw (and/or jig saw), drill press, jointer and possibly a lathe.

Floor plan #2 shows how each of these tools may be efficiently placed. Note that the circular saw and jointer are placed near the center of the workshop for free movement when working with long boards or large panels.

The band saw is also placed in the fairway, but off center to avoid interference with nearby machines. The other power tools—the lathe and drill press—may be located against the wall since you work to these machines and not beyond them.

Ample wall workbench and counter space is like-

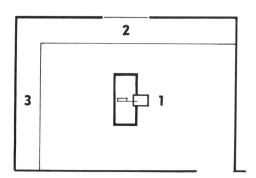

Floor Plan Number 1. 1. Combination power tool; 2. Workbench (hand tool storage and incidentals); 3. Lumber and stock storage.

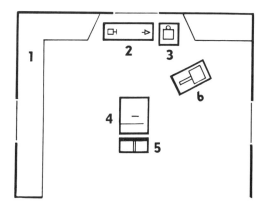

Floor Plan Number 2. 1. Workbench and storage cabinets; 2. Lathe; 3. Drill press; 4. Circular saw; 5. Jointer; 6. Jig saw.

wise included. Here you can store hand tools, portable power tools and lumber.

For the Maximum-Space Shop. The homeowner who has a very large shop area need have no inhibitions about the type or number of power tools which may be installed. If you have at least 12' by 16', you can use this "open planning."

Here the problem resolves itself into efficient organization of maximum space. One area that can be set off from the rest is the finishing bench and its surrounding space. Here you can leave pieces to dry after they have been painted or stained without fear of dust settling on them.

With plenty of space, take advantage of outside doorways for delivery and storage of lumber or supplies. By setting lumber storage off near the door, it is possible to add supplies without interfering with the shop itself.

Floor plan #3 shows the ideal location of many different power tools in the shop. The circular saw,

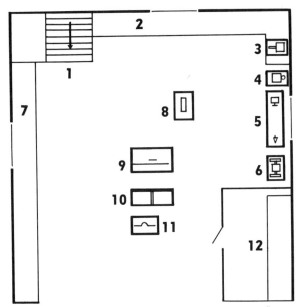

Floor Plan Number 3. 1. Entrance to cellar; 2. Workbench and storage area; 3. Jig saw; 4. Drill press; 5. Lathe; 6. Grinder; 7. Lumber storage; 8. Band saw; 9. Circular saw; 10. Jointer; 11. Shaper; 12. Finishing bench.

jointer and band saw are placed as they were in the medium-size shop in layout #2. The jig saw, drill press, lathe and grinder can be placed along the wall, near a window if possible. With this size shop, it is also possible to add a storage cabinet for the keeping of portable power tools and special equipment. The finishing bench can be set as far back as possible or in a separate, dust-free compartment or room.

A SIMPLE STORAGE RACK

After you acquire power tools, you begin to accumulate odds and ends of plywood and lumber that are too large to throw away. A material storage rack will save these treasures, keep your work area uncluttered and preserve the straightness and dryness of new materials. Too, it is an economy to buy large sizes and cut your own. This rack will hold full sheets of standard size plywood—4' × 8'—and has two shelves for lumber above. Then, too, it will fit behind a workbench against the wall in limited space. Begin construction by fitting and installing the 2" × 3" risers to the wall. Very little fastening has to go into the wall on these, since the heaviest load will be taken by a full-length 2" × 3" cleat against the ceiling, as shown in the drawing. Set up your new power saw and cut the diagonal braces and cross-pieces for the top lumber rack with the 45° angles where indicated. These brackets should be solidly nailed into the wall risers. The rectangular separators for the plywood rack are identical in construction and are nailed to the 1" × 10" "floor" and top cleats, after nailing blocks between risers at the back to facilitate sliding plywood sheets into the rack. The cleats at the top of the rack should be level for they form your second lumber shelf. More risers and brackets, identical in construction, may be added at each end of the storage rack so that very long lengths may be stored, if desired.

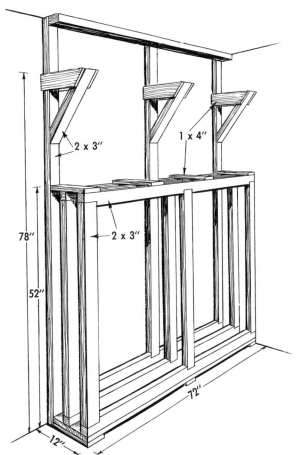

HOW TO CHOOSE POWER TOOLS

From the abundance of power tools available, there are three categories from which to choose. Each has its own particular appeal.

1. Multi-purpose, single-unit power tools may be installed advantageously in the small home workshop where space is at a premium. There are several different types in this category but they have certain basic characteristics in common. All have an individual motor and all occupy a limited amount of floor area. One, for example, combines a circular saw, jointer, sander and drill press in a single unit. Another is actually a radial arm saw to which you can connect various attachments to convert it into a lathe, drill press, sander, shaper, router, grinder, jointer or buffer. While these complete and compact power plants fit into a small space and perform the work of many individual machines, there is always a time loss while you convert the machine from one purpose to another. This is not a major obstacle for the average homeowner, but for the "production worker" who wants to save time while going from one operation to the next, this type is not really adequate.

2. Single-purpose power tools with individual motors are ideal for quick access to every operation. For the heavy production man, there is no substitute for the single-purpose power tool. The traditional idea of adding self-contained, single-purpose tools to the home workshop—as you need them and can afford to buy them—is a wise practice, particularly if you want all of your power tools ready for instant action. However, this is undoubtedly the most expensive way of going about building a power tool workshop.

3. Single-purpose tools with only one "quick change" motor provide the advantage of individual units and, at the same time, eliminate the cost of buying a separate motor for each tool. If you have the space, you can have a single-purpose power tool shop plus economy. That is, if you use a "quick change" motor. Special mounting brackets on the motor make it easy to shift from one tool to another. The one motor runs them all and the change-over takes less than a minute.

When you buy power tools, your choice will be guided by the type and quantity of the work you plan, the amount of space available and the amount of money you want to spend. Fortunately, all power tools of standard make are so well designed and constructed that it would be almost impossible to go wrong.

Selecting the Right Motor for Power Tools. The best power tool is only as efficient as the motor that runs it. It is most important to have a motor strong enough to do the required job. Of the many types of motors available, only three are commonly used in the home workshop.

1. The universal motor, so called because it can be operated on AC as well as DC current, runs at variable speeds and is generally used for small loads. If operated without a load, that is, not doing any work at all, it will accelerate to a very high speed. This type of motor is generally found in a tool where the motor is an integral part. The universal motor is usually used in electric drills.

2. The split phase motor, which runs only on AC, is used with power tools which do not impose a heavy starting load on the motor. For example, a split phase motor is used with a jig saw or a drill press. The split phase motor has what is technically called a low starting torque (the tendency of a force to rotate the body on which it acts). This type of motor may require five to seven times more current for initial starting than for operating.

3. The capacitor start motor which, like the split phase motor, operates only on AC, is used with power tools having a heavy starting load. It is used,

THE RIGHT MOTOR FOR EACH TOOL

Tool	Split phase		Capacitor start		
	1/4	1/3	1/3	1/2	3/4
Saw					
8″ tilting arbor				×	
10″ tilting arbor					×
8″ tilting table				×	
Drill press *					
1/4″ drill chuck		×			
1/2″ drill chuck		×			
Jig saw					
18″ throat	×				
24″ throat		×			
Band saw					
8″ model	×				
10″ model			×		
12″ model			×		
12″ 3-wheel model			×		
Jointer					
4 3/8″ blades				×	
6″ blades					×
Lathe			×		
Grinder—6″ wheel			×		
Shaper				×	
Belt sander					
4″ belt				×	
6″ belt					×

* Make sure motor will operate properly in a vertical position.

for example, with tilting arbor saws and jointers. It has a high starting torque and generally needs about four times as much current for starting as it does for running.

Most motors of $\frac{1}{4}$ HP and over are made so that, with the proper internal wiring, they can operate on either 110 or 220 volts. If both are available, it is better to use the 220-volt current for power tool motors. The higher voltage will cut the amperage, or current needs, in half and put less load or strain on the electrical wires to the motor. In addition, the higher voltage will result in less heating of the motor, enabling you to operate it for longer periods of time.

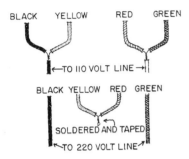

Motors capable of running on 110 or 220 volts come with 4 wires. Here is the proper way to wire them for use with either current.

The most important consideration in connecting a motor to the source of electricity is the wire size. *Lamp wires should not be used.* If the wire is too small, it will overheat and there will be a loss of voltage. A drop in voltage may cut the speed of the motor, overheat it and even burn out the motor wiring. The minimum size of wire for the normal workshop motor, according to the National Board of Fire Underwriters, is a # 14. That is, a 14-gauge wire will be sufficient to support a running load of any motor up to 12 amperes. If you have a very large basement with considerable wiring, you might

The following table gives the *maximum* fuse size as recommended by the Fire Underwriters' Board:

Motor Amperage	Maximum Fuse Size
1 to 5	15
6	20
7 to 8	25
9 to 10	30

need to use a larger wire. If you have more than 100 feet of wire running from your fuse box to the power tool motor, use a # 12 wire.

Another important consideration in connecting the motor to the electrical line is to have the correct size of fuse in the circuit. It is best to use a time-lag (also called a thermal or delay) type of fuse. Momentarily, this type can carry a high amperage or load required for starting but will "blow" if it is continually overloaded. For example, a $\frac{1}{2}$ HP motor which is rated (generally printed on the name plate on the motor) at 3.5 amperes, will draw a considerably heavier load when it starts. If it is a split phase type, it may draw from 14.5 to 17.5 amperes. A capacitor-start type may draw about 14 amperes to start. Therefore, a normal 5 or 10 or even 15 ampere fuse is likely to "blow" as soon as you switch on the motor.

THE CIRCULAR POWER SAW

When the home handyman graduates from simple hand tools to ownership of an electrical circular saw, a whole new field of activity and attainment opens up. Many projects can be undertaken which would have been almost impossible with hand tools. First, though, you must learn the do's and don'ts of operating your power saw and postpone any complicated sawing until you are completely at ease with the saw. Practice by performing simple ripping and cutting operations. Use waste lumber for this and do only ripping (cutting along the grain) on sufficiently wide stock and cross-cutting on narrow boards, using the gauge to become familiar with its usefulness.

Through these very first steps, you will become acquainted with several basic safety rules. For one thing, always stand a little to one side instead of directly behind the blade so that you will be out of the way of "kick-backs" caused by the work being twisted or squeezed against the blade and thrown back by the force of the saw. Another good rule to follow is to avoid pushing a narrow piece of wood into the blade with your fingers. Use a "pusher stick"—a block shaped to hold the work to the table—and push it along from behind. You can make a pusher yourself. One more beginner's rule: never try to rip short pieces of lumber by using the molding fence unless the fence is faced with a smooth board running its length and bolted or clamped to it. The reason for this is that any object between the blade and the fence may be pulled into the saw if the work binds against the fence. Your fingers may be pulled in with it or the wood being cut may be hurled back in your face. Like every machine, the power saw has its quirks and characteristics. The average blade operates on $\frac{1}{3}$ to $\frac{1}{4}$ HP at about 3,400 R.P.M. As a result, the saw packs a terrific wallop and any accidents happen quickly.

The following are techniques which make professional-type work not only possible, but commonplace.

Ripping. This is actually the simplest operation of all. The wood is fed to the saw blade, which cuts along the grain and reduces it to the desired widths.

1. Always measure the size of the cut by allowing for the saw kerf, the thickness of the blade while it's rotating. Measure from inside of blade to the rip fence. Make certain switch is off or motor disconnected from outlet.

2. Adjust height of blade to thickness of wood being cut. Keep 2 saw teeth above top surface of wood. If blade is too low, it will raise grain. If blade is too high, it is dangerous —there may be a kick-back of the wood.

3. Periodically check to see that blade is tight on the arbor. Do not jam blade when tightening. Instead, hold belt to prevent arbor from rotating. Always disconnect motor from outlet when working on blade.

4. Keep control knob in working order. When finished working, brush dust off mechanism. Periodically, every 60 days for the average homeowner, lubricate wheel controls with graphite.

$\rightarrow$

The Home Workshop **437**

5. For greater accuracy in cross-cutting (cutting against the grain), add a wood fence to your miter gauge. It gives you more support, greater protection, and results in more accurate cutting of lumber.

6. If you have to cut a number of pieces all of the same length, this simple jig is your answer. Merely clamp a block to the fence of the miter gauge and rest the work against it. Distance from block to saw remains the same.

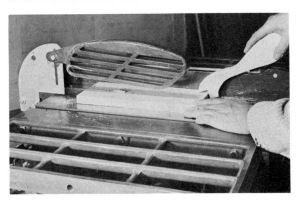

7. When ripping (cutting along the grain) a wide piece of wood, protect yourself and increase the accuracy of your cut by straddling the rip fence with the fingers of your hand as shown in this photograph.

8. When ripping narrow pieces of wood, however, keep your fingers away from the blade. Use a pusher stick to guide and push the wood through between the saw blade and rip fence. The stick is easy to make, as shown below.

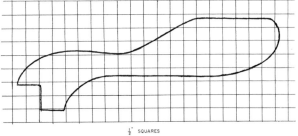

½″ SQUARES

9. When cutting a bevel on a tilting arbor saw, you can make a more exact cut by lining up the edge with the rip fence and pushing stock through with the miter gauge. Adjust rip fence after saw blade has been tilted to proper angle.

10. Here are the plans for a pusher stick. Draw this pattern to scale on any piece of 1″ stock and then cut to shape with a coping or jig saw. Sand edges smooth and keep pusher handy next to your circular saw.

The fence is set in advance so that the distance between fence and blade is the width of the finished piece of the work. Operate the saw with the guard in position and feed the lumber smoothly with both hands until nearing the end, when only the hand on the fence finishes the run-through. Where the board is longer than the table, use a sawhorse or other suitable support to assist in holding the work flat on the table. Several teeth of the blade should protrude above the wood for this operation.

Cross-cutting. Square cross-cutting is done with the use of the miter gauge for applying pressure toward the blade. Gauge and work are advanced at the same rate. If the board is so wide that no room is left on the table for the gauge, either reverse the gauge or build a cutting box, as illustrated. The wood held against the gauge must be straight or it will twist the blade and be thrown back.

Miter-cutting. The miter-gauge has a swivel setting to obtain any angle of cut. For greater accuracy and to eliminate "creep" (a sideways sliding of the work due to the angle at which it meets the blade), use special clamps fitted with points to hold the work tightly in place.

Dado-cutting. There are several ways in which this operation may be performed with a power saw. A group of cutters set in place of the standard saw blade and equipped with special outside blades per-

mits you to cut grooves and rabbets in varying widths. Special washers for use with the standard blades are also available which, when in position, rotate the saw at an angle that cuts a wider-than-normal—actually a dado—groove. When cutting a dado groove with the grain, wood is held against the fence. When making this cut across the grain, the miter-gauge is used. Depth of the dado groove is governed by adjusting the height to which the saw teeth protrude above the table.

Rabbeting. This actually consists of making two cuts at right angles to each other. If the two sides of the rabbet are the same size, the operation is simple. The first cut is made slightly shallower, then the blade is adjusted and the second cut clears the waste material away completely. Where the two sides are unequal, the blade must be set correctly for the second cut, the first one always being the shallow cut.

Special cutting. Taper ripping, tenoning, pattern sawing, abrasive-wheel cutting and cutting molding shapes are all operations requiring special skill and the use of extra safety precautions. They should not be undertaken until considerable experience has been gained.

WAYS TO RUN YOUR POWER SAW EFFICIENTLY

Right: Rabbet cut in long end of board. Clamp an extra length of squared lumber against fence if it is too close to blade.

Below, left: Dado blades are set to thickness and depth of desired cut. When cutting with grain, hold stock against fence. Use miter gauge for cross-grain dado cutting.

Below, right: Dado blades used for rabbeting edge of board.

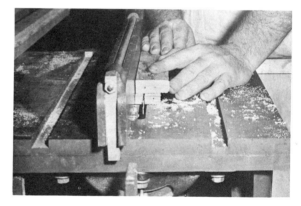

THE BAND SAW

For all-around work, such as building closets, cabinets, shelves and rough construction, the circular saw is the primary tool. But if you plan any fancy work such as valances, lawn furniture, toys and novelties, the band saw is a better choice.

The band saw slices through thick blocks of wood with no effort. It will not "throw" the work at you, and the safety guard exposes only the working part of the blade. In fact, the band saw is one of the safest of all power tools.

The general impression is that a band saw is limited to curved lines and cut-outs. In actual practice, however, a band saw can be equipped with a fence and used for straight ripping and cross-cutting. With a tilting table, the band saw will cut bevels and compound miters as well as its speciality, curves.

It is essential that the saw be properly set up before work is begun. Its cover is first removed, then the long blade fitted over the top wheel. The tension adjustment knob is loosened and the saw slipped over the bottom wheel. The blade passes through a slot in the table top and between two guides. The teeth must always point downward from the upper wheel to the table. Then the tension is restored to its maximum by means of the tension knob, then loosened slightly. There should be a slight "give" when the blade is pressed between the fingers. Now, by rotating the lower wheel by hand, check the blade to see that it rides properly on both upper and lower wheels.

The band saw blade passes between two sets of guides, one located above the work, one beneath the table. The purpose of the guides is to prevent the blade from twisting, which would distort the cut. Guides are adjusted by first loosening the set screws, then bringing the guides back to the blade to a point

Left: Location of switch below work table is an important safety factor in band saw operation.

Below, left: Use of fence, as in circular saw work, adds to versatility of band saw in rough lumber cutting.

Below, right: Free hand cutting of all varieties is readily learned with little practice. Rigid cutting edge assures good control.

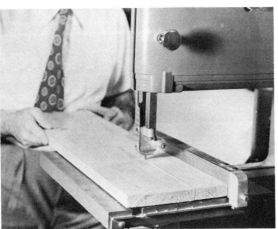

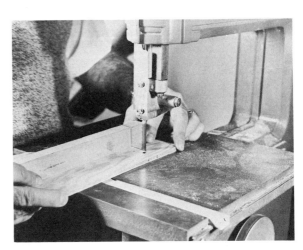

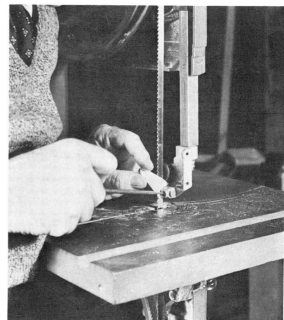

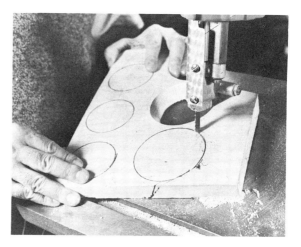

Above, left: Band saw's endless length is slipped over top and bottom wheels, through guides.

Above, right: Guides should be thickness of stiff paper from blade.

Right: Narrow blades are best for cutting small circles, intricate curves and into tight corners.

where the clearance is that of a piece of stiff paper. By holding a slip of paper against the saw blade and slowly bringing up the guide on each side, the adjustment can be made easily. Check this clearance each time you use the saw in case the guides become loose in operation. If the clearance is too great, the blade will twist and cut poorly. If the clearance is too small, the blade will strike the guides in running and the teeth will be ruined.

Unlike the circular saw, lumber can be fed to a band saw by freehand without a fence. For curved work, the pattern can be scribed directly on the wood or on paper pasted to the work. Since the band saw will cut up to five or six inches of material, you can cut identical pieces by clamping lumber together.

To make long, narrow slots, first drill a hole at one end, cut in along the side lines to clear away excess stock, then clear the corners by turning the wood at right angles. Use narrow ¼″ or ⅜″ blades for sharp radius turns and the more rigid ½″ and ¾″ blades for straight ripping and cross-cutting.

THE RADIAL ARM SAW

With the attachment of a "portable" power saw to an overhead arm, a new idea in shop-tool safety was created, the radial arm saw. The weight of the saw is carried on the arm on which it slides back and forth. The arm, too, is mobile. And the saw, plus its motor and shaft, can be revolved on an axis. This triple-movement gives the saw complete mobility in any direction. At the same time, the operator of the saw doesn't have to hold any weight. Also, the saw itself holds down wood. This last is the ideal

First step in all cutting, reducing boards to desired length, involves a cross cut. With the radial arm saw, press board against fence and pull saw across board toward you at proper depth.

safety feature since kick-back and up-thrust are eliminated. While many users of powershop equipment are inclined to consider this all-purpose tool useful for sawing wood only, it is practical to learn all that the unit can do. In this way, its usefulness is multiplied and it becomes what it was originally intended to be—an all-purpose tool.

While upward of 20 cuts may be made with the saw in its different positions, the addition of a few supplemental knives and devices makes the radial arm saw capable of virtually any shop job—except that of driving nails.

To get acquainted with the radial arm saw and what it can do, examine the accompanying photographs. They represent but a fraction of its total capacity. You will undoubtedly develop some original techniques of your own.

Since the saw and its motor are adjustable in vertical direction, depth of cut can be controlled. A ¼″ ply table covering is all the protection the permanent table needs.

Cuts at any angle, including the often-used 45° miter cut, are made by locking the saw in position and drawing it across the board as for the simple cross cutting operation.

When making a bevel miter cut, a job almost impossible with a hand saw, tilt motor and blade ,lower to needed depth, then set the angle required for the miter cut.

To make a straight rip, the saw is turned at right angles to the fence, locked, and the stock pushed into the saw blade. Kick-back stopper prongs do not mar the wood.

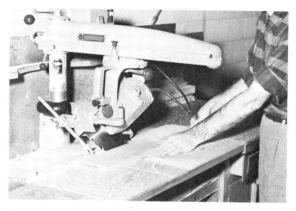

It's possible, too, to rip at beveled angles by setting the saw in proper angled position, then lowering it to the necessary depth. Note that line is visible from any point.

Ripping wide stock, particularly plywood sheets, is often a problem. The 2′ span of the radial arm permits cutting down the centerline of full-size standard stock.

With the saw lowered until the cut is only to a pre-measured depth into the stock, dado grooves can be made quickly, with dado cutting head or with saw blade in several cuts.

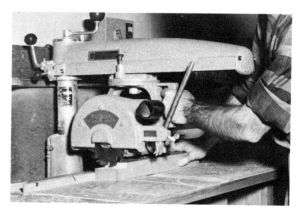

Rabbeting is simplified to a matter of two cuts; with the saw placed horizontally and set to depth of rabbet, then with the saw reset to vertical position to cut away the scrap cleanly.

VARIOUS ATTACHMENTS FOR THE RADIAL ARM SAW

With the wide assortment of additional cutter heads, knives and shaping tools which may be operated by different methods of attachment, the radial arm saw develops its true versatility. You can literally set up your own planing mill from rough log to finished stock, if you wish, or from simple trim, tongue-and-grooved non-standard stock, to intricate moldings and routed patterns.

  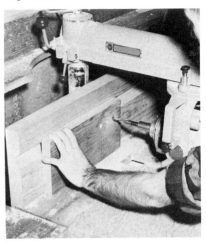

1. Shaper heads, in assorted patterns, take the place of the saw blade. The motor is placed in the horizontal position. Lock the carriage, lower the guard and feed stock through from the right-hand side at even speed.
2. A sanding disc is a time-saving gadget, taking the drudgery out of a large sanding job. Butt-end sanding, as well as all other sanding work, prepares wood for final finish when done this way.
3. When the radial arm saw is transformed into a drill, its horizontal action will surprise you. Not only is hole depth easily controlled by the glide along the arm, but angled holes are as easily drilled as those at 90°, an advantage for mitered doweling when miter cuts are off the usual 45°.

4. Drum sanders are not usually considered of great value—even though indispensable for inside curves—but when partial fence is used and wood slipped past it, drum sander cleans flat surfaces, too.
5. Besides wood-cutting blades, try the metal-cutting type for all metals. An abrasive disc will cut plastic sheets easily and will score flagstone for easy breaking to neat-edge patterns and pieces.
6. Routing delights hobbyists who like to write their names on boards, but has a serious job in making louver cuts, mortising, blind dado cuts, as well as its ornamental chores on inside beading.

THE MULTIPLE-DUTY DRILL PRESS

A precision tool capable of doing many jobs quickly and accurately, the drill press is as much at home working on wood as on metal. An example is the ordinarily tedious job of wood joining. With a drill press, you can make mortise-and-tenon and dovetail joints, not to mention precise drilling of dowel holes. In addition, the drill press uses special attachments and accessories to do routing, shaping, milling, tapping, polishing, planing, sanding, grinding, fluting and buffing. Unlike most other workshop tools, a drill press has no particular speciality. You can use it to drill glass and marble, cut keyways in metal, do scratch-brushing or mix paint.

This all-around tool consists of a heavy iron base on which is mounted a thick, round column. This column has an adjustable "head" at the top, holding the motor in the back and the drilling assembly at the front. These last two are connected by a belt on variable speed pulleys. Also mounted on this column is the iron work table, which can be fixed in any position on the column by means of a clamp.

The typical motor for workshop use is rated at $\frac{1}{3}$ HP, 1,750 R.P.M. The pulleys, known as cone pulleys, allow drill speeds from approximately 600 through 1,300 and 2,400 to 4,000 R.P.M. The motor should be of the capacitor type with sealed ball-bearing shafts.

A spindle, which holds the drill chuck or other tools, is fitted and locked inside a movable sleeve called a quill. A feed lever at the side of the head moves the spindle down to the work at any desired pressure, and a coil spring returns the spindle upward when the lever is released. The quill can be locked in any position by means of a clamp.

For regular wood boring, the drill press uses many styles of bits and twist drills. Holes are bored through the work at any desired depth by means of a gauge built into the press. They may be drilled at an angle by using a device called a set square which is a tilting device clamped to the table. By using a stop pin as a guide, holes can be drilled in series. A special V-block holds round work, and straight holes can be drilled up to 8 or more inches deep, depending on the capacity of the drill. Expansive bits are used for drilling holes 2 inches or more in diameter.

Where auger bits have the usual screw points, it is best to first grind the threads off to eliminate the tendency to pull the work upward. This grinding can be done right on the drill press by holding a file in a V-block lightly against the tip while the drill is turning.

Mortising is done with a mortising bit set inside a hollow square chisel which is attached to the quill with a special adaptor. A fence clamped to the table guides the work for accurate cutting. A hold-down bracket, a part of the fence, lets the work slide along the fence but keeps it in place when you raise the spindle. The cut is started at the end of the mortise, then continued with successive strokes of the chisel, each cut being slightly over-lapped. A depth gauge

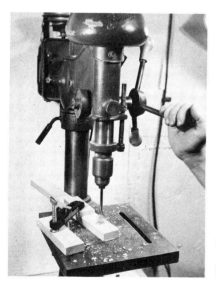

Feed lever brings wood bit down to work with even pressure. Gauge regulates hole depth.

Round work must be held in vise fitted with V-grooves to prevent turning under drill or bit.

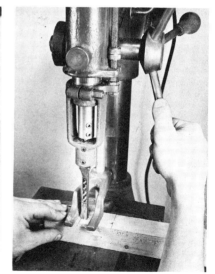

Hollow square chisel with matched twist drill can make an easy job of mortise cutting.

Completed mortise. First cuts shape ends of mortise, then center section is cut away.

is essential in keeping the bites uniform.

Routing is done with small bits in various shapes which cut on the side to form grooves and notches and which will do rabbeting, pattern curves, fluting and carving. The press is run at high speed, and a fence or guide should be clamped to the table to prevent sudden twisting. Free-hand work can be done only with extremely small router bits, not over ⅛″ in diameter.

The shaping operation requires the same cutters used in a standard shaper, operated at about 5,000 R.P.M. The press can be operated in regular position, or the head can be inverted so that the spindle comes through the center hole from below the table. Work must always be carefully supported with a fence or jig and hold-downs during a shaping operation. Only moderate side pressure is used, so several passes along the cutters are necessary. The table is raised as close as possible to the quill. Glass is drilled with either a brass tube, slotted at the end, or a triangular file ground to a long, tapering point. With the brass tube, Carborundum is the abrasive used, held with a circular dam of putty. Turpentine or kerosene is the cutting lubricant.

Dovetail joints, as shown in the photograph, are cut with a ¼″ dovetail router. Both sides of the work are mounted together in a dovetailing fixture. The bit will cut into both a drawer front and side at the same time, so the attachment is designed to offset one section of the work the width of a single cut. The parts then can be lined to and will join perfectly if the calculations of the cut are correct.

Planers, sanding drums, polishing and buffing wheels are similar to those used in other tools. Such work is done at slow speeds and can be held without a fence or guide.

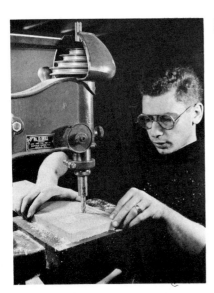

Routing bits operating at 5,000 R.P.M. make light of fancy work. Hold-down is imperative.

Special dovetail jig and bit hold both parts of joint in position for accurate cutting and matching.

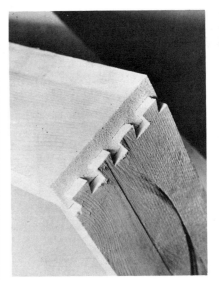

Strong dovetail joint, laborious by any other system, is quick work for versatile drill press.

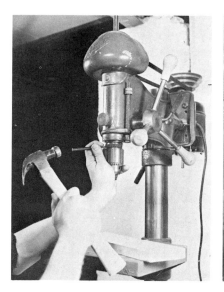  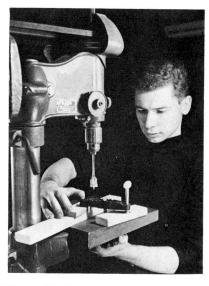

When removing chuck, hold finger underneath to prevent damaging fall. Drift pin loosens collar.

To set chuck on spindle, recess chuck jaws and rest on upturned wood block to support weight.

Universal hold-down clamps work to table. Board against column holds work against spin.

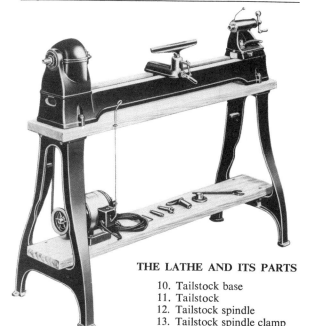

THE TURNING LATHE

There are few tools a handyman can own which will give as much satisfaction and pleasure as a turning lathe. Wood turning is an old and fascinating art. And, like all art, the only limit is that of talent and experience.

Essentially, the lathe takes a piece of wood and rotates it. You—with some sharp implement to press against the turning wood—knock off chips until the piece is the desired shape. The lathe is a relatively safe tool. About the only hazards are, first, that you might get your clothing wound up on the wood—so roll up your sleeves and don't wear a necktie—and, second, chips flying in all directions might get in your eyes—working well away from the turning wood and at a normal rotating speed will minimize this

THE LATHE AND ITS PARTS

1. Pulley guard
2. Headstock
3. Headstock spindle
4. Index pin
5. Lathe bed
6. Tool rest base
7. 12-in. tool rest
8. Tool rest base clamp
9. Tool rest clamp
10. Tailstock base
11. Tailstock
12. Tailstock spindle
13. Tailstock spindle clamp
14. Tailstock feed handle
15. Tailstock clamp
16. Set-over screw
17. Headstock wrench
18. 4-in. tool rest
19. Spur center
20. Cup center
21. Allen wrench
22. 3-in. faceplate
23. Motor belt

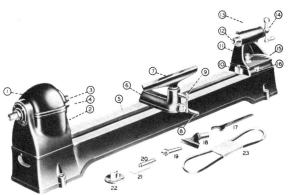

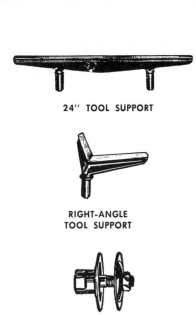

24″ TOOL SUPPORT

GRINDING WHEEL

RIGHT-ANGLE TOOL SUPPORT

SANDING DISC

SCREW-ON ARBOR

WIRE BRUSH

SINGLE SCREW CENTER

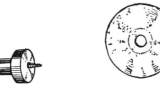

BUFFING WHEEL

SANDING DRUM

STEADY REST

Accessories for various kinds of lathe work.

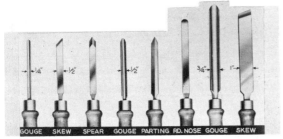

GOUGE SKEW SPEAR GOUGE PARTING RD. NOSE GOUGE SKEW

Standard wood turning chisels. For a start, the ¾″ gouge, the 1″ skew, and the parting tool are enough. Add others later as you learn.

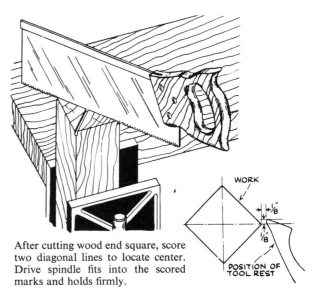

After cutting wood end square, score two diagonal lines to locate center. Drive spindle fits into the scored marks and holds firmly.

WORK

POSITION OF TOOL REST

Position tool rest to provide clearance of ⅛″ between rest and work, and set head of rest ⅛″ above centerline of work.

possibility and, of course, protective goggles will eliminate it entirely.

Lathe sizes are always given in two dimensions—the "swing" and the "distance between centers." The swing is twice the distance from the center of the drive spindle to the top of the lathe bed; this limits the diameter of pieces being turned. The distance between centers limits the length of pieces being turned. Once you have learned the art of wood turning, you can graduate to points beyond these limits. For instance, you can turn larger diameter pieces on the outboard side. And you can overcome the handicap of short lengths by joining two or more lengths dowel-fashion, making the end of one piece a dowel and drilling a hole to fit it in the next piece to be added. The implements used to cut the wood are mainly chisels of assorted shapes and perhaps a wood rasp and sandpaper for finishing touches. The chisels are held on a rest and slipped slowly forward for contact with the wood.

All work that is turned between centers is called spindle turning. A candle stick, a baseball bat, a bowling ball or a chair leg—all are called spindles. For this type of turning, use clear, knot-free wood a bit longer than the finished piece is to be. Cut both ends square. Mark, then lightly score both ends with a back saw, forming an X on each end. Set one end against the spur drive so that the teeth of the spur match the notches you cut, and tap the wood into the teeth. Center and set the other end and pull up tight. Then turn the wood *by hand* a few times to see that it is firmly held between centers. Move the tool

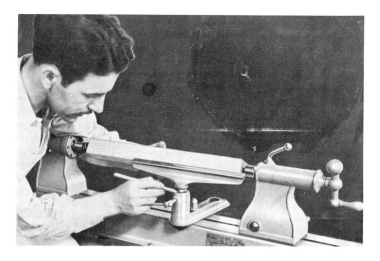

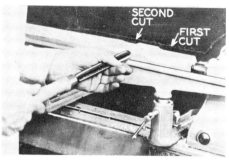

Left: Turn tail end spindle until work is firmly in position; rotate wood by hand to test firm hold, then position tool rest.

Above: Make first cut about 3″ from end and continue to end. Start next cut back about 3″ to 4″ and merge into first cut, then continue.

rest parallel to the wood and allow about ⅛″ clearance. The top of the tool rest should be about ⅛″ above the center line of the wood. Turn again by hand a few times to be sure that no part of the wood stock touches the tool rest. Use a gouge to rough-round the stock. Keep a firm grip on the gouge and all other chisels used. Do not try to turn the piece down to its intended size all at once—take off a little at a time. Reset the tool rest closer to the work—maintaining the ⅛″ clearance—as you reduce the diameter of the stock. It's much safer to work with the rest near the work.

The large gouge used for rough-rounding is intended to do the hard work—that of cutting sharp corners off blocks of wood. Start about 3″ from the tail end of the stock (away from the drive end) and work left, up to the end. Start the next cut about 3″ from the tail end and work to that end. No rough-cutting should be done in one continuous movement. Make short cuts and merge them. The wood can split if you don't, or the chisel may "grab" and be torn out of your hand. The marking of patterns on the wood and the proper selection of chisels for cutting and finishing are easily learned.

Simple finishing is fun on a lathe and, with a little experimenting, can be varied considerably. The easiest, of course, is a wax finish. Apply paste wax to the work, let it dry about ten minutes. Then start the lathe and at slow speed hold a soft cloth against the work. If a higher finish is wanted, apply a second coat and repeat. Bees wax or paraffin gives an even higher gloss when handled in this way. By using mahogany paste wax or a little brown paste shoe polish added to paste wax, you get color as well as finish. A satin-smooth finish without high gloss is obtained with linseed oil, painted on, then buffed as the wood turns slowly. For salad bowls, use salad oil—or olive oil in which a garlic clove has been crushed. For a shellac finish, apply one coat with a brush as you turn the work by hand. Let it dry for ten minutes. Then sand lightly with worn finishing paper (fine garnet is best) and rub with a cloth pad (lint free, such as an old sheet) about ½″ thick, moistened with shellac thinned 3 to 1, adding 2 or 3 drops of machine oil. Apply to slowly revolving work and when polished to desired finish, rinse with water.

Don't be afraid to experiment with your lathe. For instance, try using a wood rasp on the rough-round operation. Tear strips from a belt sander abrasive belt and "shoe shine" the work as it turns. Strips from aluminum oxide open-coat abrasive paper will do as well. Or, for a more permanent finishing tool, glue a whole sheet of abrasive paper to a strip of hardboard and use it to smooth cylindrical work that has no beading. A length of wire held between the hands and pressed firmly on the work will make a clear, sharp line on a fast turning spindle. Repeat at marked intervals for fine design effects.

WOOD TURNING: LATHE SPEEDS	Diameter of Work	Roughing Off	General Cutting	Finishing
	Under 2 in.	900 to 1300 R.P.M.	2400 to 2800	3000 to 4000
	2 in. to 4 in.	600 to 1000 R.P.M.	1800 to 2400	2400 to 3000
	4 in. to 6 in.	600 to 800 R.P.M.	1200 to 1800	1800 to 2400
	6 in. to 8 in.	400 to 600 R.P.M.	800 to 1200	1200 to 1800
	8 in. to 10 in.	300 to 400 R.P.M.	600 to 800	900 to 1200
	Over 10 in.	300	300 to 600	600 to 900

The Home Workshop 449

THE JOINTER-PLANER-MOLDER

The jointer-planer-molder is a power tool which—by a change of its cutting knife or head—can perform an unlimited number of wood-working functions. While a saw cuts to length and a drill makes holes, the jointer-planer reduces wood to exact thickness and shape.

Since it can perform so many varied functions, the tool itself is known by a great many different names. You may already know it as a molding cutter, a thickness planer, a jointer or a jointer planer—but basically, they're all the same tool. Among its many accomplishments are jointing (making edges interlock or preparing them for gluing), surface planing (smoothing wood or reducing its thickness), rabbeting, bevel cutting and taper cutting, shaping moldings and edging cut-outs.

Jointing, one function of this tool, is a great time saver. It eliminates hours of hard planing and, in effect, makes a motorized plane of the tool. The jointer planes smooth the surfaces and edges of pieces of wood for joining with glue, and it prepares lumber for a final sanding on exposed surfaces. In many jointers, the wood is pushed along a divided table and over rapidly whirling cutters which pro-

trude a measured distance above the tables. The front table, on which the wood starts its trip, is separated from the rear table (which is elevated above the front table) by the whirling knives. The cutter head is usually somewhat cylindrical, and the knives are inserted into it. As the blades wear down, the rear table can be adjusted to compensate.

All jointers have a fence or guide which can be set at any desired angle. Auxiliary fences can be added, which will help when jointing wide boards on the edges. A spring-tensioned guard protects the operator from the knives. *Don't remove the guard!*

In making use of the machine, never cut deeper with one pass of the wood than $\frac{1}{8}$", particularly on softer woods. A setting of $\frac{1}{16}$", or even as little as $\frac{1}{32}$", does a better job—just as hand planing is better done with fine rather than deep strokes.

The most common function of this power tool is edging for jointing. The fence is set square to the table at 90°. The depth of cut is set— $\frac{1}{16}$" to $\frac{1}{8}$"— and the best face of the wood is set against the fence. Press the wood against the fence and lightly upon the front table. Hold the wood with both hands and move it forward across the cutter head. As the wood passes over the knives, hold it with the right hand, advance the left without passing it directly over the

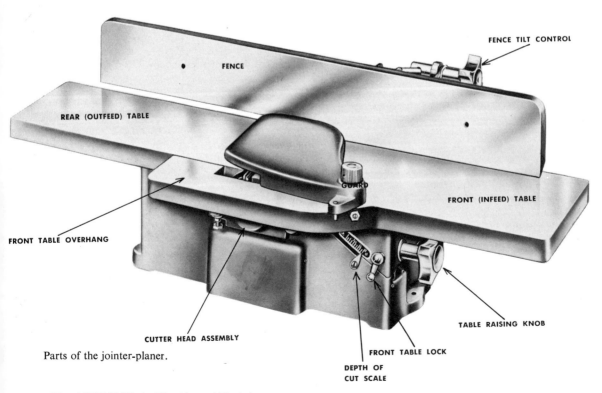

Parts of the jointer-planer.

Check fence with square edge before use since incorrect fence angle will distort joint.

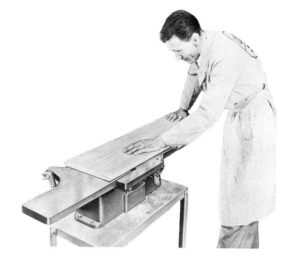

For wider boards, remove fence and guard and pass outer edges, then center, over cutters.

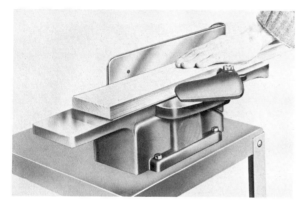

Correct positioning of hands, guard and fence in surface planing of boards.

In pushing material over cutters, all parts of hands and fingers should be above the table.

head and grasp the wood on the opposite side. As you near the end of the piece, use both hands to press the wood down on the rear table to keep the end from being depressed and knicked at the lower corner.

To plane end grain (which also may frequently become part of a joint), feed the work into the cutter head halfway, remove it and push it through the other end halfway. This reduces the chance of splitting along the grain—just as in hand planing.

The limit of the board width may be decided by the size jointer you have— 4″ or 6″. The purpose is to smooth the flat and wide surface. Lay the board flat, hold it with both hands against the fence and the table. At *no* time must any part of the hands or fingers extend over the edges of the board: use a pusher stick to advance the work. When planing a board wider than the surface of the jointer, remove the fence and make several passes across the cutter

heads, thus covering the entire board surface. Make the first two passes on the outer 3″ of the two sides, then the center passes.

For bevel cuts, instead of tilting the table, tilt the fence to the desired angle. Lock the fence in place securely. Wherever possible, tilt the fence to a closed angle—less than 90°. You'll have better control of the work when feeding it into the closed angle. In most cases, this work will require several passes across the cutter heads, reducing the stock a little more each time across, until full depth of the bevel is reached.

Rabbeting is the only operation where the guard must be removed. Remove the guard and set the fence for the width of the rabbet and the front table for the depth of the rabbet. Hold the wood firmly and feed it slowly. If the cut is to be deep, make several passes across the cutters. In making rabbets across the end grain—a common form of jointing—

In cutting a rabbet, cut-out section is on underside, and fence side, of piece being cut.

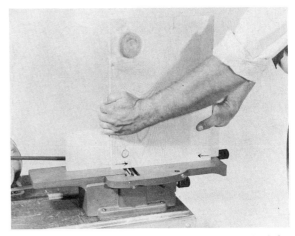

Bolt on fence addition for longer pieces as required for grain-end rabbets and smoothing.

lay the edge to be cut down and against the fence. Use a form of pusher if at all possible.

Taper jointing is one of the most interesting jobs your jointer will do. While it's possible to cut a 9″ taper on a 9″ piece of wood, it's better to start out with wood which is longer than the taper. All taper cuts start with one end of the piece of wood resting on the rear table, which is raised above the front (feed-in) table. The height of the rear table is set to produce the desired angle of taper. When the length of the taper to be cut is shorter than the in-feed table, use the following method: to taper 9″ of a 15″ table leg ¼″, mark the work and set the in-feed table ¼″ lower. Clamp a stop-block to the in-feed table 9″ from the cutter. Then rest the end to be tapered against the stop-block, press down on this

end and feed in. If more than one side is to be tapered, as with a table leg, for instance, repeat on all the sides to be tapered. Eventually, as you become more proficient, you can omit the stop-block and start from the marked line without it. If you see that the taper is going to end up longer than the front table, do the following: divide the taper into two equal sections—each 10″ long for a 20″ taper. Supposing the taper is to be ¼″ deep. Lower the feeding table half the depth of the taper—in this case, ⅛″ only. Make the first cut, starting at the 10″ marker point, toward the end of the marked area. Make the second cut, starting this time at the 20″ mark and running the full 20″ length. Repeat for the other sides of the taper.

The jointer will also, with selected cutter heads, convert plain stock to tongue-and-grooved stock. And, with combination cuts, you can make other interlocking joints for connecting two pieces of wood permanently with the addition of glue only.

Thickness planers are often in a class by themselves. Molder-planers can be converted to other uses, such as jointers, by the addition of other blades. They can also be used to make moldings of various types with these knives. Basically, however, the molder-planer is a thickness planer, a small machine to pass boards through rather than over, in order to reduce thickness. A curious feature of the molder-planer is that its opening is twice its rated capacity so that, by reversing the board and passing it through twice on opposite sides, a double width board may be handled. It can create from raw stock such materials as door and window casings, baseboards and their trim, tongue-and-grooved boards, knotty pine and other ornamental panel stocks (such as V-grooved boards for random width work) and

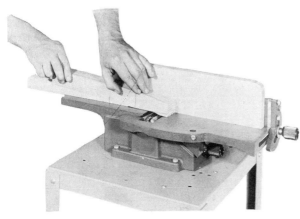

Eventually, you can manage without the stop-block, but it's still good for cutting multiple pieces.

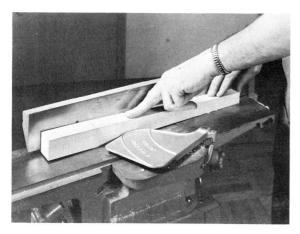

Long taper needs no block, runs through from high to low end, is repeated on all sides.

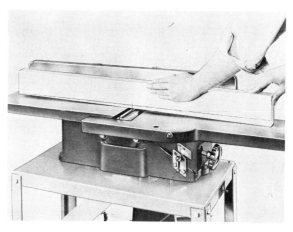

Full length long taper (guard removed to show technique). Note halfway mark on work.

similar, well-known shapes. All of these can be created from rough stock of irregular thickness and shape. The main limitation is in the amount of wood that can be removed from stock as it passes through the machine and over the knives.

The thickness planer, similar to the others in many respects, is used almost exclusively in making thick wood thinner. Naturally, this suggests the salvaging of wood. If all nails are removed, you can salvage second-hand lumber with this device at great saving, but you must remember that old paint is partly metallic and may, therefore, raise cain with the blades. It's better to remove old paint and old nails before reducing the wood to desired thickness.

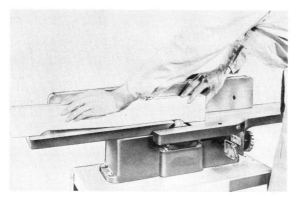

More intricate work on tapering can also be handled—here is a cut-out made as a taper.

Honing jointed cutter heads with cutter locked in place. Use fine abrasive stone with heavy kraft paper taped around it.

ATTIC AND BASEMENT: OPPORTUNITIES FOR EXPANSION AND IMPROVEMENT

Probably no projects around the home will pay such dividends in sheer living comfort as the finishing of your basement and attic. Such projects enable you to obtain highly usable and desirable space—even glamorous space—at a cost that is amazingly low.

In your basement, you already have rough flooring, walls and ceiling. You can finish them yourself with modern and attractive surface materials. You have plumbing, heating and electrical wiring nearby, so additions can be made relatively easily.

By making full use of both your basement and attic, you can double or even triple the living space of your home. Finishing the attic and utilizing the areas under the eaves for storage can add almost 100 per cent to the amount of storage space you already have.

However, it is not just space that most homeowners are seeking . . . it is space properly planned and located, areas that allow for privacy or for crowds, retreats for reading or music, recreation rooms for family and friends. The first thing to determine, then, before you outline your first plan, is the primary use or uses to which you want to put your new-found space.

The entire space under the rafters was utilized in this attic. Walls and ceiling are fir plywood given a modern finish with a tinted clear varnish.

THE ATTIC

Your attic need not be a place to merely store old trunks and letters. With a little planning and work, you can turn it into a highly attractive and useful area.

Often homeowners are confronted with the problem of which to finish first, the basement or the attic. Of course either one adds to the living space of the home, but a finished attic tends to increase the value of the home more than does a finished basement. Furthermore, it is often easier to finish the attic and to gain more room for living even if you have the same usable area in both basement and attic.

The photographs on these pages show a few examples of successful treatments which you may want to develop or adapt in planning your own attic rooms. You will find that there are dozens of different ways to finish an attic, and the way you choose will depend entirely upon what your own tastes and budget happen to be.

An "open staircase" effect is achieved here by means of a distinctive floor-to-ceiling bookshelf. The "open attic" was designed for use by college students.

Stairs from the main floor are also left open in this attic. This treatment enables the window to provide light for both the attic room and the stairs.

Luxurious effects can be achieved with wood block floors and pre-decorated wood-grained gypsum wallboard, the wall material illustrated here.

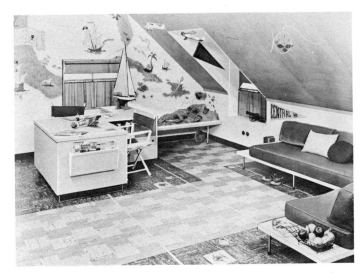

Vinyl tile floor makes this youngster's room easy to keep clean. A pirate's map makes a pictorial scene of one entire gable. Note window treatment.

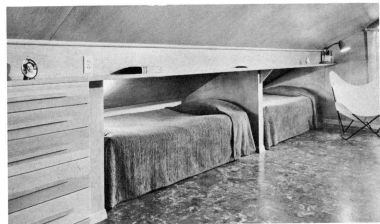

Beds built in under a bookshelf provide a distinctive "Pullman" touch.

How to use the space in a small dormer? Here's one suggestion: Build in a small table for books, flowers and pictures. Overhead lighting is an unusual idea.

PLANNING AND FINISHING AN ATTIC

In the initial stages, it is best to work with paper and pencil. Measure your attic and make a floor plan on paper, outlining areas to a scale of 1″ equaling 1′. How you divide this attic space depends upon your personal needs. There is virtually an unlimited number of layouts you can plan for your attic. Show in your scale drawing the placement of partitions, lights, doors, windows, wall outlets, plumbing fixtures and heating facilities. Your blueprint need not be professional, but from it you will be ordering materials, so the measurements should be accurate.

Basic to all attic planning is the inclusion of built-ins. Since attics vary widely in size and shape, all built-ins are necessarily "custom-made." Between the attic room side walls and the outer edges of a sloping roof there is waste space, known as knee wall space, which can be used most advantageously. In fact, by use of built-in units in the knee wall areas, you can increase your floor space by as much as one-third. Storage closets, desks, book shelves, vanities, even whole music walls, can fit nicely into these otherwise lost areas. "Primer for Built-ins" in Chapter 7 details general construction methods.

In most expansion attics, the builder has brought all heating, plumbing and electrical lines up to the attic. If, however, your attic has not been prepared for finishing, certain phases of this work should be left to the professionals, particularly if:

1. You have to bring heat up from the basement to the attic. Not only is it necessary to install new pipes or ducts in the walls, but it is essential that your heating system's capacity be checked to see if it can deliver the additional heat required.

2. You wish to install a bathroom in the attic. Breaking into the drain pipes and adding vents is not a job easily or happily tackled by the average home handyman. However, if a plumber brings the lines up to the proposed bathroom, the homeowner can add the fixtures to complete the job.

3. You desire more headroom and light and want to add a shed or gable dormer. A shed dormer provides more headroom and light than does a gable type. Construction of either means that the roof must be opened and the interior exposed to the elements until the new addition is closed in.

Usually, in the unfinished attic, there is a bare stairway, naked studs with or without insulation between them, a rough floor or just a cat walk across the joists that support the ceiling of the floor below.

If the upstairs space is to be used by children romping at play, it may be desirable to provide acoustic insulation to reduce the noise level in the rooms below. This is easily accomplished by placing loose fill, batts or other acoustic material between

joists before laying any flooring (see Chapter 3).

If there is only a cat walk or a few loose boards run down the center of the joists, you must provide a rough flooring on which to work. This can consist of the usual 6 or 8″ rough tongue-and-grooved lumber, nailed to the joists with 6-penny nails or, better still, it may be of ¾″ plywood panels, 4 × 8. Plywood can be put down faster, it won't curl or warp, and later it can be used as a base for the finish floor material, thus realizing a worthwhile saving. Nail the plywood across the joists with 8-penny flooring nails, spaced 8″ apart. Once the rough floor is laid, there is no danger of injury to the ceiling below.

Now you can move about and further plan the room or rooms you want. Lay out the guide lines for the knee walls, using a tape measure and chalk line. The knee walls should be located so that they measure at least 4′ in height. Plan exactly what you are going to do with this knee wall space so you can frame the areas accordingly. The first actual construction step is the nailing in of studs for walls. The studs are nailed to rafters and floor joists except in the case where the floor has been run all the way to the eaves. In the latter case, nail a 2 × 4 to the floor in the line of each partition wall, cutting it out only for doorways, and toe-nail the studs to this plate. Use 6-penny nails for this job. Toe-nail the knee wall studs to the base plate and to the rafters to form the attic side walls. Where the walls turn in a direction parallel to the rafters, they should also have a top plate which is fastened to 2 × 4 blocking nailed between the rafters as shown in the lower left-hand sketch on page 462. Use a level to make certain that the studs are perfectly vertical before you nail them into place.

Next, nail all of the collar beams to the rafters as shown in Step 1. The height from the subfloor to the

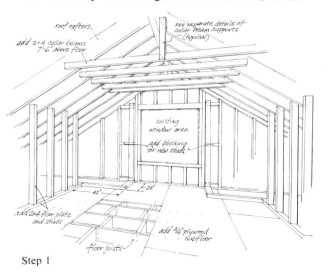

Step 1

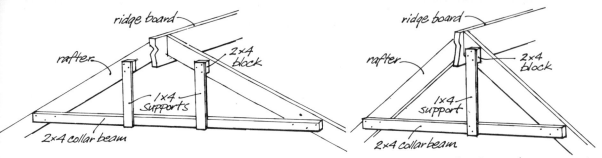

Collar beams over eight feet require two supports.

Collar beams over four feet require one support.

joists should be 7½' (a building code requirement in many communities). Use 2×4's for the collar beams and secure them to the rafters with 16-penny nails. Use your level frequently to be sure that the ceiling parallels the floor. If these beams are to be over 4' long, nail 1×4's between the beams and rafters as additional support (shown above). If they are longer than 8', use a pair of 1×4 supports for each beam.

The next step is to consider the subject of insulation. If this matter has already been taken care of, well and good. If not, it's wise to put in the insulation now before walls interfere with work. (See Chapter 3 for a general discussion of insulation.)

There are three attic areas which should be insulated: (1) the floor between the knee walls and the outside of the house, (2) the end walls, knee walls and the sloping rafter walls, and (3) over the ceiling.

It is also a good idea to consider now the question of whether an attic-type of fan should be installed to cool the home. Such construction is more easily done now than later when new walls and ceilings have to be cut through to install the fan. (See Chapter 3, page 199.) If louvers were not inserted in the gable ends, now is the time for that work, too, since they will be above the new ceiling and virtually inaccessible after the ceiling is put up.

INSTALLING ATTIC INSULATION

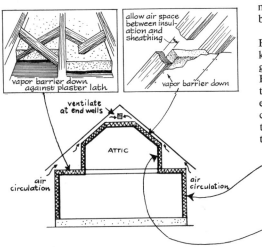

Right: The space between the knee walls and the outside of the house can be insulated with granule insulation material as shown or with batts laid between the studs.

Below: Mineral wool batts or blankets should be butted closely together in the stud or rafter space. Both should be trimmed to fit exactly the space to be insulated. Most modern mineral wool batts or blankets come with flanges which are stapled to joints and rafters to provide a tight vapor barrier.

AUTOMATIC ATTIC VENTILATORS

Attic ventilators are commonly regarded as a blessing in the summer and an evil in the winter as far as comfort is concerned. During warm weather, they let hot air out of the attic and help cool the whole house by creating a rising current of air that pulls cooler air in from the ground floor. But in the winter, the wind blowing through these ventilators often chills the attic enough to cause the temperature in the rest of the house to drop to an uncomfortable level. Since a blanket of relatively warm air trapped in the attic helps insulate the house, cutting down fuel bills, some homeowners block off their attic ventilators with plywood or other sheet material when it gets cold.

However, the most important function of attic ventilators is to provide an escape path for excess attic moisture. Blocking off these ventilators only invites unseen but serious trouble for the homeowner. When moisture accumulates in the attic, it condenses on rafters and the framing members—encouraging rotting. It forces its way through the siding—causing paint blisters; and it often soaks the house insulation—rendering it ineffective. Besides, simply sealing off the attic ventilators doesn't provide for the alternation of warm and cold days during the spring and fall. Therefore, use the type of ventilators consisting of metal louvers which are automatically opened and closed by a thermostatically controlled mechanism which responds to temperature changes, keeping the ventilator open when the weather is warm and closing it when the temperature drops. While the louvers close tightly enough to reduce heat losses and provide substantial fuel savings, they are not airtight, so the attic can "breathe," equalizing humidity with the outside and preventing moisture condensation. These louvers are not electrical but use a simple mechanical thermostat which is completely self-contained and requires no wiring, servicing or maintenance. A bonus safety feature is that they snap shut automatically in case of fire, so the attic ventilators do not create a draft to intensify the fire. These ventilators are available in a range of standard sizes to fit gable-end ventilator openings, roof vents, soffit vents and also for crawl space installation. They come with outer deflectors and insect screening, or the automatic louver unit may be purchased separately for mounting behind existing, non-adjustable louvers.

Before installation, it is necessary to attach the operating mechanism to the louvers. This is done by means of drive rivets and a control rod which links the operating mechanism and louver assembly. Next, the existing ventilator openings (if any) are completely framed out with 2 × 4's as shown. Each louver unit is then simply nailed in place over the framed opening, and your automatic ventilators are in operation. Where there are no ventilators in the attic, cut one or more openings in each gable end to accommodate the new louvers. Use a sabre saw to cut through sheathing and siding, then insert the ventilator from the outside and nail it to the siding. A special model is available for this type of application, and it requires none of the inside framing work shown here. After it is nailed into place, calk around the edges of the flange.

1. Rivet operating mechanism to frame.

2. Control rod links mechanism to louver blades.

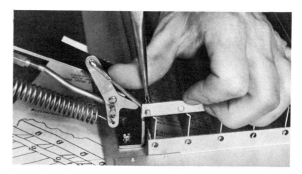

3. Retaining clip completes the assembly.

4. Existing ventilator is framed out with 2 × 4's.
5. Louver assembly is nailed to frame.

At this stage of construction, it is best to have a local electrician come in to do the electrical wiring needed to provide adequate light and service in the attic. Refer to Chapter 4, "Adequate Wiring," to determine your wiring needs. All wiring will, of course, be governed by your local ordinances in regard to its installation. Give your electrician a sketch indicating the location of all switches, light fixtures and convenience outlets. Plan on at least one light fixture in every room and every walk-in closet. Keep light switches near the doors and be generous in your placement of convenience outlets. Have the electrician bring new electrical lines from the main fuse box to the attic, if necessary, and install all fixture, outlet and junction boxes. The only remaining electrical work should be the connection of the lighting fixtures themselves, which you can do after the walls and ceilings have been covered with paneling and tiles.

If your attic is exceptionally dark, with uncomfortably low ceilings, you can gain more daylight and serviceability by adding a shed dormer, plans for which should be incorporated into your original attic-finishing project.

Heating pipes or ducts should also be put in place at this point. In considering the heating arrangements, it would be best to consult your heating contractor or service man. Your furnace may or may not be able to handle the extra work of heating these new rooms. It may have been installed with this expansion in mind, and then again maybe not. Now is the time to be sure. Should expanding the attic mean also expanding the furnace, it may be

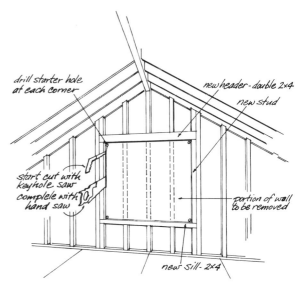

Procedure for installing a window.

more economical to consider heating by electricity through radiant glass panels. These are installed in the walls and take up no floor space.

You are now ready for the finish walls and the ceiling, application of which will suddenly give your rooms substance. In putting up wall materials, you will usually discover that the windows are unfinished (lacking trim) or inadequate; or maybe there are no windows. Adding one is relatively simple. First, remove the studs in the area where the window is to be located. Add a doubled 2×4 header and framing, as shown above, allowing a minimum of 1″

Before (above): Typical attic end-wall window looks like this. There is enough wall space here to accommodate a window opening almost three times as wide.

After (left): In this remodelled attic room, the end-wall window is considerably wider than the average. It lets in so much light and air that construction of a dormer with additional windows is unnecessary.

clearance between the framing members and the outside dimensions of the window you purchase. Next, cut out the sheathing and siding within this area and insert the new window in the opening. Level the window, using scraps of wood wedged between the window and the framing to keep it in position, and nail it securely to the framing. To prevent cold air from filtering in around the trim, be sure your insulation is packed into the space around the window before the wall finish is applied. Close the gap between the window and the outside siding with wood trim. Next, add a strip of copper flashing (slip one edge up under the siding, bend the remainder over the top of the window frame and tack into place) and fill all joints with calking material so that no water can penetrate the outside wall. On the inside, the wall paneling butts against the window frame and the joint is covered with a molding strip.

Should you prefer not to install a window in the gable end, but still desire to create an open feeling, you can cover this space with photo-mural wallpaper applied over wall paneling. Thin strips of wood mold-

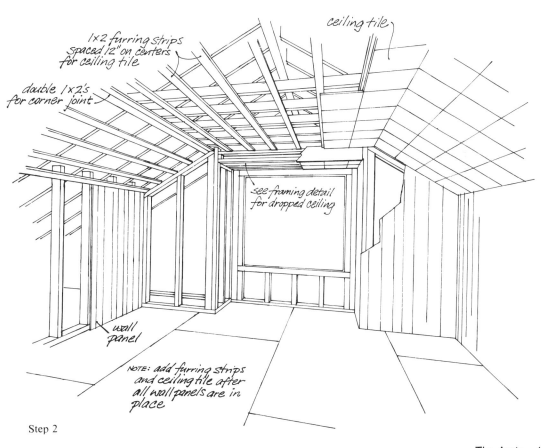

Step 2

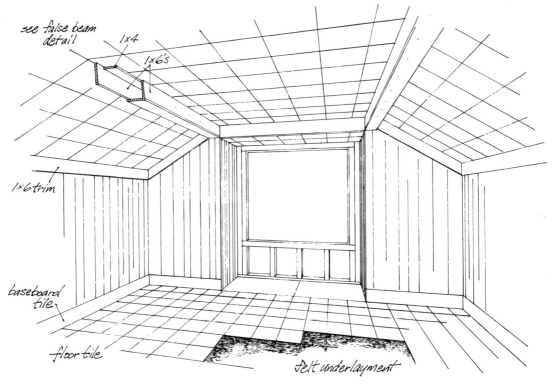

see false beam detail

1×4

1×6's

1×6 trim

baseboard tile

floor tile

felt underlayment

Step 3

ing nailed over the mural can be used to create the effect of a window which overlooks the scene depicted in the photograph on page 461.

Next, install the ceiling framework at the gable end. After basic construction has been completed—all ceiling and wall framing—and the electrical wiring is in, you can proceed with the wall paneling and

then the floor and ceiling tiles (see Steps 2 and 3). Chapter 2 gives you the details of both operations.

You may want to install false beams for an air of casual charm. Study the sketches below. To make the construction and installation of the false beams easy, first assemble them completely on the floor, leaving only the bottom board loose to provide access for nailing the beams to the ceiling. Finishing the beams with a dark stain before you put them up will save a great deal of time and effort. This also applies to the matching trim boards along the top edge of the walls. The exposed nail heads in the false beams and the trim boards need not be concealed with wood putty since they add to the rustic effect of this type of construction.

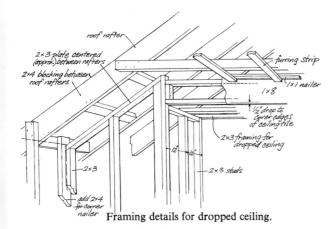

roof rafter

2×3 plate centered (approx.) between rafters

2×4 blocking between roof rafters

furring strip

1×1 nailer

1×8

½" drop to cover edges of ceiling tile

2×3 framing for dropped ceiling

2×3

12" 12"

2×3 studs

add 2×4 for corner nailer

Framing details for dropped ceiling.

¾ × 5⅝ × 4⅝ spacer blocks at ends and every 48" along beam.

add bottom last

False beam detail.

ATTIC BUILT-INS

Shallow Storage Units. Even in attics with extremely low knee walls and shallow under-the-eaves space, built-ins are possible. You can use sliding doors in place of the low wall, or you can build open shelves or drawers right into the wall.

Once you have decided upon the location and type of built-in you wish, leave an opening in the knee wall and do not set any studs in place. However, cut two short studs and attach them to the rafter and a floor plate to form the other three sides of the built-in (see Sketch A).

Add any wall surfacing material across the rafters inside this unit from the front edge of the unit to the short studs in back. This seals off the top of the built-in. An easy way to add shelves, if they are to be later covered with sliding doors, is to make a framed unit of ⅜″ or ½″ plywood (see Sketch B). Here, however, do not include the baseboard or lowest shelf. The sides are attached to the shelves with #8 flathead screws 1½″ long. The back, of hardboard or ¼″ plywood, is attached in the same way. If the unit is to be installed has open shelves, one modification is necessary. There has to be a bottom shelf, the top of which is flush with the top of the baseboard you will use in the room (see Sketch B). If you plan to con-

One method of using under-the-eaves space is the making of open shelves and drawers to fit into the knee-wall. However, where the space between the knee-wall and outside edge of the roof is greater, use cabinets instead of open shelves.

ceal these shelves behind sliding doors, make the entire unit 1½″ shallower than the depth of the under-the-eaves closet to allow for the doors and track.

Another possibility is to turn open shelves into drawers. Make the basic frame (Sketch B) and the drawers fit into this. For ease of handling and appearance, certain drawer proportions should be followed: (1) if the drawer is less than 4″ deep, it can be made up to 18″ wide; (2) but if the drawer is between 4″ and 7″ deep, make it no more than 14″ wide; (3) and if the drawer is up to 12″ deep, make it no more than 12″ wide.

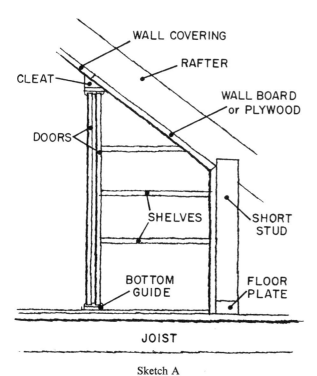

Sketch A

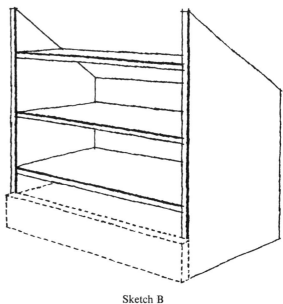

Sketch B

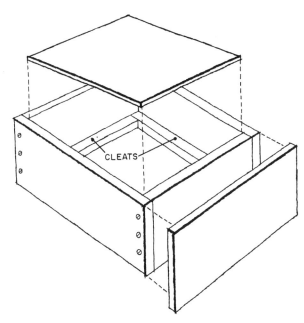

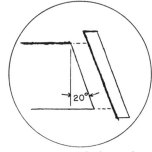

Sketch C. A contemporary-style drawer is made in the same manner as the traditional style except that sides are cut at a 20-degree angle (see detail above). Drawer front is cut to size; top and bottom edges are planed to a matching angle and the top is then set into place. Drawer face is likewise planed to a 20-degree angle.

tional framing, considerably simplifying construction.

The basic plan shows a unit 7′ long, more than 3′ deep and 7′ to 8′ high, depending upon the slope of the ceiling. However, it is a flexible plan that can be arranged according to your individual requirements. You can lengthen it or deepen it to get more space in any direction. This unit has been deepened 2′ in back to take advantage of the extra space under the rafters.

The closet section is 3′ wide, allowing plenty of

A side view of the unit, showing how the space is utilized. Doors make suitcases, out-of-season sports equipment, etc., easy to reach.

Using ½″ plywood, cut two sides and the front and back panels. Join these pieces as shown (Sketch C) with #6 flathead screws 1¼″ long, countersinking the heads. Space the screws 3″ apart, using at least three at each corner. Then cut ½ × ½ cleats to fit inside this frame flush with the bottom edge. Hold the cleats to the sides with #6 flathead screws ¾″ long, spaced 2″ apart and with heads countersunk. The bottom of the drawer fits inside this frame and rests on the ½ × ½ cleats. Cut the bottom out of ¼″ plywood for drawers up to 12×24″; for larger drawers, use ⅜″ or ½″ plywood for the bottom. Secure the bottom with #17 brads ¾″ long.

The face plate of the drawer, made of ¾″ plywood, is cut so that it extends ¼″ on all four sides. Secure it to the front panel by screws from inside the drawer. Use #6 flathead screws 1″ long spaced about 4″ apart along the top and bottom. Countersink all heads.

An Under-the-Eaves Storage Unit. This three-section, all-purpose built-in storage unit was designed especially for attics, story-and-a-half homes and older houses. It will enable you to turn that hard-to-use, bump-your-head area under a sloping ceiling or pitched rafters into well-planned, built-in storage. It provides space for clothing, accessories, linen, bedding, desk supplies and out-of-season or seldom-used items such as luggage and bulky sports equipment.

There are no mitered corners and every joint is a simple butt joint. There are no dadoes or rabbets requiring power tool equipment. Full-size fir plywood partitions and facing panels eliminate conven-

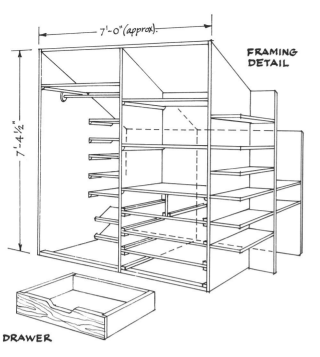

FRAMING DETAIL

7'-0" (approx.)

7'-4½"

DRAWER

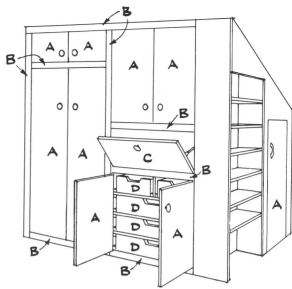

A, doors; B, facing strips; C, drop front desk; D, drawers.

space for clothes hangers. It is deep enough to leave room for shelves where you can put boxes, hats and other items that are not used frequently. Shoes go in at the bottom, and over this section is a small unit for everyday hats.

The second section is also about 3' wide. Here there is room in the cabinets above for bedding, linen, towels and other similar items. In the center

is a drop-leaf desk and beneath this is a series of drawers for accessories, folded garments and desk supplies. Part of this section provides floor-to-ceiling shelves for books, a table radio and other items.

At the rear of this section is a deep space, 4' to 5' high, depending on the ceiling slope, for luggage and boxes. It is reached through a door in the side. In most homes this can be widened by extending it

Right: Extra rear door, being installed here, enables you to make use of wasted space under eaves.

Below: This entire unit goes together without fancy carpentry. Plywood goes into place easily.

The Attic   465

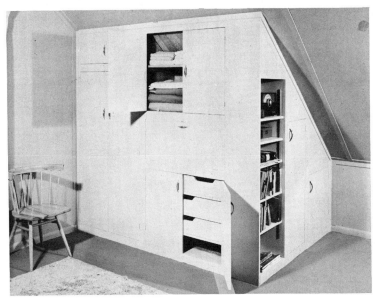

A front view of the unit. By cutting the sides to the proper angle, it can be made to fit any ceiling slope.

further back under the eaves. This leaves room for items such as water skis, tennis rackets, golf bags, luggage, boxes and other dead or seasonal storage.

Most of the unit, except for parts like the cabinet drawers, is built from an economical "one-good-side" grade of fir plywood. The remaining parts are built with a similar grade that looks well on both sides. The unit can be finished in the way that best suits your decorative scheme (see Chapter 7, "Wood Finishing").

BILL OF MATERIALS

FIR PLYWOOD			
No.	Size	Grade	Where used
7 panels	$4' \times 8' \times \frac{3}{4}''$	Interior A-A, DPA	Partition, doors, front sides, shelves, drawer sides and back, desk front
2 panels	$4' \times 8' \times \frac{1}{2}''$	Ply panel (A-D)	Interior partitions, back, shelves
1 piece	$4' \times 4' \times \frac{1}{4}''$	Ply panel (A-D)	Drawer bottoms

LUMBER		
Item	Quantity	Where used
$1\frac{1}{4}''$ diameter	3 feet	Clothes pole
$1'' \times 2''$	90 feet	Alternate handles, trim, shelf cleats, drawer guides, miscellaneous

HARDWARE		
$1\frac{1}{2}'' \times 3''$ butt hinges	12 pairs	Doors
Bullet catches	10	Doors
Pulls	10	Doors
Metal chains	2	Drop shelf
$\frac{1}{2}'' \times 1\frac{1}{2}'' \times 1\frac{1}{2}''$ angle irons	3	To anchor unit

Attic Knee-Wall Vanity and Chest. Here is a delightful built-in that adds the stamp of luxury to an attic room and fulfills the need for extra storage space at the same time. Simple, easy-to-follow details take all of the complexity out of the framing job so that anyone with moderate skill can build the entire unit.

The first step, after deciding on the location, is to measure off and indicate with chalk lines exactly where the framing will be located. The framing must be aligned properly so that it can be nailed directly to the studs and rafters within the wall and ceiling (see Sketch 1 on the next page). The studs and plates that are nailed to the ceiling must be cut at an angle that matches the slope of your ceiling. Construct the side partitions first, then proceed with the lighter framing work for the lower drawers, as shown in Sketch 1.

The framing work for the upper drawers should be started after the ¾″ plywood countertop is nailed into place. A ¾″ half-round molding, nailed and glued over the exposed edge of the plywood, provides a neat and protective edging for the countertop. The upper drawer framing is similar to that of the lower drawers, except that additional members are added to support the side mirrors so that they make a 45° angle with the wall. The framework for furring down the ceiling extends the full length between the side partitions.

Cover all of the framework, except where the mirrors are to be attached, with ⅛″ hardboard. The mirror framework should be covered with ¼″ plywood.

The molding under the center section of the countertop is cut from ½″ clear pine wood with a scroll saw or sabre saw. It should be fastened in place with countersunk screws driven through the top of the counter and by toe-nailing to the drawer sections through the back of the molding. Fill all of the screw and nail holes in the countertop with wood putty and sand them smooth. Extend the floor molding around the base of the side partitions to match the existing floor molding. The base of the built-in and the inside corners of the center section are then trimmed with ¾″ quarter-round molding.

The final construction step is the making of the drawers. Use ½″ plywood for the bottoms and ½″ clear pine for the sides. All drawer joints are butted and fastened with screws and glue. The front face of each drawer should overlap ½″ on all sides. Select the drawer pulls to match the room decor and mount them after the drawer fronts have been sanded smooth and painted. Paint the entire built-in, including the side partitions, one color. This treatment heightens its dramatic effect and makes it an integral part of the surroundings.

Mounting the mirrors is the last operation. Have all four mirror sections cut to size at a local glazing shop from ¼″ plate glass mirror stock, and have all the edges ground smooth. The sections can be mounted on the plywood backing with either standard mirror clips or screws, as shown in the photograph.

If you're planning an attic bedroom, this built-in makes a useful addition that will put your wasted attic space to work.

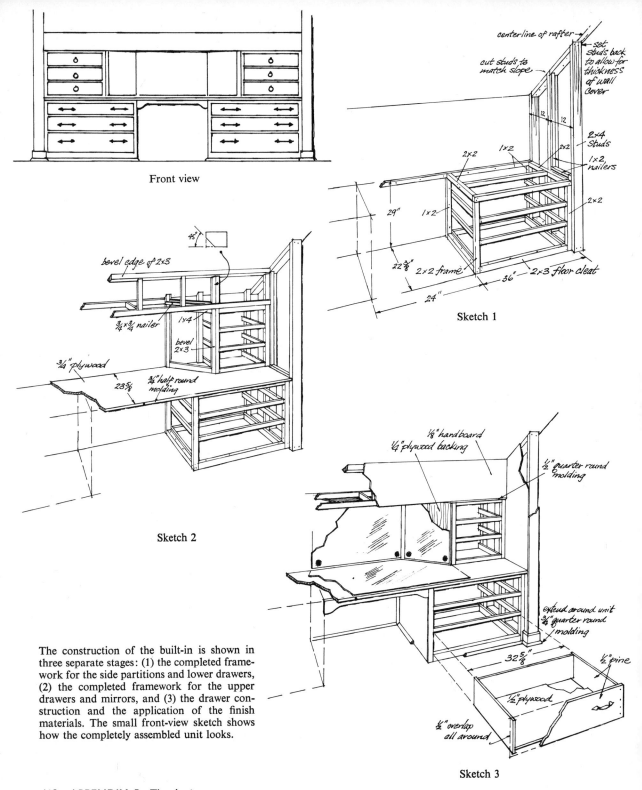

Front view

centerline of rafter

set studs back to allow for thickness of wall cover

cut studs to match slope

2×4 Studs

1×2 nailers

2×2

2×2

1×2

12   12

29"

2×2

1×2

22 3/8"

2×2 frame

36"

24"

2×3 floor cleat

Sketch 1

45°

bevel edge of 2×3

3/4×3/4 nailer

1×4

bevel 2×3

3/4" plywood

23 5/8"

3/4" half round molding

Sketch 2

1/8" hardboard

1/4" plywood backing

1/2" quarter round molding

extend around unit 3/4 quarter round molding

32 5/8"

1/2" pine

1/2" plywood

1/2" overlap all around

Sketch 3

The construction of the built-in is shown in three separate stages: (1) the completed framework for the side partitions and lower drawers, (2) the completed framework for the upper drawers and mirrors, and (3) the drawer construction and the application of the finish materials. The small front-view sketch shows how the completely assembled unit looks.

A Space-Saving Attic Closet. One of the features which adds a touch of luxurious order to a home is a cedar-lined closet. It is ideal for storing your out-of-season clothes because clothes-eating moths do not like the incense of cedar.

Such a closet is also desirable for clothes you do not wear often, and of course it is equally suitable for storing everyday garments.

This closet combines the moth-repelling qualities of cedar with space-saving utilization of the area under the eaves. The framing is simple. Frame the knee walls under the rafters, then nail cedar strips to the wall studs and to the rafters up to the front of the closet. Make certain that your closet door fits tightly in its frame.

A completed cedar-lined closet in an attic room. Room paneling is knotty western pine.

After cedar lining is in place in the rear and top of the closet, the sides and front are framed.

Doors are simple to make from paneling. Panels exactly match those in wall section above door.

The Attic   469

THE BASEMENT

For too many years, the basement has been the stepchild of the house. Though it may be well finished and dry, it has usually existed as the catch-all for various and sundry miscellany which the family doesn't quite want and yet can't quite discard—the outmoded sofa, the "almost" antique desk and the table that "might be useful some day." It has been left in its unattractive loneliness downstairs, used only occasionally and then, at best, as a last resort.

However, no other room in the house will allow you to "be yourself" as completely as will the basement. Because it is bonus space in every sense of the word, you can use it to your heart's desire and adapt it for almost any hobby or interest for your leisure time.

Often a basement is long enough for bowling, shuffle-board or even rifle practice. It's a good place to practice short golf putts. It provides ample storage space for fishing gear, skis and all kinds of sports equipment.

Photographers find that the basement is ideally suited for a photo dark room because running water is usually available. The basement can be used as a clubhouse for hobby enthusiasts, as a greenhouse (if you open it up to enough light), for little theater groups and as a library or a den.

Many mail order businesses are operated from homes. Basements provide office floor area which would cost many hundreds of dollars each year if rented as business space.

If you keep in mind all the possibilities basements offer, you will enjoy planning yours and turning it into one of the most lived-in and valued areas in the house.

Center girder and lally columns can be boxed in attractively so that they blend perfectly with the rest of the room. Knotty pine cabinets make an attractive room divider.

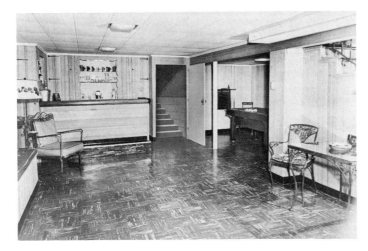

A basement recreation room that is easily accessible to the outdoors, as is the room shown here, is more useful to every member of the family.

Simple materials give this basement room a rich and elegant look. Heavy timbers, wood paneled ceiling, tile floor and "old English" walls combine to make it a cozy place for entertaining.

A resilient tile floor with a built-in shuffleboard court and the colorful walls of attractive insulation plank make this room easy to clean.

Imagination pays off in basement planning. Plastic panels make a handsome room divider. Rope is threaded into treads to achieve different stair arrangement.

Music, reading, sewing, family games—whatever your interest, you probably can indulge it in a basement room. A piano (left) and a game table (right) are basic furniture that help turn a basement into a family room.

Plastic-surfaced hardboard was used as the wall finish of this inviting basement room. Light and dark planks on the far wall create a stunning checkerboard effect.

This playroom is for the children by day and for the adults by night. The train table folds up into the wall. Deep, rich walnut is the wall paneling.

BASEMENT PLANNING

Before you begin the actual work of renovating your basement, it will be well to sit down with pencil and paper and plan carefully what you want to do with the space you have available.

There are two basic reasons for this suggestion:

1. By following a plan, you can get more out of your space. Generally, the basement occupies the same amount of area as does the first floor of your home. If five or six rooms are on the first floor, you should be able to make five or six rooms of approximately the same size in the basement. But only by planning the utilization of the basement as carefully as you would plan the main part of your house will you be able to find the space for rumpus room, handyman workshop, photo darkroom, laundry, den, office or whatever other rooms you might wish to have.

2. You can save money by following a plan. Suppose you are thinking of turning one section of your basement into a photo dark room, where a primary requisite is running water. There are already water supply and waste disposal lines running to and from parts of the first floor area. If you plan ahead to locate the photo dark room in a corner where it will be a relatively simple matter to hook into these lines, you may save a hundred dollars or even more.

The importance of "room planning" the basement is recognized by many architects. Often, when they design a new home, they draw a sketch illustrating how various basement rooms can be fitted into the overall plan. By vizualizing future uses for the basement in this way, they enable homeowners to realize the maximum potential from basement space at the lowest possible cost. The drawings illustrate how a basement can be planned to fit in with the upstairs plan. Keep in mind the following suggestions in basement planning:

1. Make your recreation room easy to reach from the main floor. Preferably it should be at the foot of the stairs so that people will not be required to walk through any unfinished areas in order to reach it. Also, it should be accessible to the outdoors so that the youngsters will not track through the house.

2. Plan your layouts, if possible, so that areas to be used for recreational purposes will not have heating ducts, plumbing lines, etc., open to view when the rooms are completed. These utility lines often can be placed in the area between the first floor joists and they will be hidden from sight when the ceiling is installed.

3. The basement bathroom should be convenient to the outdoors and located close to the existing plumbing lines. In homes with kitchens or bathrooms facing the rear, the best location for these new basement rooms probably will be the rear—near the back yard.

4. The "natural" partition line for basement rooms generally will be found to be directly under the center girder. By erecting a partition wall here, you can cover up the girder and lally columns.

5. Remember your electrical needs. Suppose that you will want a 220-volt drier for your laundry and 220-volt power tools for your workshop. Running power lines from the main entrance box may be costly, so locate your equipment to minimize long runs.

The foundations of most modern homes are waterproofed carefully when the house is built. If the builder of your house took a few simple precautions —like placing a membrane coating and drain tiles on

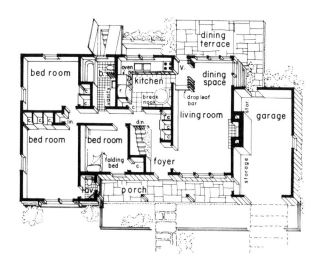
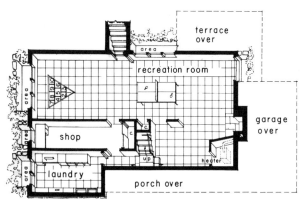

Left: First floor plan of a typical one-story home. Note location of utility lines. Right: Basement plan of the same house. Stairs go to recreation room. Laundry is under first floor lavatory. Furnace is boxed off.

the outside of the foundation wall—you probably have a dry basement which you will be able to enjoy to its fullest the whole year round. Basements of older homes usually can be effectively waterproofed from inside. (See Chapter 5, "Cures for a Damp Basement.")

Once you are ready to begin your basement improvement projects, be sure to plan for adequate light, air, and access. There is no longer any reason for dark, dank basements. Modern designers agree that a basement can still be bright and convenient even though below grade all the way around.

For example, windows larger than the conventional basement sash can be used with recessed areas outside to admit as much light as possible. A big triple window brightens the entertainment or workshop areas.

A separate basement entrance to the outdoors eliminates tracking through the house. It also increases the basement's usefulness for hobbies, garden tool storage, laundering, and other activities. It is a convenience greatly appreciated when bulky things like screens or lawn furniture need to be taken in or out, or as a route that minimizes noise and dirt when the children take over the basement for play.

Glamorizing the basement with large exterior wall openings is easier than it might seem. By using a hand hammer and chisel on concrete block or an electric hammer on a poured concrete foundation, the average handyman usually experiences no difficulty in enlarging a basement window area.

In the usual house, wide openings can be made in the two foundation walls which run in the same direction as the floor joists. These walls are necessary to the structure for only a few feet in the center where they hold up the girder.

In the bearing walls—where the first floor joists rest

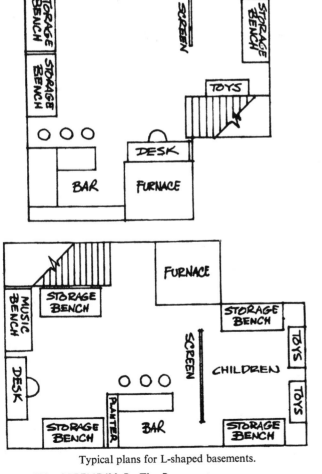

Typical plans for L-shaped basements.

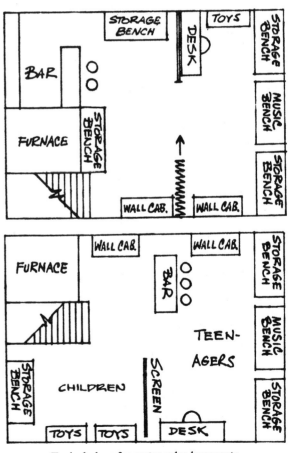

Typical plans for rectangular basements.

Before you cover the basement ceiling with furring strips and acoustical tile, record the location of all plumbing and electrical conduit with a sketch or a photograph so that you can refer to it in the future if alterations or repairs have to be made.

High basement windows simplify the placement of furniture as in this light and charming bedroom.

—average window and door-sized openings usually can be made without disturbing the structure. Larger openings may require placing a girder at the top of the opening. Many building codes specify that habitable living areas must have minimum openings for light equal to 10% of the room's floor area. To meet that standard, a 12 by 20′ playroom (240 square feet) needs 24 square feet of glass opening—the equivalent of about six standard basement sash windows 32″ wide, 18″ deep. These requirements should be borne in mind if you wish to use rooms for bedrooms in the future.

CONCEALING UNSIGHTLY UTILITY EQUIPMENT

Basement Pipe Enclosures. One problem that often emerges when a homeowner undertakes to finish his basement is the concealment of ugly pipes. There are usually some such pipes in even the best planned basement because of the necessity of making connections from the upstairs plumbing fixtures to the outside sewer or septic tank. One way to hide the pipes is to create a false closet of attractive wood paneling. Another design provides useful storage space for books and other items. Construction of both is relatively simple.

This closet, when open (photo at left), reveals the cast-iron sewage disposal pipes which would be an eyesore if exposed to view in the recreation room. Closed (at right), the closet of western pine paneling fits the room's decor.

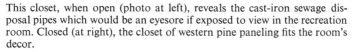

For the enclosure illustrated, first nail 2×2 framing cleats to the floor, walls and ceiling of the basement, as shown in the sketch. Next, fasten the ¼" plywood panels over the framing. The front plywood panel should have a cut-out to accept the cabinet and an extra 2×2 stud at the side of the cut-out to support the cabinet hinges. Use ¾" plywood for the back, sides and shelves of the cabinet and 1×4 lumber for the surrounding frame.

The hinges for the frame are attached to the cabinet on the opposite side of the hinges that support the cabinet itself. This accordion type of hinging permits the frame to overlap and conceal the opening for the cabinet.

If there is a baseboard molding at the floor level, continue it around the enclosure as a finishing touch.

The front frame of the cabinet is hinged and closes over it to conceal cut-out edges.

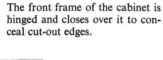

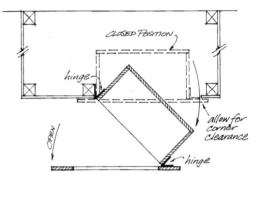

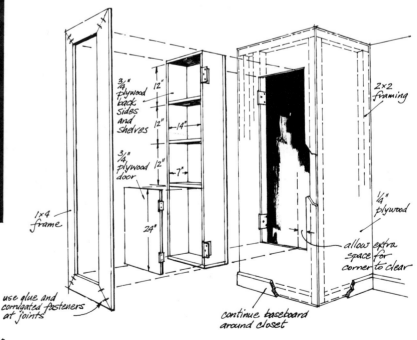

Enclosing the Furnace. The potential which your basement holds for enjoyable relaxation is difficult to visualize when a furnace mars the picture. If you're faced with this problem in your basement, the situation can be easily remedied by erecting a stud wall enclosure for your heating plant as shown in the accompanying sketches. Keep the walls of the enclosure at least 2' away from the furnace and be sure to line the opening around the smoke pipe with asbestos as a safety precaution.

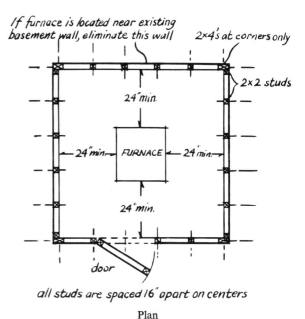

If furnace is located near existing basement wall, eliminate this wall

2x4's at corners only

2x2 studs

24" min.

24" min. ← FURNACE → 24" min.

24" min.

door

all studs are spaced 16" apart on centers

Plan

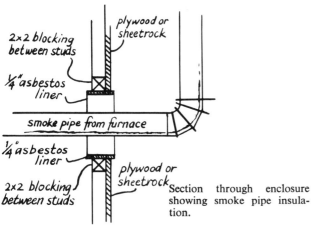

plywood or sheetrock

2x2 blocking between studs

¼" asbestos liner

smoke pipe from furnace

¼" asbestos liner

2x2 blocking between studs

plywood or sheetrock

Section through enclosure showing smoke pipe insulation.

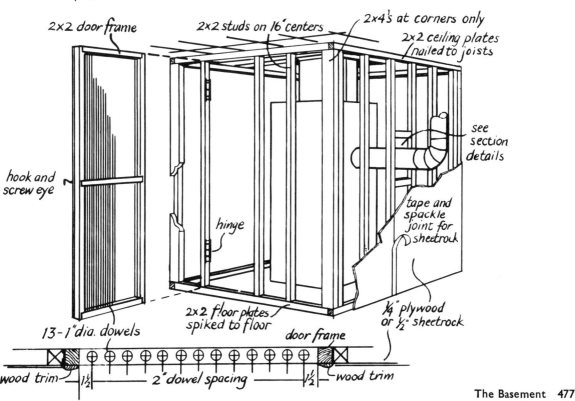

2x2 door frame

2x2 studs on 16" centers

2x4's at corners only

2x2 ceiling plates nailed to joists

hook and screw eye

see section details

hinge

tape and spackle joint for sheetrock

2x2 floor plates spiked to floor

door frame

¼" plywood or ½" sheetrock

13 - 1" dia. dowels

wood trim — 1½ — 2" dowel spacing — 1½ — wood trim

Meter Mask. Here is a handsome cabinet that not only hides the meter but becomes an integral part of the decor—and also provides handy storage shelves and cubby holes. The dimensions given are based on a 7' ceiling height. However, the space between the full-width shelves can easily be changed to compensate for a different floor-to-ceiling measurement.

Construction is simple. Except for the toe plate and door, the wood is 1×10 knotty pine shelving. The horizontal members butt against the vertical supports and are nailed through them.

The space at the top is enclosed with scraps of the same random-width paneling used on the walls, to form a soffit. The crown molding is extended around the top to visually tie the cabinet construction to the room. The other edges of the soffit can be trimmed with corner beads, as shown in the sketch. Also, the full-length uprights have been dressed up by bradding strips of ⅜" half-round molding to the leading edges.

The door that masks the meter is a ¾" panel of knotty-pine-faced plywood and has a ⅜" lip that overlaps the edges of the opening.

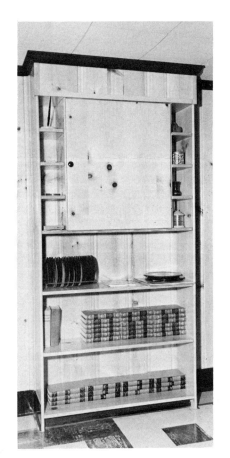

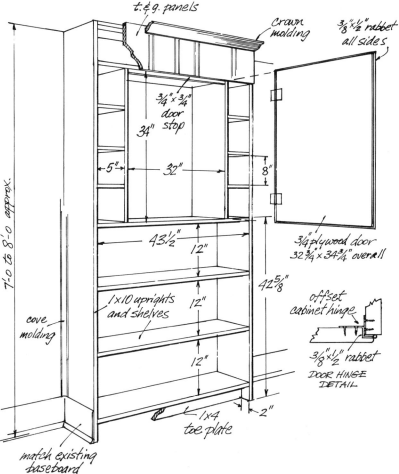

BASEMENT STORAGE UNITS

Double Built-in Storage Sofas. The built-in storage sofa shown here and in the sketches on the next page uses the same type of paneling for its base framework as is used on the walls, thereby tying the unit into the room and minimizing its size. It also simplifies construction and provides a surface requiring little sanding. The use of prefinished paneling would lessen the work still more. And almost every cubic foot does double duty; both the identical sofas and the corner table between them are lift-lid chests providing a wealth of storage space. The plywood tops of the two "end table" units are stationary but may be cut out to recess planter boxes.

Before adapting this plan to your own space, it's advisable to have the planter boxes and your up-

Hinged lids on lounges and table provide access to storage areas. See sketches on the next page for construction plan.

holstery units on hand since they influence the overall dimensions. The unattached cushioning may be of rubberized hair lounge pads, felted cotton bunk mattresses or—if you are prepared to invest a little more money—3″ or 4″ foam rubber mattresses. Such units usually measure about 30″ by 75″. Buy the double bolsters (the wedge type is best here) at the same time. The flush door, which serves as the supporting lid, will most likely require shortening to fit these units. The door should be padded on its upper face and edges with a layer or two of upholstery cotton or other padding and covered with the same type of cloth used for the mattress and bolster sleeves. This material is pulled taut around the panel and the edges are folded under and tacked.

The upper face of the frame that supports the lid should be at least 1′ above the floor; the exact height is determined by the thickness of your door and cushioning and by whether or not you prefer low or normal (17–19″) seating.

The edges of the plywood table tops are covered with ¾″ cove molding mitered at the outside corners. The 29″ square top for the corner table has this molding secured in place before the front corner is sliced off to form the lift-up lid. This triangular piece is then reattached with the proper length of continuous (piano) hinge.

After the framing is enclosed with paneling and a finish has been applied (sealer and paste wax, penetrating stain wax or paint, depending on the paneling used and the effect desired), each upholstered door is secured to its wall with two 4″ butt hinges located so the door rests firmly on the cleats when closed. If desired, the planter boxes may be omitted and the tops of these end sections may be hinged to provide additional storage space.

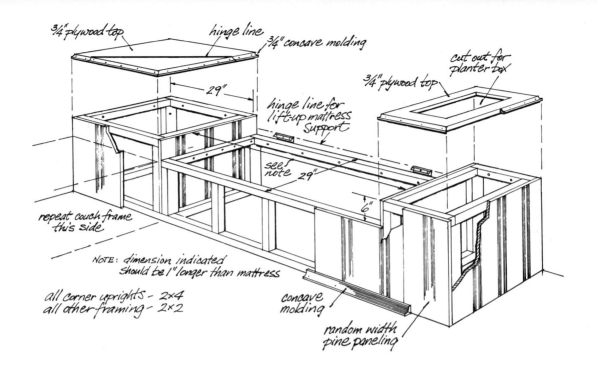

¾" plywood top
hinge line
¾" concave molding
cut out for planter box
¾" plywood top
29"
hinge line for lift-up mattress support
see note 29"
6"
repeat couch frame this side
NOTE: dimension indicated should be 1" longer than mattress
all corner uprights – 2×4
all other framing – 2×2
concave molding
random width pine paneling

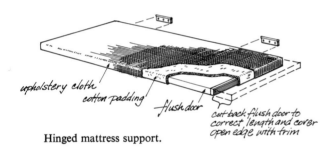

upholstery cloth
cotton padding
flush door
cut back flush door to correct length and cover open edge with trim

Hinged mattress support.

Under-the-Stairs Storage Areas. A stairway to an unfinished basement can usually be called nothing more than an oversized ladder. The banister, if any, is a 2×3 on top of a couple of posts. The steps themselves are nailed to a couple of stringers. There may or may not be risers; if not, the resemblance to a ladder is even stronger. The space beneath the stairs often becomes a depository for the odds and ends that every family seems to accumulate.

The plans outlined here show you how to convert this cluttered area into an orderly, spacious closet, and the drawings show the method of construction. The large sketch on the facing page illustrates the framing that is the start of the job. 2×3's fastened to the floor on edge or on the wide side, as shown, are used for plates. If the floor is concrete, they may

This bright, cheerful recreation room was once a cold and dismal cellar. Enclosing the stairway and paneling the walls started the job.

be spiked into place with steel cut nails or, if you have a masonry bit for your electric drill, drill into the concrete and set lead anchors in the holes. Then the plates can be secured in place with lag bolts screwed into the anchors. Start at the bottom step and work toward the large closet end (from right to left in the sketch). Fasten the first short length, then

set in the first vertical 2×3 that extends from plate to banister, nailing through its side into the plate just placed.

Continue construction by setting plates and posts alternately until all are in place. Then cut and fit the banister and the 2×3's that parallel it along the stringer. Be sure to fit 1×2 cleats in place, as indicated, before going on to the next step.

Horizontal members are nailed in next. In the smaller portion of the closet, they act as shelf supports. Elsewhere they provide a nailing surface for the covering material. When framing is completed, place all shelves. These may be made of common boards of ½" plywood cut to fit, with corners notched out for uprights wherever necessary.

Paneling is the next step. First decide on the material. Here random width, knotty pine boards, tongue-and-grooved are used. Hardboard, plywood, wallboard—any of these are equally suitable (see Chapter 2, pages 111 to 114). Nail the paneling to the frame, cutting it so that a door opening is left. To make sure that doors will fit properly, cut each piece of panel to the overall length needed, then cut it again. Of the two pieces resulting, one will be nailed on as siding while the other will become part of the door.

When all paneling is completed, the doors may be nailed together and hung. All doors are of board-and-batten construction, hung on sturdy butt hinges. Magnetic catches may be used so that no hardware will be seen to destroy the illusion of an unbroken surface when the doors are closed.

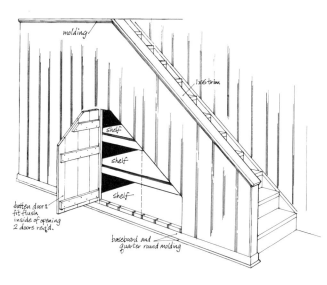

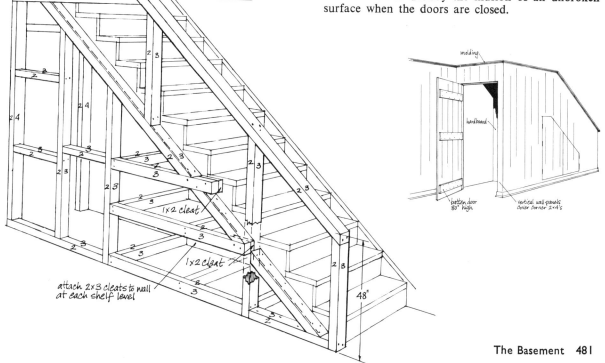

A Full-size Storage Wall. Here is a case where a plan to use the under-stairs space grew until it became a complete storage wall. It includes two general utility areas, a pantry closet for extra canned goods and bottled beverages and, to complete it, a clothes closet. Shelves run through the pantry and the utility unit to its left. The smallest part, under the foot of the stairs, has no shelves because of its limited height. Overall dimensions and shelf heights must be determined by existing conditions, but framing methods may follow the sketch.

Start with floor cleats and 2×2 nailing strips on the underside of the stringer, add the posts and shelf

cleats, then set in the shelves. The 1″ facing board nailed over the stringer brings out the side of the stairway so that the doors are flush when closed. The doors, which swing on H-L hinges, are standard board-and-batten construction, using tongue-and-grooved stock.

Cover the outer faces of the posts with a strip of lumber of the same thickness as the stock used for the doors. When all the doors are shut, the entire surface will be flush.

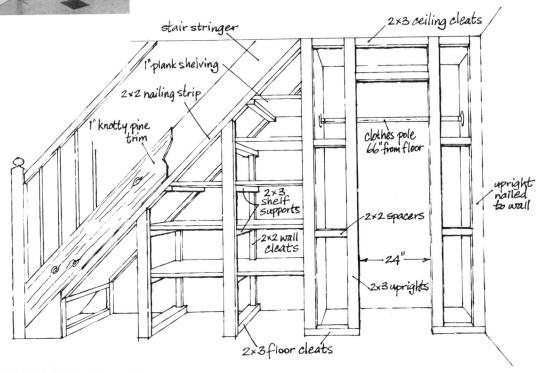

Sliding Storage Cabinets. For this unique unit, the working procedure is simple, even if you have to remove a portion of wall under the steps. If you are faced with this problem, first remove all molding or baseboard alongside the stairway. (A floor or glazier's chisel comes in handy for the job of prying; you will be able to salvage the wood removed without splintering it.) Then remove all wall covering between the stringer (which supports the stairs) and the floor. Wallboard may be pried loose with a glazier's chisel; use a hammer and cold chisel on plaster and then remove the lath. At this point any electrical wiring in the way, or pipes, will have to be shifted to a new position.

Studs should be 24″ apart on centers. You may be able to use the old studs if they fit this pattern, so check carefully before tearing out any (see Sketches A and B). To remove studs, saw them through the center and then knock them out with a hammer. Remove all nails remaining in the floor plate and the stringer overhead.

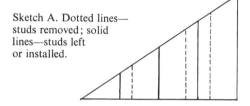

Sketch A. Dotted lines— studs removed; solid lines—studs left or installed.

Sketch B

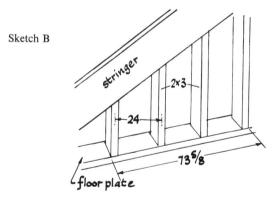

For the basic framing, cut new studs so that there will be one on each side of each sliding cabinet (see Sketch A). Determine the correct bevel for each stud by placing it against the stringer and marking the angle with a pencil; then cut along this line. Each stud should fit snugly under the stringer so that stud, stringer and floor plate are all flush (see Sketch B). Next, nail the studs into place, toe-nailing at the bottom to the plate and at the top into the stringer. Use 8d common nails.

Measure the depth from the rear edge of the plate to the wall at the back and cut two pieces of 2×3 for each cabinet. These will be nailed at right angles to the plate to hold the drawer slides to support and guide the cabinets (see Sketch C). Toe-nail into the

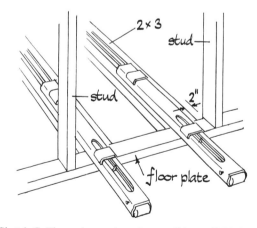

Sketch C. The under-carriage drawer slide, available in most hardware stores, will carry a weight of up to 50 lbs. per pair. The cabinets may be removed by pulling them out to the full length of the slides and lifting slightly.

plate and anchor to the floor, 2″ from vertical studs. Attach the slides with screws provided with the hardware to these 2×3's and to the plate so that the front end is 1″ from the outside edge of the plate.

To make the cabinets, use simple butt joints (Sketch D). Each cabinet is 22⅛″ wide, fitting between the studs with ⅛″ clearance on each side. The cabinet's depth should be two-thirds the distance from the front edge of the floor plate to the rear wall. This is done because the cabinets do not slide out all the way and it would be difficult to reach small items at the rear.

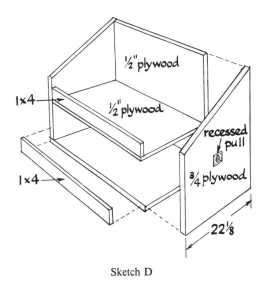

Sketch D

Cut the cabinet sides out of ¾″ plywood to the shape of each of the three areas bordered by studs, stringer and plate (Sketch B); cut each base to size out of ¾″ plywood. Use ½″ plywood for the back panel, then assemble with 8d finishing nails (Sketch D). If shelves are needed, cut these out of ½″ plywood and nail into place. To prevent items from falling off the shelves, add strips of 1×4 to the shelf fronts between the sides.

Add a recessed drawer pull, available in most hardware stores, in the center of each unit (Sketch D) so that it will be easy to pull out the cabinets. To do this, you mark the location of the drawer pull, drill a series of small holes and chisel out the opening.

Finally, extend the slides of the cabinets and set the units in place. Mark the positions for screw holes; then turn the units on their sides and drill pilot holes for the screws. Disengage the slide extensions, attach them to the base of the cabinets, engage them again and slide the cabinets back under the stairs. The project is now ready for use.

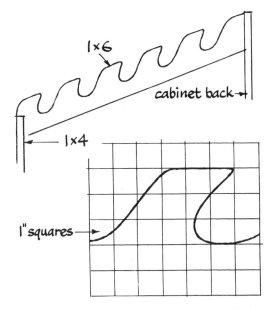

Pattern for umbrella rack fitted into lowest cabinet is shown above. Use 1 × 6 stock, cut with a keyhole saw and attached to the front and back panels with 6d finishing nails.

Basement Storage Cabinets. There's room to spare for all your hobby, play and sports equipment in these three spacious cabinets.

Cabinet 1. The first step in construction is to nail cleats of 1×2 stock to the ceiling, floor, and walls to which the large panels of plywood will be nailed. Cleats in back and at ends will be concealed by the plywood, but the floor cleats also act as baseboards and add a pleasant appearance when painted.

Assemble the large panels as follows: the ¼″ plywood back goes on first, followed by the ¾″ plywood ends and partition. The partition is notched to fit the ceiling nailing cleat and the door stop strip, both of which butt against the inside surfaces of the end panels. Spacing of the shelves is optional; it is not permanent because the shelves merely rest on shelf brackets, as shown. Since these brackets require only ¼″ holes in the ends and the partition for installation, a good trick is to drill a row of holes 2″ apart so that no further work is required when you later re-space the shelves. Be sure to use a wood block over your drill point as a depth gauge when drilling holes in the ends so that the drill does not come through.

The front trim of the cabinet (which also acts as the door casing) is made from 3½″ stock. Cut four doors, two for each opening, to fit; then build the framed storage bins on back of each before hanging. Note that the hinges called for are double offset.

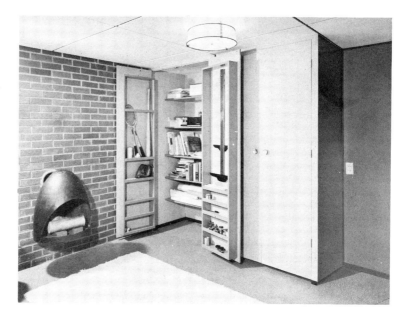

Cabinet 1. The two-by-eight foot area of this floor-to-ceiling cabinet with adjustable shelves holds a lot of material without looming too large in your basement.

These resemble butt hinges when the doors are closed, but since they are bent so that the screws go through them into the *back* of the plywood, they hold much more securely.

Use heavy, spring-type friction catches at the top of each door, with the companion parts of the catch located on the door stop. Your choice of door pulls and a paint job complete this capacious cabinet.

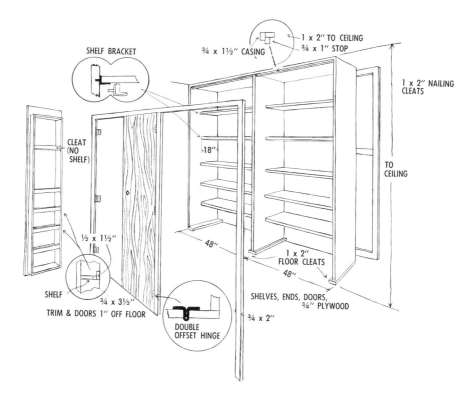

Cabinet 2. This cabinet is excellent for storing fishing and hunting gear. For a neat job, rabbet the edges of the sides where they meet the back and top. If you do not have a power saw, use 1×1 corner strips for nailing. The shelves and partitions are cut narrower than the depth of the cabinet, as shown, to allow space for the storage door to close. The shelf immediately under the drawers is cut back the thickness of the drawer front, as is the partition between drawers, so that the drawer fronts may lap them. The drawers are conventional in construction but no space need be allowed for runners or slides since they fit between members of the cabinet around them. Build a frame and bins on the back of the ¾″ plywood door, as shown. Then cement sheet cork to the upper section for your lures. Cup hooks should be used near the top of the door to hang your poles, and depth of the bins may be varied to your own particular purpose.

The door is hung with three offset hinges, and a friction catch will hold it closed. A hasp and padlock may be added on the outside of the cabinet to keep its contents completely safe.

COAT HANGER ROD

¼″ PLY BACK

20″

SHEET CORK LINER

84″

7″

4½″

9¼″

13¼″

13″

4½″

5″

7″

10¼″

4″

8 x ½″ DOWELS 6″O.C.

22¼″

10″

3½″

2″

3¼″

2″
6″
2″
6″
7″
4½″

17″   17″   24″   24″

OFFSET HINGE

Cabinet 2. This cabinet will hold all your rods, reels, lures, poles, waders, etc., very comfortably, secure against damage and deterioration.

Cabinet 3. The major difference between this cabinet and cabinet 2 is the gun rack. In order to make room for the guns, the coat hanger is omitted and the drawers are set lower, as indicated in the drawing below. Rubber sheeting is cemented to the shelf that takes the slotted stock rack, and the rack is nailed *through* the sheeting to the shelf. The barrel rack is made in two pieces, the outer one hinged so that the guns will be secure. The inside of the door is the same on both cabinets. If you elect to build both, have one open to the left, the other to the right.

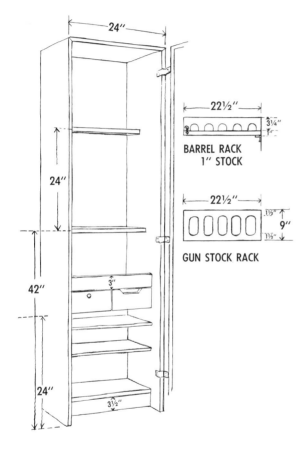

BARREL RACK
1" STOCK

GUN STOCK RACK

Cabinet 3. If your taste runs to hunting and fishing, a few simple changes in the interior design make ample room for rod, reel and rifle. But perhaps you enjoy both sports. Then by all means build both cabinets.

MUSIC WALLS

A basement recreation room or family room is bound to be more enjoyable if it has music. Compact, built-in units along one wall provide a place for hi-fi, radio, phonograph and records. No floor space is lost and all your equipment is attractively housed in one place.

Music Wall 1. Because of its many different functions, this music wall is designed as built-in units, then set into place. It is possible to rearrange the units to your floor plan and to add additional bookcases or magazine racks as space allows. If you do not have a piano, you may extend the end bookcase 24″ in length and eliminate the closed front storage bin. The choice, in other words, is yours; a complete study of the drawings will save time in construction.

Begin by cutting the partitions for all units, since they are similar in size. Add cleats wherever shelf ends meet partitions.

All fronts are cut and assembled to the units before the tops, which extend over them, are put in place. The smaller drawing on the next page shows how a table-like shelf raises to set on blocks, thus bringing records to a convenient height. A standard wire

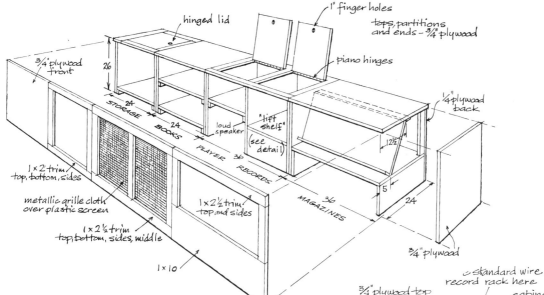

record rack rests on the top of this shelf. The shelf table is built and installed before the top is fastened into place. Other construction is conventional and the hardware standard.

This multi-unit music wall blends well with game floors and rough textured walls.

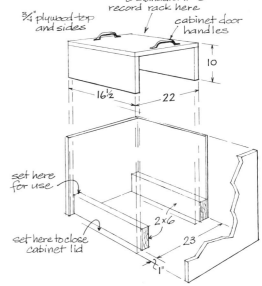

Detail of "lift-shelf" for records.

Music Wall 2. The first step in building this music wall is to locate the most suitable place for it, bearing two important considerations in mind:

1. Acoustics. Generally speaking, an end wall in a long, narrow room or the middle of the most unbroken (by window or door openings) wall in a square, or nearly square, room is best.

2. Wall Structure. A wall with a closet behind it, such as the one in the photograph, is ideal. Since the wall to be cut into is on the average about 5" deep, the net depth the closet loses is less than 8". How-

ever, if the first consideration—acoustics—rules out some wall that is not backed by a closet, consider whether the cabinet back can extend into another room. By extending the ends and running shallow shelves between, it could very well become a knick-knack case in the other room.

Before cutting into any wall, make certain there are no pipes or heating ducts in the way. You can usually get around wires by pulling enough slack to detour around one side of the enclosure. Make sure you turn off the house current before touching the wires.

Begin construction by cutting out the plaster or other wall surfacing back to the studs that limit the width of the opening. The middle stud is cut off high enough to allow for the header above the desired height of the cabinet. Try to align the top of the opening with other doors in the room. The 2×4 plate is left on the floor, and another short 2×4 laid behind it, as shown. If it is hard to work in back of the cabinet space, you can assemble the main parts of it before installing. The plywood back should be screwed to the sides to obtain the best results from your speaker, and all joints must fit well to cut down vibration. Note that the sides of the speaker box

This complete hi-fi takes space—besides existing wall—of less than 8″ × 32″ × 80″ out of the end of an outsize closet next to the stairs.

are lined with vibration damping (sound-absorptive) material. The small, square, box-like opening below the speaker, called the port, should be as deep as the speaker magnet for best results. The front panel that holds the speaker is screwed in from the front so that it may be removed as needed.

Tracks are mounted on one shelf to match slides on the bottom of the record player base. Shelves and openings in the front must be arranged to accommodate the size of hi-fi components you select.

Louver doors, conventionally hinged to each side of the cabinet, and a casing and baseboard in front complete the built-in hi-fi.

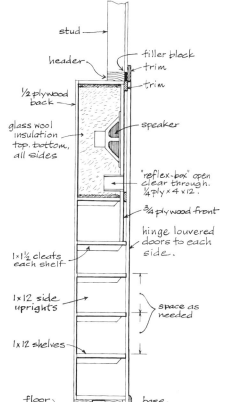

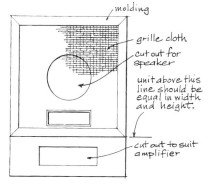

Left: Section through unit.

Right: Front view of speaker and amplifier section.

BASEMENT BARS

Food and drink go hand in hand with entertainment, and since your finished basement may often be the center for parties and festivities, you must provide ample storage for all the ingredients. You'll find it here in either of these two easy-to-build bars, one Colonial, the other contemporary.

Colonial Bar. First lay out full-size lines on the floor for the framework of the bar, using the dimensions indicated. By laying the different parts of the 2×2 sills across the intersecting lines, you can mark the exact angles to be cut. One post must be of 2×4 stock since one edge of it is to be planed to the 135° angle of the front. The other posts are square. Shelves are cut and installed next, then knotty pine facing at front and end. Follow the facing with a 2×2 spacer and 1×6 trim board at the front and end to make a 3″ overhang. The top is of ¾″ hardwood plywood, with the moldings and baseboard applied last.

Colonial in design, this knotty pine bar stores all the ingredients you'll need.

¾ hardwood plywood top

overhang 3″ at end and front

135°

18

18

¾ plywood shelf   42

54

18

2×2 spacer

1×6 trim

random width shiplap pine

1″ dia. ¾ round
1½ dia. ½ round

2×4 post planed to 135° - all other framing of 2×2 stock

base to match room baseboard

3″

Section-detail of bar-top overhang.

Contemporary Bar. Two different plywood patterns —"one-eleven" outside, "brushed" inside—give this folding bar a striking appearance and ample strength without heavy framing. Cut all parts for the back of the bar to the sizes indicated and assemble it first, since the swinging front must fit it accurately. Clearance must be allowed for the bar, with the top folded, to swing under the lowest shelf. When building the lower portion, allow space under it for the casters on which it rolls. Doors on the upper part must lap down over the top of the bar, when closed, to meet the matching front. Invisible (recessed) hinges are used in the bar top, offset hinges for doors and to swing the bar in. Build the flower and lighting recess as shown in the detail. Place shelves and partitions to suit your individual needs. All ends, shelves, partitions and the bar top are of ¾" plywood for strength and rigidity.

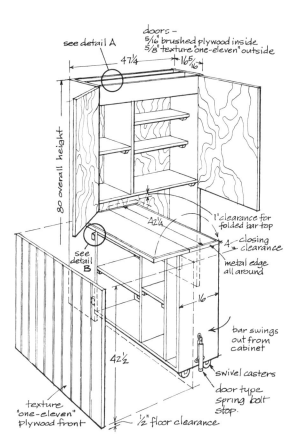

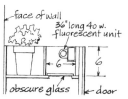

Detail A. Fluorescent lighted plant box at top.

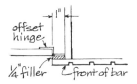

Detail B. Hinge arrangement for swing-out bar.

The clean lines of this fold-away bar make it particularly attractive.

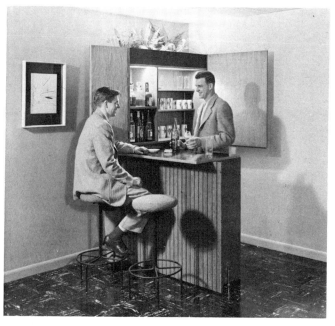

CREDITS

All photographs and diagrams in this book have appeared in *The Family Handyman* magazine. Many of the photographs were provided originally by manufacturers and are credited as follows:

Adjustable Clamp Co., p. 31; Alsco Inc., p. 288; American Walnut Manufacturers Association, p. 472; Armstrong Cork Co., Inc., pp. 122, 458, 471, 472, 475; Babock & Co., p. 46; The Borden Co., p. 37; Black & Decker Manufacturing Co., pp. 57, 58; The Celotex Corp., p. 101; Chicopee Manufacturing Corp., p. 150; Douglas Fir Plywood Association, pp. 287, 454, 455; The Dow Chemical Co., p. 281; Du Fast Inc., p. 46; The Forsberg Manufacturing Co., p. 58; Marlite Wallpanels, pp. 114, 472; Monsanto Chemical Co., p. 371; The National Plastic Products Co., p. 14; Owens-Corning Fiberglas Corp., pp. 123, 186; Pittsburgh Plate Glass Co., Inc., pp. 142, 143, 347, 353, 354, 356, 361, 362, 363, 372, 373; Red Devil Tools, p. 24; Reynolds Metals Inc., pp. 13, 147; Skilsaw Inc., p. 54; Structural Clay Products Institute, p. 288; Sylvania Electric Inc., p. 225; Synchro Corp., p. 55; Union Carbide & Carbon Corp., p. 375; U. S. Expansion Bolt Co., p. 119; Western Pine Association, pp. 112, 113, 398, 399, 400, 469, 475; The Wiremold Co., p. 224.